Economic Development and Environmental Sustainability

THE INITIATIVE FOR POLICY DIALOGUE SERIES

The Initiative for Policy Dialogue (IPD) brings together the top voices in development to address some of the most pressing and controversial debates in economic policy today. The IPD book series approaches topics such as capital market liberalization, macroeconomics, environmental economics, and trade policy from a balanced perspective, presenting alternatives and analyzing their consequences on the basis of the best available research. Written in a language accessible to policymakers and civil society, this series will rekindle the debate on economic policy and facilitate a more democratic discussion of development around the world.

OTHER TITLES PUBLISHED BY OXFORD UNIVERSITY PRESS
IN THIS SERIES

Fair Trade for All

Joseph E. Stiglitz and Andrew Charlton

Stability with Growth

Joseph E. Stiglitz, José Antonio Ocampo, Shari Spiegel,
Ricardo Ffrench-Davis and Deepak Nayyar

Economic Development and Environmental Sustainability

New Policy Options

Edited by

Ramón López
and
Michael A. Toman

OXFORD
UNIVERSITY PRESS

OXFORD
UNIVERSITY PRESS

Great Clarendon Street, Oxford OX2 6DP

Oxford University Press is a department of the University of Oxford.
It furthers the University's objective of excellence in research, scholarship,
and education by publishing worldwide in

Oxford New York

Auckland Cape Town Dar es Salaam Hong Kong Karachi
Kuala Lumpur Madrid Melbourne Mexico City Nairobi
New Delhi Shanghai Taipei Toronto

With offices in

Argentina Austria Brazil Chile Czech Republic France Greece
Guatemala Hungary Italy Japan Poland Portugal Singapore
South Korea Switzerland Thailand Turkey Ukraine Vietnam

Oxford is a registered trade mark of Oxford University Press
in the UK and in certain other countries

Published in the United States
by Oxford University Press Inc., New York

British Library Cataloguing in Publication Data

Data available

Library of Congress Cataloging in Publication Data

Data available

Typeset by Newgen Imaging Systems (P) Ltd., Chennai, India
Printed in Great Britain
on acid-free paper by
Biddles Ltd., King's Lynn, Norfolk

ISBN 978–0–19–929799–3
ISBN 978–0–19–929800–6 (Pbk.)

10 9 8 7 6 5 4 3 2

Acknowledgements

This book is derived from the work of the Initiative for Policy Dialogue (IPD) Environmental Economics and Sustainable Development Task Force. IPD is a network of some two hundred-fifty economists, development researchers, and practitioners throughout the developed and developing world, who are committed to furthering the understanding of the development process. (For more information about IPD and the Environmental Economics and Sustainable Development Task Force, see the IPD website at www.policydialogue.org.)

The IPD environmental program is overseen by Joseph Stiglitz, IPD Executive Director, and Shari Spiegel, IPD Managing Director, with additional assistance from Lauren Anderson, Shana Hofstetter, Sylvia Wu, Siddhartha Gupta, and Ariel Schwartz. We would like to thank all the task force members for their efforts in furthering the work of the task force. We would also like to thank our editor at Oxford University Press, Sarah Caro, and also Jennifer Wilkinson, for their help in bringing this book to fruition.

Finally, we would like to thank the Charles Stewart Mott Foundation for supporting IPD's environmental program. Additional support was received from the Swedish International Development Cooperation Agency (SIDA), the Ford Foundation, and the John D. and Catherine T. MacArthur Foundation.

Contents

Contents

List of Figures

List of Figures

List of Tables

List of Boxes

Foreword

Joseph E. Stiglitz

The objective of development is to improve and sustain the well-being of those living in developing countries. It is not just to increase GDP. Sustainable increases in living standards require that resources—including all aspects of the environment—be managed well. Resource depletion and environmental degradation are potential threats to sustainable development. Too often, those entrusted with shaping economic policy have put too little attention on the consequences of the policies for natural resources and the environment, and devoted even less attention to shaping policies that might actually improve the quality of the environment and resource management.

At the Millennium Summit of the United Nations, the attention of the world was directed towards the reduction of poverty, setting goals to be attained by 2015—some concrete, others more general. It was noteworthy that among the targets was 'ensuring environmental sustainability, including integrating the principles of sustainable development into country policies and programs; reversing the loss of environmental resources; and reducing by half the proportion of people without sustainable access to safe drinking water.' Yet, it has become increasingly clear that bad environmental policies have particularly adverse effects on the poor.

It is essential, if we are to have sustainable, equitable development, that we have a better understanding of how to improve resource management and the environment in developing countries, and how various policies affect the environment. That is one of the central objectives of the essays collected in this volume. But the essays address an even deeper question, which policies must be attacked if we are to have sustainable reforms: why is it that so many countries have not managed their resources well? What are the political forces at play?

Nothing illustrates the complexity of the issues at hand more than the resource paradox: the fact that countries with large endowments of natural resources seem, on average, to perform more poorly than those without resources. Examples of poorly performing resource-rich countries, like Congo and Sierra Leone, leap to mind; as do examples of successful countries without resources, like Korea and Singapore. There are, of course, examples of successful resource-rich countries—Malaysia and Botswana, among the most rapidly growing countries of the last three decades—and these show that the resource curse is not inevitable. But the fact that so many resource rich countries have not done well (and have corrupt and dictatorial political regimes) suggest that there may be some causal links.

This illustrates the importance of political economy concerns, as does another paradox: in principle, because there are no distortions associated with taxing rents, at least purportedly democratic resource-rich countries should have more equalitarian distributions of income than those where national incomes are dependent on individual efforts, where progressive taxation might have adverse incentives. Yet, on the contrary, resource-rich countries are marked by high degrees of inequality. They are rich countries with poor people.

The essays in this volume repeatedly emphasize the political dimension of the environmental problem. The misuse of the environment reflects broader problems of governance in developing countries. But the problems of governance are, in many ways, endogenous. Those seeking access to resources at the lowest possible prices—maximizing profits for their shareholders—often find they can do so best by bribing government officials, rather than paying full market prices. Even advanced industrial countries have found the pressures from natural resource lobbyists, with their bounteous campaign contributions, irresistible. The United States even gives away its mineral resources to anyone who stakes out a claim: attempts by President Clinton to garner for American citizens the value of these resources through competitive auctions were beaten back by the mining companies.

There are complex interlinkages between economic policies, the environment, and governance: high interest rates (often associated with the structural adjustment programs of the IMF), for instance, encourage more rapid resource depletion; but they also encourage asset stripping as opposed to wealth creation, and with more firms and individuals having a stake in asset stripping rather than wealth creation, there is less support for the creation of a rule of law supportive of wealth creation and sustainable development.

Globalization by itself need not be bad for the environment and the protection of natural resources; but as practiced it often has been. Globalization has been associated with high levels of volatility—and with IMF programs which have raised interest rates to very high levels; these crises and the way they have been managed have not been good either for the conservation of natural resources or the protection of the environment. When poor people can't afford kerosene, they turn to forests to obtain the fuel they need. When countries face hard times, they are more likely to have a fire sale—use up their resources—to keep themselves going. Very high interest rates mean that it is rational not to pay much attention to the future consequences.

While today, most multinational mining companies have websites which portray themselves as keepers of the environment—and they may be more sensitive to public relations than privately held companies—the track record is worrisome: their profit maximizing incentives to keep costs down naturally lead to attempts not only to get the resources at as low a price as they can, but also to neglect the environment—and to exert what political pressure they can to limit environmental regulations. Nowhere was this more evident than in Chapter 11 of the North American Free Trade Agreement, where foreign investors succeeded in getting an agreement to being compensated for adverse effects on profitability by environmental regulations, no matter how well conceived and no matter how well designed—a 'regulatory takings' provision that had been repeatedly rejected by the U.S. Administration, courts, and Congress for domestic investors.

At one time, there was a worry that limitations on resources meant that there simply could not be sustainable, long-term growth. The ability of technology to stretch our resources further, to allow us to do with less, has reduced these concerns—though not completely alleviated them, since there remain concerns over the consequences of greenhouse gas emissions. As resources become depleted, countries can substitute other forms of capital, so their total 'natural plus physical plus knowledge' capital stock grows.

One difficulty in implementing sustainable growth policies is the accounting frameworks that are conventionally used. Accounting provides information that can be helpful in guiding decisions; but poorly designed accounting frameworks can provide poor guidance. The accounting frameworks used, for instance, for measuring national output do not take into account the depletion of natural resources or the degradation of the environment. Governments are given high marks if GDP goes up, even if the country is actually poorer, as a result of its depletion of its resources, and even if, as a result, the growth is not sustainable. When I was chairman of the Council of Economic Advisers under President Clinton, I pushed for introducing Green GDP accounting frameworks that reflected this. The potential importance of the new accounting framework was highlighted by the political pressure that was exerted, for instance, by representatives from coal mining states, to stop this initiative by withholding all funding for it.

For developing countries, the 'good news' is that their environmental and natural resource policies are often so bad that there are reforms which would be both good for the economy and good for the environment. The elimination of open and hidden subsidies, for instance, which have the effect of encouraging excessive use of energy and water would simultaneously provide the government with more money to spend on alternative, more productive development projects and lead to a better environment.

These are only a sampling of the important topics touched upon by the papers in this volume. There is a simple message. Environmental sustainability requires an integrated set of policies, not just environmental policy. Perhaps it requires most of all a reform in political processes in both the North and the South, which have provided particular interests an opportunity to advance their own interests at the expense of the environment and of the long term well being of those in the developing world.

Overview

Sustainable Development: Towards a Broader Policy Agenda

Ramón López and Michael A. Toman

Over the last few decades, economic growth in developing countries has been, with some exceptions, slow; social equity has either not improved or worsened; and environmental degradation in many places has been significant. In numerous countries, economic development has not been environmentally sustainable.[1]

A central message of this volume is that the failure to achieve environmental sustainability has been the result of a systematic underinvestment in public goods by governments. Since in many respects the environment is a public good, the low priority assigned by governments to supplying public goods implies a tendency to waste natural resources. This volume consistently identifies poorly functioning environmental institutions as well as other inadequate environmental regulation and enforcements such as ill-defined property rights. The failure to implement high yield environmental protection investments is a key source of environmental degradation. Complementary, cross-cutting problems such as weaknesses in legal systems, underinvestment in human capital, weak financial capital markets, corruption, and rent-seeking often exacerbate the failure of environmental institutions.

Most developing country governments attach low priority to spending public resources on developing or enforcing property rights for natural

---

[1] A renewed commitment to attacking these interlocking problems of economic progress, social development, and environmental sustainability by the world community as affirmed in the 2000 United Nations Millennium Declaration and the subsequent Millennium Development Goals (MDGs) in 2002 (see UNDP 2003) is in place (see Appendix). Though the means and policies that will be used to achieve these goals are not mentioned in the documents, the goals have merit because they incorporate not just environmental objectives and targets (Goal 7, Targets 9–11) but also a variety of other intertwined economic and social-development objectives. The environmental objectives are not just important in their own right (i.e. as a source of direct value added), but they also contribute to the achievement of other goals (e.g. improved health and productivity). Similarly, achievement of other MDGs (e.g. poverty reduction) may contribute to environmental protection.

resources. The chapters in this volume report consistent government failures to impose environmental regulation and to effectively prevent encroachment and wasteful illegal exploitation of ecosystems that are nominally protected. Even countries that have sophisticated institutions and highly effective property rights regimes often fail to define and enforce property rights for the poor. Such countries are also reluctant to spend resources on defending ecosystems that are legally designated as protected. This may mean that the environmental failures identified in this volume are not simply a result of governments' lack of means and information. Powerful political economy motivations must be at work given the massive resources governments divert from high return environmental projects to endeavors of dubious social value.

The lack of environmental sustainability is only one symptom of the malaise that affects public policy priorities. The same government programs that dedicate little to basic and secondary education, such as those identified by Dreze and Sen (1995), also neglect policies and investments that could prevent environmental destruction and yield large social pay-offs. Moreover, as Dasgupta (1993) and other authors have shown, the losses created by environmental degradation are disproportionately paid by the poor, whose income is often most dependent on natural resources. In other words, the inadequate supply of public goods essential to environmental sustainability combines with the under-provision of other public goods to worsen poverty and social inequity.

In this introductory chapter, we first briefly review recent developments in economic growth and the environment to provide a general context for the chapters that follow. We then move through a series of common themes developed from various perspectives in the chapters. These themes include governance and political economy, the under-supply of non-environmental public goods, international trade issues, fiscal and structural adjustments, and the under-supply in terms of quantity and quality of specific environmental goods. In the concluding section of this chapter, we draw together key overarching lessons not just to better understand environment and development linkages, but also to better manage such linkages at both micro sectoral and macro economy-wide levels.

Modern Growth Theory and the Environment

The literature on (endogenous) economic growth and the environment has shown that environmental sustainability can be consistent with sustained economic growth if certain conditions are met. Positive economic growth that is achieved along with environmental degradation may impose several costs to society: (i) the degradation of the environment directly affects the welfare or utility function of people, so that the welfare benefits of economic growth are at least in part undermined; (ii) in countries where growth itself is significantly dependent on natural resources, environmental degradation is likely to directly hurt economic growth at least over the medium run; (iii) for countries where growth is not directly resource-dependent, continuous economic growth may be feasible, at least over the short run, but the degradation of the environment may, in the long run, lead the economy to approach certain critical environmental thresholds, which would compromise the health and even the life of important segments of society; (iv) environmental degradation may involve serious social-equity effects, since the costs of environmental degradation are not evenly shared among groups in society. The poor may suffer an inordinate share of the negative consequences of environmental destruction, whereas the wealthy are likely to obtain most of the short-run benefits of such destruction.

Modern growth theory shows not only that environmental sustainability is potentially compatible with positive economic growth but also, and perhaps more importantly, that failure to achieve environmental sustainability may become an obstacle to sustained economic growth. That is, a lack of environmental sustainability may entail non-monetary costs to society—this is effect (i) above. It may also make growth infeasible in countries where the economy is highly dependent on natural resources—this is effect (ii). Moreover, even in countries that are not resource-dependent, a lack of environmental sustainability may, according to effect (iii), prevent further growth once the economies approach critical environmental thresholds. This means that, even for policymakers who only focus on GDP growth as a measure of economic success, environmental sustainability is a relevant goal, at least over the long run. In addition, there is mounting empirical evidence that (iv), the negative-social-equity effect, is a feature of a lack of environmental sustainability. Modern (sustainable) economic growth theory integrates the effects of environmental degradation on social welfare and utility, medium-run economic growth, and the risk of approaching environmental thresholds within an *optimal* dynamic framework by fully accounting for the trade-offs between them and the speed of long-run, or 'balanced,' economic growth. Growth theory is generally mute about the social equity effects of environmental degradation, since it mostly sticks to the representative–agent approach and thus assumes away any distributional consequences.

Growth theory has been used in the context of sustainable development in two ways: as a tool to improve our measures of economic growth and as a conceptual instrument to understand the feasibility of, and policies needed for, sustainable growth. The paper in this volume by Hamilton and Hassan (see Ch. 2) focuses on the measurement of economic growth. It encapsulates a number of the measurement issues and challenges that arise in addressing the above issues of utility and medium-run economic growth [(i) and (ii)]. The authors study how growth theory can be embedded in an extension of the standard national-income-accounting framework under the so-called weak sustainability hypothesis. Under weak sustainability, environmental and natural-resource

3

assets, or natural capital, can affect both production and utility, but there can also be trade-offs between these assets and other forms of capital. The theory admits the possibility of declining natural assets with sustainable income, at least for some period of time, provided there is offsetting capital accumulation in other parts of the economy's wealth portfolio. The net value of all changes of capital is referred to in this literature as 'genuine saving.' Negative per capita net saving must necessarily imply some eventual decline of per capita income over time.

A good empirical measure of genuine saving that includes environmental wealth, then, would serve as a valuable early warning indicator for an economy in decline. For the concept of genuine savings to be valid, however, environmental and man-made assets must be correctly valued. Each asset price must, in other words, reflect its true marginal contribution to welfare over time. Another way of stating this is that substitution between environmental and man-made assets cannot be linear. As environmental assets, for example, become scarcer relative to man-made assets, the shadow price of environmental assets should increase. Thus, any further substitution of natural capital needs a greater increase of man-made assets to compensate the welfare losses caused by environmental degradation. The second part of Chapter 2 by Hamilton and Hassan shows not only what has been accomplished in this arena, which is substantial, but also how much further we need to go to impute reliable values to changes in natural capital. As might be expected, the more qualitative or intangible the impact, the more difficult it is to value. We may have some success attributing values to soil loss, for example, but data and measurement problems make the valuation of pollution in national accounts difficult and biodiversity more difficult still.

Now we turn to the conditions required for sustainable growth. According to most growth models, the conditions for environmentally sustainable economic growth are strong even if we assume a benign and fully informed social planner that is able to fully internalize all environmental values. These are very special conditions not only in terms of what the social planner should do to regulate and steward the growth process towards sustainability but also in terms of assuming certain conditions about the representative agent's utility function and about the production technology that may be implausible (Aghion and Howitt, 1998).

Most growth models are extremely aggregative not only in terms of relying on a representative agent but also in their assumption of a single production sector and two or three inputs, including labor, capital, and the environment. To obtain sustainable growth, some models rely on exogenous technical change, which is simply assumed to allow ever-decreasing pollution to output intensity (Stokey, 1998). Other models allow for endogenous technical change. They assume that progressive tightening of environmental regulation, as income grows, stimulates pollution-saving technical change and, hence, decreases pollution intensities along the growth process (Bovenberg and Smulders, 1996). Still other models rely on a change of the input composition that increases the human capital (a 'clean' input) to physical capital (the 'dirty' input) ratio (Aghion and Howitt, 1998). Less-aggregative endogenous growth analyses, using two-sector models, find that structural change from commodity production towards production of services and from physical to knowledge inputs, in conjunction with investments in environmental and natural-resource protection, yield feasible sustainable economic growth (López, et al., 2004).

The assumption of a benign social planner who is able to internalize all environmental effects is obviously unrealistic. As noted by Smulders (2005), in a market economy—as opposed to the idealized optimal social planner case—the ability of endogenous innovation to support sustainable growth depends critically on the institutional backdrop. This backdrop can allow greater or lesser degrees of internalizing market failures, such as open access problems and pollution spillover effects. Also, endogenous innovation may in some cases increase the ability to exploit a scarcer resource (e.g. declining fish stocks) rather than serve as a way to reduce depletion.

Even under the unrealistic assumptions of full internalization of environmental effects and optimal institutions, there is another important condition for sustainable growth highlighted by all sustainable-growth models: the steady-state or 'balanced' rate of economic growth cannot exceed a certain *maximum* level. This maximum rate of growth in most analyses depends on society's discount rate, the elasticity of the marginal utility of consumption (the rate at which the marginal utility of consumption or income falls as income increases, often called the Frisch coefficient or coefficient of risk aversion in other contexts), and the elasticity of substitution in production between man-made capital and pollution. That is, regulation and investments in protecting the environment required by sustainable growth lead to an equilibrium (long-run) rate of economic growth. This rate is slower than it would be if the environmental 'problem' did not exist. Environmental sustainability requires partially sacrificing economic growth even under most optimistic assumptions, not only in the short run but also over the long run.

In the highly stylized world of growth models, sustainable growth thus may not be feasible if the conditions regarding production technology and the preferences of the representative agent are not satisfied. In this case, environmental sustainability would be 'technically' incompatible with positive long-run growth. If, however, these conditions are satisfied, then the planner is always wise enough to maximize welfare with environmental sustainability. Yet, it may be worthwhile to ask the following question: If we assume that the technology and preferences conditions are met, what potential errors on the part of the planner could conceivably lead to a failure to achieve environmental sustainability? This question is, in a sense, outside the realm of growth theory because it allows for the possibility that the social planner makes mistakes (or, alternatively, in the market interpretation of the model, that all markets do not exist or are not perfect). Nonetheless, this question could help guide a more empirically relevant analysis of sustainability.

Two possible mistakes of the planner may cause failure to achieve optimal (welfare-maximizing) sustainable growth. One, the planner shoots for too rapid a growth rate. That is, he or she invests too little in the mechanisms required to prevent continuous environmental degradation. The trade-off between economic growth and environmental sustainability is not optimally balanced and the result is an excessively high rate of growth over the short run in exchange for too much (vis-à-vis what is socially an optimum) environmental degradation. As a consequence of this imbalance, the economy fails to achieve its (environmentally constrained) maximum rate of welfare growth over the long run. Two, the planner may sacrifice too much growth for the sake of avoiding environmental degradation and thus forgo too much economic growth in the short run.

In the real world, however, economic growth is often sacrificed not for the sake of environmental sustainability, as postulated by optimal- or sustainable-growth theory, but for more prosaic reasons. Economic stagnation or semi-stagnation is almost always associated with government policy failures, including misallocation of public revenues, failure to correct market imperfections, and failure to promote the development of certain basic institutions and other public goods. Behind these policy failures, one does not typically find only ignorance or a lack of financial means and capacity building. Many policy 'mistakes' have political-economy roots as well.

But before discussing these political economy issues, it is important to emphasize that the diversion of economic growth to benefit economic elites or other special interest groups often makes environmental sustainability even harder to achieve. If income grows slowly, the demand for environmental services also expands slowly (the marginal utility of consumption decreases more slowly over time); the social discount rate may remain too high as a large segment of the population continues to live in poverty; and, most importantly, structural change (changes of the output and input composition towards cleaner outputs and inputs) is delayed.

When the potential for economic growth is wasted, there is a negative effect on most of the mechanisms that growth theory has taught us are important for achieving environmental sustainability. Moreover, in addition to exacerbating the sacrifice of environmental sustainability for growth in the short run, low growth rates entice policy-makers to misuse natural resources in a usually futile effort to expedite growth. Finally, for countries where the economy is highly dependent on natural resources, this scenario results in a further reduction in the rate of economic growth over the medium run. For economies that are not resource-dependent, this feedback effect may not happen until the health of the population is significantly impacted by environmental degradation. At this point, the full consequences of unsustainable economic growth are felt.

Thus, many slow-growing countries do not fit the mold assumed by neoclassical growth models: they are not really facing a trade-off between the rate of economic growth and the degree of environmental sustainability, as assumed by growth models. With the right policies and institutions, such countries could simultaneously achieve both faster economic growth and a better environmental performance, thus allowing for sustainable growth over the long run. Unfortunately, however, the win–win policies that may lead to such a desirable outcome are likely to hurt powerful economic interests that benefit from the current policies.

There are, however, at least a handful of important developing countries that more closely fit the neoclassical sustainable growth models, which consider the trade-off between the speed of economic growth and environmental sustainability. India and, most especially, China and Korea have been able to maintain extremely rapid rates of economic growth for a significant time period. Recent studies have documented the astounding destruction of the environment in China over the last decade.[2] It is indeed difficult to expect that a country growing at 9–10 percent per annum can do so while sustaining the environment. The largely autocratic regime in China apparently has accepted an extreme trade-off entailing very rapid economic growth and large environmental losses (though some localized environmental improvements have been realized). In this case, growth theory would most likely suggest that this is not an optimal strategy and that the welfare of the 'representative' Chinese citizen could be enhanced by a slower growth rate accompanied by less environmental degradation or even no net degradation over the long run.

Finally, we must examine the important question, for whom are policies optimal? Reliance on the representative agent implies that growth models simply ignore this crucial question. Here, distributional factors come into play, across both space and time (i.e. across generations as factors that determine policies and institutions that affect growth). The tension between sustainability, inter-generational distribution, and optimality is illustrated by a simple bio-economic model of optimal fishery exhaustion. Even though the resource base in this case is renewable, impatient and egoistic individuals today may prefer inter-generational unsustainable consumption paths.[3] The inter-generational issue may be regarded as a problem of choosing the right discount time rate in general and thus may not be inherently associated with optimal growth

---

[2] See, for example, Economy (2004) and Elvin (2004) for dramatic accounts of the massive increases of water and air pollution that are causing severe effects on the health of a large segment of the population and of the destruction of a large portion of rural ecosystems. Economy reveals that China's environmental protection agency has a staff of 300 to deal with environmental regulation, monitoring, and enforcement for the whole country of 1.2 billion people!

[3] For relatively recent compendia on these subjects see Pezzey and Toman (2002) and Simpson, Toman and Ayres (2005).

theory. But the issue of distribution within generations has not been tackled by growth theory; and constitutes one of its key remaining weaknesses.

Governance and Political Economy

Most chapters in this volume conclude that excessive natural-resource and environmental degradation is associated with institutional failures and market imperfections, both of which impede the full internalization of the true social value of the environment in economic decision-making. In addition, several chapters provide evidence suggesting that governments mostly exacerbate, rather than manage, such market and institutional imperfections: 'Rather than correcting market imperfections governmental intervention often aggravates them' (Bulte and Engel, p. 18).

A dramatic illustration of this phenomenon is provided by the so-called perverse subsidies, including energy subsidies, water subsidies, and credit and fiscal incentives for activities such as livestock and land conversion in forest areas. This is an issue discussed at length by Deacon and Mueller, López, and Strand in Chapters 4, 5, and 3 respectively. The conclusion is that, despite some reforms, notably in energy, these subsidies often continue to be massive and pervasive. In addition to their microeconomic efficiency costs and the environmental consequences of induced resource over-use, these subsidies have been, for the most part, counterproductive—even as instruments to accelerate aggregate economic growth or to spread its benefits. Their main effects have been to redistribute wealth in favor of the economic elites as well as to exacerbate environmental degradation. Large subsidies, according to several analyses, constitute a heavy fiscal burden (on average, they have absorbed about 25 percent of total government revenues in non-OECD countries), crowding out the supply of many important public goods from the fiscal budget.[4] Thus, subsidies may not only cause economic inefficiency and greater resource degradation but also greater social inequity.

It would be naive to assume that these subsidies persist merely because of policy-makers' lack of information and lack of clear understanding about their deleterious effects. By now, the long-run effects of subsidies are more or less known, given the significant dissemination (even through mass media) of evaluative studies. It would, however, also be an exaggeration to blame the subsidies' permanence entirely on corruption and political contribution patterns

---

[4] Alternatively, subsidies may be financed through higher taxes instead of through lowering the provision of public goods. The efficiency costs of higher taxes are well known, but the social-equity effects of taxation are also often undesirable because of the high degree of tax evasion and the great reliance on indirect taxes in developing countries, which make them socially regressive (World Bank, 2004). In reality, non-social subsidies are financed through a combination of both lower investment in public goods and higher taxes.

that permit the economically powerful, the greatest beneficiaries of the subsidies, to 'buy' public subsidies. After all, very diverse countries around the world, some of them with sophisticated and highly democratic political regimes and with seemingly low indexes of corruption, have these subsidies in place.

There can also be an *ideological bias* among policy-makers and politicians, which is partly due to factors that do not exactly correspond to the level of corruption and bribery: policy-makers are under significant pressure to attain 'good' economic performance, as measured over a short time period by conventional national account indicators. The fate of current policymakers and politicians once they abandon office does not depend so much on decreases in pollution or deforestation as on increases in GDP, declines in unemployment, and the corporate friendly nature of a given administration. The ability of former policymakers and politicians to obtain lucrative positions in the private sector and in international organizations, as well as to command profitable lecture fees and other significant benefits, are likely to be a potent incentive for politicians and policymakers to promote policies which are heavily biased in favor of economic elites. In the short run, such policies contribute to sustaining employment levels and boosting GDP as measured by conventional national accounts, however, the absence of an accepted system of 'genuine' national accounts is certainly a factor that conspires to preserve this ideological bias. As Hamilton and Rashid suggest in this volume (see Ch.2), we are still far from the time when genuine accounts can be widely accepted and used.

Under-supply of Non-Environmental Public Goods

The insufficient supply of non-environmental public goods in most developing countries is thoroughly documented by the literature (The World Bank, 2004; Dreze and Sen, 1995; Baland and Kotwal, 1998). Among the many *public goods* that most governments under-provide, the development of property-right institutions is one that is emphasized by several chapters in this volume. At issue are a lack of recognition and a lack of enforcement of informal property rights of the poor, especially in rural areas, which sometimes makes such property rights vulnerable to external challenges from big commercial interests and often leads to expropriation or 'enclosure' of the poor. These issues are discussed by Barbier and López in Chapters 1 and 5 of this volume. In addition, unlike the enclosures in Western Europe more than two centuries ago, the property-right issue in today's developing countries is often not solved through expropriation. The beneficiaries of these usurpations rarely obtain legal rights, and are often simply content to mine the resources—especially during commodity booms. Even if these beneficiaries do obtain legal rights, the newly acquired rights are often not secure, in part because of the illegitimate means used to obtain them.[5] The lack of development and subsequent enforcement of property rights is also a cause of massive illegal extraction of natural resources, including expensive woods and rare animal and plant species.

Another important non-environmental public good that appears to be heavily under-supplied is human capital. The literature systematically reports extremely high and persistent rates of return over time for investments in education, R&D, and other forms of human capital and knowledge-enhancing investments. The under-investment in human capital may significantly affect the potential for environmental sustainability. As discussed earlier, structural change is one of the most important vehicles for environmental sustainability. The slow investment in human capital and related knowledge assets delays structural change. The reason is that clean inputs mainly consist of such assets, while production of clean outputs is generally knowledge and human-capital intensive. Thus, if environmental sustainability is to be achieved, it needs to rely much more on instruments that are blunt, costly, and politically difficult to implement, such as regulation and taxation instead of structural change. The net result is that such instruments are rarely implemented to the extent needed; thus, the chances for environmental sustainability are considerably diminished.

The under-supply of human capital also worsens poverty, since the poor are the most affected by the insufficient public support of human capital formation. The poor are affected not only by the insufficient provision of public goods but also by the *composition of the public goods* provided by governments, which is generally biased against them. For example, the emphasis on tertiary education in many countries subtracts from the already limited budgets such countries have to invest in primary and secondary education, the component that is most beneficial to the poor. In addition, the composition of public goods tends to prioritize large physical infrastructure (roads, dams, etc.) to the detriment of social public goods, such as welfare and social-security services. Thus, governments not only under-provide public goods, but they often bias this low supply toward physical infrastructure and against human and social public goods. Recent studies have shown that countries with autocratic and corrupt governments tend to supply fewer public goods. Additionally, the composition of available public goods in these countries is biased in favor of large infrastructure projects (Deacon, 2002).[6]

The consequence of such priorities is that poverty is more widespread and deeper than it would otherwise be. Barbier, in this volume, and several

[5] The challenges through occupation and other means faced by many owners of lands that were originally usurped from native communities in Latin America (Deacon and Mueller, Ch. 4 Alston et al., 1999) are an interesting illustration of the fragility of property rights when they are acquired through illegitimate means.

[6] It may also be, as Sterner and Somanathan's paper (Ch. 7) and others in the volume indicate, that in the environmental and resource sphere an additional problem is one of supplying the wrong kinds of infrastructure.

other studies have shown that poverty worsens the degradation of certain environmental resources such as forests, particularly in heavily populated countries. Governments frequently use development policies at the extensive margin, through colonization–settlement projects (often poorly conceived and poorly funded) into remote frontier areas, as ways to relieve the political pressures of the poor in already settled areas. That is, frontier expansion in land-rich countries plays the role of anti-poverty policy, substituting for social programs. However, as Barbier shows, frontier expansion has rarely contributed to economic development and has even more rarely led to significant poverty reduction. It has, however, contributed quite massively to deforestation, habitat loss for many species, and other environmental losses.

International Capital Mobility and Trade Issues

Apart from the obvious effects of corruption and apart from the less obvious ideological biases that motivate politicians, there are also international developments that may play an important role in promoting such environmentally perverse subsidies. Competition among countries and even among states within countries to attract *foreign capital* can be another important motivating factor for such subsidies. The studies reviewed by Copeland and Gulati in Chapter 6 show that the pollution-haven hypothesis is not empirically supported. However, many countries try to persuade multinational corporations to establish operations in their countries by giving away natural resources for free and by providing other subsidies and tax exemptions (see Chapter 5 by López, in this volume, and Oman, 2000). Although empirical evidence suggests that subsidies to attract foreign investment are very large in certain countries (Calmon, 2004; Oman, 2000), there are no studies showing that these subsidies have indeed played an important role in affecting the location of foreign investment. But there is increasing empirical evidence demonstrating that the fiscal costs of these apparently futile efforts to attract foreign investment ('race to the bottom') are significant.

Has *trade openness* worsened the tendency to waste scarce fiscal resources and natural resources through subsidies? According to Copeland and Gulati in Chapter 6, trade openness has not played an important role in countries that do not already have comparative advantages in activities that are natural-resource intensive. For such countries, a weak domestic environmental policy, although contributing to increased pollution in general, has not been a decisive factor in attracting 'dirty' industries. The authors point out however, that emerging empirical evidence suggests that countries that are natural resource-intensive exporters with weak domestic institutions are vulnerable to increased natural capital degradation from trade liberalization. In these countries, trade liberalization may also lead to increased pressures on policy-makers to 'liberalize' corporate access to natural resources and to increase the 'incentives' (e.g. subsidies) for corporations to become more competitive in world commodity markets.

The size of perverse subsidies appears to be even larger among natural resource-abundant countries, the countries affected by the so-called resource curse. As Deacon and Mueller point out in Chapter 4, evidence suggests that natural resource abundance is associated with poor governance and poor institutions. In turn, earlier works by Deacon (2002), as well as by others, have shown that poor governance, lack of democracy, and lack of participation of civil society increase the tendencies of governments to under-provide public goods and to waste public revenues in non-social subsidies (including perverse ones), which are mostly directed to the economic elites.

Copeland and Gulati (Ch. 6) do not explicitly deal with *trade in services*. A relatively recent development has been the promotion of free trade in services, especially between North and South. A fundamental consequence of the liberalization of service sectors is the freeing of the service sectors from limitations on foreign ownership. This usually occurs after privatization of service sectors that were previously in public hands. Once foreign ownership is established, the foreign investment agreements are often governed by GATTS rules as established by WTO or by more ad hoc Regional or Bilateral Free Trade Agreements (Mann, 2004). The overwhelming aim of these rules is to protect foreign investment against policy changes that were not foreseen at the time the investment took place. Moreover, complaints from foreign investors are mainly subject to international arbitral decisions, not to appeal in any national court of law. Mann (2004) points out that 'it is questionable whether such arbitration tribunals would apply human rights and environmental laws when considering the scope of a state's rights and obligations' (p. 14).

The consequences for host countries that decide to change some of their policies are becoming increasingly more serious. Argentina is facing lawsuits for $16 billion (6% of its annual GDP) from several foreign firms in reaction to state policy changes—mainly the exchange rate devaluation that took place in 2002, which may have affected the firms' profits (Solano, 2004). Other countries, including Mexico, Chile, and Nicaragua, are facing similar legal challenges, though perhaps none so costly as those faced by Argentina (Mann, 2004; Solano, 2004). Some countries have had to turn back important environmental regulation because foreign firms have threatened to bring their cases to international arbitration. Governments face obvious losses when forced to divert money from social and environmental programs to pay compensation to foreign investors. The tight grip of foreign capital may significantly restrict the scope of countries to implement reforms that reduce subsidies and change policies. This factor may militate against sustainable development.[7]

The failure of the international community to develop mechanisms to compensate developing countries for *global services*, such as retention of carbon and other climate-changing gases, and for services related to biodiversity preservation is another important international factor that worsens the chances of environmental sustainability. The rich countries, presumably because of their high income, are more able than developing countries to value and to afford paying for such services (Albers and Ferraro, see Ch. 12). Yet the international institutions that could make the development of trade in environmental services possible are, at best, at an incipient state of development. As Albers and Ferraro point out, the failure to develop adequate international trade mechanisms (in environmental services) is related not only to failures at the international negotiation level, but also to property-rights imperfections and government failures in developing countries. Successful trade in environmental services needs the assurance of compliance with international contracts, which can only be guaranteed if domestic institutions that assign responsibility for contract enforcement are in place.

Fiscal and Structural Adjustments

In addition to openness to trade and capital inflows, another important international influence affecting developing countries is the policy role played by international organizations such as the World Bank and the IMF. On the one hand, fiscal adjustment (monetary and fiscal policies to induce macroeconomic stability and to correct for internal and external disequilibria) has been a main mechanism used by the IMF to influence short-run policies. On the other hand, structural adjustment (trade, factor market, and financial liberalization, privatization, and others) has been a key vehicle to influence long-run policies by the World Bank and associated international institutions. Despite that the policy agenda promoted by international organizations is hardly concerned about environmental sustainability—or, perhaps, because of this fact—this agenda has significantly affected the environmental consequences of economic growth, as López argues in this volume. The demands from the IMF for the reduction of fiscal deficits have generally been met through the further

---

[7] The case of NAFTA and the current US Model Bilateral Investment Treaty are particularly worrisome. NAFTA and other US bilateral free-trade pacts use a top-down approach, where foreign investment in all sectors is considered covered by the investment protection agreement unless specific exclusions are negotiated. This may be particularly risky to poorer countries, which have little capacity to negotiate exclusions. The result is that poorer countries are exposed to great losses if their policies need to be changed.

reduction of the supply of public goods, including the supply of environmental public goods, which worsens environmental distortions. In addition, structural adjustments gave only scant technical and financial support to the development of environmental institutions and regulation.[8]

At the same time, international institutions, mainly through structural adjustment, demanded that developing countries integrate themselves into world commodity and financial markets very rapidly. As economic openness increased, so too did the need to develop measures to prevent the significant market and institutional imperfections that affect the environment from undermining, or even negating, the gains from globalization (Copeland and Gulati, Ch. 6). Thus, precisely when environmental institutions and regulation were most needed, structural and fiscal adjustments further discouraged such endeavors.

The narrowness of the international financial institutions' policy agenda has been the greatest setback to sustainable development. There has been a strong preoccupation with preventing governments from interfering with markets. The removal of government-induced market distortions in some cases was a single-minded objective. This narrow approach does not address distortions that result from market imperfections and from government-induced distortions through mechanisms other than market intervention. The public sector expenditure allocation, which encompasses subsidies to the rich and the under-supply of public goods, is among the often overlooked non-market distortions. As long as the subsidies are provided through mechanisms that are not openly distorting markets, they have often not been a matter of concern to fiscal and structural adjustments. Massive financial grants, land gifts, and natural resource transfers given for free, as well as special tax exemptions, are usually enjoyed by rich individuals and corporations. Financial bail-outs of unregulated banks and other financial institutions are rarely mentioned as a concern in the structural-adjustment reports.[9] It is now clear that fiscal tightening coupled with the protection of expenditures on non-social subsidies is bound to cause an even graver under-supply of public goods, including environmental protection, human capital, and social anti-poverty programs. Such policies drastically affect the potential for sustainable development.

---

[8] For his part, Strand notes that the direct impacts of a domestic economic crisis will depend on its nature; for example, a drop in a commodity export price could lead to less extraction, unless the state itself raises extraction rates to compensate for lost revenue. However, the indirect effects resulting from a general drop in incomes could be as serious as any direct effects; for example, more intensive land exploitation with a return to subsistence agriculture or state efforts to enhance competitiveness through relaxed controls on resource use and environmental degradation.

[9] The case of the recent bailout of one bank and its few but highly influential customers by the government of Dominican Republic is an important illustration. The almost $2 billion spent by the government in this endeavor (more than 25% of the country's GDP) practically ruined the country and triggered a massive economic recession in 2003. International financial institutions, often ready to advise against market interference by governments, were conspicuously complacent about this particular interference.

Under-supply of Natural Resource and Environmental Goods

A number of the chapters are consistent with the hypothesis of under-investment in natural capital advanced above. They identify several investments that improve natural and environmental resources management and exhibit high social rates of return. Nevertheless, these investments are not implemented. Investments in water supply, watershed protection, soil conservation, and in other environmental resources of national or domestic value have large rates of return, yet governments often attach relatively low priorities to their realization. Given the theory of international public goods and international agreements for their protection (e.g. Barrett, 2003), resources of global value, such as biodiversity conservation and carbon retention services are, not unexpectedly, of even lower priority. In addition to domestic institutional failures, inadequacies of international institutions largely prevent the compensation of developing countries for the provision of such services, and, consequently, this international institutional failure becomes an important additional source of environmental distortion.

The chapters by Dinar and Saleth and by Barnes and Toman (Chs 9 and 8 respectively) address the problem of chronic under-supply of water and energy in many developing countries. Both of these resources figure prominently in the Millennium Development Goals, which is not a coincidence given their important influence on economic growth and social development. The *quality* of water is also of obvious importance and is addressed in Chapter 10 by Markandya. Both the Dinar-Saleth and Barnes-Toman chapters focus on issues identified in previous chapters. Problems of resource availability just as often reflect difficulties in the provision of adequate and appropriate delivery infrastructure as they do basic problems of material scarcity. However, countries with limited water, or the need to import large quantities of expensive energy, face additional challenges.

Infrastructure problems in turn reflect a variety of market and institutional distortions. Government agencies that provide these services usually have little incentive to be efficient or provide reliable services, and may be biased toward larger but less cost-effective investments. Private provision of infrastructure may in turn be impeded by government regulations that limit entry or distort investment choices. Both public and private provisions face problems related to the political economy of these services, especially the desire to hold down prices in an effort to benefit the poor. Revenue shortfalls can undermine the financial, and therefore the economic, sustainability of the services and can drain funds badly needed to remedy poorly targeted subsidies in the public budget.

In their analysis of energy and, in particular, electricity-service provision, Barnes and Toman (Ch. 8) advance two arguments. First, increased availability of modern energy services is an important driver of social and economic development. Secondly, greater attention to the social value of increased energy availability and to the cost of service provision is needed in overall energy policy and planning. Flexibility in the ways these services are provided is also needed. In many cases, smaller-scale systems, especially renewable-based systems, are the best practical option though theoretically, such systems are less technically efficient than larger scale, grid-based electricity (which may take years to arrive). These systems can be combined with targeted subsidies of fixed capital and connection costs to benefit the poor without creating the costly and distorting effects of usage subsidies.

Dinar and Saleth (Ch. 9) address similar issues in their analysis of water-resources provision, though, given the long and difficult history of water allocation in all societies, their conclusions are somewhat different. They note that although the standard economic prescription of more efficient water tariffs and of greater involvement of the private sector is conceptually sound and has been effective in improving water allocation, in practice, this advice has been taken relatively infrequently. Their diagnosis of the problem echoes themes of political economy, property rights, and endogenous institutional constraints identified in previous chapters. Specifically, they argue that institutional transactions costs and idiosyncratic linkages of water reforms to other issues (e.g. public debt, crises in agriculture or electricity sectors) influence the practical capacity to implement standard economic prescriptions for efficient pricing. Reforms, they conclude, must be designed to incorporate these endogenous constraints and the political interests of powerful interest groups.

The chapters by Albers and Ferraro (Ch. 12) and Bulte and Engel (Ch. 13) consider natural and environmental resources, such as forest landscapes and, more generally, terrestrial protected areas. These resources provide multiple potential benefits and involve substantial quality as well as quantity components. Bulte and Engel summarize the many causes of deforestation, from the direct effects of weak property-rights regimes and rent-seeking to the induced effects of increased returns to agriculture in land clearing or incentives to mine forests for cash flow in the face of debt problems. The resulting social costs of such excessive tropical deforestation range from reduced yields of timber and non-timber forest products to reduced benefits of a variety of ecosystem services, such as erosion control and carbon sequestration. It is perhaps surprising, however, that the *marginal* value of these losses is in some cases relatively low—not large enough *per se* to trump economic gains from forest clearing.

Bulte and Engel's chapter (Ch. 13), and the chapter by Albers and Ferraro (Ch. 12) on protected-areas management emphasize two additional critical points. First, there is a large degree of uncertainty surrounding efforts to economically value the ecosystem services in question. Moreover, there needs to be a way to realize the value of protecting these ecosystems as a way of reducing the risk of adverse economic and social impacts, even if the expected values of conservation or protection benefits seem a bit low. A corollary observation is the essential need for more primary research on the valuation of local and national benefits of ecosystem services in developing countries and of the global benefits of services like biodiversity and carbon sequestration. Albers and Ferraro sketch some promising directions for such work, drawing on recent developments in spatial economic analysis as well as interdisciplinary assessments of ecosystem functions.

The second critical point is the need to undertake practical measures for conservation and protection that reflect the incentives and institutional conditions present. Both chapters describe sometimes quixotically hopeful efforts to engineer increased protection as an indirect co-product of ostensibly sustainable local land- and resource-development programs. Often, such efforts deliver neither the desired protection outcomes, due to indirect and weak incentives, nor the local benefits of sustainable resource development. Two other alternatives explored in the chapters involve direct financial transfers for protection (e.g. compensation for foregoing access to sensitive areas) or direct local participation in reaping financial rewards of conservation (e.g. local participation and benefit sharing in game protection for ecotourism). In principle, these approaches should have stronger, more direct incentive effects. In practice, institutional weaknesses in monitoring and enforcing conservation requirements and outcomes can undermine these activities by means of 'paper parks' or other forms of encroachment and opportunistic rent seeking. Once again, a key issue in designing effective policies is the recognition that institutions matter and that their performance is endogenous to the economic rewards and costs present.

The same problem arises in connection with activities to reduce net-greenhouse gas emissions by limiting fossil fuel combustion and changes in land cover. Neither the Convention on Biodiversity nor the Framework Convention on Climate Change currently offers solid mechanisms for monetizing and rewarding the global value of efforts in developing countries to produce these global public goods. The beginnings of such mechanisms are evident under the Kyoto Protocol to the Framework Climate Convention through the adoption by industrialized ('Annex B') countries of limits on greenhouse-gas emissions and through the ability of developing countries to earn revenues by producing 'carbon emission reduction credits' (CERs). But this mechanism remains weakened by uncertainties about developed country commitments to their Kyoto targets and by uncertainties about negotiations of future targets. This lowers the economic reward to sustainable energy and land management beyond the softness of nominal emission targets under Kyoto and beyond any domestic obstacles to more environmentally sustainable management.[10]

That there are weaknesses in international commitments to produce global public goods is not surprising since, theoretically, we know such agreements

---

[10] Despite criticism by many environmentalists on this point, it is not necessarily bad.

have a tendency to be weak and fraught with free riding. It is also not surprising from a political economy perspective that the developed world would decry unsustainable resource management in the developing world while also participating or acquiescing in weak international commitments themselves. Two facts remain: first, there are win–win opportunities for jointly deriving local/national and international benefits from more sustainable management. Secondly, given richer countries' greater ability to pay and the need for developing countries to focus on raising living standards without undermining natural capital, greater success in the production of international environmental public goods still depends on the leadership—not just piety—of richer countries in bearing the burdens.

The last three chapters emphasize the valuation and management of environmental goods that have a strong quality dimension, in particular clean air and water. The chapter by Sterner and Somanathan (Ch. 7) embeds this discussion in a larger context by noting first that although some of the needs of the poor in developing countries are similar to those for residents of richer countries—such as clean air and water to protect human health—other needs of the developing country poor are more distinctive. For example, the developing country poor need access to, and the protection of, basic land fertility. This contrasts with the pursuit by richer countries of environmental recreational opportunities. Sterner and Somanathan use examples to suggest that the variety of institutional and political economy problems already identified above—including a concentration of political power that masks social preferences and causes a misallocation of social investment as well as more conventional concerns with corruption—need to be addressed through the construction of effective environmental policies in developing countries. Additionally, they argue that in designing environmental protection instruments, the tools used must reflect the institutional capacities for design, monitoring, and enforcement. The role of market-based instruments may be more circumscribed. For example, even though these instruments can be very cost-effective, broader market distortions or lack of effective monitoring may impede the operation of economic incentives.[11]

The chapter by Markandya (see Ch. 10) takes up one of the central challenges of the Millennium Development Goals: the provision of clean water for human use and, more generally, the treatment of waterborne effluents to protect both water sources for human use and inland aquatic ecosystems. Markandya summarizes both the compelling health evidence in support of safe water provisions and ecological protection. The economic valuation of

---

[11] In comparing incentive-based instruments to alternatives such as traditional technology or performance standards, it is important to avoid comparing the actual with the ideal. It is well known that incentive-based instruments are not a substitute for effective environmental laws, effectively implemented. However, lack of monitoring or enforcement capacity will undercut the effectiveness of the more traditional instruments as well.

these resources is at the cutting edge of environmental valuation research and practice.

The conclusions of the chapter may be somewhat surprising. The MDGs call for halving (by 2015) the number of people without access to safe drinking water and for reducing significantly those without access to modern sanitation. Assuming a 50 percent cut in those without access to sanitation as well, Markandya concludes that available evidence on benefits and costs supports these twin objectives. However, the achievement of the sanitation goal is several-fold more expensive than the achievement of safe water access, which may be accomplished in several ways without necessarily resorting to greatly expanded sanitation investments.[12] When one looks separately at the two objectives of safe water and sanitation, the economic case for water is much stronger than for sanitation. Subject to the caveat that in some cases sanitation may indeed be the best or even the only way to ensure safe local water supply (along with investments to increase the safety of the water delivery system), this finding is of considerable relevance for decision-makers in developing countries that must set priorities in the use of very scarce investment resources.

Markandya also underscores that the limited evidence available suggests that poor as well as rich households have a willingness to pay well above current water prices for safe water. The price is sufficient to provide a financial base for enhancing household water quality, especially if poorer households receive well-targeted subsidies for connection in lieu of more poorly targeted consumption subsidies from richer to poorer users. This indicates once again that the challenge is political and institutional (e.g. are people willing to pay without more assurance that existing municipal authorities will actually deliver the goods?) rather than a matter of costs-versus-benefits.

The economic evidence on the value of cleaning up water bodies for other uses is even more limited and equivocal. Looking at a number of case studies, Markandya concludes that, although river basin clean-up may be a priority in many environmental agendas, the overall economic benefits (including all amenity and other values) may not be sufficient to justify the costs. This holds true unless the water body has special cultural significance, or it is very costly to turn to other sources. Water bodies with significant biodiversity potential also generate global public benefits, but, as already noted, the capturing of these benefits in payment streams to those who would incur the costs of clean-up remains somewhat elusive.

Many similar issues arise in the assessment by Krupnick, in Chapter 11 who discusses the health effects from urban (outdoor) air pollution and options for

---

[12] Safe water could be provided by tapping more remote clean sources that are protected through an upstream-integrated-river-basin management plan. Moreover, investment in ensuring that the delivery system is not subject to contamination, without necessarily investing in greatly expanded downstream municipal-household effluent treatment, will also provide safe water.

ameliorating these impacts.[13] Drawing on similar sources of information in linking pollution to health and in evaluating the health impacts, Krupnick notes that, from an economic perspective, it is important to set priorities and target policies. Fine particulates from various sources have been implicated as a much more serious health threat than some other pollutants, causing, for example, chronic lung disease and other illness as well as premature death. Airborne lead from gasoline also has been implicated as a serious health problem, and, although this threat has been abated in many countries, it still lingers notably in Africa. These problems, although smaller in the aggregate than the health problems associated with water contamination, are significant enough in the overall hierarchy of threats to human health in developing countries to warrant serious policy attention.

After establishing these points, Krupnick reviews recent policy attempts to ameliorate urban airborne pollutants. The examples he gives echo the point made by Sterner and Somanathan (Ch. 7) about the need to craft policy to fit circumstances. Krupnick provides a variety of examples, especially in Asia, of the potential for the use of incentive-based instruments for pollution control. In some cases, these instruments may be less direct and therefore less efficient than a direct attack on a pollutant—for example, a fuel tax in lieu of a direct measure for controlling diesel-based particulates. Nevertheless, even indirect incentive-based policies may offer opportunities to improve on the performance of more command-and-control-based measures.

Concluding Comments

In these final comments, we would like to try to highlight four cross-cutting messages that we believe are especially important for decision-makers seeking to strengthen environmental policies individually and the environmental sustainability of economic growth generally. The first point is the need to broaden the discussion of environmental sustainability. Contrary to what many believe, environmental sustainability is not achieved merely through environmental policy or even through optimal environmental policy. Optimal environmental policy in the context of economy-wide policies that consistently discriminate against the poor and that under-provide non-environmental public goods, such as human capital, would amount to pressing the brake and the accelerator at the same time. Such policy would assure neither sustained nor environmentally sustainable economic growth. We need not only to see the environment as an important value, for which the evidence is compelling, but also to address the interactions between

[13] Indoor air pollution, mainly from smoky fuels in poor households, also is a serious health concern. This problem is addressed in the energy chapter by Barnes and Toman (see Ch. 8).

under-provision of environmental and non-environmental economy-wide policies. This calls for a more holistic and integrated approach to policy in which some of the most important actions in support of environmental values may focus on, for example, financial markets or human capital. At the same time, the contributions of good environmental policy to sustainable development must be addressed.

The second point is the pervasiveness of the political economy challenges resulting from weak or opaque property rights in many spheres. By this we mean not just the problems directly plaguing governance of environmental resources, but also the problems citizens face in exerting a collective demand for less corruption, more efficient and fair taxation. Having noted the problem, we are left somewhat humbled by the chapters in this volume regarding proposed solutions. In some cases, the authors have indicated that innovative solutions involving different strategies of decentralization and public participation can be effective. But in other instances, such solutions are ineffective; solutions must be based on solid evidence of promise, not on quixotic wishes.

Our third point is that, although expanded trade may sometimes exacerbate the lack of environmental sustainability, there is, at this time, no broad and deep evidence that international trade itself has become an obstacle for environmental sustainability. Though trade liberalization is often analyzed separately from the liberalization of capital flows, it is clear that liberalizing trade of services is closely linked to foreign investment expansion. While foreign investment has at times contributed to economic growth, increasing evidence points to the emergence of biased legal international institutions that limit independent policy-making and environmental regulation by the states. The effects of domestic fiscal and structural adjustment programs, on the other hand, seem more worrisome, though here again, the empirical record is not entirely clear. It is clear, however, that fiscal and structural adjustment programs have previously missed an opportunity to help address many of the key issues that have contributed to slow long-run growth, inadequate social equity, and environmental degradation in a large number of developing countries.

The fourth and last point we wish to underscore is a corollary of the first three: there is a desperate need for more and better empirical work on environment and development issues and on policies in developing countries. There is also a need for international economic institutions to broaden their policy advice and act in favor of a more balanced political economy. Such steps would induce governments to give a greater weight to the needs of the poor and to environmental sustainability in their policy agendas. At the global level, a need exists for greater balance in the role of international institutions so that emerging global arrangements take the interests of the developing countries more seriously.

References

Aghion, P. and P. Howitt (1998), *Endogenous Growth Theory*. MIT Press, Cambridge.

Alston, L. Lbecap, G. and B. Mueller (1999), *Titles, conflicts and land use: The development of property rights and land reform on the Brazilian Amazon frontier*. The University of Michigan Press, Ann Arbor.

Barrett, S. (2003), *Environment and Statecraft: The Strategy of Environmental Treaty-Making*. Oxford University Press, Oxford.

Bovenberg, A. and S. Smulders (1996), 'Transitional Impacts of Environmental Policy in an endogenous growth model', *International Economic Review*, 37 (4): 861–93.

Calmon, P. (2004), 'Notes on subsidy evaluation in Brazil', Unpublished the World Bank, Washington, DC.

Dasgupta, P. (1993), *An Inquiry into well-being and destitution*. Oxford University Press, New York.

Deacon, R. (2002), 'Dictatorship, Democracy, and the provision of public goods'. Unpublished, Department of Economics, University of California, San Diego.

Dreze, J. and A. Sen (1995), *India: Economic opportunity and social change*. Oxford University Press, Oxford.

Economy, E. (2004), *The river runs black: The environmental challenge to China's future*. Cornell University Press, New York.

Elvin, M. (2004), *The retreat of the elephants: an environmental history of China*. Yale University Press, New Haven, CT.

López, R., G. Anriquez, and S. Gulati (2004), 'Sustainability with unbalanced growth: The role of structural change'. Unpublished, University of Maryland at College Park.

Mann, H. (2004), 'International Economic Law: Water for Money's Sake?'. Paper presented at the First Latin American Seminar on Water Policies, Brasilia (September 22–25).

Oman, C. (2000), 'Policy Competition for Foreign Direct investment.' OECD Development Centre, Paris.

Pezzey, J. C. V. and Toman A. (eds) (2002), *The Economics of Sustainability*, International Library of Environmental Economics and Policy.

Simpson, R. D., M. A. Toman, and R. U. Ayres (eds), 'Scarcity and Growth Revisited: Natural Resources and the Environment in the New Millennium' Resources for the Future, 2005.

Smulders, Sjak. (2005). *Endogenous Technical Change, Natural Resources, and Growth*, In R. David Simpson, M. Toman, and R. Ayers (eds) *Scarcity and Growth Revisited*, Washington, DC, Resources for the Future.

Solano, M. (2004), ' Contratos y Acuerdos Internacionales de Inversión'. Paper presented at the First Latin American Seminar on Water Policies, Brasilia (September 22–25).

Stokey, N. (1998), 'Are there limits to growth?', *International Economic Review*, 39 (1):1–31.

United Nations Development Programme (2003), *Millennium Development Goals: A Compact Among Nations to End Human Poverty*. Human Development Report 2003. New York: Oxford University Press for UNDP.

World Bank (2000). *The Quality of Growth*. The World Bank and Oxford University Press.

—— (2004), *Inequality in Latin America: Breaking with history?*, The World Bank, Washington DC.

1

Natural Capital, Resource Dependency, and Poverty in Developing Countries: The Problem of 'Dualism within Dualism'

Edward B. Barbier

Introduction

The purpose of this chapter is to explore the problem of resource degradation and poverty in developing countries. As this is a potentially huge topic—over 1 billion people in the world live on less than $1 per day and most are dependent on some form of resource use—any meaningful analysis of the linkage between resource degradation and poverty must be organized around a consistent theme. In this chapter, the theme is 'dualism within dualism'. That is, there are currently two types of 'dualism' in patterns of resource use within developing countries that are very much relevant to the problem of resource degradation and poverty.[1]

The first 'dualism' concerns aggregate resource use and dependency within the global economy. Most low- and middle-income economies are highly dependent on the exploitation of natural resources. For many of these economies, primary product exports account for the vast majority of their export earnings, and one or two primary commodities make up the bulk of exports. Moreover, recent evidence suggests that increasing economic dependence on natural resources is negatively correlated with economic

---

[1] It should be noted that, given the topic of resource degradation and poverty, the focus of the proposed chapter will be on natural resource use and economic development in present-day low- and middle-income countries in Africa, Asia, and Latin America. Many themes explored in this chapter are addressed in fuller detail in a book by the author on natural resources and economic development (Barbier, 2005b).

performance. The implications for low-income countries is that the 'take off' into sustained and structurally balanced economic growth and development is still some time away, and thus the dependence of their overall economies on natural resources will persist over the medium and long term.

The second 'dualism' concerns aggregate resource use and dependency within a developing economy. A substantial proportion of the population in low- and middle-income countries is concentrated in marginal areas and on ecologically 'fragile' land, such as converted forest frontier areas, poor quality uplands, converted wetlands and so forth. Households on these lands not only face problems of land degradation and low productivity but also tend to be some of the poorest in the world. Although most studies of resource degradation and poverty tend to focus on the problems posed by the second type of dualism, a major innovation of the proposed chapter is to show how this dualism is linked to the first. Hence, the sub-title of the chapter is 'Dualism within Dualism'.

Specifically, the chapter seeks to demonstrate the following processes. First, most low- and middle-income economies are highly dependent on the exploitation of their natural resource endowments for commercial, export-oriented economic activities. Secondly, the major investors in export-oriented resource-based economic activities, whether in commercial agriculture, mining, timber-extraction or other activities, tend to be relatively wealthier households. These households generally have education and skilled labor advantages that allow them to attain higher income levels, accumulated wealth available for investment, and the collateral for, and access to, formal credit markets for financial loans. Thirdly, the process of resource exploitation in resource-dependent developing economies tends to involve the following 'cumulative causation' cycle.

Development in low- and middle-income economies is accompanied by substantial resource conversion. In particular, expansion of the agricultural land base in these economies is occurring rapidly through conversion of forests, wetlands and other natural habitat. In addition, many developing regions of the world are also placing greater stress on their freshwater resources as a result of increasing population and demand. Although it is commonly believed that poor rural households are mainly responsible for much of this resource conversion, what is often overlooked is that inequalities in wealth between rural households also have an important impact on resource degradation processes. Moreover, such problems are exacerbated by government policies that favor wealthier households in markets for key resources, such as land.

The consequence is that resource-dependency of developing economies is usually accompanied by excessive resource conversion, and the benefits of this conversion are inequitably distributed. That is, the abundance of land

and natural resources available in many developing countries does not necessarily mean that exploitation of this natural wealth will lead either to sustained economic growth, widespread benefits, or substantial rural poverty alleviation. The increased concentration of the rural poor in marginal land and resource areas continues, and this in turn will generate the conditions for additional resource conversion through a process called 'frontier resource expansion'.

This chapter explores this 'dualism within dualism' link between resource degradation and poverty in developing countries in the following way. The first section examines four key structural features, or 'stylized facts', of natural resource use underlying the two types of dualism in developing economies. The subsequent section elaborates on how resource exploitation in resource-dependent developing economies produces these 'dualism within dualism' characteristics. The fourth section focuses on the economy-wide implications of this pattern of resource use: increased frontier resource expansion and conversion, disappointing economic performance and persistent, widespread rural poverty. The final section examines the potential role of policies in reversing this 'cumulative causation' cycle.

Natural Capital and Developing Economies: Four 'Stylized Facts'

Economists now recognize that, along with physical and human capital, the natural and environmental resource endowment of a country should be viewed as an important economic asset, which can be called natural capital. Moreover, it is also accepted that management of this 'natural capital' stock is critical to the country's ability to attain sustainable economic development. This is particularly relevant to low- and middle-income, or 'developing', countries, many of which have abundant stocks of environmental and natural resources that they must exploit efficiently and sustainably if these economies are to develop successfully (Barbier, 2003).

In order to determine whether present-day developing economies are exploiting successfully their natural capital stocks to achieve sustainable development, it is useful to examine some of the key patterns of natural resource use in these economies. Such an examination reveals four key structural features, or 'stylized facts', of natural resource use in these economies.

Stylized Fact One: The Majority of Low- and Middle-Income Countries have Resource-Dependent Economies

Most low- and middle-income economies today are highly dependent on the exploitation of their natural resource endowments for commercial, export-oriented economic activities. For these economies, primary product exports—and often one or two main commodities—account for nearly all export earnings.

Appendix 1 depicts the export concentration in primary commodities for 95 low- and middle-income economies.[2] As indicated in the appendix, 72 of the countries—more than three-quarters—have 50 percent or more of their exports from primary products, and 35 countries—more than a third—have an export concentration in primary commodities of 90 percent or more.[3]

Appendix 1 also indicates the share in total exports of the two main primary commodities for each country. For those low- and middle-income countries with an export concentration in primary products of 50 percent or more, two commodities account for most of these exports and for a large share, if not the majority, of total exports. On average, for countries with a primary product export share of 50 percent or more, the two main commodities accounted for about 60 percent of total exports. For those countries with a primary product export share between 10–50 percent, the two main primary commodities still account for over 25 percent of total exports.

Although since the 1960s, some low- and middle-income countries have reduced their resource-dependency, there are important regional differences. Figure 1.1 shows the average regional changes from 1965 to 1990/99 in primary product export concentration for Sub-Saharan Africa, North Africa and the Middle East, Latin America and the Caribbean, and Asia and Oceania. In 1965 low- and middle-income economies in all four regions had on average 85–92 percent of their exports based on primary commodities, but regional trends have varied considerably over the next 30 years. In the 1990s, African countries still remained highly dependent on primary product exports (85%), and North African and Middle Eastern countries also maintained high resource dependence (73%). Latin American and Caribbean economies reduced their

---

[2] As indicated in Appendix 1, the designation of 'low- and middle-income countries' in Africa, Latin America, Asia and Oceania, is based on the World Bank's definition. The World Bank lists a total of 142 such countries in these regions. However, many of the countries not included in Appendix 1 are small island states and nations (e.g. Antigua and Barbuda, Gaza Strip, Cook Islands, Kiribati) or countries for which export data are not readily available (Democratic Peoples Republic of Korea). The 95 economies listed in the table have GDP per capita in 1994 at 1987 constant purchase power parity US dollars of less than $10,500 with an average of $2,691 and a median of $1,604.

[3] For all the low- and middle-income countries depicted in Appendix 1 for which the data are available (88 countries), the average export share of GDP is 31.4%. For those countries with a primary product share of 50% or more, the export share of GDP is 29.6%. As the importance of exports across low- and middle-income economies is fairly stable across these countries, around 30% of GDP, this suggests that the percentage share of primary products to total exports is a fairly good indicator of the degree of resource dependency of these economies. In fact, the importance of exports increases slightly with the degree of resource dependency. For economies with an export concentration in primary products of 70% or more, the export share of GDP is 30.7%; for those countries with a primary product export concentration of 90% or more, the export share rises to 34.6%.

26

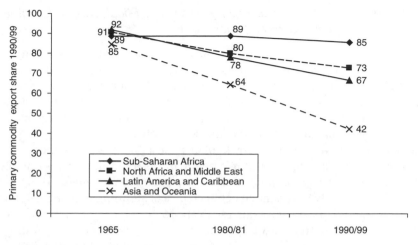

Figure 1.1 Regional trends in resource dependency
Source: See Appendix 1.

primary commodity export share much more, but still have a relatively high export share (67%). Only in Asia and Oceania has resource-dependency fallen dramatically over the 30-year period, to less than half of all exports (42%).

The World Bank has attempted to measure recently the extent to which the overall 'wealth' of an economy consists of natural capital. For low- and middle-income countries dependent on export revenues from primary commodities (other than petroleum), 20 percent of their national wealth comprises natural capital (World Bank 1997). These economies are typically located in the Caribbean, East and Southern Africa, the Middle East, South Asia and West Africa. As a comparison, natural capital accounts for only 5 percent of wealth for developed economies in North America, and 2 percent for developed economies in the Pacific and Western Europe. The most important source of natural capital in resource-dependent low- and middle-income countries is agricultural land, especially for economies without substantial petroleum reserves. For example, in the poorest countries, agricultural cropland comprises around 80 percent of the natural capital.[4]

---

[4] Although the vast majority of the low- and middle-income countries listed in Appendix 1 can be considered resource dependent, in terms of 50% or more of their exports are primary products, the latter countries do not contain the majority of the developing world's population. For example, the total population estimate (in 1999 or nearest year) for 94 of the countries listed in Appendix 1 is just under 4.52 billion, whereas the population in resource-dependent economies totals around 1.33 billion (30% of the total). That is because five of the most populous developing countries, China, India, Brazil, Pakistan and Bangladesh, in the world cannot be classified as resource-dependent as each has less than 50% of the exports from primary products.

27

Stylized Fact Two: Resource-dependency in Low- and Middle-Income Countries is Associated with Poor Economic Performance

Low- and middle-income countries tend to be dependent on their natural resource endowments for economic growth and development because in poor economies natural capital may be the only source of capital readily available to them. Moreover, many countries are fortunate to have abundant natural resources to exploit, although as we have just seen, the most likely form of natural capital available to the poorest countries is likely to be land.

Given the importance of natural capital to sustainable development, one might conclude that greater resource abundance should improve economic performance. That is, economies that have a greater endowment of natural resources must surely have a much better chance of attaining higher economic growth rates and prosperity than relatively resource-poor economies. This must be particularly true with respect to low- and middle-income countries, whose economies are generally more dependent on exploiting their natural capital stock in the transition to developing industrial and service sectors and the 'take off' into higher and more balanced rates of long-run growth.

As we shall discuss further below, it has been difficult to determine from the empirical evidence whether greater resource abundance, in terms of a larger natural resource endowment or stocks, is associated with lower long-run growth in developing economies. However, recent evidence does provide some evidence that resource-dependency may be associated with poorer economic performance.[5] For example, many low- and middle-income economies that can be classified as highly resource-dependent today in terms of primary product export share, as shown in Appendix 1, also currently display low or stagnant growth rates (Barbier, 1999). Cross-country analysis has confirmed that countries with a high ratio of natural resource exports to GDP have tended to grow less rapidly than countries that are relatively resource poor (Sachs and Warner, 1997; Rodríguez and Sachs, 1999). Economies with a high primary product export share of GDP in 1971 also tended to have low growth rates during the subsequent period 1971–89 (Sachs and Warner, 1995). This finding

[5] Recent claims of a 'resource curse' hypothesis, i.e. that resource-abundant economies grow less fast than resource-poor ones, are based largely on empirical estimations by Jeffrey Sachs and colleagues. However, these authors use primary products exports as a percentage of GDP as the measure of a country's 'resource abundance'. Strictly speaking, such a variable cannot be a true indicator of 'resource abundance' *per se*, as it is not a measure of the total resource endowment or stocks of a country. Instead, throughout this chapter, indicators such as primary products exports as a percentage of GDP or of total exports will be referred to as measures of a country's *resource dependency*, as in Appendix 1 and subsequent figures, as these indicators are really a measure of the degree to which an economy is dependent on natural resource-based exports. Hence, the second stylized fact is stated in terms of the correlation between resource dependency, and not abundance, with poor economic performance in low- and middle-income countries.

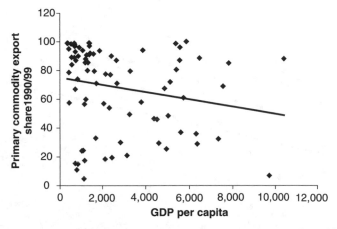

Figure 1.2 Resource dependency and GDP per capita in low- and middle-income economies

Notes: Primary commodity export share is the average export share 1990/99 for low- and middle-income countries in Appendix 1. GDP per capita in 1994 at 1987 constant purchase power parity $, from World Bank Development Indicators. Correlation coefficient, $r = -0.205$. Number of observations = 82.

is confirmed for the 1970–90 period, even when direct controls for the influence of geography, climate and growth in the previous decade are included (Sachs and Warner, 2001). There is also evidence that low- and middle-income economies that are more resource-dependent tend to have lower levels of GDP per capita. Figure 1.2 indicates this relationship. The average export share of primary commodities in the total exports of low- and middle-income countries over 1990/99 appears to be negatively correlated with the real GDP per capita of these countries in 1994.[6]

Finally, low- and middle-income economies that are more resource-dependent tend to have higher poverty levels. Figure 1.3 illustrates this association. Resource-dependency appears to be positively correlated with the proportion of the population living in poverty.

[6] As indicated, the relationship depicted in Figure 1.2 is for the low- and middle-income developing economies listed in Appendix 1 and for the 1990s. Rodríguez and Sachs (1999) appear to obtain the contradictory finding that GDP per capita is positively associated with 'resource abundance'. However, the latter relationship is established by regressing the log of GDP per capita in 1970 on exports of natural resources, in percent of GDP, also in 1970. Clearly, the results of Rodríguez and Sachs are for a different era, just before the oil and commodity price boom of the 1970s and early 1980s. In addition, as the authors indicate, their data set includes predominantly mineral and energy exporting countries, and countries other than the low- and middle-income economies listed in Appendix 1.

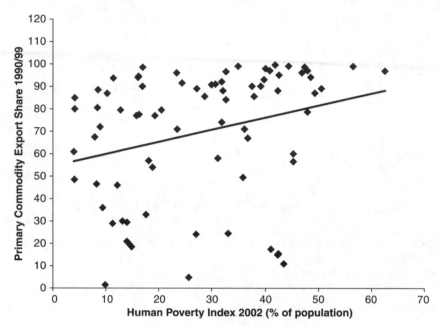

Figure 1.3 Resource dependency and poverty in low- and middle-income economies

Notes: Primary commodity export share is the average export share 1990/99 for low- and middle-income countries in Appendix 1. Human Poverty Index 2002 from the United Nations Development Program, *Human Development Report 2002*. Correlation coefficient, $r = 0.275$. Number of observations = 77.

Stylized Fact Three: Development in Low- and Middle-Income Economies is Associated with Increased Land Conversion and Stress on Available Freshwater Resources

As noted above, in developing economies, especially those without oil and natural gas reserves, the most important source of natural wealth is agricultural land. In these economies, expansion of this agricultural land base is occurring rapidly through conversion of forests, wetlands and other natural habitat. In addition, many developing regions of the world are also placing greater stress on their freshwater resources as a result of increasing population and demand. This trend for greater land and water use appears to be occurring in all low- and middle-income countries, regardless of their resource-dependency or economic performance.

López (1998) identifies most of Sub-Saharan Africa, parts of Asia and the tropical forests of South America as regions with 'abundant land' and open-access resource conditions that are prone to agricultural expansion. Widespread land and resource conversion is also occurring in Central America, parts of

Mexico and tropical South America and some East and South-East Asian countries, mainly due to the high degree of integration of rural areas with the national and international economy as well as population pressures. Agricultural land expansion in many tropical regions is also spurred by the prevailing structural conditions in the agricultural sectors of many developing countries, such as low irrigation and fertilizer use as well as poor crop yields (FAO, 1997).

A study by the Food and Agricultural Organization (FAO, 1995) indicates the long-run dependence of developing countries on agricultural land expansion for crop production. Over 1970–90 increased harvested area accounted for 31 percent of the additional crop production in these countries, and over 1990–2010 this contribution is expected to rise to 34 percent. However, some of the increase in harvested area is likely to come from cropping intensity (i.e. multi-cropping and multiple harvests on the same land area). Although improvements in cropping intensity and yields are expected to reduce the developing world's dependency on agricultural land expansion over 1990–2010, about 19 percent of the contribution to total crop production increases in poorer economies are likely to be derived from expansion of cultivated land. Cropland expansion is expected to be particularly prevalent in Sub-Saharan Africa, East Asia (excluding China) and Latin America (including the Caribbean).

Fischer and Heilig (1997) combined the results of the FAO (1995) study with recent UN population projections to estimate the demand for additional cultivated land in developing countries in 2050. Their results suggest that all developing countries are expected to increase their demand for cultivated cropland considerably, leading to extensive conversion of forests and wetlands. Throughout the developing world, cultivated land area is expected to increase by over 47 percent by 2050, with about 66 percent of the new land coming from deforestation and wetland conversion. Recent hydrological projections of the world's freshwater resources have pointed to an emerging global threat, the dwindling supply of freshwater relative to the growing demand for water worldwide (Falkenmark et al., 1998; Revenga et al., 2000; Rosegrant et al., 2002; Vörösmarty et al., 2000). According to various scenarios, water scarcity is expected to grow dramatically in some regions as competition for water increases between agricultural, urban and commercial sectors. The cause of this global water crisis is largely the result of population growth and economic development rather than on global climate change (Vörösmarty et al., 2000). The problem is expected to be particularly severe in low- and middle-income countries, especially in selected river basins within those countries (Rosegrant et al., 2002).[7]

---

[7] Hydrologists distinguish two concepts of water use: water withdrawal and water consumption (Gleick, 2000: 41). Withdrawal refers to water removed or extracted from a freshwater

A study by Rosengrant et al. (2002) provides global projections over 1995 to 2025 for total water withdrawal and the share of withdrawal to renewable water supply.[8] Already, developing countries account for 71 percent of global water withdrawal. Water demand in these countries is expected to grow by 27 percent over 1995 to 2025. The ratio of water withdrawals to total freshwater resources per year is often referred to as relative water demand or the water 'criticality ratio'. Hydrologists typically consider criticality ratios for a country or a region between 0.2 and 0.4 to indicate medium-to-high water stress, whereas values greater than 0.4 reflect conditions of severe water limitation (Cosgrove and Rijsberman, 2000; Vörösmarty et al., 2000). Although criticality ratios are projected to remain low across all developing countries, there are important regional exceptions. By 2025 Asia is expected to show signs of medium to high stress (see Rosengrant et al., 2002). West Asia/North Africa is currently facing severe water limitation, and this problem is expected to reach critical levels by 2025.

As shown in the Rosegrant et al. (2002) study, the problem of water stress and scarcity is likely to be worse for key developing countries and regions. The two most populous countries of the world, China and India, together account for around 35 percent of global water withdrawal. Both countries are already displaying medium-to-high water stress, which is expected to worsen by 2025. However, the problem is worse still for specific river basin regions within these two countries. Some of these river basins have, or will have, in coming years criticality ratios exceeding 100 percent, suggesting chronic problems of extreme water scarcity.[9] Other countries facing worsening water stress and scarcity include Pakistan, the Philippines, South Korea, Mexico, Egypt, and virtually all other countries in West Asia and North Africa.

Increasing land conversion and stress on freshwater resources in developing countries may be symptomatic of a more general correlation between environmental deterioration and growth in these economies. A World Bank

---

source and used for human purposes (i.e. industrial, agricultural or domestic water use). However, some water withdrawal may be returned to the original source, albeit with changes in the quality and quantity of the water. In contrast, consumptive use is water withdrawn from a source and actually consumed or lost to seepage, contamination, or a 'sink' where it cannot economically be reused. Thus water consumption is the proportion of water withdrawal that is 'irretrievably lost' after human use. For example, in 1995 total global freshwater withdrawals amounted to 3,800 km^3, of which 2,100 km^3 was consumed.

[8] These reported projections correspond to the 'business as usual' baseline scenario in Rosegrant et al. (2002).

[9] According to Rosegrant et al. (2002, Table B.3), by 2025 the Huaihe, Haihe, Huanghe, and Inland Regions in China will display criticality ratios higher than 100%, whereas in India the Cauvery Region will have a criticality ratio of 91% and the India-Coastal-Drain and the Mahi-Tapti-Narmadi Regions will have criticality ratios well over 100%.

study noted that GDP growth and higher incomes in developing economies are associated with better sanitation and improved water supply, as well as investments in cleaner technologies (Thomas et al., 2000). However, the same study tested for a correlation between growth and an overall environmental quality change index (EQI) across developing countries, where the EQI was constructed by attaching equal weights to changes in indicators of water quality, air quality and deforestation. For 56 developing economies, the study found a statistically significant negative correlation ($r = -0.27$) between EQI and growth rates over 1981–98. Countries with higher growth rates displayed deteriorating overall environmental quality.[10]

Stylized Fact Four: A Significant Share of the Population in Low- and Middle-Income Economies is Concentrated on Fragile Lands.

Between the years 2000 and 2030, the world's population is expected to increase by more than a third, from 6.06 billion to 8.27 billion (Population Division of the United Nations, 2001). Virtually all of this population growth will occur in the less developed regions, and mainly in urban areas. Rural populations are expected to fall in more developed regions over 2000–2030, from 0.29 billion to 0.21 billion. Only a modest rise in rural populations will occur in less developed regions over the same period, from 2.90 billion to 3.08 billion.

However, these aggregate trends in world population obscure two important facts concerning rural populations in developing countries. First, rural population growth is much higher for those low- and middle-income economies that are more resource-dependent, and secondly, a large share of the rural populations in these economies are concentrated on poor, or 'fragile', lands.

Figure 1.4 illustrates that rural population growth rates are positively correlated with the degree of resource-dependency in low- and middle-income economies. The trend line in the figure indicates that, on average, rural populations are expanding at 1 percent per year in developing economies that have a primary commodity export share of 70 percent or higher. In contrast, for those economies with a primary product export share of 25 percent or less, rural populations are stagnant or even declining.

The World Bank has launched a major study of the concentration of rural populations in developing economies on 'fragile lands', which they define as 'areas that present significant constraints for intensive agriculture and where the people's links to the land are critical for the sustainability of communities,

---

[10] Controlling for per capita income in 1981 also yielded a correlation coefficient of -0.27 that was significantly significant at the 95% confidence level.

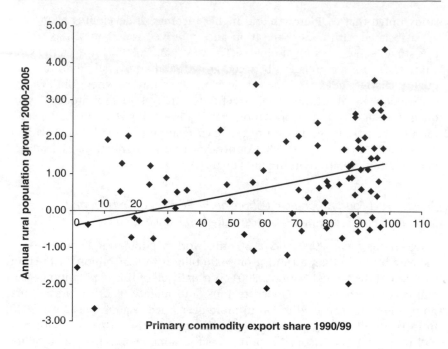

Figure 1.4 Resource dependency and rural population growth in low- and middle-income economies

Notes: Primary commodity export share is the average export share 1990/99 for low- and middle-income countries in Appendix 1. Annual rural population growth 2000–2005 from Population Division of the United Nations Secretariat, World Urbanization Prospects: The 2001 Revision. Correlation coefficient, $r = 0.465$. Number of observations = 94.

pastures, forests, and other natural resources' (Word Bank, 2003, p. 59). The main findings of the study are:

- Since 1950, the estimated population on fragile lands in developing economies has doubled.
- Currently one-quarter of the people in developing countries—almost 1.3 billion—survive on fragile lands. More than 1.2 billion people on fragile lands are in the developing regions of Latin America, Africa, and Asia.
- The developing country populations on fragile lands include 518 million living in arid regions with no access to irrigation systems, 430 million on soils unsuitable for agriculture, 216 million on land with steep slopes and more than 130 million in fragile forest systems.
- These populations living on fragile land in developing countries account for many of the people in extreme poverty, living on less than $1 per day.

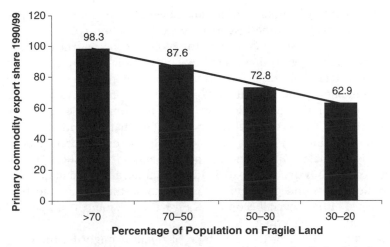

Figure 1.5 Resource dependency and share of population on fragile lands in low- and middle-income economies

Notes: Primary commodity export share is the average export share 1990/99 for low- and middle-income countries in Appendix 1. Share of population on fragile land is from World Bank, *World Development Report 2003*, Table 4.3. Fragile land is defined in the report as 'areas that present significant constraints for intensive agriculture and where the people's links to the land are critical for the sustainability of communities, pastures, forests, and other natural resources' (p. 59). Number of observations = 72, of which 2 (>70%), 8 (70–50%), 33 (30–50%) and 29 (20–30%).

The World Bank study also identified specific developing countries with significant shares of their populations on fragile lands, that is, from 20–30 percent of their population, to 30–50 percent, to 50–70 percent to over 70 percent (World Bank, 2003, Table 4.3). Seventy-two low- and middle-income economies from Appendix 1 can be grouped into these four categories.

The results are indicated in Figure 1.5, which shows that resource-dependent low- and middle-income economies contain large concentrations of their populations on fragile lands. Moreover, greater resource-dependency is associated with a larger percentage of population on fragile land. For example, as the concentration of populations on fragile lands in low- and middle-income economies increases from 20–30 percent to 30–50 percent to 50–70 percent to over 70 percent, the average share of primary products in exports rises from 62.9 percent to 72.8 percent to 87.6 percent to 98.3 percent, respectively.

The 'Dualism within Dualism' Pattern of Resource Use

Together, the four 'stylized facts' suggest that there are currently two types of 'dualism' in patterns of resource use within developing countries that are very much relevant to the problem of resource degradation and poverty. The first 'dualism' is revealed by the first two stylized facts, and concerns aggregate resource use and dependency within the global economy. For example, the first stylized fact suggests that most low- and middle-income economies are highly dependent on the exploitation of natural resources. For many of these economies, primary product exports account for the vast majority of their export earnings, and one or two primary commodities make up the bulk of exports. The second stylized fact suggests that currently, for developing countries, increasing economic dependence on natural resources is negatively correlated with economic performance. The implications for low income countries is that the 'take off' into sustained and structurally balanced economic growth and development is still some time away, and thus the dependence of their overall economies on natural resources will persist over the medium and long term.

Thus, one indicator of this first type of dualism might be the degree of resource-dependency of an economy, as measured by the share of primary commodities in total exports. For instance, an economy with a primary product export share of 50 percent or more would be considered highly resource-dependent and more susceptible to this first type of dualism.

The second 'dualism' is revealed by the last two stylized facts, and concerns aggregate resource use and dependency within a developing economy. The third stylized fact suggests that economic development in low-income countries is associated with high rates of land conversion and degradation as well as increased stress on available freshwater resources. However, the fourth stylized fact suggests that many poor people in rural areas may not necessarily be benefiting from this increased resource use. Instead, a substantial proportion of the population in low- and middle-income countries is concentrated in marginal areas and on ecologically 'fragile' land, such as converted forest frontier areas, poor quality uplands, converted wetlands and so forth. Households on these lands not only face problems of land degradation and low productivity but also tend to be some of the poorest in the world.

Two indicators of this second type of dualism might be the share of the total population concentrated on fragile lands, as defined by the World Bank (2003: 59) and discussed above (p. 35), and the share of the rural population living under conditions of absolute poverty. Combining these two indicators gives us an approximate benchmark, or '20–20 rule', for the degree of rural poverty-resource use dualism within a developing economy: a country with 20 percent or more of its population concentrated on fragile land and 20 percent or more of its rural population living in rural poverty shows evidence of the second type of dualism.

Table 1.1 combines the above two sets of indicators to show the extent of 'dualism within dualism' for 72 low- and middle-income economies. The countries are grouped in terms of their degree of resource-dependency, as

Table 1.1 Selective countries displaying 'Dualism within Dualism' characteristics

	Share of Population on Fragile Land ≥ 50%	Share of Population on Fragile Land 30–50%	Share of Population on Fragile Land 20–30%
Primary Product Export Share ≥90%	Burkina Faso (61.2) Chad (67.0) Congo Dem. Rep. (NA) Laos (53.0) Mali (72.8) Niger (66.0) Papua New Guinea (NA) Somalia (NA) Sudan (NA) Yemen A.R. (19.2)	Algeria (30.3) Angola (NA) Benin (33.0) Botswana (NA) Cameroon (32.4) Comoros (NA) Eq. Guinea (NA) Ethiopia (31.3) Gambia (64.0) Guyana (NA) Iran (NA) Mauritania (57.0) Nigeria (36.4) Rwanda (51.2) Uganda (55.0)	Ecuador (47.0) Congo, Rep. (NA) Liberia (NA) Zambia (88.0)
Primary Product Export Share 50–90%	Egypt (23.3) Zimbabwe (31.0)	Central Af. Rep. (66.6) Chad (67.0) Guatemala (71.9) Guinea (40.0) Kenya (46.4) Morocco (27.2) Senegal (40.4) Sierra Leone (76.0) Syria (NA) Tanzania (51.1)	Bolivia (79.1) Burundi (36.2) Côte d'Ivoire (32.3) El Salvador (55.7) Ghana (34.3) Guinea-Bissau (48.7) Honduras (51.0) Indonesia (15.7) Madagascar (77.0) Mozambique (37.9) Myanmar (NA) Panama (64.9) Peru (64.7) Togo (32.3) Trinidad & Tobago (20.0)
Primary Product Export Share <50%		Costa Rica (25.5) Haiti (66.0) Lesotho (53.9) Nepal (44.0) Pakistan (36.9) South Africa (11.5) Tunisia (21.6)	China (4.6) Dominican Rep. (29.8) India (36.7) Jamaica (33.9) Jordan (15.0) Malaysia (15.5) Mexico (10.1) Sri Lanka (20.0) Vietnam (57.2)

Notes: Primary commodity export share is the average export share 1990/99 for low- and middle-income countries in Appendix 1. Share of population on fragile land is from World Bank, *World Development Report 2003*, Table 4.3. Figure in parenthesis is the percentage of the rural population below the national poverty line, from World Bank, 2002 World Development Indicators.

measured by the share of primary products in total exports, and the extent to which their populations are concentrated on fragile land. The figure in the parentheses by each country also indicates the percentage of the rural population below the national poverty line. According to the table, 56 out of the 72 economies have a primary product export share of 50 percent or more, and therefore display evidence of the first type of 'dualism', that is, resource-dependency within the global economy. All the economies have 20 percent or more of their population on fragile land and all but seven also have 20 percent or more of the rural population living in absolute poverty. Thus by the '20–20 rule', virtually all the economies listed in Table 1.1 show signs of the second type of dualism, that is, a high incidence of rural poverty-resource degradation linkage within the economy. What is more striking is that, with the exception of the Yemen Arab Republic and Indonesia, all 56 highly resource-dependent countries also satisfy the '20–20 rule'.[11] That is, three-quarters of the countries listed in Table 1.1 show considerable evidence of 'dualism-within-dualism' characteristics.

Of the 16 countries that do not show strong signs of the first type of dualism, that is, they have a primary product export share of less than 50 percent, many of the countries nevertheless show a high degree of the second type of dualism. For example, Haiti, Lesotho, Nepal and Pakistan have 30–50 percent of their populations on fragile land and display an incidence of rural poverty of 30–70 percent. The Dominican Republic, India, Jamaica, and Vietnam have 20–30 percent of their populations living in fragile areas and around 30–60 percent of their rural populations in poverty. Only China and Mexico, and to a lesser extent Jordan and Malaysia, do not conform very strongly to the second type of dualism, according to the '20–20 rule' for population concentrated on fragile land and the degree of rural poverty.

In sum, the 'dualism within dualism' characteristics of most developing countries suggest that the process of resource-based development undertaken by these economies is not yielding widespread benefits. Agricultural land expansion, and natural resource exploitation by primary sector activities more generally, appears to be a fundamental feature of economic development in many of today's poorer economies. Yet, as we have seen, many developing economies have a large concentration of their populations on fragile land and high incidence of rural poverty. Also, developing countries that are highly dependent on exploiting their natural resource endowments tend to exhibit a relatively poor growth performance. This poses an intriguing paradox. Why is it that, despite the importance of natural capital for sustainable economic development, increasing economic dependence on natural resource exploitation appears to be a hindrance to growth and development in today's low- and middle-income economies?

Conventional explanations suggest that the comparatively poor growth performance of low-income countries can be attributed to failed policies and weak institutions, including the lack of well-defined property rights, insecurity

---

[11] In fact, with over 50% of its population in fragile areas and with a rural poverty incidence of 19.2%, Yemen shows distinct signs of the second type of dualism. Indonesia is also not far off from satisfying the '20–20 rule', given that the country has over 20% of its population on fragile land and 15.7% of its rural population in absolute poverty.

of contracts, corruption and general social instability (Pack, 1994; World Bank, 1992). More recent explanations have focused on the *resource curse hypothesis*, that is, the poor potential for resource-based development in inducing the economy-wide innovation necessary to sustain growth in a small open economy, particularly under the 'Dutch disease' effects of resource-price booms (Matsuyama 1992; Sachs and Warner, 1995). Other theories have suggested an *open access exploitation hypothesis*, that is, opening up trade for a developing economy dependent on open access resource exploitation may actually reduce welfare in that economy (Brander and Taylor, 1997 and 1998).

While elements of these conventional explanations are relevant to explaining the paradox, the rest of this chapter develops an alternative explanation as to why current efforts of resource-based development are not more successful for low- and middle-income economies.

Resource-Based Development and Frontier Expansion

Once again, an important clue to unravelling the paradox of the poor economic performance of today's resource-based developing countries can be found in the four 'stylized' facts of natural resource use in these economies. For example, the first three stylized facts suggest that developing countries today are embarking on a pattern of resource-dependent development that culminates in frontier resource exploitation, particularly in the form of agricultural land expansion and chronic stress on freshwater resources, but the end results do not yield much in the way of sustained economic progress. In fact, stylized fact four indicates the 'symptoms' of malaise associated with frontier land expansion and resource-based development today. In many developing economies, a significant proportion of extremely poor households are concentrated on fragile lands, and both rural population growth and the share of population on fragile lands seem to increase with the degree of resource-dependency of a developing economy. That is, frontier land expansion appears to be serving mainly as an outlet for the rural poor in many developing countries.

But why should frontier land expansion be associated with 'unsustainable' resource-based development in many low- and middle-income countries today? Historically, this has not always been the case. For instance, finding 'new frontiers,' or 'reserves,' of natural resources to exploit became the basis of much of global economic development for the past 500 years (Cipolla, 1976; di Tella, 1982; Findlay and Lundahl, 1994; Webb, 1964). Such frontier-based economic development can be characterized by a pattern of capital investment, technological innovation and social and economic institutions dependent on 'opening up' new frontiers of natural resources once existing ones have been 'closed' and exhausted (di Tella 1982; Findlay and Lundahl 1994). Particularly noteworthy is the period 1870 to 1913, which is often dubbed the 'Golden Age' of resource-based development, because so many resource-dependent economies with unexploited 'frontier' natural resources benefited from exporting primary products to the 'industrial' core of the booming world economy (Findlay and Lundahl, 1999; Green and Urqhart, 1976; Taylor and Williamson, 1994; Schedvin, 1990). This was also the era of rapid migration of settlers and inflows of foreign capital into the 'Great Frontier' regions identified by Webb (1964): temperate North and South America, Australia, New Zealand, and South Africa. The economies of these regions therefore also expanded as a consequence of the world economic boom. Finally, a number of primary-producing 'developing' or 'periphery' regions, also experienced considerable growth as a consequence of growing world demand for raw materials and food. These included not only temperate Argentina but also a number of tropical countries that exported cash and food crops to the rest of the world.[12]

In addition, it has been argued that the origins of rapid industrial and economic expansion in the U.S. over 1879–1940 were strongly linked to the exploitation of abundant non-reproducible natural resources, particularly energy and mineral resources (Romer, 1996; Wright, 1990). Other examples of successful mineral-based development have been cited for today's economies (Davis, 1995; Wright and Czelusta, 2002). In the developing world, most prominent have been the mineral-led booms in the 1990s in Peru, Brazil, and Chile, although Davis (1995) identifies up to 22 mineral-based developing economies who appear to have fared comparatively well compared to other developing countries.

Recent reviews of successful resource-based development, both past and present, have pointed to a number of key features critical to that success (David and Wright 1997; Wright and Czelusta, 2002). First, the given natural resource

---

[12] Findlay and Lundahl (1994 and 1999) suggest that five types of developing economies benefited from resource-based growth over 1870–1914: regions of recent settlement (Argentina), plantation-based tropical economies (Brazil), peasant-based tropical economies (Burma, Siam, Gold Coast), 'mixed' peasant and plantation-based economies (Colombia, Costa Rica, Ceylon, and Malaya), and finally, mineral-based economies (Bolivia, Chile, South Africa). As suggested by Findlay and Lundahl, the economic development in these four types of economies conform largely to the 'staples thesis', which has argued that the development of many countries and regions has been led by the expansion of export sectors, and in particular, natural resource exports, and the 'vent for surplus' theory, which suggested that trade was the means by which idle resources, and in particular natural resources in poor countries, were brought into productive use (Chambers and Gordon, 1966; Myint, 1958; Smith, 1976; Southey, 1978; Watkins, 1963). A common theme in both the staples and vent for surplus is the existence of excess resources—'land' and 'natural resources'—that are not being fully exploited by a closed economy. The function of international trade is to allow these new sources of natural resources that previously had no economic value to be exploited, for increased exports and growth. Thus, as both the staples and vent for surplus theses have been mainly concerned with 'surplus' natural resources as the basis for the origin of trade and export-led growth, it is not surprising that both theories derived their inspiration from the Golden Age of Resource-Based Development.

endowment of a country must be continuously expanded through a process of *country-specific knowledge in the resource extraction sector*. As argued by Wright and Czelusta (2002: 29 and 31): 'From the standpoint of development policy, a crucial aspect of the process is the role of country-specific knowledge. Although the deep scientific bases for progress are undoubtedly global, it is in the nature of geology that location-specific knowledge continues to be important... the experience of the 1970s stands in marked contrast to the 1990s, when mineral production steadily expanded primarily as a result of purposeful exploration and ongoing advances in the technologies of search, extraction, refining, and utilization; in other words by a process of learning.'

Secondly, there must be *strong linkages between the resource and other, more dynamic economic sectors* (i.e. manufacturing). 'Not only was the USA the world's leading mineral economy in the very historical period during which the country became the world leader in manufacturing (roughly from 1890 to 1910); but linkages and complementarities to the resource sector were vital in the broader story of American economic success.... Nearly all major U.S.-manufactured goods were closely linked to the resource economy in one way or another: petroleum products, primary copper, meat packing and poultry, steel works and rolling mills, coal mining, vegetable oils, grain mill products, sawmill products, and so on' (Wright and Czelusta, 2002: 3–5).

Thirdly, there must be *substantial knowledge spillovers* arising from the extraction and industrial use of resources in the economy. For example, David and Wright (1997) suggest that the rise of the American minerals economy can be attributed to the infrastructure of public scientific knowledge, mining education and the 'ethos of exploration'. This in turn created knowledge spillovers across firms and 'the components of successful modern-regimes of knowledge-based economic growth. In essential respects, the minerals economy was an integral part of the emerging knowledge-based economy of the twentieth century .... increasing returns were manifest at the national level, with important consequences for American industrialization and world economic leadership' (David and Wright, 1997: 240–1).[13]

However, there are two important caveats attached to the above conditions for successful resource-based development. First, all of the past and present examples of development with the above three features are clearly based largely on minerals-based development (David and Wright, 1997; Wright and Czelusta, 2002). There is little evidence to date that a small open economy dependent on frontier agricultural land expansion is likely to foster the above conditions for successful resource-based development. In fact, there is some

[13] Wright and Czelusta (2002: 17) cite the specific example of the development of the U.S. petrochemical industry to illustrate the economic importance of knowledge spillovers: 'Progress in petrochemicals is an example of new technology built on resource-based heritage. It may also be considered a return to scale at the industry level, because the search for by-products was an outgrowth of the vast American enterprise of petroleum refining.'

evidence that agricultural-based development based on land expansion may be negatively correlated with economic growth and development (Barbier, 2003 and 2004; Stijns, 2001).

Secondly, the existence of policy and market failures in the resource sector, such as rent-seeking behavior and corruption or open-access resource exploitation, will mitigate against successful resource-based development. Unfortunately, it is well documented that resource sectors in many developing countries are prone to problems of rent-seeking and corruption, thus ensuring that natural resource assets, including land, are not being managed efficiently or sustainably (Ascher, 1999; Tornell and Lane, 2001; Torvik, 2002).[14] Several studies have also noted the rent-dissipation effect of poorly defined property rights, including the breakdown of traditional common property rights regimes, in developing countries (Alston et al., 1999; Baland and Plateau, 1996; Bromley, 1989 and 1991; Deacon, 1999; Ostrom, 1990). Brander and Taylor (1997 and 1998) note that over-exploitation of many renewable natural resources—particularly the conversion of forests to agricultural land—occurs frequently in developing countries if property rights over a resource stock are hard to define, difficult to enforce or costly to administer. They demonstrate that opening up trade for a resource-abundant economy with an open access renewable resource may actually reduce welfare in that economy over the long run.

Many studies of resource-rich countries emphasize how political economy factors more generally, in particular the existence of policy and institutional failures that lead to myopic decision-making, fail to control rent-seeking behavior by resource users and weaken the political and legal institutions necessary to foster long-run growth (Ascher, 1999; Auty, 1994 and 1997; Broad, 1995; Gylfason, 2001; Karl, 1997; Ross, 1999 and 2001; Stevens, 2003; Torvik, 2002). If 'bad' policies and institutions lie at the heart of translating resource abundance and windfall gains into negative economy-wide effects, then 'good' policies and institutions may explain why some developing economies with resource wealth may have avoided the 'resource curse.' In other words, 'the natural resource curse is not necessarily the fate of resource abundant countries.... sound economic policies and good management of windfall gains can lead to sustained economic growth' (Sarraf and Jiwanji, 2001: 3). However, judging by the outcome—sustained economic growth—very few resource-abundant developing economies have achieved such success. For example,

---

[14] There is also an obvious link between rent-seeking activities in frontier areas and the lack of government enforcement of efficient regulation of these activities For example, Ascher (1999: 268) points out: 'The weak capacity of the government to enforce natural-resource regulations and guard against illegal exploitation is an obvious factor in many of the cases reviewed. In every case of land and forest use, illegal extraction and failure to abide by conservation regulations reduce the costs to the resource exploiter and induce overexploitation, while failing to make the exploiter internalize the costs of resource depletion and pollution.'

Gylfasson (2001b, 566) examined the long-run growth performance of 85 'resource-rich' developing economies and concluded: 'Of this entire group there are only four resource-rich countries which managed to achieve (a) long-term investment exceeding 25 percent of GDP on average in 1965–98, equal to that of various successful industrial states lacking raw materials, and (b) per capita economic growth exceeding 4 percent per year on average during the same period.... These countries are Botswana, Indonesia, Malaysia, and Thailand. The three Asian countries achieved this success by diversifying their economies and by industrializing; Botswana without doing so.'[15]

Botswana is a particularly interesting case because its economy has remained heavily dependent on mineral export earnings, principally diamonds, and has experienced substantial commodity export booms and windfalls periodically since the 1970s, yet since 1965 the country has one of the highest rates of long-term growth in the world and in the 1990s the highest ratios of government expenditures on education to GDP (Gylfason, 2001). Botswana's success in managing cycles of resource booms and busts is attributed largely to its adoption of appropriate and stable economic policies, including managing the exchange rate to avoid excessive appreciation during boom periods, using windfalls to build up international reserves and government balances that provide a cushion when booms end, avoiding large-scale increases in government expenditure and instead targeting investments to public education and infrastructure, and finally, pursuing an economic diversification strategy that has led to modest increases in labor-intensive manufactures and services (Hill, 1991; Sarraf and Jiwanji, 2001). However, such long-term policies for stable management of the economy are only possible if legal and political institutions function well. Compared to most African countries, Botswana has had considerable political stability and lack of civil conflict. In addition, the government has an international reputation for 'honest public administration,' and overall Botswana is generally rated the least corrupt country in Africa (Gylfason, 2001).

In many developing economies, inequalities in wealth between rural households also have an important impact on land degradation and deforestation processes, which may explain why so many poorer households find themselves confined to marginal lands (Barbier, 1999). There is also increasing evidence in developing countries that more powerful groups use their social and economic power to secure greater access to valuable environmental resources, including land, minerals, energy, gems, water, and even fuelwood, (Alston et al., 1999; Barbier, 1999; Barbier and Homer-Dixon, 1999; Binswanger and Deininger, 1997; Fairhead, 2001; Homer-Dixon, 1999; Lonegran, 1999;

---

[15] However, Gylfason (2001: 566 n. 12) maintains that Indonesia should at best be considered only a qualified success, given the widespread corruption in the country and because Indonesia has recovered much less well from the 1997–8 Asian crisis compared to Malaysia and Thailand.

Swain, 2001). Such problems are exacerbated by government policies that favor wealthier households in markets for these key natural resources, and especially land. For example, 'rural elites' in developing countries are often 'able to steer policies and programs meant to increase rural productivity into capital-intensive investment programs for large farms, thus perpetuating inequality and inefficiency' (Binswanger and Deininger 1997: 1996).

First, poorer households are often unable to compete with wealthier households in land markets for existing agricultural land. The result is two segmented land markets: the wealthier rural households dominate the markets for better quality arable land, whereas the poorer and landless households either trade in less productive land or migrate to marginal lands. Secondly, although poorer households may be the initial occupiers of converted forest-land they are rarely able to sustain their ownership. As the frontier develops economically and property rights are established, the increase in economic opportunities and potential rents makes ownership of the land more attractive to wealthier households. Because of their better access to capital and credit markets, they can easily bid current owners off the land, who in turn may migrate to other frontier forest regions or marginal lands. Thirdly, because of their economic and political importance, wealthier households are able to lobby and influence government officials to ensure that resource management policies favorable to them continue. This means that policy reform is very difficult to implement or sustain. For example, in Colombia, distortions in the land market prevent small farmers from attaining access to existing fertile land (Heath and Binswanger, 1996). That is, as the market value of farmland is only partly based on its agricultural production potential, the market price of arable land in Colombia generally exceeds the capitalized value of farm profits. As a result, poorer smallholders and of course landless workers cannot afford to purchase land out of farm profits, nor do they have the non-farm collateral to finance such purchases in the credit market. In contrast, large land holdings serve as a hedge against inflation for wealthier households, and land is a preferred form of collateral in credit markets. Hence the speculative and non-farming benefits of large land holdings further bid up the price of land, thus ensuring that only wealthier households can afford to purchase land, even though much of the land may be unproductively farmed or even idled.

Similarly to Colombia, land titling, tax and credit policies in Brazil generally reinforce the dominance of wealthier households in credit markets and the speculative investment in land as tax shelters (Alston et al., 1999; Mahar and Schneider, 1994). Because poorer households on the frontier do not benefit from such policies, their ability to compete in formal land markets is further diminished. This reinforces the 'sell out' effect of transferring frontier land ownership from poorer initial settlers to wealthier and typically urban-based arrivals, forcing the poorer households to drift further into the frontier, or enter into land use conflicts with wealthier landowners (Alston et al., 1999; Schneider, 1994).

Throughout the developing world, the ability of poor farmers to obtain credit for land improvements is limited either by restrictions on the availability of rural credit for this purpose, or because insecure property rights mean that poor farmers are not eligible for credit programs. In particular, legal land titles prove to be significant in helping alleviate liquidity constraints affecting the purchase of working inputs, as well as land improvements generally, yet many smallholders do not have legally recognized titles to their land (Feder and Onchon, 1987; López and Valdés, 1998). In any case, often the only asset available to poor rural households for collateral is their land, and this may not always be allowed as the basis for acquiring loans (Zeller et al., 1997). In addition, for many poor rural households, 'imperfect insurance markets, spatial dispersion, and covariant incomes add to the difficulties of obtaining access to credit' (Binswanger and Deininger, 1997: 1971; see also Hoff and Stiglitz, 1990; Stiglitz, 1987). Thus even if formal credit is available in rural areas, poor smallholders usually are not eligible or unable to take advantage of it to finance the inputs needed for improved land management and productivity (Binswanger and Deininger, 1997; Feder, 1985). Estimates suggest that only 5 percent of farmers in Africa and around 15 percent in Latin America and Asia have access to formal credit. Moreover, around 5 percent of all borrowers receive 80 percent of all credit (Hoff et al., 1993). A study across five countries in Latin America indicates that access to either extension assistance or credit for input purchases by smallholders ranges between 13 percent and 33 percent (López and Valdés, 1998). Of the rural producers surveyed across Mexico who received rural credit, only 9.6 percent had holdings of 0–2 ha (Deininger and Minten, 1999). In Malawi, although approximately 45 percent of rural smallholders have holdings of less than 1 ha and over 21 percent are 'core poor' households with less than 0.5 ha, only 17 percent of medium-term credit is allocated to households with less than 2 ha of land (Barbier and Burgess, 1992). Many poor smallholders in developing countries are therefore forced to meet both consumption and input needs by borrowing from informal credit sources, often at much higher effective rates of interest (Binswanger and Sillers, 1983; Chaves and Sánchez 1998; Zeller et al., 1997).

Economy-Wide Implications: The Frontier Expansion Hypothesis

Having provided evidence that the significant frontier land expansion accompanying resource-based development is not leading to sustainable economic development in poor economies, we now must try to explain why. We refer to this explanation as the *frontier expansion hypothesis*.[16] This hypothesis is based

[16] Further elaboration of the frontier expansion hypothesis and a formal model illustrating the hypothesis can be found in Barbier (2005a). See also Barbier (2005b) for further discussion of the frontier expansion hypothesis in the overall context of natural resource use in economic development in low- and middle-income economies.

on four key observations of the process of frontier-based development in developing economies today (Barbier, 2003 and 2004).[17]

First, frontier land expansion and resource exploitation may be associated with poor economic performance in resource-dependent developing countries but not necessarily a cause of it. That is, frontier-based development is symptomatic of a pattern of economy-wide resource exploitation that: (a) generates little additional economic rents, and (b) what rents are generated are not being reinvested in more productive and dynamic sectors, such as manufacturing.

Secondly, one important reason that frontier land expansion is unlikely to generate much rents is that, as such expansion results largely from conversion of forest, wetlands and other natural habitat, it is likely to yield mainly 'marginal' or 'fragile' land exhibiting low productivity as well as significant constraints for intensive agriculture (World Bank, 2003). This in turn implies that very little effort is invested, either by poor farmers working this land or government agricultural research and extension activities, in developing *country-specific knowledge* in improving the productivity and sustainable exploitation of frontier land and resources.

Thirdly, in contrast to past and present examples of successful minerals-based development, there are unlikely to be *strong linkages between more dynamic economic sectors* (i.e. manufacturing) and the economic activities responsible for frontier land expansion (Wright and Czelusta, 2002). This in turn limits the opportunities for *substantial knowledge spillovers* arising from the exploitation and conversion of frontier resources, including land. Thus frontier-based economic activities are unlikely to be integrated with the rest of the economy. There are two reasons for this. First, as noted above, frontier land expansion appears to be serving mainly as an outlet for the rural poor in many developing

---

[17] As noted earlier, successful resource-based development in the U.S. was largely mineral-based development. In fact, there is increasing evidence that the considerable frontier agricultural expansion that did occur in the North America in the late nineteenth century had many of the features associated with frontier expansion occurring in developing economies today: it served mainly as an outlet for relatively poor smallholders, and what little rents were available were generally dissipated. For instance, the classic case of the 'race for property rights' that often accompanies frontier agricultural expansion was the 'land giveaways' and homesteading that opened up both the Canadian and United States West in the nineteenth century (Anderson and Hill, 1975 and 1990; Southey, 1978). As described by Anderson and Hill (1990: 177): 'When property rights and the rents therefrom are "up for grabs", it is possible for expenditures to establish rights to fully dissipate the rents, leaving the efficiency gains from privatization in question.' In the case of homesteading, individual farm families could establish freehold title by occupying and developing their land. In the case of land and natural resource giveaways (or grants), land and other natural resources were given away to large-scale landowners (e.g. railroad companies, ranchers, mineral exploiters) by the government as a reward for initiating development (e.g. building railways, establishing ranches, initiating mining operations). However, as argued by Southey (1978: 557) the latter activities could be considered 'simply homesteading on a grand scale'. The result is that competition among homesteaders for the best land, and large-scale landowners for the best resource grants, will lead to premature development, as well as the complete dissipation of all net capitalized rents.

countries, which suggests that much of the output is either for subsistence or local markets. Second, by definition, frontier areas are likely to be located far away from urban and industrial centers.

Fourthly, as discussed in the previous section, policy and market failures, such as rent-seeking behavior and corruption or open-access resource exploitation, are prevalent in the resource sectors of many developing economies. Frontier land expansion and resource exploitation is especially associated with open access.[18] In addition, many large-scale resource-extractive activities, such as timber harvesting, mining, ranching and commercial plantations, are often responsible for initially opening up previously inaccessible frontier areas (Barbier, 1997). Investors in these activities are attracted to frontier areas because of the lack of government controls and property rights in these remote areas mean that resource rents are easily captured, and thus frontier resource-extractive activities are particularly prone to rent-seeking behavior (Ascher, 1999).

All of these factors combine to ensure that frontier-based economic development is unlikely to lead to high rates of sustained economic growth. In essence, all frontier resources, including land in forests and wetlands, are 'reserves' that can be exploited potentially for economic rents. However, as we have seen, conversion of frontier land 'reserves' tends to produce fragile agricultural land that is largely an outlet for absorbing poor households. Such frontier land expansion does not generate substantial rents, and any resulting agricultural output will increase mainly consumption of non-tradable goods (food for subsistence or local markets). Frontier resource-extractive activities may yield more significant rents, but the rent-seeking behavior associated with these activities will mean that these rents will be re-invested into further exploitation of frontier resources. This process will continue until the economically accessible frontier resource 'reserves' are exhausted and all rents are dissipated.

The lack of integration of frontier-based economic activities with the rest of the economy also decreases the likelihood that any rents generated by these activities will be reinvested in more productive and dynamic sectors, such as manufacturing. In essence, the frontier sector operates as a separate 'enclave' in the developing economy. As already noted, frontier-based land expansion will result mainly in small-scale agricultural production that increases domestic, non-traded consumption. In contrast, more large-scale, frontier resource-extractive activities, such as mining, timber extraction, ranching and plantations, may generate increased resource-based exports. Such exports are more likely to result in either imported consumption or imported capital goods that are employed predominantly in the frontier resource-extractive industries. There are two reasons for this outcome. First, large-scale resource-extractive

---

[18] In this regard, the frontier expansion hypothesis shares many similarities with the open access hypothesis of Brander and Taylor (1997 and 1998). However, as noted, the open access problem is only part of one of the four key features of the frontier expansion hypothesis.

activities tend to benefit wealthier households in the economy, who have a higher propensity to consume imported goods. Secondly, as explained above, the re-investment of resource rents into further exploitation of frontier extractive reserves will require specific investments in imported capital goods for this purpose, such as mining machinery, milling equipment, road-building and construction tools, and other. It follows that, although frontier-based economic development can lead to an initial 'economic boom,' it is invariably short-lived and the economic benefits are quickly dissipated. If the additional frontier 'reserves' are used mainly to expand domestic consumption and exports (in exchange for imported consumption), then there will be little additional capital accumulation outside of the frontier resource-extractive sector. This implies that any economic boom will continue only as long as the frontier resource reserves last. Once resource rents are dissipated and the frontier is effectively closed, there will be no long-term take off into sustained growth for the economy as a whole.

If, during the frontier expansion phase, some rents are invested in capital accumulation in other sectors of the economy as well, then the initial boom period will coincide with increased growth. However, this growth path cannot be sustained. The additional capital accumulation is unlikely to overcome the poor linkages between other economic sectors (i.e. manufacturing) and frontier-based economic activities, and is therefore unlikely to yield substantial economy-wide knowledge spillovers. As a result, any additional growth generated by this capital accumulation will last only as long as frontier expansion continues. Once the frontier is 'closed' and any reserves of land and natural resources available to an economy have been fully exploited or converted, some economic retrenchment is inevitable, and an economic bust will occur.

In sum, the structural economic dependence of a small open low- or lower-middle income economy on frontier land and resource expansion precipitates a 'boom and bust' pattern of development that is simply not conducive to sustained and high rates of long-run economic growth. Resource dependency, frontier-land expansion and populations concentrated on fragile lands are all indications that a developing economy is not exploiting its natural capital efficiently and sustainably. The result is a poor overall growth and development performance, and the 'dualism within dualism' pattern of resource use and development described above.

Reversing the Cycle: The Role of Policy

If this 'vicious cycle' is to be reversed, there are essentially two roles for policy reform within developing economies. First, specific policies must be aimed at overcoming the structural features of 'dualism within dualism' in resource-use patterns. Secondly, policies must also be introduced that improve the overall success of resource-based development that is accompanied by frontier land expansion. As we shall see, these two sets of reform are inherently interrelated.

One straightforward, but often politically difficult, approach to reducing 'dualism within dualism' is economy-wide land reform. As noted by Binswanger and Deininger (1997: 1972), 'where rural capital markets are highly imperfect and the distribution of wealth is unequal, a one-time redistribution of wealth, such as a land reform, may largely eliminate the need for distortionary redistributive policies later. As the authors point out, the experience of Japan, South Korea and Taiwan indicate that land reform is also likely to alter the growth path of the economy and lead to permanently higher levels of growth. Finally, the 'greater wealth' arising through land reform 'also increases the ability of the poor to directly participate in the political process' (Binswanger and Deininger 1997: 1999).

A related, but equally difficult, task is reform of tax, credit and other economic policies that generally reinforce the dominance of wealthier households in natural resource and land markets and promote the speculative investment in these resources as tax shelters. According to López (2003: 271) such policies in Latin America over the past 50 years are symptomatic of the general economic policy failure in the region that has 'focused on the generation of an expensive and often incoherent system of short-run incentives to promote investment in physical capital . . . by undertaxing capital income and wasted in massive subsidies to the corporate sector in a futile effort to promote investment and economic growth'. This has had two overall consequences on the land degradation and deforestation process in the region. First, as described above, the resulting market and tax distortions promote this process directly, in a deliberate strategy of 'wasting natural resources as a way of enticing investors' (López, 2003: 260). Secondly, Latin American governments are dissipating scarce revenues and financial resources 'instead of concentrating their efforts in raising enough public revenues to finance the necessary investment in human and natural capital and the necessary institutional capacities to effectively enforce environmental regulations' (López, 2003: 271).

Finally, the third structural problem associated with 'dualism within dualism' is the under-investment in human capital in rural areas, particularly by those poor households concentrated on fragile land. As noted above, these households generate insufficient savings, suffer chronic indebtedness and rely on informal credit markets with high short-term interest rates. As a result, private investment in human capital improvement is a luxury for most poor rural households, and similarly the lack of education and marketable skills limits not only the earning potential of the rural poor but also their political bargaining power relative to wealthier rural and urban households. As argued by Binswanger and Deininger (1997: 1988–9), 'Primary education and health services, especially for the poor, rural inhabitants, and women, are important not only because they foster growth and help reduce poverty through several well-known channels, but also because they reduce income inequality, and thereby enhance the collective action potential of the poor.'

Clearly, if resource-dependent development in poor economies is associated with frontier land expansion and resource exploitation, then the critical issue for these economies is how to improve the sustainability of such development. Based on our previous discussion, the key to sustainable economic development will be improving the economic integration between frontier and other sectors of the economy, targeting policies to improved resource management in frontier areas and overcoming problems of corruption and rent-seeking in resource sectors. Better integration between frontier-based activities and more dynamic economic sectors means a greater commitment to promoting 'agro-industrialization' generally. As argued by Reardon and Barrett (2000), such a strategy comprises three related sets of changes: (a) growth of commercial, off-farm agro-processing, distribution and input provision activities; (b) institutional and organizational change in relations between farms and firms both upstream and downstream, such as marked increases in vertical integration and contract-based procurement; and (c) related changes in product composition, technologies, and sectoral and market structure. Such an integrated approach to agro-industrialization is essential for developing *country-specific knowledge* in improving the productivity and sustainable exploitation of land resources, *strong forward and backward linkages* between more dynamic economic sectors (i.e. manufacturing) and agricultural activities, and finally, the opportunities for *substantial knowledge spillovers* from the farm to firm level.

However, frontier-based agricultural activities will be largely left out of the development of such agro-industrial capacity in low- and middle-income economies unless specific policy reforms are aimed at improving resource management and productivity of frontier lands, and targeted especially at poor rural households farming these lands. Nevertheless, recent economic analyses are beginning to indicate what kind of policy reforms may be necessary to improve the incentives for better land management in the frontier areas and marginal farmlands of developing countries. The good news is that overall agricultural sector policy reforms that reduce price distortions, promote efficient operation of rural financial markets, and make property rights enforceable, should support these incentives (Barbier, 1997). In some countries, there may be a 'win–win' situation between general macroeconomic and sectoral reforms and improved land management. For example, in the Philippines it was found that reducing import tariffs and export taxes may also reduce the rate of upland degradation (Coxhead and Jayasuriya, 1995). Similarly, in Indonesia reducing fertilizer, pesticide and other subsidies for irrigated rice could be compatible with improved investment and credit strategies for the uplands of Java (Pearce et al., 1990).

However, other economy-wide and sectoral reforms may have unknown—and possibly negative—aggregate impacts on land and resource use strategies of rural households. It may therefore be necessary to complement these reforms with specific, targeted policies to generate direct incentives for improved rural resource management. The main purpose of such policies should be to increase the economic returns of existing as opposed to frontier lands; improve the access of poorer rural households to credit and land markets; and alleviate any remaining policy biases in these markets that favor relatively wealthy farmers and individuals (Barbier, 1997). In some cases, specific non-price transfers in the form of targeted subsidies could reduce significantly the incentives for land degradation and forest conversion in developing countries. This is particularly true for expenditures that aimed to improve access by the rural poor to credit, research and extension, investments to disseminate conservation, information and technologies to smallholders, and investments in small-scale irrigation and other productivity improvements on existing smallholder land. For example, in Mexico there is some evidence that a land improvement investment program for existing rain-fed farmers, particularly in states and regions prone to high deforestation rates, could provide direct and indirect incentives for controlling deforestation by increasing the comparative returns to farming existing smallholdings as well as the demand for rural labor (Barbier, 2002; Barbier and Burgess, 1996).

Targeting public investment and expenditure to the agricultural sector to provide effective credit markets and services to reach poor rural households, while continuing to eliminate subsidies and credit rationing that benefit mainly wealthier households, may be important in achieving a more efficient pattern of land use—and a less extensive one—in many developing countries. An important inducement for many poor smallholders to invest in improved land management is to establish proper land titling and ownership claims on the land they currently occupy. To improve land tenure services in areas where frontier expansion is occurring it may be necessary to develop more formal policies for smallholder settlement, such as a policy to allocate preferentially public land with fully demarcated ownership and tenure rights to smallholders.

In addition, policies that have increased processes of land degradation and deforestation as an unintended side effect should be mitigated. For example, expansion of the road network in frontier areas has been identified as a major factor in opening up forestlands and thus making these lands artificially cheap and abundantly available. Tax policies that encourage the holding of agricultural land as a speculative asset not only artificially inflate the price of existing arable land but promote much idling of potentially productive land.

Finally, in many developing countries policy reform will have to be complemented by investments in key infrastructural services. Several have been mentioned already—availability of rural credit, conservation and general extension services, land tenure and titling services, and irrigation and other land improvement investments for existing smallholder land. However, other services may also be important. For example, in most rural areas there needs to be a general development of adequate post-harvest and marketing facilities targeted to smallholder production, in order to ensure that such production participates in an overall agro-industrial development strategy. In frontier areas, there is a need not only to increase credit and extension services to initial settlers but also more basic services such as improved community, education and health-care services.

Perhaps one of the greatest challenges for policy reform in developing countries will be to reduce the propensity for corruption and rent-seeking in resource-based sectors. The institutional 'failures' that promote such practices appear to be deep-seated and endemic, and will be difficult to change. Nevertheless, as argued by Ascher (1999: 299) there is some hope for reform even in this difficult area: 'The fact that some government officials may intend to sacrifice resource-exploitation soundness for other objectives does not mean that they will necessarily have their way, even if they are chiefs of state. Prior arrangements, public outcry, and adverse reactions by international institutions can raise the political or economic costs too high. Other officials may be in a position to block their actions, especially if the structures of natural-resource policymaking reveal policy failures for what they are.'

References

Alston, Lee J., Gary D. Libecap and Bernardo Mueller (1999), *Titles, Conflict, and Land Use: The Development of Property Rights and Land Reform on the Brazilian Amazon Frontier*. The University of Michigan Press, Ann Arbor.

Anderson, Terry L. and Peter J. Hill (1975). 'The Evolution of Property Rights: A study of the American West.' *The Journal of Law and Economics* 18: 163–79.

—— and —— (1990), 'The Race for Property Rights.' *The Journal of Law and Economics* 33: 177–97.

Ascher, W. (1999), *Why Governments Waste Natural Resources: Policy Failures in Developing Countries*, Johns Hopkins University Press, Baltimore.

Auty, Richard M. (1994), 'Industrial Policy Reform in Six Large Newly Industrializing Countries: The Resource Curse Thesis.' *World Development*, 22(1) (January) pp. 11–26.

—— (1997), 'Natural Resource Endowment, the State and Development Strategy,' *Journal of International Development* 9(4) (June) pp. 651–63.

Baland, Jean-Marie and Jean-Philippe Plateau (1996), *Halting Degradation: Is there a Role for Rural Communities?* Clarendon Press, Oxford.

Barbier, Edward B. (1997), 'The Economic Determinants of Land Degradation in Developing Countries,' *Philosophical Transactions of the Royal Society of London, Series B* 352: 891–9.

—— (1999), 'Poverty, Environment and Development,' in J. C. J. M. van den Bergh (ed.), *The Handbook of Environmental and Resource Economics*, Edward Elgar, London. pp. 731–44.

—— (2002), 'Institutional Constraints and Deforestation: An Application to Mexico,' *Economic Inquiry* 40(3): 508–19.

—— (2003), 'The Role of Natural Resources in Economic Development,' *Australian Economic Papers* 42(2): 259–72.

—— (2004), 'Agricultural Expansion, Resource Booms and Growth in Latin America,' *World Development*, 32(1): 137–57.

—— (2005*a*). 'Frontier Expansion and Economic Development,' *Contemporary Economic Policy* (in press).

—— (2005*b*), *Natural Resources and Economic Development*. Cambridge University Press 410 pp.

—— and Burgess, J. C. (1992), 'Malawi—Land Degradation in Agriculture.' Environment Department, Divisional Working Paper No. 1992–37, The World Bank, Washington DC.

—— and Joanne C. Burgess. (1996), 'Economic Analysis of Deforestation in Mexico,' *Environment and Development Economics* 1: 203–40.

—— and Homer-Dixon, Thomas (1999), 'Resource Scarcity, Institutional Adaptation, and Technical Innovation,' *Ambio* 28(2): 144–7.

Binswanger, Hans P. and Klaus Deininger (1997), 'Explaining Agricultural and Agrarian Policies in Developing Countries,' *Journal of Economic Literature* 35: 1958–2005.

—— and Sillers, D. A. (1983), 'Risk Aversion and Credit Constraints in Farmers' Decisionmaking: A Reinterpretation,' *Journal of Development Studies* 22: 504–39.

Brander, James A. and M. Scott Taylor (1997), 'International Trade and Open-Access Renewable Resources: The Small Open Economy,' *Canadian Journal of Economics* 30(3): 526–52.

—— and M. Scott Taylor (1998), 'Open Access Renewable Resources: Trade and Trade Policy in a Two-Country Model,' *Journal of International Economics* 44: 181–209.

Broad, Robin (1995), 'The Political Economy of Natural Resources: Case Studies of the Indonesian and Philippine Forest Sectors,' *The Journal of Developing Areas* 29: 317–40.

Bromley, Daniel W (1989), 'Property Relations and Economic Development: The Other Land Reform.' *World Development* 17: 867–77.

—— (1991), *Environment and Economy: Property Rights and Public Policy*. Basil Blackwell, Oxford.

Chambers, E. J. and D. F. Gordon (1966), 'Primary Products and Economic Growth: An Empirical Measurement,' *Journal of Political Economy* 74(4): 315–32.

Chaves, R. A. and Sánchez, S. M. (1998), 'Poverty, Entrepreneurs and Financial Markets in the Rural Areas of Mexico,' In R. López and A. Valdés (eds), *Rural Poverty in Latin Amercia*, The World Bank, Washington DC.

Cipolla, C. M. (1976), *Before the Industrial Revolution: European Society and Economy, 1000–1700*. Metheun, London.

Cosgrove, William J. and Frank R. Rijsberman (2000), *World Water Vision: Making Water Everybody's Business*. World Water Council and Earthscan Publications, London.

Coxhead, Ian and Sisira Jayasuriya (1995), 'Trade and Tax Policy Reform and the Environment: The Economics of Soil Erosion in Developing Countries,' *American Journal of Agricultural Economics* 77: 631–44.

David, Paul A. and Gavin Wright (1997), 'Increasing Returns and the Genesis of American Resource Abundance,' *Industrial and Corporate Change* 6: 203–45.

Davis, Graham A. (1995), 'Learning to Love the Dutch Disease: Evidence from the Mineral Economies,' *World Development* 23(1): 1765–79.

Deacon, Robert T. (1999), 'Deforestation and Ownership: Evidence from Historical Accounts and Contemporary Data,' *Land Economics* 75(3): 341–59.

Deininger, Klaus and Bart Minten (1999), 'Poverty, Policies and Deforestation: The Case of Mexico,' *Economic Development and Cultural Change* 47(2): 313–44.

di Tella, G. (1982), 'The Economics of the Frontier,' in C. P. Kindleberger and G. di Tella, (eds) *Economics in the Long View*. Macmillan, London: pp. 210–27.

Fairhead, James (2001), 'The Conflict over Natural and Environmental Resources,' in E. W. Nafziger, F. Stewart, and R. Väyrynen, (eds) *War, Hunger, and Displacement: The Origins of Humanitarian Emergencies. Volume 1: Analysis*. Oxford University Press, Oxford: pp. 147–78.

Falkenmark, Malin, Wolf Klohn, et al. (1998), 'Water Scarcity as a Key Factor Behind Global Food Insecurity: Round Table Discussion,' *Ambio* 27(2): 148–54.

Feder, G. (1985). 'The Relation between Farm Size and Farm Productivity: The Role of Family Labor, Supervision and Credit Constraints,' *Journal of Development Economics* 18: 297–313.

—— and Onchan, T. (1987), 'Land Ownership Security and Farm Investment in Thailand,' *American Journal of Agricultural Economics* 69: 311–20.

Findlay, Ronald and Mats Lundahl (1994), 'Natural Resources, "Vent-for-Surplus", and the Staples Theory.' In G. Meier (ed.), *From Classical Economics to Development Economics: Essays in Honor of Hla Myint*. St. Martin's Press, New York: pp. 68–93.

—— and —— (1999), 'Resource-Led Growth — a Long-Term Perspective: The Relevance of the 1870–1914 Experience for Today's Developing Economies.' UNU/WIDER Working Papers No. 162. World Institute for Development Economics Research, Helsinki.

Fischer, Günther and Gerhard K. Heilig (1997), 'Population Momentum and the Demand on Land and Water Resources,' *Philosophical Transactions of the Royal Society Series B* 352(1356): 869–89.

Food and Agricultural Organization of the United Nations (FAO) (1995), *World Agriculture:Towards 2010 — An FAO Study*. Rome and New York: FAO and John Wiley & Sons.

——. (1997), *State of the World's Forests 1997*. Rome: FAO.

Gleick, Peter H. (2000), *The World's Water, 2000–2001: The Biennial Report on Freshwater Resources*. Island Press, Washington DC.

Green, Alan and M. C. Urquhart (1976), 'Factor and Commodity Flows in the International Economy of 1870–1914: A Multi-Country View,' *Journal of Economic History* 36: 217–52.

Gylfason, Thorvaldur (2001), 'Nature, Power, and Growth,' *Scottish Journal of Political Economy* 48(5): 558–88.

Heath, John and Hans Binswanger (1996), 'Natural Resource Degradation Effects of Poverty and Population Growth are Largely Policy-Induced: The Case of Colombia,' *Environment and Development Economics* 1: 65–83.

Hill, Catherine B. (1991), 'Managing Commodity Booms in Botswana,' *World Development* 19(9): 1185–96.

Hoff, Karla and Joseph E. Stiglitz (1990), 'Introduction: Imperfect Information and Rural Credit Markets—Puzzles and Policy Perspectives,' *World Bank Economic Review* 4(3): 235–50.

——, Avishay Braverman, and Joseph E. Stiglitz, (eds) (1993), *The Economics of Rural Organization: Theory, Practice and Policy*. Oxford University Press, New York.

Homer-Dixon, Thomas F. (1999), *Environment, Scarcity, and Violence*. Princeton University Press, Princeton.

Karl, Terry L. (1997), *The Paradox of Plenty: Oil Booms and Petro-States*. University of California Press, Berkeley.

Lonegran, Steven C. (1999), *Environmental Change, Adaptation, and Security. NATO ASI Series*. Kluwer, Dordrecht.

López, Ramón (1998), 'Where Development Can or Cannot Go: The Role of Poverty-Environment Linkages,' In *Annual Bank Conference on Development Economics 1997*, (eds), B. Pleskovic and J. E. Stiglitz. Washington DC: The World Bank: pp. 285–306.

—— (2003), 'The Policy Roots of Socioeconomic Stagnation and Environmental Implosion: Latin America 1950–2000,' *World Development* 31(2): 259–80.

—— and Alberto Valdés, (eds) (1998), *Rural Poverty in Latin Amercia*, The World Bank, Washington DC.

Mahar, Dennis and Robert R. Schneider (1994), 'Incentives for Tropical Deforestation: Some Examples from Latin America,' in Katrina Brown and David W. Pearce, (eds), *The Causes of Tropical Deforestation*, University College London Press, London: pp. 159–70.

Matsuyama, Kimoru (1992), 'Agricultural Productivity, Comparative Advantage, and Economic Growth,' *Journal of Economic Theory* 58: 317–34.

Myint, Hla. (1958), 'The Classical Theory of International Trade and the Underdeveloped Countries,' *Economic Journal* 68: 315–37.

Ostrom, Elinor (1990), *Governing the Commons: The Evolution of Institutions for Collective Action*. Cambridge University Press, Cambridge.

Pack, Howard (1994), 'Endogenous Growth Theory: Intellectual Appeal and Empirical Shortcomings,' *Journal of Economic Perspectives* 8(1): 55–72.

Pearce, David W., Edward B. Barbier, and Anil Markandya (1990), *Sustainable Development: Economics and Environment in the Third World*. Edward Elgar, London.

Population Division of the United Nations Secretariat (2001), *World Urbanization Prospects: The 2001 Revision*. United Nations, New York.

Reardon, Thomas and Christopher B. Barrett (2000), 'Agroindustrialization, Globalization, and International Development: An Overview of Issues, Patterns, and Determinants,' *Agricultural Economics* 23(3): 195–205.

Revenga, Carmen, Jake Brunner, Norbert Henninger, et al. (2000), *Pilot Analysis of Global Ecosystems: Freshwater Systems*. World Resources Institute, Washington DC.

Rodríguez, Francisco and Jeffrey D. Sachs (1999), 'Why Do Resource-Abundant Economies Grow More Slowly?' *Journal of Economic Growth* 4: 277–303.

Romer, Paul M. (1996), 'Why, Indeed, in America? Theory, History, and the Origins of Modern Economic Growth', *American Economic Review* 86(2): 202–12.

Rosegrant, Mark W., Ximing Cai, and Sarah A. Cline (2002), *World Water and Food to 2025: Dealing with Scarcity*. International Food Policy Research Institute, Washington DC.

Ross, Michael L. (1999), 'The Political Economy of the Resource Curse.' *World Politics* 51: 297–322.

—— (2001), *Timber Booms and Institutional Breakdowns in Southeast Asia*. Cambridge University Press, Cambridge.

Sachs, Jeffrey D. and Andrew M. Warner (1995). 'Natural Resource Abundance and Economic Growth.' *National Bureau of Economic Research Working Paper* No 5398 (December).

—— and —— (1997), 'Fundamental Sources of Long-Run Growth.' *American Economic Review* 87(2): 184–8.

—— and —— (2001), 'The Curse of Natural Resources.' *European Economic Review* 45: 827–38.

Sarraf, María and Moortaza Jiwanji (2001), 'Beating the Resource Curse: The Case of Botswana.' *Environmental Economics Series*. The World Bank Environment Department. The World Bank, Washington DC.

Schedvin, C. B. (1990), 'Staples and Regions of Pax Britannica.' *Economic History Review* 43: 533–59.

Schneider, Robert R. (1994), *Government and the Economy on the Amazon Frontier.* Latin America and the Caribbean Technical Department, Regional Studies Program, Report No. 34. The World Bank, Washington DC.

Smith, S. (1976), 'An Extension of the Vent-for-Surplus Model in Relation to Long-Run Structural Change in Nigeria.' *Oxford Economic Papers* 28(3): 426–46.

Southey, C. (1978), 'The Staples Thesis, Common Property and Homesteading,' *Canadian Journal of Economics* 11(3): 547–59.

Stevens, Paul (2003), 'Resource Impact: Curse or Blessing? A Literature Survey,' *The Journal of Energy Literature* 9: 3–42.

Stiglitz, Joseph E. (1987), 'Some Theoretical Aspects of Agricultural Policies,' *World Bank Research Observer* 2(1): 43–53.

Stijns, Jean-Phillipe C. (2001), 'Natural Resource Abundance and Economic Growth Revisited.' *Mimeo.* University of California at Berkeley.

Swain, Ashok (2001), 'Water Scarcity as a Source of Crisis.' In E. W. Nafziger, F. Stewart, and R. Väyrynen (eds), *War, Hunger, and Displacement: The Origins of Humanitarian Emergencies. Volume 1: Analysis.* Oxford University Press, Oxford: pp. 179–206.

Taylor, Alan M. and Jeffrey G. Williamson (1994), 'Capital Flows to the New World as an Intergenerational Transfer,' *Journal of Political Economy* 102(2): 348–71.

Thomas, Vinod, Mansoor Dailami, et al., (2000), *The Quality of Growth.* Oxford University Press, New York.

Tornell, A. and P. R. Lane (2001), 'Are Windfalls a Curse?' *Journal of International Economics* 44: 83–112.

Torvik, Ragnar (2002), 'Natural Resources, Rent Seeking and Welfare.' *Journal of Development Economics* 67: 455–70.

Turner, F. J. (1986), 'The Significance of the Frontier in American History.' In F. J. Turner, *The Frontier in American History.* University of Arizona Press, Tucson: pp. 1–38.

Vörösmarty, Charles J., Pamela Green, et al. (2000), 'Global Water Resources: Vulnerability from Climate Change and Population Growth,' *Science* 289 (14 July): 284–8.

Watkins, M. H. (1963), 'A Staple Theory of Economic Growth.' *The Canadian Journal of Economics and Political Science.* 29(2): 141–58.

Webb, W. P. (1964), *The Great Frontier.* University of Nebraska Press, Lincoln.

World Bank (1992), *World Development Report 1992.* World Bank, Washington DC.

—— (1997), *Expanding the Measure of Wealth: Indicators of Environmentally Sustainable Development.* The World Bank, Washington DC.

—— (2003), *World Development Report 2003.* World Bank, Washington DC.

Wright, Gavin (1990), 'The Origins of American Industrial Success, 1879–1940,' *American Economic Review,* vol. 80(4): pp. 651–68.

—— and Jesse Czelusta (2002), 'Exorcizing the Resource Curse: Minerals as a Knowledge Industry, Past and Present.' *Mimeo.* Department of Economics, Stanford University.

Zeller, M., Schneider, G., von Braun, J., and Heidhues, F. (1997), *Rural Finance for Food Security for the Poor.* Food Policy Review No. 4, International Food Policy Research Institute, Washington DC.

APPENDIX 1

EXPORT CONCENTRATION IN PRIMARY COMMODITIES FOR LOW AND MIDDLE INCOME DEVELOPING ECONOMIES

	Export Share 1990/99 a/	Export Share 1980/81 b/	Export Share 1965 b/	Main Export Commodities c/ 1		2	
	90–100%						
Yemen A.R.	100	49	100	Fisheries	31.3%	Petroleum	14.1%
Botswana	100 c/	NA	NA	Diamonds	92.7%	Beef	5.3%
Angola	99	NA	82	Petroleum	77.1%	Coffee	2.6%
Nigeria	99	99	97	Petroleum	94.2%	Cocoa	2.5%
Mali	99	83	97	Cotton	41.9%	Groundnuts	0.8%
Ethiopia	99 d/	99	99	Coffee	66.6%	Sugar	1.1%
Iran	99 c/	NA	96	Petroleum	98.1%	Fisheries	0.2%
Rwanda	99 c/	99	100	Coffee	68.8%	Tea	8.4%
Eq. Guinea	99 c/	91	NA	Cocoa	53.5%	Timber	38.0%
Sao Tome & Pr.	99 d/	100	NA	Cocoa	95.5% d/	Copra	1.8%
Yemen PDR	99 d/	NA	94				
Burkina Faso	98 d/	85	95	Cotton	27.3%	Livestock	26.8% d/
Zambia	98 c/	99	100	Copper	93.3%	Zinc	1.8%
Liberia	98 c/	98	97	Iron Ore	60.4%	Rubber	20.4%
						Oilseed	
Sudan	97	99	99	Cotton	30.0%	Cake	1.6%
Niger	97	98	95	Ores/Metals	67.0%e/	Food	29.0%e/
Uganda	97	100	100	Coffee	95.8%	Cotton	1.6%
Mauritania	97 d/	99	99	Fisheries	41.9%	Iron Ore	37.0%
Algeria	96	99	96	Petroleum	34.9%	Phosphate	0.2%
Benin	96	96	95	Cotton	26.0%	Cocoa	16.0%
Malawi	95	93	99	Tobacco	53.5%	Tea	15.4%
Libya	95	99	100	Petroleum	90.5%		
Iraq	95 c/	NA	99	Petroleum	94.4%	Tobacco	0.1%
Somalia	95 d/	99	86	Bananas	18.6%	Fisheries	3.5%
Ecuador	94	93	98	Petroleum	43.6%	Fisheries	15.8%
						Groundnut	
Gambia, The	94	NA	NA	Groundnuts	17.2%	Oil	12.0%
Guyana	94 c/	NA	NA	Bauxite	39.5%	Sugar	35.7%
Congo, Dem. Rep. (Zaire)	93 d/	94	92	Copper	35.9%	Coffee	14.3%
Nicaragua	92	92	94	Coffee	40.9%	Cotton	21.2%
Comoros	92 d/	86	NA	Cloves	41.7% d/	Vanilla	33.3% d/
Cameroon	91	97	94	Petroleum	48.1%	Coffee	13.1%
Congo, Rep.	91 c/	94	37	Petroleum	83.2%	Timber	5.7%
Saudi Arabia	90	99	99	Petroleum	88.5%e	Food	1.0%e/
Papua N.G.	90	100	90	Copper	31.0%	Coffee	15.2%
Lao PDR	90 d/	100	94	Timber	51.7% d/	Electricity	19.0%

57

Edward B. Barbier

continued

	Export Share 1990/99 a/	Export Share 1980/81 b/	Export Share 1965 b/	Main Export Commodities c/ 1		2	
	80–89%						
Burundi	89 c/	96	95	Coffee	83.5%	Tea	4.2%
Venezuela	89	NA	98	Petroleum	55.7%	Aluminum	3.7%
Myanmar	89	81	99	Timber	40.3%	Rice	28.1%
Chad	89 d/	96	97	Cotton	33.2%	Oilseed	0.2%
Oman	88	96	NA	Petroleum	90.0%	Fisheries	0.7%
Cote d'Ivoire	88 d/	90	95	Cocoa	30.5%	Coffee	18.5%
Paraguay	87	NA	92	Cotton	16.4%	Soybeans	14.9%
Gabon	87 c/	NA	NA	Petroleum	70.5%	Manganese	8.1%
Guinea-Bissau	87 d/	71	NA	Fisheries	13.9%	Groundnuts	10.4%
Togo	86	85	97	Phosphate	31.7%	Cotton	11.8%
Ghana	86	98	98	Cocoa	49.2%	Aluminum	11.3%
Chile	85	90	96	Copper	42.9%	Fisheries	11.6%
Tanzania	84	86	87	Coffee	44.1%	Cotton	11.3%
Panama	81	91	98	Fisheries	31.3%	Bananas	22.5%
Honduras	80	89	96	Bananas	35.4%	Coffee	28.0%
Peru	80	83	99	Copper	17.3%	Zinc	12.3%
Guinea	80	NA	NA	Bauxite	72.8%	Aluminum	19.4%
Cuba	80 c/	NA	NA	Sugar	74.9%	Fisheries	2.3%
	70–79%						
Mozambique	79 c/	NA	NA	Fisheries	55.7%	Sugar	7.1%
Bolivia	78	100	95	Tin	18.6%	Zinc	3.4%
Syrian Arab Republic	77	NA	90	Petroleum	40.1%	Cotton	7.9%
Maldives	77 d/	70	NA	Fish	57.1% d/		
Kenya	74	88	94	Coffee	31.7%	Tea	22.2%
Colombia	72	72	93	Coffee	46.7%	Bananas	4.1%
Zimbabwe	71	63	85	Tobacco	19.7%	Cotton	6.7%
Guatemala	71	71	86	Coffee	39.2%	Bananas	6.5%
	60–69%						
Argentina	69	84	94	Oilseed	9.5%	Wheat	8.7%
Trinidad and Tobago	68	86	93	Petroleum	41.7%	Sugar	1.3%
Madagascar	67	92	94	Coffee	36.8%	Fisheries	8.8%
Uruguay	61	70	95	Beef	12.0%	Wool	8.5%
Senegal	60	81	97	Fisheries	39.9%	Phosphate	8.5%
	50–59%						
Egypt	58	92	80	Petroleum	39.3%	Cotton	7.4%
Sierra Leone	58 c/	57	39	Bauxite	18.0%	Cocoa	16.3%
El Salvador	57	63	83	Coffee	63.6%	Sugar	3.0%
Central African Republic	57 c/	74	46	Coffee	26.0%	Timber	18.0%
Indonesia	54	96	96	Petroleum	31.1%	Rubber	4.7%
Morocco	50	72	95	Phosphate	16.9%	Fisheries	11.9%
	40–49%						
Costa Rica	49	68	84	Coffee	31.4%	Bananas	20.0%
Jordan	47	57	81	Phosphate	22.1%	Wheat	0.3%
Brazil	46	59	92	Coffee	8.5%	Iron Ore	6.6%
Malaysia	33	80	94	Petroleum	12.5%e/	Food	10.0%e/
Sri Lanka	33	79	99	Tea	28.7%	Rubber	7.3%

continued

	Export Share 1990/99 a/	Export Share 1980/81 b/	Export Share 1965 b/	Main Export Commodities c/			
				1		2	
30–39%							
South Africa	37	26	68	Ores/metals	16.0%e/	Petroleum	8.5%
Mexico	36	73	84	Petroleum	49.6%	Coffee	3.3%
Thailand	30	68	95	Fisheries	10.7%	Rice	9.0%
Jamaica	30	40	69	Aluminum	34.5%	Bauxite	16.5%
20%–29%							
Mauritius	29	69	100	Sugar	38.7%	Fisheries	1.5%
Tunisia	26	56	82	Petroleum	32.5%	Fisheries	3.1%
India	25	47	51	Tea	4.6%	Iron Ore	4.2%
Vietnam	24 c/	NA	NA	Fisheries	10.3%	Rubber	4.0%
Dominican Rep.	21	81	98	Sugar	20.6%	Nickel	15.4%
Philippines	20	49	95	Coconut Oil	7.0%	Copper	5.1%
10%–19%							
China	19	43	NA	Petroleum	12.5%	Cotton	1.7%
Pakistan	18	36	64	Cotton	12.1%	Rice	8.4%
Bangladesh	16	39	NA	Fisheries	12.5%	Jute	12.5%
Haiti	15	NA	NA	Coffee	15.5%	Cocoa	1.8%
Nepal	11	48	NA	Rice	3.6%	Oilseed	1.6%
0%–9%							
Korea, Rep.	7	9	40	Fisheries	3.1%	Sugar	0.2%
Lesotho	5 c/	NA	NA	Wool	4.8%		
Lebanon	2 c/	NA	66	Tobacco	1.3%	Wool	0.2%
Total No. of Countries			95				
Avg Export Share of All Countries			71				
Median Export Share of All Countries			84				
Countries with Export Share > 90%			35				
Countries with Export Share > 50%			71				

Notes: Low- and middle-income countries in Africa, Latin America, Asia and Oceania, based on World Bank defini-tion (countries with GDP per capita in 1994 at 1987 constant purchase power parity $ of less than $10,500 and an average of $2,691).

a/ Based on United Nations Conference Trade and Development (UNCTAD), *Handbook of International Trade and Development Statistics, 2001* unless otherwise stated.

b/ Based on various editions of the following World Bank documents: *World Development Report, Trends in Developing Economies, Commodity Trade and Price Trends* and *African Economic and Financial Data.*

c/ Based on World Bank, *Commodity Trade and Price Trends, 1989–91 Edition.*

d/ Based on World Bank, *Commodity Trade and Price Trends, 1989–91 Edition.*

e/ Based on World Bank Development Indicators.

2

Measuring Development Prospects by 'Greening' the National Accounts

Kirk Hamilton and Rashid Hassan

Introduction

The principal aggregates of the System of National Accounts—GDP or GNI—are essential indicators for measuring economic performance and guiding macroeconomic policymaking. Almost from the inception of modern systems of national accounting in the 1940s by Kuznets and Stone, however, there have been vigorous debates about the extent to which the accounts can, or should, measure social welfare. The elevation of environmental issues in the policies of the developed world in the 1970s helped to fuel these debates along several dimensions.

The chief environmental criticisms of standard national accounting, as voiced in Ahmad et al. (1989),[1] fall under two main headings: (i) standard measures of income and product do not account for the depletion of natural resources; (ii) national income measures the goods but not the 'bads' (polluting byproducts, for example) inherent in economic activity. The publication of the Brundtland Commission Report in 1987 added a third dimension to the environmental critique: standard national accounts, because they ignore depletion and degradation, do not provide indications of the sustainability of economic development.

Since the 1980s, there has been a concerted effort by economists and national statisticians to clarify the conceptual issues linking environmental resources to national accounting, and to construct empirical estimates of environmental stocks and flows within, or in parallel to, the System of National Accounts. This effort is motivated first by a supposition that environmental factors

---

[1] The authors are with the Environment Department, The World Bank, and the Centre for Environmental Economics and Policy in Africa, University of Pretoria, respectively.

unmeasured or obscured in the national accounts are significant, and secondly, by the belief that more complete national accounting systems will support better management decisions concerning the environment and natural resources and their inter-linkages with the broader economy.

This chapter briefly reviews income and welfare measurement, then moves to the central topics of assets and sustainability, appraising the key conceptual and theoretical literature. Methods of asset accounting are outlined, followed by presentation of selected empirical results from 'greening' the national accounts. Linkages to policy are explored, followed by broad conclusions on some basic questions: To what extent has the promise of environmental accounting been realized? Which approach has the greatest policy significance? And where is environmental accounting likely to be most useful?

Income or welfare?

The canonical definition of income was by Hicks (1946), who defined 'Income No. 1' as: 'Income . . . is thus the maximum amount which can be spent during a period if there is to be an expectation of maintaining intact the capital value of prospective returns . . .; it equals consumption plus capital accumulation.' From this it is clear that income is a net concept—we can measure gross income in an economy as the sum of all payments to production factors, for example, but to arrive at the true measure of income we need to net out the depreciation of assets that has occurred over the accounting period. The extension of Hicksian notions of income to environmental accounts is straightforward. All that is required is to extend the range of assets whose value is being maintained in aggregate to include natural resources or, as an example of a 'bad' (pollution) stock. 'Green' national income is therefore regular national income less the value of depletion of resource stocks and the disamenity value of growth in pollution stocks.

It is worth asking why, if income is a net concept, the key indicator used by policymakers and reported in the press is Gross Domestic Product, or growth in GDP. There are two answers. First, because there are no direct measures of depreciation of assets (these are usually modeled by statistical agencies), there is a question of the accuracy of measurement of Net Domestic Product— the national accounting identity no longer constrains the range of estimates. Secondly, many of the key macro variables which are the target of policy (inflation and unemployment, to name the most obvious) correlate well with gross activity measures or the growth rates of these measures.

For those concerned with measuring economic progress there remains, however, the question of measuring welfare versus measuring income.

Because national income measures both consumption and the net change in assets, it is clear that it cannot be a direct measure of the welfare derived from consumption. The more difficult problem with national income as a welfare measure concerns what is excluded—healthfulness, for example, or the enjoyment of natural amenities. Moreover, there may be productive activities in an economy that, because they occur outside of the market, are not captured in the accounts. Household work is one such example, and we will look briefly at the harvesting of timber and non-timber products in the empirical section below.[2]

The most comprehensive attempt to extend the national accounts is the work of Robert Eisner, summarized in Eisner (1988). The 'Total Income System of Accounts' (TISA) imputes non-market production, including that in households, re-defines government expenditures on police and defense as intermediate consumption (as well as commuting and other costs associated with work), and expands measures of investment to include R&D, education and health. The TISA measure of income for the U.S. in 1981 exceeds the standard measure of GNP by about 60 percent.

Nordhaus and Tobin (1973) were the first to include adjustments for changes in the environment and natural resources in their Measure of Economic Welfare. Their approach has much in common with Eisner, including adjustments under the three broad headings of imputing non-market production, redefining intermediate production, and expanding measures of investment. An important point to bear in mind is that measuring income is not the same as measuring sustainability. This is the topic of the next section.

Income, assets and sustainability

The year 1989 was a watershed in terms of work in greening the national accounts. Repetto et al. published their landmark study on adjusting the GDP of Indonesia to include resource degradation and depletion, the United Nations and World Bank started research on applied environmental accounting in several countries (reported in Lutz (1993)), and a symposium volume by Ahmad et al. presented conceptual work dealing with the environment in the national accounts.

What is striking about the papers in Ahmad et al. (1989) is the extent of disagreement about quite fundamental issues. To give just one example, different papers in the volume suggest (i) increasing the measure of gross product by the value of environmental degradation; (ii) decreasing the value of net product by

---

[2] This is sometimes termed 'environmental income.'

the difference between current levels of 'defensive' expenditures and the cost of restoring the environment to the level of quality at the beginning of the accounting period; and (iii) modifying gross product to account for services provided by the environment. These are very different approaches to dealing with the issue of environmental degradation in national accounts.

The key to eliminating conceptual confusion in green accounting lay in Weitzman (1976). This paper made the critical link between growth theory and national accounting when Weitzman asked why we measure national product as consumption plus investment when the economic goal, at its simplest, is to consume. The answer lies in Weitzman's proof that the present value of current NNP (held constant) is just equal to the present value of consumption along the optimal growth path for a simple economy—net national product (NNP) is the 'stationary equivalent of future consumption.' The first environmental applications of the growth-theoretic approach to national accounting appeared in Hartwick (1990) and Mäler (1991). These papers examined a variety of pollution and natural resource problems, and showed what adjustments were required to NNP to reflect these issues.

While the growth-theoretic approach provided clear guidance on income measurement, the link to sustainable development remained to be explored. Pearce and Atkinson (1993) made a first attack on the problem by employing basic intuitions concerning assets and sustainability. They argued that sustainability can be equated to non-declining values of all assets, including natural resources. The consequence of this conceptualization is that changes in asset values, measured by net saving, should signal whether an economy is on a sustainable path. Pearce and Atkinson presented empirical results on net saving for a range of developed and developing countries using values published in the green accounting literature. This approach was used in World Bank (1997), which estimated total wealth and genuine[3] saving (net saving adjusted for resource depletion, CO_2 damages and human capital formation) for nearly 100 countries.

More recent theoretical work on income and savings has firmly established the linkage between net savings, social welfare and sustainable development. The saving link, explored further below, was established in Hamilton and Clemens (1999)[4] for an optimal economy, and Dasgupta and Mäler (2000) for non-optimal economies (with suitable definition of shadow prices). Asheim and Weitzman (2001) show that growth in real NNP (where prices are deflated by a Divisia index of consumption prices) indicates the change in social welfare in the economy.

---

[3] The term 'genuine' was applied in order to distinguish this aggregate from the traditional measure of net saving in the national accounts, which accounts only for depreciation of produced assets.

[4] A longer exposition of many of these issues is in Atkinson et al. (1997).

The basic theoretical insight of Hamilton and Clemens (1999) is to show that genuine saving G, utility U, social welfare V, marginal utility of consumption λ, and pure rate of time preference ρ are related as follows:

$$V = \int_{t}^{\infty} U(C, \ldots) \cdot e^{-\rho(s-t)} ds$$

$$G = \lambda^{-1} \frac{dV}{dt}$$

This just says social welfare is equal to the present value of utility, and that genuine saving is equal to the instantaneous change in social welfare measured in dollars. The utility function can include consumption C and any other set of goods and bads, while genuine saving must include the change in all stocks (assets) in the economy valued at current shadow prices. Assets can include bads such as stocks of pollution.

This result says that the path for social welfare can be determined by policies aimed at altering genuine savings levels in an economy. If policymakers wish to ensure continuously increasing social welfare, then the policy prescription must ensure positive genuine saving. By implication, policies affecting net investment in all the assets of an economy, including produced capital, natural resources, pollution stocks, and human capital, can play a role in achieving increases in social welfare.

Hamilton and Clemens (1999) go on to show that negative levels of genuine saving must imply that future levels of utility over some period of time are lower than current levels—that is negative genuine saving implies unsustainability. Similar implications hold for the approaches of Dasgupta and Mäler (2000) and Asheim and Weitzman (2001).

These approaches to 'greening' the accounts, and the models that underpin them, are agnostic on the question of the degree of substitutability between different assets, in particular between produced and natural assets. An important strand of the sustainability literature, dating back to Pearce, Markandya and Barbier (1989), looks at the question of *strong* versus *weak* sustainability. Weak sustainability assumes that there are no fundamental constraints on substitutability, and it is clear that the recent literature on saving and changes in real NNP is consistent with weak sustainability. If, however, some amount of nature must be conserved in order to sustain utility—the strong sustainability assumption—then these models need to be modified to incorporate the shadow price of the sustainability constraint.

A formal approach to the strong vs. weak sustainability problem has been explored in the 'Hartwick rule'[5] literature. Dasgupta and Heal (1979) and

[5] Hartwick (1977) showed that consumption is sustainable (in fact constant) in a fixed technology economy with an essential exhaustible resource if: (i) net saving is everywhere 0;

Hamilton (1995) show that if the elasticity of substitution between produced capital and natural resources is less than 1, then the Hartwick rule is not feasible—eventually production and consumption must fall, implying that the economy is not sustainable under the rule.

On the question of thresholds, it is clear that the saving approach to measuring sustainability and changes in social welfare is applicable under certain assumptions. A typical example of this problem is the potential existence of ecological thresholds—crossing a certain boundary may produce catastrophic results, such as the re-routing of the Gulf Stream as a result of global warming, or the death of most plankton in the ocean as a result of ozone layer destruction. As long as marginal damages are smooth and unbounded as a threshold is approached, the saving approach will give correct signals concerning sustainability, since approaching the threshold will eventually result in negative savings. If the marginal damage curve is not smooth and becomes vertical at the threshold, then the saving rule may not indicate unsustainability as the threshold is approached. There is clearly an important question of the science of threshold problems, since we do not know a priori what the shape of the marginal damage curve is for many important problems.[6]

The theoretical literature on national accounting has yielded important insights into the proper way to construct green national accounts, and has elucidated the linkages between expanded national accounting systems and questions of social welfare and sustainability. It has not, however, eliminated some of the practical difficulties in constructing green national accounts, which is the subject of the next section.

Asset accounting

A lot has been learned since 1989 on how to actually construct greener national accounts. The main problems in environmental accounting revolve around the fact that many of the relevant asset values are not observed in the marketplace. For the most part, natural resources are owned by governments and there is no market in resource assets. For issues like pollution damages, the effects of many of these damages are already reflected in the national accounts—human health damages reduce productive working days, for example—but they do not appear explicitly.

In the absence of market information, the analyst is reduced to constructing estimated accounts built upon two foundations: (i) measuring shadow prices

---

(ii) the elasticity of substitution between resources and produced capital is 1; and (iii) the elasticity of output with respect to produced capital is greater than the corresponding elasticity for the resource.

[6] See also Pearce et al. (1996).

for resources and pollutants—that is, the net contribution to dollar-valued social welfare resulting from an extra unit of the asset in question; and (ii) making assumptions about the future stream of benefits from the assets in question. We examine the accounting issues for specific assets below, focusing on the general principles rather than detailed formulae.

Exhaustible resources

The value of an exhaustible resource stock is the present value of the total resource rents generated by the stock up to the point of exhaustion. To actually calculate this, however, assumptions about future prices, extraction costs and the path of extraction must be made. A real market for resource assets would, in effect, embody an agreed set of assumptions on these factors.

The value of resource depletion is directly linked to assumptions about the future as well. Assuming some physical quantity q of a resource is depleted then the value of depletion is the change in the asset value of the resource stock before and after q is extracted. The literature contains what are more or less polar cases in terms of valuing depletion, as Hartwick and Hageman (1993) show. If extraction is optimal, so that scarcity rents (price minus marginal extraction cost) rise at the rate of interest—the Hotelling rule—then the value of depletion is just the current unit scarcity rent times q. This reduces to the valuation used by Repetto et al. (1989), unit total rent (price minus average cost of extraction) times q if marginal and average costs of extraction are equal. If q is constant to the point of exhaustion and unit total rents are also constant, then the El Serafy (1989) formula results—depletion equals the present value of the final quantity q extracted valued at the unit total rent.

If resource stocks are large relative to extraction, or if the discount rate is high, these two approaches to valuing resource stocks and depletion will yield very different results. On the other hand, if resource lifetimes are less than 20 years (a typical number) and social discount rates of 3–4 percent are used, the divergence is smaller. Underlying each approach, however, is a very different assumption. The Repetto et al. alternative requires optimality, and so we should observe resource prices rising at near-exponential rates (which we do not) if we wish to apply this approach. The El Serafy approach eschews optimality, and so underestimates the value that a profit maximizing owner would place on the resource stock. The two alternatives presumably bracket how a functioning market would value resource stocks.

If the value of resource depletion is 'model-dependent,' this is equally true for the treatment of resource discoveries. Hartwick (1993) presents one of the main approaches. If it is assumed that the cost of resource discovery is an increasing function of both the quantity discovered and cumulative discoveries (so that resource discovery becomes progressively more expensive), then resource discoveries should be valued at their marginal discovery cost. The assumed dependence of discovery cost on cumulative discoveries ensures that this marginal discovery cost will be less than the scarcity rent. As a practical matter, standard national accounting practice is to treat most discovery costs as investment—as long as there is no large divergence between marginal and average discovery costs, therefore, no explicit adjustment need be made to net saving to reflect resource discoveries.

Living resources

Setting aside for the moment the question of the age structure of stocks of living resources, simple models of living resources yield accounting approaches that are not fundamentally different from the approach to valuing exhaustible resources. The key differences are that living resources grow, and that they do not need to be discovered. The value of living resource stocks is equal to the present value of net harvest (harvest minus growth) over a potentially infinite time horizon. If optimal management is assumed, then the value of depletion of living resources is equal to unit scarcity rent times net harvest. In practice, many studies assume no wide divergence between marginal and average harvest costs, and so value assets and their depletion on that basis.

Note that, rather than depletion, there may be a net augmentation of the value of living resource assets if harvest is less than growth. From an accounting perspective, it is important to be sure that the regions where net growth is occurring are in fact regions where the resource has commercial value—this can be an issue with forest accounting in particular. If harvest exceeds growth, and can be assumed to continue to do so, the forest accounting problem reduces to the exhaustible resource problem.

Since living resource stocks have distinct cohorts of individuals born or germinated in a given year, this can introduce complications for accounting if, for example, only individuals within a given range of ages have commercial value. Vincent (1999a) shows how to account for forest depletion in such a situation. In addition to accounting for the harvest of commercial cohorts, it is necessary to account for the increasing value of younger cohorts according to how many years they are from having commercial value.

Deforestation

Deforestation offers a particular challenge in green accounting because it requires estimation of land values under alternative uses—first, when land is under forest (and can be assumed to remain so), and secondly, when the land is cleared for alternative uses such as crops or livestock. The difference between these two land values represents the net creation or destruction of wealth as a result of deforestation—destruction can occur, of course, when there are significant externalities or market or policy failures which distort private decisions to deforest.

The basic approach to the valuation of deforestation is to compare the total economic value of the land under the alternative uses. For agriculture this can be measured as the commercial land value or, where there are market distortions, the present value of land rents under agriculture. For forests, as Vincent (1999b) shows, this entails valuing local and global willingness to pay for standing forests, external benefits provided by these forests, net carbon sequestration, plus the value of rents generated by sustainable harvest of timber and non-timber products or non-extractive uses such as tourism.

Pollution

The principles of accounting for pollution in environmental accounts are clear enough, but practical issues abound. The main distinction that needs to be made is between flow pollutants, which cause instantaneous damage to assets (such as human lungs in the case of particulate emissions), and stock pollutants, which cause damage to assets over time and which typically dissipate naturally. The valuation approach for stock pollutants involves taking the present value of damages to assets over the period of time that they are exposed to the stock of pollution.

Valuing pollution in the national accounts is in some aspects different from how total pollution damages are valued in the environmental health literature. An accounting of total pollution damages from acid rain, for instance, would include damage to assets (human lives, buildings, soils, lakes, etc.), willingness to pay to avoid health damages, and lost production (from human illness, crop damages, and so on). Environmental accounting would consider only the damage to assets, in part because this is what theory suggests, but in part because many of the other values are already reflected in GDP—GDP is already *lower* than it would otherwise be because of the lost production.

Damage to human health dominates most accounting estimates of pollution damages (see, for example, Hamilton and Atkinson (1996)). Valuing these damages involves several difficult and controversial steps. Typically a dose-response function needs to be specified (linking how many deaths and illnesses are associated with a given pollution exposure). Then illness has to be valued on the basis of willingness to pay,[7] an area where there is still relatively

---

[7] An accounting approach would value only chronic illness, since this is notionally the depreciation of a stock of healthfulness, part of human capital.

little research. And then deaths have to be valued. Two approaches to the latter are typically applied, the 'human capital' approach which values lost wages as a result of premature death, and the willingness to pay approach, which employs an estimated 'value of a statistical life.'

Another difficulty in dealing with pollution concerns trans-boundary effects. Here the question arises as to which assets are damaged, and who owns them. The solution to the accounting problem lies in assumptions about property rights. If countries have the right not to be polluted by their neighbors, then pollution damages can be accounted for as if each country had to pay compensation for damages caused to all their neighbors. Thus there would be a deduction from saving corresponding to the damage that domestic pollution does to domestic assets plus the value of damage done to assets in other countries. In other words, damage to domestic assets from foreign pollution is assumed to be completely offset by compensatory payments by the foreign countries emitting the pollution.

Alternatively, if no such property right exists and compensation for pollution damages is not owed, then accounting for pollution consists simply of accounting for total damage to domestic assets associated with both domestic and foreign emissions. Depending on the nature of the pollutant (regional or global), on whether a country is up-wind or down-wind of major emissions, and on whether the pollutant is harmful or beneficial to a given country (some northern countries may benefit from global warming, for example), these two accounting approaches can clearly lead to very different values of adjustments to savings.

Exogenous change

Many economic variables affecting individual countries are determined exogenously—the classic example of this is the small exporting country, where world prices for the country's exports are determined by a global market which the country cannot influence in any substantial way.

Vincent et al. (1997) explore the accounting issues for a small resource exporter. The basic conclusion of their analysis is that saving should be adjusted to reflect exogenous price change by including the present value of future changes in world prices times the quantity of resource produced. This presents an obvious problem to the green accountant, since it requires a forecast of world prices. Possible approaches to this problem include extrapolating world prices based on past trends, but this is clearly fraught with large uncertainties.

Weitzman and Löfgren (1997) show how exogenous change in technology, as measured by total factor productivity, could be treated similarly in adjusted national accounts.

Conclusions on asset accounting

A major resource for practitioners has been provide by the United Nations (2004) in their handbook on *Integrated Environmental and Economic Accounting*. This presents a full set of asset and flow accounts in physical and value terms and deals with issues beyond what are presented above, such as linking physical flow data to input–output accounts.

The main conclusion to be drawn on asset accounting is that the lack of market prices for environmental assets makes virtually all environmental accounting results model-dependent. This was mentioned above, but requires emphasis. Practitioners need to specify their assumptions about the future. Some assumptions may be viewed as biasing valuations above or below what 'real' markets would produce—as argued above the Repetto et al. (1989) valuation of resource depletion is probably biased to the high side, while the El Serafy (1989) approach is probably low. But all valuations of environmental assets and changes in asset values must be considered to be contingent upon the assumptions made—there are right approaches but no 'right answer.'

Empirical experience

The empirical literature on green national accounting is by now enormous, and it would be fruitless to try to summarize the work that has been carried out to date. Hamilton and Lutz (1996) present an overview of the work accomplished by the middle of the last decade. What the following section offers is, first, a critical examination of the seminal empirical work by Repetto et al. (1989), second a sampling of cross-country empirical results based on the World Bank (2003) data base, and finally an example of the application of green accounting in southern Africa, a region where environmental accounting can have a real impact on policies.

Repetto et al. (1989) was the first comprehensive attempt to include natural resource and environmental issues in national accounts. They studied Indonesia, a country with a high degree of resource dependence. The analysis focused on oil depletion, forest depletion and soil degradation as shown in Table 2.1.

The results are striking, and helped to establish the empirical significance of green national accounting. In peak years, when oil prices were high, the value of depletion and degradation as a share of regular GDP was over 20 percent. Soil degradation exceeds 1 percent of GDP for many years, while forest depletion approached 7 percent. The results are clearly dominated by petroleum depletion, and here the results are particularly sensitive to the choice of accounting methodology.

Because Repetto et al. (1989) count oil discoveries as additions to product (see the discussion of this issue in the preceding section), NDP actually exceeds

Table 2.1 Comparison of Indonesian GDP and NDP, constant 1973 Rupiah (bn.)

Year	GDP	Petroleum	Forestry	Soil	Net change	NDP
1971	5,545	1,527	−312	−89	1,126	6,671
1972	6,067	337	−354	−83	−100	5,967
1973	6,753	407	−591	−95	−279	6,474
1974	7,296	3,228	−553	−90	2,605	9,901
1975	7,631	−787	−249	−85	−1,121	6,510
1976	8,156	−187	−423	−74	−684	7,472
1977	8,882	−1,225	−405	−81	−1,711	7,171
1978	9,567	−1,117	−401	−89	−1,607	7,960
1979	10,165	−1,200	−946	−73	−2,219	7,946
1980	11,169	−1,633	−965	−65	−2,663	8,506
1981	12,055	−1,552	−595	−68	−2,215	9,840
1982	12,325	−1,158	−551	−55	−1,764	10,561
1983	12,842	−1,825	−974	−71	−2,870	9,972
1984	13,520	−1,765	−493	−76	−2,334	11,186
Average Annual Growth	7.10%				4.00%	

Source: Repetto et al. (1989). Note that NDP excludes depreciation of fixed capital.

GDP from 1971 to 1974. This in turn has a significant impact on calculated growth rates from 1971 to 84, as reported in Table 2.1. If we exclude the data from 1971 to 1976, a period when petroleum discoveries were particularly strong in Indonesia, the growth rates in GDP and NDP from 1977 to 1984 are virtually identical. The 'headline' result in this study, the divergence in growth rates reported in Table 2.1, is therefore highly dependent on the choice of accounting methodology. Alternative assumptions yield very different results. If depletion and degradation are roughly constant as a proportion of GDP, as they were from 1977 to 1984 in Indonesia, then GDP and NDP growth rates are indistinguishable.

Quite aside from this question of model-dependence in the Indonesia results, it is also worth reflecting on questions of sustainability as derived in the paper by Asheim and Weitzman (2001). These authors show that the instantaneous change in real NDP, using a Divisia price index, is the correct indicator of sustainability, rather than any longer run growth rate in NDP, or indeed any comparison of NDP and GDP growth rates.

Cross country patterns of saving

The World Bank has been publishing estimates of genuine saving for roughly 150 countries since 1999 in the *World Development Indicators*. As an example of this work, Table 2.2 shows the composition of genuine saving in Latin America in 2001.

Table 2.2 Composition of saving in Latin America, 2001, percentage of GNI

	Gross saving	Education	Depreciation	Energy Depletion	Mineral Depletion	Net Forest Depletion	CO2 Damage	Genuine saving
Argentina	12.8	3.2	12.0	2.6	0.1	0.0	0.3	1.0
Bolivia	9.4	5.5	9.3	7.3	0.7	0.0	1.0	−3.4
Brazil	17.0	4.8	10.9	2.3	1.0	0.0	0.4	7.2
Chile	20.3	3.4	10.0	0.3	4.8	0.0	0.6	8.0
Colombia	14.7	3.1	10.3	6.6	0.1	0.0	0.5	0.3
Costa Rica	15.1	5.1	5.8	0.0	0.0	0.4	0.3	13.7
Ecuador	22.9	3.2	10.6	19.0	0.0	0.0	0.9	−4.4
El Salvador	14.9	2.2	10.3	0.0	0.0	0.6	0.3	5.9
Guatemala	10.4	1.6	9.9	0.8	0.0	1.0	0.3	0.0
Honduras	26.0	3.5	5.6	0.0	0.1	0.0	0.5	23.3
Mexico	18.1	4.6	10.6	5.2	0.1	0.0	0.4	6.4
Panama	24.3	4.8	7.9	0.0	0.0	0.0	0.6	20.6
Paraguay	10.6	3.9	9.5	0.0	0.0	0.0	0.4	4.6
Peru	16.8	2.6	10.3	1.0	1.2	0.0	0.3	6.6
Uruguay	10.9	3.0	11.5	0.0	0.0	0.2	0.2	2.0
Venezuela	22.4	4.4	7.2	23.1	0.3	0.0	0.6	−4.4

Source: World Bank (2003).

These estimates are based on some necessarily crude assumptions, given data limitations. Current education expenditures are treated as gross investment in human capital and there is no depreciation of human capital. Depreciation of produced assets is as reported by the United Nations, with some modeling of missing values. Energy and mineral depletion are estimated as total resource rents (price minus average extraction costs times quantity extracted). Cost data are derived from a variety of sources (Hamilton and Clemens (1999) list the principal sources) and regional average costs are often used to fill in gaps. Net forest depletion is calculated as average unit rent times the excess of harvest over natural growth—if growth exceeds harvest, then net depletion is set to 0 on the assumption that much of this growth is in non-economic (remote or inaccessible) forest stocks. CO_2 damages are really a place-holder for other pollutants, and represent the present value of global damages incurred by each ton emitted.[8] Genuine saving is calculated as gross saving plus education expenditures (these are in effect re-classified from consumption to investment) minus depletion and CO_2 damages.

The results in Table 2.2 show, first, that negative genuine saving is more than a theoretical possibility. The big energy exporters all display negative saving rates. Secondly, the adjustments to saving are sizable in many countries, particularly the mineral and energy producers. Finally, large resource endowments do not automatically lead to lower saving rates—sound policies, such as in

---

[8] The approach taken by the World Bank is to assume that countries have the right not to be polluted by their neighbors—under this regime compensation for damages would be paid by emitters, and genuine saving would be adjusted to reflect the value of these payments to other countries, as well as the damage done to the country's own assets from its own emissions.

Chile, lead to relatively robust levels of genuine saving (and therefore wealth creation) in spite of heavy dependence on minerals.

The next three figures display different aspects of the distribution of genuine saving across countries. Figure 2.1 scatters genuine saving as a percent of GDP against income measured by GDP per capita. The first point to note is that in 1999 there were many countries with negative genuine savings rates. Some of the observed negative savings rates are a result of extremely low rates of gross saving, rather than any environmental adjustments per se. There is a clear upward trend in the scatter—the rich are getting richer while the poor are getting poorer. It is also notable that roughly half the countries under $1000 per capita income have negative saving rates. The results are even more striking when population growth is factored into the analysis, the subject of Figure 2.2.

Population growth introduces a Malthusian aspect to environmental accounting. The fact that there are x% more people in a country in a given year as a result of population growth means that existing assets, including environmental assets, must be shared with these new citizens. Hamilton (2002) extends the World Bank saving data set to examine the effects of population growth. The basic insight is that, for exogenous population growth rate g, population P and total wealth W, genuine saving per capita is measured as,

$$\Delta\left(\frac{W}{P}\right) = \frac{\Delta W}{P} - g \cdot \frac{W}{P}$$

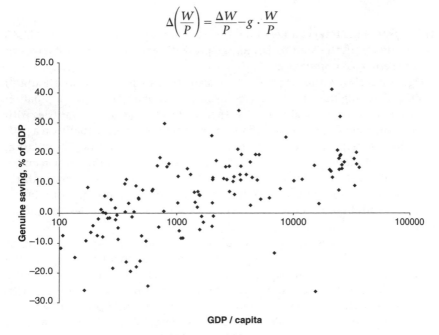

Figure 2.1 Genuine saving vs. GDP/capita, 1999

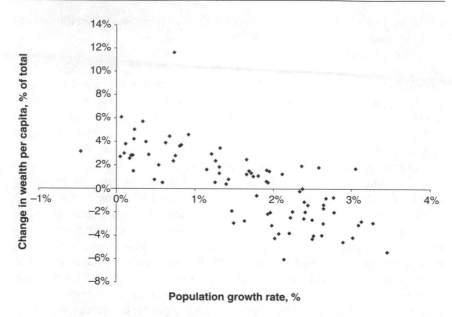

Figure 2.2 Change in wealth/capita vs. population growth rate, 1999

This says that the total change in wealth per capita equals genuine saving (ΔW) per person minus the Malthusian term representing the sharing of total wealth over the enlarged population.

Figure 2.2 shows the result of this calculation as presented in Hamilton (2002), scattering the change in total wealth per capita against the population growth rate. It is empirically the case that the great majority of countries with population growth rates greater than 1.5 percent per year are actually on a path of declining wealth per capita. To put this in context, the average population growth rate in low-income countries in 2001 was 2.1 percent, 2.6 percent in the Middle East and North Africa, and 2.7 percent in Sub-Saharan Africa. However, it is important to note that there is a not-insignificant number of countries with high population growth rates where sound policies are leading to increases in wealth per capita.

Figure 2.3 explores the question of whether countries are consuming or investing natural resource rents by scattering genuine saving rates against the share of mineral and energy rents in GNI.[9] The Hartwick rule states that a sustainable constant consumption path is possible in countries with exhaustible resources if resource rents are invested in other productive assets. If countries were in fact following such a sustainability rule, the scatter in

[9] Only countries where exhaustible resource rents make up more than 1% of GNI are shown.

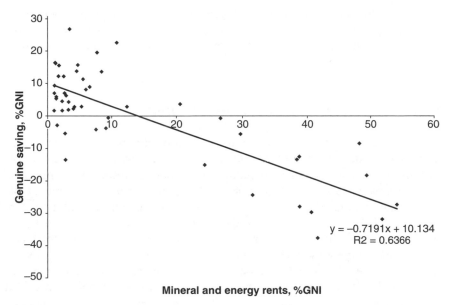

Figure 2.3 Genuine saving vs. exhaustible resource share, 2000

Figure 2.3 should exhibit no trend. In fact we observe a distinct downward trend, and the fitted line suggests that, looking in cross-section, for each additional per cent of GNI that is derived from exhaustible resource rents, roughly 0.72 of this is being consumed. A very significant proportion of the marginal resource endowment is therefore not being invested. It should be noted, however, that this result is largely driven by the countries with very large resource dependence, typically the oil states.

Finally, while the theory on genuine saving is very clear, there is the important empirical question of whether genuine saving rates do in fact predict changes in social welfare. Ferreira, Hamilton, and Vincent (2003) derive a means to test this using the World Bank's genuine saving data base. They show that saving in the current period should just equal the difference between current consumption and a weighted average of future consumption.[10] This is then tested over rolling 10-year periods and over a 28-year period. The conclusions are that (i) for some specifications of the test, more comprehensive measures of saving (including natural resource depletion) increase the ratio of current saving to future consumption; (ii) looking across countries and using a 28-year time horizon, each dollar of genuine saving is in fact converted into an incremental dollar of average future consumption; and (iii) looking along time

[10] To be precise, the weighted average is equal to the interest rate times the present value of consumption.

paths of individual countries over 10-year time periods, genuine saving is a good predictor of future consumption for poor countries but not for rich—for rich countries it seems that something more than capital deepening is determining future consumption.

Recent empirical results from Southern Africa

The past few years have seen major efforts to apply environmental accounting in selected countries in Southern Africa, which analysed critical aspects of sustainable management and exploitation of natural resources. A number of studies were carried out to evaluate the experiences and performance of Namibia, Botswana and South Africa (SA) in managing their natural resources in pursuit of economic expansion and growth (Lange et al., 2003). While these studies focused mainly on the performance of key resource sectors, they have also produced preliminary assessments of changes in the level and composition of total wealth and hence aggregate welfare. This section provides a critical review and syntheses of the results and experiences documented in these studies.

Dependence on natural resource endowments

The extent of dependence on natural resources in Botswana, Namibia and SA can be seen from the fact that primary production (agriculture, forestry and fisheries) and processing of primary products (food, timber and minerals) contribute about one-third of total value added (VAD) and more than 70 percent and 40 percent, respectively, of the total value of exports in Namibia and Botswana and SA (Lange et al., 2003). While the three countries have rich mineral endowments, mining is the mainstay of the economy of Botswana as it supplies 33 percent of GDP and 74 percent of exports, compared to shares of less than 6 percent of GDP and less than 34 percent of exports in SA, which has a more diversified economy. Namibia falls between these extremes. Prudent exploitation and management of these natural assets is accordingly critical for the future well-being of the people of the three countries.

Performance in managing key resource sectors

Physical and monetary asset accounts have been constructed for a number of key natural resource sectors to examine the state of these resources and trends in their exploitation and development in Namibia, Botswana, and SA. In addition to generating detailed accounts of the physical state and trends in extraction and consequent changes in stocks, these studies produced very valuable information and analyses of the way that resource rents from liquidating these natural assets have been managed to compensate present and future generations for depletion of their natural wealth. This is of crucial importance particularly in the case of exhaustible resources such as subsoil assets, which constitute a significant share of total wealth and provides the main source of income and foreign exchange for financing investment and economic growth in the three countries.

Experiences with managing subsoil assets in Southern Africa

While all three countries are endowed with rich mineral resources, interesting variations exist between them in the type, reserve levels and historical patterns in the extraction and use of these assets. Gold and coal contribute more than 70 percent of the mining income in SA while more than 90 percent of mining VAD come from diamonds in Botswana. On the other hand, diamonds and recently uranium are the major minerals produced by Namibia. Mining is relatively older in SA and Namibia dating back to the nineteenth century, compared to Botswana where development of commercial mining only started in the 1960s. Accordingly, mining made significant contributions to financing early investments in diversifying economic activity through the development of the manufacturing, services, and other sectors that currently dominate the economies of SA and Namibia, whereas the economy of Botswana remains highly dependent on diamond mining (Lange and Hassan, 2003; Blignaut and Hassan, 2002).

The physical asset accounts indicate that extraction of diamonds has been on a steady increase in Botswana over the past 20 years growing by fourfold, from 5.1 to 20.7 million carats production per year between 1980 and 1999. As a result, about 25 percent of known diamond reserves in Botswana have been extracted over the past 20 years, which appears to be relatively rapid. On the other hand, SA has slowed down its gold extraction over the same period by about 30 percent, dropping from 675 to 464 ton production per year by 1998. At the same time, SA has increased its extraction of coal by 150 percent over the same period from 115 to 290 million tons production per year by 1998. In spite of that, SA remains with about 80 percent and 90 percent of its gold and coal reserves, respectively (Figure 2.4). Extraction of diamonds fluctuated around one million carats and uranium production dropped from 5.5 to 3.3 tons per year in Namibia between 1980 and 1998 (Lange and Hassan, 2003).

Considerable resource rents have been generated in the three countries during the 20 years of extraction described above. Generated rents have reached highs of more than US$ 3 billion in the mid-1980s but dwindled to low levels of less than $1 billion in the 1990s in SA as world gold prices

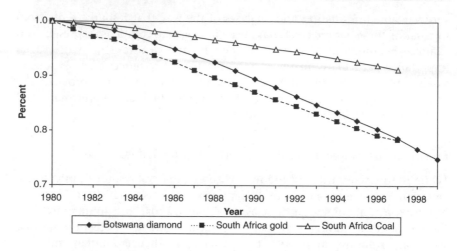

Figure 2.4 Mineral reserves in Botswana and South Africa, 1908–1998 (Index 1980 = 1)

declined. On the other hand, mineral rents in Botswana continued to rise, reaching more than $2 billion by the late 1990s with increased extraction of its diamond resources. Mineral rents in Namibia fluctuated around $150 million per annum during the period as the countries high-value diamond resources have been depleted and the recent revival through gold and offshore diamond discoveries.

How the generated rent was managed and used is critical to assessing progress toward sustainability in these countries. The first question in this regard is who received the generated mineral rent? The Botswana government was the most successful of the three countries in recovering minerals rent through taxes and royalties, which averaged about 76 percent over the reported period, followed by Namibia where rent recovery fluctuated around 50 percent (Figure 2.5). Least successful in minerals rent recovery was SA, which only after the 1980s managed to recover an average of 45 percent of the rent compared to almost zero rents in the 1970s. This is in part a reflection of the variation in minerals' property rights regimes in the three countries as the state has been the owner of subsoil assets in Botswana and Namibia, whereas private rights dominated mining in SA in the past, a situation revised in the new mining policy (RSA, 1998) to vest all minerals rights in the state (Blignaut and Hassan, 2002).

While success in recovering rents is certainly a necessary prerequisite, it is not a sufficient condition for sustainable management and exploitation of natural resources. Sustainability requires that sufficient shares of the recovered rent be reinvested in other forms of capital to compensate current

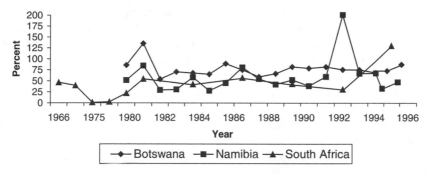

Figure 2.5 Recovery of mineral rent, 1966–1996 (percent)

and future generations for liquidation of their natural capital. When rent recovery by the state is low, private extractive companies enjoy a windfall in rents, which often forms an incentive for over-exploitation and sub-optimal extraction regimes. On the other hand, the private sector is often considered more efficient than the government in investing the generated rents. However, the nature of public and private investments generally differs as public investment targets social development (infrastructure and basic services) while private investment builds commercial and industrial capital. Nevertheless, both forms of capital add to total wealth and hence the more relevant question becomes what shares of the rent accruing to public or private hands are reinvested (i.e. public versus private saving rates) and in what forms of capital?

Although it was possible to estimate public and private shares in total minerals rent, data were inadequate to allow calculation of rates of reinvestment of minerals rent by private or public sectors. Nevertheless, a few indicators were constructed to evaluate progress toward sustainability in managing mineral resources in these countries. The first indicator was the Sustainable Budget Index (SBI) used by Botswana to monitor the manner in which revenues from liquidation of its mineral resources have been converted into other forms of capital assets (Lange and Hassan, 2003). The SBI calculates the ratio of non-investment spending to recurrent non-mineral revenue.

If the SBI is less than one, this indicates that all current government consumption is financed from non-mineral revenues and hence all mineral revenues are invested, ensuring sustainability. A value of SBI greater than one thus means that part of current consumption is financed from mineral revenues, an indication of unsustainable consumption. According to the SBI, Botswana has performed well in reinvesting minerals rent with a SBI value of less than 1 up to the late 1990s when SBI began to approach the value of 1 (Lange and Hassan, 2003).

The other indicator of sustainability in managing subsoil assets was constructed for SA based on El Serafy's 'user cost' approach for calculating resource depletion (El Serafy, 1989) described in an earlier section. The user cost of mineral extraction was accordingly calculated for the 1996–93 period and compared to capital formation in the mining industry (total mining investments) of SA. The results indicated that the mining sector in SA invested more than twice the user cost of mineral extraction, which means that the user cost has been fully reinvested in alternative forms of capital (Blignaut and Hassan, 2002).

The forest and woodlands of SA

While the arid lands of Namibia and Botswana support few forest resources, SA manages extensive forest plantations and other woody resources. Forests cover about 2 percent of the land in SA, one-third of which is under natural forests and the rest is cultivated plantations (Hassan, 2002). Natural forests are relatively small in SA compared to the extensive forest plantations, which make about one-fifth of the total land under industrial plantations in Africa (Hassan, 2002). Based on its cultivated plantations, SA has developed an advanced timber industry that currently supplies a large share of the world's pulp and paper products. Moreover, woodlands and thicket occupy about 40 percent of the total land area in the country. The economic contribution of these resources however, is seriously underestimated in the current national accounts, as only the commercial output of cultivated forests is reported. This is especially true for measures of wealth, which currently exclude the value of all forest assets including cultivated plantations (Hassan, 2000).

Comprehensive physical and monetary asset accounts recently constructed for SA revealed that forests and woody resources contribute significantly to the country's total wealth. The official measure of SA's NDP for 1998 increased by more than 2 percent when adjusted for the missing value of net accumulation of carbon and timber stocks in standing forest and wooded land resources (Hassan, 2002). This 'environmental income' is important in South Africa.

The Fisheries of Namibia

Unlike Botswana and SA, fisheries represent an important sector in Namibia that contributes significant shares of GDP, exports and employment. During the 1960s, before fish stocks began to collapse in Namibia, fisheries contributed about 10 percent and 15 percent of GDP and exports, respectively (Lange, 2003a). As a result of the predominantly open access to foreign fleets before independence, the stock of the country's main commercial species were seriously depleted, falling from 14 million tons to about 2 million tons by the late 1980s. This was reflected in the much lower production and hence smaller contribution of only 2 percent to GDP and exports by 1980.

Namibia however, introduced new policy and control measures over the exploitation of its fisheries after independence in 1990. The new measures were successful and effective in halting the decline of the country's fisheries, which has since then seen stable stocks and was set on a recovery course. By 1998 fisheries contributions to the national economy have significantly improved reaching levels of 9 percent and 30 percent, respectively of GDP and value of exports. However, the government has been relatively unsuccessful in recovering the resource rent from fisheries as private companies continue to collect about 75 percent of the rent (Lange, 2003a). At the same time, this situation indicates the huge potential for fisheries to contribute to future revenues and fiscal improvements in Namibia, with better rates of recovery and prudent use of the resource rent. The contribution of fisheries to the total wealth of Namibia after corrections were made through fisheries resource accounts starting in 1990 is discussed in the next section (Figure 2.6(c)).

Aggregate performance and measures of national wealth in Southern Africa

In addition to assessing the performance of Namibia, Botswana, and SA in managing selected natural resource sectors, environmental accounts were developed and used to correct aggregate measures and indicators of sustainability. The conventional asset accounts of these countries do not include any of the above natural resource assets as part of national wealth and hence provide misleading information on the performance in managing the total asset portfolio and consequently sustainability of the path of development. Natural resource asset accounts have been compiled for minerals, forests, and fisheries and used to correct measures of total wealth in the three southern African countries. Table 2.3 shows the extent by which conventional measures of national capital may underestimate actual total wealth. The magnitude of miss-measurement is very high in the case of Botswana where subsoil assets alone account for close to half of actual total wealth. For a country that has diversified its asset portfolio away from natural resource endowments like SA, natural capital (in this case only minerals and plantation forests) constitutes a relatively smaller portion of total wealth, but nevertheless large in magnitude (about 4 percent of total wealth of more than R trillion). The exclusion of minerals and fisheries alone reduces total wealth in Namibia by more than 10 percent in recent years.

The preliminary resource asset accounts of the three countries also reveal the degree of relative dependence and hence vulnerability of the different countries to careful exploitation and management of their natural capital.

Table 2.3 Components of total wealth in Namibia, Botswana, and South Africa (1981–1996)

Year	Botswana (Billion 1993 Pula)		South Africa (Billion 1993 Rand)		Namibia (Billion 1990 N$)	
	Total Wealth	% Natural capital	Total Wealth	% Natural capital	Total Wealth	% Natural capital
1981	15.2	53.1	1028	2.4	25.0	7.1
1982	20.0	62.1	1079	2.8	25.3	6.4
1983	25.4	67.2	1120	2.8	25.3	6.1
1984	29.8	68.6	1160	3.0	25.1	5.8
1985	31.7	63.2	1188	3.0	25.6	7.5
1986	34.1	60.1	1201	3.1	26.2	10.3
1987	36.5	57.5	1213	3.2	26.6	11.4
1988	41.9	57.4	1226	3.2	27.2	13.1
1989	44.9	53.6	1245	3.1	27.6	14.1
1990	50.8	53.5	1272	3.8	29.0	17.3
1991	52.5	49.4	1279	3.5	28.5	15.7
1992	53.2	47.1	1293	3.9	28.9	15.5
1993	53.2	43.7	1302	4.2	29.1	14.8
1994	56.2	43.5	1313	4.2	29.4	13.7
1995	59.4	44.2	1330	4.3	28.9	10.3
1996	64.5	42.7	1221	4.9	29.7	10.6

Botswana provides a typical case of very high dependence on the natural component of its total wealth. The country however, has significantly reduced its reliance on its mineral wealth in the recent past by converting that wealth into alternative forms of capital, namely investments in produced and financial assets (Lange and Hassan, 2003). On the other hand, the share of natural capital in Namibia's total wealth has increased over the past few years, mainly due to new discoveries of additional mineral wealth and recognition of the value of the country's important fisheries resources in the mid-1990s.

Figures 2.6(a) to 2.6(b) show how the value of total wealth has changed in the three countries over the past two decades. Again the dependence of Botswana on its mineral wealth is evident from the fact that change in total wealth has closely followed the pattern of change in mineral wealth (Figure 2.6(a)). It is also clear from Figure 2.3(a) that Botswana has managed to top its mineral wealth with a build up of a significant share of other forms of capital. SA displays a similar pattern, although with a significant slow-down of building alternative forms of capital (Figure 2.6(b)). This is also observed in Namibia, apart from erratic patterns of asset values in the late 1980s and early 1990s (Figure 2.6(c)).

Results of the above reviewed efforts to green the national accounts in southern Africa indicate the high margin of error in measuring economic performance and developing sustainability indicators when environmental values and depletion of natural capital are not properly accounted for. Valuable insights were also gained into the varied experiences of the studied countries in managing their natural wealth in pursuit of economic growth and how successful were their different resource use regimes and policies in keeping

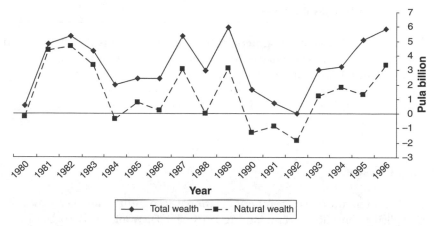

Figure 2.6(a) Change in value of assets in South Africa, Botswana, and Namibia (1980–1996)

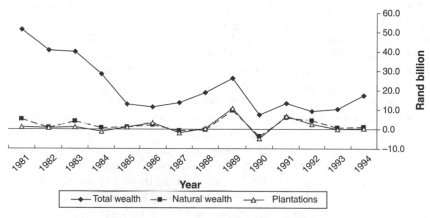

Figure 2.6(b) Change in value of assets in South Africa (1981–1994)

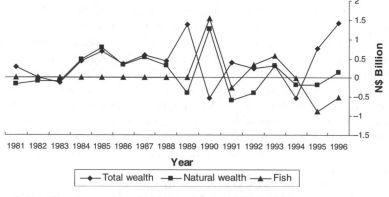

Figure 2.6(c) Change in value of assets in Namibia (1981–1996)

them on a sustainable development path. A major lesson is that, while high dependence on natural resource endowments, especially non-renewable assets such as diamonds in Botswana is a source of economic risk and vulnerability, prudent resource use policies in terms of adequate recovery and reinvestment of resource rents provide critical insurance against future declines in social welfare.

Policy linkages

The 1980s literature on environmental national accounting embodied a more or less explicit assumption that measuring a greener NDP would lead to better, more environment-friendly, policymaking. The development of both the theory and the practice of environmental accounting casts some doubt on this question.

The practical issue is that a green NDP is simply an adjustment in the level of measured income. From this information alone it is difficult to draw any policy conclusions, particularly with regard to sustainability. As the discussion of the Repetto et al. (1989) study hints, there is no information with regard to sustainability in the relative growth rates of adjusted and unadjusted NDP. If depletion and damage to the environment were constant from year to year, then the growth rate of green NDP would be greater than regular NDP; if depletion and damage were the same proportion of NDP from year to year, the growth rates would be precisely the same.

Asheim and Weitzman (2001) show that for a particular NDP deflator, a Divisia price index, the growth rate of real NDP indicates whether social welfare is rising or falling. While this is elegant in theory, in practice there do not seem to be examples of empirical application. Regarding the policy linkages of this approach, there is the thorny problem of trying to link policy levers to the rates of change of individual components of real NDP. As an alternative to greener NDP, the analysis of genuine saving offers a more direct route to policy issues. First, the sign and magnitude of genuine saving offers a clear indicator of the extent to which social welfare is increasing, and whether the economy is on an unsustainable path. Secondly, the decomposition of genuine saving into its component parts permits relatively direct linkages to be established between saving and particular policy levers. If a country experiences low or negative net saving at a point in time, policy responses to the effect that 'we need to boost saving' are clearly not operational. Decomposition of genuine saving permits a more practical response, falling into two broad categories: (i) what policies will boost gross saving; and (ii) what policies will affect the series of additions and subtractions that comprise genuine saving?

The determinants of gross saving can in turn be broken down into two broad components, public sector and private. For the public sector, the level of government dis-saving is typically the issue, and this is directly amenable to alteration by fiscal policies. Policies linked to private saving tend to be more indirect, involving tax incentives, maintenance of positive real interest rates, and the depth and stability of the financial system. For many developing countries a focus on government dis-saving is likely to be the most important issue.

The other components of genuine saving are linked to specific sectors. Policies to boost these components of saving include: increasing education expenditures and other investments in human capital; reducing incentives to over-exploit natural resources by, for example, ensuring rent capture and enforcing concessions and quotas; and reducing excess pollution emissions through monitoring, enforcement and provision of economic incentives. For natural resources and the environment, the key is not to stop exploitation or completely eliminate pollution, but rather to ensure efficient use of these resources. Since natural resources are often over-exploited in developing countries, and pollution emissions are excessive in the newly industrializing countries, better resource and environmental policies in the developing world will generally boost genuine saving.

The theory presented under the heading 'Income, assets and sustainability' on p. 62 shows that the policy rule for increasing social welfare is to maintain positive genuine saving. For countries that are exploiting natural resources, this implies that the value of resource depletion is being offset by other invest-ments, which in turn are, notionally at least, financed by the resource rents being generated. This raises an important question about the effectiveness of public investment. If resource rents are being invested in 'white elephant' projects with low social returns, then increases in social welfare cannot be guaranteed, even if the policy rule is being followed.

Conclusions

There is by now a decade and a half of experience with environmental accounting, and the theoretical underpinnings of this work are firmly estab-lished. Most OECD countries, and many developing countries, are carrying out work on resource and environmental accounts. The United Nations (2004) has codified the methodologies to be employed in practical environmental accounting. This is a good time to ask whether the promise of environmental accounting has been realized.

Lange (2003b) provides an exhaustive description of the potential and actual uses of a range of environmental accounts. This chapter highlights some of the applications in southern Africa, including the Sustainable Budget Index in Botswana. But, as the previous section noted, there was a sense in the 1980s literature that if we could just 'green' GDP, then better policy would automatically follow. Certainly these expectations have not been met. It may be that the earlier emphasis on adjusting income, rather than accounting for changes in asset values, was a blind alley, both in terms of policy application and links to sustainability. Simply handing a Finance Minister an adjusted measure of income does not answer two critical questions: is there a problem? and what should be done about it? This is not to deny, however, that better measures of income are important.

This chapter has argued, and the literature largely supports the argument, that adjusted measures of saving have the greatest policy significance. Savings measures are also quite sensitive to environmental adjustments: if gross saving is 15 percent of GDP, and resource depletion 1.5 percent of GDP, then net saving will be reduced by 10 percent when the environment is taken into account. In many instances the adjustments made to savings will be large—as Table 2.1 suggests, the Finance Minister of Ecuador presumably thinks that the country's saving rate is nearly 23 percent of GNI, whereas in net terms it is actually less than −4 percent. For the most resource-dependent countries the standard national accounting aggregates may be seriously misleading.

The empirical evidence on environmental accounting strongly suggests that this work will be of greater importance in developing than in developed countries. The greatest significance will be observed in low income resource exporters, 'oil states,' and rapidly industrializing countries.

It is important to note that the decision to consume resource wealth, which will manifest itself in low or negative genuine saving rates, represents an opportunity not taken. Resource assets represent a sort of frozen development finance which some countries (Malaysia, Botswana) have used to good effect. Other countries choose to consume resource rents, which, while it boosts short-run welfare, does so at the cost of future welfare. The starting level of income is relevant in this instance. It is one thing for Saudi Arabia, at $8500 per capita GNI, to choose to forgo future welfare; it is another matter entirely for Nigeria at $290 GNI per capita.

Sustainability rules may seem like an irrelevance for low-income countries under stress, such as the Democratic Republic of the Congo. In extreme circumstances consuming wealth is the correct policy option, when the alternative is starvation. But this should serve as a clear signal to the international community that some of these countries are not only poor but getting poorer.

While this chapter has emphasized the greening of national accounts, it is worth noting in conclusion a key insight from the theoretical literature on income and asset accounting: it is the change in value of all assets that determines the prospects for social welfare and sustainability. This implies that, beyond greening, a series of further adjustments to saving—human capital accumulation, both in terms of knowledge and healthfulness, reclassifying R&D as investment, net accumulation of social and institutional capital—are ideally required in order to assess development prospects.

References

Ahmad, Y., S. El Serafy, and E. Lutz (eds) (1989), 'Environmental accounting for sustainable development', Washington, DC, World Bank.

Asheim, G. B., and M. L. Weitzman (2001), 'Does NNP Growth Indicate Welfare Improvement?' *Economics Letters* 73 (2001): 233–9.

Atkinson, G., R. Dubourg, K. Hamilton, M. Munasinghe, et al. (1997), 'Measuring Sustainable Development: Macroeconomics and the Environment'. Cheltenham: Edward Elgar.

Blignaut, J. and R. Hassan (2002), Assessment of the performance and sustainability of mining subsoil assets for economic development in SA. Ecological Economics, Vol. 40, Issue 1: 89–101.

Dasgupta, P., and Heal G. (1979), *Economic Theory and Exhaustible Resources*, Cambridge: Cambridge University Press.

—— and K.-G. Mäler (2000). Net national product, wealth, and social well-being. Environment and Development Economics 5, Parts 1&2: 69–93, February & May 2000.

Eisner, R. (1988), 'Extended Accounts for National Income and Product', *Journal of Economic Literature*, vol XXVI: 1611–84. http://ideas.repec.org/a/aea/jeclit/v26y1988i4p1611-84.html

El Serafy, S. (1989), 'The proper calculation of income from depletable natural resources', in Y Ahmad, S. El Serafy, and E. Lutz (eds).

Ferreira, S., K. Hamilton and J. Vincent, (2003). Comprehensive wealth and future consumption. Mimeo.

Hamilton, K. (1995), Sustainable Development, the Hartwick Rule and Optimal Growth. *Environmental and Resource Economics* 5, 393–411.

—— (2002), 'Sustaining per capita welfare with growing population: theory and measurement.' Presented at Second World Congress of Environmental and Resource Economists, Monterey, California, June 27–30.

—— and Atkinson, G. (1996), 'Air Pollution and Green Accounts, Energy Policy', vol. 24 no. 7: 675–84.

Hamilton, K., and Atkinson, G. (1996), 'Measuring Sustainable Development: Progress on Indicators, Environment and Development Economics 1: 85–101.

——, and M. Clemens (1999), 'Genuine Saving in Developing Countries', *World Bank Economic Review*, 13: 2, 333–56.

—— and E. Lutz (1996), 'Green National Accounts: Policy Uses and Empirical Experience'. Environment Department Technical Paper No. 39. Washington: World Bank.

Hartwick, J. M. (1977), 'Intergenerational equity and the investing of rents from exhaustible resources'. *American Economic Review*, 67 (5): 972–4.

—— (1990), 'Natural Resources, National Accounting and Economic Depreciation', *Journal of Public Economics* 43: 291, 304.

—— (1993), 'Notes on economic depreciation of natural resources stocks and national accounting', in A. Franz and C. Stahmer (eds), *Approaches to Environmental Accounting*. New York: Springer-Verlag.

——, and A. Hageman (1993), 'Economic depreciation of mineral stocks and the contribution of El Serafy' in Lutz (ed.) 1993.

Hassan, R. M. (2000), 'Improved measure of the contribution of cultivated forests to national income and wealth in South Africa, Environment and Development Economics', Volume 5: 157–76.

—— (ed) (2002), 'Accounting for Stock and Flow Values of Woody Land Resources: Methods and results from South Africa. Centre for Environmental Economics and Policy', in Africa (CEEPA), University of Pretoria, Pretoria.

—— (2003), 'Forestry accounts: capturing the value of forest and woodland resources', in Lange, Hassan, and Hamilton.

Hicks, J. R. (1946), 'Income' = Chapter XIV of *Value and Capital* (2nd edn, Oxford Clarendon Press, 1946), reprinted in Parker, R. H., Harcourt, G. C., and Whittington, G., *Readings in the Concept and Measurement of Income* (2nd edn Deddington, Oxford, Philip Allan, 1986).

Lange, G. M. (2003*a*), 'Fisheries accounts: management of a recovering fishery', in Lange, Hassan, and Hamilton.

—— 2003*b*, 'Policy Applications of Environmental Accounting. Environment Department Papers', Environmental Economics Series No. 88. Washington: The World Bank.

—— and R. Hassan (2003), 'Mineral accounts: Managing an exhaustible resource', in Lange, Hassan, and Hamilton.

——, —— and K. Hamilton (2003), 'Environmental Accounting in Action: Case Studies from Southern Africa'. Cheltenham: Edward Elgar.

Lutz, E. (ed) (1993), 'Toward Improved Accounting for the Environment, World Bank, Washington DC.

Mäler, K.-G. (1991), National Accounts and Environmental Resources, Environmental and Resource Economics 1: 1–15.

Moss, M. (ed) (1973), 'The Measurement of Economic and Social Performance'. Conference on research studies on income and wealth, vol. 38, Columbia University Press for NBER.

Nordhaus, W., and J. Tobin (1973), 'Is Growth Obsolete?', in Moss (ed.).

—— and Kokkelenberg, E. C. (eds), (1999), 'Nature's Numbers: Expanding the National Economic Accounts to Include the Environment', Washington DC, National Academy Press.

Pearce, D. W., A. Markandya and E. Barbier (1989), 'Blueprint for a Green Economy', London, Earthscan Publications.

—— and Atkinson, G. (1993), 'Capital Theory and the Measurement of Sustainable Development: An Indicator of Weak Sustainability', *Ecological Economics* 8: 103–8.

Pezzey, J. (1989), 'Economic Analysis of Sustainable Growth and Sustainable Development', Environment Dept. Working Paper No. 15, The World Bank.

Repetto, R., Magrath, W., Wells, M., Beer, C., and Rossini, F. (1989), 'Wasting Assets: Natural Resources in the National Accounts', Washington, World Resources Institute.

Republic of South Africa (RSA) (1998), 'The New National Mining Policy', *Government Gazette*, Pretoria

Solow, R. (1974), 'Intergenerational equity and the exhaustible resources', *Review of Economic Studies*, Symposium, 29–46.

United Nations (2004), 'Integrated Environmental and Economic Accounting. New York' (forthcoming).

Vincent, J. R. (1999*a*), 'Net Accumulation of Timber Resources', Review of Income and Wealth, 45(2): 251–62.

——— (1999b). 'A framework for forest accounting,' *Forest Science* 45(4): 1–10.

Vincent, J., Panayotou, T., and Hartwick, J. (1997), 'Resource Depletion and Sustainability in Small Open Economies,' *Journal of Environmental Economics and Management* 33, 274–86.

Weitzman, M. L. (1976), 'On the Welfare Significance of National Product in a Dynamic Economy,' *Quarterly Journal of Economics* 90 (1): 156–62.

———, and Löfgren, K-G. (1997), 'On the Welfare Significance of Green Accounting as Taught by Parable,' *Journal of Environmental Economics and Management* 32: 139–53.

World Bank, (1997), 'Expanding the Measure of Wealth: Indicators of Sustainable Development,' ESD Studies and Monographs Series No. 17, Washington: The World Bank.

World Bank (2003), World Development Indicators 2003. Washington: The World Bank.

3

Impacts of Macroeconomic Policies on the Environment, Natural Resources, and Welfare in Developing Countries

Jon Strand and B. Gabriela Mundaca

Introduction

The purpose of this chapter is to explore relationships between macroeconomic conditions and policies on the one hand, and the environment, natural resources and population welfare in developing and emerging countries on the other. It is a broad and complex topic, and the literature dealing with the relationships between macroeconomic policy, and environmental and resource management and performance so far is small and typically not focused on direct links. Our objective here is to try to sum up some lessons from the literature so far, not the least with the aim to guide future investigations in this area.

An early discussion of relevant issues is found in Munasinghe (1996), in particular the chapter by Mäler and Munasinghe (1996). Broader discussions of the relationships between alternative economic policies, and environmental and resource degradation and management, are provided by Dailami and ul Haque (1998) and Weiss (1995). Dasgupta and Mäler (1996) and Pearce (1996) focus on more specific relationships between macro policies and environmental and resource degradation, with an emphasis on the possible causes of market failure, that is, the factors that lead to deviation from efficiency.

In what follows, our discussion is limited to a small set of issues that are in different ways macroeconomic:

1. Taxes and subsidies, such as those affecting sectors that extract natural resources or strongly influence the environment, and the environmental and resource/welfare effects of these. At a sector level these are often considered microeconomic given their implications for relative prices and

allocation efficiency, but given their importance and their link to a country's overall fiscal policy we include them here.

2. Domestic investment, including infrastructure investment affecting costs of resource extraction and environmentally degrading activities, clean-up and other environmental equipment, and the inclination to invest in projects that have long-run versus short-run consequences.

3. Monetary policy, in particular exchange rate and interest rate policy, with focus on exchange rate regime.

4. Issues related to the functioning of the financial sector, including control and regulation of credit and financial markets (hereunder regulation of banks and other lending institutions), the degree to which foreign direct investment (FDI) and foreign ownership are encouraged and regulated, and the actual flows of funds.

5. The implications of stress situations such as financial crises and disasters with major impact on GDP, employment and balance of payments, and policy responses to crises.

Points 1 and 2 are largely directed at particular sectors or even firms. Points 3 to 5 deal more with core macroeconomic policy issues, in combination with financial markets issues. Our discussion of points 3 and 4 will be focused more on principles than on empirical detail and verification, as data here are scant.

Our focus forces us to ignore, or downplay, a number of macroeconomic issues that are potentially important for environmental and resource developments. These include fiscal policy directed at short-run stabilization (hereunder budget deficit policy), for many the very heart of macroeconomics; growth and other long-run issues; and issues related to international trade or exports. The latter two topics are discussed in depth in other chapters of this book. The exclusion of fiscal policy issues is made mainly for brevity and in order to keep the focus of this chapter on financial (including monetary) policy.

We consider a wide set of environmental and natural resource impacts and management issues. Particular attention will however be paid to resource extraction issues, with tropical deforestation and factors causing it as a prime example. There are several reasons for this focus. First, a number of good and relevant studies now exist dealing with mechanisms behind tropical deforestation. Secondly, for many regions of the developing world, deforestation is a key environmental and natural resource problem, at least when viewed from a global perspective. In our view, forest management can also in many countries be considered as a good indicator of more general environmental management practices and principles.

As a basic principle of economics, efficient environmental policy implies that marginal costs and benefits of additional pollution reduction or natural resource improvement be made equal. In most developing countries today, such principles are far from being met. Sometimes the necessary legal framework does exist, and attempts are made, even by the private sector (as when environmental certification is required), to move in the direction of soundness in environmental and resource policy. Very often, however, the institutional capacity and incentives imply that little is done to enforce formal regulations.

The broader relationships between macroeconomic activity, environment and natural resource pressure, and population welfare are complicated and will not be analysed in detail here (work that discusses and analyses such issues includes the so-called Kuznets curve literature, see Grossman and Krueger (1995), Shafik (1994), Stern (1998), and Torras and Boyce (1998)). Direct quantitative income effects of environmental and resource availability and quality have been studied in the literature only to a limited extent, though they can be very significant. Studying 14 cities in Central America, Strand and Walker (2003) found that the average real disposable income of households without current tap water access (who are typically poor) would rise from 62 to 75 percent of the average income of households with initial access, if tap water access were provided to all. The supply is greatly affected by macroeconomic policies of types considered here (such as improper subsidies or lack of such, government public goods supply, and macro policies affecting government budgets). Failures in several sectors simultaneously (a typical situation) will compound and magnify the welfare effects identified here.

The concept of a 'macro economy' is in itself ambiguous. In standard macroeconomics as taught in universities and practiced by central banks and governments, GDP (or NDP) is taken as the basic measure of macroeconomic activity, and as the basis for analysis. More recently, views of what constitutes macroeconomic analysis has changed in several respects. The introduction of 'green national accounting' and related themes (Dasgupta (2001), Dasgupta and Mäler (1996), see also Hamilton and Hassan (this volume)), implies the alternative view that the value of, and change in, the environment and resources are part of the calculation of national product, on a par with society's output of more traditional goods and services. It is still unclear how the various effects ought to be embedded into standard macroeconomic policy. Few countries have so far even tried to implement the green GDP concept in the sense of putting numbers to the effects. Secondly, macroeconomic analysis has over time taken a gradually more micro-oriented form, implying that one also may consider sectoral and more partial effects, via the behavior of particular economic agents, in response to particular macroeconomic instruments. This is the approach we will take in the following.

1 Taxes, subsidies and government investment

Ideally, taxes and subsidies on commodities and economic activities ought to reflect the need for government financing, in combination with the need to address externalities by corrective taxes or subsidies. The current consensus however seems to be that, in many or most developing countries, too many taxes and subsidies work 'perversely' in promoting resource extraction and excessive pollution, instead of the opposite (whereby pollution and unwanted extraction are prevented by such policies). As documented by Clements et al. (1998), the level of government subsidies follows particular patterns that are not closely related to economic efficiency, but rather to other political and economic factors (such as the size of government and the composition of industry, with particularly high subsidy rates when government and the manufacturing sector are both big).

The concept of a 'subsidy' here needs some further clarification. Moor and Calamai (1997) (see also Beers and Moor, Table 3.1.) discuss two categories of such subsidies, namely direct on-budget subsidies (government funds are paid out directly to producers or buyers of particular commodities), and more indirect, off-budget subsidies that still normally have budgetary implications for the government. The second category can take many forms such as tax credits or reductions; public provision below cost (including insufficient resource rents for natural resources); capital cost subsidies (preferential loans and debt forgiveness); domestic-oriented market-based subsidies (through price regulation and procurement policies); and trade-oriented market-based subsidies (tariffs and non-tariff barriers). A third and more controversial category implies that a commodity charged a price that covers production cost but is not corrected for possible negative externalities (such as when the pump price of gasoline covers production cost but not road and pollution externalities). In many cases the issue of whether a commodity is 'subsidized' or not may then be controversial, since the level of the optimal tax correcting the externality very often is controversial.

Subsidies to, or under-taxation of, environmentally harmful activities has three main implications. First, too little care is taken by economic agents, to improve the environment and reduce excessive resource use. Perverse resource overuse may even be directly encouraged (such as with subsidies to clear-cutting for ranching purposes in the Brazilian Amazon, and with virtually cost-free limited-time logging concession in East Asia). Secondly, government revenues are reduced, leaving room for fewer highly productive government expenditures. Thirdly, it may have adverse distributional implications as in most cases only the wealthier population groups are able to exploit the subsidies, as with gasoline and electricity subsidies, and even often water subsidies.

Consider first subsidies to activities and goods that have a direct environmental and natural resource nature or have strong impact on the use of the environment and resources. Subsidy schemes of this type can take different forms in different sectors of the economy, and affect different users differently. Production subsidies lead to higher production of the subsidized good, and greater use of inputs into its production. Similarly, consumption subsidies lead to higher consumption of the relevant goods, assuming market clearing and production mainly for a domestic market. Such stimulus can be socially desirable if it corrects a market failure, or externality that implies that the activity level is otherwise sub-optimal. Much more typically, however, the subsidy is detrimental to efficiency. Since some of the relevant inputs are environmental and natural resource goods, subsidies lead to overuse and deterioration of these goods.

'Subsidies' can, as noted, also take the form of under-pricing for particular buyers, in cases where markets are not allowed to clear or the good in question is produced or procured by the government. Subsidies of this type will often go hand in hand with rationing of the resources among users, and with a number of further inefficiencies related to under-provision, such as poor maintenance and upkeep of necessary infrastructure, and poor incentives for system expansion. Important examples of such inefficient policies, involving natural resource allocation, can be found in the (urban and rural) water and sanitation sectors of many developing countries, as noted below.

The effects of subsidies on the environment and natural resources depend critically on institutional structure, in particular ownership structure, and on the time horizon of producers. With permanently high prices and secure ownership relationships, it is not always obvious that high producer prices, pushed up by subsidies, need to imply environmental over-exploitation (see e.g. Barbier et al., 1995 and Bohn and Deacon, 2000). When high prices by contrast are expected to be short lasting, ownership or control relationships insecure, or there is substantial illegal logging, the pressure toward over-exploitation is typically much greater (see Amacher, Koskela and Ollikainen, 2004a,b).

Beers and Moor (2001) discuss a range of environmental and resource implications of different sectoral subsidy groups, where subsidy is defined as the two first categories discussed above ('subsidies' that are due to a failure to correct for externalities are not included). They focus on eight economic sectors which all enjoy substantial subsidies worldwide: agriculture, water, forestry, fisheries, mining, energy, road transport and manufacturing. Table 3.1 below gives an

Table 3.1 Global annual public subsidies by sector, group of countries, 1994–1998, billion USD

Sector	OECD	Non-OECD	Total
Agriculture	335	65	400
Water	15	45	60
Forestry	5	30	35
Fisheries	10	10	20
Mining	25	5	30
Energy	82	162	245
Road transport	200	25	225
Manufacturing	55	Small	55
Total	725	345	1070
% of GDP	3.4	6.3	4.0

Source: Beers and Moor (2001).

overview of subsidy levels within these sectors, for both OECD and non-OECD countries, as annual averages for the years 1994–98. (The table shows that OECD country subsidies are far greater overall than non-OECD ones, and are concentrated in the agriculture and road transport categories.)

For the non-OECD group, which is of most interest here, direct subsidies to agriculture are rather limited (the largest single item being implicit subsidy in the form of cheap irrigation water). Instead, massive subsidies to agriculture in rich countries tend to push world market food prices down toward levels that make it difficult for most developing-country producers to compete. The main effect of the massive agricultural subsidies in OECD countries for poor countries is to seriously depress production of cash crops (of the types competing with developed-world agriculture). While hardly a favorable situation for the developing world, an effect of these may be to reduce environmental and resource exploitation, at least in the short run. Angelsen and Kaimowitz, in surveying a large number of studies (see Angelsen and Kaimowitz (1999), Kaimowitz and Angelsen (1998)), conclude that lower agricultural prices overall tend to reduce tropical deforestation. The main driving factor behind this conclusion seems to be that the pressure on the frontiers of agricultural expansion in forest-rich regions is thereby reduced.

In the water sector, developing country subsidies take three main forms: as irrigation subsidies (according to Beers and Moor (2001) about half of the total), as general underpricing, and in the form of unsanctioned illegal connections. These subsidies have three main effects. The first, and quantitatively most important, is that following from real subsidization of water-intensive irrigated agriculture, with zero or near-zero user prices of irrigation water, with often extremely low productivity in irrigated water use (as in Mexico as discussed in Asher (1999)). The second is inefficient water use within households, whereby water is over-used by tap households whose water rates are below government provision costs, and under-used by non-tap households, typically also with very adverse income distribution effects. The third is inefficient provision of water and sewage services by authorities. Utilities then have little incentives to maintain or expand the water and sewage systems (since utility revenue would then typically fall), and often lack even incentives to collect revenue properly (since greater revenue collection might lead to further budget tightening from above). Striking examples of such problems are found in Central American cities; see Strand (2000), Walker et al. (1999) and Strand and Walker (2004). The general problem is however ubiquitous, found also in African (Whittington et al., 1990) and Asian (Altaf et al., 1993) contexts as well. A related set of problems exist in the irrigation water sector (see e.g. Asher, 1999).

In fisheries, subsidies are largely a developed country problem, except in China which today subsidizes the sector substantially. Subsidies here take both on-budget and off-budget forms; the most important off-sector subsidies are investment subsidies and the private capturing of public resource rents; see

Milazzo (1997) for a further discussion. Fishery subsidies are particularly damaging in the long run, in particular when not accompanied by imposed production restraints or quotas, in that they tend to lead to excessive harvesting rates of ocean fish stocks, which are already seriously depleted in many ocean waters. This is a serious global resource problem for the long term, and a possible pollution problem for the short term. China today in particular appears to suffer from these problems, exacerbated by the subsidies from the 1970s on: despite more intensive fishing activity catch rates are only about half of those experienced in the 1950s. The long-run consequence may be to undermine the livelihood of regions currently relying heavily on ocean resources. The short-run effect of subsidies may in some cases be 'beneficial' in allowing the maintenance of incomes for local fishermen. Note however again that the overwhelming amount of subsidies are paid out in rich countries. Poor countries' welfare is then of course further reduced through the reduction in catch rates of their (largely unsubsidized) fisheries.

In forestry, subsidies comprise support policies both within and outside the forest sector. The most common type of support within the forest sector takes the form of inefficient capture of resource rents, mainly through low stumpage fees to logging companies, for the right to harvest timber over a given concession period (see e.g. the examples discussed by Asher (1999), from Cameroon, Costa Rica and Malaysia). Such under-pricing is particularly harmful when concession periods are short, or possible renewal of current concessions uncertain. Timber companies with concession then have strong incentives to harvest as much as possible within the area and time frame for the concession. Such practices have been, and are still widespread, in large regions in particular in South-East Asia and Africa. Beers and Moor (2001) calculate that prices paid by concessionists in most of the country cases studied (such as Indonesia, Russia and a number of African countries) only are in the range 5–25 percent of resource rents. In Latin America (notably Brazil) the main problem has rather been a large more direct subsidization of the forestry sector, in particular through investment credits for logging companies, and the payment of direct subsidies for the establishment of cattle ranches on previously forested lands. In many cases this has had a devastating effect on forest lands, and a double negative effect: first, widespread clear-cutting of forest for agricultural expansion; and secondly, little actual use of the forest resources lose (apart from selective exploitation of valuable tree species), as entire forest tracts are simply burned off.

Among the sectors covered by Beers and Moor (2001), the energy sector seems to be the most heavily subsidized sector in the developing world, with overall subsidies estimated at about 160 billion USD annually over the period 1995–98, as indicated in Table 3.1. Table 3.2 breaks these subsidies down by more specific energy sector. We see that more than half of the subsidies concern fossil fuel use, where subsidies often are particularly harmful, as fossil fuel use

Table 3.2 Public energy subsidies, 1994–1998 averages, billion USD

Sub-sector	OECD	Non-OECD	Total
Coal	30	23	53
Oil	19	33	52
Gas	8	38	46
Electricity	(included in fossil fuel subsidies)	48	48
Nuclear	16	Small	16
Renewables	9	Small	9
Total	82	162	245
Per capita (USD)	88	35	44
Share of BNP	0.4	5.5	1.8

Source: Beers and Moor (2001).

instead ought to be taxed for efficiency and fiscal reasons (as it is in many OECD countries, notably in Europe), see Dixit and Newbery (1984), Newbery (1985) and Gupta and Mahler (1994) for discussions with particular relevance to developed economies. While most subsidies in developed countries here go to production (which spurs output of fossil fuels but not necessarily domestic consumption), in developing countries most subsidies go to consumption, which increases consumption more directly. The most quantitatively important such subsidies are in the form of lower prices of gasoline and kerosene. Such subsidies are particularly high in many resource-rich (especially petroleum-rich) developing countries. A thorough documentation of such phenomena is found in Wunder's (2003) detailed study, focusing on deforestation, of eight oil-exporting countries (Gabon, Venezuela, Cameroon, Ecuador, Mexico, Nigeria, Indonesia, and Papua New Guinea).

In the case of subsidies to fossil fuels, the categories of 'subsidy' covered by Beers and Moor (2001) are clearly insufficient to describe the inefficiencies involved. From a social efficiency point of view, a 'net subsidy' or 'net tax' ought to be calculated relative to a socially optimal tax or subsidy. For fossil fuels this may lead to great differences in optimal subsidy rates, both by fuel type and by location of users. Two important and rather opposite examples may here be mentioned. The first is gasoline consumption, which often involves substantial (congestion, road use, accident and pollution) externalities that by themselves warrant substantial taxes. A further point is that gasoline is over-consumed by wealthier households, making a gasoline tax highly progressive in most developing countries. A zero tax on gasoline is then in reality a significant subsidy. There may here in addition be substantial geographical variation (both across and within countries) in the optimal tax due to differences in magnitudes of externalities and in willingness to pay to avoid these. As argued by, for example, Gupta et al. (2002) and Hossain (2003), for kerosene used in households the situation is often the diametrical opposite. Such fuels are consumed by poorer households, typically replacing fuelwood for cooking and heating. Subsidizing kerosene use may then have positive externality effects by leading to less pressure on local forests in the vicinity of concentrations of poorer households, a factor that is particularly significant in Africa.

Another important subsidy category is for electricity users, typically firms or wealthier households. Many of the effects are here similar to those for water, namely inefficient and inequitable use of limited overall electricity supplies, and often sub-optimal rates of expansion of new electricity capacity. The latter problem follows because the rate of capacity expansion often is a function of public utility net revenue, which tends to be low when electricity prices are kept artificially low.

A study by the International Energy Agency (1999) attempts to derive potential efficiency gains and reductions in CO_2 emissions, when energy subsidies are removed in selected countries. These figures are given in Table 3.3. These calculations are based on a framework developed by Shah and Larsen, (1992) and Larsen, (1994), and involves two main steps (see International Energy Agency (1999): 86–7). In the first step, overall subsidy rates to energy in the different countries are assessed by calculating 'reference prices' for the respective energy goods, that is, the prices that would have prevailed in the absence of subsidies. The second step uses assessed values of country- and energy-type-specific demand elasticities, to compute the respective energy demand responses, as well as the Harberger triangle inefficiency measures associated with the subsidies. We see that gains can be substantial, on average CO_2 emissions can be reduced by 16 percent in these countries (among which are the two most important emitters in the developing world, China and Russia), and the average potential GDP gain is close to 1 percent. One should further note that the IEA study does not consider the further gains that could be reaped, when scarce government funds are freed for other high-value uses when these subsidies are eliminated. (Such costs can however be roughly calculated using a range of values for the marginal cost of public funds).

Table 3.3 Calculated efficiency gains and environmental effects of removing subsidies on energy consumption, 1997–1998, selected countries

Country	Subsidy rate, %	Relative efficiency gain, %	Relative CO_2 reduction, %
Russia	33	1.5	17
China	11	0.4	13
Iran	80	2.2	50
India	14	0.3	14
Venezuela	58	1.2	26
Indonesia	28	0.2	11
Kazakhstan	18	1.0	23
South Africa	6	0.1	8
Average	21	0.7	16
Average, non-OECD			10
Average, world			5

Source: International Energy Agency (1999).

A pending question is what can be done to remove unwanted subsidies, and what factors are responsible for their presence. Beers and Moor (2001) point to two main factors in this context, namely rent-seeking behavior and adjustment costs. The World Development Report 1992 (World Bank, 1992), in its analysis of these issues a decade ago, identified a range of perverse subsidies that inflict strong and unnecessary harm on the environment and natural resource base, and at the same time wastes resources in other ways, strongly recommending their removal. In a recent follow-up study, Acharya and Dixon (2002) discuss the practical possibilities for removing perverse subsidies. They point out that relatively little has so far actually been done in this regard. Main reasons for the inaction are institutional weaknesses in the affected countries, and coalition formation and consolidation among key groups actually benefiting from subsidies. In almost all cases, no matter how perverse or misguided subsidies are, some parties will lose from their removal. Typically, these are parties with considerable political power who are able to exploit the respective institutional weaknesses to their advantage. In some cases, however efficiency gains have been made. One example is the extent of petroleum subsidies benefiting the general public, which seems to be dropping in some of the countries.

A main problem in this area for many developing countries is one of under-taxation of activities that are harmful to the environment and to the resource base. Most developing countries do have a formal legal apparatus for dealing with environmental and resource problems. Still, most have no institutional structure permitting the implementation and collection of the appropriate taxes. Hydrocarbon exploitation is an important case in point. Hydrocarbon resources for many countries represent wealth that in many cases naturally has a national ownership, with the potential to provide substantial government revenue. Yet this potential is often not exploited. This may be identified as a subsidy (in the third sense discussed above) of the parties consuming the resources. A prominent case is Russia, where Speck and Martussevich (2002) argue that hydrocarbon exploitation is in this sense seriously undertaxed The problem is often worsened by, and goes hand in hand with, corruption and excessive government complexity. The scope for corrupt activity and revenue is often magnified by large potential and actual resource rents; in fact this appears to be a main ingredient in the 'resource curse' problem to be discussed below at p. 103 Acharya and Dixon (2002) present several examples of cases where a multitude of government ministries and agencies are often in charge of implementing particular laws (as in their concrete examples from Zimbabwe, Botswana, and India), typically without much or even any coordination, and often with conflicting interests.

2 Domestic investments and environmental and resource interactions

In this section, we discuss briefly public investments and their interactions with environmental and resource problems. Some public investments clearly put greater burdens on the environment, such as those requiring large increases in aggregate energy consumption (such as the construction of coal fired power plants or certain heavy manufacturing). Similar effects may be found from direct government investment in, or support of, agricultural expansion (such as agro-business investments or directed programs for settlement in agricultural frontier regions), and infrastructure investment that lowers the costs of resource extraction, such as the building of roads into forested areas and mining areas. Such investments tend to be high in countries with substantial export income, for example, from resource exports. Wunder (2003) found little direct evidence in the eight countries that he studied (which are rich both in tropical forest and mineral resources), in favor of increased resource extraction pressure due to agricultural expansion stimulated by the central government. Investments in roads into forested regions however typically lead to large increases in deforestation. In Wunder's study such effects were found for the three Latin American countries included (and similar effects are strong all over Latin America), in addition to Cameroon. Counter-examples were however also found: In Venezuela before 1950, and in Gabon and Cameroon at the oil export peak in 1979–1985, greater road building reduced deforestation pressure, mainly by facilitating migration out of the rural areas and into the cities. These latter cases are however neither typical nor representative.

Certain government investments by contrast tend to reduce overall environmental and resource burdens, for example, by reducing energy requirements or directly reducing pollution loads. Examples are the instalment of air or water pollution cleaning equipment, sewage treatment plants, and the building of hydroelectric power capacity (as least when such expansion does not in itself have grave environmental consequences).

A key issue is the time frame of government investment projects, whether largely directed toward prevention of long-run problems, or solving short-run ones. This in turn involves at least two issues. First, chronically high interest rates (or high implicit interest rates for investors resulting from widespread credit rationing) tend to bias activities and investments in the direction of short-run solutions, as investment with long-term returns typically become less attractive. These are typical situations for poor countries where credit and other financial markets are poorly developed (see e.g. Munasinghe (1996), chs 1 and 2; see also our discussion in section 4 below p. 106). As is well known, this biases government preferences in the direction of taking short-run instead of long-run positions, thus putting less priority on environmental and resource consequences far into the future such as deforestation, desertification, species extinction, overfishing, long-term pollution issues, and global warming. Effects should be less serious for shorter-term problems such as reductions in local air and water pollution and current provision of water resources. The second aspect is that interest rates typically correlate with general competitiveness: economies with high resource export value, and high income and export levels, tend to have low real interest rates, not in little part due to good access to international credit. It may then be difficult to isolate effects of interest rates from that of resource wealth, on the environment and resource use. Theoretically, lower interest rates ought to reduce deforestation and resource extraction rates, increasing the attractiveness of immediate resource extraction relative to conservation. They also ought to increase general public concerns for the longer term, which ought to be favorable for the environment.

Under-investment can also be a source of inefficiency in managing the environment and natural resources. One possible such inefficiency, indicated by Asher (1999), is under-capitalization of government-owned companies in resource extracting sectors, notably the petroleum sector, in Latin American countries such as Mexico, Venezuela, and Peru. The argument here is that the respective governments were overly concerned with the short-run net revenue flow from resource exploitation, which lead to the companies not getting access to sufficient investment funds to extract optimally from given (opened or as of yet non-opened) resource fields. It is an unusual type of policy failure in this context: too little is extracted, as extracting additionally from the given fields would cause little environmental harm, but could yield considerable additional benefits to the respective countries' governments.

3 Monetary policy

'Monetary policy' is, in this context, taken to mean exchange rate and interest rate policies, with a particular focus on the former (what one may denote international monetary policy). In modern economies with high degrees of capital mobility, expansionary or contractionary monetary policy has come to be closely associated with central bank interest rates being set at 'low' or 'high' levels. In addition, exchange rates and interest rates are closely related. Under perfectly flexible capital markets these two variables are, at least in theory, bound together by an (uncovered) interest rate parity condition whereby the domestic interest rate equals an international (outside) rate corrected for expected exchange rate appreciations or depreciations. 'Monetary policy' is typically understood as the use of exchange and interest rate policy for short-term macroeconomic regulation purposes. In our context, the issue is whether changes in monetary policy have systematic effects on resource use and on the environment, when considered either at the macroeconomic or sector level.

For the greater part of recent history a majority of developing countries have opted for regimes with 'fixed' exchange rates, by officially pegging the home currency to one particular outside currency (for most countries this has been the U.S. dollar). We identify several types of unfavorable economic effects of such policies relevant to natural resource sectors. First, many developing countries have kept this peg at a rate that systematically overvalues the currency, hurting the export sector. Secondly, less foreign capital attracted, as a result of an overvalued currency (which may trigger a fear of future devaluation) may imply less than efficient investment in extraction. An overvalued exchange rate could imply less direct pressure to export the commodity, since the price obtained in the domestic currency is lower than otherwise. Thirdly, trying to cling to unrealistic pegs can have negative overall consequences for the stability of the country's financial and economic system. Fourthly, low domestic commodity prices through high exchange rates may adversely affect domestic agents' degree of care for the resource, for example, through establishment of property rights. Note that while the former two of these arguments are likely to reduce natural resource extraction, notably deforestation (by making resource exports as well as general agricultural expansion less attractive), the two last are likely to increase it. A fifth point is, as Reinhart and Rogoff (2004) have documented, that 'fixed' exchange rates have in most developing countries caused the creation of parallel exchange markets, with often extremely different exchange rate levels from the official ones. The existence of parallel markets typically dampens the adverse impacts of the (wrongfully) fixed rates, but has the adverse implication of distorting economic activity, between transactions taking place in the official and the parallel market.

A volatile exchange rate may have serious negative implications for resource extraction. A weak rate may lead to strong pressures and incentives to extract in the short run, in anticipation of a strengthening of the future rate (and a reduction in profitability of extraction in domestic currency terms). This pressure is likely to be exacerbated when there is illegal logging or uncertain property relationships, as exposed in recent theoretical work by Amacher, Koskela and Ollikainen (2004a,b), and in empirical studies by Gray (2000).

Most available empirical evidence indicates that the negative effects on deforestation of a high exchange rate dominates, at least in the short run. Pandey and Wheeler (2001) have found that a 10 percent devaluation typically increases forest extraction by about 2 percent, with greatest effects in Asia. Angelsen and Kaimowitz (1999), surveying more than 100 studies, found that devaluation increases deforestation, mainly via increased agricultural expansion. The effect on logging via timber prices is less clear, but the tendency is to increase deforestation rates. Note here the important distinction, stressed by Wunder (2003), between deforestation and logging. While deforestation in most cases is caused by land clearing for agricultural, or other land purposes, logging is typically selective and in most tropical-forest contexts only involves about 10–20 percent of the standing biomass, which leaves the main forest, although not necessarily its biodiversity, intact. Wunder concludes that currency appreciation typically reduces pressure on forest resources, for several reasons. One is a reduction in agricultural activity, leading to re-growth of abandoned agricultural land, and to reductions in the amount of new land clearing in forested areas (and thus reduced deforestation); and via reductions in logging for export. He goes so far as to claim that, in the case of logging for export only, the real exchange rate ought to be the only important variable. Empirically, he finds a negative relationship between deforestation and real exchange rates, in all eight countries in his study. In all these countries the effects were felt both through reduced agricultural expansion (or periodic agricultural contraction coupled with forest regrowth in Venezuela and Gabon), and in reduced logging activity for export. He in fact finds that the real exchange rate, together with national output, account for a full 70–80 percent of the country-specific variance in deforestation, over the period of study (for most countries, 1970–98).

The general relationship between natural resource extraction and exchange rates is however more complex, and can in some cases have an opposite sign. The Cameroon experience in 1986–94, to be discussed further in section 5 below on p. 114, is an important case in point. An extremely overvalued exchange rate here caused a depression that forced people back to the countryside, putting pressure on nearby forest areas. A different class of cases is comprised of countries where resources contribute substantially to wealth. High resource extraction rates may then have 'Dutch disease' implications, with high domestic spending pressure, loss or relaxation of government control of revenues and expenditures, and appreciated exchange rates. The 'resource curse' hypothesis, put forth by Auty (2001), Ross (1999), Sachs and Warner (2001) and Stevens (2003), claims that greater natural resource revenues may even tend to make the respective countries poorer over time as their growth is reduced. While the partial effect of the resulting appreciated exchange rate has a general dampening effect on deforestation as described above, the effect of resource wealth on income can in principle turn this relationship around. Wunder (2003) finds for the Latin American countries in his sample (Ecuador, Mexico and Venezuela), that the appreciated exchange rate following from oil wealth went hand in hand with higher deforestation rates, at least in periods with high income growth. The reason seemes to be a rapidly growing domestic demand for forest products, for furniture and construction purposes. In Brazil, 86 percent of timber production is demanded domestically and not exported (Smeraldi and Verissimo, 1999), and similar relationships exist in most other Latin American countries. It is not strange then that the real exchange rate is after all far from being the sole dominant factor behind changes in deforestation.

Explanations are found in a nexus of political economy issues. Wunder (2003) points to the lack of central government accountability to political constituencies when most revenues are provided from resource rents and not from local taxes; high degrees of corruption and rent-seeking activity triggered by the resource rents; and reduced labor supply and a less highly educated work force, as all contributing to a lack of government control over their own resources. Overvalued exchange rates are clearly a main factor here.

Trying to cling to unrealistic pegs can also increase the risk of financial crises (more about this will be said in section 5 and conclusions below (pp. 111 and 116), with negative consequences even in non-crisis situations. A large literature in international macroeconomics deals with such issues. 'First-generation' theories of exchange rate crises (Krugman, 1979) indicated that an overvalued currency cannot be maintained indefinitely in a rational expectations equilibrium: it tends to trigger an exchange rate crisis which in turn leads to a breakdown of the initial equilibrium. The 'second-generation' literature (see Obstfeld, 1996) adds to this by demonstrating that an exchange rate crisis whereby a pegged exchange rate system is attacked and the peg subsequently is abandoned (with possibly devastating consequences for the country subject to attack), can be triggered even in the absence of adverse changes in fundamentals, merely by a shift in expectations among exchange rate market participants.

Importantly here, even when a direct crisis does not occur, lack of credibility of a country's exchange rate policy can be harmful, for example, by increasing interest rates beyond levels otherwise prevailing, or forcing central banks to intervene to support their currencies, thus depleting foreign-exchange reserves.

4 The role of financial markets

The characteristics of a country's financial markets have implications for how economic fluctuations develop and unfold, and what are their implications for the environment and resources. Key financial markets are the bond market; equity markets; markets for foreign exchange; markets for international and domestic credit; and markets for risk allocation such as derivatives and options markets. We here also include real assets such as corporate takeovers and foreign direct investment (FDI). Openness of these markets involves the degree to which the relevant instruments are traded, within and across countries, the costs involved in such trading, and the range and quality of institutions supporting or hindering the markets. The strength of financial institutions, institutional structure, and market 'openness' all impact on the functioning of these markets. The term 'openness' is here imprecise. It has formal aspects via the degree of government regulation and formal transactions rules. It also has a real or empirical side through the amounts of international transactions actually taking place, between the country and the rest of the world.

Our aim in this section is, with a couple of exceptions, limited to fundamental effects of financial-sector openness on developing-country environment and resources, and less to presentation of hard evidence on the issue. Relatively little such evidence is available today, although data do exist on properties of FDI and corporate equity investment, presented below.

Financial market openness has implications for environmental and resource policy in developing and emerging economies in at least two ways. First, financial market openness is likely to create more frequent and deeper crises, as argued below. As we will also document, such crises often lead to increased stress on the environment and resources. Secondly, greater reliance on international financial markets, and an increased range and availability of financial instruments, makes it easier for international investors to take advantage of opportunities to extract resources from developing countries, and thereby exploit the environment and resources in poor host countries to their short-run advantage.

Openness in financial markets creates possibilities for firms and individuals to hedge risk, obtain credit and other funding, and implement international transactions, in ways that are otherwise not feasible, thus potentially leading to large welfare gains. As widely recognized, a high degree of financial openness entails costs resulting, for example, from loss of control and vulnerability to crises. Many economists still hold the view that the gains from openness outstrip any potential losses (see e.g. Obstfeld and Rogoff, 1996). Several other leading economists, among them Joseph Stiglitz (see e.g. Stiglitz, 2002) and Paul Krugman (in several newspaper and web columns), are however urging for greater caution in letting market forces go unchecked at least under current international arrangements of financial institutions (or 'financial architecture').

A possible negative effect results from international investments aiming at targets where environmental and resource protection concerns are relatively low, thus possibly adding to the pressure on the environment and resources. This need not be particularly bad if such country policies reflect a real long-run concern for citizen welfare, whereby a (temporary) deterioration in environmental conditions are traded off against higher economic growth made possible by the added investment. However, often a lack of environmental and resource control is more the result of weak or selfish governments that tend to ignore or misrepresent population preferences. In such cases openness can be a bad thing, by adding greatly to global environmental and resource pressure.

A number of features of an economy and its financial sector impact on the degree to which a country is affected by international shocks. General 'financial architecture' deals with common rules and institutions for managing the global financial system (see Eichengreen, 2002, Stiglitz, 2002, and Tirole, 2002 for recent elaborations). Another feature is 'fundamentals' of the individual country and its financial institutions, namely the degree of diversity of its economy and financial strength of its enterprises; the financial strength of its banks and other financial institutions; the degree and quality of government control, leadership and legislation; and the financial strength of government itself such as the size of its debt and its ability to raise tax revenue. Finally, the degree of imposed controls, for example, on the short-run movement of capital and currency into and out from the country. This issue also has implications for the degree to which, for example, short-run resource extraction opportunities can be exploited by international investors and entrepreneurs, often with little concern for the host country's environment and resources in the long run (and often with backing from the host country government). These topics will be detailed further in the next section.

The problem of capital market incompleteness is particularly serious for poor households in developing countries, who often do not have access to bank credit or other forms of formal-sector financing, and often do not even have formalized relationships with banks. Such households experience a 'worst of both worlds': the downside of financial-market openness in terms of high volatility of prices and income, and a poor ability to hedge against such volatility. An implication may be increased pressure on natural resources, in particular in times of extreme stress when harvests or external income possibilities fail, something that is confirmed in our empirical cases considered in section 5 on pp. 114–15. This situation creates an increased need, and potentially far bigger role, for effective systems of micro-finance (e.g. of the Grameen Bank type). So far however the total importance of such sources is limited. Morduch (1999) discusses in detail the successes and potentials of micro-finance schemes, and finds that they have had substantial positive impact where they have been implemented so far (in countries such as Bangladesh, Bolivia, and Indonesia), and in addition an enormous potential future impact. A main source of this impact is the alternative monitoring mechanisms that reduce lending risks and make it feasible to extend credit to new classes of borrowers. Murdoch argues that such microfinance schemes are generally not the solution for the very poorest households (at least not in the absence of substantial subsidy), but more for the poor with some minimum amount of resources. Moreover, microfinance schemes have given a new and expanded role for NGOs with their typically greater ability and desire for experimentation and direct problem solution. NGOs are often, more than traditional aid institutions, able and willing to see the direct relationships between environmental and resource degradation and the microsolutions to be sought out to avoid them.

Another important aspect of financial markets in this context is availability of short- and long-term financing for small businesses. This depends on both borrower risk and general availability and price of credit. Tight credit is likely to imply both that many small profitable investment projects are not carried out, and that small agents will have difficulty smoothing consumption in face of cyclical fluctuations. This may have conflicting effects on environment and resource extraction. Clearly, it depends for one thing on what types of investment projects are precluded: whether these contribute to, or prevent, environmental or resource problems. This can be clarified only in each particular case.

A second type of effect is more clear, namely that individuals who are shut off from the credit market will tend to cope with a particularly stressful situation by using whatever resources they have available, hereunder natural resources. This is likely to lead to unwanted and excessive resource extraction during such periods, as also found by Sunderlin et al. (2001) in their Indonesian case study of deforestation during the East Asian crisis, and as discussed further below, on page 115.

Market volatility, representing the degree to which effects of a crisis are propagated to a given economy through financial markets, is a key issue. It is here of some importance to study what types of financial instruments are likely to contribute most to an overall volatile situation. Kaminsky and Reinhart (2002) have considered the degree of co-movement of yields in different types of markets, and find that government bond yields (indicating the possibility of country sovereign debt default) is the asset type that co-varies most across developing countries, followed by equities. Domestic interest rates on credit seem to be least affected by international shocks. This indicates that the market for government bonds is the most internationalized and open (this market also mainly has large institutional investors, who make placements across country borders), while domestic credit markets are the most 'closed' or autonomous (which may also be natural as these are the markets here most directly subject to individual macroeconomic policy; governments may thus want to shelter these markets from impacts of common international fluctuations). The correlation of bond yields might however also indicate that government default risk as perceived by international investors is highly correlated between countries, in particular in times of crisis. Aspects related to the functioning of international credit markets contribute to such a correlation.

The ease with which equity investments can be made in developing countries by international investors (largely from richer countries) is also important. Equity investments take two forms, namely foreign direct investment (FDI) by international corporations, and portfolio investments in equity assets, made by individuals, governments or corporations, and by larger institutional investors. Rich-country FDI in developing countries has a long history (dating back to early colonial times), but has increased rapidly, in leaps and bounds, as a result of capital market liberalization over the last 20 years (with major setbacks during the Latin American crisis in the 1980, and the East-Asian crisis in 1997–8). Financial equity investments have grown even more rapidly, exploding in certain parts of the world over the last 15 years (particularly in Latin America), in line with local governments' increased willingness and pressure to finance their budget deficits through sales of domestic real assets, and the more efficient functioning of local equity markets. Overall, the level of international capital flows from rich to poor and emerging countries increased from 44 billion U.S.D in 1990, to 244 billion in 1996 (and then suffered a setback in 1997–8 before again rising to previous levels by around 2000). Out of this total in 1996, 110 billion was FDI, and 46 billion equity investments (see French, 1998).

Investors' willingness to invest in a given country depends on various features of the country, including its economic policies and legal regime. In particular, exploitable natural resources, such as mineral ores and petroleum, are obvious FDI targets. Lax environmental and labor laws have traditionally tended to promote FDI, as they lower investors' operation costs. On the other hand, a transparent legal system, including secure property rights and low corruption levels, also represents important factors for investors. Such features are typically associated with stronger regimes where environmental and labor laws are more strictly enforced. Firms may thus be viewed to face a tradeoff, between 'weak' and 'strong' regimes, each with attractive and less attractive features for FDI investors.

When FDI is encouraged by relaxing environmental standards, it likely comes at a cost of environmental and resource degradation. Undoubtedly, much FDI has had such implications. Foreign companies typically have incentives to exploit available resources rapidly (e.g. because their tenure relations may be viewed as less secure), thus often pushing governments to the limits in terms of environmental and resource pressure. Good examples are from the forest sector in many African countries (including Cameroon and Liberia), where foreign companies have been behind more than 80 percent of timber extraction and where the loss of valuable timber has been very serious. French (1998) also points out that, from 1991 to 1997, international spending on metals exploration grew by six times in Latin America, by four times in East Asia and doubled in Africa, mainly as a result of regimes' more liberal attitude to FDI.

It is still far from obvious whether higher levels of FDI in developing countries significantly increases the global pressure on the environment and natural resources. The so-called 'pollution haven hypothesis', stating that pollution is 'exported' to developing countries as a result of specialization across countries whereby the rich countries avoid environmentally harmful production activities, is not strongly confirmed in the data so far (see also the chapter by Copeland and Gulati in this volume). As Copeland and Gulati document, a number of factors make this issue very complex. First, even if the 'pollution haven' hypothesis were true, global pressure may not increase as activity is shifted from rich to poor countries (although particular groups in poor countries may suffer), or more generally as trade is expanded. One may even visualize positive environmental effects for some developing countries when multinationals with cutting-edge technologies and cleaning equipment set up shop there, out competing inefficient and highly polluting domestic firms, although little hard empirical evidence is currently available on this issue. It should also be noted that most FDI today is made by large international corporations with increasing consideration for the environmental and resource implications of their activities. This occurs not mainly because of host government pressure to perform, but instead, out of self-interest, for various reasons. French (1998) argues that most large multinationals currently adhere to roughly uniform environmental policies throughout their worldwide operations (see also UNCTAD, 1996). This may serve a variety of purposes for the multinationals, such as streamlining their overall management practices, the avoidance of potential lawsuits (that may be filed both by the host countries, or by the corporations' home countries against transgressions overseas), and general image building. Worldwide adherence by many large corporations to the ISO 14000 system or similar certification systems (and the requirement that their suppliers adhere to this system), underlines this trend.

As noted, there has recently been a tendency for developing-country governments to sell off government-owned companies and exploration rights to natural resources. Such selling-off is typically triggered by short-run financing needs (as typically imposed by creditors) and leads to one-time cash gains for the selling country, in return for foregoing the potential net asset returns in future periods. When the responsibility and accountability of governments are limited, such gains can lead to wasteful initial spending booms (either directly in utilizing the added cash, or in extending credit lines), and to resource management problems further down the line.

5 Short-run responses to crises

We will now look a bit more carefully at cases where a country is hit by an 'economic crisis' which causes a substantial reduction in national output, and what then happens to the country's environment and resources. The overall effects of economic crises has become a central issue in the recent economic policy debate following several severe events, notably in East Asia, Russia, Mexico and Argentina. Accumulated output losses have here in all cases been large, up to more than 50 percent of current GDP in cumulated value. Typically, a crisis is triggered by a shock, often with an 'initial' external component (such as an exogenous negative shock to the trade balance, to import or export prices, or to firms' costs), and/or an (endogenous) domestic component, often in interaction with some particular negative features of the country, including its institutions and financial markets. In many cases the situation leading to a crisis can be described by mechanisms familiar from the celebrated Diamond and Dybwig (1983) framework, where actors in the financial system 'panic' and trigger the very crisis (or at least cause an already started crisis to become more serious). Real impacts of such a scenario are significantly higher (potential or actual) bankruptcy rates for domestic firms, the drying up of credit and finance lines for investors and entrepreneurs, and reductions in investment and output.

Several related adverse components often enter into a crisis. One is capital flight whereby international investors withdraw assets from countries in crisis. There are also internal components resulting from financial instability and liquidity scarcity, whereby domestic funds become severely rationed or over-priced; and a debt component whereby foreign-denominated debt increases in value when the country is forced to devalue its currency. Eichengreen and Hausmann's (1999) 'Original Sin Hypothesis' states that countries with weak financial systems or adverse histories for failures, must finance their investments by borrowing abroad. Private sector agents may want to hedge their exposures, especially the ones denominated in foreign currency, but may be unable to do so. Financial markets incompleteness, representing far more serious problems in less-developed than in developed countries, are thus accentuated in economic crises.

Table 3.4, taken from Summers (2000) (see also the related discussion in Tirole, 2002), represents principal factors behind the crises in Mexico, 1994, East Asia, 1997, Russia, 1998 and Brazil, 1999. The table shows that initially pegged exchange rates, financial-sector weakness and short-term foreign debt were important, and that pegged exchange rates seemed important in all cases. The table also suggests that exchange rate and 'financial' crises (representing the other items in the table) were highly related, as in all cases both types of causes figure simultaneously.

A domestic economy 'crisis' may have the following components:

- A reduction in GDP below capacity
- A higher firm bankruptcy rate, in particular those with heavy borrowing
- Reduced private consumption

Table 3.4 Subjective ratings of potential factors behind recent international crises affecting developing countries

Source of distress	Brazil	Indonesia	South Korea	Mexico	Thailand	Russia
Pegged exchange Rate	1	0	0	1	1	1
Currrent-account Deficit	0	2	3	1	1	3
Fiscal deficit	1	3	3	3	3	1
Financial-sector Weakness	3	1	1	1	1	1
Government short-term debt	1	3	3	1	2	1
Total short-term foreign debt	2	1	1	2	1	1
General governance	2	1	2	2	2	1

Source: Summers (2000).
Explanation of figures: 0 = extremely serious, 1 = very serious, 2 = serious, 3 = not serious.

- Higher import and export prices as the exchange rate is devalued; or opposite, real exchange rate revaluation leading to reduced real export prices.

- Increased interest rates and reduced financial flows to (possibly rationing of) prospective investors and borrowers.

- Capital flight from the domestic economy as foreign investors withdraw their financial holdings.

The crisis typically has two main economic effects, namely a general basic reduction in economic activity, and thus GDP, and a reduction in population consumption and welfare.

To understand how the first affects the environment and resource extraction, consider a crisis that is caused mainly by a large initial shock to the domestic economy, such as exogenous falls in prices or quantities of key export goods, or simply poor macroeconomic management, and that triggers a devaluation of the local currency. The immediate (production) effect is then most likely to reduce pressure on the environment and resources, at least to the extent that pressure depends rather directly on economic activity (such as air and water pollution levels). GDP is reduced for two different reasons. First, certain businesses are knocked out directly from the shock (which again is influenced by the bailout strategies followed by the country). The effects of this on the environment will depend heavily on the energy and resource intensities of the businesses mainly affected, in terms of their inputs and outputs. Secondly, there will be a general reduction in private-sector demand, where the effect is likely to be more general and across the board. Both effects should work to reduce pollution and the extraction of resources that depends directly on economic activity. Note that this process is different from just moving along a given long-run output-environment relationship (or EKC curve (see footnote 1 for references), as technologies, both for production and for pollution control, are already established and will generally not deteriorate over time; thus movement will not be one back along the established EKC curve but rather to a lower level of pollution and resource load. On the other hand, resource extraction for export should increase as the real exchange rate is devalued. Overall, the theoretical effect on deforestation is generally ambiguous.

A second type of crisis is driven largely by a fall in export prices of one or several important natural resources, as exemplified by the Cameroon crisis in 1986–94. The pressure on the natural resource then ought to be less than under the first type above, simply because the resource price falls. The main effect should then be that both export volume and price drop. Certain factors may however confound such a pattern. In some cases one may try to compensate for the loss of export revenue by increasing the amount of extraction, thus leaving the overall effect on extraction more or less the same as in the first case. The crisis itself may then create incentives to act more myopically with respect to its natural-resource use. This is probably most relevant when the government itself is directly in charge of natural-resource extraction; or when private extractors are given strong direct incentives to increase it (by the government directly, or indirectly, e.g. via higher interest rates or an excessively devalued exchange rate) (see e.g. Rauscher (1990) and Barbier and Rauscher (1994) for analyses of such situations). Similar effect on natural resource extraction may follow when the export price fall is sufficiently strong that households are forced back to local subsistence on rural natural resources, with corresponding increases in deforestation rates (as in the Cameroon example). The degree of efficiency or inefficiency of general environmental and resource policy, as dealt with in the Soma and Sterner chapter of this volume, here is very consequential.

A third category is crises-driven mainly by a real revaluation of the local exchange rate (as when the country is a member of a currency union with no independent exchange rate policy, and experiences a serious terms-of-trade worsening). The pressure on resources is then likely to be minor but still perhaps non-negligible as households' immediate needs may increase.

The consumption and welfare effect of crises may have feedback effects on the environment and resources through separate mechanisms, and particularly so in countries where the population relies heavily on natural resources for their livelihoods. Effects are likely to be severe when the consumption reduction largely hits the poor (as when prices of basic foods rise substantially), and the consequences for them can be dramatic in the absence of compensating 'coping' mechanisms that would permit a minimum livelihood standard to be met. One coping mechanism is the harvesting of natural resources that otherwise would be preserved. Among natural resources ripe for immediate over-harvesting are forest land and trees close to populated areas, other vegetation that normally have erosion preventing roles, and groundwater supplies known to be scarce. These will often be viewed as reserves that can be run down in times of excessive stress.

Some empirical evidence is available on the relationships between crisis-induced contractions and increases in poverty. Cline (2002), citing in particular the World Development Report 2000–01 (World Bank, 2001), assesses the poverty elasticity with respect to income at about -2. On this basis about 40–60 million additional persons were put in poverty as a result of the financial crises in Mexico, Brazil, Argentina, Russia, and the Far East over the 1995–2000 period. As documented by Barbier (this volume), in poorer and less developed countries, a large share of the population depends directly on natural resources for their livelihood. Thus, the poorer the country that is hit by a financial crisis, and the greater the degree to which poor households' incomes are reduced, the greater one should expect the pressure on natural resources to be.

There are also typically government policy responses to a negative shock. This response may in, and of itself, have environmental and resource implications.

Such responses can take many different forms. One possible response is that environmental regulations may be relaxed as more firms are in danger of bankruptcy, if the government's philosophy is that less stringent environmental regulations may help to 'save' more firms or make room for further firm establishment. (Such effects may be magnified in cases where the shocks hit several countries at the same time, and some of the countries act to relax their environmental policies; this may provide additional domestic arguments for policy relaxation, thus increasing environmental loads both directly and indirectly from neighbors.)

For resource-rich countries facing serious liquidity and debt problems, bailouts (or debt forgiveness in various forms) may play a constructive role in preventing excessive natural resource extraction. Theoretical models by Strand (1995, 1997) show that providing unconditional debt forgiveness is likely to do relatively little to prevent excessive resource extraction, on a dollar-by-dollar basis, but is more helpful when it also helps to reduce debtor-country borrowing costs. It is however a much more potent instrument when debt forgiveness can be tied directly to the saving of resources, or when debt is purchased in return for such saving ('debt-for-nature swaps' (see Hansen, 1989).

A controversial issue is whether 'bailouts' ought to be used to minimize the consequences of crises. Two main types of bailouts are relevant: first, governments may bail out domestic agents in financial distress; and secondly, international institutions (principally the IMF) may bail out governments in danger of defaulting. Two different views prevail in the literature. Some authors emphasize the negative effects of bailouts on 'moral hazard' by leading economic agents to set their 'efforts' at sub-optimal levels, or take excessive risks, in anticipation of future bailouts when things go wrong (see e.g. Corsetti, Pesenti, and Roubini (1999), Burnside, Eichenbaum, and Rebelo (2002), and Mundaca (2002). The second, more positive, view is that bailouts can have favourable consequences once a crisis has already materialized and is unfolding, by softening its effect on the overall economy and avoiding systemic risk (see e.g. Mundaca, 2003a, b). Typically the government is severely weakened both by the loss of export and tax revenue, by the direct costs of bailouts, and by the inability to attract foreign investment.

Bailouts can be conditioned on environmental and resource policies implemented in the country that receives funding. This is particularly relevant when the party responsible for the bailout is an outside IFI or a (developed) 'donor' country (or group of such countries).

Some countries affected by financial crises may find it advantageous to impose additional financial market regulations or controls, for example, to prevent an excessive outflow of short-run financial assets placed in the country in the aftermath of a negative shock. (A practical example is the control on outgoing short-run capital from Malaysia imposed in 1998 as a response to heavy investment withdrawals from that country; which however were lifted in the spring of 1999, see Rogoff, (1999)). Such tightening may backfire in the longer run, by triggering retaliatory effects by the international community, for example, in the form of reduced international credit lines, for domestic company borrowing or for overall imports, or greater pressure to immediately repay international debts. Some possible implications of such reactions for environmental and resource extraction may be visualized. One is a cash-strapping effect in the form of reduced public investment. This in turn can take several forms. We may have less instalment of pollution-reducing equipment, leading to more pollution than otherwise. We may also have less investment in industries and enterprises that put direct pressure on the environment and natural resources (and in turn either domestically or foreign financed), thus reducing environmental and resource loads. Finally, the degree of immediate stress on domestic natural resources that can be exported or used domestically as import substitutes (forest resources, easily available petroleum or mineral reserves), may increase. Overall, the picture is complex, and only good case studies can determine the empirical net effects. A couple of such studies will be presented at the end of this section.

Two further issues here need to be discussed. First, to what degree does a country's initial environmental and resource situation make it prone to shocks, and how does this affect the magnitude of a given shock. Secondly, to what degree is the country's environmental and resource situation able to insulate it from the adverse effects of a shock.

We will now go into a more practical discussion of country cases that illustrate the basic principles put forth so far, with emphasis on deforestation issues where the evidence is most ample. Two country cases, both taken from the list of Wunder's (2003) eight case studies, are particularly illustrative, namely the Cameroon crisis in 1986–94; and the Indonesia crisis in 1997–99.

The Cameroon crisis was extremely serious with a drop in GDP by 30 percent and a halving of real per-capita incomes. It was triggered by a dramatic terms-of-trade deterioration, by 65 percent from 1985 to 1987, combined with a pegging of the local currency to the French franc (this peg was retained until 1994) and at the same time revaluation of the franc against the U.S. dollar by 40 percent, and a drop in oil output by a third. A strong over-valuation of the local currency was thus in a large part to blame for the crisis. From arguments in sections above, the prima facie effect of a real exchange rate revaluation ought to be to reduce deforestation pressure as well as extraction of other natural resources, mainly by reducing the incentives for resource exports, but also possibly to reduce incentives for illegal extraction such as timber logging. Other mechanisms were, however, also at play. Forestry exports did decline substantially during the crisis. But, as documented in separate studies by Mertens et al. (2000), Sunderlin and Pokam (2002), and Wunder (2003), the deepness of the crisis increased unemployment dramatically in major cities, and forced parts of the population back to the countryside. This in turn caused substantial increased deforestation pressure in areas at the agricultural margin, through agricultural land clearing. In fact, Wunder (2003) argues that the main, often overwhelming, factor behind deforestation is just marginal land clearing for agricultural expansion. Here, this factor far dominated any negative impacts on deforestation, from reduced illegal logging or timber exports.

The Indonesian crisis was almost as deep as that in Cameroon, but far shorter lasting. During 1967–97, Indonesia's economy increased by an average of 6.5 percent annually. In 1998, it contracted by 13.6 percent. Taking the long-run growth path as the benchmark, the output drop in 1998 was thus 20 percent below capacity, an astonishing one-year drop, and by far the greatest of any of the countries experiencing the 1997–8 East-Asian debt crisis. For good or bad, it can be viewed as an interesting natural experiment. One main difference from Cameroon was that the Indonesian currency was devaluated almost immediately, and dropped to a level only about one-fourth of its initial value, as an average for the period 1997–9. The crisis was not, as in Cameroon, stretched out as a consequence of an exchange rate imbalance. The Indonesian economy was thus able to recuperate relatively quickly after the crisis. The impact on deforestation was however more direct and dramatic, as documented, for example, by Holmes (2000). First, the dramatic devaluation increased the profitability of both timber and food exports, causing a surge in deforestation, mainly due to increased logging, but also as a result of short-run agricultural expansion. The fall in output, together with the devaluation and resulting inflation, also had the consequence that incomes were dramatically reduced, in particular for the urban populations. A strong surge of urban-to-rural return migration took place, putting additional pressure on forest lands.

An interesting case study by Sunderlin et al. (2001), of small-farmer households in five outer island provides of Indonesia (Riau/Jambi, Lampung, West Kalimantan, East Kalmantan, and Central Sulawesi), showed that about 70 percent of the households cleared additional forest land over the 1997–9 period. Forest clearing for domestic food consumption increased only slightly over this period. Clearing for cash and export cropping however increased dramatically, in particular in the last part of the period. A reason for this pattern may be that, in the first part of the period, reduced real income forced farmers to care about short-run survival concerns, making it important to sustain consumable food production. As farmers adapted to the more protracted downturn, however, a longer-run view was taken, and more trees were planted for cash crops. The main factor, as agued by Sunderlin et al. (2001), was the increased uncertainty caused by the crisis, which triggered a response to attempt to sustain stable long-run incomes. This basic factor was the same as in the Cameroon case. The overall deforestation pressure was however greater in the Indonesian case, since here also the pressure on logging for export increased greatly, something that did not happen in Cameroon (where the real exchange rate appreciated during the crisis).

The bottom line in this section is that a financial and economic crisis can impose severe stress on a country, with serious potential consequences for environmental and resource management. Some of the main factors may be summed up. First, it causes the country to lose grips with its initially established policy regime. Secondly, it leads to stresses (e.g. in the form of increased unsustainable resource use) as households and firms try to cope with the resulting deteriorated situation. There are also countervailing factors, in particular, the reduced economic activity may reduce short-run pollution or extraction for consumption by domestic-market firms. In the examples we have offered, these are however of lesser importance relative to those leading to deterioration.

Final comments

We conclude the discussion with just a few final remarks, that at the same time serve to sum up some of the most important conclusions from our review above. First, subsidies of non-renewable natural resource use, in particular fossil energy, are typically wasteful and can add pressure to the environment and lead to too rapid resource extraction. Examples of wasteful subsidies are offered, but we also offer examples of ways in which subsidies can be structured such that environmental and resource efficiency and preservation is promoted. Secondly, government investments have the potential to greatly improve the environment and resource use, but also here care must be taken. One particularly sensitive area for investments is road building in previously inaccessible areas, which almost invariably leads to greater pressure to extract resources and convert land to agricultural uses. Thirdly, changes in monetary policies by weakening exchange rates and increasing interest rates can have substantial negative implications for resource use, in particular by promoting short-run exports and illegal extraction when tenure relations are uncertain. Fourthly, increased foreign direct investment resulting from liberalization of capital markets can add environmental and resource pressure, but the evidence here is less clear, in particular as international corporations seem to take their environmental concerns more and more seriously. Fifthly, financial crises very often have negative consequences for environmental and natural resource management, as the worsening (upsetting) effects in most cases seem to outweigh the dampening effects.

As noted in the introduction, this presentation only barely scratches the surface of the basic problem complex. Little that is systematic is known today, and much needs to be done in the future, in acquiring and assembling such knowledge.

References

Acahrya, G. and Dixon, J. (2002), 'No one said it was going to be easy! An analysis of the recommendations made by the 1992 World Development Report and the experience in the last decade'. Background paper for the World Development Report, 2003.

Altaf, A. et al. (1993), 'Rethinking rural water supply policy in the Punjab, Pakistan'. Water Resources Research, 29 1943–1954.

Amacher, G. S., Koskela, E. and Ollikainen, M. (2004a), 'Socially optimal royalty design and illegal logging under alternative penalty schemes.' CESifo working paper no. 1131.

——, —— and ——. (2004b), 'Deforestation, production intensity and land use under insecure property rights.' CESifo working paper no. 1128.

Angelsen, A. and Kaimowitz, D. (1999), 'Rethinking the causes of deforestation: Lessons from economic models.' The World Bank Research Observer, 14: 73–98.

Asher, W. (1999), Why governments waste natural resources—policy failures in developing countries. Baltimore: Johns Hopkins Press.

Auty, R. M. (2001), 'The political economy of resource-driven growth.' European Economic Review, 45: 39–46.

Barbier, E. (2003), 'Natural capital, resource dependency and poverty in developing countries: the problem of dualism within dualism' (ch. 1 in this volume).

—— and Rauscher, M. (1994), 'Trade, tropical deforestation, and policy interventions.' Environmental and Resource Economics, 4: 74–90.

——, Bockstael, N., Burgess, J., and Strand, I. (1995), 'The linkages between timber trade and tropical deforestation,' The World Economy, 18: 411–442.

Beers, C. V. and Moor, A. D. (2001), 'Public subsidies and policy failure.' Cheltenham: Edward Elgar.

Bohn, H. and Deacon, R. (2000), 'Ownership risk, investment, and the use of natural resources,' American Economic Review, 90: 526–49.

Burnside, C., M. Eichenbaum, and S. Rebelo (2001), 'Prospective deficits and the Asian currency crises,' Journal of Political Economy.

Clements, B., Rodriguez, H. and Schwartz, G. (1998), 'Economic determinants of subsidies.' IMF working paper 98/166.

Cline, W. (2002), 'Financial crises and poverty in emerging market economies.' Center for Global Development Working Paper no. 8.

Copeland, Gulati (2004) (Ch. 6 in this volume).

Corsetti, G., Pesenti, P. and Roubini, N. (1999), 'Paper tigers? A model of the Asian crisis,' European Economic Review, 45: 1211–36.

Dailami, M. and ul Haque, N. (1998), 'What macroeconomic policies are "sound" ?' Working paper, World Bank.

Dasgupta, P. (2001), 'Human well-being and the natural environment.' Oxford: Oxford University Press.

Dasgupta, P. and Mäler, K. G. (1996), 'Environmental resources and economic development,' in Lundahl and Ndulu (1996): 176–202.

DEFRA (2001), 'International financial institutions: Enhancing their role in promoting sustainable development.' Report by the Royal Institute for international Affairs and Forum for the Future, London.

Diamond, D. and Dybwig, P. (1983), 'Bank runs, deposit insurance, and liquidity,' *Journal of Political Economy*, 91: 401–19.

Dixit, A. K. and Newbery, D. (1984), 'Setting the price of oil in a distorted economy,' *Economic Journal*, 1984, supplement, 77–82.

Eichengreen, B. (2002), 'Financial crises and what to do about them.' Oxford: Oxford University Press.

Eichengreen, B. and R. Hausmann (1999), 'Exchange rate and financial fragility.' NBER working paper #7418, Cambridge, Massachussetts.

French, H. F. (1998), 'Investing in the future: Harnessing private capital flows for environmentally sustainable development.' Working paper 139, Worldwatch Institute, Washington DC.

Gray, J. (2000), 'Forest concessions, policies and revenue systems: Country experience and policy changes for sustainable tropical forestry.' World Bank Technical Paper, Forest Series. Washington DC.: The World Bank.

Grossman, G. M. and Krueger, A. B. (1995), 'Economic growth and the environment.' *Quarterly Journal of Economics*, 112: 353–77.

Gupta, S. and Mahler, W. (1994), 'Taxation of petroleum products: Theory and empirical evidence.' IMF working paper, 94/32.

Gupta, S. et al. (2002), 'Issues in domestic petroleum pricing in oil-producing countries.' IMF working paper 02/140.

Hamilton, K. and Hassan, R. (2003), 'Measuring development prospects by "greening" the national accounts.' (Ch. 2 in this volume).

Hansen, S. (1989), 'Debt-for-nature swaps: Overview and discussion of key issues.' *Ecological Economics*, 1: 77–93.

Holmes, D. (2000), 'Deforestation in Indonesia: A review of the situation in Sumatra, Kalimantan and Sulawesi,' Draft report, The World Bank.

Hossain, S. M. (2003), 'Taxation and pricing of petroleum products in developing countries: A framework for analysis with application to Nigeria.' IMF working paper 03/42.

International Energy Agency (1999), 'Looking at energy subsidies: Getting the prices right.' World Energy Outlook, Paris: IEA.

Kaimowitz, D. and Angelsen, A. (1998), 'Economic models of tropical deforestation: A review.' Bogor, Indonesia: Center for International Forestry Research.

Kaminsky, G. L. and Reinhart, C. M. (2002), 'Financial markets in times of stress.' *Journal of Development Economics*, 69: 451–70.

Krugman, P. (1979), 'A model of balance-of-payments crises.' *Journal of Money, Credit and Banking*, 11: 311–25.

Krupnick, A. (2003), 'Urban air pollution, health, and policy instruments,' (Ch. 11 in this volume).

Larsen, B. (1994), 'World fossil fuel subsidies and global carbon emissions in a model with interfuel substitution.' Policy Research Working Paper 1256, Washington DC.: The World Bank.

Lundahl, M. and Ndulu, B. J. (1996), 'New directions in development economics.' London: Routledge.

Mäler, K. G. and Munasinghe, M. (1996), 'Macroeconomic policies, second-best theory, and the environment,' in Munasinghe (1996): 111–23.

Mertens, B. et al. (2000), 'Impact of macroeconomic change on deforestation in South Cameroon: Integration of household and remotely-sensed data.' World Development, 28: 983–99.

Milazzo, M. J. (1997), 'Subsidies in world fisheries: a re-examination.' World Bank Technical Paper 406, Fisheries series. Washington DC: The World Bank.

Moor, A. D. and Calamai, P. (1997), 'Subsidizing unsustainable development: undermining the earth with public funds.' The Hague/Costa Rica: Institute for Research on Public Expenditure/Earth Council Report.

Munasinghe, M. (1996), 'Environmental impacts of macroeconomic and sectoral policies.' Washington DC.: The World Bank.

Mundaca, B. G. (2002), 'Moral hazard effects of bailing out under asymmetric information.' Proceedings of the 2002 North American Summer Meetings of the Econometric Society (http://www.econometricsociety.org/meetings/vol1/money.html).

Mundaca, B. G. (2003a), 'Optimal bailout during currency and financial crisis: A sequential game analysis.' Working paper, Department of Economics, University of Oslo.

Mundaca, B. G. (2003b), 'Will provision of liquidity be effective if conditioned on performance?' Paper presented at the 2003 ASSA-International Economics and Finance Association Meetings, Washington DC., 3–5 January.

Murdoch, J. (1999), 'The microfinance promise,' Journal of Economic Literature, 37, no. 4 1569–1614.

Newbery, D. M. (1985), 'Efficiency criteria and equity criteria in energy pricing with practical applications to LDCs in Asia,' in C. Siddayao (ed.): 'Criteria for energy pricing policy.' London: Graham and Trotman: 65–88.

Obstfeld, M. (1996), 'Models of currency crises with self-fulfilling expectations,' European Economic Review, 40: 1037–47.

Obstfeld, M. and Rogoff, K. (1996), 'Foundations of international macroeconomics.' Cambridge, Ma.: MIT Press.

Pandley, K. and Wheeler, D. (2001), 'Stuctural adjustment and forest resources: The impact of World Bank operations.' Policy Research Working Paper 2584. Washington DC.: The World Bank.

Pearce, D. (1996), 'The capture of global environmental value,' in Lundahl and Ndulu (1996): 224–49.

Rauscher, M. (1990), 'The optimal use of environmental resources by an indebted country.' Journal of Institutional and Theoretical Economics, 146: 500–16.

Reinhart, C. M. and Rogoff, K. S. (2004), 'The modern history of exchange rate arrangements: A reinterpretation,' Quarterly Journal of Economics, 119: 1–48.

Renner, M. (2000), 'Working for the environment: A growing source of jobs.' Working Paper 152, Worldwatch Institute, Washington DC.

Rogoff, K. S. (1999), 'International institutions for reducing global financial instability.' Journal of Economic Perspectives, 13: 21–42.

Ross, M. L. (1999), 'The political economy of the resource curse.' World Politics, 51: 297–322.

Sachs, J. D. and Warner, A. M. (2001), 'The curse of natural resources.' European Economic Review, 45: 827–38.

Shafik, N. (1994), 'Economic development and environmental quality: an econometric analysis.' *Oxford Economic Papers*, 46: 757–73.

Shah, A. and Larsen, B. (1992), 'World energy subsidies and global carbon emissions.' Background paper for World Development Report 1992. Washington DC.: The World Bank.

Smeraldi, R. and Verissimo, J. A. (1999), 'Hitting the target: Timber consumption in the Brazilian domestic market and promotion of forest certification.' São Paulo: Amigos da Terra and IMAFLORA.

Somanathan and Sterner, Ch. 7 of this volume.

Speck, S. and Martussevich, A. P. (2002), 'Taxation Policy Reform in the Russian Federation: Challenges and Obstacles for Implementation of Environmentally Related Taxes.' Unpublished report.

Stern, D. L. (1998), 'Progress on the environmental Kuznets curve?' *Environment and Development Economics*, 2: 173–96.

Stevens, P. (2003), 'Resource impact: curse or blessing? A literature survey,' *Journal of Energy Literature*, 9: 3–42.

Stiglitz, J. E. (2002), 'Globalization and its discontents.' New York: Norton.

Strand, J. (1995), 'Lending terms, debt concessions, and developing countries' resource extraction.' *Resource and Energy Economics*, 17: 99–117.

Strand, J. (1997), 'Developing-country resource extraction with asymmetric information and sovereign debt: A theoretical analysis.' *Environment and Development Economics*, 2: 265–89.

Strand, J. (2000), 'A political economy analysis of water pricing in Honduras' capital, Tegucigalpa,' in A. Dinar (ed.), *The Political Economy of Water Pricing Reform*. New York: Oxford University Press: 237–58.

Strand, J. and Walker, I. (2003), 'The value of water connections in Central American cities: A revealed preference study.' Working paper, University of Oslo.

Strand, J. and Walker, I. (2005), 'Water markets and demand in Central American cities,' *Environment and Development Economics*, 10: 313–35.

Summers, L. H. (2000), 'International financial crises: Causes, preventions, and cures,' *American Economic Review*, 90 (papers and proceedings): 1–16.

Sunderlin, W. D. et al. (2001), 'Economic crisis, small farmer well-being, and forest cover change in Indonesia.' World Development, 29: 767–82.

Sunderlin, W. D. and Pokam, J. (2002), 'Economic crisis and forest cover change in Cameroon: The roles of migration, crop diversification, and gender division of labor,' *Economic Development and Cultural Change*, 50: 581–606.

Tirole, J. (2002), 'Financial crises, liquidity, and the international monetary system.' Princeton, N.J.: Princeton University Press.

Torras, M. and J. K. Boyce (1998), 'Income, inequality, and pollution: a reassessment of the environmental Kuznets curve,' *Ecological Economics* 25: 147–60.

UNCTAD (1996), 'Self regulation of environmental management: An analysis of guidelines set by International Industry Associations for their member firms.' New York: United Nations.

Walker, I. et al. (1999), 'Reform efforts in the Honduran water sector,' in W. Savedoff and P. Spiller (eds): *Spilled Water*. Washington DC.: IADB—Latin American Research Network,: 35–88.

Weiss, J. (1995), 'Economic policy in developing countries.' London: Prentice-Hall.

Whittington, D., Laria, D. T. and Mu, X. (1990), 'A study of water vending and willingness to pay for water in Onitsha, Nigeria.' World Development, 19: 179–98.

World Bank (1992), *World Development Report 1992. Development and the Environment.* Oxford: Oxford University Press.

—— (2001), *World Development Report 2000–2001: Attacking poverty.* Washington DC.: Oxford University Press.

Wunder, S. (2003), 'Oil wealth and the fate of forests.' New York: Routledge Press.

4

Political Economy and Natural Resource Use

Robert T. Deacon and Bernardo Mueller

Introduction

Comparing how countries with diverse political systems use their natural resources suggests that systems of governance have important effects on resource use. Norway and Nigeria make for a stark comparison.[1] Both countries were endowed with extensive forests in prehistoric times, but the fractions of these forests that remain intact are very different. In Norway over 90 percent of the country's original forest cover remains today, while the figure for Nigeria is less than 11 percent. The forests that do remain are used in very different ways in the two nations. In Norway, 95 percent of timber harvested goes to industrial uses such as sawn wood and paper; only 5 percent is used for fuel. In Nigeria the shares are roughly reversed: 8 percent is destined for commercial uses, while 92 percent is used for fuel and most of this is gathered from forests lacking firm ownership rights. In Norway, the acreage of land in legally protected natural areas represents about 20 percent of the country's original forestland. In Nigeria, the fraction is roughly 7 percent. Norway and Nigeria are both major oil producers and, as others have noted, there are marked differences in the ways they use their petroleum endowments.[2]

This is admittedly 'straw man' comparison. Norway and Nigeria differ radically in their non-political attributes, for example, in their income levels, cultural heterogeneity, and religious beliefs, so their differences in natural resource use may stem from several sources. Still, the general pattern just sketched is broadly consistent with basic economic reasoning about how political economy affects the use of natural resources.

---

[1] The following data on forest use and forest cover are taken from World Resources Institute (1999) and generally refer to the year 1995.   [2] Karl (1997, Ch. 4) provides comparisons.

Let us look at four ways in which a nation's political system is linked to the way its natural resources are used. First, when property rights to resources are weak, competition to acquire them can be wasteful and be characterized by rent-seeking and violent conflict. The link to political systems comes about because ownership claims are most likely to be weak or ambiguous in countries where the rule of law is not well established. Secondly, when a country's political system is unstable or non-representative, the individual's claim to a resource stock's future return can be rendered insecure. This reduces the payoff to natural resource conservation, leading to more rapid depletion of resource stocks. When tenure insecurity is a general feature of an economy, however, it can have the secondary effect of raising the cost of resource extraction, rendering some stocks uneconomic and slowing rates of depletion. Thirdly, when a country's natural resources are capable of generating significant rents, but institutions of democratic governance and the rule of law are not well established, corruption by government officials responsible for resource management can encourage rent-seeking, dissipating the benefits those resources would otherwise confer. Fourth, the mix of private vs. public good outputs produced by a nation's natural resources may be affected by its political system. A resource such as a forest can provide either non-exclusive, public good outputs such as habitat and watershed, or appropriable, private good outputs such as salable timber. When a country's government does not represent the interests of the entire population, but rather acts on behalf of a select group, the use of resource stocks to provide public good amenities may be under-emphasized. In what follows we present evidence on each of the first three links from political systems to natural resource use. At present there is little evidence on the fourth link, hence this point is discussed only as a topic for future research in the conclusions.

We begin in Section 1 by examining how ownership institutions are created and how these institutions affect and are affected by the use of resources. A central point here is that property rights are created by economic agents in response to the costs and benefits of creating them. Creating property rights that provide incentives for efficient use of natural resources, and optimally adapting these rights as conditions change, requires that economic agents be able to cooperate and coordinate, and that the State be able to coerce in order to overcome market failures and opportunistic behavior. The ability to cooperate, coordinate and coerce, however, depend on the political institutions that determine who has a say and how they make decisions on natural resource use. Another essential ingredient is a commitment mechanism to facilitate these actions, for example an independent and well-functioning judiciary.

Political institutions also determine whether the State's ability to coerce will be used to achieve efficient resource use, that is, maximizing net benefits to the population at large, or to benefit specific groups while shifting costs to the rest of society. In the absence of appropriate political institutions, property rights may not provide incentives for efficient use and, as observed repeatedly throughout the world, this situation may persist despite the existence of obvious superior alternate arrangements. These themes, and empirical evidence on the associated resource allocation effects, are examined in Section 2.

Empirical evidence on the linkage between governance institutions and natural resource use is examined in Sections 3 and 4. The medium whereby governance affects resource use is property rights, so the hypothesized causal chain postulates that political institutions affect property rights, and property rights in turn affect resource use. Some of the work on this chain examines only the second link, testing for systematic relationships between property rights structures and resource use. Others approach the problem by testing for direct associations between political institutions and resource use, effectively skipping the middle step.[3]

Emerging evidence on a phenomenon called the 'natural resource curse' is examined in Section 4. This literature raises the novel possibility that a nation's natural resource endowment may influence the political system it adopts. Some observers conclude that the presence of abundant natural resource stocks, particularly at the time when a country's governance institutions are being formed, can lead to the adoption of autocratic, non-democratic, elitist political systems. Resource stocks that are concentrated in space, such as oil or minerals, appear most strongly associated with this unfortunate outcome. While this possibility is based on evidence that is still evolving, it brings the analysis full circle in the sense that causal links between politics and natural resources may operate in both directions.

Finally, in Section 6 we review the phenomenon of 'perverse subsidies,' the prevalence in many countries of natural resource subsidies that have environmentally degrading effects. The discussion questions why governments wishing to effect transfers to specific groups choose to use such wasteful mechanisms. It is argued that making transfers through subsidies related to natural resources is attractive to governments because it reduces transparency and political transaction costs, leading to less opposition and confrontation to those transfers, which more than compensates the losses due to environmental degradation.

1 Property Rights to Natural Resources

Property rights are key determinants of natural resource use (Alston and Mueller, 2003). When a natural resource is not scarce relative to the existing demand, rights to use it are generally irrelevant. If changes occur that render the resource economically scarce, however (for example, shifts in preferences, technology or demographics) rights to use the resource begin to matter and

---

[3] The rationale for taking this approach is discussed later.

a process whereby property rights evolve may be set in motion. It is useful to think of this process in terms of demand and supply forces.

The demand for property rights arises when groups or individuals realize that their welfare would be enhanced if the current property rights system were changed. Imagine a renewable natural resource used by a village under open access conditions, but where demand is low relative to the yield the resource can sustain, so common pool losses are minimal. An exogenous change then occurs that dramatically increases demand, for example, a technological innovation or trade liberalization that creates a demand for the resource as an input. If open access persists, each individual's increased use of the resource would now adversely affect use by others, causing welfare losses. Users now have an incentive to 'demand' a change in the property rights system, to a form that avoids these losses (Demsetz, 1967). This observation applies more generally: most market failures, such as externalities, public goods and asymmetric information, afford the possibility to increase efficiency through changes in property rights.[4]

Nothing guarantees, however, that the demanded change in property rights will be automatically supplied. In fact, casual observation indicates that inefficient situations that could readily be improved by obvious changes in property rights are rife. An important reason for this is that property rights are created, or 'supplied,' by a political process. Political economy considerations are thus crucial for understanding the actual arrangements that emerge in any given situation. The groups that control the political process will not consider the costs and benefits to society as a whole that arise from a change in property rights, but only those relevant to themselves (Deacon, 2003). The property rights that emerge in an ideal democracy, where the controlling group is the entire voting population, will therefore tend to be different to those that would emerge if policies were controlled by an elite minority.

To expand on this point, consider as a benchmark a world where the Coase Theorem applies to the political realm (Coase, 1960; Acemoglu, 2002). In this benchmark, political property rights are well defined, individuals are well informed on the costs and benefits of alternative courses of action, and there are no political transaction costs. In such a world, natural resources would always be used efficiently, regardless of who owns them. If optimality requires a change in resource use that would harm the politically powerful, costless compensations could be arranged to allow the change to take place. That is, welfare enhancing property rights would always emerge. The fact that societies routinely chose policies and institutions that lead to inefficient use of natural resources indicates that these benchmark conditions are not satisfied in the real world. Property rights that are conducive to better economic performance may fail to emerge because informational problems lead citizens to be

---

[4] Demand for a change in property rights may also arise from purely redistributive motivations, where one group seeks to increase its welfare at the expense of other groups.

unaware or to disagree as to which changes are optimal (Alston and Mueller, 2003). Even when losses under an existing arrangement are obvious, free-riding and other problems of collective action may prevent changes from being accomplished.

More importantly, when political property rights are insecure it is difficult for politicians and citizens to make credible, long term commitments to compensate those who would lose from the change in resource use. It may be impossible to assure them that promised side-payments will actually be made and will not be altered or reversed in the future, or that the gains will not be eroded by corruption or incompetence. If the costs of carrying out such political transactions are prohibitively high, sub-optimal property rights arrangements may persist even in the face of obviously superior alternatives.

The Landless Peasant Movement (MST) in Brazil is a case in point. The MST has practiced a successful strategy of land invasions to force the government to expropriate land in their favor (Alston, Libecap, and Mueller, 1999a, 1999b, 2000). This strategy for land reform has led to high levels of rural violence and has been shown to give incentives for both landowners and squatters to clear forests prematurely, so as to solidify property rights. Clearly, this property rights arrangement has been wasteful. The government has tried to persuade the MST to cease invading by promising in exchange to accelerate the pace of land reform. It has also tried to dissuade invasions by passing a law that invaded properties will not be the object of State expropriations. Neither of these policies have had the intended effect, however, because the government cannot credibly commit to continue land redistribution in the absence of invasions or to desist from intervening when an invasion attracts the electorate's attention. The MST is consequently unwilling to accept any form of compromise that involves ceasing invasions, and the waste continues (Alston, Libecap, and Mueller, 2003).

While stable political conditions and a well-established rule of law are conducive to the creation of efficient ownership institutions, they by no means guarantee it. Libecap's (1989) analysis of bargaining for changing property rights over fisheries, crude oil, and federally owned range and timber land in the United States makes this point. In all four cases, initial property rights institutions led to common pool losses and attempts were made to change these to more efficient regimes. Attempts to mitigate these losses by forming new property rights arrangements generally met with little success, however. Although significant potential gains were widely acknowledged, issues of 'the distribution of wealth and political power that are part of the transition to the proposed rights structure [remained] a source of dispute.'[5]

In the case of oil, for example, the common-law rule of capture granted property rights to oil upon extraction. This created incentives for multiple owners

---

[5] Libecap (1989: 5).

of land over a single reservoir to embark in a race to drill and drain, even though this led to excessive capital costs and increased extraction costs due to losses of pressure. Unitization, whereby a single firm operates the field in a profit maximizing fashion with the net returns divided among the claimants according to a pre-specified formula, would have avoided these losses. Although this seems a straightforward fix for rampant common pool losses, the fraction of oil reservoirs successfully unitized has been surprisingly low (Libecap and Wiggins, 1985). Reaching agreement over individual shares has proved diffi-cult, particularly when the parties are heterogeneous with respect to location and the productive potential of their leases. Agreements often took several years to reach and frequently broke down when conditions changed. As these examples illustrate, the probability of reaching wealth-enhancing agreements to change property rights is crucially determined by transaction costs.[6]

Transaction costs are likely to be low in small, stable, homogeneous commu-nities. Accordingly, prospects for achieving cooperation and coordination for more efficient use of natural resources are greatest in these circumstances. Ostrom's (1990) work on communal resource management systems implicitly makes this point. Ostrom (1990) criticizes the presumption in much of the policy literature that communal governance of natural resources is inefficient, as well as the resulting policy prescriptions that optimal use requires either government intervention or private property rights. She argues that the simple models that underlie this presumption, the 'tragedy of the commons' (Hardin, 1968; Gordon, 1954), prisoner dilemma, and the logic of collective action (Olson, 1965), do not necessarily apply to all common property situations. She provides several examples of groups using natural resources under common property arrangements who create new rules that essentially change the game they face to avoid inefficiencies. The individuals in these cases overcame both the free-rider problems inherent in communal use and the second-order dilemma of supplying the institutions that enabled credible commitments and mutual monitoring.

It is worth reiterating that the groups examined in these case studies were generally small, stable, and relatively homogeneous, so the transaction costs of adapting institutions were relatively low. Also, the question remains as to how successful these arrangements were in a quantitative sense in overcoming com-mon pool incentives to overuse communal resources. While a community may exercise a degree of control through customs, social penalties, and taboos, the penalties for inefficient use by an individual are arguably sharper under private ownership. Accordingly, the costs and benefits of individual resource use deci-sions are (arguably) more loosely linked under communal ownership than

---

[6] That is, agreement will be less likely the greater (i) the aggregate gains to be shared, (ii) the number and heterogeneity of the bargaining powers involved, (iii) the extent of limited and asymmetric information, and (iv) the distributional issues involved, all of which depend as well on the physical nature of the resource (Libecap, 1989).

Robert T. Deacon and Bernardo Mueller

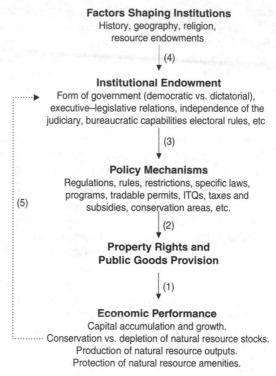

Factors Shaping Institutions
History, geography, religion,
resource endowments

(4)

Institutional Endowment
Form of government (democratic vs. dictatorial),
executive–legislative relations, independence of the
judiciary, bureaucratic capabilities electoral rules, etc

(3)

Policy Mechanisms
Regulations, rules, restrictions, specific laws,
programs, tradable permits, ITQs, taxes and
subsidies, conservation areas, etc.

(5)

(2)

**Property Rights and
Public Goods Provision**

(1)

Economic Performance
Capital accumulation and growth.
Conservation vs. depletion of natural resource stocks.
Production of natural resource outputs.
Protection of natural resource amenities.

Figure 4.1 Political institutions, policy mechanisms, and property rights

under private ownership. Studies of bush fallow and forest biomass use in Côte d'Ivoire and Ghana support this point (López, 1997, 1998). At least in these communities, common ownership has apparently increased cultivation and reduced forest cover well beyond what strict profit maximization would dictate.

The discussion in this section is framed by a central proposition: a country's political institutions, by determining transaction costs, shape the pattern of property rights that emerge and the way natural resources are used.[7] Figure 4.1 provides a simple framework that relates institutions and policy mechanisms to property rights, and these in turn to economic performance. These two links represent the two major lines of research in the property rights literature (Alston and Mueller, 2003; Libecap, 2002).

Research that takes property rights as given and seeks to understand how their specific structure affects the allocation and use of resources is depicted by

[7] There has been increasing interest in the effect of political institutions on economic outcomes. Several authors have been applying the notion of transaction costs economics (Williamson, 1985, 1991) to politics, in what has been termed transaction cost politics (Dixit, 1996; North, 1990b; Levy and Spiller, 1996; Spiller and Tommasi, 2003).

link (1). Insecure property rights lead to rent dissipation by providing incentives to usurp, defend and lobby for more secure rights. More importantly, insecure rights prompt claimants to excessive or premature investment in the hopes of strengthening their claims (Anderson and Hill, 1990), they prevent the holder from using a resource as collateral, and they reduce potential gains from exchanging assets.[8] In Section 3 we qualify this point by noting that insecure property rights discourage investment in produced capital, and explain how this can have countervailing effects on both the depletion of natural resource stocks and the production of natural resource outputs.

An illustration of this effect in action is provided by research indicating that the use of forests is affected by whether or not the user has an adjudicated land claim. Ownership of cleared land is generally more secure than forested land, which has the effect of rendering forest biomass highly insecure. Adjudicating a land claim is an alternative way to securing ownership rights, hence one should expect forest clearing to be less extensive on adjudicated lands, and forest stocks more plentiful. This has been shown in Ecuador, where the relative frequency of land claim adjudication across cantons is negatively correlated with rates of land clearing.[9] In Brazil, applicable property laws, land reform policies, and conservation programs have a similar effect, rendering rights to forest biomass highly insecure, and this is cited as an important cause of deforestation.[10]

Research depicted by links labeled (2) and (3) in Figure 4.1 examines how property rights evolve and investigates why inefficient arrangements can persist when more efficient alternatives are readily available. This line of inquiry has been the main topic of this section, and has been described in terms of the demand and supply of property rights.[11] Both institutional endowments and policy mechanisms form the 'rules of the game' that restrict agents' behavior (North, 1990a). The difference between the two is that institutional endowments change very slowly over time so that they can be taken as exogenous, whereas political or policy mechanisms can be altered in a shorter time frame and can thus be considered as choice variables of the political actors. Institutional endowments include the type of government, for example, parliamentary or presidential, democratic or dictatorial, legislative–executive relations, the independence of the judiciary, the level of bureaucratic capabilities, electoral rules, and so forth. These institutions determine who are the players, what are their payoffs for cooperating or deviating, what are their horizons, where and how frequently they interact, who initiates legislation, who has a vote, who can veto, and in what sequence these decisions are made.

---

[8] Sub-optimal use of forested land due to property rights insecurity has been analyzed by Alston, Libecap, and Mueller (1999a, 1999b, 2000), Besley (1995), Deacon (1999), Feder and Feeney (1991), Place and Hazell (1993), Migot-Adholla et al. (1991), and Southgate et al. (1991).

[9] Southgate, Sierra, and Brown (1991) p. 1146. In Ecuador, individuals seeking to acquire land in tree covered areas must clear those lands in order to acquire formal property rights.

[10] Alston, Libecap, and Mueller, 2000, pp. 169–72.

[11] The work by Libecap (1989) and Ostrom (1990) cited above are examples of this literature.

Policy mechanisms are rules, regulations and restrictions that policy imposes on resource users. They can come in the form of a law or a program devised by policymakers. A program for implementing individual tradable quotas (ITQs) for solving the common pool problem in a fishery is an example of a policy mechanism that affects property rights. Other examples are Pigouvian taxes, conservation areas and eco-labeling. Institutional endowments partially determine the success of any given policy mechanism in promoting more efficient property rights. The use of ITQs, for example, has lead to disappointing results in some circumstances, despite elegant theoretical underpinnings (Johnson, 1999). Where failure occurs, it is often due to a mismatch between the extant institutional endowments and those required to resolve distributional issues, provide credible commitments against expropriation, and assure effective monitoring.

Although we assumed above that institutional endowments are fixed, Figure 4.1 suggests that economic performance and other factors such as history, geography, religion and resource endowments do in fact determine those institutions and lead to change over time. The arrows linking economic performance (5) and these other factors (4) to institutional endowments are dashed to indicate that these effects work slowly over time. In Section 4 we review research on one of these links, a connection between resource endowments, economic growth, and governance, which is attracting increasing attention in the literature.

2 Political systems, ownership risk, and natural resource stocks

One aspect of property rights that has been studied in the empirical literature on political economy and natural resource use is the link between insecure tenure and incentives to conserve resource stocks such as forests, fish, oil, minerals, etc. The intuition that underlies this connection is straightforward. If the current owner of a resource stock faces a risk that his or her claim to the stock or its future return may be lost, the effect on the choice between consuming vs. conserving the resource is similar to the effect of discounting it.[12] The necessary ingredients for this choice are: R_0, the return from immediate consumption, R_1, the return from consuming the asset one year hence, r, the rate of interest, and π the probability that the owner's claim to the resource is lost before R_1 is received. The expected present value of the owner's claim on next year's return is $R_1(1-\pi)/(1 + r)$. Comparing this to R_0 captures the current owner's consumption vs. conservation decision. An increase in r will tilt the comparison in favor of immediate consumption; an increase in π, the probability of ownership loss, has the same effect.

---

[12] Besley (1995) calls this the 'security argument' for why property rights affect asset conservation and investment decisions. He also presents two other arguments for why property rights and conservation and investment decisions could be linked. One is based on using an asset as collateral for a loan to obtain investment funds; the other emphasizes the importance of transfer rights to exploiting an asset's complete productive potential.

The free access fishery is an extreme example. Any fish purposely left uncaught by an individual fisher to grow to a larger size during the coming year will, with virtual certainty, be caught by someone else, so $\pi \cong 1$ in this case. Whatever R_1 may be, the expected present value return from conserving the stock is essentially zero to the individual fisher. By this reasoning, the incentive to conserve stocks of fish, groundwater, game, and forests is diminished by insecurity in the owner's claim on their future returns.[13] Similar reasoning implies that insecure ownership diminishes the incentive to conserve non-renewable resource stocks for future consumption. In some of these cases, insecure ownership is partly due to the resource's fugitive or hidden nature, which makes monitoring and enforcement more difficult.

Of particular relevance here is the fact that a country's political system can induce ownership risk. When a country's government is either unstable or authoritarian, incentives to conserve natural resource stocks are likely to be weak. For example, conserving biomass in a forest rather than consuming it immediately is an act of investment, and the investor's return might be an enhanced stock of nutrients to support agriculture or a larger biomass for commercial timber to be harvested later. The user will not sacrifice current consumption without an assurance that he or she will receive the future benefit. Such assurances are normally provided by legal title, a third party enforcement mechanism, and an impartial judiciary to resolve disputes.

When government lacks the power, stability, and popular support needed to enforce legal claims, enforcement will fail. Even resource stocks that are nominally owned by government may be subject to free access use if government cannot control what goes on in the countryside or if the political system does not provide incentives for government officials to monitor and enforce the State's claims.[14] Evidence on illegal logging and forest clearing in forest land nominally owned by government is illustrative. Illegal logging can involve logging inside national parks or outside concession areas and cutting of restricted species. According to widely cited estimates, the percentage of wood harvested illegally exceeds 80 percent in Bolivia, Cambodia, Myanmar, and Brazil (Smith 2002). Each of these countries ranks relatively low on standard 'rule of law' indexes.

Even when the government's enforcement powers are adequate, the individual's claim to a resource will be insecure if the country's legal system cannot be relied upon to provide predictable interpretations of property laws. In countries ruled by autocrats and dominant elites, rather than by anonymous laws and

---

[13] For π near zero the expected present value approximately equals R_1 discounted by $r + \pi$, which reinforces the point that ownership risk affects natural resource use in much the same way as a higher interest rate.

[14] In Colombia more than 35% of land designated as national parks is actually held by private owners, 20% is occupied by untitled squatters, and another 10% is disputed by other parties. Enforcement of land ownership claims is hindered more generally by drug smuggling, the actions of revolutionary bands, and conflicts among native groups (Deacon and Murphy, 1997, p. 6.)

institutions, the individual's claim to an asset can depend crucially on remaining in favor with those in power. Being in compliance with the written law may be of little consequence. Even those in favor with the political elite face ownership risk because the elite might be deposed, and the structure of ownership claims realigned as a consequence. Accordingly, incentives to conserve natural resource stocks are likely to be weak in countries subject to the rule of individuals rather than the rule of law.

Instability in a country's policies can affect incentives to conserve resource stocks in similar ways. Consider the effect of a hypothetical trade liberalization policy, one that would shift the terms of trade in favor of agriculture, on a nation's agricultural soil. In a country where policies tend to be stable and government promises are kept, some farmers will rationally invest in greater soil conservation, reasoning that enhanced agricultural output in the future will more than repay the initial outlay. In a country where government policies change frequently, the opposite might occur. Farmers might rationally conclude that the best course is to farm intensively in the short run, while the policy is in force, anticipating that it will be dismantled in the future. The net effect could be accelerated soil depletion in this case and the driving force is not the policy itself, but rather the fact that it is unstable.

The preceding discussion suggests a simple, intuitive proposition: insecure ownership diminishes the conservation of resource stocks for future use. This simple aphorism does not apply universally, however. When ownership insecurity is induced by a country's political system, ownership claims to all assets, natural resource stocks and ordinary goods alike, may be rendered uncertain. This can have the secondary effect of increasing the cost of, or diminishing the return from, appropriating natural resources. Stripping biomass from a forest again provides a convenient illustration. One reason for removing a forest's biomass is to gain access to the land it occupies, possibly for farming or ranching. If forest biomass cannot be owned with any degree of certainty, the incentive to maintain it, let alone nurture it, clearly is diminished. If rights to the agricultural land one would obtain by clearing the forest are also uncertain, however, then the incentive to incur the cost of land clearing is similarly diminished. This is a case where insecure ownership, as a general feature of an economy, diminishes the return from consuming the natural resource stock. If this secondary effect is sufficiently strong, the net effect could be larger stocks of standing forest biomass under insecure ownership.

The same net result can occur in cases where the act of harvesting or accessing a natural resource requires produced capital, for example, where a road, truck, or specialized logging equipment is required to remove forest biomass. Generalized insecure ownership, by creating uncertainty in claims to harvesting capital, effectively makes harvesting more costly. Again, the net result can be diminished forest use if this effect is strong enough to outweigh the diminished incentive to conserve forest stocks. This point is pursued in more detail later.

In cases where these secondary effects are deemed to be small, a simple, testable hypothesis suggests itself: renewable resource stocks will tend to be low in countries with political systems that induce insecure ownership, for example, where government is ineffective, unstable, or autocratic, and the rule of law is not well established. One empirical strategy is to test for direct relationships between political conditions and resource use, without examining the intermediate link in the causal chain—property rights institutions. One advantage of this approach is the availability of well-documented data sets on governance institutions, sources that cover virtually all independent states in the world over long time frames. Data on property rights institutions are not available at anything close to this level of detail and coverage. A second advantage is the importance of knowing which aspects of governance matter to the formation of property rights and to the use of natural resources.

This strategy has been applied to cross-country data on political attributes and changes in forest cover (Deacon, 1994, 1999). The presence of the secondary effects just described means that the existence and direction of a relationship between the two is an empirical question. In parts of the world where deforestation is most pronounced the deforestation process most often involves little capital, so it is reasonable to expect that the direct effect dominates. Political instability is indicated by frequencies of events that signal potential political change, for example, guerrilla warfare, revolutions, coups d'etat, and major constitutional shifts. Rule by elites rather than by impersonal laws and elected representatives is indicated by whether or not the chief executive was elected, whether or not a legislature exists and has significant powers, and whether political competition is tolerated. Overall, the results on deforestation broadly support the hypothesis: forest stocks tend to be relatively depleted in countries with unstable, non-representative systems of governance. The estimated effects are large: a one standard deviation change in an index of ownership security, described later, accounts for about three-fourths of the mean reduction in forest stocks observed in a sample of 62 countries.

The fact that insecure ownership due to political conditions applies to produced capital as well as natural resource stocks suggests a related hypothesis: the political factors affecting natural resource stocks should also affect stocks of produced capital. A similar cross-country empirical procedure found that the specific political variables that are associated with depleted levels of forest cover also affect country-wide investment rates (Deacon, 1994, 1996). This adds corroboration to the claim that ownership risk is what drives the correlations between deforestation and the political attributes of countries.

3 Interactions between produced capital and resource stocks

In a country that suffers from generalized ownership risk, the cost of capital, including capital used for natural resource extraction, will be relatively high.

As noted earlier, this diminishes the incentive to exploit natural resource stocks that require significant extraction capital, such as petroleum, natural gas, and metallic minerals.[15] This effect can partially or completely offset the direct 'discounting' effect that ownership risk has on a resource's future return, an effect that tends to hasten consumption.

Ownership risk diminishes the return from both immediate and future consumption of a resource and this can render uneconomic some stocks that would be profitable to exploit if ownership were secure. Mineral deposits that would otherwise be profitable might be left unexploited where ownership is uncertain because extraction requires an up-front investment and ownership of the capital created might be lost.[16] A higher extraction cost also changes the payoff to immediate versus future consumption for stocks that remain profitable to extract. For a non-renewable resource the effect is generally to slow the rate of extraction, increasing the amount conserved for the future.[17] Recall that the effect of ownership risk on a resource with fixed returns is to hasten extraction. Thus the two effects work against one another, and the effect of ownership risk on the timing of extraction for a capital-intensive non-renewable resource becomes an empirical question.

These hypotheses have been examined empirically using a two-step procedure. The first step is identifying the political factors that affect ownership security and their relative contributions. One way to do this is to estimate a model of economy-wide investment, controlling for economic variables such as the openness of the economy, education levels, and business cycle terms. Including political variables believed to be correlated with ownership risk enables one to identify the political determinants of investment. Regarding these political effects as resulting from ownership risk, one can then use the estimated coefficients to form an index of politically-induced ownership risk, an index that varies across countries and over time (Bohn and Deacon, 2000). This index can then be used to test for associations between politically induced ownership risk and natural resource use.

Petroleum provides a natural context for examining the effect of generalized ownership risk on capital intensive natural resources. Up-front outlays for exploration, production wells, processing equipment, and transportation infrastructure are typically large relative to revenues, and are generally incurred many years before production begins. Both of the effects postulated above— the tendency for ownership risk to render marginal resources uneconomic and to affect the rate of production for stocks that are exploited—were found to be

---

[15] The primary source for the following discussion and empirical results on capital intensive resource stocks is Bohn and Deacon (2000).

[16] If one regards abandoned stocks as being 'conserved', then economy-wide ownership risk can cause more conservation of capital intensive resource stocks.

[17] Intuitively, this occurs because pushing the higher extraction costs toward the future reduces their present value.

important.[18] Higher ownership risk reduces exploration activity and the effect is statistically significant and large. A one-standard deviation increase in the ownership risk index is associated with a 68 percent decrease in drilling. There is also a strong empirical relationship between the ownership risk index and production rates, measured as the ratio of annual production to the current reserve.[19] Production from a given reserve was found to be systematically slower in countries with relatively high ownership risk, indicating that the tendency for ownership risk to raise extraction costs swamps the effect of applying a higher effective discount rate to future returns. Again, the effect is large: a one-standard deviation increase in the risk index is associated with a 28 percent decrease in the extraction rate. Additional evidence on this general question comes from examinations of forest products production. Forestland can be used for shifting cultivation, fuel wood gathering, and commercial timber harvesting, and the last of these is clearly more capital intensive than the others. Production of industrial timber requires up-front expenditures for roads, logging camps, equipment, and port or rail facilities in some cases. If the current owner's claim to future income from logging is uncertain, the incentive to use a marginal tract of forest for commercial logging is diminished, rendering other less capital intensive uses more attractive. In this fashion, insecure ownership can potentially shift forest use away from capital-intensive activities such as commercial logging.

Ferreria and Vincent (2003) examine a model of forest allocation decisions made by a 'leader,' a possibly autocratic ruler who is able to appropriate the rents from the forest, but faces the possibility of being deposed. The model thus includes elements of insecure ownership, but also entertains the possibility of corruption in the appropriation of forest rents. The leader can enhance his probability of surviving in office, and thus receiving the forest's future return, by sharing forest income with the citizenry. Harvesting the forest requires an initial outlay of capital and is less attractive the lower the probability of surviving to reap the return.

With this motivation, Ferreira and Vincent (2003) examine relationships between timber harvests and indices of corruption, the rule of law, and other indicators of governance.[20] When their governance indicators are aggregated into a single variable, 'lower quality' governance is strongly associated with smaller timber harvests. This mirrors the finding for petroleum. The individual governance indicators are found to have different effects, however. In keeping

---

[18] Empirical analysis used a cross-country panel of observations on petroleum drilling activity, production rates, and current reserves. Drilling rates were specified to depend on price, the physical attributes and geologic abundance of a country's oil resources, OPEC membership, and ownership risk.

[19] Conditioning variables included price, the physical attributes of oil reserves and OPEC membership.

[20] They control for factors such as forest area, the stock density of forests, and relevant prices.

135

with expectations, forest harvests are consistently smaller when the risk of expropriation is high and the quality of the bureaucracy is low. (A low-quality bureaucracy is highly politicized and inefficient in providing public services.) Surprisingly, however, forest harvests tend to be higher where there is greater corruption and the rule of law is absent.[21] In a counterfactual simulation aimed at seeing how harvests would change if governance institutions for countries in the sample were changed to levels prevailing in the U.S., they found that 'better' institutions would increase harvests by 10–20 percent.

The evidence reviewed in the preceding sections demonstrates a causal link from a country's political and governance institutions to its pattern of natural resource use. This politics-to-resource link operates through the ability (or inability) of a country's government to form an efficient system of property rights. In simple situations, insecure tenure for resource stocks leads to premature and excessive depletion. When resource extraction is capital intensive, however, insecure ownership can raise extraction costs and diminish or eliminate the incentive to deplete resource stocks. While there is ample evidence showing that governance and property rights affect natural resource use, no simple 'tag line' adequately describes how the effect works—in some cases weak property rights hasten resource exploitation and in other contexts they hinder it. The presence of a politics-to-resources link seems evident, however, even if its form is not simple. The following section reviews exploratory evidence that an effect may operate in the opposite direction, evidence that a country's natural resource endowment may affect the political institutions it adopts.

4 Politics and the Natural Resource Curse

It is not uncommon to find a population that is poor, unhealthy, and politically oppressed inhabiting a country that is rich in natural resources. This seems paradoxical: as a matter of common sense and basic economic reasoning, natural resource abundance should confer prosperity. Yet examples of slow growth accompanying resource abundance abound. Nigeria's per capita GDP in 2000 was actually 30 percent lower than in 1965, despite oil revenue receipts of roughly $350 billion over that period.[22] Venezuela's performance was only slightly better. Saudi Arabia's GDP per capita was lower in 1999 than it was in 1970, before the jump in oil prices. Gylfason (2001, 848) reports that OPEC as a whole experienced per capita GNP decreases of 1.3 percent per year during 1965–98, while income increased at an average rate of 2.2 percent per year in all lower- and middle-income countries. Many resource-rich countries have avoided the curse of slow growth, of course, including Botswana, Chile (after

[21] The authors provide no explanation for the difference in results for different aspects of governance.

[22] Oil revenues, after payments to foreign companies, are reported by Sala-i-Martín and Subramanian (2003, p. 4). Information on income is from Summers and Heston (2002).

Pinochet), Malaysia and Norway. Overall, however, recent research indicates that resource abundance is systematically associated with slow growth, hence the term 'natural resource curse.'

Recently, preliminary evidence has come to light that the effect of natural resources on growth may operate through political institutions, that is, resource endowments may affect governance. The factors that determine a country's political institutions presumably are numerous and diverse, and none seems to be well understood at present. In what follows we examine evidence suggesting that resource abundance is one of these determinants.

Formal empirical evidence on the resource curse first emerged from the empirical literature on economic growth. Sachs and Warner (1997, 2001) examined cross-country data on growth in per capita income between 1970 and 1990 and related these growth rates to initial (1970) income, openness to trade, the share of investment in GDP, and other variables. They included the 'primary products' share of a country's exports in 1970 as a measure of natural resource abundance and found that subsequent growth was slow in countries where this export share is large. Primary products include food, agricultural products, fuels, and minerals; hence their export variable clearly is a flow measure and represents a mixture of heterogeneous resource products. Sachs and Warner (1997, 2001) tried including additional explanatory variables and experimented with alternative measures of resource abundance, but concluded the basic resource curse result is robust. The magnitude of this effect is substantial: according to Sachs and Warner (1997) a one-standard deviation increase in a country's primary products export share reduces the growth rate of per capita GDP by 0.6 to 1.5 percentage points.

Early explanations for this phenomenon made use of conventional economic arguments—stressing the role of markets rather than processes that operate through political institutions. One such explanation is the 'Dutch disease,' a theory offered to explain the poor economic performance of the Netherlands following the discovery of North Sea oil.[23] According to this theory, a natural resource boom causes a country's exchange rate to appreciate, reducing its manufacturing exports. The predicted effect is slow growth if, as Dutch disease proponents argue, manufacturing is more conducive to economic growth than resource extraction due to learning-by-doing and other external effects.[24] Others postulate that natural resource development diverts a country's attention away from activities that have higher long-term payoffs. Gylfason (2001) argues that resource-rich countries tend to neglect education, essentially because they see their natural resource wealth, not human capital, as the key to the future.[25] Another market-based explanation stresses volatility in

[23] This explanation is stressed by Sachs and Warner (1997, 2001).

[24] The assumption that manufacturing is an engine of growth, whereas resource extraction is not, is largely untested.

[25] Gylfason shows that investment in education is systematically lower for countries with capital concentrated in natural resource stocks. The resource measure does not capture

natural resource prices, which leads to frequent boom–bust cycles and exchange rate fluctuations. This is said to impair economic performance by hindering investment planning and effective government policy (Stevens 2003, 12). Others argue that a volatile exchange rate directly hinders exports and prospects for export-led growth (Gylfasson et al., 1999).

Significantly, it appears that the curse operates in some political contexts, but is absent in others. Moreover, the curse plagues some types of natural resources, while other resources seem largely immune. Neoclassical explanations, such as the Dutch disease, do not predict these regularities. Perhaps for this reason, theories stressing political economy considerations such as rent-seeking and forms of governance have gained prominence.[26] There is substantial case study evidence that the availability of rents from abundant natural resources can lead to rent-seeking and corruption in government, particularly in countries where the rule of law is not well established. Some observers argue that natural resource rents impair growth by attracting a country's entrepreneurial talent away from its productive sectors, for example, manufacturing, and into socially non-productive attempts to enhance one's share of the large resource pie (Torvik, 2002). This is particularly likely if resource rents are nominally captured by government, but are subject to private appropriation by those willing to engage in lobbying, corruption, and the like. In equilibrium the returns to both lines of work will be equalized, hence a boom in the resource sector will draw talent away from the economy's productive sector.

This theory does not explain why some resource-rich economies fall prey to the curse while others seem to escape it, however. Botswana, Chile, Malaysia, and Norway are all resource rich, and all achieved very attractive growth rates during 1965–2000, based significantly on natural resource industries. Over the same period Bolivia, Nigeria, Saudi Arabia, and Venezuela, also resource rich, all languished. One possibility is that institutional differences across countries cause variations in the efficacy of rent-seeking, and therefore differences in the degree to which resource rents hinder growth (Mehlum, Moene, and Torvik, 2002.) According to this theory, resource abundance will be a curse in a country whose political institutions are receptive to rent-seeking, because the diversion of entrepreneurial energy away from productive activities will be severe. The diversion of entrepreneurship will be modest and natural resource wealth will be a blessing, however, where government is immune to rent-seeking.

Recently available indicators of institutional quality, including measures of the rule of law, bureaucratic quality, expropriation risk, and other governance

abundance, however, but rather the degree to which total capital is concentrated in resources. Birdsall, Pinckney, and Sabot (2001) also draw a link with education, but argue that the effect operates through a country's political system.

[26] Stevens (2003, pp. 17–24) surveys several strands of this literature. Bulte and Damania (2003, pp. 3–6) review this literature and related work on economic growth, emphasizing theoretical contributions.

attributes allow straightforward tests of these predictions. In one recent study the results are remarkably clear: natural resource abundance retards growth when institutional quality is low, that is, when government is prone to rent-seeking, confiscation, and corruption.[27] For a country with good institutions, however, resource abundance has a mildly positive (though statistically insignificant) effect on growth.[28] If resource abundance and weak governance both tend to be found in the same countries, countries typically suffering poor economic performance, might resource abundance and governance be somehow causally linked? There is considerable anecdotal evidence for such a link. Civil wars in Angola, Nigeria, Sierra Leone, and Zaire have been attributed to struggles to control resources, particularly resources that are spatially concentrated such as diamonds, oil, and metallic minerals. Sales of diamonds, cocaine, and timber can provide rebel groups with the financial resources necessary to pursue their aims, whether ideological or mercenary. This suggests that resource abundance might contribute to the determination of at least one political attribute, political instability. Indeed, systematic study of available evidence has demonstrated that the probability and duration of civil wars in a cross section of countries is strongly correlated with resource abundance, measured as the share of primary products in a nation's total exports (Collier and Hoffler, 1998, 2002).

One can also find anecdotal evidence of resource wealth affecting the distribution of power between central and regional governments.[29] In Nigeria a concentration of resource wealth in one region, and attempts by other regions to gain a share of it, contributed to the breakup and eventual re-establishment of centralized political power. In post-Soviet Russia, resource-rich regions have sought to enhance their own political power vis-à-vis the center in order to obtain more complete control of resource wealth.

The notion that resource abundance might influence governance gains plausibility from an empirical regularity in the resource curse literature: the curse seems most prevalent when the resources involved naturally occur in dense concentrations. Such 'point' resources can arguably be controlled by a strong State mechanism, while resources that are 'diffuse,' or evenly distributed over

---

[27] See Mehlum et al. (2002). They estimate an empirical model of economic growth that includes both a resource abundance measure and an interaction between resource abundance and institutional quality. This allows for different economic growth responses to resource abundance under different governance regimes. Bulte and Damania (2003) pursue a similar empirical strategy and find that the curse holds for autocratic regimes, but not for democracies.

[28] A somewhat different theory, based on the composition of political power in a country, reaches a similar conclusion. Where a number of groups vie for political power, a resource windfall is predicted to set off a feeding frenzy. This is said to cause inefficiency in the allocation of capital because intensified rent-seeking causes government to raise revenues, which are supported in part by taxes on the more productive sectors. The result can be a slow-down in economic growth. However, the size and direction of the effect depends on the number of groups competing for government largesse. See Tornell and Lane (1999), who provide evidence on the economic growth consequences of natural resource booms in Venezuela, Nigeria, Mexico, Costa Rica, Côte d'Ivoire, and Kenya.

[29] We are indebted to Joseph Stiglitz for these examples.

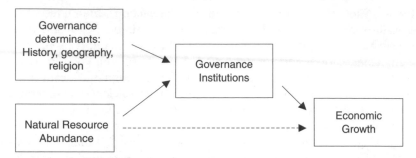

Figure 4.2 Resource abundance, governance, and growth

the landscape, cannot. From this observation, it does not take a heroic leap to hypothesize that countries with abundant point resources will tend to evolve governance structures based on centralized agglomeration of power, power directed at controlling those resources, and that their histories will be replete with struggles to retain that control.[30]

This reasoning suggests that the effect of resource abundance on economic growth is indirect: resource abundance leads to 'bad' or unproductive governance institutions, and these institutions in turn lead to poor economic performance. This chain is illustrated in Figure 4.2. It recognizes that factors such as history, religion and geography may well contribute to a nation's governance system, as indicated by the upper left solid link. The empirical literature on economic growth has established the solid link from repressive, corrupt, or unstable government to slow economic growth to the satisfaction of most observers. Hence those seeking to evaluate political economy explanations for the resource curse must address two questions: Does resource abundance systematically lead to unproductive governance institutions, that is, does the lower left solid link exist? If so, does resource abundance have an additional direct effect on economic growth, for example, due to Dutch disease effects, terms of trade effects, and so on? The latter possibility is illustrated by the dotted link in Figure 4.2.

Motivated by these questions, recent research on the resource curse has distinguished 'point' resources, such as fuels and minerals, from 'diffuse' resources such as and food and agricultural products. Empirical models have also begun to allow for the possibility that resource abundance influences governance institutions.[31] One way to combine these considerations is to specify a two-part

[30] Woolcock, et al. (2001) reach the same general conclusion by a different path of reasoning. They argue that point source resources, including such plantation crops as sugar, cotton, and tobacco, are associated with highly concentrated ownership and, consequently, wealth inequality. They see this inequality as a source of political conflict that hinders the adoption of productive public policies.
[31] Leite and Weidmann (1999), Bulte et al. (2003), Isham et al. (2003), and Sala-i-Martín and Subramanian (2003) are examples of this work. See also Woolcock et al. (2001) for a less formal empirical exercise that has the same flavor.

empirical model. In the first part, institutional quality is hypothesized to be a function of natural resource abundance, with a distinction drawn between 'point' and 'diffuse' resources. Here, the consistent finding is that an abundance of point resources in an initial period is associated with bad institutions later on, while diffuse resources show no such effect. Additional variables that may exert separate influences on institutions are included as controls, however the association between point resource abundance and undesirable governance appears robust.[32]

The second step involves determining whether or not resource abundance exerts a separate, direct effect on economic growth, once the effect of governance institutions is controlled. This involves specifying a model of GDP growth that includes, as determinants, governance, income in an initial period (to allow for convergence in growth rates), and additional economic variables thought to determine economic growth. A strong link between governance and economic growth rates, familiar from the empirical growth literature, is confirmed here. This establishes an indirect link between natural resource abundance and economic growth, where the resource effect is conveyed through an influence on institutions. One can then test for an additional direct link between resource abundance and growth by adding resource abundance as a separate determinant of growth rates (Sala-i-Martín and Subramanian, 2003). Evidence reported to date indicates that no additional direct effect is present, implying that the entire natural resource curse arises from the impact of resource abundance on governance.

Standard econometric approaches to testing the direction of causation between resources and institutions with cross country panel data can be unconvincing because governance institutions tend to be highly persistent. This fact enhances the value of case studies of individual resource-rich countries as a supplement to formal statistical analysis. The available case study evidence generally supports the proposition that point resource abundance leads to weak political systems and consequent economic disadvantage, but there are important exceptions.

At first glance Bolivia seems to fit the model well.[33] Bolivia is rich in hard minerals and petroleum, with mineral rents equaling 16–25 percent of GDP and minerals accounting for roughly 90 percent of exports during the 1970s and early 1980s. During most of this period Bolivia suffered from political instability, factional strife, autocratic rule, and a lack of social and political freedoms.[34]

---

[32] The controls examined include: language fractionalization to allow for difficulty in attaining consensus on public policy questions, settler mortality rates in former colonies to allow for differences in the form of governments set up by the former colonial powers (Acemoglu et al. 2001), school enrolment rates and per capita incomes at an historic date to allow for differences in attitudes toward governance, regional dummy variables, latitude or location in the tropics, openness to trade, and life expectancy at birth in an historic year.

[33] See Auty and Evia (2001).

[34] Political factionalization and instability characterized governance in Bolivia in the years after the 1952 revolution. Instability was particularly acute after the mid-1970s, with nine

Economic growth during this period was negative. Potential economic advantages were squandered on unproductive social investments and on protection for inefficient manufacturing enterprises—all seemingly consistent with the theory linking concentrated resource stocks to bad governance and economic demise. The full story is more nuanced, however. A severe economic crisis occurred in the early 1980s, with inflation reaching 20,000 percent at one point and private investment collapsing to 3 percent of GDP. This event precipitated an abrupt political transition. The earlier political factionalization gave way to a more consensual democracy and improvements in the quality of governance. These gains have largely persisted to the present, despite Bolivia's resource wealth.[35]

According to Abidin (2001), a similar crisis allowed Malaysia to escape, or at least mitigate, the resource curse. Malaysia is rich in rubber, tin, petroleum, and natural gas. Through the 1950s and 1960s it suffered from factionalized politics and civil strife. In 1969, race riots between the numerically dominant ethnic Malays and economically dominant Chinese fed fears that the country would descend into chaos. This is broadly consistent with predictions that natural resource abundance leads to strife and poor governance. In Malaysia's case, however, the crisis that resulted led to a political compromise and a restructuring of the nation's economic policy. In the new order, emphasis was placed on improving the position of ethnic Malays through education and investments in rural infrastructure. Since 1970 Malaysia's governance system has received higher rankings for governance than other resource-rich states, although they are certainly not distinguished when compared to non-resource-rich states. During the 1990s, Malaysia has enjoyed relatively rapid growth.

Saudi Arabia is perhaps *the* model for a State rich in point resources, and its political and economic history are much more in conformance with the curse hypothesis. Outwardly it is a benevolent monarchy, yet inequalities in the distribution of income, education, and human development are clearly radical. At a deeper level, Saudi Arabia might be better described as a predatory autocracy in which the elite transfer a small share of natural wealth to the masses to prevent them from rebelling. Saudi Arabia's political institutions have been 'perfectly autocratic' since the country was formed.[36] Over the last three decades it has suffered the curse of slow growth. Per capita income was actually lower in 1999 than it was in 1971, before the major oil price shocks occurred.

changes of government occurring between 1978 and 1982 (Auty and Evia, 2001, 182–4.) Regarding social and political capital, Bolivia had a decidedly low rating on political and civil freedoms and a low rating for democratic governance during the same period (Freedom House, 2003 and the Polity IV data base.)

[35] After 1983, Bolivia's political and economic freedoms ratings and democracy score improved dramatically.

[36] As judged from the Polity IV data base, Saudi Arabia has received a 'perfect' 10 out of 10 score on the index for autocratic governance.

Given the numerous and diverse sets of factors that presumably determine the economic and political development paths of individual countries, any theory that attempts to explain events on such a grand scale clearly will have a large error term. Such a theory will remain valuable, however, if it can predict broad regularities in political and economic development patterns. Here, the comparative case-study evidence compiled by Karl (1997) is illuminating. She studied the history of economic and political development in Algeria, Indonesia, Iran, Nigeria, Venezuela, and, for purposes of comparison, Norway. While the historical record is filled with nuances and idiosyncrasies, the central themes Karl identifies resonate with the stylized theories linking resource abundance to unproductive governance. When minerals are a nation's key source of wealth and mineral rents accrue directly to the State, the framework for decision making in government is altered, including goal formation, the locus of authority, and the types of institutions adopted (Karl, 1997, 44, 45). Because minerals tend to be concentrated in space, the European colonists (or western commercial interests, if colonization never formally occurred) who first exploited them could extract rents by controlling only specific mining and export sites. There was no need to set up a governing apparatus to collect taxes, extract rents, and control populations throughout the country. In other words, it was not necessary to extend civil authority and the rule of law to the countryside (Karl, 1997, 60–1). In Venezuela, the dominance of oil in the economy led to a blurring of the worlds of commerce and State policy, an outcome that promoted a rent-seeking culture and a patron–client system of governance. With this legacy and the ongoing importance of concentrated mineral stocks in the country's economy, the persistence of autocratic, strong man rule, and the tendency for entrepreneurial talent to be directed toward rent-seeking, is unsurprising.

A hardwood timber boom in Southeast Asia had a similar effect on the governments of the Philippines, Indonesia, and the Malay states of Sarawak and Sabah (Ross, 2001). Two of the three countries inherited strong, professional forestry management institutions upon independence. A boom in timber prices caused timber to become a dominant force in the economies of all three countries. In each case, though most strongly in the Philippines and Malaysia, the jump in timber prices led to a change in the structure of governance (Ross, 2001, 32ff.) Political elites altered institutions to acquire a greater control over resource rents—a process Ross (2001) terms 'rent-seizing.' Once the control of resource rents was secured, the political elite allocated this wealth to political supporters, family, friends and campaign donors. The overall effect was a general increase in corruption and a concentration of political power among the elite.

5 Natural Resources and Perverse Subsidies

Natural resources generate substantial rents. World Bank data cited by Auty and Gelb (2001) for 1994 put the average share of natural resource rents in GDP at 15 percent.[37] In most cases, access to these rents is directly or indirectly determined by the government. This implies that in general, but especially in resource-rich countries, there will be plentiful opportunities for rent-seeking related to natural resources. In this section we describe one of the main mechanisms through which this rent-seeking manifests itself, a phenomenon known as 'perverse subsidies.' In this literature the term 'perverse subsidies' refers specifically to a subsidy that has unintended, harmful effects on the environment.[38] This is an important topic for this chapter as perverse subsidies illustrate particularly well the political and institutional determinants of natural resource use.

Perverse subsidies come in a variety of forms, and are often linked to policy that is not directly related to the environment.[39] A direct transfer to producers or consumers of a good or service that uses environmental inputs can lead to increased degradation. The same effect can result from a tax exemption. But perverse subsidies are not only budgetary. They can involve provision by government of complementary goods and services, such as infrastructure and technology. Other forms taken by perverse subsidies are price controls, import and export tariffs and other non-tariff barriers, all of which can protect consumers and producers of goods and services that degrade the environment. In addition, the government can provide subsidized credit for activities that have important environmental consequences, such as subsidized agriculture leading to increased deforestation, erosion and pesticide use. A more covert form of perverse subsidy comes about through the non-internalization of environmental externalities in regular economic activities. Because the private costs of the activity diverge from the social costs, too much of that activity will be undertaken in terms of social welfare. Any form of production or consumption that generates an environmental externality is in effect being under-priced and is consequently implicitly subsidized. It is as if the government is making a transfer by not charging externality generators for these social costs. Finally, a common type of perverse subsidy occurs when the government charges less than the full economic rent for the right to use or extract a given natural resource. This is revenue that the government could bring to its own coffers but opts to grant to certain groups and individuals.

The distortions brought about by all these forms of subsidies are perverse (environmentally degrading) for several reasons (Porter, 1998). They can lead

---

[37] These numbers consider only pasture, cropland and minerals so that actual natural resource rents must be even higher. The shares varied from 9.86% for small resource-poor countries to 21.22% for small oil-exporters.

[38] Subsidies may also have other harmful side effects, for example on trade, competition, and equity. Subsidies can also have beneficial effects, correcting market failures. A more precise term that focuses on the environmental effect of the subsidies is 'environmentally damaging subsidies' (EDS) as used by Beers and Bergh (2001). We will stick with 'perverse subsidies,' nevertheless, as this is the term that predominates in the literature.

[39] For different typologies and classifications see Beers and Bergh (2001), Moor (1997) and Myers (1998).

to an over-capitalization of natural resource sectors, bringing resources into production or consumption that would not otherwise be used. Related to this, subsidies often encourage the use of technologies that use environmental inputs more intensively and less efficiently. In addition they encourage over-consumption of natural resources as prices are brought below levels that would prevail in the absence of the subsidies. Finally, subsidies generally come at a cost to the government, which is deprived of resources that could be used for monitoring and enforcing more sustainable resource use.

Given the various forms taken by perverse subsidies, as well as their often hidden nature, it is difficult to quantify how pervasive they actually are. Some studies have nevertheless attempted to do so. De Moor and Calamai (1997) put the total cost of subsidies per year in the mid-1990s at $950 billion, with the main effects coming through agriculture and fisheries (36.3%), transport (23.7%), energy (21.5%), water (6.3%). These subsidies affect the environment by contributing to soil erosion, acid rain, depletion of fish stocks, water and air pollution, emission of greenhouse gases, among others (Beers and Bergh, 2001). Myers (1998) estimates the total value of subsidies for the whole world at $1,110 billion per year, considering only agriculture, fossil fuels, nuclear energy, road transport, water, and fisheries. He identifies a further $785 billion of implicit subsidies derived from environmental externalities whose costs are not borne by those who generate them, thus leading to a total of $1,895 billion per year. Of this total he estimates that $1,450 billion are perverse subsidies, that is, they have negative environmental consequences. Clearly these calculations are debatable and can be contested on many levels, from definitions of what should actually be counted as a subsidy, to the non-inclusion of counter-vailing effects, to the credibility of the various data used.[40] Whatever one may think of this estimate, however, the important point is that subsidies are pervasive and sometimes have environmentally damaging consequences.

If subsidies often have such deleterious environmental effects, why do governments implement them in the first place and then allow them to persist? According to Ascher (1999) one misleading answer to this question is that government officials are often unaware of their consequences or are unable to devise more sensible policies. Another is that policy is often initially sound, but when conditions change, governments are unable to make the necessary adjustments. The problem with both of these explanations is that the rents involved are typically very large and it is hard to believe that governments would systematically allow them to be dissipated instead of trying to appropriate them. Instead, Ascher (1999) suggests that environmentally damaging natural

---

[40] Deacon (1995) develops a general equilibrium model to analyze the relationship between government policy, characterized as taxes and subsidies on an economy's inputs and outputs, and deforestation. In some instances, predictions from that model disagree with some of the more popular claims in the case study literature on the deforestation effects of government policies.

resource policies are often adopted purposefully, and not for reasons related to natural resource use, but rather as a tool for sustaining or increasing their political power. The aim of these policies is to capture part of those resources directly, or to grant them to groups who will reciprocate with political support and contributions. They can also be used to finance development programs that are important to the government.

In Indonesia, for example, President Suharto, subsidized private commercial loggers through low stumpage fees, leading to over-harvesting and deforestation.[41] While on the surface the government appeared to be relinquishing an important source of revenues, private loggers where actually channeling much of those funds back to the President by financing a petrochemical industry and the state aircraft industry. Both of these were pet projects of the President, but were highly contested within government. The use of perverse logging subsidies was thus purposefully chosen by the President to get around institutional restrictions within his own government.

Another example is the subsidies given by the Brazilian government for private ranching and other development projects in the Amazon. The military government's intent with these subsidies in the 1970s was to promote the occupation of the Amazon so as to assert Brazilian sovereignty. These subsidies were maintained after the return to civilian government in 1985, despite the fact that practically none of the projects ever became productive. Each subsequent administration has maintained the program despite irrefutable evidence of corruption, environmental degradation and waste of public resources. At first sight this persistence of faulty government policy seems to be simply incompetence, malfeasance and inertia, however consideration of the working of Brazilian politics reveals other motivations. Alston and Mueller (2003) argue that the process of economic reform and policy-making in Brazil is based on a strong President who provides patronage (jobs in government and budgetary transfers) to members of Congress in exchange for support. The President, who has a stronger incentive than members of Congress to pursue sound economic policy for the nation as a whole, uses resource subsidies to accomplish the political exchanges necessary to enact those policies. The persistence of perverse subsidies for projects in the Amazon can be traced to the fact that this is an effective mechanism to realize transfers to local politicians, as they are given the power to determine which projects will be approved and therefore are the ones who ultimately receive those rents. As long as Brazil's political institutions remain unchanged, and there is a strong Presidency- and coalition-based government, all Presidents will have an incentive to use this established mechanism to garner support.

Although it is intuitive that governments will want to transfer resources to supporting groups, it is not obvious why this is so often done through subsidies

---

[41] This case is detailed in Ascher (1999), who examines 16 cases where resource policy in developing countries led to a squandering of natural resources.

related to natural resources when there are always more direct and less wasteful instruments for affecting these transfers. The two examples above illustrate the importance of considering a country's political and institutional context when seeking to understand perverse subsidies. In both cases it would be less costly to make direct transfers that would not have the collateral effect of degrading the environment. Becker (1983) argued that when governments decide on transfers between interest groups they take into consideration not only the support and opposition the transfers will generate but also the cost of these policies in terms of the inefficiencies they engender. Given that these ineffi-ciencies are large in the case of natural resource subsidies, one would not expect this to be a common method of making transfers. However, natural resources have several countervailing advantages for a government confronted with political transaction costs involved in redistributing income. The effi-ciency losses involved in natural resource-related subsidies tend to be incon-spicuous, as they are usually far from the electorate and difficult to apprehend and quantify, many times because the losses will only be incurred by future gen-erations or by the poor (Ascher, 1999). In addition, natural resource subsidies can often be portrayed as being good for the economy, growth and employ-ment as well as being patriotic. Thus the lack of transparency that pervades perverse subsidies may make it rational for governments to choose wasteful methods of transfers so as to economize on the political confrontation that would be involved in a direct and explicit transfer.

The discussion of perverse subsidies in this section can be put into the con-text of Figure 4.1. What has been argued here is that a country's institutional endowment plays an important role in the existence of perverse subsidies. Political institutions determine both the government's motivation to redistribute wealth among different groups as well as the restrictions it faces in doing so. The subsidies themselves are choices made by government (policy mechanisms) that are conditioned by those motivations and restrictions. The subsidies in turn affect how the natural resources are ultimately used. What this discussion highlights is that recommendations to correct the inefficient use of natural resources brought about by perverse subsidies must not concentrate exclu-sively on the particular subsidies themselves, such as suggesting an increase in stumpage fees. They should also focus on the institutional factors that motiv-ate governments to adopt those policies in the first place and to persist with them despite environmental losses.

Conclusions

The economic literature on natural resource use in developing countries has now explored a number of ways in which a country's political system interacts with its use of natural resource. At a fundamental level, a nation's system of governance forms the institutional context within which property rights to natural resources evolve. The ability and inclination of those in political power to facilitate the cooperation and coordination needed to overcome opportunistic behavior by individuals is a key factor in forming property rights systems that encourage incentives to use natural resources efficiently. Where the State's power resides with individuals, rather than in impersonal laws and institutions, resources will be used to benefit specific groups and costs will be borne by the rest of society. The stability or instability of a country's political system is a specific political attribute that has been shown to have significant effects on natural resource use. Where political systems are volatile, individual ownership claims to the future returns to resource conservation actions tend to be uncertain. This uncertainty dilutes the individual's incentive to undertake resource conservation actions and encourages depletion of resource stocks. However resource exploitation sometimes requires the individual to incur up-front costs, for example, for extraction capital or access to resource stocks. If uncertainty over claims to future returns is a general feature of an economy, affecting ordinary investment as well as resource conservation, it can deter resource exploitation by weakening incentives to make the up-front investments necessary to exploit resource stocks. On balance, then, the effect of generalized ownership risk on the depletion of resource stocks is an empirical question.

Research aimed at understanding why countries rich in natural resources tend to suffer from slow economic growth has provided preliminary evidence indicating that natural resource abundance may affect political institutions. Countries that are rich in concentrated point resources have been observed to suffer from political systems wherein power is similarly concentrated, among small groups of political elites who use the returns from resource wealth to accomplish their own ends. While progress on the link between political economy and resource use is evident, the research agenda is still evolving and there are clear needs for further empirical and theoretical work. Research on the 'natural resource curse' is in a particularly early stage and additional research may uncover flaws in the methods or alternative explanations for the empirical relationships now in evidence. Better measures of natural resource abundance clearly would be desirable. The most common measures used are flow measures of production net of domestic consumption. Stock measures of oil, gas, coal, forests, water, aggregated by value, would better capture what is generally meant by abundance. A related issue is that the 'non-renewability' of the resources involved, a feature that clearly should affect their impact on economic growth, typically has been ignored in this research. An additional concern is that the data examined to date vary primarily across countries, rather than within countries over time. This fact, combined with the strong persistence of governance institutions over time, makes it difficult to test statistically the direction of causation between resources and institutions.

One resource use/political economy link that arguably deserves further examination concerns the way a country's political system affects the mix of private vs. public good outputs its natural resources produce. As mentioned in the introduction, a forest can be used to provide habitat, watershed, and scenic amenities, all of which are a public good that benefit society at large. A forest can also provide living space for forest dwellers, who typically lack political power.[42] Alternatively, a forest can be managed to produce private goods that have market value that can be appropriated, such as timber or agricultural land. When the State's policy decisions are dominated by a small group of political insiders, it is likely that natural resources will be used primarily to provide salable private goods that can be captured by the politically powerful. The use of resources to provide either non-excludable public goods, or to benefit the politically weak, is likely to occur only when a country's system of governance is based on the rule of law and represents the broad interests of society in general. This general phenomenon, under-provision of public goods under non-democratic systems of government, has been observed in the provision of ordinary public goods (Deacon, 2003). It has not, however, been incorporated into the study of how natural resources are allocated.[43] The ways in which detailed attributes of governance structures affect natural resource use is not well-understood at present, and arguably deserves greater attention. Corruption, rule by elites, political instability and other political attributes are often lumped together and described collectively as 'bad' or unproductive governance institutions. There is no reason to believe, however, that these different aspects of political life will have similar effects on natural resource use.[44] At this juncture the task of 'unbundling' political institutions, and developing theoretical models and empirical tests of their separate effects on natural resource use, deserves to be high on the research agenda.

Finally, we draw a novel policy message from evidence that natural resource abundance can lead to breakdowns in governance: the method whereby the State establishes property rights to natural resources can have important, unrecognized, efficiency effects.[45] Simply giving resources away to private interests in order to enable their exploitation and enhance economic growth tends to encourage rent-seeking as a general form of political activity. Less directly, but of possibly greater importance, the precedent of giving away resources to private interests encourages the political elite to modify governance

[42] Ross (2001) points out that the rights of forest dwellers and swidden farmers were nullified in the political scramble to acquire timber rents during the hardwood timber boom in Southeast Asia.

[43] A related but more far-reaching observation is that property rights systems are themselves public goods. Accordingly, they may also be under-provided by autocratic, or non-representative political systems, or if they are provided, they may be made available primarily to those who hold political power.

[44] See Ferriera and Vincent (2003) for evidence that the effects can be diverse.

[45] We are indebted to Joseph Stiglitz for this point.

structures in ways that enhance their ability to bestow such gifts on political allies, that is, to adopt more corrupt political systems. Advising resource-rich developing countries simply to establish secure property rights to resource stocks could be counter-productive if the method of assignment is seen to be illegitimate, serving only the interests of those in power.

References

Abidin, Mahani Zainal (2001), 'Competitive industrialization with natural resource abundance: Malaysia,' in Auty, R. M. (ed.), Resource Abundance and Economic Development, Oxford: Oxford University Press.

Acemoglu, Daron (2002), 'Why not a Political Coase Theorem? Social Conflict, Commitment and Politics,' Working Paper 02–44, MIT.

——, Simon Johnson, and James A. Robinson (2001), 'The Colonial Origins of Comparative Development: An Empirical Investigation,' *American Economic Review*, 91, 5, 1369–1401.

Alston, L., Libecap, G. and Mueller B. (1999a), 'A model of rural conflict: Violence and land reform policy in Brazil,' *Environment and Development Economics*, 4: 135–60.

——, —— and —— (1999b), 'Titles, conflict and land use: The development of property rights and land reform on the Brazilian Amazon frontier,' Ann Arbor: The University of Michigan Press.

——, ——, and —— (2000), 'Property rights to land and land reform: Legal inconsistencies and the sources of violent conflict in the Brazilian Amazon,' *Journal of Environmental Economics and Management*, 39(2): 162–88.

Alston, Lee J. and Bernardo Mueller (2003), 'Democratization and Exploiting the Gains from Trade: Executive and Legislative Exchange in Brazil,' Working Paper Universidade de Brasilia.

Anderson, Terry L., and Peter J. Hill (1990), 'The Race for Property Rights,' *Journal of Law and Economics*, 22 (April).

Ascher, William (1999), *Why Governments Waste Natural Resources: Policy Failures in Developing Countries*, Johns Hopkins University Press.

Auty, R. M. and Gelb, A. H. (2001), Political economy of resource-abundant states. In Auty, R. M. (ed.) Resource Adundance and Economic Development, Oxford: Oxford University Press, 126–44.

——, and J. L. Evia (2001), 'A growth collapse with point resources:Bolivia,' in Auty, R. M. (ed.), *Resource Abundance and Economic Development*, Oxford: Oxford University Press.

Becker, Gary, S. (1983), 'A Theory of Competition among Pressure Groups for Political Influence,' *Quarterly Journal of Economics*, 98(3): 371–400.

Besley, Timothy (1995), 'Property Rights and Investment Incentives: Theory and Evidence from Ghana,' *Journal of Political Economy*, 103: 903–37.

Birdsall, Nancy, Thomas Pinckney, and Richard Sabot (2001), 'Natural Resources, Human Capital, and Growth,' in R. M. Auty (ed.), *Resource Abundance and Economic Development*, Oxford: Oxford University Press.

Bohn, H., and R. T. Deacon (2000), 'Ownership risk, investment, and the use of natural resources,' *American Economic Review*, vol. 90, No. 3, (June): 526–50.

Bulte, Erwin H., Richard Damania, and Robert T. Deacon (2003), 'Resource Abundance, Poverty and Development,' Working Paper, Department of Economics, University of California, Santa Barbara, CA.

—— and —— (2003), 'Resources for Sale: Corruption, Democracy and the Natural Resource Curse. Working Paper, School of Economics, University of Adelaide, Adelaide, Australia.

Coase, R. (1960) 'The Problem of Social Cost,' 3 *Journal of Law and Economics*, October: 1–44.

Collier, P., and Hoeffler (1998), 'On the Economic Causes of Civil War,' *Oxford Economic Papers* vol. 50: 563–73.

——, and —— (2002), 'On the Incidence of Civil War in Africa,' *Journal of Conflict Resolution*, vol. 46 No. 1: 13–28.

de Moor, André P. G. (1997), 'Perverse Incentives, Subsidies and Sustainable Development: Key Issues and Reform Strategies,' Hague, Institute for Research in Public Expenditure.

—— and P. Calamai (1997), 'Subsidizing Unsustainable Development: Undermining the Earth with Public Funds,' Ioo/the Earth Council.

Deacon, Robert T. (1994), 'Deforestation and the rule of law in a cross section of countries,' Land Economics, vol. 70, No. 4 (November): 414–30.

—— (1995), 'Assessing the Relationship between Government Policy and Deforestation,' *Journal of Environmental Economics and Management* 28: 1–18.

—— (1996), 'Deforestation, Investment, and Political Stability,' 1996, in Michelle R. Garfinkel and Stergios Skaperdis (eds), *The Economics of Conflict and Appropriation*, Cambridge University Press: 131–57.

—— and P. Murphy, (1997), 'The Structure of an Environmental Transaction: The Debt-for-Nature Swap,' *Land Economics* 73(1) (1997): 1–24.

—— (1999), 'Deforestation and ownership: Evidence from historical accounts and contemporary data,' *Land Economics*, 71(3) (August): 526–49.

—— (2003), 'Dictatorship, Democracy, and the Provision of Public Goods,' Working Paper, Department of Economics, UCSB.

Demsetz, Harold (1967), 'Towards a Theory of Property Rights,' *American Economic Review*, 57 (May, No. 2): 347–59.

Dixit, Avinash K. (1996), 'The Making of Economic Policy: a Transaction-Cost Politics Perspective.' Cambridge, Mass, MIT Press.

Feder, Gershon and David Feeny (1991), 'Land Tenure and Property Rights: Theory and Implications for Development Policy,' *World Bank Economic Review*, 3: 135–53.

Ferriera, Susana, and Jeffrey R. Vincent (2003), 'Corruption and Global Timber Supply,' *Mimeo*, Department of Economics, University of California, San Diego.

Freedom House (2003), Freedom in the World. Data available at: www.freedomhouse.org/ratings/index.htm.

Gordon, H. S. (1954), 'The Economic Theory of a Common Property Resource: The Fishery,' *Journal of Political Economy* 62: 124–42.

Gylfason, T. (2001), 'Natural resources, education, and economic development,' *European Economic Review* 45 847–59.

Gylfason, T., T. T. Heberson, and G. Zoega (1999), 'A Mixed Blessing: Natural Resources and Economic Growth,' *Macroeconomic Dynamics* 3: 204–25.

Hardin, G. (1968), 'The Tragedy of the Commons,' *Science* 162: 1243–8.

Isham, Jonathan, Michael Wookcock, Lant Pritchett, and Gwen Busby (2003), 'The Varieties of Resource Experience: How Natural Resource Export Structures Affect the Political Economy of Economic Growth,' Middlebury College Discussion Paper 03–08, Middlebury, Vt.

Johnson, R. N. (1999), 'Rents and Taxes in an ITQ Fishery,' *Individual Transferable Quotas in Theory and Practice*, R. Arnason and H. H. Gissurarson. Reykjavik, Iceland, The University of Iceland Press: 205–13.

Karl, Terry Lynn (1997), *The Paradox of Plenty: Oil Booms and Petro-States*, Berkeley, University of California Press.

Leite, C and J. Weidmann (1999), 'Does Mother Nature Corrupt? Natural Resources, Corruption and Economic Growth,' Working Paper of the International Monetary Fund, IMF Working Paper WP/99/85.

Levy, B. and Spiller, P. T. (1995), 'The Institutional Foundations of Regulatory Commitment: A Comparative Analysis of Telecommunications Regulation,' Cambridge University Press.

Libecap, Gary D. (1989), *Contracting for Property Rights*, New York: Cambridge University Press.

—— (2002), 'Contracting for Property Rights,' in Terry L. Anderson and Fred S. McChesney, *Property Rights: Cooperation, Conflict and Law*, Princeton University Press.

—— and Steve N. Wiggins (1985), 'The Influence of Private Contractual Failure on Regulation: The Case of Oil Field Unitization,' *Journal of Political Economy*, 93: 690–714.

López, Ramón (1997), 'Environmental Externalities in Traditional Agriculture and the Impact of Trade Liberalization: The Case of Ghana,' *Journal of Development Economics* 53: 17–39.

—— (1998), 'The Tragedy of the Commons in Côte d'Ivoire Agriculture: Empirical evidence and implications for evaluating trade policies,' *World Bank Economic Review*, 12(1): 105–31 (January).

Mehlum, H., K. Moene and R. Torvik (2002), *Institutions and the Resource Curse*. University of Oslo, Department of Economics, *Mimeo*.

Migot-Adholla, Shem, Peter Hazell, Benoit Blarel and Frank Place (1991), 'Indigenous Land Rights System in Sub-Saharan Africa: A Constraint on Productivity?' *World Bank Economic Review* 5: 155–75.

Myers, Norman (1998), 'Lifting the Veil on Perverse Subsidies,' *Nature*, 392: 327–8.

North, D. C. (1990a), 'Institutions, Institutional Change and Economic Performance,' New York: Cambridge University Press.

—— (1990b), 'A transaction cost theory of politics,' *Journal of Theoretical Politics* 2(4): 355–67.

Olson, Mancur (1965), *The Logic of Collective Action. Public Goods and the Theory of Groups.* Cambridge, Mass.: Harvard University Press.

Ostrom, Elinor (1990), *Governing the Commons: The Evolution of Institutions for Collective Action.* New York: Cambridge University Press.

Place, Frank and Peter Hazell (1993), 'Productivity Effects of Indigenous Land Tenure Systems in Sub-Saharan Africa,' *American Journal of Agricultural Economics* 75: 10–19.

Porter, Gareth (1998), 'Natural Resource Subsidies, Trade and Environment: The Cases of Forests and Fisheries,' APEC http://www.nautilus.org/papers/enviro/tepp/porterTEPP.html.

Ross, Michael L. (2001), *Timber Booms and Institutional Breakdown in Southeast Asia.* Cambridge: Cambridge University Press.

Sachs, J. D. and A. M. Warner (1997), 'Natural Resource Abundance and Economic Growth.' Working paper, Center for International Development and Harvard Institute for International Development (November).

—— (2001), 'The curse of natural resources,' *European Economic Review* 45: 827–38.

Sala-i-Martín, Xavier, and Arvind Subramanian (2003), 'Addressing the Natural Resource Curse: An Illustration from Nigeria,' Cambridge Mass.: National Bureau of Economic Research, Working Paper 9804.

Smith, Wynet (2002), 'The global problem of illegal logging,' *Tropical Forest Update*, vol. 12, No. 1: 3–6.

Southgate, Douglas, R. Sierra, and L. Brown (1991), 'The causes of tropical deforestation in Ecuador: A statistical analysis,' *World Development* 19(9): 1145–51.

Spiller, Pablo T. and Mariano Tommasi (2003), 'The Institutional Foundations of Public Policy: A Transactions Approach with Application to Argentina,' *Journal of Law Economics and Organization*.

Stevens, Paul (2003), 'Resource Impact: Curse or Blessing?—A Literature Survey,' *Journal of Energy Literature*, vol. IX (1) (June) 3–42.

Summers, Robert, Alan Heston, and Bettina Aten (2002), 'The Penn World Table Version 6.1.' Center for International Comparisons, University of Pennsylvania (CICUP) (October).

Tornell, Aaron, and Philip R. Lane (1999) 'The Voracity Effect' *American Economic Review*, vol. 89(1) (March) 22–46.

Torvick, R. (2002), 'Natural Resources Rent Seeking and Welfare,' *Journal of Development Economics*, 67: 455–70.

van Beers and C. J. M. van den Bergh (2001), 'Perseverance of Perverse Subsidies and their Impact on Trade and Environment,' *Ecological Economics* 36: 475–86.

Williamson, Oliver (1979), 'Transaction Costs Economics: The Governance of Contractual Relations,' *Journal of Law and Economics.* 22: 233–61 (October).

—— (1985), *The Economic Institutions of Capitalism.* New York: Free Press.

Woolcock, Michael, Lant Pritchett, and Jonathan Isham (2001), 'The Social Foundations of Poor Economic Growth in Resource-Rich Countries,' in R. M. Auty (ed.), *Resource Abundance and Economic Development.* Oxford: Oxford University Press: 76–94.

World Resources Institute (1999), *World Resources: A Guide to the Global Environment.* New York: Oxford University Press.

—— (2003), 'World Resources 2002–2004: Decisions for the Earth: Balance, Voice and Power.' World Resources Institute.

5

Structural Adjustment and Sustainable Development

Ramón López

Human capital and technology are important factors of production and are essential for economic growth. The preservation of natural capital (environment and natural resources) at adequate levels, on the other hand, is important to prevent long run growth from becoming unsustainable. The role of research and development (R&D), besides that of education and healthcare, in allowing for continuous increases in productivity and growth has been shown by a large number of empirical growth studies (Krueger and Lindahl, 2001; Barro and Lee, 1994). Perhaps even more importantly, human capital accumulation inherently increases welfare and, moreover, economies that base growth on an adequate balance of human and physical assets are more likely to sustain growth in a context of social equity.

Adequate investments in human knowledge and other forms of human capital ultimately allow for the persistence of high rates of return to private investments in physical assets and, hence, preserve the incentives to continue investing over time. The decreasing marginal returns to private investments can be prevented by expanding human assets that are complementary to physical assets. Economic growth over the long run is thus feasible. Countries that fail to promote sufficient human capital, and rely too heavily on physical capital accumulation for growth, tend to be affected by biased income distribution, more poverty, and greater environmental degradation (World Bank, 2000). All this conspires against the chances of sustaining economic growth itself.

Human and natural assets have certain intrinsic properties that are important to assure social equity. There is a key asymmetry between human and environmental assets on the one hand, and physical capital on the other: human assets, unlike physical assets, tend to disperse more easily across the population. This is in part due to the decreasing marginal productivity of education and health investment in one single individual as a consequence of the limited span of human life. By contrast, human capital may have increasing returns at the aggregate as it is dispersed across the population. Accumulation of human capital naturally leads to its dispersion across the population.[1] This dispersion effect is largely responsible for the positive income distribution effects of human capital accumulation. By contrast, physical capital can be almost endlessly concentrated in a few firms or individuals, especially large firms and wealthy individuals that face few restrictions in capital markets and are able to exploit the considerable economies of scale at the firm level that are often available.

The positive social equity effect is also valid for natural capital. The literature has shown that most of the costs of the degradation of natural capital are primarily paid by the poor, whose income is most dependent on such capital (Dasgupta, 1993). In general, while the wealthy can substitute environmental losses with more private goods, the poor can do this only to a limited extent (López, 2005). Thus, investing in the protection of natural capital is most beneficial to the poor and tends to promote more social equity. In addition, more human capital-driven growth is generally less environmentally demanding than growth based more on physical capital accumulation (World Bank, 2000). Thus, an adequate balance of investments in human assets and physical capital not only tends to be socially equitable but also environmentally friendly, with additional pro-poor secondary effects. Finally, human and environmental assets are likely to play a direct role in welfare in addition to their indirect welfare effect via economic growth. Improving human capital in a context of a clean environment is a goal by itself beyond its economic growth effect.

Another important feature of human and environmental assets is that they are much more heavily affected by market and institutional failures than physical assets. The vast positive externalities associated with investments in R&D are certainly well recognized in the literature. Human capital accumulation, apart from also generating positive externalities, is affected by other important market failures especially in developing countries. In particular, common failures in the capital markets and the inherent difficulties in collateralizing human capital means that, in the absence of government intervention, much of the population needs to rely on their own savings to finance even highly profitable investments in human capital. This means that most of the

---

[1] The dispersion effect of education is empirically documented by studies that show the normally rapid decline of inequality in education as the average level of education increases. Thomas, Wang and Fan (2000) examine the experience of 85 countries over the period 1960–95 showing that 81 of them have experienced a decline of the education Gini coefficient at a rapid pace. China, for example, experienced over the period 1975–95 a 40% decline in the education Gini while the distribution of physical capital became considerably more concentrated. In Korea the education Gini fell by more than 50% over the same period.

155

population in poor countries do not have the capacity to implement such investments without public support, even if they have high private rates of return. Similarly, the market failures affecting the environment and natural resources associated with inherent difficulties of defining property rights and developing other environmental institutions are also well understood (World Bank, 2003). Of course ill-defined property rights on natural resources are even more pervasive in poor than in rich countries.

All this gives human (including R&D) and environmental assets a public or semipublic good character. The rate and patterns of investment in human and environmental assets are largely dependent on the state. It is mainly through the support of the accumulation of these assets where public policies become most crucial. If the State does not directly or indirectly invest sufficiently in these assets, it is going to dramatically affect the rate as well as the quality of growth. What 'sufficiently' is is something that we consider below.

The significant degree by which market and institutional failures negatively impinge upon the investments in human and environmental assets, and the consequent direct or indirect reliance on the government for the provision of such assets, may lead one to hypothesize that there is a tendency to under invest in them.[2] This presumption is strengthened by certain political economy considerations: the State tends to be controlled by economically powerful groups that are likely to lobby governments more for private goods (e.g. subsidies) that benefit them directly than for the provision of public goods of which they share only a fraction of their benefits. Thus there is a risk that spending government financial, human and institutional resources in human and environmental public goods is 'crowded out' in favor of government spending in private goods.

In the first part of this chapter, we provide empirical evidence for developing countries showing that this crowding out phenomenon is indeed relevant for most of them. Also, we present evidence suggesting that under-investment in public goods is in many countries a major distortion that at least in part explains the triple curse affecting the vast majority of the developing countries over recent decades: slow growth, large social inequities and poverty, and environmental destruction.

In the second part, we examine the contribution of structural adjustment at the light of the above framework. Structural adjustment, as conceived and promoted by the World Bank and the IMF since the mid-1980s, encompasses several policy changes: (a) Macroeconomic stabilization (fiscal deficit reduction, tighter monetary policies), exchange rate adjustments, and opening the

---

[2] By contrast, accumulation of physical assets, although also affected by externalities and market failures, is more market-driven depending much more on the private sector than on governments.

economy to short-term and long-term capital flows. (b) Privatization of state enterprises and, more generally, a significant downsizing of the role of the state in the economy. (c) Increased role of the markets in resource allocation through the removal of price distortions, where trade liberalization and other domestic commodity and factor market price reforms play key roles.

Rather than analyzing how each of the reforms may affect the environment, we instead focus on the following questions

1. Is structural adjustment likely to correct the under investment in human capital and environmental capital discussed above?

2. Can we identify specific policies within structural adjustment that are likely to particularly affect such under investment?

We certainly do not try to be comprehensive in our evaluation of the reforms; we intend, instead, to provide certain insights of, in our judgment, important aspects that previous studies have tended to overlook. The idea is that since behind environmental destruction there is a common policy denominator that also causes social inequities, poverty and slow long-run economic growth, focusing on how structural adjustment affects such a common denominator is probably quite useful. In the analysis we will focus mostly on the macro component of the reforms while we shall consider the remaining reforms mostly on a tangential form.

Under-Investment in Human and Environmental Assets

Empirical studies show extraordinarily high rates of return to investments in human and environmental public goods. The literature reports such high returns with an amazing degree of consensus for many countries around the world. Investments in formal education (especially in secondary education), R&D (both in agriculture as well as in other sectors), agricultural extension, air and water pollution abatement, and investments in the management of certain natural resources are reported to have very high rates of return. The permanence of such high returns per se does not necessarily reflect under investment mainly given the existence of significant non-convexities. Non-convexities may imply that the marginal returns to these assets do not necessarily fall or decrease only very slowly with their accumulation. Thus, if this is the case, even a rapid accumulation of the assets would do little to reduce their rates of return. However, given such high returns, one would expect a great emphasis of governments in investing in such assets. Yet, as we shall see, this is not the case. In fact, in the overwhelming majority of the developing countries, investment in human and environmental assets has not even kept up with population growth. That is, per capita human and environmental wealth appears to be declining.

Returns to Education

Two recent surveys, one by Psacharopoulos (1994) and another one, an update of such survey by Psacharopoulos and Patrinos (2002), report findings of hundred of studies around the world that have used a great variety of methodologies and diverse types of data and time periods over the last three decades or so. Despite this variability in data, countries and methodology, there is a high degree of homogeneity of the results for most countries. In fact, the calculated rates of return found in the great majority of the countries analyzed are high. The average private rate of return for investment in primary education is about 20 percent, while the average social rate of return was about 30 percent.[3] Only in a handful of countries are the returns to primary and secondary education both below 15 percent. In addition, from the evidence for countries that have more than one study, it follows that in the vast majority of them the rates of return to education have not declined over time.

It is hard to imagine discount rates even near these rates as shown by the large number of projects that are implemented with much lower *ex-ante* rates of return in developing and developed countries alike. Despite these large rates of return, in most developing countries one encounters massive school drop-out rates, especially at the late primary and high school levels. Even in middle income countries such as Chile, Brazil and Mexico, high school drop-out rates reach 40 percent to 50 percent (World Bank, 2000). Even primary school drop-out rates were also high in the 1990s: Chile, 23 percent; Mexico, 28 percent; Indonesia, 23 percent; Philippines, 30 percent. Similarly, public expenditure per student as a percentage of GDP per capita was extremely low. According to the World Bank (2003) public expenditure per student in primary school was about 8 percent of per capita GDP in Argentina, 9 percent in Chile, 7 percent in Mexico and 2 percent in Venezuela. This compared to 23 percent in Korea or the United States.

The high rates of return of schooling and the also high rates of school desertion may be mutually consistent if liquidity constraints prevent parents from being able to afford to give children education, even if it is 'freely' provided by the State. This issue becomes more acute when children have an opportunity cost in the child labor market or in subsistence family operations. In fact, certain government programs that reduce the opportunity cost of attending school by children at working age (above 10 or 11 years-old) and that reduce commuting time to school by increasing public school density especially in rural areas, have been quite successful in increasing school attendance. Making

---

[3] Examples of most recent studies: Brazil, 35.6% for primary and 21% for higher education; Uganda, 66% for primary and 28.6% for secondary; Morocco, 50% for primary and 10% for secondary; Taiwan, 27.7% for primary and 17.7% for higher; India, 17.6% for primary and 18.2% for higher. These are social rates of return, with the exception of India. Private rates are even higher.

parents more aware of the value of education and increasing their participation in their children's education is another effective mechanism to promote more school enrollment. All this, however, requires a greater allocation of government resources to education, including not only public financial resources, but also human and institutional resources. In the context of a usually tight availability of such resources, this additional allocation of government resources to education obviously needs hard choices in terms of cutting other expenditures or increasing public revenues. Based on the available data on government expenditures per student as a proportion of per capita income, governments in developing countries are not opting for such choices. They seem to have other priorities.

R&D and Farm Extension

A survey by Alston et al. (2000) reviewed almost 300 studies that evaluated private and social rates of return to agriculture R&D and farm extension in about 95 countries. The methodologies and data used varied dramatically across the many studies. The simple mean (social) rate of return for agricultural research among all studies in developing countries was over 50 percent while the mean rate of return for public expenditures in agricultural extension was even higher—of the order of 80 percent. In most countries these rates rarely fall below 30 percent, still obviously a fantastic payoff. The authors, exploiting the fact that there are many countries for which there is more than one comparable study available, concluded that, as in the case of returns to education, there is no evidence to support the view that the rates of return have declined over time. Despite this great social profitability, studies often report that with few exceptions countries are not expanding agricultural R&D and many have indeed drastically cut them back.[4]

R&D in non-agricultural contexts, especially those that emphasize research on the adaptation of foreign technologies also seem to yield very large returns. Countries that are able more rapidly to incorporate new industrial technologies into the productive system have been shown to grow faster than countries that are slower to do so. Although, unlike agricultural research, much industrial R&D is often directly done by the private sector itself, the large positive externalities of such research are by now well documented. Yet well-structured and systematic public programs to support industrial R&D by the private sector are seldom encountered in developing countries.

---

[4] The case of Peru is illustrative. In the mid-1990s the government decided to privatize agricultural research. The government sold 21 agricultural experiment farms where most of the agricultural research in the country was performed. The result, by the year 2000 20 of the 21 experiment stations had been transformed into commercial farm operations. Only one remained as an experimental farm. Agricultural research in Peru practically became extinct.

Returns to Public Investment in Pollution Abatement and Natural Resource Management

World Bank (2000) examines a great number of studies that report the health benefits of reducing air and water pollution in developing countries. As with the case of the other public goods discussed above, the dollar value of pollution reduction vis-à-vis its cost is highly favorable even if one uses a relatively high time discount rate. Cost benefit analyses for controlling air pollution in many large cities in Asia and Latin America have consistently yielded extremely high rates of returns to such investments (World Bank, 2000; O'Ryan et al., 2001). The same is true for investments in decreasing urban water contamination, including sewage treatment plants and related investments. For example, according to various World Bank studies cited in World Bank (2000), in China a $40 billion investment in clean water within a 10-year period would yield a present value benefit of $80 to $100 billion. In Indonesia a $12 billion investment would give benefits of the order of $25 to $30 billion in terms of present value. Some studies for investment in air pollution control in various countries provide estimates even more favorable than the clean water investment. In China, for example, according to the World Bank, a $50 billion investment for selected cities could return benefits of the order of $200 billion in reduced illness and death.

Despite the high rates of return to investments in urban water and air pollution abatement, such investments do not seem to have received a high priority as shown by available indicators for cities in developing countries. For example, according to a sample of cities with per capita income below $2500 for the year 1998, less than 40 percent treated their waste water, and less than 60 percent of the population had water or sewage connections (World Bank, 2002).

High Returns but Low Investment in Human and Environmental Assets

The emerging literature on genuine savings is providing a clearer picture of the real changes in wealth over time. The World Bank has provided estimates of genuine investment for many countries by adding net investment in human and natural capital to estimates of net investments in physical capital (Hamilton, 2002). Apart from extending the analysis to more than 110 countries, an important modification over previous estimates of genuine savings done by the World Bank is that now measures of change of net wealth are expressed on a per capita basis. Per capita rather than total wealth change is an adequate and consistent measure of welfare change (Dasgupta and Maler, 2002). The measure of per capita genuine savings as defined by Hamilton in his country estimates equals net investment in manufactured or physical capital minus depletion of natural resources plus net investment in education, health and R&D.

The estimates for the year 1997 show that out of 90 low- and middle-income countries in Asia, Africa and Latin America, 71 (or about 80% of them) exhibit negative per capita changes in wealth. While these estimates cover a large sample of countries the fact that they refer only to one year raises the question of how representative this year might be. An analysis using the same definition of wealth as Hamilton, but which covered a 20-year period, was performed by Dasgupta (2005). Five Asian countries (Bangladesh, India, China, Nepal, and Pakistan) and Sub-Saharan countries over the period 1973–93 were considered. This analysis shows similar results to Hamilton's. Not only Sub-Sahara Africa has experienced decreased per capita net wealth, but four of the five Asian countries also show negative per capita wealth changes. The only exception is China, which, as in Hamilton's analysis, has managed to accumulate wealth in advance of its population growth.

The overwhelming majority of the countries considered by Hamilton and Dasgupta show positive per capita growth rates for physical capital, implying that the reason for the negative growth rates of total wealth is that human, knowledge, and environmental assets are growing at a rate below that of population. That is, as a minimum, 80 percent of the countries considered are experiencing reductions in their per capita human and environmental wealth. Since at least some countries may be compensating the declines of human and environmental assets with positive per capita growth of physical assets, the number of countries experiencing declines in human–environmental assets may be even larger.

By combining the data provided by Hamilton with national account data on gross (physical) capital formation, I calculated the implicit per capita changes in human and environmental assets for the 10 largest economies in Latin America as well as Uruguay and Costa Rica (Table 5.1).[5] In calculating rates of capital growth from gross capital formation data, I assumed a 5 percent depreciation rate and followed the common practice of assuming that the physical capital stock/GDP ratio is 3. Over the period 1990–2001 as well as in 1997, all of them except Colombia experienced positive rates of growth for physical capital per head. In nine out of twelve countries total net wealth per head declined. Only Chile, Costa Rica and Uruguay experienced increases of per capita total wealth. In all ten large countries the rate of growth of per capita human (including R&D), plus environmental assets was negative, with some countries such as Ecuador, Venezuela, Bolivia and Paraguay showing dramatic reductions in excess of 2 percent per annum. Even Chile, which was the only country among the ten large ones having positive per capita total wealth change, appears to reduce human–environmental assets per capita slightly. Only the two smaller economies, Costa Rica and Uruguay, experienced positive changes in per capita human and environmental wealth, with the former showing an impressive 1 percent gain and Uruguay a slight increase of 0.2 percent per annum.

[5] I subtracted estimates of per capita net physical capital formation from the change in total net wealth per capita to obtain estimates for the growth of per capita human and environmental assets.

Ramón López

Table 5.1 Per capita annual asset and GDP growth rates for selected countries in Latin America (1990–2001)

	Growth of Physical Capital per Capita	Growth of Human & Environmental Assets per Capita	Growth of Net Total Wealth per Capita	Per Capita GDP Growth
Mexico	2.0%	−0.6%	−0.1%	1.5%
Paraguay	1.6%	−1.8%	−1.0%	−0.6%
Chile	3.0%	−0.6%	0.2%	4.9%
Ecuador	3.5%	−2.6%	−1.3%	−0.4%
Costa Rica	1.4%	1.0%	1.1%	3.0%
Peru	1.8%	−0.8%	−0.2%	2.6%
Uruguay	0.0%	0.2%	0.1%	2.2%
Argentina	0.0%	−0.5%	−0.4%	2.4%
Colombia	−0.6%	−0.7%	−0.7%	0.8%
Bolivia	1.0%	−2.0%	−1.6%	1.4%
Brazil	2.0%	−0.6%	−0.1%	1.4%
Venezuela	1.5%	−4.0%	−1.5%	−0.6%
Comparators				
Korea	3.5%	1.2%	1.8%	4.7%
Ireland	2.7%	1.7%	2.0%	6.8%

To contrast these numbers with two successful countries, I also present in Table 5.1 the corresponding estimates for Korea and Ireland. As can be seen, in sharp contrast with the Latin American countries, both Korea and Ireland show positive per capita increases of both physical assets and human–environmental assets. Interestingly, these countries show human–environmental capital growing at a slower pace than physical assets. However, the ratios between the growth rates of human–environmental assets and those of physical capital are less than one-to-three in Korea, and less than one-to-two in Ireland. We could speculate that perhaps these ratios may be considered an approximation of what 'balanced' growth might be to assure sustained economic growth. Also interesting is the fact that Costa Rica is completely atypical to Latin America in this respect. In fact, it is closer to the case of Ireland.[6]

[6] Using the data in Table 5.1, I run a regression to explain average annual economic growth of per capita GDP (Gy) over a ten-year period as a function of annual average growth of physical capital per head (Gk) and growth of per capita human and environmental assets (Gh). The results are the following (t-statistics in brackets):

$$Gy = 0.024^{***} + 0.46^* \, Gk + 1.21^{***}Gh \qquad N = 12; \ Adj.R = 0.74; \ F = 10.47$$
$$(4.49) \qquad (2.09) \qquad (5.86)$$

Thus a 1 percentage point increase of the rate of growth of human–environmental capital seems to have a much more powerful effect on long-term economic growth than a similar acceleration in the rate of growth of physical capital. This would suggest that the slow or negative growth of human–natural capital that so many developing countries have experienced may have implied a considerable loss in terms of long-term growth. Of course this is a highly limited and simplistic exercise; it does suggest, nonetheless, that it might be worthwhile pursuing more thorough econometric work using the data emerging from the genuine savings literature.

We thus have an important paradox. Despite the apparently large rates of return to human and environmental assets, the emerging literature on genuine savings is showing that the overwhelming majority of the developing countries are reducing the per capita availability of such assets.

Under Investment, Government Financial Constraints, and Public Expenditure Priorities

The preceding analyses in this chapter show that most developing countries under-invest in public human and environmental goods. Of course the failure of the private sector to exploit these large rates of return is explained by the market and institutional failures affecting these assets that we already discussed. The issue is why governments have not either themselves invested or provided the conditions for the private sector to invest in them. The fact that, according to so many studies, these assets have extremely high rates of return and that public investment in them have, nevertheless, been so sluggish may reflect a significant policy failure associated with failing to exploit such investment opportunities. Could it be that governments in developing countries face such strenuous financial constraints (in part due, for example, to the fact that the countries are poor and have little access to international lending sources) and are thus forced to forgo such dramatic investment opportunities?

It turns out that governments in most LDCs spend public resources in dubious investments and unproductive and even perverse subsidies, mostly to the benefit of the rich. Van Beers and de Moor (2001) estimate that developing countries (non-OECD) spend more than 25 percent of their government revenues and more than 6 percent of their GDP in such subsidies (Table 5.2).[7] Ascher (1999) also describes massive subsidies and policy failures in eight developing countries that are not only financially onerous to the public sector but also promote unsustainable use of natural resources and worsen poverty. Just eight countries (Russia, China, India, Iran, Venezuela and Indonesia, South Africa, and Kazakhstan) annually spend more than $17 billion or 0.7 percent of their GDP (or almost 4 percent of their government revenues) just in across-the-board subsidies of energy prices (World Bank, 2003).

More evidence on the importance of public subsidies to corporations and to rich producers is emerging in some countries as improved data on public finances is becoming available. A study for Brazil, for example, shows that in 1998 the federal government alone spent more than 6 percent of GDP and almost 30 percent of the total federal government revenues in this type of subsidies, including credit subsidies to corporations, financial grants, tax holidays and others (Calmon, 2003). Additional subsidies are also provided in the form of

---

[7] To compare, OECD countries spend about 15% of government budgets and 3.4% of GDP in similar subsidies.

Table 5.2 The global costs of public subsidies per year, 1994–98 (US$ billion)

	OECD	Non-OECD	World
Natural Resource Sectors			
Agriculture	335	65	400
Water	15	45	60
Forestry	5	30	35
Fisheries	10	10	20
Mining	25	5	30
Subtotal	390	155	545
Energy and Industrial Sector			
Energy	80	160	240
Road Transport	200	25	225
Mining Industry	55	—	55
Subtotal	335	185	520
Total	725	340	1065
Total in % GDP	3.4	6.3	4.0

Source: Van Beers and de Moor (2001).

forgone government revenues related to publicly owned land, natural resources, and other patrimonial assets belonging to society given free of charge or for a nominal fee to powerful economic groups with government connections. In addition, it appears that state governments in Brazil also provide important subsidies.[8] It is quite clear that most of these subsidies are not particularly geared to positive technological or other desirable spillovers associated with firms' investments. A recent study has shown that much of the tax incentives provided to corporations in Brazil do not, in fact, promote investments (Estache and Gasper, 1995). They generate rents instead.

A recent study looks at the allocation of public expenditure in rural areas and its consequences for the rural development in 10 Latin American countries (López, 2004). The study shows that over the period 1985–2000, on average the countries spent about 55 percent of their total government budget for the rural sector in private goods or subsidies mainly to the wealthy (commodity programs, investment subsidies, credit subsidies, and others). Only about 40 percent of the rural government budget was spent on public goods including education, health, R&D, roads and the environment.

---

[8] There is no systematic data on subsidies provided by state governments in Brazil. The little evidence available, however, shows that they have not stayed much behind the federal government in their generosity towards big business. According to Alves (2001), three agreements made by Mercedes-Benz with the state of Minais Gerais, General Motors with Rio Grande do Sul, and Renault with the state of Parana had a total fiscal cost of about US$850 million in terms of soft loans, tax exemptions, financial grants, land grants and others. These investments yielded between 4,500 and 5,500 new jobs at a fiscal cost to Brazil of US$150,000 and US$190,000 per job. According to Alves, most subsidies were the result of states competing among each other to attract the investments, which would have been made in Brazil anyways even without subsidies. The subsidies were a payoff to a common strategy by large corporations to stimulate 'tax wars' among states.

That corporate subsidies, at least in the form in which they are usually allocated, do not generally promote investment or more R&D has been shown by several studies in various countries. Empirical studies using detailed firm level data by Bregman et al. (1999) for Israel, Fakin (1995) for Poland, Lee (1996) for Korea, Harris (1991) for Ireland and several others have shown that subsidies and corporate tax concessions are at best ineffective to promote investment and technological adoption and, in some instances, even counter-productive. Crowding out of private investment as a consequence of the subsidies may occur. Firms that do not receive the subsidy (in most cases the subsidy is received by a subset of the firms in an industry, not by all), may easily postpone profitable investments if they believe that with some more lobbying they may persuade the government to give them an investment subsidy in the future.

The above findings are econometrically corroborated in the López (2004) study for the rural sector in Latin America. He found that increasing the share of non-social subsidies in rural government expenditures greatly reduces agricultural per capita GDP, increases rural poverty and promotes a pattern of agricultural growth that is based more on agricultural land expansion than on intensification. In countries where there are forests remaining, this extensive pattern of growth means a greater expansion of the agricultural frontier causing more deforestation. That is, subsidies in rural areas are detrimental for long-run growth of agriculture, social equity and the environment; this can be called the 'triple curse' of non-social subsidies.

The previous discussion allows us to discard the explanation that governments in developing countries fail to invest more in high yielding public goods such as human capital, technological innovation and the environment because they are poor or because of tight financial constraints. Governments under-invest in assets that have such high rates of return while, at the same time, spend a large portion of their revenues in low yielding or even counter-productive subsidies. So this is a problem of wrong priorities rather than of poverty. It is therefore natural to search for governance failures as an explanation for this phenomenon.

Governance Failures

An important study by Deacon (2002) sheds light on the issue of how certain categories of governance affect the provision of public goods. Using a sample of 90 countries over the period 1972 to 1992 (with the following breakdown of the observations: 36% democracies, 54% dictatorships and 10% mixed), Deacon shows that the provision of several public goods including secondary school enrolment, access to safe water and sanitation, lead in gasoline and roads dramatically improves in democracy vis-à-vis dictatorship and other intermediate forms of governance. These results were obtained controlling for per capita income and population size.

165

The magnitude of the governance effect on the provision of public goods is impressive: Full democracy relative to dictatorship means an almost 30 percent increase in the portion of population having access to safe water and 40 percent increase in sanitation. Secondary school enrolment increases by about 10 percent in democracy vis-à-vis dictatorship but, even more importantly, the income elasticity of enrolment is twice as high in democracy relative to dictatorship (0.40 versus 0.20). Similar results hold for lead in gasoline, which decreases over time at a much faster rate under democracy than under dictatorship. Using more continuous indicators of democracy, Deacon shows a monotonic relationship towards greater supply of public goods, *ceteris paribus*, as the form of governance moves from dictatorship towards full democracy. Thus, these results suggest that under-investment in public goods is at least in part explained by governance failures associated with lack or insufficient degree of democratization.

Why can the style of governance be such a crucial factor to affect the supply of public goods? A plausible hypothesis is that the more democratic a regime is, the greater is the involvement of the civil society in controlling how governments use public resources and that a dictatorial regime is much more prone to be manipulated by small power groups in their favor than democracies. This study distinguishes among fairly broad categories of governance. One may further hypothesize, however, that even within full democracy one may find a variety of regimes more or less prone to yield to special interest groups. Government accountability and the ability of the civil society to monitor and supervise the allocation of public resources appears to be an important factor in determining the extent of the under-investment in public goods.

When we return to Table 5.1, where we report annual growth estimates of per capita human, technological and environmental assets for the Latin American countries, it can be seen that the four worst cases correspond to Venezuela, Ecuador, Paraguay, and Bolivia (all of which show rates of decrease of at least -2%). Although all countries in this sample may be considered to have democratic regimes, it is clear that these four are among the countries in the region where the degree of manipulation of the state by power groups is most acute. These are countries where adequate channels for the civil society are least perfected and, consequently, where the degree of accountability and transparency of the government has been most inadequate. Interestingly, three of these four countries (Paraguay, Ecuador, and Venezuela) were the only countries in this sample that experienced negative annual growth rates per head over the period 1990–2001 (Ecuador, -0.4%; Paraguay, -0.6%; Venezuela, -0.6%) despite that all four showed positive and comparatively large growth rates in physical capital per head (Ecuador, 3.5%; Paraguay, 1.6%, Venezuela, 1.5% and Bolivia, 1.0%). In addition, the study by López mentioned above finds that Ecuador, Paraguay and Venezuela were among the countries that spent the greatest share of their public rural budget in non-social subsidies over the period 1985–2000.

Structural Adjustment and Under Investment in Human and Environmental Assets

Structural adjustment has focused mostly on macroeconomic stability and on increasing economic efficiency, especially of price efficiency. Specific objectives were the reduction of the role of the state in the economy and replacing the state allocation of resources with a more market-oriented allocation. Liberalization and deregulation of the capital account, trade liberalization, and elimination of price controls and privatization of state enterprises were the main mechanisms used to achieve the above objectives. The pre-adjustment situation was typically characterized by widespread price controls, high trade protection and extreme inefficiency of state enterprises. In addition, several countries were affected by significant macroeconomic instability and endemically high inflation rates. In this context it is not surprising that at least some of the reforms may have contributed to reduce price inefficiency. Moreover, certain reforms (perhaps most prominently trade liberalization, the elimination of price controls and the eradication of hyperinflation and other forms of macroeconomic disequilibria) may have contributed to set up conditions that are at least necessary to enable more rapid economic growth over time. However, from the post-reform experience of many countries that implemented structural reforms (among the most faithful reformists were the Latin American countries that we have considered above with some detail), it follows that the structural changes were not indeed sufficient to promote sustained and sustainable economic growth over time.

In fact, we argue below that while some reforms did contribute to generate conditions for economic growth over the long run, a few of them have apparently been counterproductive. More importantly, we postulate that the conception of structural adjustment used an unnecessary narrow definition of efficiency, focusing mostly on price efficiency. The emphasis was on static efficiency gains that provide mostly once-and-for-all increases in income (although such gains can be distributed over a number of years appearing as faster growth). Much less emphasis was placed on dynamic efficiency gains that may generate the conditions for faster economic and sustainable economic growth over the long run and even less emphasis was placed on social equity.

The vital issue regarding the efficiency in the allocation of public resources was largely neglected. In particular, the allocation of government resources to public goods and to overcoming market imperfections vis-à-vis allocations to private goods were mostly ignored or simply took a back seat in the reform advice from international organizations. The low priority that governments give to investing in public goods is a major dynamic inefficiency that conspires against rapid productivity growth, private investment and, ultimately sustainable growth. Judged from this perspective, some of the reforms, in particular those that promoted sweeping cuts in fiscal deficits without giving much

167

attention on how to cut the deficit, and the abrupt liberalization of capital inflows and outflows, have apparently contributed to exacerbate the deep imbalances that have historically characterized the allocation of public resources in most developing countries. That is, they have contributed to consolidate rather than eradicate the 'triple curse' effects.

Cutbacks of the Fiscal Deficits

One of the pillars of structural adjustment was the rapid reduction of government deficits as part of the macroeconomic stabilization program. While the goal of reducing unsustainable deficits as a necessary component to achieve macroeconomic stability was obviously essential, the mechanisms used to achieve it had important consequences. The usual approach was to cut those public expenditures that were easiest to do. Almost inevitably the public programs that were cut, or drastically reduced, were those which had the weakest political constituencies. Cutting subsidies to the rich or closing important tax loopholes, or reducing tax evasion, was politically difficult as the groups that benefited out of all this were those able to lobby and bribe politicians most effectively. Reducing investments in public goods was easier than cutting both current expenditures and, especially subsidies to the well-off. Similarly, reducing social expenditures and safety nets favoring the poorest and least influential sectors was also easier. Cutting the existing rather mild environmental programs that helped manage and supervise the environmental impact of large energy, mining, irrigation and other projects was particularly easy and politically convenient. These resources are often controlled by powerful economic groups which are pleased to see such 'regulatory nuisances' out of their way.

The literature that evaluates structural adjustment illustrates the process by which fiscal accounts are brought into equilibrium. A study by ECLAC Economic Commission for Latin America (1989) evaluates structural adjustments taking place in the early and mid-1980s in several countries in Latin America. It concludes that adjustment policies failed to protect social expenditures as fiscal austerity was imposed to stabilize the economy. Moreover, the adjustment policies pursued in the 1980s led to cutbacks in current expenditure allotments for managing and supervising investment in sectors such as infrastructure, irrigation, mining and energy. The fiscal adjustment reduced the already limited funds available for environmental impact assessments and the supervision of projects to control their environmental impacts.

Other studies attributed the enormous increase in air pollution in many cities in Latin America to reductions in expenditures in cleaner public transportation while at the same time retaining heavy subsidies on the use of gasoline and other petroleum-derived fuels (Ten Kate, 1993). A study by the World Bank (1994) for African countries that have undertaken adjustment, found significant declines in government social expenditures, including expenditures in education and health, despite that in the pre-reform period such expenditures were already quite low by comparison to other countries of similar levels of development. Similarly, Stryker et al. (1989) found that in Sudan and other African countries, fiscal adjustment led to reduced funding for institutional reform such as land titling and other measures to improve property rights as well as to a reduction of public resources available for forest protection and reforestation.

A recent evaluation of fiscal adjustments by the IMF itself gives at least partial support to the above points (IMF, 2003). This report uses both a cross-country sample of 146 countries for the period 1985–2000 as well as detailed desk studies for 15 specific IMF-supported programs. The cross-country econometric analysis concludes that, after controlling for other factors, the presence of IMF-supported program does not reduce public spending in either health or education.[9] However, the detailed country specific study shows a different picture. It finds that only one-third of these programs even considered social programs that need protection, '. . . Performance criteria were rarely used to support social measures . . .' and '. . . spending categories most critical to vulnerable groups come under pressure and are likely to be pre-empted by other expenditures . . .' (p. 16). In addition the report recognizes that on the revenue side little attention was granted to income tax evasion reduction, curtailing discretionary exemptions (i.e. subsidies) and improved tax administration. Next we quote an extraordinary recognition that the fiscal adjustment in the way it is usually implemented may contribute to worsening the overall orientation of the public system to favor vested interests to the detriment of the provision of public goods:

This evaluation finds that efforts in this area (curtailing discretionary exemptions and reducing tax evasion) by the IMF have not been forceful enough, both in the context of programs and in surveillance, **particularly if they affect powerful vested interests**. Often tax administration reforms have focused on the technology side rather than on politically more difficult actions, such as legislation to empower agencies to pursue tax evasion forcefully and for the system to be less prone to political interference (IMF, 2003, p. 18 (highlighted by author).

The reduction of investments in public goods as well as social and environmental public expenditures that fiscal adjustment tend to impose upon most countries undergoing structural adjustment, appear to magnify the under-investment in human, technology, and environmental assets that often

[9] The cross-country data base includes a great variety of programs, some at least formally targeting poverty reduction: Enhanced Structural Adjustment Facility and the Poverty Reduction and Growth facility, Stan-By arrangements and Extended Fund Facility Arrangements. They include not only fiscal deficit reduction typical of structural adjustment programs, but also other types of programs. In fact, according to the report, in 40% of the cases, the fiscal deficit was allowed to widen. This heterogeneity of the cross-country data may explain why the econometric exercise failed to capture an effect for education and health public expenditures.

existed prior to the reforms. Macroeconomic stability is doubtless a necessary condition for achieving sustained economic growth and welfare improvements. However, reliance on cutting public goods as well as social and environmental public expenditures to reach fiscal equilibrium imposes an unnecessary cost to achieve such a goal. This added cost is not only a social cost. It means worsening a distortion that, as we have seen before, is one of the causes of long-term economic stagnation and environmental degradation in most developing countries. Instead of inducing governments to cut the fiscal deficit by eliminating unproductive subsidies and transfers to corporations and rich individuals and instead of increasing tax revenues by improving collection and charging rents and royalties for access to natural resources belonging to society at large, governments were prompted to reduce key expenditures in public goods with deleterious long-term welfare effects. That is, the fiscal adjustment missed the opportunity of integrating the conventional short run goals (fiscal equilibrium) typical of fiscal adjustment with desirable long-term objectives (reallocate public sector priorities from supplying private goods to providing more public goods).

To be sure, as macroeconomic stability is achieved, it is possible to reactivate social programs and, in fact, a few of the countries that underwent adjustment have done so in a limited way. But the failure to use better fiscal tools to cut public deficits has meant increased poverty, a more degraded environment and, in general, a worsening of the private good–public good supply distortion. Even more important, the approach used to some extent validated an even more unbalanced control of the state by economic elites that now obtain powerful external support to their objectives of reducing state environmental supervision and lowering the weight of social expenditures in the fiscal budget, which means a greater share of subsidies targeted to them. As 'normal' times return and governments gradually are able to increase public expenditures again, the new more favorable (to the economic elites) shares in the public budget are easy to preserve. Thus the short run dynamics of fiscal adjustment leaves at least one permanent effect: the system by which public resources are allocated becomes even more biased toward subsidies and other private goods directed to the wealthy. The control by small but economically powerful elites of the state is consolidated thanks to the implicit and, at times explicit, external support that such elites receive through the way in which fiscal adjustment was implemented. The new political economy conditions mean that under-investment in public human and environmental goods now becomes more difficult to address.

Liberalization of the Capital Account and Interest Rate Policies

Many countries were induced to eliminate most controls on capital movements. This naturally has had positive effects on foreign direct investment and technological transfer. But the insistence of international donors in reducing or eliminating even mild restrictions on financial capital movements causes further macroeconomic consequences that have been discussed at length by several analysts (Stiglitz, 2002). One of the consequences of this has been a large increase in economic instability, which now has a different origin from the old macroeconomic instability, but nonetheless is not less pernicious. As has been well documented by the experience of Latin American countries such as Argentina, Brazil, Mexico, and others over the last two decades, serious macroeconomic crises have taken place at least twice every decade. That is, the historical pattern of periodical balance of payments-cum-exchange rate crises has not been broken. It appears that the lack of control of speculative capital mobility has replaced fiscal imbalances and the consequent cumulative monetization of fiscal deficit as a major factor in promoting these crises.

Moreover, recent structural adjustment programs have encouraged developing countries to adhere to international (i.e. GATS and WTO), regional (through NAFTA and others) and bilateral agreements that protect the profitability of foreign investment. One of the chief mechanisms used in making these adjustments is arbitration tribunals. In general, they have powers to dictate resolutions that supercede those of domestic courts. Arbitration is often non-transparent, and in the main not subject to appeal, and it is often biased in favor of protecting foreign investors (Mann, 2004). In particular, Mann shows that recent arbitral rulings have been motivated by the principle that 'legitimate and reasonable expectations' of investors must be protected.

The consequence of this has been to limit the countries' right to set macro-economic, environmental and social policies that could result in foreign investors attaining profits below their 'legitimate and reasonable' expectations at the time of investing. The result is that many countries, which have introduced economy-wide policies that violate such expectations, are now being subjected to international demands for compensation in arbitral tribunals. According to Solanes (2004), Argentina is facing damage demands from foreign firms amounting to a total of $16 billion as a consequence of the exchange rate devaluation which caused reduced profits mainly to utilities and other foreign firms. The same author describes several less dramatic examples of other countries also facing large demands for compensation as a consequence of changes in general policies.

In part, as a consequence of the almost unlimited openness to speculative capital, countries tend to become dependent on them during 'good times' so that they are deeply affected by the inherent cyclical fluctuations of these financial speculative flows (Griffith-Jones, 1998). The implication of this is that every few years they need a new fiscal and monetary adjustment. Many of the issues concerning the impact of fiscal and monetary adjustment discussed earlier apply again. In addition to the fiscal adjustment discussed earlier, a usual response to the crises is a drastic tightening of monetary policy and consequent exorbitant increases in interest rates in a usually vain effort to make the country again attractive to financial capital. That is, any possible progress made in reducing the under-investment in public goods that could take place when the economy is normalized, is quickly lost when the new fiscal and monetary adjustment becomes necessary again. Thus, two issues arise: first, an environment of periodical macroeconomic imbalances is maintained; and second, such imbalances are corrected using inadequate means. The continuous short run macro adjustments effectively impede real progress to correct the massive distortion associated with under-investment in public goods.

Apart from macroeconomic instability, the unrestricted opening to speculative capital brings about a tendency among the countries to offer increasingly beneficial conditions to foreign capital. A 'race to the bottom' may in part be intensified by the increased openness of individual countries to foreign financial capital inflows. This phenomenon is empirically documented by an OECD study that looks at the experience of several countries (Oman, 2000). The increased dependence of developing countries upon short-term financial flows raises the market power of foreign capitalists willing to invest in developing countries vis-à-vis the individual countries. This, in turn, means more favorable conditions to foreign capitalists and smaller benefits for the host countries, including less tax revenues. Even Chile, which had successfully implemented a mild tax on speculative foreign capital for many years decided to eliminate it. After the latest crisis affecting foreign capital inflows in Latin America, Chile decided that it had to be more competitive in attracting foreign capital, which required that Chile become more in tune with the majority of the other countries in the region, which impose no restrictions whatsoever. The move was, however, costly to the government as the tax, despite being in place for several years was still, at the time that it was eliminated, yielding important tax revenues (Agosin, 1997). What are going to be the costs in terms of increased macroeconomic instability associated with greater susceptibility to international financial fluctuations remains to be seen.

Although capital openness leads to easier access to international funding sources for the government in the short run, the increased frequency of macroeconomic crises and the reduced benefits to host countries that such capital inflows bring about, means that over the long run fiscal revenues may, in fact, decrease. This, in turn, implies a restricted availability of fiscal resources for public goods and consequently may induce a worsening of the under-investment in public goods, including reduced investment in the management, and the protection of natural capital. In addition, the frequent crises and the policy responses unquestionably reduce the potential for economic growth. A dramatic example: the 35 percent increase in per capita income of Argentina during 1990–8, the 'miracle years', was more than completely wiped out in the ensuing crisis over the next 4 years. So Argentina has had two lost decades. The 1980s was lost as a consequence of massive economic inefficiency caused by price distortions and extreme macroeconomic instability associated with the prevailing pre-adjustment policies. The 1990s was lost too in large part because of misguided macro policies largely induced by adjustment policies.

In a context where the under-investment in public goods is worsened, it is not surprising that the likelihood of further environmental degradation, and slower, or even negative, improvements of human capital and knowledge is enhanced. The decline of per capita human and environmental wealth and the slow rates of economic growth in the Latin American countries may in part be a reflection of the increased dependence on financial capital inflows and of the misguided policy response to macroeconomic crises built in the very conception of structural adjustment.

The New Emphasis on Poverty and Social Equity of Structural Adjustment

Over the 1990s the World Bank and other international institutions began to focus on poverty reduction and even on measures to reduce inequality and increase education expenditures (World Bank, 2004). Unfortunately the prompting of governments to spend more on social programs and education has not been coupled with an advice to reduce non-social subsidies as well. In fact, governments with the tacit or explicit support of international organizations have continued to protect a great volume of financial, human, and institutional resources devoted to the supply of subsidies to the wealthy.

Thus the strategy of expanding education and social programs while keeping subsidies intact can be financed only if: (i) a reduction in the provision of other public goods is curtailed; (ii) taxes are increased; (iii) government borrowing and thus more debt; (iv) any combination of the above. Alternative (i) obviously implies that the overall issue of under-provision of public goods is not solved and, therefore, much of the 'triple curse' remains in place. Alternative (ii) may help solve the under-supply of public goods, but its efficiency, and even its net equity effect are questionable. The reason is that the tax system in most developing countries is very inefficient and socially regressive as a consequence of high levels of tax evasion and extreme reliance on indirect taxes (World Bank, 2004). Finally, alternative (iii) may attempt against the sustainability of growth and cause over the long run an even greater restriction on the supply of public goods. Increasing government borrowing (often in the international markets) may be adequate as a short-run strategy. However, relying too much on such an approach increases the debt service thus restricting the availability of government resources to finance public goods. Worse still, it could easily trigger a severe financial collapse once international conditions become tighter such as during the 1997 Asian crisis which affected most Third World countries. In the end, strategy (iii) may cause recession, unemployment and the collapse of the programs themselves.[10]

Conclusion

With the important exception of China and a handful of other countries, mainly in Asia, the vast majority of the developing countries have been affected, over the last two decades, by a rather dismal performance. Slow economic growth, deep social inequities and persistent poverty, and rapid environmental degradation have been features characterizing the experience of most countries. We have argued that behind the three evils of economic stagnation, social inequity and environmental degradation there is a massive policy failure that is rarely discussed in this context, namely that successive governments have failed to invest enough in public goods such as R&D, human capital and the management of the environment despite such investments having very high rates of return. Instead they continue to spend a significant part of their resources in subsidies and other private goods of dubious economic value. The available empirical evidence strongly suggests that in most developing countries there is serious under-investment in public goods. The availability of certain important public goods has not kept pace with population growth in the overwhelming majority of developing countries. This decline in publicly supplied wealth per head, which has not been offset by the generally positive growth rates of privately supplied assets (mostly physical capital), appears to explain, at least in part, the dismal performance of a large number of developing countries.

We suggest that evaluating structural adjustment within this framework is appropriate. One conclusion is that while structural adjustment has allowed the correction of certain distortions existing prior to the reforms, in general the adjustment has failed to set up the conditions for sustained and environmentally sustainable growth. The early reforms focused too narrowly in addressing one form of economic efficiency, price efficiency, and in reducing macroeconomic imbalances without adequately protecting both social spending and, more generally, the supply of vital public goods that were already under-provided before the reforms. The more recent structural reforms have promoted investments

[10] Argentina over the first half of the 1990s is a good example of the borrowing approach; Argentina increased during such period both social programs and non-social subsidies quite rapidly, using mostly foreign borrowing as a key mechanism to finance the ever increasing fiscal expenditures (with the enthusiastic approval and support of the IMF and the World Bank). Once the financial crisis arrived, Argentina eventually faced the drying-up of foreign funds, and with the need to service a huge foreign debt thus triggering devaluation and one of the deepest economic depressions ever seen in Latin America. The crisis brought a great worsening of poverty and social equity.

in poverty alleviation and human capital. However, by not simultaneously promoting enough cuts of government subsidies to support the financial, human and institutional costs that such programs entail, the effectiveness of such an approach has been limited, in fact, and in some cases, have contributed to unsustainable public debt and economic collapse.

Ultimately, far from addressing under-investment in public goods, structural adjustment contributed to a worsening of such under-investment. Moreover, it also contributed to create political economy conditions that make it even more difficult to change the traditional government approach. A strategy of reducing government expenditures in private goods, including unproductive subsidies, as a necessary step to expand investments in public goods, may be more difficult as a consequence of the political economy legacy of structural adjustment.

References

Agosin, M. (1997), 'Managing Capital Inflows in Chile'. *Estudios de Economía* 24, 2 (December): 297.

Alston, J., M. Marra, P. Pardey, and P. Wyatt (2000), 'Research Return Redux: A Meta-Analysis and the Returns of R&D', *Australian Journal of Agricultural Economics*, 44: 1364–85.

Alves, M. (2001), 'Guerra Fiscal e Financas Federativas no Brasil: O Caso do Sector Automotivo,' Instituto de Economia, Universidad de Campinas, Campinas, Brazil.

Ascher, W. (1999), *Why Governments Waste Natural Resources—Policy Failures in Developing Countries*. Baltimore: Johns Hopkins University Press.

Barro, R. and J. Lee (1994), 'Losers and Winners in Economic Growth,' in *Proceedings of the World Bank Annual Conference on Development Economics 1993*. World Bank, Washington, DC.

Bregman, A. Fuss, M., and Regev, H. (1999), 'Effects of Capital Subsidization on Productivity in Israeli Industry,' *Bank of Israel Economic Review*: 77–101.

Calmon, P. (2003), 'Notes on Subsidy Evaluation in Brazil.' Unpublished, World Bank, Washington, DC.

Dasgupta, P. (1993), *An Inquiry into Well-Being and Destitution*. Oxford: Clarendon Press.

—— (2005), 'Sustainable Economic development in the world of today's poor'. In R. Simpson, M. Toman, and R. Ayres (eds) Scarcity and Growth Revisited, RFF Press, Washington, DC.

—— and K-G Maler (2002), 'Decentralization Schemes, Cost–Benefit Analysis, and Net National Products as a Measure of Social Well-Being.' *Environment and Development Economics*, 5, pp. 69–93.

Deacon R. (2002), 'Dictatorship, Democracy, and the Provision of Public Goods.' Department of Economics, University of California, San Diego.

Economic Commission for Latin America, ECLAC (1989), 'Crisis, External Debt, Macroeconomic Policies and their Relation to the Environment in Latin America and the Caribbean.' Paper prepared for the meeting of Experts on Regional Cooperation in Environmental Matters in Latin America and the Caribbean, UNEP, Brasilia.

Estache, A., and Gaspar, V. (1995), 'Why tax Incentives do not Promote Investment in Brazil,' in A. Shah (ed.), *Fiscal Incentives for Investment and Innovation*. Baltimore: Oxford University Press.

Fakin, B. (1995). 'Investment Subsidies During Transition,' *Eastern European Economics*, Sept/Oct.

Griffith-Jones, S. (1998), 'How to Protect Developing Countries from Volatility of Capital Flows.' *Institute of Development Studies*.

Hamilton, K. (2002), 'Dictatorship, Democracy, and the Provision of Public Goods.' The World Bank, Environment Department, Washington, DC.

Harris, R. (1991). 'The Employment Creation Effects of Factor Subsidies: Some Estimates for Northern Ireland' *Journal of Regional Science* 31: 49–64.

IMF, Independent Evaluation Office (2003), 'Fiscal Adjustment in IMF-Supported Programs.' International Monetary Fund, Washington, DC.

Krueger, A., and Lindahl, H. (2001), 'Education for Growth: Why and for Whom?' *Journal of Economic Literature*, 39.

Lee, J. W. (1996), 'Government Intervention and Productivity Growth', *Journal of Economic Growth*, 1(3), 392–415.

López, R. (2004), 'Why governments should stop Non-Social Subsidies: Measuring their Consequences for Rural Latin America,' University of Maryland, College Park.

—— (2005), 'Intragenerational vs Intergenerational Equity: Views from the South'. in Simpson, D. and M. Toman (eds), *Scarcity and Growth*, Resources for the Future, Washington, DC.

Mann, H. (2004), 'International Economic Law: Water for Money's sake?' Paper presented at the I Seminario Latino-Americano de Políticas Públicas, Brasilia.

Oman, C. (2000), 'Policy Competition for Foreign Investment.' OECD Development Centre, Paris.

O'Ryan, R., S. Miller, and C. de Miguel (2003), 'A CGE framework to evaluate policy options for reducing air pollution emissions in Chile', Environment and Development Economics, vol. 8, pp. 285–309.

Panayotou, T. and C. Sussangkarn (1991), 'The Debt Crisis, Structural Adjustment and the Environment: The Case of Thailand.' Paper prepared for the World Wildlife Fund Project on the Impact of Macroeconomic Adjustment on the Environment, October.

Psacharopoulos, G. (1994), 'Returns to Investment in Education: A Global Update,' *World Development*, 22(9), 1325–43.

—— and H Patrinos (2002), 'Returns to Investment in Education: A Further Update.' World Bank Policy Research Working Paper #2881, Washington DC.

Solanes, M. (2004), 'Contratos y acuerdos internacionales de inversión'. Economic Commission for Latin America, Santiago, Chile.

Stiglitz, J. (2002), 'Development Policies in a World of Globalization.' Paper presented at the Seminar 'New International Trends for Economic Development,' BNDES, Rio de Janeiro, Brazil.

Stryker, J., et al. (1989), 'Linkages Between Policy Reform and Natural Resource Management in Sub-Saharan Africa.' Unpublished, Fletcher School, Tuft University, June.

Ten Kate, A. (1993), 'Industrial Development and the Environment in Mexico.' Policy Research Working Paper #1125, World Bank, Washington DC.

Thomas, V., Y. Wang, and X. Fan (2000), 'Measuring Education Inequality: Gini Coefficients of Education.' Working Paper, World Bank Institute, Washington, DC.

Van Beers, C., and de Moor, A. (2001), *Public Subsidies and Policies Failures*. Northampton, MA: Edward Elgar.

World Bank (1994). Adjustment in Africa: Reforms, Results and the Road ahead. Oxford Econ. Press, New York.

—— (2000), *The Quality of Growth*. Oxford University Press, Washington, DC.

—— (2003), *World Development Report 2003. Sustainable Development in a Dynamic World*. World Bank and Oxford University Press, New York, NY.

—— (2004). Inequality in Latin America: Breaking with History? The World Bank, Washington, DC.

6

Trade and the Environment in Developing Economies

Brian R. Copeland and Sumeet Gulati

Introduction

The linkage between trade and the environment has become an important policy issue in the last few years. Some environmentalists claim that international trade increases environmental degradation across the world, and in developing countries in particular. Business lobbyists in developed countries are concerned that strict environmental regulations reduce their competitiveness and shift pollution intensive industries to developing countries. Policymakers in developing countries fear that links between trade and environmental policy will be used as another avenue for rich countries to erect barriers to imports.

This paper explores the interaction between international trade, capital mobility, and environmental quality in developing countries. The central concern is how increased international trade and investment affect environmental quality. Changes in the scale of economic activity, the environmental impact of economic activity, the institutions which manage environmental quality, and the composition of economic activity all affect environmental outcomes. Much of our focus will be on the latter two channels. Although increases in growth (the scale effect) can cause environmental problems, economic growth is a key objective for developing countries. To distinguish the effects of trade from other sources of growth, we need to determine whether trade moves the growth path in a direction that systematically favors or harms various aspects of environmental quality—that is, does the composition effect of trade harm the environment? And because the environmental effects of either growth or changes in the composition of output depend on the policy regime, we address the interaction between trade and environmental policy in some detail.

The 'pollution haven hypothesis' has dominated much of the discussion of the composition effects of trade between rich and poor countries on the environment. The strong form of the pollution haven hypothesis is that trade liberalization shifts environmentally intensive industries to countries with relatively weak environmental policy. We argue that there is little empirical evidence to support the pollution haven hypothesis: differences in environmental policy are not the principal determinants of the direction of trade. Although this is still an active area of research, the current evidence suggests that other factors, such as capital abundance, technology differences, infrastructure, or distance to major markets seem to be much more important than environmental policy in determining trade patterns. However, even if the pollution haven hypothesis fails to hold, trade liberalization will nevertheless shift the development path towards environmentally-intensive activity in some developing countries. Countries may have a comparative advantage in environmentally intensive goods for reasons that have nothing to do with environmental policy.

The second major issue is the distinction between environmental problems associated with industrial pollution emissions, and those that affect stocks of natural capital, such as fisheries, soil, forests, and other renewable resources. Environmental problems stemming from industrial pollution are often characterized as trade-offs between income and pollution: the issue is whether the benefits of increased real income from trade are more than offset by the costs of increased pollution. Moreover, because environmental quality is a normal good, there is some evidence that increased income will stimulate the development of institutions to implement and enforce more stringent environmental policy. Increased income can therefore act as a check on environmental degradation in the future. This has been the subject of much debate in the Environmental Kuznets Curve literature, which examines the relation between per capita income and environmental quality.

On the other hand, environmental problems involving natural capital are fundamentally different. If economic activity is based on natural capital, and if trade leads to a deterioration of stocks of natural capital, then it is possible that trade could lead to a decline in both environmental quality and in the long run real income. If this is the case, there is a possibility that trade could contribute to a downward ecological spiral in which increased pressure on the environment reduces resource stocks, which reduces income, which weakens institutions protecting resource stocks, which leads to further environmental degradation and income loss. This is the basis of theoretical arguments in Daly (1993), Chichilnisky (1994), Brander and Taylor (1997a), and Copeland and Taylor (1997, 1999). There is relatively little cross-country empirical evidence on the interaction between trade and natural capital; however there are a number of suggestive case studies which we discuss.

The third major issue we discuss is the effects on developing countries of linkage between trade policies and environmental concerns. There are a variety of issues here, but many center around market access issues. There has been much attention given to the possibility that a 'race to the bottom' in environmental standards might occur if countries weaken their environmental policy in response to freer trade to shelter their industry from international competition. This has led to proposals to either harmonize environmental policy, impose 'eco-duties' to 'level the playing field' by ensuring that importers bear the same types of environmental compliance costs as domestic producers, or to make market access contingent on meeting certain environmental standards. We review the empirical evidence first on whether or not environmental policy affects trade flows, and second, on whether or not freer trade affects governments' willingness to implement and enforce tough environmental standards.

Other motives for linkage arise from an attempt by one country to affect the environmental quality in another country, particularly when the particular environmental problem has some global implications. Several recent trade disputes (such as the tuna/porpoise and shrimp/turtle cases) involve a rich country (the U.S.) attempting to make imports contingent on the environmental practices used in harvesting renewable resources. We discuss the implications of current trade rules on these issues for developing countries.

The paper is organized as follows. In Section 1, we discuss the role of the environmental policy process and institutions and how they interact with the trade regime. In Section 2, we review the empirical evidence on the effects of environmental policy on trade patterns; and the evidence on the effect of trade on environmental quality. Section 3 considers policy issues, and the final section concludes.

The Policy Regime and Institutions

Trade affects the environment through a variety of channels: it changes the overall level of economic activity (a *scale effect*); it changes the type of economic activity (a *composition effect*), and it can lead to change in the environmental intensity of production (a *technique effect*).[1] Each of these channels is affected by the interaction between market forces and a country's policy regime. This section discusses the role of the policy regime.

A country's environmental policy regime is critical in determining how increased international trade or investment affects the environment. If, for

---

[1] See Grossman and Krueger (1993) and Copeland and Taylor (1994) for further discussion of this decomposition.

example, a country adjusts policy to enforce an ambient air quality standard, then increased economic activity or a shift to industrial manufacturing need not have any effect on air quality. The regulator could adjust emission standards to accommodate the changes in economic activity and aggregate pollution need not change. Similarly if a regulator enforces binding harvest quotas in a fishery, an export-driven increase in the price of fish need not lead to deterioration of the stocks—it would simply increase resource rents. Conversely, if there is no environmental regulation in place, a shift to manufacturing is likely to increase pollution, and increased opportunities to export fish are likely to lead to stock depletion. The regulatory regime and institutions that affect resource management are critical because they can help explain the heterogeneity across countries in their response to the pressures and incentives arising from increased access to international markets.

Income Effects

Environmental regulations differ across countries, and especially between rich and poor countries. The most popular explanation of this difference is based on income effects in the demand for environmental quality. If environmental quality is a normal good, and if environmental regulation is responsive to consumer demand, then the stringency of environmental regulation increases with improvements in income. This hypothesis forms the theoretical basis of most explanations for the environmental Kuznets curve (EKC). The EKC postulates that pollution rises in the early stages of development and falls as countries get richer.[2]

The existence and magnitude of an income effect has been the subject of extensive empirical work. Macro-level studies typically regress cross-country environmental indicators on various specifications of income.[3] This approach does not test directly for the income effect discussed above, but rather looks for a reduced-form relation between pollution and per capita income. In these studies the effects of per capita income on the demand for environmental quality cannot be disentangled from the effects of scale and composition on environmental outcomes. Some of these studies find an EKC for specific environmental indicators, while others do not. Recently Harbaugh et al. (2002) and Stern and Common (2001) have shown that the relation between pollution and income is sensitive to the sample of countries or time period chosen. Copeland and Taylor (2004a) argue that this lack of robustness points to a misspecification of the macro-level EKC. Using a simple theoretical model they demonstrate how different sources of growth will lead to different paths in

---

[2] See López (1994) for an early formal model incorporating the role of the income effect, and Copeland and Taylor (2003) for a recent treatment.
[3] See Copeland and Taylor (2004a) and Stern (1998) for surveys.

environmental quality. They argue that there is no reason to expect a simple stable relationship between pollution and income across countries. They suggest a more structural approach to calculating the effect of growth on the environment, one that allows for differences in the source of pollution across different countries. Antweiler et al. (2001) adopt such an approach, and estimate the effects of increases in per capita income on sulphur dioxide concentrations in a sample of cities in both rich and poor countries, while holding the trade regime, scale of economic activity, capital abundance, and other factors constant. A key aspect of their approach is that the effects of per capita income can be isolated from the effects of scale of economic activity on environmental outcomes. They find strong evidence of an income effect: all else equal (in particular, when controlling for scale), higher per capita income is associated with lower SO_2 concentrations.

A potentially more promising method to test the effect of increasing income on demand for environmental quality is to use micro-level data. Chaudhary and Pfaff (1998) use a household level dataset on income and fuel use from Pakistan to estimate the relationship between household income and indoor air quality. Using plausible assumptions regarding emissions implied by fuel use, the authors estimate the implied relationship between indoor air quality and household income. They find an inverted-U-shaped relationship between household income and air quality and attribute this relationship to the income effect discussed earlier.

There is also a large literature which uses survey methods to estimate the willingness to pay for various types of improvements in environmental quality.[4] Kristom and Riera (1996) and Hökby and Söderqvist (2003) review several studies from Europe and find that the income elasticity of willingness to pay for improvements in environmental quality is in almost all cases positive, but on average is less than one. These results suggest that environmental quality is a normal good, but not a luxury good.

Other approaches try to estimate how changes in income affect responses to risks. Several studies estimate the income elasticity of the value of a statistical life (VSL). The VSL measures the marginal rate of substitution between income and the risk of death in a given period of time. Hammitt et al. (2000) note that many studies either compare estimates from separate studies across countries, or else use survey methods. The estimates from these studies tend to be positive but less than one. Hammitt et al. (2000) use data on work-place fatality risk and wages from Taiwan over the period 1982–97 to estimate how the VSL responded to changes in income during a period of rapid economic growth. They obtain estimates of the income elasticity of the VSL which range between 2 and 3, which are much larger than previous studies have indicated.

A more direct test for our purposes would be to look at the relation between the stringency of environmental policy and income. By analyzing the country

---

[4] These are often known as contingent valuation studies.

reports prepared for the United Nations Conference on Environment and Development, Dasgupta et al. (1995) develop comparable cross-country indicators for environmental policy across 31 countries. They find a strong positive relationship between stringency of environmental policy and per capita income across countries. Magnani (2000) shows that second order moments (capturing income inequality) are important in determining the impact of income on environmental policy. She shows that improvements in income across her sample of OECD countries leads to an increase in environmental spending. However, increases in income inequality can dampen the increase in environmental spending. Pearce and Palmer (2001) review data on public expenditures on environmental protection in OECD countries and find an income elasticity of 1.2, suggesting that public expenditure on the environment as a fraction of income rises with national income.

Overall, the empirical literature provides some support for the existence of an income effect on environmental policy. This has two important implications for the effects of trade on the environment. First, we should expect the stringency of environmental standards to vary across countries, and be more stringent in rich countries than in poor countries. Second, if trade helps facilitate increases in real incomes, then that can lead to an increase in the demand for environmental quality and increased support for more stringent environmental policy. The short- and long-run effects of trade on the environment may therefore be different if environmental policy responds only after the increases in income are secured.

Property Rights

While environmental regulations are a key factor affecting pollution emissions, the effects of trade on natural resources issues is often dependent on the property rights regime. A significant proportion of income derives from exploitation of natural resources in several regions of the developing world (Dasgupta, 1993). Examples of such resources include forest tracts, fishing grounds, grazing areas, and irrigation waters. However, despite (and sometimes because of) their importance, natural resources in developing countries are often exploited under poorly defined property rights.[5] Some argue that property rights are more insecure in developing countries than in developed countries (see World Bank, 1992; ch 3). Reasons cited include weak judicial and political systems, inadequate income to devote to costly enforcement of property rights, and a breakdown of traditional common property controls (like tribal or village level

---

[5] Brown (2000) argues that poorly defined property rights are a consequence of the characteristics of most renewable natural resources. Most renewable resources do not respect political boundaries, making private ownership difficult. Renewable resources often have non-use values making it difficult to set up efficient markets. Ecological complexity and dramatic time lags between action and consequences often obscures their true benefits and costs.

institutions) caused either by the stress of population pressure or economic development.

As Gordon (1954) and others have pointed out, imperfect property rights can lead to excessive pressure on renewable resource stocks. Each resource harvester or user imposes a negative externality on other users. For example, in a fishery, an individual who harvests a fish reduces future fish stocks, which drives up harvesting cost for other harvesters. Moreover, individuals lack the appropriate incentives to invest in the resource. An individual who chooses not to harvest a fish today so that it can grow and reproduce will not reap the full benefits of the investment because some other fisher may harvest the fish instead. If these externalities are not internalized, excessive resource depletion can result.

Losses from poorly defined property rights are significant. López (1998c) estimates the loss from non-cooperative behavior on common property lands at the village level in Côte d'Ivoire. He finds that farmers do not internalize the external costs of biomass use in their land allocation decisions. Estimates of the loss in income from such behavior put their value as high as 14 percent of village income. Similar estimates for the loss in income from imperfect controls over common property resources in the developing world are provided by López (1997). Also using data at the village level in Côte d'Ivoire, Ahuja (1998) provides estimates of internalization of the costs of land (and associated biomass) use as an agricultural input. Using a scale where 0 represents the case where there is no internalization, and 1 represents complete internalization, the author finds estimates ranging from 0.07 to 0.27 in the three regions analyzed. The author concludes that there is substantial inefficiency in land use due to imperfect property rights.

The existence of poorly defined property rights can have important implications for how trade affects the environment.[6] McRae (1978), Chichilinsky (1994), and Brander and Taylor (1997) develop theoretical models to investigate the interaction of trade and renewable resources under open access.[7] They find that resource exporting counties may lose from freer trade. When the country opens up to trade at a resource price higher than the domestic price, the short term returns to harvesting the resource increase. This attracts entry. In the short term there may be real income gains, but in the long run there is stock depletion. In short, trade exacerbates the negative production externality. Brander and Taylor (1997a) provide a simple example in which the resource

[6] See Anríquez (2002) for a survey.
[7] Also see Karp et al. (2001) for a model with a richer set of possible outcomes. They model the non-cooperative behavior between an exogenously fixed number of resource extractors. If there is only one extractor, there are complete (static) property rights. As the number of extractors increases, the property rights regime tends to open access. Modeling trade between countries with different exogenously given numbers of extractors, Karp, et al. (2001) argue that both, an increase, or a decline in steady state utility is possible. They show that the gain or decline in utility is conditional on the resilience of the environmental stock present in the trading country.

exporting country must suffer a real income loss from access to international trade. Moreover, Chichilnisky notes that the country's comparative advantage in resource extraction may only be apparent—a side effect of excessive entry in the industry due to the lack of well-defined property rights.

An important distinction between imperfect property rights in renewable resources and imperfect pollution regulation is in the income effect. In the case of industrial pollution, an exporter of pollution-intensive goods may face an increase in pollution due to poor environmental regulations. However, if the expansion of the manufacturing sector leads to an increase in real income, then the increased income can lead to an increased demand for environmental quality which can lead to improved environmental regulations. The income effect may dampen the adverse environmental consequences of the expansion of manufacturing.

In the case of renewable resources, the reverse may occur. In the Brander/ Taylor and Chichilnisky models, a resource exporter suffers a fall in long run real income if trade leads to a depletion of natural capital. Trade both reduces income and environmental quality. This can also be a consequence if industrial pollution damages natural capital. Copeland and Taylor (1997) explicitly model this process in a model of cross-sectoral pollution. In their model, exports of manufactures leads to increased pollution, which damages natural capital. If the decline in natural capital is sufficiently severe, the fall in income leads to weaker pollution policy (via the income effect), which exacerbates the pollution problem and leads to further destruction of natural capital and further income loss. The country gets caught in low-income, low-environmental quality trap.[8]

If property rights (or their enforcement) are endogenous,[9] then changes in the trade regime may induce changes in the property rights regime. Hotte et al. (2000) analyze the interaction between international trade and the stock of natural resources in an economy where there are private costs for enforcing property rights. They find plausible conditions under which higher prices gained by international trade encourage greater enforcement of property rights and higher stocks of the natural resource.[10] Margolis and Shogren (2002)

[8] Similar problems could occur if industrial pollution causes human health problems— increased pollution could lower labor productivity, which could then both increase environmental damage and lower real income.

[9] This has previously been emphasized in economic literature (see Anderson and Hill, 1975; Field, 1989; and Hotte, 1997). See Cohen and Weitzman (1975), De Meza and Gould (1994), and Long (1994) for models where property rights are endogenously determined.

[10] However the authors also show that this increase in enforcement need not always result in higher welfare for the economy. Agents in the model increase private enforcement if higher profits result from such an action. However, increased enforcement involves an increase in unproductive enforcement expenditures. The authors show that due to the unproductive enforcement expenses, an increase in profits can be smaller than the reduction in deadweight loss from open access.

consider a model of endogenous enclosure of resource stocks where agents can build a fence for a fixed cost. They show that international trade can induce increased enclosure by raising the value of the resource. However, they find that real income may still fall because the enclosure costs can offset other gains.[11]

Institutions and Informal Mechanisms

Social institutions play an important role in enforcing property rights and preserving natural resources. Formal institutions include legal and legislative institutions. These institutions determine the responsiveness of public policy to concerns about the environment. They also determine the enforcement of public policy.

Ferreira (2004) is one of the few empirical studies that analyze the interaction of openness and government institutions in determining resource depletion. Using data for a cross-section of countries she studies the impact of openness on deforestation in 1999–2000. She finds that once income and resource abundance are taken into account, openness by itself does not have a statistically significant impact on deforestation. Openness has an impact on deforestation only through its interaction with institutional variables. In particular she finds that variables reflecting bureaucratic quality and government fulfillment of contracts influence the impact of openness on deforestation.

Besides government institutions, self-organized and voluntary institutions (sometimes formal, and sometimes informal) also determine the preservation of the environment. Ostrom (2000) argues that self-organized resource governance regimes exist across the world. She also argues that within these institutions, participants invest in monitoring and sanctioning to prevent free riding by other participants (also illustrated in Ostrom, 1990). Baland and Platteau (1996) highlight the role of rural communities in the preservation of natural resources. Other examples of the role of rural communities in resource management are provided in Bardhan (2000) and McCarthy et al. (2001).[12]

Using village level data on land use, Ahuja (1998) analyzes community land management in Côte d'Ivoire. In the area analyzed, land ownership rests with the village, and the village chief acts as a land manager. Ahuja provides estimates of inefficiency in land use and finds significant differences across the three regions analyzed. In a subsequent analysis explaining these differences, he finds that all else being equal, larger villages tend to be less efficient in

[11] While raising the value of the natural resource might encourage enclosure, or other investment which leads to preservation, Swanson (1994) shows even under socially optimal control, a reduction in the value of a natural resource can lead it to being harvested to extinction. The author shows that a reduction in value of natural capital (resulting from an exogenous reduction in the price of the resource intensive good) reduces the economy's incentive to invest costly resources required for its survival, and can lead to eventual extinction.

[12] McCarthy et al. (2001) discuss the community based cooperative management of common property land in Mexico's ejidos (communally owned farm and grazing lands).

managing common land and its associated biomass. Further, while ethnic homogeneity facilitates management, income heterogeneity in the village does not seem to have any impact.

Another example of informal policy control is citizen activism. One of the most interesting applications is Pargal and Mani (2000). Using data on the location of new industrial plants in India, Pargal and Mani (2000) find that activism measured through the propensity to complain, vote, or join interest groups, translates into pressure for cleaner production on the plant. Due to this pressure, firms take into account the potential for collective action while deciding on a choice of location. Based on their results the authors argue that the potential for collective action is an effective informal regulation on pollution.[13]

Using data from China, Dasgupta, and Wheeler (1996) investigate citizen complaints as informal regulation. They provide several examples where regulatory authorities rely on citizen complaints to investigate environmental transgressions. They find that while citizen complaints are correlated with benefits and to the exposure of highly visible pollutants, they are not affected by harmful pollutants which are less visible. They also find that basic education has a strong, independent effect on propensity to complain. This implies that a reliance on complaints alone results in an inappropriately low allocation of inspection resources to less-educated and relatively 'silent' regions. Dasgupta and Wheeler argue that imperfect information is a key problem in environmental regulation, and that regulators who rely on citizen complaints should consider large-scale environmental education programs which pay special attention to communities with lower levels of education. Besley and Burgess (2002) also demonstrate how greater information, and electoral accountability increase government responsiveness. Using data from India the authors show that higher newspaper circulation and electoral accountability in an area encourages state governments to be more responsive to agriculture-related natural calamities.

Some authors argue that formal and even informal institutional quality is positively correlated with development. Using subjective measures of institutional quality from the *International Country Risk Guide*, published by IRIS, University of Maryland including government repudiation of contracts, risk of expropriation, corruption, rule of law, and the quality of bureaucracy, Ferreira (2004) finds that richer countries have higher institutional quality (also see Hall and Jones, 1999; and Easterly and Levine, 2002 for similar results).

---

[13] Pargal and Mani (2000) is a follow up of Pargal and Wheeler (1996). Using plant level data from Indonesia Pargal and Wheeler (1996) demonstrated the importance of community–factory interactions as an informal regulation of pollution. Using data from Southern India, Santhakumar (2003) verifies that citizen activism can block the establishment of new factories in an area. However, the author argues that citizen activism is not very effective in controlling pollution from existing factories.

While the institutions analyzed differ, the common conclusion drawn is that communities or countries differ in their control of pollution or management of resources. In communities where resources are managed well, opportunities to export can lead to real income gains, while in communities where resources are not managed well, the reverse can occur.

Copeland and Taylor (2004b) present a theory of endogenous resource management which reflects the above intuition. They argue that cross-country differences in the effectiveness of resource management can derive from differences in production technology, resource growth rates, and demographic characteristics such as population density, and expected life spans. They also find that access to international markets encourages some countries to effectively manage their natural resources through institutional reform. However, this is not true for all countries. In some countries (especially those with vulnerable slow-growing resources), efficient management is never feasible. They show that for such countries exporting the resource intensive good, trade liberalization reduces long-run steady state income.

Political Economy and Corruption

Several papers analyze the impact of trade liberalization on environmental policy and the environment using political economy models.[14] Governments can use environmental policy as a means to redistribute income to politically influential groups. If trade liberalization reduces income and output in the polluting industry, and if the polluting industry is politically powerful, then the government may face pressure to weaken environmental policy to help shelter the industry from the forces of international competition. The opposite may occur if trade increases income and output in the polluting sector.

There is little empirical work that explicitly incorporates political economy considerations while studying the impact of trade liberalization on the environment. However, there are a few studies that discuss the relationship between trade liberalization and corruption. Krueger (1974) argues that quantitative trade restrictions shift resources from directly productive activities to rent-seeking activities, such as corruption. If that is to be believed, trade liberalization should reduce corruption. In fact, several empirical studies do find such a relationship between trade liberalization and corruption.[15] However, more recent work casts doubts on the robustness of these results.[16] These studies find that the reduction of corruption from trade liberalization is sensitive to the choice of corruption indicator and to sample selection bias. Knack and Azfar (2003) argue that most available corruption indicators only provide ratings for

[14] See Bommer and Schulze (1999), Fredriksson (1999), Gulati (2003), McAusland (2002), Schleich (1999), and Yu (2000).
[15] See Ades and Di Tella (1999), Treisman, (2000), and Wei (2000).
[16] See Knack and Azfar (2003) and Torrez (2002).

those countries in which multinational investors have the greatest interest. These countries usually include almost all large nations and relatively well-governed small nations. They find that the relationship between corruption and trade intensity disappears if they use new corruption indicators and increase country coverage. Nevertheless, there seems to be consensus on a negative correlation between trade intensity and corruption for the sample of larger and relatively richer developing countries. Economies with higher levels of corruption are also likely to have lower flows of Foreign Direct Investment.[17]

All things being equal, an economy with higher levels of corruption is likely to have higher levels of pollution per unit of output (see López and Mitra, 2000). If we combine this with work that suggests that more open economies are less corrupt, this suggests another channel through which trade liberalization may affect environmental quality by way of endogenous changes in the policy process. But until such further work materializes, such a conclusion must remain speculative.

Environmental Policy and the Pattern of Trade

We now consider how market forces interact with the policy regime to determine the effects of trade on the environment. We focus mainly on composition effects. Although trade can also be expected to generate scale effects (by affecting an economy's growth rate), these are an unavoidable consequence of virtually any type of economic development. Composition effects, however, force us to ask whether trade induces a country to shift towards more or fewer environmentally intensive activities.

Much of the literature has been pre-occupied with the possibility that the composition effects of trade will cause pollution-intensive industry to shift from rich to poor countries because of differences in the stringency of environmental regulation. This is often referred to as the 'pollution haven hypothesis'. If the pollution haven hypothesis were correct, a number of implications would follow. First, if poor countries lack adequate and enforceable environmental regulations, then trade liberalization driven by pollution haven forces is likely to increase total world pollution and may lower welfare in low-income countries. Secondly, such a process could justify concerns raised in richer countries about the possibility of a 'race to the bottom.' That is, if industry migrates to countries with relatively weak environmental policy, then concerns about the effects of environmental regulation on international competitiveness could lead governments in rich countries to weaken their environmental policy. Finally, if pollution-haven-driven international trade has been an important part of the adjustment process to more stringent environmental

---

[17] See Fredriksson et al. (2003), and Smarzynska and Wei (2001).

189

policy, then the experience of high income countries in adjusting to more stringent environmental policies may not be a good predictor for poor countries. If rich countries have dealt with environmental problems by shifting dirty goods production to poor countries, then eventually the world will run out of new places to which it can shift such production. Long run abatement costs would therefore increase, and poor countries may not be able to grow their way out of environmental problems.

The literature on pollution havens has focused on two separate hypotheses that are often blurred together. This has led to some confusion in interpreting the empirical evidence. Copeland and Taylor (2004a) suggest that we distinguish between a 'pollution haven effect' and the 'pollution haven hypothesis'.

A pollution haven *effect* exists if, given world prices, a tightening of environmental policy in a particular country leads to a decline in net exports (or increase in net imports) of pollution intensive goods from that country. In the context of capital mobility, a pollution haven effect exists if tightening pollution regulations leads to a capital outflow in the affected industries. The presence of a pollution haven effect simply indicates that environmental regulations have an influence on trade volumes, plant location decisions, and capital flows.

The pollution haven *hypothesis* is stronger. According to the pollution haven hypothesis, the pollution haven effect is strong enough to be the principal determinant of the direction of trade and investment flows. That is, the pollution haven hypothesis asserts that liberalizing trade barriers will induce polluting industry to migrate (at the margin) to countries with relatively weaker environmental policy. Countries with weaker environmental policy will have a comparative advantage in pollution intensive goods. Moreover, such countries will also attract foreign investment in these sectors.

The theoretical case for the existence of the pollution haven effect is quite strong. The premise is simply that environmental regulations are costly, and that (at the margin), higher costs in a particular jurisdiction tend to make that jurisdiction a less attractive location for production of the affected goods. Two caveats have, however, been suggested. Porter (1991) argues that stricter environmental regulation may actually lower costs by encouraging an industry to be more innovative. Eskeland and Harrison (2003) note that more stringent environmental policy could increase the optimal scale of a firm and thereby increase capital inflows.[18] While these caveats raise the possibility that one might not expect to find evidence of a pollution haven effect in all industries, it is nevertheless fair to say that there is a strong theoretical presumption in its favor.

[18] They consider only a single firm with no entry and exit and so do not consider the offsetting effects of the increase in average cost implied by environmental regulations that would tend to work in favor of a pollution haven effect. However, in industries with entry barriers, their analysis raises the possibility that the effects of more stringent environmental regulations on trade and investment flows could be ambiguous.

In contrast, theoretical support for the pollution haven hypothesis is considerably weaker. Differences in pollution policy are only one of many factors that determine trade patterns. Resource endowments, technology, infrastructure, distance, and many other factors all interact with pollution policy differences to determine the trade pattern. The pollution haven hypothesis asserts that pollution policy is the critical factor determining trade patterns. An alternative hypothesis is that other factors are more important. Unless countries are otherwise very similar, or pollution control costs are very high, the theoretical support for the pollution haven hypothesis would seem to be rather weak.

Finally, we should note that developing countries may nevertheless have a comparative advantage in some types of polluting goods even if pollution policy is not an important determinant of trade patterns. If polluting goods are relatively intensive in the use of factors in which developing countries are relatively abundant, then developing countries will be net exporters of these goods and trade liberalization could lead to a shift of polluting production to these countries. That is, even if there is no evidence of a pollution haven effect, trade could still shift some types of dirty good production to poor countries.

Renewable Resource Policy and the Pattern of Trade

The logic of the pollution haven hypothesis has sometimes also been applied to trade in renewable resources. Chichilnisky (1994) considers a world in which North and South each have a stock of renewable resources. The countries are identical except that the North fully internalizes property rights while the South does not. She argues that the lack of property rights internalization will give the South a 'false' comparative advantage in renewable resources. Trade will induce entry into the renewable resource sector in the South, and increase pressure on their already over-extended resource stock. In the North, on the other hand, trade reduces pressure on resource stocks.

The distinction between pollution 'effect' and 'hypothesis' is relevant to renewable resources as well. Comparative advantage in renewable resources is determined by more than just the property rights regime. Differences in technology, capital availability, the natural growth rate of the resource, and other factors may more than offset the effects of differences in property rights.

However, there are several ways in which trade patterns in renewable resources are different from those for polluting goods. The first is that for many types of renewable resources, productivity relies on the health and viability of the natural environment supporting the resource stock. If property rights are not internalized, then an open access resource can become severely depleted. Depletion of the resource will reduce a country's supply and lead to a comparative *dis*-advantage in the resource. Brander and Taylor (1997b) distinguish between mild and severe over-use cases. They consider countries identical except for the property rights regime. In the mild over-use case, they obtain

191

Chichilnisky's result: weak property rights leads to excessive harvesting, which pushes out the supply curve. However, in the severe over-use case, excessive harvesting depletes the stock and the country with weak property rights enforcement is a resource importer. In this case, openness to trade takes pressure off the resource in the country where it is most depleted. This is the exact opposite in spirit to pollution haven scenarios: trade in such cases is both good for the environment and raises real incomes.

Another way in which composition effects of trade can be different for renewable resources than for polluting goods production, arises when there are competing uses for the habitat that supports the resource. Suppose a country has a comparative advantage in agriculture and a comparative disadvantage in forestry. Trade can then take pressure off the forest resource. However, if agriculture and forestry compete for the same land, then a trade-induced shift away from forestry towards agriculture can lead to depletion of the forest as land is cleared for agricultural purposes (Barbier and Schulz, 1997).

Similar effects can occur when there are cross-sectoral pollution externalities. A trade-induced shift from agriculture to manufacturing can take pressure off soils and reduce pesticide use. However, pollution from manufacturing can also lead to soil contamination. Once again, a composition effect that may at first seem to take pressure off a resource may ultimately do the reverse.

Empirical Evidence: 'The Pollution Haven Effect'

Empirical work in this area has been hampered by data limitations. Good data on the stringency of environmental regulations does not exist for most countries. Moreover, to account for unobserved heterogeneity it is necessary to have both time series and cross-sectional variation in the data. This further compounds the data limitation problem. As a consequence of this, a disproportionately large number of studies use U.S. data. Much of this work exploits variation in the stringency of environmental policy across states or counties within the U.S. This is not ideal, given the focus of this paper on developing countries. Nevertheless, we will review the results from some of these studies, as the methodological lessons learned in that literature will likely have wider applications.

We begin by considering studies that test for the presence of a pollution haven effect. That is, these studies try to estimate the effect of variations in the stringency of pollution policy on trade flows, plant location decisions, or direct foreign investment flows. The first wave of work in this area (up until about 1997) used mainly cross-sectional data, and the results were almost universally negative. Jaffe et al. (1995) and Levinson (1996) surveyed this work and concluded that there was little or no evidence that environmental policy had a significant effect on trade flows, plant location or investment flows. This was a striking finding for three reasons. First, it is at odds with the predictions of most theoretical models. Second, if correct, it would suggest that the pollution haven hypothesis is likely to be false as well: if environmental policy does not affect trade flows, then there is little reason to be concerned that freer trade will systematically shift polluting industry to regions with weak environmental policy. And third, it called into question the basis of much of the debate on 'race to the bottom.' If environmental policy does not affect competitiveness, then there is no reason for governments to be more reluctant to tighten up environmental policy as markets become more internationally integrated.

The results came from several different types of studies. Tobey (1990) used data on factor endowments and a measure of environmental policy stringency to explain net exports of pollution intensive goods for a sample of 23 countries. In all of his regressions, the environmental policy variable was not significant. This result has been widely cited; however, the conclusion is somewhat tenuous. Although the environmental policy variables were not significant, neither were most of the factor endowment measures.

Several other studies of trade flows focus on variation across industries, rather than across countries, mostly using U.S. data. Kalt (1988) and Grossman and Krueger (1993) regress net exports in a sample of U.S. industries on industry characteristics (such as tariffs, shares of various factors in costs, measures of pollution abatement costs (which is meant to capture the importance of environmental policy), and other control variables. These and similar studies tend to find that either that the abatement cost variable is insignificant or that it has the wrong sign. Kalt (1998) finds that higher pollution abatement costs are sometime associated with increased export success. Similar results were found in the literature on plant location. Levinson (1996), for example, found that differences in the stringency of environmental policy across states in the U.S. had little, or no effect on plant location decisions.

A number of explanations for these findings have been suggested. Most authors pointed out that pollution abatement costs were low in most industries (typically less than 5% of costs). Some authors took the sometimes positive association between environmental policy stringency and plant location decisions or net exports as evidence in support of the Porter hypothesis. However, a third explanation is that there were some serious econometric problems (in part driven by data limitations) with earlier studies. A recent group of studies has provided evidence that unobserved heterogeneity across locations and endogenous pollution policy are important enough to bias results if they are not carefully accounted for.

Suppose the North is both capital abundant and high income, so that it has relatively stringent environmental policy. Moreover, suppose the capital abundance effect dominates so that the North exports the pollution intensive good despite having relatively stringent environmental policy. If we ran a regression of trade flows on pollution policy (and failed to account for capital abundance), we would find a positive association between the stringency of pollution policy and net exports. The regression would not reveal a pollution haven effect, even though one is operative (an increase in the North's pollution tax would shift its supply of the dirty good inward and reduce its exports). Of course, we could rectify this by controlling for capital abundance, but there are many other location-specific factors that could affect trade flows for which we may neglect to account. In a cross-section framework, we will be unable to account for this type of unobserved heterogeneity; however if we have both time series and cross sectional variation in the data, then the use of fixed effects can help.

Another possibility is that via the political process, pollution policy responds to the pressures of international competitiveness. Suppose that as trade is liberalized, governments try to shelter import-competing industries from foreign competition by relaxing environmental policy. Then (even if stringent pollution regulations do in fact encourage imports) we would find a negative association between net imports and the stringency of environmental policy. Paradoxically, in cases where there really is the potential for a 'race to the bottom', we may be unable to measure a pollution haven effect.

In the context of trade, Levinson (1999) used panel data on hazardous waste trade flows between states in the U.S. using data on both trade flows and taxes on hazardous waste disposal, he first used a simple OLS regression and found that higher waste taxes were associated with *higher* import flows of hazardous waste into a state. He notes, however, that states which have attractive sites for hazardous waste processing are more likely to have to respond to waste inflows with stricter environmental regulations. After taking into account the endogeneity of pollution regulations, he finds that, all else equal, higher waste taxes deter waste imports.

Ederington and Minier (2003) use cross-sectional time-series data on net imports in U.S. manufacturing from 1978–92. They treat pollution policy (abatement costs) as endogenous and responsive to political pressure. Using industry fixed effects, they find a small positive effect of pollution policy on imports. However, after correcting for endogeneity, they find a large positive effect. Levinson and Taylor (2003) also use data on U.S. imports. Using industry fixed effects, they find a small significant and positive effect of higher abatement costs for net imports from Canada and Mexico. The effect is also positive for trade with non-OECD countries, but not significant. However, when they also account for the endogeneity of pollution policy, they find a large and significant effect of abatement costs on net imports, as would be predicted if there were a pollution haven effect.

Several recent studies on plant location, mostly in states in the U.S. have also found evidence supporting a pollution haven effect. Becker and Henderson (2000) use a panel of county-level U.S. data to investigate the effects of federal air pollution regulations on location decisions for new manufacturing plants in the U.S. Previous studies had found no significant effect. They had both a better measure of environmental policy, and they were able to control for unobserved heterogeneity across locations. They found a large and significant negative impact of increased stringency of environmental regulations on new plant births. Kahn (1997), Greenstone (2002), and List et al. (2003) have all confirmed these results.

Keller and Levinson (2002) find similar results using data on inward foreign direct investment in U.S. states from 1977–94. Using a pooled OLS regression, they replicate earlier studies which found that abatement costs do not have a significant effect on investment flows. However, when they include state-level fixed effects to account for unobserved heterogeneity, they find that abatement costs have a statistically significant negative effect on foreign investment.

Gray and Shadbegian (2002) use data on the allocation of production across plants in different states in the U.S. in the paper and oil industries during 1967–92. They find evidence that firms shift production to states with less stringent environmental regulations. The results are stronger for the paper industry than for the oil industry. One possible explanation for this difference is that paper is more easily transportable. They note that paper shipments travel an average of 238 miles, while oil shipments travel an average of 79 miles. This suggests that transport costs or other measures of 'tradability' may be an important factor which is often unaccounted for in cross-industry studies, a conjecture which receives support from the work of Ederington, Levinson and Minier (2003), who present evidence that pollution abatement costs tend to be higher in industries which are relatively less mobile. If not properly accounted for, this effect can bias results.

While there is now an emerging body of work which finds that pollution regulation does affect trade and investment flows, much of this work has focused on the U.S. There are as yet almost no studies which attempt to account for issues of endogeneity and unobserved heterogeneity in attempting to determine how pollution regulations may affect trade or investment in developing countries.

Ederington, Levinson and Minier (2003) look at U.S. trade flows, but divide their sample into OECD and non-OECD countries. Their hypothesis is that variations in the stringency of U.S. environmental regulations are likely to be highly correlated with other OECD countries, and so if there is a pollution haven effect, it is more likely to be detected in trade with non-OECD countries. They find evidence in support of this: abatement costs do not have a significant effect on U.S. net imports from OECD countries (the sign of the coefficient is in fact negative). However, abatement costs have a positive and statistically significant effect on net imports from non-OECD countries.

Eskeland and Harrison (2003) consider direct foreign investment across a sample of industries in four developing countries (Côte d'Ivoire, Morocco, Mexico, and Venezuela). As with the earlier work on foreign investment, they find little or no evidence that U.S. abatement costs affect the flow of foreign investment to these countries. However, although this study does control for unobserved heterogeneity across regions, it does so by restricting the number of regions to only four.

Smarzynska and Wei (2001) use a firm level data set on investment in 24 transition economies in Eastern Europe and the former Soviet Union. They find some weak evidence that countries with more participation in international environmental treaties are less likely to attract pollution intensive foreign investment. However, their result is not robust to other measures of the stringency of environmental regulation. This study does control for differences in corruption across countries, but is not able to control for unobserved heterogeneity across countries.

To summarize, there is currently very little explicit evidence that environmental policy affects trade and investment flows between rich and poor countries. However, virtually all of the available evidence comes from studies which do not account for the endogeneity of pollution policy and unobserved heterogeneity. This omission is likely to be critically important because there is an emerging body of evidence that plant location within the United States, and U.S. trade and investment flows with the rest of the world are affected by environmental policy. These recent studies account for the endogeneity of pollution policy and unobserved heterogeneity across locations. This suggests that it is premature to conclude that there is no evidence for a pollution haven effect. In fact, if there is a pollution haven effect within the United States, it is reasonable to conjecture that such an effect will also be operative in the context of trade and investment between rich and poor countries because of greater variation in the stringency of environmental policy. However, a definitive answer to this question will require more research.

Empirical Evidence: 'The Pollution Haven Hypothesis'

In our terminology, the pollution haven hypothesis is that trade liberalization will shift pollution intensive industry to countries with relatively weak environmental policy. In contrast to the relatively large number of studies on the pollution haven effect, there have been few studies that explicitly test the pollution haven hypothesis. Several studies have examined changes in the share of dirty goods in exports from developing countries over time. That is, they study changes in revealed comparative advantage. Low and Yeats (1992) is an early well-known study of this type. They looked at the composition of manufacturing exports and found that over the period 1965–1988, developing countries were increasing their comparative advantage in pollution intensive manufactures. Mani and Wheeler (1997) found similar results. While these types of results are suggestive, they do not establish whether trade liberalization was responsible for changes in the pattern of industrial production, or whether other factors were more important. Copeland and Taylor (2004a) suggest that capital accumulation or other forms of economic growth in developing countries could also account for the same trends.

An alternative approach is to try to estimate the composition effect of openness to trade directly. Antweiler et al. (2001) use the GEMS data on sulphur dioxide concentrations to estimate the scale, technique and composition effects of trade. They hypothesize that the composition effect will depend on both per capita income (which will affect the stringency of environmental policy) and capital abundance (which gives countries a comparative advantage in SO_2-intensive industry. They define the composition effect of trade as the per cent increase in SO_2 concentrations arising from a 1 percent increase in openness to trade, while controlling for scale, techniques, and other factors. If the pollution haven hypothesis is correct, the composition effect should be decreasing in per capita income: it should be positive for low income countries and negative for high income countries. In fact, they find the reverse. This suggests that higher income countries have a comparative advantage in SO_2-intensive industries, so that trade liberalization would shift SO_2-intensive polluting industry to richer countries. This is consistent with results from Grossman and Krueger's (1993) study of NAFTA which drew upon CGE simulations of the effects of trade liberalization on trade flows and concluded that NAFTA would, at the margin, shift pollution intensive industrial production to the U.S. It is also consistent with the existing pattern of trade, in which pollution intensive industry is heavily concentrated in high income countries.

Much of this work has focused on industrial pollution; however trade may also shift production based on natural capital between countries. If trade increases pressure on renewable resources in countries which do not have institutions that internalize externalities in these industries, then the effects of trade may be potentially more devastating than in the case of the industrial pollution haven hypothesis. This is because excessive pressure on natural capital can both reduce environmental quality and reduce long-run real income. Most of the work on of the effect of trade liberalization on sectors intensive in natural capital has been case studies. Consequently, we do not yet have good evidence as to whether trade liberalization has systematically shifted production in these sectors to countries with weak property rights.

López (1997) and (2000) calculates composition and scale effects for agriculture in Ghana and Côte d'Ivoire respectively, using an empirical general equilibrium framework. He finds that price movements brought about by trade liberalization in Ghana encourage the expansion of agriculture. This expansion is achieved by pushing the area cultivated into forests. In other words, the composition effect has a negative impact on the environment. Contrary to the case in Ghana, López (2000) finds that Côte d'Ivoire has a comparative advantage in tree crops that are not land intensive. Thus the composition effect of trade liberalization implies that agriculture as a whole becomes less land intensive, and reduces damages to the local biomass.[19]

A potential problem with the composition effect is the implicit assumption of input mobility. Composition effects usually assume smooth structural adjustment. Labor and materials used in the production of the declining industry are assumed to find employment in the expanding industry. However, this is not always true. Labor in developing economies is typically not very mobile. This lack of mobility can be caused by the absence of well-defined credit markets, and/or the inaccessibility of education and labor training facilities. Barbier (2000) provides an example where landless, near-landless workers, and the rural poor displaced by agro-industrialization migrate to forest frontier regions and marginal lands. This displacement can potentially nullify the reduction in deforestation gained from agro-industrialization. Similar effects are pointed out in López (1998c) and Barbier and Burgess (1996).[20]

Measuring the Effects of Trade on Environmental Outcomes

The net effect of trade on the environment depends on the sum of scale, composition, and technique effects. Since we can expect heterogeneity across countries in both the direction and magnitude of these effects, we should also expect to see considerable differences across countries in the net effect. It is useful to think of several different types of countries, classified by their comparative advantage and property rights regime:

I *Natural-capital-intensive exporters with weak property rights regimes*. These countries are potentially vulnerable to increased environmental degradation from trade liberalization. Trade will place increasing pressure on their natural resources. This can lead to both resource depletion and real income losses. Trade may make it harder for such countries to escape from a poverty trap.

II *Natural-capital-intensive exporters with strong property rights regimes*. These countries should be able to experience real income gains from trade liberalization without suffering severe resource depletion.

---

[19] Like López (1997), Benhin and Barbier (2001) also study deforestation in Ghana. The authors analyze the impact of economy-wide reforms on deforestation in the country. They find that a rise in the price of cocoa, or a decline in input prices leads to an expansion of land employed in cocoa, inducing deforestation. Their analysis is different from López (1997) in that it does not estimate composition effects from trade liberalization.

[20] Barbier and Burgess (1996) study the effect of reforms induced by the North American Free Trade Agreement on maize production and subsequently deforestation in Mexico. They find that while trade liberalization and economic growth tend to reduce agricultural expansion, return migration to the rural areas during the transition is likely to have an opposite effect. They find that this return migration in the short run can outweigh the positive effects of liberalization and cause overall negative effects on the forest cover.

III *Low income pollution-intensive manufacturing exporters.* These countries will have a comparative advantage in pollution intensive industries and may have relatively weak environmental policy because of their low income. Trade will stimulate pollution intensive production, and will increase industrial pollution. If trade helps to increase real income, improved environmental regulation may emerge, depending on the responsiveness of government. Policy improvements may or may not dampen the deterioration of environmental quality.

IV *Low income exporters of relatively clean goods.* These countries will also have relatively weak environmental policy, but with a comparative advantage in relatively clean production, both real income and environmental quality may improve with trade. However, increases in real income will increase consumption of pollution intensive goods such as automobiles, and this can also lead to an increase in pollution.

Relatively few studies undertake a comprehensive accounting of the effects of trade on the environment. Applied general equilibrium studies come closest to doing this. Their advantage is that they can be used to run counterfactuals to isolate the pure effects of trade from other effects. Moreover, they can also isolate composition effects, and they can take into account a wide range of different environmental incomes. The disadvantage of these types of studies is that they are simulations and so do not measure actual outcomes.

Some studies investigate the impact of trade liberalization on natural resources (examples are López, 1997 and López, 2000; and Bandara and Coxhead, 1999). Others investigate the impact on air and water pollution (examples are Strutt and Anderson, 2000, and Unteroberdoerster, 2003). Results often vary across countries and types of resources.

López (1997) finds that trade liberalization has a negative effect of biomass in Ghana. This may be an example of a type I country in our classification above. In contrast, López (2000) finds that trade liberalization has a positive effect on biomass in Côte d'Ivoire. As explained earlier, the main difference between these two studies lies in the composition effect resulting from trade liberalization. Similarly to López (2000), Bandara and Coxhead (1999) find that the composition effect of trade liberalization increases demand for tea production (a relatively less erosive sector) in Sri Lanka. In other words, they too find that trade liberalization has positive effects on the environment. These latter two countries may be examples of our type IV countries above.

Unteroberdoerster (2003) studies the impact of trade liberalization on the environment in countries that make up the Asia Pacific Economic Cooperation (APEC). He finds that trade liberalization does not worsen the environment in these countries. He also finds that an increase in environmental standards by trading partners also has an insignificant impact on pollution in these countries. The primary reason is the favorable composition effect from trade liberalization in most of these countries.

Strutt and Anderson (2000) undertake a comprehensive applied general equilibrium analysis of both WTO-based trade policy reform, and trade policy reform slated for Indonesia under the APEC. They first simulate a base case scenario in which Indonesia grows over the next decade under the current trade regime. Pollution rises. This reflects a combination of industrialization and growth in the context of a relatively weak environmental policy regime. They then simulate a scenario in which Indonesia grows in the context of trade policy reforms. Pollution still grows, but less than in the previous scenario. Moreover, there is less depletion of natural resources. This is because the composition effects of trade liberalization on pollution are negative. Trade liberalization shifts the growth path to relatively cleaner production.

Among empirical analyses of trade reform on the environment, Vukina et al. (1999) examine the relationship between policy reforms and composition of pollution in output in the former Centrally Planned Economies. They use information on 13 pollutants and the energy intensity of output. They find, 'policy reforms affecting price liberalization, trade and the foreign exchange system had a beneficial effect on the composition of manufacturing output steering it towards less-polluting sectors.' The authors link this improvement in composition to environmental policy reforms that accompany trade reforms. It is important to note the large and negative scale effect in most of these countries. The authors find that in addition to policy induced reduction in pollution; large scale decreases in economic activity also lead to large decreases in pollution.

Another approach to measuring the effect of trade on the environment is to ask whether there is a systematic relationship between openness to trade and environmental quality. Several of the Environmental Kuznets Curve studies (e.g., Grossman and Krueger, 1993 and Gale and Mendez, 1998) include openness to trade as an explanatory variable to explain pollution levels. These studies typically find that openness is either insignificant or else has a positive effect on environmental quality. Frankel and Rose (2005) use a similar approach, but control for the endogeneity of openness to trade. They also find a positive effect of openness on environmental quality.

These studies suggest that on average, trade does not systematically worsen environmental quality. However, they have a couple of important weaknesses. First, they typically focus on only a small number of pollutants. Second, they do not account for heterogeneity across countries in the response of the environment to trade. If some countries have a comparative advantage in dirty goods, and others in clean goods, then we may well find that on average, trade does not have much of an effect on the environment. But this may mask significant effects on individual countries.

Antweiler et al. (2001) used data on sulphur dioxide pollution to estimate scale, technique and composition effects of trade. They allowed composition effects to vary across countries because of differences in comparative advantage. When they add up the scale, technique and composition effects, they find that trade is good for the environment (as measured by SO_2 concentrations) for the average country in their sample. However, they also find heterogeneity across countries. The composition effect tended to be negative (pollution-reducing) for poorer countries (reflecting a comparative disadvantage in SO_2 intensive industry) and positive for richer countries.

Policy Issues

Much of the work on trade and environment has been stimulated by policy issues. From a developing country perspective, these fall into two major categories: internal domestic policies for developing countries; and the implications of policies adopted by other countries and/or their implementation via multilateral trade organizations such as the WTO, the European Union, and such others.

Internal Policies

If all countries had efficient domestic environmental policies and well-defined property rights for natural capital, then (with the exception of transboundary or global environmental problems), there is a strong theoretical case for avoiding links between trade policies and the environment. The major insight here comes from the policy targeting literature (Bhagwati, 1971): environmental distortions are best dealt with via environmental policy, and once externalities are internalized, the optimal trade policy is independent of environmental concerns (Bhagwati and Srinivasan, 1996).

However, most (and perhaps all) countries do not fully internalize environmental distortions for many different reasons, including information problems, political pressures and a lack of institutional capacity. The problem is particularly acute in many developing countries. Given this reality, the case for pursuing trade policy reforms independently of environmental concerns is considerably weaker. Copeland (1994) considers trade policy reform in the presence of exogenous environmental distortions. If the export sector is on average intensive in its use of environmental inputs, then broad-based trade policy reform can reduce welfare by exacerbating environmental distortions. On the other hand, if the import-competing sector is environmentally intensive, then broad-based trade policy reforms can yield a double dividend—they yield both gains from trade and shift resources out of environmentally damaging activities. Copeland also shows how trade reform in the presence of capital mobility can exacerbate the strength of these effects.

It is always possible to design trade policy reforms that improve welfare (Copeland, 1994 and Beghin et al., 1997): such reforms attempt to stimulate clean industries and depress dirty industries. One can think of trade policy as a second best instrument of environmental policy since it implicitly taxes or subsidizes various production activities in the economy. However, the information requirements for such reforms are significant.

A better strategy is to consider coordinated trade policy reforms and environmental policy reforms. That is, if broad-based trade policy reform will stimulate the environmentally intensive sectors, then a reform of environmental policy directed towards those sectors can mitigate possible problems. While such a strategy will work in theory, it may not be feasible in practice because of institutional constraints and political problems. This raises the issue of timing. Should environmental policy reform be a precondition for trade policy reform?

The sequencing of policy reform is best dealt with in a model with endogenous environmental policy. Here the literature on income effects and the political economy of protection is relevant. First consider our type III countries, which export goods intensive in industrial pollution. If trade raises both income and pollution, then we may expect the income effect to increase support for improved environmental policy in countries where governments are responsive to consumer preferences. This suggests that for these types of countries, making environmental policy reform a pre-condition for trade policy reform could be counter-productive.

The situation is quite different for our type I countries which are heavily dependent on natural capital exports but which also have weak property rights regimes. Trade policy reform in these countries may not raise long run real income, and hence the case for coordinating environmental and resource management reforms with trade policy reforms is quite compelling. Unfortunately such reforms may be difficult in the presence of poverty and with vulnerable natural capital.

When environmental policy fails to fully internalize externalities, the instruments used to control pollution can be important. This suggests that when reforms are implemented, and policymakers anticipate that they may not be able to fully internalize externalities, the choice of instruments can have implications for the consequences of future trade policy reforms. Copeland (1994) and Copeland and Taylor (2003) note that pollution quotas (if they are enforced), ambient standards and tradable permits all do a better job than exogenous taxes or emission standards of protecting the economy from increased pollution when trade liberalization stimulates pollution-intensive activities. Although there is a strong efficiency-based case for market-based instruments such as pollution taxes, these policies require an active and flexible regulator to adjust their levels in responsive to increased pressure on the environment arising from export expansion or other sources of growth. If such flexibility is not going to be politically feasible, they lose some of their attractiveness.

External Policies

Much of the debate about linkages between trade and environmental policies in a multi-country context revolves around issues of market access. Environmentalists concerned about environmental problems in other countries often propose to make the right to import certain products contingent on meeting certain environmental standards. Those concerned about the competitiveness aspects of environmental policy often propose to either 'level the playing field' by tying participation in trade agreements to the adoption of environmental standards, or by using 'eco-duties' to force foreign firms in countries with weak environmental policy to bear the same environmental cost as domestic firms subject to stringent regulation.

Issues of Competitiveness

Environmentalists fear that without international coordination, governments will sacrifice environmental quality and the welfare of their citizens to become globally competitive (see Nader et al.,1993). This is often referred to as the 'race to the bottom' hypothesis.[21] Wheeler (2001), Vogel (2000) and others argue that there is little empirical support for this hypothesis.[22] The evidence is of two types. First, early work (as surveyed by Jaffe et al., 1995) found little empirical support for the pollution haven effect. If differences in environmental regulations do not affect trade flows, then there is little justification for governments to weaken environmental policies to subsidize domestic firms. However, as we have discussed earlier in the paper, recent work suggests that while there is little evidence for the strong form of the pollution haven hypothesis (pollution policy is not the principal determinant of trade patterns), there is emerging evidence that changes in environmental policy do affect plant location and production decisions at the margin. If environmental policy does affect competitiveness, then the 'race to the bottom' issue is not likely to go away.

---

[21] See Daly (1993, 1997) and Anríquez (2002). For theoretical examination of this issue, see Rauscher (1995) and Markusen et al. (1995) and Oates and Schwab (1988).

[22] In obvious contrast to the 'race to the bottom hypothesis' Vogel (2000) also informally discusses the 'race to the top hypothesis.' By *race to the top* he implies that economic openness and capital mobility might have encouraged nations to enact standards higher than they would have in absence of increased economic interdependency (also termed the *California Effect*). One of the reasons presented for race to the top is alliances between domestic producers and environmentalists. If both groups are politically influential, and domestic producers are relatively more efficient at incorporating environmental standards than their foreign competitors the government might raise standards instead of lowering them. He cites the example of strict German automobile emission controls in the 1980s. The author says that these emission controls protected the domestic market share of German automobiles as Italian and French car manufacturers found the controls too costly to comply with (see Vogel, 1995 for other examples).

The second type of evidence looks at actual government behavior. Wheeler (2001) points to evidence of improvements in air quality and other environmental indicators in the face of increased trade. He suggests that this is inconsistent with a weakening of environmental policy in response to increased pressures of trade. However there have been very few studies that attempt to explicitly measure the policy response of governments to freer trade. The two recent studies that do attempt such an exercise find some evidence in support of the hypothesis. Eliste and Fredriksson (2002) and Ederington and Minier (2003) find evidence of the use of environmental regulation as a secondary means to provide protection to domestic industries.

Even if there does turn out to be some evidence that shows that concerns about competitiveness do affect environmental policy, the possibility of a literal race to the bottom seems highly unlikely. The main reason is that weak environmental policy is an inefficient way to subsidize domestic firms— environmental control costs are relatively small, and weakening environmental policy imposes costs on others and encourages green lobbies to become more active. Instead it is more likely that competitiveness issues may act as a damper on the aggressiveness of environmental policy in some industries in high income countries.

What are the implications for developing countries? The major effects are likely to be that the 'race to the bottom' issue increases political support for demands for linking environmental standards to trade agreements, and in some cases for policy harmonization. There is some support for including labor and environmental agreements in the World Trade Organization (WTO) (see Suranovic, 2002). Such agreements might require minimum environmental and labor protection across all countries and allow countries to punish violations with import restrictions.

The logic for linkage arises mainly from a concern that when the use of traditional barriers to trade is increasingly restricted, environmental policies can be used as a substitute for trade policies. Ederington (2001) and others have shown that in such cases, the first best solution can be obtained if countries agree to expand the trade agreement to restrict environmental policy as well. The difficulty with this approach is that for such an agreement to be efficient, environmental standards will in general have to be different across all countries. Efficient environmental policy should reflect local marginal damages and local marginal abatement costs. These vary with income, factor endowments, the sensitivity of the local environment, and many other factors. The information requirements for setting such standards efficiently are enormous. Moreover, policy in most high-income countries is set via a political process and not necessarily in a way that is socially efficient. Consequently, an attempt to enforce such linkage on a global basis would introduce so many inefficiencies that it is likely to be unworkable. There is more potential for such an approach to work in regional trade agreements (such as in the EU), where countries are similar in income and in their institutional capacity to deal with environmental problems.

Current WTO practices distinguish between trade measures that target the characteristics of products that enter a country (such as automobile emission standards) and those that target the process by which an imported good is produced in a foreign country. The former are allowed, subject to a national treatment rule (and some other conditions) while the latter tend to not be allowed. This is a distinction which is not ideal, but which is probably reasonable from the perspective of developing countries.

The regime is not ideal because it is inconsistent in the way that subsidies are treated. Explicit export subsidies are vulnerable to countervail duties under WTO rules. But implicit subsidies because of weak environmental regulations are not. This seems anti-environment because it takes the norm to be the market outcome (no explicit subsidies) while in the case of pollution and other environmental problems, the non-interventionist market outcome is not efficient. However, because of the information problems discussed above, opening the door to process standards or 'green countervail' would create so many opportunities for disguised protectionism that it is unlikely to generate wide support. Hence a norm that does not allow trade-related process standards or green countervail is in the interests of both developing countries and developed countries.

The current rules on product standards do allow countries some room to manipulate standards to protect local industry, mainly by 'raising rivals' costs' (Salop and Sheffman, 1983). If it is easier for local firms than foreign firms to adopt a standard, then the implementation of a more stringent standard will benefit local firms at the expense of foreigners. That is, disguised protectionism is possible even under a national treatment regime. The WTO has moved beyond national treatment, however, by requiring some scientific justification for standards. This has angered some environmentalists, but from the perspective of developing countries reduces the scope for disguised protectionism.

Finally, although most developing countries tend to oppose harmonization across the entire spectrum of environmental policies, it is worth noting that in some cases, harmonization in sanitary and phytosanitary standards across developed countries might actually be beneficial for developing countries. Wilson et al. (2003a; 2003b) argue that the unilateral food safety standards are economically inefficient as they create very high transaction costs for exporters. Using data on global trade patterns for certain food products, the authors find that if standards recommended by Codex Alimentarius Commission (a commission created by the Food and Agricultural Organization) were to be adopted, there would be large increases in world trade in the food products analyzed. They also find that the largest gainers from such a harmonization would be developing countries.

Targeting Foreign Pollution

A second market access issue arises from attempts by policymakers or environmental groups to influence environmental policy in developing countries. Many of theses issues involve natural capital such as rain forests, endangered species, and biodiversity issues.

These types of issues have been the subject of some high-profile GATT and WTO cases. In the tuna–porpoise case, the U.S. banned imports of tuna from Mexico unless Mexican fishers adopted certain practices that prevented porpoise deaths during harvesting (the issue is that porpoises get caught in the fish nets). Mexico filed a complaint with GATT arguing that this was an unfair restriction on imports. The GATT panel sided with Mexico. Although the panel decision was never adopted, it created an uproar among environmentalists because it was taken as a signal that GATT was not environment-friendly.

In the shrimp-turtle case, the U.S. banned imports of shrimp from some Asian countries because of the possibility that endangered sea turtles were killed during harvesting. The U.S. made adoption of U.S. fishing practices (which involve the use of turtle excluder devices) a condition of market access. India, Malaysia, Pakistan, and Thailand complained to the WTO that this was an unfair restriction on imports. The WTO panel ruled against the U.S. Again, environmentalists were unhappy. However, in this case, the WTO panel went to some length to emphasize that it did not rule out the possibility that actions by the U.S. to protect sea turtles (perhaps with trade policy) might be GATT-consistent. Rather it argued that the implementation of the U.S. policy was discriminatory because it treated different members of the WTO differently (Caribbean fishers were subject to different rules from Asian fishers).

These cases have received a great deal of attention. In both cases, the GATT/WTO ruled against the attempts by the U.S. to impose its environmental standards in other countries. The shrimp–turtle ruling is not a clear test of the whether such extra-territoriality is WTO-legal because of the discriminatory aspects of the U.S. policy. However, even if more such policy initiatives are implemented by the U.S. or other countries in the future, it is worth noting that the amount of trade involved is very small, the number of cases so far is small, and the trade impact of such cases pales in comparison to other trade-distorting practices of high-income countries (such as agricultural subsidies, restrictions on textile trade, etc.).

Global Environmental Problems

Non-cooperative behavior between jurisdictions will lead to inefficiently low levels of environmental regulation when environmental problems are inter-jurisdictional. Some examples include acid rain, depletion of the ozone layer, shared fisheries, biodiversity issues, and global warming. Here there exists a justification for either multilateral or bilateral coordination in setting the environmental policy. While coordination is desirable in the case of several global environmental problems, it is usually hard to achieve. Global environmental agreements are a possible solution. In order for the solution to work, many complexities need to be dealt with (see Barrett (2002) for an excellent discussion of international environmental agreements). Some of these include enforcement of the agreement, the terms that would achieve participation, and others. Ideally these agreements would be self-enforcing and elicit large-scale participation by most countries. More often than not even after longs periods of negotiation large-scale participation is hard to achieve.[23]

As an alternative, several authors argue that environmental agreements should be linked with trade agreements. Some environmental agreements contain trade sanctions. Examples are the Montreal Protocol on Substances that Deplete the Ozone Layer, or the Convention on International Trade in Endangered Species that bans trade of certain endangered species and by-products like ivory and furs. In contrast, the WTO usually does not accept differences in environmental policies as grounds for trade sanctions.

Linkages between trade and environmental agreements can increase incentives necessary to encourage enforcement of agreements on global environmental problems (see e.g., Limão, 2002; Ederington, 2001; Abrego et al., 1997; Cesar and Zewe, 1994; and Runge, 1994). The basic intuition behind all these studies is that when trade and environmental policies are strategic complements, linking the two agreements creates incentives for greater cooperation in both issues. Linking the two agreements might allow greater reductions in tariffs and improvements in environmental standards, and thereby raise world welfare.

Nevertheless, there are also several arguments against linkage. The most pertinent one is that linkages will cause a large increase in trade disputes. Looking at recent trends this argument might be important. From 1994 to 1999, the number of trade disputes involving non-trade issues tripled as compared to the previous four years (Limão, 2002). This increase was largely caused by intellectual property issues. Non-trade issues are typically harder to prove, and increase the cost of litigation in any dispute. Thus while linking trade and environmental agreements might encourage greater adherence to both agreements, it might also make the task of dispute settlement in these agreements harder.

From a developing country perspective, whether or not such agreements are in their interest depends on the terms negotiated. If pressure on the global environment is proportional to consumption, and if willingness and ability to pay for environmental quality is an increasing function of income, then it is

---

[23] Barrett (2002) classifies the agreements into two types, broad but shallow (where there is broad participation but little is achieved by the agreement), and narrow but deep (narrow participation with stricter requirements).

both efficient and fair for higher income countries to bear a larger share of the costs of implementing international environmental agreements.

Conclusion

Increased international trade between rich and poor countries is not incompatible with improvements in environmental quality. The effect of trade on the environment depends on the interaction between the pattern of trade and the institutions in place to manage environmental policy.

While there is some evidence that differences in environmental policy do affect trade and investment flows, there is no evidence that it is one of the major factors. Also there is little convincing evidence that trade liberalization leads to pollution havens. However, even if environmental policy is not an important determinant of trade flows, some countries will nevertheless have a comparative advantage in environmentally intensive industries, and trade will lead to increased pressure on their environment. Whether or not this leads to excessive deterioration of environmental quality depends on the policy regimes and the institutions in place to manage resources and the environment. If there is good domestic environmental policy in place, there is no reason for increased trade to cause environmental problems—in fact it can yield benefits by providing increased access to environmentally friendly technology from other countries.

In countries with weak environmental policy regimes, trade can lead to increases in pollution and degradation of natural capital. If trade also contributes to income growth, there is some evidence that the increase in income will increase the demand for environmental quality and can lead to improved environmental policy. However countries with weak property rights regimes that are heavily dependent on natural capital exports can potentially suffer increased environmental degradation without offsetting income gains. In such countries, improvements in resource management and environmental policy may be an important pre-condition for broad-based trade policy reform.

There has been some support for linkages between trade policies and environmental policies in global trade negotiations. This has roots in concerns about both competitiveness and environmental quality. To deal with competitiveness issues, the WTO currently bans explicit export subsidies. However, it tolerates implicit export subsidies arising from weak environmental policy. While this is inconsistent, an attempt to make market access contingent on meeting environmental standards would lead to disguised protectionism. Consequently, this type of linkage at the global level is in the interests of neither developing nor developed countries.

Linkage to address issues of environmental quality is more likely to occur. Currently only a small amount of world trade is affected by such measures.

However, there is likely to be pressure for more such linkage in the future, and developing country interests may be best served if these issues are dealt with within a multilateral forum rather than on a unilateral basis.

References

Abrego, L. E., C. Perroni, J. Whalley, and R. M. Wigle (1997), 'Trade and Environment: Bargaining Outcomes from Linked Negotiations,' *NBER Working Paper 6216*.

Ades, Alberto and Rafael Di Tella (1999), 'Rents, Competition, and Corruption,' *American Economic Review*, 89(4), 982–3.

Ahuja, Vinod (1998), 'Land Degradation, Agricultural Productivity, and Common Property: Evidence from Cote d'Ivoire', *Environment and Development Economics*, 3(1998): 7–34.

Aidt, Toke S. (1998), 'Political Internalization of Economic Externalities and Environmental Policy.' *Journal of Public Economics* 69(1): 1–16.

Anderson, T. L. and P. J. Hill, (1975), 'The evolution of property rights: a study of the American West,' *Journal of Law and Economics:* 18: 163–79.

Andreoni, James and Arik Levinson (2001), 'The Simple Analytics of the Environmental Kuznets Curve,' *Journal of Public Economics*, 80: 269–86.

Anríquez, Gustavo (2002), 'Trade and the Environment: An Economic Literature Survey,' *Working Paper 02–16, Department of Agricultural and Resource Economics*, University of Maryland, College Park.

Antweiler, W., B. R. Copeland, and M. S. Taylor, (September 2001), 'Is Free Trade Good for the Environment?' *American Economic Review*, 91(4): 877–908.

Baland, J. M. and J. P. Platteau (1996), *Halting Degradation of Natural Resources: Is there a role for Rural Communities*, Clarendon Press, Oxford, U.K.

Bandara, Jayatilleke S. and Ian Coxhead (1999), 'Can Trade Liberalization Have Environmental Benefits in Developing Country Agriculture: A Sri Lankan Case Study,' *Journal of Policy Modeling*, 21(3): 349–74.

Barbier, E. B. (2000), 'Links between Economic Liberalization and Rural Resource Degradation in the Developing Regions,' *Agricultural Economics*, 23: 299–310.

—— and J. C. Burgess (1996), 'Economic Analysis of Deforestation in Mexico,' *Environment and Development Economics*, 1: 203–40.

—— and C-E. Schulz (1997), 'Wildlife, biodiversity and trade,' *Environment and Development Economics*, 2: 145–72.

Bardhan, P. (2000), 'Irrigation and Cooperation: An Empirical Analysis of 48 Irrigation Communities in South India,' *Economic Development and Cultural Change*, 48(4), 847–65.

Barrett, S. (2002), 'The Strategy of Treaty Negotiation: "broad but shallow" versus "narrow but deep",' in B. Kriström, P. Dasgupta, and K Löfgren (eds), *Economic Theory for the Environment: Essays in Honour of Karl-Göran Mäler*, Edward Elgar Publishing, Cheltenham, UK.

Baumol, W. J. (1967), 'Macroeconomics of Unbalanced Growth: The Anatomy of Urban Crisis,' *American Economic Review*, 57(3): 415–26.

——, S. A. B. Blackman, and E. N. Wolff (1985), 'Unbalanced Growth Revisited: Asymptotic Stagnancy and New Evidence,' *American Economic Review*, 75(4): 806–17.

Becker and Henderson (April 2000), 'Effects of Air Quality Regulations on Polluting Industries,' *Journal of Political Economy*, 108(2): 379–421.

Beghin, J. and M. Potier (1997), 'Effects of Trade Liberalisation on the Environment in the Manufacturing Sector,' *The World Economy*, 20(4): 435–56.

——, D. Roland-Holst, and D. Van Der Mensbrugghe (1997), 'Trade and Pollution Linkages: Piecemeal Reform and Optimal Intervention,' *Canadian Journal of Economics*, 30(2): 442–55.

Benhin, J. K. A. and E. B. Barbier (2004). 'Structural Adjustment Programme, Deforestation and Biodiversity Loss in Ghana.' *Environmental and Resource Economics* 27: 337–66.

Besley, Timothy, R. Burgess (2002), 'The Political Economy of Government Responsiveness: Theory and Evidence from India,' *Quarterly Journal of Economics* 117, no 4: 1415–51.

Bhagwati, J. (1971), 'The Generalized Theory of Distortions and Welfare,' in J. R. W. Bhagwati, Jones, R. Mundell, J. Vanek, (eds), *Trade Balance and Payments and Growth. Papers in International Economics in Honor of Charles P. Kindleberger*. North Holland, Amsterdam.

—— and V. K. Ramaswami (February 1963), 'Domestic Distortions, Tariffs, and the Theory of the Optimum Subsidy,' *Journal of Political Economy*, 71(1): 44–50.

—— and T. N. Srinivasan, 'Trade and the Environment: Does Environmental Diversity Detract from the Case for Free Trade?' In *Fair Trade and Harmonization: Prerequisites for Free Trade?* edited by J. Bhagwati and R. Hudec. 159–224. MIT Press, 1996.

Bommer, R. and G. G. Schulze (1999), 'Environmental Improvement with Trade Liberalization,' *European Journal of Political Economy*, 15: 639–61.

Brander, J. and M. Taylor (1997a), 'International trade and open access renewable resources: The small open economy case,' *Canadian Journal of Economics*, 30(3): 526–52.

—— and M. Taylor (1997b), 'International trade between consumer and conservationist countries,' *Resource and Energy Economics*, 19: 267–97

Brown, M. G. Jr, (2000), 'Renewable Resource Management and Use without Markets,' *Journal of Economic Literature*.

Cesar, H. and A. de Zewe (1994), 'Issue Linkage and Issue Tie-in in Multilateral Negotiations,' *Mimeo*. Warwick University.

Chaudhuri Shubham and Alex Pfaff (March 1998), 'Does Indoor Air Quality Fall or Rise as Household Incomes Increase?' *Departmental Working Paper*, School of International and Public Affairs, Columbia University.

Chenery, H. B. (1960), 'Patterns of Industrial Growth,' *American Economic Review*, 50: 624–54.

Chichilnisky, G. (1994), 'North–south trade and the global environment,' *American Economic Review*, 84(4): 851–74

Cohen, J. S. and M. L. Weitzman (1975), 'A Marxian Model of Enclosures,' *Journal of Development Economics*, 1: 287–336.

Copeland, B. R. (1994), 'International Trade and the Environment: Policy Reform in a Polluted Small Open Economy,' *Journal of Environmental Economics and Management*, 26(1), 44–65

—— (1994), 'North–South Trade and the Environment,' *Quarterly Journal of Economics* 109(3): 755–87.

—— (1995) 'Trade and Transboundary Pollution,' *American Economic Review*, 85(4), 716–37.

—— (1997), 'The Trade-Induced Degradation Hypothesis,' *Resource and Energy Economics*, 19: 321–44.

—— (1999), 'Trade, spatial separation, and the environment,' *Journal of International Economics* 47: 137–68.

—— and (2004a), 'Trade, Growth and The Environment,' *Journal of Economic Literature*, 42(1): 7–71.

—— and M. S. Taylor (2004b), 'Trade, Tragedy and the Commons,' NBER Working Paper No 10836.

—— and (2003), *Trade and the Environment: Theory and Evidence*. Princeton University Press.

Cohen, J. S. and M. L. Weitzman (1975), 'A Marxian Model of Enclosures.' *Journal of Development Economics* (1): 287–336.

Coxhead, I. and S. Jayasuriya (2003), *The Open Economy and the Environment: Development, Trade and Resources in Asia*, Edward Elgar, Cheltenham, UK.

Daly, Herman (1997) 'Reconciling Internal and External Policies for Sustainable Development,' in Andrew Dragun, Kristen Jakobsson, (eds), *Sustainability and Global Environmental Policy: New Perspectives*, Edward Elgar, UK.

—— (1993), 'The Perils of Free Trade,' *Scientific American* 269: 24–9.

Dasgupta, P. (1993), '*An Inquiry into Well-Being and Destitution*.' Clarendon Press, Oxford.

—— Susmita and David Wheeler (November 1996), 'Citizen Complaints As Environmental Indicators: Evidence From China.' *PRDEI Working Paper*, The World Bank.

——, Ashoka Mody, Subhendu Roy, and David Wheeler (1995), 'Environmental Regulation and Development: A Cross-Country Empirical Analysis,' *World Bank, Policy Research Department Working Paper, No. 1448*, April.

De Meza, D. and J. Gould (1994), 'The Social Efficiency of Private Decisions to Enforce Property Rights,' *Journal of Political Economy* 100(3): 561–80.

Dean, J. M (2002), 'Testing the Impact of Trade Liberalization on the Environment: Theory and Evidence,' *Canadian Journal of Economics* 35.

Easterly, W. and R. Levine (2002), 'Tropics, Germs and Crops: How Endowments Influence Economic Development,' *NBER, Working Paper No. 9106*.

Echevarria, C. (1997), 'Changes in Sectoral Composition Associated with Economic Growth,' *International Economic Review*, 38(2): 431–52.

Ederington, J. (2001), 'International Coordination of Trade and Domestic Policies,' *American Economic Review*, 91(5), 1580–93.

—— and J. Minier (2003), 'Is environmental policy a secondary trade barrier? An empirical analysis,' *Canadian Journal of Economics* 36: 137–54.

——, A. Levinson, and J. Minier (2003), 'Footloose and Pollution-Free' NBER Working Paper 9718 (May).

Eliste, P. and Fredrikkson, P. G. (2002), 'Environmental Regulations, Transfers and Trade: Theory and Evidence,' *Journal of Environmental Economics and Management*, 43(2): 234–50.

Eskeland, G. S. and A. E. Harrison (2003), 'Moving to Greener Pastures? Multinationals and the pollution haven hypothesis,' *Journal of Development Economics* 70: 1–23.

Ferreira, S. (May 2004), 'Deforestation, Openness and Property Rights', *Land Economics* 80(2): 174–93.

Field, B. C. (1989), 'The evolution of property rights,' *Kyklos* 42, 319–45.

Frankel, J. A. and A. K. Rose (2005), 'Is Trade Good or Bad for the Environment? Sorting out the Causality,' *Review of Economics and Statistics* 87: 85–91.

Fredriksson, P. G. (1997), 'The political economy of pollution taxes in a small open economy,' *Journal of Environmental Economics and Management* 33(1), 44–58.

—— (1999), 'The Political Economy of Trade Liberalization and Environmental Policy,' *Southern Economic Journal*, 65(3), 1999: 513–25.

—— and Noel Gaston (2000), 'Environmental Governance in Federal Systems: The Effects of Capital Competition and Lobby Groups,' *Economic Inquiry* 38(3): 501–14.

——, J. A. List, and D. L. Millimet (2003), 'Bureaucratic corruption, environmental policy and inbound USFDI: theory and evidence' *Journal of Public Economics*, 87(7–8): 1407–30 (Aug.).

—— and R. Damania, and J. List (2003), 'Trade Liberalization, Corruption, and Environmental Policy Formation: Theory and Evidence,' *Journal of Environmental Economics and Management*, 46(3): 490–512.

Gale, L. R. and J. A. Mendez (1998), 'A note on the relationship between trade, growth, and the environment,' *International Review of Economics and Finance*, 7: 53–61.

Gordon, H. S. (1954), 'The Economic Theory of a Common Property Resource: The Fishery,' *Journal of Political Economy*, 63(2): 124–42.

Gray, W. B. and R. J. Shadbegian (2002), 'When do firms shift production across states to avoid environmental regulation?' NBER Working Paper 8705 (January).

Greenstone, M. (2002), 'The impacts of Environmental Regulations on Industrial Activity: Evidence from the 1970 and the 1977 Clean Air Act Amendments and the Census of Manufactures', *Journal of Political Economy*, 110: 1175–219.

Grossman, Gene M. and Alan B. Krueger (1993), 'Environmental Impacts of a North American Free Trade Agreement,' in Garber, Peter M., (ed.), *The Mexico–U.S. free trade agreement*, Cambridge and London: MIT Press, 13–56.

Gulati, Sumeet (2003), 'The Effect of Free Trade on Pollution Policy and Welfare,' *Food and Resource Economics Working Paper 2003–02*, University of British Columbia.

Hall, E. and C. I. Jones (1999), 'Why do some countries produce so much more output per worker than others?' *The Quarterly Journal of Economics* 114: 83–116 (February).

Hammitt, James K., Jin-Tan Liu, and Jin-Long Liu, 'Survival is a Luxury Good: The Increasing Value of a Statistical Life,' Presented at the NBER Summer Institute Workshop on Public Policy and the Environment, Cambridge, Ma, August 2000.

Harbaugh, W., A. Levinson, and D. Wilson (2002), 'Re-examining Empirical Evidence for an Environmental Kuznets Curve,' *Review of Economics and Statistics*, 84.

Hettige, H., R. E. B. Lucas, and D. Wheeler (1992), 'The Toxic Intensity of Industrial Production: Global Patterns, Trends and Trade Policy,' *American Economic Review Papers and Proceedings*, 82, 478–81.

——, P. Martin, M. Singh, and D. Wheeler (1995), 'IPPS: The Industrial Pollution Projection System,' *Policy Research Working Paper*, The World Bank, Washington DC.

Hokby, S. and T. Soderqvist (2003) 'Elasticities of Demand and Willingness to Pay for Environmental Services in Sweden,' *Environmental and Resource Economics*, 26: 361–83.

Hotte, L. (1997), 'Natural resource exploitation with costly enforcement of property rights,' *Working Paper 2697, CRDE*, University Montreal.

Hotte, L., N. Van Long, and H. Tian (2000), 'International trade with Endogenous Enforcement of Property Rights,' *Journal of Development Economics*, 62(1), 25–54.

Israel, Debra, and Arik Levinson (2002), 'Willingness to Pay for Environmental Quality: Testable Empirical Implications of the Growth and Environment Literature,' *Department of Economics Working Paper 02–09*, Georgetown University.

212

Jaffe, A., S. Peterson, P. Portney, and R. Stavins (1995), 'Environmental Regulation and the Competitiveness of U.S. Manufacturing: What Does the Evidence Tell Us?' *The Journal of Economic Literature*, 33: 132–63.

Kahn, M. E. (1997), 'Particulate Pollution Trends in the United States,' *Regional Science and Urban Economics* 27: 87–107.

—— (1995), 'Micro Evidence on the Environmental Kuznets Curve,' *Mimeo*. Columbia University (April).

Kalt, J. P. (1988), 'The Impact of Domestic Environmental Regulatory Policies on U.S. International Competitiveness, in A. M. Spence, and Heather A., Hazard, (eds), *International competitiveness*. Cambridge, Ma.: Harper Row, Ballinger: 221–62.

Karp, Larry, S. Sacheti, and J. Zhao (2001), 'Common Ground Between Free-Traders and Environmentalists,' *International Economic Review*, 42(3): 617–47 (August).

Keller, W. and Levinson, A. (2002), 'Pollution abatement costs and foreign direct investment inflows to US states,' *Review of Economics and Statistics* 84: 691–703.

Knack, Stephen, and Omar Azfar (2003), 'Trade Intensity, Country Size, and Corruption,' *Economics of Governance* 4(1): 1–18 (February).

Kongsamut, P., S. Rebelo, and D. Xie (2001), 'Beyond Balanced Growth,' *Review of Economic Studies*, 68(4): 869–82.

Kristom, B. and P. Riera (1996), 'Is the Income Elasticity of Environmental Improvements Less than One?' *Environmental and Resource Economics*, 7, 45–55.

Krueger, Anne (1974), 'The Political Economy of the Rent-Seeking Society,' *The American Economic Review*, 64, 291–303.

Kuznets, S. (1957), 'Quantitative Aspects of the Economic Growth of Nations II,' *Economic Development and Cultural Change*, Supplement to Volume V(4): 3–11.

Laitner, J. (2000), 'Structural Change and Economic Growth,' *Review of Economic Studies*, 67: 545–61.

Levinson, A. (1996), 'Environmental Regulations and Industry Location: International and Domestic Evidence,' in *Fair Trade and Harmonization: prerequisites for free trade*, J. N. Bhagwati and R. E. Hudec (eds), Cambridge, Ma: MIT Press.

—— (1999), 'State Taxes and Interstate Hazardous Waste Shipments,' *American Economic Review*, 89: 666–77.

—— and S. Taylor (2003), 'Trade and the Environment: Unmasking the Pollution Haven Effect,' *Mimeo* (July).

Lewer, Joshua J. and Hendrik Van den Berg (2003), 'How Large is International Trade's Effect on Economic Growth?' *Journal of Economic Surveys*, 17(3): 363–96.

Limão, N. (2002), 'Trade Policy, Cross-border Externalities and Lobbies: Do Linked Agreements Enforce More Cooperative Outcomes?' *UMD Center for International Economics WP 02–01*, University of Maryland at College Park.

Lipsey, R., and K. Lancaster (1956), 'The General Theory of Second Best,' *Review of Economic Studies*, 25, 11–32.

List, J. A., W. W. McHone, D. L. Millimet, and P. G. Fredriksson (2003), 'Effects of Environmental Regulations on Manufacturing plant births: evidence from a propensity score matching estimator,' *Review of Economics and Statistics*. 85(4): 944–52.

Long, N. V. (1994), 'On optimal enclosure and optimal timing of enclosure,' *Economic Record*, 70, 141–5.

213

López, R. (1994), 'The Environment as Factor of Production: The Effects of Economic Growth and Trade Liberalization,' *Journal of Environmental Economics and Management* 27(2), 163–84.

—— (1997), 'Environmental Externalities in Traditional Agriculture and the Impact of Trade Liberalization: The Case of Ghana,' *Journal of Development Economics* 53(1): 17–39.

—— (1998a), 'Where Development Can or Cannot Go: The Role of Poverty-Environment Linkages,' in B. Pleskovic and J. Stiglitz (eds), *Annual Bank Conference on Development Economics* 1997, The World Bank Press, Washington, DC.

—— (1998b), 'Agricultural Intensification, Common Property Resources and the Farm-Household,' *Environmental and Resource Economics*, 11: 443–58.

—— (1998c), 'The Tragedy of the Commons in Côte d'Ivoire Agriculture: Empirical Evidence and Implications for Evaluating Trade Policies,' *The World Bank Economic Review* 12(1): 105–31.

—— (2000), 'Trade Reform and Environmental Externalities in General Equilibrium: Analysis for an Archetype Poor Tropical Country,' *Environment and Development Economics* 5(4): 377–404.

—— and S. Mitra (2000), 'Corruption, Pollution and the Kuznets Environment Curve,' *Journal of Environmental Economics and Management*, 40(2), 137–50.

Low, P. and A. Yeates (1992), 'Do "dirty" Industries Migrate,' in P. Low, (ed.), *International Trade and the Environment*, World Bank discussion paper, No. 159: 89–104.

Lucas, D. Wheeler and H. Hettige, 'Economic Development, Environmental Regulation and the International Migration of Toxic Industrial Pollution: 1960–88, in P. Low, (ed.) *International Trade and the Environment*, World Bank Discussion Paper, No. 159.

McAusland, Carol (2002) 'Voting for Pollution Policy: The Importance of Income Inequality and Openness to Trade,' *Forthcoming Journal of International Economics*, University of California at Santa Barbara (August).

McCarthy, N., E. Sadoulet, A. de Janvry (2001), 'Common pool resource appropriation under costly cooperation,' *Journal of Environmental Economics and Management*, vol. 43, no. 3, 297–309.

McGuire, Martin C. (1982), 'Regulation, Factor Rewards and International Trade,' *Journal of Public Economics*, XVII: 335–54.

McRae, James J. (1978), 'Optimal and competitive use of replenishable natural resources by open economies', *Journal of International Economics*, 8 (1): 29–54 (February).

Magnani, E. (2000), 'The Environmental Kuznets Curve, Environmental Protection Policy and Income Distribution,' *Ecological Economics*, 32(3): 431–43.

Mani, M. and D. Wheeler (1997), 'In search of pollution havens?: dirty industry migration in the world economy,' World Bank Working Paper No. 16 (April).

Margolis, M. and J. Shogren (2002), 'Unprotected Resources and Voracious World Markets,' *Discussion Paper, Resources for the Future*, Washington DC.

Markusen, James, Edward Morey, Nancy Olewiler, (1995), 'Competition in Regional Environment Policies When Plant Locations Are Endogenous,' *Journal of Public Economics* 56(1), 55–77.

Nader, Ralph (ed.), William Greider, Margaret Atwood, David Philips, and Pat Choate (1993), *The Case Against Free Trade: Gatt, Nafta and the Globalization of Corporate Power*. Earth Island Press.

214

Oates, W. E. and R. M. Schwab, (1988), 'Economic Competition Among Jurisdictions: Efficiency Enhancing or Distortion Inducing?' *Journal of Public Economics*, 35, 333–54.

Ostrom, E. (1990), *Governing the commons: The evolution of institutions for collective action.* Cambridge University Press.

—— (2000), 'Collective Action and the Evolution of Social Norms,' *Journal of Economic Perspectives*, vol. 14, No. 3, 137–58.

Otsuki, Tsunehiro and John S. Wilson (2001), 'Global Trade and Food Safety: Winners and Losers in a Fragmented System,' *Policy Research Working Paper: 2689* (October). The World Bank, Washington DC, http://econ.worldbank.org/files/2469_wps2689.pdf.

Pargal, S. and M. Mani, (2000), 'Citizen Activism, Environmental Regulation, and the Location of Industrial Plants: Evidence from India,' *Economic Development and Cultural Change*, 48(4), 829–46.

—— and D. Wheeler, (1996), 'Informal Regulation of Industrial Pollution in Developing Countries: Evidence from Indonesia,' *Journal of Political Economy*, 104(6), (December.).

Pearce, D. and Palmer, C. (2001), 'Public and Private Spending for Environmental Protection: A Cross-Country Policy Analysis,' *Fiscal Studies*, 22: 403–56.

Pethig, Ruediger (1976), 'Pollution, Welfare and Environmental Policy in the theory of comparative advantage,' *Journal of Environmental Economics and Management*, II, 160–9.

Porter, M. E. (1991), 'America's Green Strategy,' Scientific American: 168 (April).

Rauscher, Michael (1995), 'Environmental Regulation and the Location of Polluting Industries,' *International Tax and Public Finance* 2(2): 229–44.

Rodriguez, F. and D. Rodrik (2001), 'Trade policy and economic growth: a skeptic's guide to the cross-national evidence,' in B. S. Bernanke, and K. Rogoff, (eds), *NBER Macroeconomics Annual 2000.* MIT Press, Cambridge. http://www.ksg.harvard.edu/rodrik/skepti1299.pdd.

Runge, C. Ford, 'Freer trade, protected environment: Balancing trade liberalization and environmental interests', Council on Foreign Relations Press, New York, 1994.

Salop, Steven and David Scheffman (1983), 'Raising Rivals' Costs,' *American Economic Review*, Papers and Proceedings, 267–71.

Santhakumar, V. (2003), 'Citizens' actions for protecting the environment in developing countries: an economic analysis of the outcome with empirical cases from India,' *Environment and Development Economics*, 8: 505–28.

Schleich, Joaquim (1999), 'Environmental Quality with Endogenous Domestic Trade Policies,' *European Journal of Political Economy*, 15(1): 53–71.

Smarzynska, B. K. and Shang-Jin Wei (2001), 'Pollution Havens and Foreign Direct Investment: Dirty Secret or Popular Myth?' *Policy Research Working Paper: 2673*, (September). The World Bank, Washington DC, http://econ.worldbank.org/files/2398_wps2673.pdf.

Stern, D. I. (1998), 'Progress on the environmental Kuznets curve?' *Environment and Development Economics*, 3: 173–96.

—— and Common, Michael S. (2001), 'Is There an Environmental Kuznets Curve for Sulfur?,' *Journal of Environmental Economics and Management*, 41(2): 162–78.

Strutt, Anna and Anderson, Kym (2000), 'Will Trade Liberalization Harm the Environment? The Case of Indonesia to 2020,' *Environmental and Resource Economics*, 17(3): 203–32.

215

Suranovic, S. (2002), 'International Labour and Environmental Standards Agreements: Is This Fair Trade?' *The World Economy*, 25(2): 231–45 (February).

Swanson Timothy M. (1994), 'The Economics of Extinction Revisited and Revised: A Generalised Framework for the Analysis of the Problems of Endangered Species and Biodiversity Losses,' *Oxford Economic Papers* 46: 800–21.

Tobey, J. A. (1990), 'The effects of domestic environmental policies on patterns of world trade: An empirical test,' *Kyklos*, 43: 191–209.

Torrez, J. (2002), 'The Effect of Openness on Corruption,' *Journal of International Trade & Economic Development*, 11(4): 387–403.

Treisman, Daniel (2000), 'The Causes of Corruption: A Cross-National Study,' *Journal of Public Economics*, 76(3): 399–457.

Unteroberdoerster (2003), 'Trade Policy and Environmental Regulation in the Asia-Pacific: A Simulation,' *The World Economy*, 26(1): 73–95.

Vogel, D. (1995), *Trading Up: Consumer and Environmental Regulation in the Global Economy*, Cambridge, Harvard University Press.

—— (2000), 'Environmental Regulation and Economic Integration,' *Journal of International Economic Law*: 265–79.

Vukina, T., J. C. Beghin, and E. G. Solakoglu (1999), 'Transition to Markets and the Environment: Effects of the Change in the Composition of Manufacturing Output,' *Environment and Development Economics*, 4: 582–98.

Wei, Shang-jin (2000), 'Natural Openness and Good Government,' World Bank Policy Research Working Paper 2411 and NBER Working Paper 7765.

Wheeler, D. (2001), 'Racing to the Bottom? Foreign Investment and Air Pollution in Developing Countries,' *Policy Research Working Paper: 2524* (January). The World Bank, Washington DC., http://econ.worldbank.org/files/1340_wps2524.pdf.

Wilson, J. S. and Tsunehiro Otsuki (2003a), 'Food Safety and Trade: Winners and Losers in a Non-harmonized World,' *Journal of Economic Integration*. 18(2): 266–87, (June).

—— T. Otsuki and B. Majumdsar (2003b), 'Balancing food safety and risk: do drug residue limits affect international trade in beef?' *Journal of International Trade and Economic Development*, 12(4): 377–402.

World Bank (1992), *World Development Report 1992: Development and the Environment*, Washington DC.

Yanikkaya, Halit (2003), 'Trade Openness and Economic Growth: A Cross-Country Empirical Investigation,' *Journal of Development Economics* 72: 57–89.

Yu, Zhihao (2000), 'Environmental Protection and Free Trade: Direct and Indirect Competition for Political Influence,' Centre for Globalisation and Labour Markets Research Paper 2000/3.

7

Environmental Policy Instruments and Institutions in Developing Countries

E. Somanathan and Thomas Sterner

Introduction[1]

Environmental economics in the industrialized countries has developed in the mold of traditional public economics which assumes a policymaker maximizing a social welfare function, most frequently not assumed to satisfy any properties except the Pareto principle. Analysis was, therefore, particularly in the earlier studies, largely confined to the design of policies to achieve Pareto-efficiency in the presence of market failures. In the last decade or two, when policies have started to be implemented on a large scale, attention has shifted to implementation efficiency, distributional consequences and political economy considerations concerning incentives for compliance, monitoring and enforcement. There is a growing literature on citizen enforcement, the use of liability, labeling and information, design for environment, and so forth. Even with these new and exciting extensions, most of this body of work tends to presume reasonably well-functioning markets and underlying economic governance systems, which may be problematic for many developing countries. A large share of research has concentrated on applications to industrial pollutants with the polluters assumed to be firms. There are other applications, of course, which have been analyzed in a developed country context, for example, vehicular pollution and solid waste management. The practice of environmental policy is generally perceived as having to some extent moved from physical and technological regulation to market-based instruments and to more sophisticated instruments such as liability and information disclosure requirements.[2]

[1] Comments from Carl Bauer and Mike Toman are gratefully acknowledged. Financial support from the Swedish International Development Cooperation Agency, Sida, is gratefully acknowledged.
[2] The literature is very large but much of it is summarized in the textbooks that have formed successive generations of students in this area: Baumol and Oates (1988), Tietenberg (1992),

In the developing countries, environmental economics, per se, is a newer and weaker discipline but its subject matter is clearly central to the concerns of most of these countries. We believe the character and mix of instruments to be chosen is quite a complex design issue that depends crucially on the type of issue and economy we are dealing with. It is not sufficient to characterize instruments as 'regulatory,' 'legal' or 'economic.' All instruments are based on laws and all imply some form of regulation that has economic consequences. We should thus adapt to the particular circumstances at hand with as wide a range of policy instruments as is needed. In practice, in developing countries, this will include the design or restructuring of a broad set of institutions including property rights, legal systems, accountability and management of the public sector, information provision systems and so forth. This is all the more important since the scope of what constitutes environmental policy is even wider in developing countries than in the developed world. The reason for this is simple: many environmental problems that have been solved in the developed world still loom large in poor countries (see Ch. 1 by Barbier in this volume). For example, waterborne diseases associated with bacterial contamination of water supplies and lack of sanitation are leading causes of death in poor countries while negligible in rich ones. Another leading cause of mortality in very low-income countries is respiratory disease associated with indoor air pollution resulting from the use of solid fuels such as wood for cooking. These two problems (water and sanitation, and indoor air pollution) are high up on the list of causes of mortality in low-income countries, together accounting for 9 percent of the 833 million disability-adjusted life-years lost in high mortality developing countries every year, not far behind the single largest risk factor, being underweight which accounts for 15 percent (World Health Organisation, 2002).[3]

Since agriculture, forestry, and fisheries constitute a much larger part of the economy in poor countries and the poor are disproportionately concentrated in these sectors, problems of resource depletion such as groundwater scarcity, inappropriate allocation of surface water, soil erosion and deforestation are all very important. In addition to having environmental problems from industry and transport, developing countries have a larger set of problems related to natural resource management and basic health.

Poor people have virtually no capital except the common property resources of the most immediate ecosystems. These provide fuel, fresh water, collection of food, firewood, construction material, material for handicraft, medicinal plants, fodder, and so on, and thus represent a much larger proportion of the asset portfolio for a poor person than the corresponding ecosystem resources do for rich people. This has serious implications for policy and it makes enclosure or privatization very problematic from a distributional and welfare

Hanley, Shogren and White (1997), and Kolstad (2000). Stavins (2001) provides a good overview of the current implementation, in industrialized countries, of market-based policy instruments.

[3] See also the Krupnick and Markandya Chapters 11 and 10 in this volume.

viewpoint—even in those cases where such enclosure does promote technical efficiency. The large number of very poor people in poor countries implies that distributional issues such as the burden of environmental problems and abatement costs become even more important than in richer countries. The fact that the distribution of costs is decisive for the political feasibility of instruments, and that it varies strongly between instruments, underlines the importance of careful instrument design. The same is true of risk management: Those who live in poverty are very risk averse and need savings or insurance to meet variations in income or in expenses. However the institutions that provide insurance and savings to the poor are often highly insufficient. This can be an important factor leading to unsustainable behavior and therefore it is important to help build such institutions as will be discussed in section 2.3 on p. 233.

Note that distributional and efficiency effects cannot be conveniently separated: they are intimately intertwined. One reason for this is an instrument that might have looked 'efficient' on the drawing board will not be efficient if its social acceptability and feasibility are low due to unacceptable distributional consequences. If, for instance, a tax implies a burden on powerful firms, they are likely to resist it and resort to lobbying against it. If the result is a much lower tax than what would have been optimal, then abatement (or resource conservation) will also be modest. Sterner (2003) shows how refunded emission payments may split the industry lobby (since a large share of firms actually gains more from the refunds than they pay in taxes). This may make it possible to implement a considerably higher fee level leading to more abatement than under a (low) tax.

Industrial, vehicular, and agricultural pollution, while increasing rapidly with industrialization, and in absolute terms generally far worse in developing than in developed countries, may still be of less importance to the majority of people in poor countries than the problems mentioned above. Over-simplifying in order to classify, it could be said that the resource depletion and allocation problems described are associated with undefined property rights, while biological contamination of water and indoor air pollution are perhaps best seen as public health issues, that is, the provision of public goods. Other air and water pollution may be analyzed as standard issues of environmental regulation although particular attention must be focused on the issues of information and monitoring and the distribution of costs and benefits.

Analysis of Some Factors Influencing Instrument Choice in Developing Countries

Most developing countries were colonized and many devastated by war and ethnic conflicts that have left geographically, politically, socially, and ethnically heterogeneous and often conflicting norms, traditions, and legal systems.

We know that a given resource, forest, lake, mangrove, coral reef, or other, could potentially be managed in a number of different ways as long as these have evolved to suit the ecology and culture. When, however, multiple principles of management and multiple legal principles are overlaid, the result is often that short-sighted rapacious interests get the upper hand over caution and sustainability.

A vital aspect of the inability of public institutions in many developing countries is the lack of a good reliable and functioning public body. This is often discussed in terms of corruption and it may be true that poverty can sometimes be a fertile ground for corruption, but we believe the most important aspects are others. One of these is the excessive concentration of power to central government. In many of the countries we have in mind, the power of local municipalities and courts is very small and virtually all power is concentrated in the hands of the state—and in fact of a small number of politicians such as the president and/or prime minister.[4] This excessive centralization is inefficient, deficient in democracy and conducive of corruption. It usually does not favor sustainable management of ecosystems.

The Provision of Public Goods

One of the effects of the deficiencies in governance structures that characterize many poor countries is an inability to provide public goods. It is even possible that it is the very difficulty in providing reasonable public goods that is the core element that makes economic development so slow. Without access to reliable electricity, water, roads, and other physical infrastructure, production is inevitably hampered. Without good public health and education, many of those born gifted but poor are not given the preconditions to develop their productive skills. Without an impartial and independent judiciary and other institutions that guarantee security and prospects for private property there will be few investments. To repeat: most environmental and resource issues are largely 'public', which implies that there tends to be insufficient provision.

Consider the issue of domestic water supply. More than a quarter of the population in South and South East Asia (including China) as well as some South American countries lack access to safe drinking water (Gleick, 1998). In large parts of Sub-Saharan Africa and some Asian countries, more than three-quarters of the population lacks access. The picture with respect to sanitation is worse.

One might suspect that inadequate domestic water supplies may be in part due to small total water supplies. In fact, this is generally not the case. In most developing countries, agricultural use is at least four times domestic and

---

[4] The IMF's Government Finance Statistics show that the size of local government as a proportion of all government, measured in terms of expenditures or revenues increases with income and democracy.

industrial use combined, so that relatively small additional transfers for domestic consumption would have little impact on agriculture (Rosegrant and Binswanger, 1994). In addition, most of the water withdrawn for domestic consumption is returned to rivers (except in coastal cities) and available for agricultural use.[5]

Another questionable hypothesis is that since the poor simply do not have the willingness-to-pay for clean water and sanitation, they do not get it. While low willingness-to-pay is part of the reason for the lack of provision, it is often misleading. The poor sometimes pay exorbitant prices for the water they buy from private vendors (Lee, 1997). This strongly suggests that municipal authorities have simply failed to provide piped safe water despite existing demand for it. This is a serious failure of governance.

Municipal water provision in the worst-affected countries is poor even for those who get it and efficiency is low. For example, 24-hour piped water from the municipality is virtually unknown in India. Pipes leak, leading to large water losses and the loss of pressure when water is not present makes contamination by sewage possible. Attempts to augment supplies by pumping more water may not result in any more reaching consumers unless pipes are monitored and repaired (Lee, 1997). The number of municipal water employees per thousand connections may be an order of magnitude higher than in countries that provide reliable safe piped water.[6]

In this area, a number of different policies and policy instruments are required. On the one hand, the systems for local supply and distribution of water are classical public goods.[7] On the other hand, as suggested above, redefining property rights in agricultural and industrial water may be important to elicit increased supply for domestic water supplies by encouraging efficiency in other sectors and enabling water transfers from them. If we take the second point first, several countries have in recent years enacted new water laws that may be fundamental in facilitating these developments. The new South African water law from 1998 focuses on providing access to the basic levels of service required to ensure health for all South Africans. At the same time, it also seeks to implement an ecosystem approach to water management. It guarantees in-stream flow necessities (minimum flow levels) and includes a campaign against invasive tree species. One of the instruments is a licensing process to limit the planting of trees.

One factor that is very important in urban water supply is the appropriate design of water tariffs. In some countries, increasing block tariffs have been used to 'guarantee' that the poor get access to affordable water. Often the tariffs for the higher blocks, and the definitions of the blocks, are such that the authority is left

---

[5] For the U.S., the figures are 83% for domestic withdrawals and 84% for industrial withdrawals (Briscoe, 1997).

[6] Personal communication from Vivek Srivastava, UN Water and Sanitation Program-South Asia.

[7] See also the chapter by Dinar in this volume concerning the economics of water issues.

Box 7.1 WATER PROVISION FOR THE POOR WITH EFFICIENT TARIFFS

Chile is, as mentioned, a country that has followed neo-liberal policies quite strictly. Water is partly privatized and partly run by autonomous public bodies. When new, more efficient, tariff structures were enacted in the early 1990s, the rate increase was dramatic for small consumers, who previously had heavily subsidized rates. To address this, a system of subsidies was created for consumers unable to pay. To achieve transparency in public affairs, this subsidy is not an automatic 'lifeline' tariff but a direct subsidy. To receive the subsidy, consumers must file a written application to the municipality proving their incapacity to pay. One condition is that the cost of 20 m^3 is more than 5% of the household's income. In 1995, just over 15% of customers received subsidies. This system might be efficient and sensitive to poverty concerns while preserving transparency in the public use of money. However, the system obviously incurs administrative costs and may be humiliating for those who are forced to apply for the subsidy.

---

with too little revenue to provide connections to everybody. In such situations, it is invariably the poor who are left out. As already mentioned, the poor often pay many times the official price of water when they have to buy it from vendors because they are still waiting for connections to the public system. Thus rhetorically 'pro-poor' policies actually end up hurting the poor. For example, Foster, Pattanayak and Prokopy (2003) find that 75 percent of the water subsidy completely fails to reach the poor in two South Asian cities, Bangalore and Kathmandu.

Higher tariffs for at least some customers are clearly needed to generate the necessary revenues to cover costs in order to improve the situation. This could improve public service without adverse impacts on welfare or perverse distributional consequences, see Box 7.1 for one, probably rather rare example where this has been at least partly successful. The political difficulty is that consumers (usually also voters) used to poor service are unwilling to pay higher charges unless service improves. Contingent valuation studies of willingness-to-pay have shown that it is highly sensitive to reliability of service (World Bank Water Demand Research Team, 1993). Ways to provide an assurance of good service are politically necessary if tariffs are to be raised.

Professionalization of the water authority and appropriate incentives for management are needed to check theft and improve efficiency. Privatization is one way of achieving this, but unless credible mechanisms for monitoring quality of service and accountability are put in place, it is risky and the public is unlikely to favor it.[8] There is a considerable risk of creating private monopolies which have no incentive to act responsibly. This requires a credible and

---

[8] McKenzie and Ray (2004) provide a brief review of studies evaluating the experience with privatization of urban water supply in several developing countries. Privatization improved access of the poor in all cases but raised water tariffs in some cases. Apart from one (spectacular) failure, the welfare of the poor appears to have improved in all cases.

independent regulator and the gradual build-up of institutions and even of culture for compliance and impartial civil service. See for instance Fischbeck and Farrow (2001) for a review of regulatory issues, Raymond (2003) on using private rights for the management of public resources and Makhaya (2001) or Ariyo and Jerome (1999) for reviews of issues concerning regulation and private/public rights in developing countries. Given the large up-front costs in repairing systems, it is not clear that private investment will always be forthcoming, even if invited. Whether reform is carried out within the public sector or not, it is clear that improvements in accountability to consumers and transparency are needed. The literature on utility management, pricing, public–private partnerships, privatization, and so forth is too voluminous to be referenced here, but Savas (2000) gives a first overview.

Property Rights Structures

Property rights are not cast in stone but continuously evolving: They started with land and have gradually been extended to more complicated assets such as water, minerals, and various natural resources and are today being extended to environmental resources such as radio frequencies, fish, genetic information, biodiversity, and clean air. The development of rights over time is often perceived as a more or less linear progression from public or common property to private property. This process is often referred to as 'enclosure of the commons.' As shown by Cole (2002), this may be quite misleading. Even in the U.S.A., various forms of public ownership account for 42 percent of all land. Cole cites authors who show that when it comes to U.S. water laws, the direction of transfer is rather in the opposite direction, from private to common property.

It is striking to see how big the variations between countries are, in the various bundles of rights applicable to land property. One example is provided by rights to water and subterranean resources: Mexico follows Spanish legal traditions and such rights are retained by the state while in the U.S., government has less power vis-à-vis individual landowners[9] and mining rights are normally part of land rights, creating greater incentives for mining. Access to land is another example. In the U.S., trespassing is highly illegal and asocial, whereas in Sweden it is a right not only to walk but even to camp and pick berries on other people's forest lands. In many developing countries, harvested fields are similarly used as a common property resource for grazing to the benefit of the poorer segments who have no private land.

The countries that have been colonized often have layers of incompatible legal systems with different perceptions and definitions of property rights.[10] In

[9] Furthermore the U.S. appears to place somewhat greater emphasis on 'prior appropriation' rights—that is the right of the first (productive) user: 'First come first served.'

[10] For instance, many countries in Africa have gone straight from a pre-feudal collective ownership to various forms of foreign dominance and state ownership.

many developing countries, common or communal property (with or without private user rights) is particularly important. In northern Ethiopia, the *rist* tenure system has predominated. Traditionally, everyone in a village had a right to land to support his or her family. Those who left the village would temporarily lose their rights but could reclaim them. Even distant descendants who can prove their lineage to village elders can return to claim land. Because of this and because of variations in family size making the average holding per person uneven, there is a tradition of periodic land reallocation. Such reallocations appear to be fairly common in many African countries and they do solve the problem of combining equity with hereditary rights as perceived. However they are completely alien to the modern notion of individual property rights and will generally not provide incentives for productive investments.

It may be a surprise to some, but African systems of land tenure with reallocation do not necessarily have a negative influence on productivity—at least not in traditional societies (Place and Hazell, 1993; Migot-Adholla et al., 1991). In a modern context, frequent reallocations do however clearly create a lack of tenure security. Now that technology and investments have become so important in financing modern agriculture and increasing productivity, the absence of tenure security and thus of investment incentives has had a significant effect on economic growth (Alemu, 1999). Peasant associations are ensnared in a seemingly impossible trap because they are responsible for conflicting tasks, namely, managing the common pool resources of the village and allocating 'individual' land lots. Difficulties are compounded by increasing population and demobilized soldiers returning so the village association often uses common pool resources, which thus effectively become privatized (Kebede, 2001).

The enclosure of the commons was a political struggle that lasted for centuries in England and was sometimes a fierce process. Today, similar struggles still take place all over the world—especially in poor countries—and the distribution of land between kinds of property has significant importance not only for the ecosystems as such but also for the distribution of wealth and welfare in society. A study of 75 villages in India found that 30–50 percent of common pool resource areas had been lost between 1950 and 1982 (Jodha, 1992).

Although a general trend toward enclosure seems to be apparent, common property is not necessarily an inferior kind of property. In some respects, a well-designed, well-functioning common pool resource is like private property (Ostrom and Schlager, 1996; Murty, 1994). Notably, it does build on the exclusion of outsiders thereby at least creating some of the necessary preconditions to avoid 'overgrazing.' In some ecological and social contexts (when the costs of protecting private property are high or when the yields are low and very variable), a common pool resource may simply have lower transaction and other costs and thus be more efficient than private property. If well-adjusted and flexible mechanisms to deal with resource allocation decisions continue to be developed, then common pool resources may continue to play an important role in the future.

When concepts of property rights clash—particularly when modern codified concepts take over from the more informal, culturally rooted, usufruct systems—the result can be an uncertainty that leads to a wasteful abuse of resources and, in many cases, to solutions that are perceived as unfair by the original users. For example, in the traditional island society of Mafia (close to Zanzibar), ownership rights are defined not to land (the so-called 'coral rag,' because it has low productivity) but to fishing sites and to coconut trees, which are valuable and belong to whomever planted them. When hotels want to buy 'land,' this implicitly includes a whole package of rights which covers exclusive rights to the land (including the beach down to the seafront) as well as water rights, vegetation and so forth. This builds on a generic international concept of property that is taken for granted by the international investor but poorly understood by locals. Negotiations tend to be uneven; hotel owners often have been successful in securing 'titles' that local residents do not understand or respect.

Although government must play a vital role as an ultimate guarantee of property rights per se, it has often failed abysmally when acting as a direct owner and manager of natural resources. This can be explained by many factors: As discussed in the previous section, the state is often rather inadequate at providing even the public goods for which it really does have a central role. When it comes to natural resources such as oil, minerals or forests, the arguments for state provision are not, in general, strong since these are activities that very well can be provided by the private sector and the role of the state is generally to control and regulate. The policymaker and civil servants will generally not have the right incentives to manage the resources in a 'welfare maximizing' fashion. In fact one might say that it would be naive to expect them to behave in such a way. The problems are compounded by poverty, poor training and other factors. In practice, matters are made much worse by the fact that many nationalizations, for instance, of forests, have been swift, affected enormous areas and failed to respect local customary rights. They were usually carried out with very limited budgets and administrative capacity to manage the resources taken over. The consequences usually are harsh, as in the central hills of Nepal, where nationalizing the forests in 1957 quickly led to deforestation because villagers no longer perceived themselves as the owners or beneficiaries of the forests.

One problem with state involvement is that the feedback mechanisms by which the people affected by poor management can influence their governments have often proved to be inadequate at national and regional scales. This suggests that decentralization of resource management to the appropriate scales may help. We discuss two examples below.

225

EXAMPLE I—SURFACE IRRIGATION

It is difficult to empirically identify the impact of decentralization since there are usually many confounding correlates. For example, Wade (1995) has argued that the superior performance of East versus South Asian irrigation systems could be due to the fact that South Asian topography favored large-scale centralized systems while ecological conditions favored decentralization in Taiwan, Korea, and Japan.

Even in large South Asian systems, however, management of the smaller field channels is left to the farmers. Because of seepage losses, farmers close to the head of a canal in a water-scarce region will often have a lower marginal value for water than those near the tail because they get more water. Monitoring and policing costs may deter farmers in such situations from actually making investments to reduce losses so that they can trade in surface water. The state can play a facilitating role in such situations by passing enabling legislation allowing water users' associations to be formed that define tradable water rights and monitor and enforce them. It is important to ensure that the legislation makes the formation and functioning of the associations consensual as far as possible, otherwise, it could lead to expropriation of de facto rights, with adverse effects on political feasibility, legitimacy, equity and transactions costs.

In Chile, legislation passed in 1981 made water rights strictly private and separate from land rights. An important factor in making the Chilean program acceptable was that rights were based on past use, thus avoiding expropriation of de facto rights. In those parts of the country where water is scarce, there has been considerable trading (Thobani, 1997; Easter, Rosegrant, and Dinar, 1999). The Chilean case with its extreme focus on neo-liberal principles has been hotly debated across the world as a model, and several other countries have passed, or considered, similar legislation. For instance, the Mexican water law introduced more limited tradable water rights in 1992. According to Bauer (2004), the Chilean model has been very successful in some respects: the legal security of private rights has led to considerable private investment in water use both in agriculture and other sectors, and there has been a certain amount of reallocation in water use from less to more productive sectors. On the other hand, the model has failed to incorporate broader environmental and social aspects in an overall river basin management. It has also failed to give advantages to the poorer segments of farmers and other users.

Market creation at the lowest level of canal irrigation systems may lead to demand for further property right definitions in canal systems, since the formation of associations can lead to trade between associations, with larger and larger federations and more trade occurring over time. The resulting rise in the value of water can act as a spur to investment, resulting in reduced losses from seepage, waterlogging, and salinization.

A bottom-up consensual approach is needed to ensure that no one is expropriated. This makes for political feasibility and makes it less likely that

---

Box 7.2 PROPERTY RIGHTS AND COMPENSATION IN WATERSHED
MANAGEMENT

Watershed management is very important both for biodiversity conservation and poverty
alleviation. The city of Chandigarh 15km downstream from a village Sukhomajri in
Haryana, N. India suffered siltation of a lake on which it depended and wanted to get villagers to reforest in order to protect the hillsides. In return, the town financed the building
of a series of small water retention dams which were useful for irrigation, particularly for
the closest farmers. These farmers were prepared to collaborate by keeping their grazing
animals off the hillside slopes. But other farmers gained little or nothing and were thus not
prepared to forgo fodder on the hillsides. Instead they demanded some share in benefits
of the dams and thus pipes were laid to all the other farms. This however did nothing for
the landless and to entice them to cooperate, a sharing mechanism was devised. First, all
citizens were given tradable vouchers for their share in water. However, the amount of
water was unknown at the beginning of the year and hence the exact value of each share
was unknown which complicated transactions considerably. A revision of the instrument
led to a price type system: All irrigators had to pay for the water they withdraw and the
proceeds are shared equally in the village which is an example of a Refunded Emission
Payment, a market-based instrument that harnesses the efficiency of the market and still
addresses the distribution of costs and assets, see further Sterner (2003).

---

newly created monopoly power will worsen the allocation. In addition, efficient
allocation at lower levels makes it much easier to reallocate water at higher levels, since valuations of agents at the lower levels have been equalized. This is
very important for equity. If water trades between groups are permitted before
trades or other mechanisms have equalized valuations within groups, then
users with less water and high valuations within a group may lose as more
powerful users within their group sell water to other groups.[11]

In larger canal systems, such as those of South Asia, management has typically been bureaucratic, with a portion of the rents being seized by state politicians and bureaucrats (Wade, 1982). Enabling legislation and success at the
lowest (field channel) level could create demand for reform at higher levels. It
is important to note that salability is important for reasons above and beyond
the usual efficiency arguments. Lack of salability provides additional incentives to lobby to re-define property rights in one's favor. This seems to happen
frequently in water disputes, the changes in water allocation on the Indus river
in the 1990s between the provinces of Punjab and Sindh in Pakistan being a
case in point.

Institutionalizing mechanisms for involving the different claimants in the
formation of legislation that defines property rights appears to be the due

---

[11] Marketability of water and forest resources is frequently opposed by advocates for the
poor or the environment since the impetus for it often comes from powerful well-endowed
groups interested in defining new rights in their favor and capturing the gains from the rise in
asset values that follows. If the rights of the poor were protected, they could gain from making
the resource salable.

process that most likely ensures that the resulting rights will be implemented successfully without non-compliance and lobbying for redefinition generating uncertainty that leads to continued rent dissipation. Most developing country governments' activities are conspicuously lacking in transparency and the drafting of legislation is no exception. While the processes suggested above may be welfare-improving for most farmers, they may eventually cut into the rents of government officials. Foreign aid can be used to induce governments to overcome resistance from within themselves, if such aid is appropriately tied. This process is clearly already at work. However, donors are often not sufficiently sensitive to the need for public consultations in the drafting of reform legislation. Typically, conditionality is applied to the content of legislation, and imperfectly so. Bureaucracies have been quite effective at undermining devolution (Lele, 2000). It would be less politically sensitive to tie it (i.e. is, aid) to the process and probably more effective if there were an insistence on public consultation and incorporation of the consensus view among stakeholders.

EXAMPLE II—FOREST MANAGEMENT

As mentioned earlier, nationalization of forests in Nepal (and elsewhere) led to drastic deforestation. During the past couple of decades, forest management has reverted back to village communities, and reforestation has been fairly rapid. It is natural to ascribe this entirely to the change in regime. Disentangling the consequences of decentralization from those of other variables is, however, difficult. Somanathan, Prabhakar and Mehta's (2005) study of the Van Panchayat (Forest Council) system for community management of village forests in the Indian central Himalayas uses geographic data to do this. They compare its performance relative to state management of neighboring forests. They find that while the village council forests had the same or higher crown cover (an indicator for forest stocks), they cost less than one-tenth as much to administer as the state forests. This suggests that while decentralized management may not improve the condition of forests, it can lead to substantial savings. It needs to be kept in mind that the system has many drawbacks. The rules do create some disincentives for villagers to invest in their forests. If these were removed, conservation might improve. It is also possible that even though village forests have crown cover that is not much higher than state forests, they might be contributing more by way of forest products like fuel and fodder due to more efficient and coordinated extraction.

Public Information and Monitoring

In the last decade, the provision and handling of public information has become a new and very powerful factor that has led to a whole new wave of policy instruments (information disclosure, labeling, certification, voluntary agreements, etc). The main common driving force behind these is the dramatic fall in the price of information gathering, processing, dissemination and even interpretation. It is reasonable to say that this process has not gotten as far in the poorer countries where wide segments of the population lack electricity not to mention computers and Internet. However, it seems that this is only a small delay and that information is indeed finding new ways to reach even less privileged recipients.

Access to appropriate information is a vital issue for the successful implementation of all policies. This includes technical and market information for local agents in the economy and, for both agents and regulators, it is important to have adequate monitoring of technology and transactions in the market. It is often asserted that costs of monitoring will be prohibitive in a developing country but we believe this argument needs to be dissected carefully. It is not acceptable to conjure up a picture of the vastness of pollution issues in say India and then say that the Pollution Control Boards are so weak and that one underpaid inspector has to deal with many hundreds of polluting firms. The reason is that if pollution problems are vast—so is the manpower supply that would potentially act as inspectors. Poverty might certainly be an aspect but then salaries are also low so poverty cannot be an explanation for the failure to supply inspection labour—rather we are speaking of the general failure to supply public goods that was the subject of the previous section. There might however, also, be a lack of sophisticated monitoring equipment, technology, and skilled manpower.

It is also important to see that there is a feedback from knowledge to preferences and consequently public demands for action on environmental issues. This leads to more environmental monitoring, that generates more environmental data and further raises public awareness of environmental issues. These feedbacks clearly operate but it is, of course, very difficult to measure them. It would be unwise, in policy formulation, to ignore them for this reason.

A very important problem for which the issue of information transmission is crucial is indoor air pollution. Such pollution is rather special because the affected are, at least partly, themselves responsible for the pollution. Therefore, it is closer to a public health problem akin to cigarette smoking than one of externalities, the traditional domain of environmental economics. This is not to say that externalities are absent. In a recent study in rural India, concentrations of respirable particulate matter in households were high (Mehta and Smith, 2002).[12] Even those who cook with gas (and hence produce no PM themselves) had approximately double the mean outdoor level for U.S. cities, for example. This suggests that the external effects of neighbors' cooking with solid fuels are not negligible. Secondly, there are intra-household externalities. Women and small children are more exposed than others in the household since they spend more

---

[12] The results for Kenya and other African countries are similar, see for instance Ezzati and Kammen (2002) who show that there are large knowledge gaps in this field despite its large significance for the health of almost half the global population.

time close to the cooking fire so that the costs of cooking with solid fuels are not uniformly distributed within the household while its benefits are. Historically, indoor air pollution disappeared as populations grew richer and were able to afford better stoves or fuels. These shifts were due to the desire to avoid the nuisance of smoke rather than to any awareness of the potentially lethal effects of emissions. Now that these effects are established, it is clear that households are making the decision to shift (or not) to more expensive cleaner fuels with inadequate information. Public education is clearly a possible tool that may be cost-effective. Similarly, research in improved stove designs has higher benefits than were thought before the results of the epidemiological studies were available.

The importance of public education and access to information reappears in the domain of drinking water and sanitation. In their study of urban India, Jalan, Somanathan, and Chaudhuri (2003) find that raising the level of schooling of the most educated woman in a household from 0 to 10 years roughly doubles willingness to pay for improved drinking water quality, which is the same as the effect of raising the household's wealth level from the first to the third wealth quartile.

Very often, this applies to other pollution problems as well. There is insufficient information available to the public about the extent, consequences and causes of various pollutants. Without such information, the demand for pollution control will be too low, relative to a hypothetical full-information situation. This suggests that government monitoring programs should be accompanied by publication of the data. In the U.S., for example, water providers are required by law to inform the public if tap water fails federal standards. Such disclosure requirements are uncommon in developing countries. In India, water quality information is rarely made public (McKenzie and Ray, 2004). In practice, the requirement to publish data may lead to lobbying to ensure that it is not collected to begin with. It is, therefore, good policy to promote capacity outside government to conduct environmental monitoring. This is best done by academic institutions.

The effect of public information programs on the incentive for polluters to clean-up has been clearly seen in the case of the U.S. Toxic Release Inventory data, where the annual publication of the data leads to stock price declines for the most polluting firms and subsequent emission reduction by the firms penalized most by the capital market (Hamilton, 1995; Konar and Cohen, 1997, Arora and Cason, 1994).[13] The stock price effect of public disclosure has now been seen in a developing country as well (Gupta and Goldar, 2003). In developing countries, the rating and labelling of industries known as PROPER in Indonesia deserves special attention.

Indonesia was long ruled by an authoritarian government in which the family and other associates of the president during the Suharto period, wielded

[13] See also Karl and Orwat (1999) or OECD (1997) for more analysis of labeling schemes in industrialized countries.

considerable power and influence in not only politics but business and administration as well. Policy making and implementation was far from transparent. Many of the owners of polluting industries were powerful and the local EPA, BAPEDAL (Badan Pengendalian Dampak Lingkungan), a relatively small and weak organization. Inevitably an EPA in this situation would be asking for trouble if they set up badly paid and ill-prepared inspectors against the most well-connected and powerful business leaders, who, if need be, could employ the best lawyers. The risks of ineffective monitoring, weak enforcement and even corruption were obvious. BAPEDAL had already tried conventional regulations with little success. They were also wary of a system of environmental charges and one of the reasons for this was that charges create a negotiation situation between the polluter and individual officers of the agency in which the latter can be tempted into corruption. They chose instead a rating or labeling system, PROPER, the Program for Pollution Control Evaluation and Rating.

The PROPER scheme was prepared very carefully and is actually more than just a labeling scheme. It is fundamentally a system for emissions reporting, for evaluation and control of the reports, for assistance, advice and in addition to this, there is grading of each industry based on the reports. A good deal of thought has been spent on designing the number of parameters to be reported and selecting these. The purpose was to have an appropriate set of parameters: not so many as to make reporting burdensome and alienate the firms; but not so few parameters that they are easy to falsify. By experience, certain problems such as stoppages cause excess release of certain—though not necessarily all pollutants. At the same time, such stoppages are related to other items the firms report, such as production, electricity use, raw material consumption, water and so forth. The PROPER team collected a large number of indicators and developed small but sophisticated programs for checking the correlation between the various data collected. This was in turn used to award labels. (See Box 7.3.)

Thus the PROPER scheme provided both technical and market information. It turned out that the power of reputation (particularly the fear of bad publicity) was stronger than expected and a rather large number of firms managed in a short time to improve their ratings. The most important sign of progress was the fact that, in the first 18 months, overall effluents from the 187 first firms was reduced by 43 per cent. (See for instance Afsah et al. (2000).)

A somewhat neglected point is that information flows even within governments may be inadequate. Tax policies are made in Finance Ministries and it may be the case that environmental implications are ignored in their making. This problem is quite acute in developing countries although it has a low-cost solution. Procedure could simply require that the environmental agency's comments on each change in the tax code be solicited before the change is made.

Another area in which information problems are of paramount importance is the regulation of run-off from farms in industrialized economies. These are

---

Box 7.3 COLOUR CODING USED BY PROPER

The choice of labels was made with great care in order to be simple, clear and understandable to citizens with little or no prior knowledge or understanding of technical and pollution issues. For simplicity a colour coding was chosen, but for coherence and credibility the colours have to have fairly precise meanings. The starting point for all of them which gives the whole system its formal legitimacy is the fact that it builds on earlier regulation. Those firms which simply comply with regulations are 'blue.' For firms that are 'proactive' and significantly exceed the legal requirements in environmental standards can be awarded a 'green' status while the 'World Class' status is gold (yet to be achieved by any firm in Indonesia). Firms that fail to meet minimum standards are 'Red'—or in the really bad cases of significant environmental damage and no effort at abatement they are Black.

---

referred to as 'non-point source pollution' since it is not possible to monitor emissions as easily as it is from a factory that has a limited number of effluent pipes and stacks. To overcome the difficulties of monitoring, a number of special instruments have been developed for the non-point source pollution case. These usually hinge on utilizing the monitoring of peers or on 'information-revealing' mechanisms of various sorts. Recently it has become apparent that these mechanisms may be usefully extended also to other contexts where monitoring is difficult or expensive. Examples include small-scale industry, agriculture and vehicles. Even quite significant industries may, for instance in many Asian countries, be comprised mainly of very small industries that have many of the characteristics mentioned here. In some cases, these industries are organized into industrial estates which may facilitate the use of certain special policies and policy instruments that can be designed for such estates. These include joint technology transfer, waste management infrastructure and educational efforts that may be channeled through the estates. These may be partly subsidized. Alternatively, the estate may be made collectively responsible for some parameters related to the ambient environmental quality (such as water quality in a river or stream that flows through the estate). This creates a two-tier pollution management issue and may help resolve the issue of incentives for monitoring. It puts the estate in the position where it has incentives to encourage its members to monitor each other. As is well known from the literature on common property, it is frequently the peers who are best placed to overcome the cost barriers to monitoring. This is an advantage and yet another advantage may be the technical collaboration (assistance) that larger firms can supply to smaller ones. Inevitably however this asymmetric interaction also implies implementation risks since the larger firms can dominate the smaller. In the case of the Ankleshwar estate in Gujarat, Kathuria, and Sterner (2006) report that one of the complaints by smaller firms was that the fees for effluent treatment and waste handling were unfair towards smaller plants since they were only partly based on actual waste volumes.

The ecosystem resources used by the poor for agriculture, fishing, grazing, or other collection are often marginal and their output low and variable due to climatic conditions such as uncertain rainfall. This variability is unacceptable for the poor who are very risk averse and thus have a demand for savings or insurance to guarantee survival in lean years. Due to asymmetric information and monitoring problems, there are however problems of adverse selection and moral hazard so that savings and insurance schemes are generally in short supply. This is a market failure that can be the cause of very unsustainable behavior. Those who cannot open bank accounts may put their savings into the only available form, which may be cattle which in turn frequently leads to overgrazing and land degradation. Similarly risk aversion may lead to the over-application of pesticides since pests, although unlikely, are an unacceptable risk in a world without crop insurance. In these cases, it is of fundamental importance to correctly judge the various underlying market failures. It is probably the case that capital market distortions (and distortions in other markets such as the labor market too) can spill over and create problems in the environmental and resource area. This is particularly a concern for developing countries where such distortions are most common. A superficial understanding might lead one to recommend taxes on cattle or pesticides when the appropriate long-run policies for sustainability might instead be the gradual build-up of small-scale insuring or banking services such as the Grameen Bank of Bangladesh. This bank is one of the pioneers in providing banking and other financial services to the rural poor. It does not look or behave like a conventional bank but it has had very large-scale success in starting savings among the poor and of extending credit for small businesses and housing and such like. There are similar schemes in a number of countries but it is clear that its success has not been easy to replicate as there are many specific cultural and social details that must be properly understood and dealt with, see http://www.gdrc.org/icm/grameen-info.html.

Incentive-Based Policies and the Costs of Pollution Control

Incentive-based policies, notably pollution charges and various types of tradable pollution permits, have turned out to be successful in many applications in the developed world not only in reducing aggregate costs, but also in increasing the acceptability of policies. It is natural therefore that the question should arise as to the conditions under which these instruments can be used effectively in developing countries. Some are enthusiastic at this prospect saying that cost efficiency is all the more important in a context of poverty. There are already a number of examples, particularly of environmental taxes or fees (sometimes paid into earmarked funds) in which they are used quite extensively in developing economies and they may well have an important role to play in some contexts.

Examples of specific pollution taxes include the fee schemes for industrial water pollution in China and Colombia and combinations of fee and regulation for management of water pollution from palm oil plants in Malaysia.[14] Other examples that are interesting in this context are the developing country experiences of taxation of goods such as fuel, energy or tobacco. These taxes may not necessarily have been instituted primarily for environmental reasons. Their operation is, however, largely independent of the original motivation and they do obviously have considerable environmental effects illustrating that environmental taxes can very well operate across a broad range of countries.

Others suggest that incentive-based policies often are not suitable for developing countries since they require special conditions to ensure compliance and effectiveness. Bell and Russell (2002) for example point to the fact that such rights are subject to all the normal hazards of commercial transactions. Sellers can default, buyers can go bankrupt and either party may try to cheat. Thus proper, reliable, transparent monitoring and accounting must exist. Furthermore, it is absolutely necessary to have some form of solid legal basis for deciding conflicts—be it a court or a public body such as an environmental protection agency. The authors further point to the fact that the participants in a pollution market need experience with market behavior. At the very least, they need to be able to ascertain their own abatement costs—which is the kind of knowledge that is best acquired after some years in a functioning regulatory system where rules really are enforced. The act of compliance is part of a whole culture of collaboration, communication, cooperation and law abidance and it may be necessary to understand this whole complex in order to understand its politics.[15]

We believe these viewpoints are important. It is definitely not possible to simply and mindlessly transfer an instrument from one type of country to another. Market-based instruments are neither universally applicable to all situations nor are they necessarily simple or automatically efficient. On the other hand, it is important to recognize that it is the very weakness of regulation in developing countries that has led to much greater heterogeneity among polluters than in developed countries where minimum standards cut off a considerable part of the distribution. This is compounded by the higher cost of capital, which results in older equipment remaining in use, and typically, polluting more. Greater heterogeneity among polluters increases the scope for cleaning up by targeting only the worst polluters. This, in turn, means that a

[14] Descriptions of these and other developing country instruments may be found in Blackman and Harrington (2000), Sterner (2003), Anderson (2002) and at the World Bank website 'New Initiatives on Pollution Regulation' at http://www.worldbank.org/nipr/commun.htm. These sources also describe interesting applications of other instruments, legal or information based in developing countries. See also the paper by Krupnick (Ch. 11) in this volume.
[15] See also Russell and Vaughan (2003). One might however also say that the argument runs both ways. The same factors that will imply difficulties for market-based instruments will also cause conventional regulatory approaches to falter.

fraction, perhaps a majority, of polluters could gain from a scheme that recycles pollution charges, whether these are implemented as permits or taxes.

Under these circumstances, the distribution of costs is just as important as their overall level for the political feasibility of any particular policy instrument. Physical regulation such as standards have a tendency of becoming manipulated by industries who will secure acceptance of special rules in favor of already existing plants. Pollution taxes would be an efficient instrument forcing heavy polluters to compensate society at the same time as they provide incentives for clean-up, but such taxes impose a burden on all polluters thus uniting them in their lobby efforts against the EPA. We are thus often pointed in the direction of earmarked charges, refunded emission or user charges and environmental funds rather than standards or general Pigouvian taxes. If the charges are related to polluting inputs (such as fuels) or outputs, the administrative costs of monitoring may be reduced making this type of instrument more feasible even in economies with limited administrative capacity.

As shown in Sterner (2003), policy instruments, be they price type or quantity-based can be configured to fit into different conceptions of property rights to the environment and thus different burden of payment. Starting with the quantity-based instruments, the permits may be either auctioned or 'grand-fathered' free of charge in proportion to earlier pollution if the polluters are considered to have ownership rights. Such a distribution may either reflect 'prior-appropriation' rights or simply be a pragmatic recognition of the pol-luters' power—either way it implies that the polluting firms get the scarcity 'rent' rather than letting society get it as with auctioned permits. Similarly for price-type mechanisms, the tax gives property rights to the state and places costs on the firms while subsidies do exactly the opposite—and refunded emission payments or tax-subsidy schemes are intermediate in this respect. It is not sufficient to say that a tax is superior to subsidy or intermediate instruments because of the excess burden of taxes. Although this argument is true,[16] it may have limited relevance if a subsidy of x $/ton is feasible while a corresponding tax of x $/ton is not. If the EPA insists on using a tax, it may find that the level actually implemented after lobbying is only a fraction of the appropriate level x $/ton. We are thus faced with a trade-off between the importance of the allocation, output and revenue effects of a given instrument. If the technical substitution effect is the most important then sometimes a subsidy may be preferable because it is effective and meets no resistance. On the other hand, with problems that have no easy technical solution but require large, long-run

---

[16] It is difficult to raise taxes but the state has many urgent needs (public goods) that are badly needed and thus each dollar of tax has an extra cost to the economy (related to the cost of collection and distortions caused). This implies that if a Pigouvian tax and a subsidy have the same effect on technology choice then the tax is likely to be superior from a welfare view-point since it also happens to contribute to the treasury whereas the subsidy in contrast requires more money from the treasury and thus more collection of conventional taxes thus further increasing the excess burden of taxation.

changes in behavior, the output substitution and revenue recycling effects will be more important and subsidies may well be expensive and inefficient and taxes thus clearly preferable.

Practical experience does show that there is scope for judicious use of a wide spectrum of instruments, and for use that can expand and evolve over time as laws, regulations, and market institutions and actors co-evolve. In China, the system of pollution charges provides an interesting example.[17] The 1979 environmental law stated, 'in cases where the discharge of pollutants exceeds the limit set by the state, a compensation fee shall be charged according to the quantities and concentration of the pollutants released' (Article 18). Today, several hundreds of thousands of factories are monitored and potentially subject to this fee. Already in 1994, more than 19 billion Yuan (more than US$2 billion) had been collected from environmental levies (NEPA, 1994). These fees are not textbook taxes, they are very low and they are put into funds accessible to industry for the finance of abatement investments. However, these departures from the Pigouvian principle are features that enhance political acceptability. The funds allay the fear that this is yet another trick from central fiscal authorities to squeeze out more money and show that the authorities actually take the environment seriously. The collaboration in the funds around the financing of abatement investments actually provides very good opportunities for the spread of information on abatement technology. The experiences from the fees paid into funds are similar in a range of other cases, from the environmental charges for water pollution in the Rio Negro (and other water sheds) in Columbia, to the systems for industrial pollution charges in Poland, and various formerly planned economies of Eastern Europe. In all these cases, the local recycling of funds for abatement appears to have helped considerably in overcoming resistance among polluters and in legitimizing the fees.

Other cases that show how useful a market-based approach can be in developing countries include the taxation of polluting inputs such as fuels and tobacco as well as the introduction of sensible tariffs for electricity, water, and similar services. Many countries are actually quite heavily dependent on fuel taxes for revenues and although the ease of collection may have been their original motivation, they clearly also reduce pollution. Also trading schemes for irrigation water can, as discussed above, be an important mechanism for equalizing marginal costs and creating incentives for efficient use. In protecting ecosystems, the market-based approaches include various mechanisms entailing payments for eco-system services from say urban centres to rural areas that protect water catchments. Examples range from New York to small towns in Costa Rica and elsewhere.

Note that the water payments scheme in Sukhomajri, described in Box 7.2 on p. 227, hinges very crucially on being sensitive to the distributional implications

---

[17] The examples discussed here are given in greater detail in Sterner (2003).

of a scheme—or to property rights. It implies equal allocation per person, not per unit of land or cattle, nor grandfathering in relation to historical patterns of use. The scheme was deemed very successful. Siltation was reduced by 95 percent, saving $200,000 in annual dredging costs. Tree and grass density increased by a factor of 100 on slopes so that managed harvests far exceed open access levels attained earlier. Livestock, crops, housing and many other indicators developed positively. However experience has also shown that replication is not easy. It appears that the initial contribution from Chandigarh was important and that sharing issues often turn out to be very complex. Sukhomajri had an unusually high degree of social equality (less than 10 percent landless) and thus arrived more easily at the equal distribution allocation.

When international competitiveness is an important issue, as it tends to be in small open economies, the selection of policy instruments needs to take particular care not to add unnecessary costs to the polluters. This is often used as a strong argument against auctioned permits and taxes. Strictly speaking this need not be the case since these instruments do not affect profitability at the margin but should mainly be seen as a windfall loss to shareholders that does not affect profitability. However, whether these income effects matter depends on how capital markets react and the political economy aspects may be quite important particularly in developing countries where the politicians hesitate to alienate powerful shareholders. If the regulator is very weak compared to commercial interests, it may start with some basic regulation and informational instruments. Also refunded payments, free permits, subsidies or regulation may be viable options. In industries with monopoly (or at least significant market power) taxes again have some undesirable side effects since they may aggravate the tendency of monopolists to over-price and under-produce. Two advantages of dealing with large multinational firms are that they often do have the requisite technology and that they are sensitive to publicity. This speaks in favour of information-based instruments such as information disclosure, labeling and voluntary agreements.

A category of environmental problems that we have not yet discussed very much are the so-called 'brown issues' that are the mainstay of environmental work in OECD countries. They include industrial pollution: air and water as well as waste issues (including hazardous wastes). They also include vehicular pollution and one could include certain types of agricultural run-off. In these areas, developing countries have a number of characteristics that make their situation distinct from that of countries in which industrialization and environmental management have a somewhat longer history. One of the differences is that there may be an advantage of being a second-mover. There is less uncertainty about the technical feasibility of abatement since decision-makers can observe and point to abatement technology in industrialized countries. They can economize on the work needed to develop such technologies and in some cases copy standards (perhaps with some time lag). In some areas, the opportunity for 'leap-frogging' may be valuable. Countries may sometimes go straight into the clean technologies and short-cut the polluting paths that led to them in the countries where they were developed.

In other respects, the developing countries face a number of disadvantages. Frequently, their environmental protection agencies are weak in relation to the industries they are set to regulate. The regulators are often poorly funded and under-staffed—partly a consequence of poverty and partly an aspect of the general failure to provide public goods that we discussed on pp. 220–4 (See also Ch. 5 by López in this volume).

The polluters tend to fall in one of two distinct categories, both of which imply problems for the regulator, although in very different ways. To be simplistic, one might say they are either very large or very small. The large polluters are very powerful compared to the environmental policymakers and this is not least the case with foreign (multinational) firms on which we will focus here. The overriding concern of most developing countries is to attract foreign investment, and multinational companies quite naturally will consider all factors (including the environmental and other bureaucratic) barriers in their choice of localization. Thus there is the risk of a 'race to the bottom' in terms of standards in order to avoid the risk of deterring investment. It is also more common for the industries in (at least smaller) Third World countries to have considerable market power. As a corollary to this, the asymmetry in information, assets and power will be particularly large when regulators meet polluters. Even in the U.S., the large firms will have better-paid staff than the Environmental Protection Agency. In a poor country with large disparities in income and training, the asymmetry of resources becomes so significant as to be a major impediment to the local regulator that may even be completely deterred from trying to regulate. This is one of the factors that make implementation difficult—particularly for some instruments that put the regulator and the firm into adversarial roles or into relationships involving the discretion over large financial transfers. Instruments such as labeling, earmarked fees, information disclosure and two-tier regulation can be designed to reduce these problems.

At the other end of the scale we have the small polluters. Typically, these will be in developing countries, small but very numerous, and poorer in both financial and other resources than their counterparts in industrialized countries. They are sometimes referred to as the 'informal' sector and, as the name suggests, may have very simplified or nonexistent routines for administration. The problem for the regulator here is not that the polluter is too powerful but that they are too many. They may in some cases be (de jure or de facto) exempt from tax payments and other regulation. It is in the nature of such polluters that they are hard to regulate by several of the conventional instruments used for bigger industries in wealthier countries. They are too poor to tax and even too poor to afford any significant abatement expense.

They also lack knowledge and organizational skills and are in fact difficult simply to locate and reach, even for informational instruments.[18]

Vehicles have many of the non-point source characteristics of small polluters but income sensitivity may be particularly high since they have individual owners. Furthermore, the distribution of emission coefficients is typically skewed so that the most polluting decile of vehicles accounts for a high fraction of urban ambient pollution. An efficient policy would be to target these vehicles (at least from urban circulation) but this is politically difficult since the worst vehicles will often belong to interests (such as truckers or taxis) that, although poor in a general sense, still have sufficient resources that they can organize and turn into rather powerful lobbies. One way around this problem, which, to the best of our knowledge, has never been tried, would be to refund payments collected from charges (or fines from random checks) within classes of vehicles. If the cut-offs are set sufficiently low, most vehicle owners within each class would end up getting a small check from the regulator, while a significant fraction of pollution would be cleaned up. Setting class-specific cut-offs reduces the scope for cleaning up but makes what cleaning up there is more politically feasible and the impact less regressive.

Conclusions Concerning the Building of Institutions and the Design of Instruments

We have in this paper highlighted four groups of factors that are essential for the design and success of environmental policymaking in developing countries: property rights, governance, information and cost distribution issues.

The absence of well-defined property rights and the resulting non-transferability of assets inhibits investment that would lead to more efficient natural resource utilization. For example, in water-scarce areas, lack of clear ownership of surface and ground water makes it difficult for urban governments to contract with rural ones to supply water for domestic and industrial use, even though the value of water in such use is much higher than in agriculture. This problem also applies to water transfers from one agricultural region to another. It leads to under-investment in water conservation and groundwater recharge measures. Investment in forest stocks suffers from a similar problem. The definition of property rights is thus a fundamental instrument on its own. Furthermore the structure of rights in a society will also condition the kinds of instruments that are applicable. In a society with a strong tradition of private,

---

[18] There is a large literature on this as on several other topics we have touched on, see for instance Blackman and Bannister (1998), Wang and Wheeler (1996), Dasgupta, Hettige, and Wheeler (2000), Hettige et al. (1996). More references are available in Sterner (2000) or Wheeler et al. (2000).

prior appropriation rights, auctioning of permits and taxation may for instance be politically harder to achieve.

A significant aspect of many developing countries is the lack of a good, reliable, and functioning public body that can provide the public goods that are important prerequisites for economic development. These include the very institutions of property, market allocation rules, legal system and the provision of many other public goods such as the rule of law and the independence of the judiciary, basic health, and education. This is often discussed in terms of poverty and corruption but we would like to emphasize the excessive centralization of information flows and formal decision-making.

One of the most important of the public goods that is relevant here is 'information'. By 'information' we mean here the whole chain from research on the states of nature to technical information on environmental issues and on technology. Other important information concerns market data and the monitoring and enforcement of peers. The technical prerequisites for cheap collection, processing and transmission of information have never been better. Unfortunately, however, many regimes feel instinctively that information should be guarded as a secret and they may well be unaware of just how damaging this can be, not only to the environment, but to economic growth in general.

Related to the issues of poor governance, lack of public goods and poor enforcement of property rights is the fact that the distribution of income and wealth is frequently uneven. With the large number of people who live on the verge of absolute poverty, risk aversion plays an important role in the determination of allocation and distribution decisions. Polluters and resource users tend to fall into one of two classes: big and very powerful, or small and so numerous as to acquire non-point characteristics. Under these circumstances, the distribution of costs and benefits is very important and the design of instruments must take this into account otherwise the instruments will end up with severe implementation problems—if in fact they get implemented at all. Heterogeneity among polluters implies that there is a greater scope for cleaning up at lower cost by targeting only the worst polluters and, naturally, poor economies are the last that can afford to pass up cost savings. This implies that instruments that recycle revenues to polluters have a better chance of succeeding. Therefore, they are to be preferred to harsher instruments, such as standards, that may provide better incentives in order to abate by inducing substitution out of a polluting activity, in addition to inducing less pollution-intensive operation of the activity. As with all generalizations, this one will have its exceptions. It bears repeating that consultation and transparency in conception and implementation of any scheme is desirable.

It follows that in spite of the considerable difficulties concerning property rights, legal systems monitoring, enforcement and other issues raised here, we believe that market-based instruments can, and should, play an important role in developing countries. In some areas, and in some ways, they may even be more suitable there than in the industrialized economies. We have already cited heterogeneity in abatement costs as one reason for this. A second reason is that low-income countries often have poor systems for income taxation. They frequently rely heavily on excise taxes already—and these can be quite distorting, except of course for the environmental taxes which instead are both corrective of externalities and revenue generating. This should not be taken to imply that the introduction of such instruments will be easy, or their efficiency properties come automatically. Quite to the contrary, very careful design will be needed for whatever instruments are chosen (irrespective of how heavily regulatory or market-based they are). Among the issues we have highlighted as particularly important are issues of distribution, information and risk management. We also may note that there are actually more interesting applications of environmental policy instruments—including market-based ones—in developing countries than is perhaps generally known (Sterner, 2003). Frequently they have somewhat different designs to the solutions chosen in OECD countries. It is not uncommon to find that several instruments are combined, that fees, if they are used, are quite low (and sometimes staggered) and that there is considerable interest in the use of the proceeds, which are quite frequently used to address informational and distributional issues as well as to finance monitoring and even abatement or clean-up.

References

Afsah, S., A. Blackman, and D. Ratunanda (2000), 'How do Public Disclosure Pollution Control Programs Work? Evidence from Indonesia', Resources for the Future, Discussion Paper 00–44, October 2000, Washington, DC.

Alemu, T. (1999), *Land tenure and soil conservation: Evidence from Ethiopia*, PhD dissertation, Department of Economics, University of Göteborg, Sweden.

Anderson, R., (2002), 'Incentive-Based Policies for Environmental Management in Developing Countries,' *RFF Policy Briefs*, 2002–07.

Ariyo, A. and A. Jerome (1999), 'Privatisation in Africa: an appraisal', *World Development*, 27(1): 201–13.

Arora, S. and T. N. Cason (1994), *A Voluntary Approach to Environmental Regulation: The 33/50 Program*. Resources for the Future (Summer).

Bauer, C. J. (2004), *Siren Songs*. Chilean Water Law as a Model for International Reform, RFF Press, Washington.

Baumol, W. J. and W. E. Oates (1988), *The Theory of Environmental Policy*, Cambridge: Cambridge University Press.

Bell, R. G. (2003), 'Choosing Environmental Policy Instruments in the Real World.' Paper prepared for the OECD Global Forum on Sustainable Development,' OECD CCNM/GF/SD/ENV(2003)10: 17–18 (March).

—— and C. S. Russell (2002), 'Environmental Policy for Developing Countries,' *Issues in Science and Technology* (Spring).

Bell, R. G. and C. S. Russell (2003), 'Ill Considered Experiments: The Environmental Consensus and the Developing World,' *Harvard International Review* (Winter).

Blackman, A. and G. J. Bannister (1998), 'Community Pressure and Clean Technology in the Informal Sector: An Econometric Analysis of the Adoption of Propane by Traditional Mexican Brickmakers,' *Journal of Environmental Economics and Management* 35: 1–21.

——— and W. Harrington (2000), 'The Use of Economic Incentives in Developing Countries: Lessons from International Experience with Industrial Air Pollution,' *Journal of Environment and Development*, 9(1): 5–44.

Briscoe, J. (1997), 'Managing Water as an Economic Good', *Water Supply*, 15(4): 153–72, reprinted in R. Maria Saleth (ed.) (2002), *Water Resources and Economic Development*, Edward Elgar, Cheltenham.

Cole, D. H. (2002), *Pollution and Property: Comparing Ownership Institutions for Environmental Protection* Cambridge University Press, Cambridge.

Dasgupta, S., H. Hettige, and D. Wheeler (2000), 'What Improves Environmental Compliance? Evidence from Mexican Industry', *Journal of Environmental Economics and Management*, 39(1): 39–66.

Easter, K. W., M. W. Rosegrant, and A. Dinar (1999), 'Formal and informal markets for water: Institutions, performance, and constraints.' *World Bank Research Observer*, 14(1): 99–116.

Ezzati, M. and D. Kammen (2002), 'The Health Impacts of Exposure to Indoor Air Pollution from Solid Fuels in Developing Countries: Knowledge, gaps and data needs,' *RFF Discussion Paper 2002*: 24 (August).

Fischbeck, P. S. and R. S. Farrow (eds) (2001), *Improving Regulation, Cases in Environment, Health and Safety*, RFF Press, Washington.

Foster, Vivien, Subhrendu Pattanayak, and Linda Stalker Prokopy (2003), 'Do current water subsidies reach the poor?' Water Tariffs and Subsidies in South Asia Paper 4, UN Water and Sanitation Program, South Asia.

Gleick, Peter H. (1998), 'Water and Human Health' in Peter H. Gleick (ed.), *The World's Water 1998–1999: The Biennial Report on Freshwater Resources*. Washington DC: Island Press.

Grossman, Sanford J. and Oliver D. Hart (1986), 'The costs and benefits of ownership: A theory of vertical and lateral integration', *Journal of Political Economy*, 94, 691–719.

Gupta, Shreekant and Bishwanath Goldar (2003), 'Do Stock Markets Penalise Environment-Unfriendly Behaviour? Evidence from India.' Working Paper # 116, Centre for Development Economics, Delhi.

Hamilton, J. T. (1995), 'Pollution as News: Media and Stock Market Reactions to the Toxics Release Inventory Data', *Journal of Environmental Economics and Management*, 28: 98–113.

Hanley, N., J. F. Shogren, and B. White (1997), *Environmental Economics In Theory and in Practice*, London: McMillan Press.

Hettige, M., M. Huq, S. Pargal, and D. Wheeler (1996), 'Determinants of Pollution Abatement in Developing Countries: Evidence from South and Southeast Asia,' *World Development* 24, (12): 1891–904.

Jalan, Jyotsna, E. Somanathan, and Saraswata Chaudhuri (2003), 'Awareness and the Demand for Environmental Quality: Drinking Water in Urban India,' Economics Discussion Paper # 03–05, Indian Statistical Institute, Delhi.

Jodha, N. S. (1990), 'Rural Common Property Resources: Contributions and Crisis.' *Economic and Political Weekly* (June 30).

Karl, H. and C. Orwat (1999), 'Environmental Labelling in Europe: European and National Tasks,' *European Environment 9*: 212–20.

Kebede, B. (2002) 'Land Tenure and Common Pool Resources in Rural Ethiopia: A Study Based on Fifteen Sites', *African Development Review* 14(1), 113–49, doi: 10.1111/1467–8268.00048.

Kolstad, C. D. (2000), *Environmental Economics*. New York: Oxford University Press.

Konar, Shameek and Mark A. Cohen (1997), 'Information as Regulation: The Effect of Community Right-to-Know Laws on Toxic Emissions', *Journal of Environmental Economics and Management*, 32(1): 109–24.

Lee, Yok-Shiu F. (1997), 'Urban Water Supply and Sanitation in Developing Countries', in R. Maria Saleth (ed.), *Water Resources and Economic Development*, Edward Elgar, Cheltenham, 2002: 215–31.

Lele, Sharachchandra (2000), 'Godsend, sleight of hand, or just muddling through: joint water and forest management in India', *Natural Resource Perspectives*, #53.

McKenzie, D. and Isha Ray (2004), 'Household Water Delivery Options in Urban and Rural India,' *Mimeo*. Stanford University.

Makhaya, G. (2001), 'Privatisation, Economic Development and the Role of the State in Developing Countries: Review Article', *International Review of Applied Economics*, v. 15, iss. 4, 460–65 (October).

Mehta, S. and K. Smith (2002), Paper presented at the Workshop on Household Energy, Air Pollution and Health—Exposure Assessment, New Delhi (January 15).

Migot-Adholla, S. E., P. Hazell, B. Blarel, and F. Place (1991). Indigenous land right systems in Sub-Saharan Africa: A constant on productivity? *World Bank Economic Review* 5(1): 155–75.

Murty, M. N. (1994), Management of Common Property Resources: Limits to Voluntary Collective Action, *Environmental and Resource Economics*, 4: 581–94.

OECD (1997), *Eco-labelling: Actual Effects of Selected Programmes*, OECD/GD(97)105.

Ostrom, E. and Schlager, E., (1996), The Formation of Property Rights, in S. Hanna, C. Folke, and K. G. Maler (eds), 1996, *Rights to Nature: Ecological, Economic, Cultural and Political Principles of Institutions for the Environment*, Island Press, Washington, DC.

Place, F. and Hazell, P. (1993). Productivity Effects of Indigenous Land Tenure in Sub-Saharan Africa. *American Journal of Agricultural Economics* 75: 10–19.

Raymond, L., (2003), *Private Rights in Public Resources*. Washington, RFF Press.

Rosegrant, Mark W. and Hans P. Binswanger (1994), 'Markets in Tradable Water Rights: Potential for Efficiency Gains in Developing Country Water Resource Allocation.' *World Development*, 22(11): 1613–25, reprinted in R. Maria Saleth (ed.) *Water Resources and Economic Development*, Cheltenham, Edward Elgar, 2002.

—— and Mark Svendsen (1993), 'Asian Food Production in the 1990s: Irrigation Investment and Management Policy,' *Food Policy* 18(1): 13–32, reprinted in R. Maria Saleth (ed.), *Water Resources and Economic Development*, Cheltenham, Edward Elgar, 2002.

Russell, C. S. and W. J. Vaughan, (2003), 'The Choice of Pollution Control Policy Instruments in Developing Countries: Arguments, Evidence and Suggestions,' *International Yearbook of Environmental and Resource Economics*, vol VII, Cheltenham: Edward Elgar.

Saleth, R. Maria, (1996), *Water Institutions in India: Economics, Law, and Policy*. New Delhi: Commonwealth Publishers.

Savas, E. S. (2000), *Privatization and Public Private Partnerships*. New York: Seven Bridges Press.

Somanathan, E., R. Prabhakar, and B. S. Mehta (2005), 'Does Decentralization Work? Forest Conservation in the Himalayas.' BREAD Working Paper #96.

Stavins, R. N. (2001), 'Experience with Market-based Environmental Policy Instruments', in Mäler K-G. and J. Vincent (2001) (eds), *The Handbook of Environmental Economics*. Amsterdam: North-Holland/Elsevier Science.

Sterner, T, (2003), *Policy Instruments for Environmental and Natural Resource Management*, Washington, DC, RFF Press, (November).

Thobani, Mateen (1997), 'Formal Water Markets: Why, When, and How to Introduce Tradeable Water Rights.' *World Bank Research Observer*, 12(2): 161–79.

Tietenberg, T. H. (1992), *Environmental and Natural Resource Economics*. HarperCollins Publishers Inc.

Vaidyanathan, A. (1999), *Water Resource Management: Institutions and Irrigation Development in India*. Oxford University Press.

Wade, Robert (1982), 'The System of Administrative and Political Corruption: Canal Irrigation in South India', *Journal of Development Studies*, 18 (3): 287–328.

Wade, Robert (1995), 'The Ecological Basis of Irrigation Institutions: East and South Asia'. *World Development*, 23(12): 2041–49, reprinted in R. Maria Saleth (ed.), *Water Resources and Economic Development*. Cheltenham, Edward Elgar, 2002.

Wang, H. and D. Wheeler (1996), *Pricing Industrial Pollution in China*. World Bank Policy Research Working Paper, 1644.

Wheeler, D. et al. (2000), *Greening Industry: New Roles for Communities, Markets and Governments*. World Bank Policy Research Report, New York: Oxford University Press.

World Bank Water Demand Research Team (1993), 'The Demand for Water in Rural Areas: Determinants and Policy Implications.' *World Bank Research Observer* 8: 47–70.

World Health Organisation 2002, *World Health Report*, Geneva.

8

Energy, Equity, and Economic Development

Douglas F. Barnes and Michael A. Toman

Introduction

We start this chapter with some observations that may be obvious to energy development experts but less familiar to others in the development field: Why focus on energy? In our view there are four reasons for doing so. The first is that increased provision of energy services, especially higher quality modern energy services such as electricity, has a demonstrated high marginal value in the context of broader economic growth and social development. Increased provision of more affordable and higher quality energy services in itself will not drive development, but it is difficult to envisage successful development without this occurring.

Second, energy services—especially higher quality services—remain physically scarce and economically costly in many parts of the developing world. This scarcity is especially evident in more impoverished areas. Whatever might be said about the causal relationships between energy scarcity and poverty, their coincidence indicates an important opportunity for poverty alleviation through reducing barriers to affordable higher quality energy services.

Third, production and provision of energy services—especially grid-supplied electricity—at a larger and more organized scale in the economy give rise to thorny issues of economic sector regulation. These problems arise in rich and poor countries alike, but they are especially acute in developing countries, and solutions must be tailored to the circumstances of those countries.

Finally, there are important and challenging energy-environment links throughout the chain of production and consumption. These include environmental damages of fossil energy extraction and transport, air pollution problems from large-scale fuel burning in power stations and industrial boilers, and highly localized (household level) health problems from indoor combustion of smoky fuels. As we know from the first principles of environmental and welfare economics, the social value of energy in economic development must account for the creation *and* amelioration of these environmental impacts, as well as the effects on household production and market production of other goods and services.

In the body of the chapter, we consider in turn the first three of these four aspects of energy and development; we also briefly consider the value of improved energy service availability on household health through improved indoor air quality in the context of the value of energy for development generally. Other issues related to air pollution are addressed in Chapter 11 by Krupnick. The specific issues related to the impacts of fossil fuel extraction are beyond our scope here. After discussing in turn these facets of energy-development linkages, we conclude the chapter with a summary of lessons learned from energy-related development activities and implications for future activities in this area.

The Value of Energy in Economic and Social Development

The linkages among energy, other inputs, and economic activity change as an economy moves through different stages of development. Barnes and Floor (1996) refer to the 'energy ladder' to describe this phenomenon (see also Smith et al., 1994; Sathaye and Tyler, 1991). Although it is described as a ladder, this does not imply a monotonic transition from one type of energy to another (see also Barnes, Krutilla, and Hyde, 2004). At the lowest levels of income and social development, energy sources predominantly tend to be harvested or scavenged biological sources (wood, dung, sunshine for drying) and human effort (also biologically powered). More processed biofuels (charcoal), animal power, and some commercial fossil energy become more prominent in the intermediate stages. Commercial fossil fuels and ultimately electricity become predominant in the most advanced stages of industrialization and development. Again, energy resources of different levels of development may be used concurrently at any given stage of economic development: electric lighting may be used concurrently with biomass cooking fires. Changes in relative opportunity costs as well as incomes can move households and other energy users up and down the ladder for different energy-related services.

In poor countries with urban per capita incomes of about $300 per year or less, approximately 90 percent of the population depends on wood and dung for cooking. But people move up the 'energy ladder' as their incomes grow, eventually switching to electricity for lighting and fossil fuels for cooking; in agriculture and industry, diesel engines and electricity replace manual and animal power. The transition to modern fuels is usually complete by the time incomes reach approximately $1,000–1,500. With technological progress and reductions in the costs of modern fuels, the income level at which people make the transition has declined. A transition that took nearly 70 years in the United States (1850–1920) took only 30 years in Korea (1950–80).

In earlier stages of the transition, alternatives to woodfuels do not come into play until woodfuel prices rise to the point that modern fuels like kerosene or coal become competitive alternatives. At later stages in the energy transition, the main issues involve the availability of modern fuels, modern appliances, and electricity, especially for the poor. Most of the rural demand for electricity comes from households that use electricity for lighting and from farms, agro-industries, and small commercial and manufacturing establishments, which use the electricity for productive purposes such as irrigation pumping, water supplies, crop processing, refrigeration, and motive power. In regions where electricity can be used both by households and for productive activities, there is ample economic justification for investment in electrification (Barnes, 1988; World Bank, 1996). Most rural electrification programs have focused on connecting rural areas to national or local grids. However, grid-supplied electricity is not the least-cost alternative under all conditions, and planners should consider other possibilities, as discussed later in the chapter.

Despite the substantial differences in energy forms and in the nature of economic activities across different stages of development, some common elements can be seen. Energy provision or acquisition is a costly activity requiring a variety of different kinds of inputs, whether that cost is denominated in terms of household labor allocated to biomass gathering or expenditures for commercial fuels and the inputs needed to provide them. Energy utilization also does not occur in a vacuum but depends on the opportunity costs of other inputs, notably various types of capital goods (be they cook stoves or electricity grids). Finally, the literature makes clear that observed patterns of energy production and utilization reflect a great deal of subtle optimizing behavior, given the constraints faced by the economic actors (Barnes and Floor, 1996; OTA 1991, 1992). Those constraints can impede better outcomes, however; and much of the work to date on energy development has been concerned with how lower-cost and more effective energy services can be delivered by alleviating or working around financing and informational barriers as well as regulatory distortions.

The energy sector also can have an impact on many different sectors. The development impact of grid rural electrification, for example, has a strong relationship with education and reading (World Bank, 2002b). Obviously, telecommunications is impossible without electricity. A point that is often made is that electricity is a necessary but not a sufficient condition for development. In rapidly developing agricultural regions, electricity helps to raise the productivity of local agro-industrial and commercial activities by supplying motive power, refrigeration, lighting, and process heating (Wasserman and Davenport, 1993). Increased earnings from agricultural and local industry and commerce then lead, in turn, to greater household demand for electricity.

The complementary nature of social infrastructure means, for example, that asking the question whether a community should have a road or electricity essentially misses the point. The two together have a much higher value than either one of them separately (World Bank, 1999a). At the same time, one must keep in mind the poor results of many past 'integrated rural development projects' in which the inflexibility of the funding plans put a constraint on the ability of rural communities to choose for themselves. If they needed a road or a school, then getting a little bit of everything did not help them to achieve their goals.

Increased energy availability could make a larger contribution to expanded economic activity in the provision of energy services or in their utilization. Before turning to specific possibilities, we illustrate the argument pictorially in Figure 8.1, which is taken from World Bank (2002b). In the diagram, we show two different schedules for the marginal value product of lighting services—lumens in providing various household benefits (longer reading time, easier reading, more security, and the like). The schedule MVP_0 represents the situation at a lower level of income, which we assume is also associated with use of lower-quality and higher-per-lumen-cost kerosene lighting. Depending on income levels, it is likely that most households already have significant

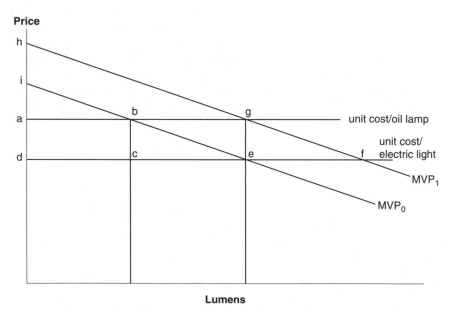

Figure 8.1 Illustration of economic effects from increased energy services utilization
Source: Adapted from World Bank (2002b).

lighting expenses involving kerosene or candles. Because of inefficiencies of kerosene and candles for producing light, the price of light for poor households actually can be higher than the price of light for wealthy households, mainly because of the efficiency gains associated with using electricity. In this regard, the poor light given off by kerosene wick lamps and candles—200 times less light than one simple electric light bulb—often makes it impossible for adults to read during the evening and children to study in the evening. At the lower level of income corresponding to MVP_0, the introduction of lower-per-lumen-cost electric lighting (with unit cost of d in the figure, versus a for oil lamp lighting) will raise total lighting used and generates an economic welfare increase measured by Area abcd (the fall in cost of inframarginal lighting usage) plus Area bce (the consumer surplus from increased lighting utilization). The schedule MVP_1 represents the marginal value product of lighting services at a higher income level induced by an increase in energy service availability—perhaps as a result of improved education capacity or ability to shift household tasks to evening hours and devote time during the day to paying work. Along this higher schedule, the additional benefits of lighting are reflected in additional benefits from baseline consumption (Area e g h i) as well as in benefits from a further induced increase in usage (Area e f g).

As modern energy systems develop, they require investments in large infrastructure-like capital like pipelines and transmission systems that show declining unit costs over a wide range of scale and utilization. Moreover, the transformation of primary energy into deliverable energy (electricity generation, petroleum refining) also exhibits increasing returns to scale, though the magnitude of increasing returns, at least in electricity generation, probably has fallen over time with technical advances (Joskow and Schmalensee, 1983; Nakicenovic, 1996; Brennan et al., 1996). Different kinds of increasing returns in lower-scale energy provision also seem to exist and may be quite important to the earlier stages of development. The energy development literature is replete with discussions of how subsistence energy systems involve large investments of household labor time, notably the time of women and children, in gathering of very low-quality fuels (OTA, 1991, 1992). An increase not just in the raw provision of energy per se, but an increase in scale that included changes in the types of energy services offered and the organization of markets to allow for greater specialization of effort, seems likely to lower considerably the effective cost of the energy services delivered. There might be a substantial threshold effect in the achievement of these economies. Unless a considerable fraction of households were above some minimum effective income level, it might not be possible to achieve the required specialization of functions at a scale and cost of energy services that could be afforded. On the other hand, raising income across such a threshold might be greatly facilitated by a reduction in the effective cost of energy services.

249

There are several ways in which increased availability or quality of energy could augment the productivity and thus the effective supply of physical and/or human capital services. The transmission mechanisms are likely to differ across the stages of development. For more advanced level industrialized or industrializing countries, increased energy availability and flexibility can facilitate the use of more modern machinery and techniques that expand the effective capital–labor ratio as well as increasing the productivity of workers (Schurr, 1982; Jorgenson, 1984). Increased energy service reliability is another key component of quality, again especially for electricity. Estimates for developed countries of the cost of electricity supply interruption per lost MWH are several orders of magnitude larger than the cost of baseload or peak electricity supply costs (OTA, 1990). A recent ESMAP report (World Bank, 2002a) provides an example from India indicating that many farmers using irrigation pay about twice the subsidized cost of electricity to use diesel for their pump sets; the authors suggest that this reflects the desire to avoid the high costs of unreliable electricity supply (since, if irrigation capacity cannot be used at critical times, the results for crop yields can be disastrous). A significant amount of capital also can be tied up in providing energy service redundancy (back-up generators) that could be otherwise and more productively deployed if the effective supply of electricity were enhanced through increased reliability.

For less advanced developing countries, factor productivity enhancement effects necessarily operate more through labor inputs. One possibility is through the development and use of human capital. Energy availability for cheaper and better lighting (in concert with the appropriate physical capital) can increase the productivity of education inputs generally and lead to an augmentation effect in human capital provision, as well as extending the length of the work day.

Within the development community recently, there has been a greater focus on indoor air pollution as a health problem. Indoor air pollution has been listed as a leading cause of death in developing countries by the World Health Organization. Smoke from cooking fires contain many particulates and carcinogens. When this smoke is contained in an indoor space, the repeated breathing of it has been related to increased incidence of respiratory illness and premature death (Smith, 1993; Smith et al., 1993; Parikh and Laxmi, 2001; Ezzati and Kammen, 2001; Ezzati, Saleh and Kammen, 2002). In India alone, there have been some recent estimates that indoor air pollution is responsible for about 400 thousand premature deaths per year (Hughes, Lvovsky, and Dunleavy, 2001).

Increased availability of different kinds of energy services also can directly or indirectly improve the health and therefore the productivity of household members and workers. Increased availability of cleaner modern energy forms can improve indoor air quality (see, e.g. World Bank, 2002c; Ezzati and Kammen, 2002;

Ezzati et al., 2002). It can also help promote access to safer drinking water (e.g. in deeper wells). By facilitating refrigeration, greater energy availability can reduce food-borne illness and the storage of medicines. By lowering costs of food production, it can make it easier for subsistence households to meet and go beyond basic dietary requirements. Finally, for countries at various stages of development, greater energy availability may interact positively with the availability of other infrastructure services. Investments in a road network that lower transportation costs and thereby increase the geographical size, scale, and efficiency of markets are the more valuable if energy is more readily available for fueling transport. The same is true for electricity availability to power more modern telecommunications and information infrastructure.

To summarize, our discussion so far suggests several possible channels through which increased energy availability (including availability of energy forms previously not available) could disproportionately affect economic development:

- Reallocation of household time (especially that of women) away from energy provision for improved education and income generation and greater specialization of economic functions.
- Economies of scale in more industrial-type energy provision.
- Greater flexibility in time allocation through the day and evening.
- Enhanced productivity of education efforts.
- With more flexible and reliable as well as plentiful energy, greater ability to use a more efficient capital stock and take advantage of new technologies.
- Lower transportation and communication costs—greater market size and access, more access to information (combined result of energy and other infrastructure).
- Health-related benefits: reduced smoke exposure, clean water, refrigeration (direct benefits and higher productivity).

This discussion of how increased energy availability may promote different stages of development also underscores the need to not think about energy development in isolation. Even if we think about the issue fairly narrowly, capital equipment (more modern stoves, refrigerators, lighting, motors, boilers, as well as marketing and delivery systems for modern fuels like LPG) and increased knowledge are required to expand energy use and increase the productivity of household and industrial labor. Attempts to expand energy availability will accomplish little if bottlenecks to such investments are not overcome.

It is necessary also to consider what happens to the labor services saved through an increase in the scale and technical sophistication of energy service provision. One option could be the expansion of other household production activities, for example, animal husbandry and micro-enterprise. The size of such benefits depends on, among other things, the status of women in society. A less direct but important potential link is through the lowering of households' opportunity cost of education, especially for children. But this requires in practice the needed investment in the capacity for increased education, not just the freeing-up of household labor time from drudge work.

Similar observations can be made about the development of social institutions that permit effective use and enjoyment of the increasing returns. If energy markets are poorly established or organized because of weak property rights, for example, then the potential benefits of economies of scale in service provision may not be realized. This would apply to the creation of both additional biomass plantations and additional electricity supply capacity. Thus, while increasing returns in the provision of energy services may offer the potential for a disproportionate effect of energy development on overall development, the fuller realization of this potential requires other economic and social development interventions as well.

Finally, whatever disproportionate effects increased energy availability may have in facilitating development on the supply-side of the economy, it is important not to lose track of direct demand-side benefits as well. Quality of life improvements stemming from better health, less drudgery, more leisure, greater communication opportunities and increased social status all have direct positive effects on the well-being of various household members, in addition to whatever effects might be enjoyed through increasing the production possibilities of the economy.

In reviewing the evidence on the development impact of energy and poverty, it should be kept in mind that there is a complementarity between energy and poverty reduction programs. In Peru, recent surveys show that the bundling of services like water, electricity, sanitation, and education has major welfare benefits for local populations. Adding a fourth service has a development impact that is about seven times greater than a second service for rural households in Peru. Such linkages also have been confirmed in the Philippines, where the combination of electricity and education appear to have an independent impact on a family's earnings (Box 8.1), as well as in urban Indonesia (Fitzgerald et al., 1990). For cooking energy, there is an energy transition, and different policies are appropriate for different levels of the transition.

The impact of electrification also can be understood by examining the use of women's time from a survey of rural areas in India (Table 8.1). The survey involved random samples from selected districts in the states, broken down by whether or not they have electricity. As indicated, the households without electricity have the advantage of reading more in the evening and having greater levels of entertainment in the form of television. Of the 60 percent of

---

Box 8.1 THE BENEFITS OF RURAL ELECTRIFICATION FOR DEVELOPMENT: THE CASE OF THE PHILIPPINES

Sometimes the benefits of certain social investments serve to enhance the benefits of other, seemingly unrelated, social investments. Thus, rural electrification generates not only direct benefits to consumers of electricity (in the form of, say, better lighting or cheaper irrigation) but also indirectly complements governmental efforts to improve education and health. The full benefit of rural electrification consists of both these direct and indirect benefits. Thus, rural electrification may be just as important in complementing other programs as in providing direct benefits to rural households.

In order to better measure the full benefits of rural electrification, the World Bank initiated a study in the Philippines to quantify all rural electrification benefits in monetary terms. Some of these benefits, such as those resulting from a cheaper source of lighting, are fairly easy to measure with conventional techniques. However, the more indirect benefits in terms of better education, more comfort, increased convenience, and improved health are not as easily measured since price–quantity relationships are more difficult to observe. In these cases, benefits can be measured by determining what individuals would be willing to pay for these benefits. For example, increased educational benefits due to electrification could be measured by the expected increases in income that are likely to result.

Based on a survey of 2000 households in the Philippines, the study finds that one year of education increases, on average, annual income by about 13 thousand pesos. However, this increase is augmented by an additional two thousand pesos if the household has electricity. The gain in income reflects the fact that electrification appears to increase the probability of participating in the labor force. More importantly, the quality of education may improve with electrification. Both the decision to read and the amount of time spent studying and reading are significantly higher in homes with electricity. Children in homes with electricity, for example, study about 30 minutes longer each day than children in households without electricity. Taken together, these findings support the notion that electricity is a complement to other rural development programs, and especially education.

Source: World Bank, 2002b.

Table 8.1 Women's time use for leisure activities, India 1966 (Household Survey of Hours Spent on Activity in 6 States)

Income Decile	HH with Electricity	Leisure (Radio & Social Activities)		Read (Studying & Homework)		TV Watching	
	Percent	No Electric	With Electric	No Electric	With Electric	No Electric	With Electric
< Rs 600	43	0.69	0.96	0.06	0.10	0.06	0.23
Rs 600–799	39	0.87	1.11	0.03	0.09	0.05	0.44
Rs 800–949	47	0.83	0.82	0.04	0.17	0.05	0.41
Rs 950–1159	47	0.87	0.85	0.01	0.14	0.05	0.45
Rs 1160–1409	52	0.78	1.01	0.03	0.13	0.05	0.47
Rs 1410–1749	61	0.98	0.77	0.04	0.18	0.06	0.64
Rs 1750–2349	70	0.94	0.95	0.05	0.21	0.01	0.79
Rs 2350–3249	79	0.74	0.89	0.04	0.22	0.07	0.96
Rs 3250–4999	82	0.79	0.99	0.02	0.28	0.13	1.18
Rs 5000+	83	0.63	0.87	0.01	0.32	0.14	1.17
Average	61	0.82	0.91	0.03	0.21	0.06	0.76

Source: World Bank, 2002a; World Bank, 2004.

households with electricity, 10 percent reported that they typically read in the course of their day. Of the remaining 40 percent of households without electricity, only one percent of the women reports that they read. Although the figures for reading appear to be low, literacy rates are also low for women in India. Some women, especially older women, cannot read because they are not literate. Women who report that they read during a typical day spend about 1 hour and 15 minutes reading. This once again underscores the complementarity of social infrastructure programs.

Energy Scarcity

At present, about two billion people do not have access to electricity in the world. An equal number rely on biomass energy for cooking (World Bank, 1996). The number of people gaining access to electricity has increased remarkably during the last 25 years, reaching over 1 billion new people. Although this may appear to be an impressive accomplishment, it is still the case that higher income households now have electricity, and the world's poorest and mostly rural households do not. For petroleum and other 'modern' fuels, the scenario is similar. The rich have access and the poor do not. The poor also often spend a significant amount of their time collecting energy for their household needs or spend a very large percentage of their income on energy. This is clearly not a problem that can be ignored.

The 'modern' fuels being used by households in developing countries include electricity, liquefied petroleum gas (LPG), and kerosene (Hosier, 1993; Leach, 1993; Reddy and Reddy, 1983; Sathaye and Meyers, 1985). The supplies of these fuels are often irregular. Policies on their use also vary, from taxation to subsidies in various countries. In many circumstances, development assistance programs have been directed towards making the supplies of these fuels more regular, reliable, and efficient. Unfortunately, the attempt to improve sector performance often does not take into consideration those who presently do not have access to such services.

In spite of poor access to modern energy services, poor people often spend a significant proportion of their scarce income on energy. In urban areas, especially those experiencing 'wood scarcities around their perimeters,' the price of fuelwood for cooking often is higher than modern fuels. Although the poor do have fewer energy expenditures than more wealthy households, energy as a percent of total expenditures is often well above 10 percent of their income. In rural areas that are experiencing wood scarcity, rural people either pay for fuelwood or switch down the energy ladder to crop residues or dung. However, it is more typical that they spend a significant number of hours per week collecting fuel, and this is often a trade-off with other productive activities. Thus, the use of traditional fuels does not mean poor people are using 'free' energy, but rather that they are paying through labor or expenditures for traditional fuels. In some circumstances, this collection of fuelwood also can have adverse environmental consequences.

From a poverty standpoint, the expenditures of the poor on the very meager amounts of energy that they use is a very important part of their overall cash expenditures. The cash income of the poor is so low that even modest changes in energy expenditures can be a real hardship for them. The poor spend less cash on energy than the more wealthy households, but the percentage of income the poor spend on energy is typically much greater (for a typical example, see Figure 8.1). The urban poor spend between 10 and 20 percent of their income on energy, whereas the wealthy spend less than 5 percent. In addition, the cost of energy services for the poor is higher than for the rich because cooking with fuelwood and lighting with kerosene are inefficient compared with cooking and lighting with modern fuels. Moreover, the poor often buy fuelwood and charcoal in small amounts, and the higher transaction costs of buying in small quantities inflate the price. Once the comparative efficiencies and transaction costs have been taken into consideration, the delivered energy for cooking often is more expensive for poor people compared to better-off households.

Over time, as urban populations and land areas grow, incomes rise, and more traditional energy sources become more scarce and costly in the urban market, changes in the composition of household energy demand can be expected. Figures 8.2 and 8.3 illustrate one case. These transitions will vary considerably with local and national conditions including policies that affect the prices of competing energy sources.

How long the transition will take in today's developing countries will vary, depending on a number of factors, including a country's economic performance and development policies, the percentage of people dependent on

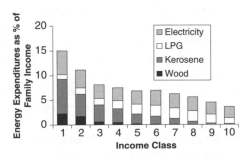

Figure 8.2 Household energy expenditures by income class, Hyderabad, 1994

Note: Income classes are in rupees per household per month and are as follows: 1 = < 185, 2 = 186–250, 3 = 251–300, 4 = 301–375, 5 = 376–498, 6 = 499–583, 7 = 584–725, 8 =726–990, 9 = 991–1480, 10 = < 1480.

Source: World Bank, 1999b.

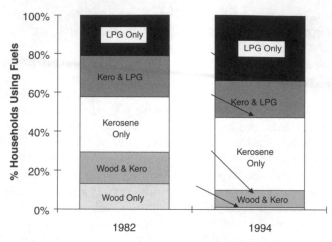

Figure 8.3 Changes in choice of household cooking fuels, Hyderabad, 1982 and 1994.
Source: World Bank, 1999b.

biomass, and the population growth rate (see Barnes, Krutilla, and Hyde, 2004). But it will not happen overnight. Even in East Asia and the Pacific, a region that has experienced rapid economic growth and significant increases in the supply of commercial energy, biomass still accounts for 33 percent of energy supplies and biomass use is expected to decrease by only 50 percent over the next 15–25 years. Therefore, while energy policies should create the necessary conditions for supplying modern fuels to those who lack them, they must also support ways to use existing biofuel energy resources more efficiently and sustainably.

Although in rural areas people spend less of the income on energy, poor people still pay a significant proportion of their income on energy. Some typical figures for India are presented in Table 8.2. As indicated, the poor pay as much as 8 percent of their very small incomes on energy, and most of it goes for kerosene for lighting purposes. As indicated, most of the cooking energy, with the exception of some wood, is generally collected from the local environment. The average time spent collecting wood or other fuels is about one hour per day in rural areas. Thus, both energy expenditures and energy collection time are important components of formal and informal expenditures by rural households.

Rural and poor people also often have difficulties affording the first costs of modern energy. For instance, the connection fees for gaining access to grid electricity in developing countries range from anywhere between 20 and 1000 dollars. A solar home system for lighting and television sets costs in the neighborhood of 500 to 1000 dollars depending on the system. Installing a community microgrid can cost a community tens of thousands of dollars. Such costs are

Table 8.2 Percent of income spent on energy in rural India, 1996

Income Decile Rs per Family per year	Wood	Charcoal	Straw	Dung	Coal	Kerosene-Ration	Kerosene-Market	LPG	Electricity	Total
< Rs575	0.9	0.1	0.2	0.5	0.0	3.0	1.0	0.1	2.1	8.1
Rs575–791	1.0	0.1	0.4	0.9	0.0	2.2	0.5	0.2	1.4	6.5
Rs792–957	1.6	0.3	0.3	0.5	0.0	2.0	0.5	0.2	1.5	7.0
Rs958–1165	1.2	0.3	0.4	0.5	0.0	1.5	0.3	0.3	1.4	6.0
Rs1166–1415	1.8	0.2	0.3	0.5	0.0	1.4	0.3	0.3	1.3	6.2
Rs1416–1740	1.3	0.1	0.4	0.5	0.0	1.1	0.3	0.3	1.7	5.8
Rs1741–2349	1.6	0.2	0.3	0.3	0.0	0.7	0.2	0.4	1.6	5.4
Rs2350–3249	1.3	0.1	0.2	0.1	0.0	0.5	0.2	0.4	1.4	4.3
Rs3250–4999	0.9	0.1	0.2	0.0	0.0	0.3	0.1	0.5	1.1	3.3
Rs5000+	0.5	0.1	0.0	0.0	0.0	0.2	0.0	0.4	0.8	2.0

Source: World Bank, 2002a.

prohibitive for rural consumers with relatively low incomes and little access to long- or even short-term credit.

As noted above, recent work on household fuel use and indoor air pollution underscores the importance for poor urban and rural people of having access to cleaner fuls such as kerosene and LPG for cooking. There are many circumstances in which cooking with LPG or kerosene is actually cheaper than cooking with wood in urban areas. Under these conditions, poor people in some countries are paying more for their cooking energy than do the wealthy.

The use of fuels in inefficient stoves appears to be at the root of this problem (Smith et al., 1993). Although the nominal price of the fuels poor people use may be less than that of modern fuels, the useful energy derived from these fuels is much, much less because of the low energy efficiency of wood stoves. The typical efficiencies of woodstoves or open fires range from 10 to 15 percent, and charcoal stoves reach up to about 25 percent. In contrast, LPG and electric stoves have efficiencies of between 55 and 75 percent. Realistic assessments of the price of energy thus must take account of energy actually delivered to cooking utensils such as pots and pans rather than the value per unit of energy.

Table 8.3 illustrates the wide variation among fuels as well as across countries in energy costs per useful energy unit for cooking. Even in the absence of subsidies, modern fuels often are less expensive than traditional fuels. Continued use of traditional fuels by the poor reflects the fact that often they do not possess the income or influence to get a service connection for LPG. The poor also buy fuels in very small quantities, which costs more than purchasing in bulk. The initial costs of cooking equipment also discourage the poor from adopting modern fuels for cooking. Finally, in some countries there are import restrictions on modern fuels, and after servicing the higher income groups, there is nothing left for the poor.

Douglas F. Barnes and Michael A. Toman

Table 8.3 The price of cooking energy in urban areas of 12 countries, 1990. (Price in US Dollars Per KgOE of Useful Cooking Energy)

Country	Income $/HH/M	Policy for Kerosene or LPG	Wood	Charcoal	Kerosene	LPG	Electricity	Coal
Thailand	99	Market	1.48	1.42	0.81	0.54	0.97	NA
Yemen	70	Market	4.35	4.92	1.55	0.61	2.41	NA
Bolivia	64	Market	1.64	1.28	0.98	0.44	0.86	NA
Haiti	59	Tax	0.87	1.12	1.41	1.19	2.16	NA
Cape Verde	54	Market	1.72	2.69	1.63	1.28	3.22	NA
Zimbabwe	51	Subsidy	1.58	2.58	1.10	0.98	1.07	NA
Philippines	32	Market	1.86	1.16	0.80	0.46	0.85	NA
Burkina Faso	29	Tax	1.63	1.99	2.10	1.90	2.18	NA
Mauritania	27	Tax	3.46	1.71	1.23	1.17	4.12	NA
Indonesia	20	Subsidy	1.18	1.11	0.41	0.54	0.94	NA
Zambia	20	Subsidy	1.14	0.55	0.66	0.50	0.28	NA
China	18	Subsidy	0.51	0.60	1.00	0.34	0.69	0.09

Note: The between-country differences can be affected by exchange rate differences, but this would not affect within-country differences. The information is based on what people actually have paid according to household surveys. The surveys were conducted in late 1980a and the early 1990s.
Source: Barnes, Krutilla, and Hyder, 2004.

Electricity Sector Structure, Regulation, and Economic Efficiency

At the earlier stages of the energy transition, much of the energy production and consumption occurs in a very decentralized fashion through household provision or localized fuel markets. As the energy transition proceeds, however, and especially as the electricity sector grows, additional problems arise in the governance of large and more centralized energy suppliers. In this section, we focus especially on electricity, given its importance in the energy transition, though the general points we make could apply as well to natural gas, the other important network-based energy resource.

All countries, developed and developing, face challenges in the governance of the electricity sector. This reflects at least partly the inherent nature of the sector. The sector is technologically complex. While individual power generating units can vary in their complexity, these units are linked together in a grid of transmission and distribution lines that must be continuously balanced to avoid outages. There are enormous economies of scale in transmission and significant economies of scale in local distribution, so competition in these stages is limited or impossible. These services must be provided either by publicly owned and managed enterprises or through some sort of privately regulated enterprises to ensure both that service is provided and that users are not subjected to the adverse effects of monopoly power.

Traditionally, power production also has been provided publicly or by regulated private enterprises. In principle, and increasingly in practice in developed countries, power generation and marketing services can be provided under

258

more competitive market conditions. But success in engendering competitive *and* efficient generation markets requires in turn a different set of regulations to ensure appropriate conditions of market access and transmission pricing, as well as structures to maintain competitive conditions in power production and purchase transactions. Moreover, while the minimum technically efficient scale of power generation facilities has fallen in the past two decades, it may still be large relative to total electricity demand in small markets, calling into question the ability to engender competition.

The above-mentioned problems are relatively generic, affecting in various ways developed and developing countries alike (Joskow, 1998, 2003). The particular circumstances of developing countries, however, can give rise to additional or more serious problems (Bacon and Besant-Jones, 2001; Wolak, 2003; Millan and von der Fehr, 2003). Weaker governance institutions and limited financial resources lead to poor economic performance of state-owned enterprises and low quality of service, even while the costs of maintaining capacity become unbearable. Indeed, it is often less a desire to improve the efficiency of resource allocation per se than the desire to lighten the financial burden on public coffers while improving service that leads to interest in privatization and sector restructuring. However, the same governance problems also can engender lack of independence and other weaknesses of sector regulators when privatization and sector restructuring are attempted. Efforts to improve financial sustainability and improve quality and efficiency of service also become entangled in debates over reforms of tariffs to reflect the real opportunity costs of services.

Against this backdrop, efforts have been undertaken by a number of developing countries to reform their power sectors for greater economic efficiency, including activities to promote privatization, entry of independent power producers, greater competition in generation, more efficient tariffs, and improved transmission efficiency (Bacon and Besant-Jones, 2001). However, these efforts have had decidedly mixed results. To some extent, the limited success may reflect efforts to implement the same kinds of reforms that have been used with success in developed countries while failing to adequately allow for the specific conditions in developing countries. To some extent, it may reflect only partial implementation of reforms in the face of political constraints. In any event, the disappointments that have been experienced seem to have weakened at least somewhat the enthusiasm for reform that was in evidence a few years ago, while leaving many developing countries still facing the dilemma of how to promote a well-functioning electricity system.

Aside from these challenges, developing countries also face the additional hurdle of how best to extend modern grid-based electricity services to currently under-served populations, especially in poorer and more rural areas. The marginal cost of grid extension typically is high, and while the relative willingness to pay of underserved populations also is significant, there is often a gap between the cost of extending service and what can be recovered efficiently even with the best designed tariffs. This is precisely the reason why alternatives to grid-based energy services are so important to consider in a broader energy and development strategy. But access to modern electricity services also provides broader development benefits, as already noted, giving it some attributes of a public good. Where the balance between the marginal social value of extending grid electricity service and its marginal cost is seen as favorable, developing countries face the practical challenge of how to most efficiently channel any public subsidies provided for such extension, given limited financial resources, in lieu of less-focused consumption subsidies based on non-remunerative tariffs that actually benefit the higher-consuming wealthy.

Improving the Energy Transition in Urban and Rural Areas

We have argued that the energy transition is an ongoing process that involves movement from the inefficient use of traditional energy to the efficient use of modern fuels for cooking, heating, lighting, and other uses. The two groups that have the greatest difficulty gaining access to energy services in developing countries are people living in rural areas, and poor people residing in urban areas. The problems of these two groups of people are somewhat similar, although the solutions to their problems can be somewhat different. Poor people in urban areas at least live near companies that provide energy services. In rural areas, the infrastructure is often totally absent.

The evidence suggests that people are willing to spend a significant portion of their incomes on higher quality energy that improves their quality of life or enables them to be more productive. It can be said with some confidence that in the long-term people will switch away from the inefficient ways of using biomass fuels and will use energy for a much wider range of services than they do now. For example, people in urban areas in Africa will eventually replace their kerosene lamps with electric lights. In Asia, the inefficient refrigerators will be replaced with more efficient models. In Latin America, cooking with electricity and LPG will become more common.

However, the long-term solution to these problems cannot be forced indiscriminately onto countries or cities regardless of their stage in the energy transition. Although there are exceptions, most people in cities will move through the energy transition slowly and in due course. Thus, it is important to address their present energy problems as well as their upcoming problems. Current problems may include stress on wood resources around some urban areas (Ravindranath and Hall, 1995), low standards of energy service, high prices for wood, and poorly functioning markets for modern fuels. Enabling consumers to choose among alternative forms of energy requires, among other things, liberalizing prices to reflect costs and adopting regulatory policies that encourage competition and level the playing field for all types of energy markets, whether they are served by public utilities, private firms, or community enterprises. Regardless of the types of assistance, the ideal should also be to expand the menu of choices available to people in rural areas.

We divide our discussion of lessons learned and recommendations for action into three broad categories: promoting efficiency in primary fuel supplies and energy efficiency; improving access to electricity for poor and rural populations; and improving the efficiency and sustainability of the modern electricity sector.

Promoting Efficiency of Primary Energy Supplies and Energy Efficiency

Many cities where fuelwood is used extensively have good access to wood resources. The problem in many cases, however, is that wood is harvested faster than it is regrown, and such harvesting cannot be kept up for long. When wood is mined from existing woodlands, the result is both fuel shortages and extensive ecological damage from deforestation.

Farm forestry and forest management have long played an important role in alleviating wood shortages and providing sustainable fuelwood supplies. Farm forestry entails planting trees, shrubs, and sometimes grasses on farmlands and crop boundaries. Because farmers outnumber foresters in most countries by several thousand to one, involving them in planting trees and shrubs can dramatically accelerate afforestation. Besides, the incentive to participate in farm forestry programs is strong in regions serving urban markets with high wood prices. In addition, trees and shrubs can supply farmers with fodder, building materials, green mulch, fruit, and other by-products that may be as valuable as the firewood itself.

While fuelwood markets themselves will provide economic signals of the benefit of increased farm forestry, experience suggests that effective management of existing forest resources also depends on letting local people take responsibility for forests or woodlands that might otherwise be open access resources with no effective management. In participatory programs in several countries, farmers can sell all the wood extracted from local woodlands; to do so, however, they must also participate in a resource-management program developed in collaboration with the national forestry department. In Niger, for example, communities were given control over natural woodlands and their products, if they participated in a program to manage the land (Foley et al., 1997).

Identification of the appropriate social unit with which to work is crucial. Several World Bank-financed community woodlot and forestry projects in the late 1970s and 1980s had disappointing results because communities had been mistakenly viewed as units of social organization when, in actuality, the interests of subgroups frequently clashed. Moreover insufficient attention was given to other complicating factors: community land was limited and the tenure of common lands uncertain; the influence of local authorities was uneven; and

261

distributional arrangements for the products were contested. Afforestation projects in which farmers themselves plant trees on farmlands have been far more successful.

For cities with extensive wood and charcoal use and relatively high energy prices, the promotion of improved stoves as well as improved fuelwood management often involves a situation in which there are no losers (World Bank, 2002c). Women spend fewer hours gathering fuelwood, so that time is released for both productive and domestic activities. Scarce cash income is saved and income generation may be promoted. The stoves give off less smoke, and thus also have health benefits since they reduce the level of indoor air pollution in homes. In areas where resources are scarce, greater efficiency also reduces aggregate wood demand, which diminishes pressure on the land surrounding urban areas.

Experience suggests that while fuelwood costs are one powerful influence on incentives to upgrade stoves, other measures typically are needed (Barnes, Openshaw, Smith, and van der Plas, 1994). In some cases with very poor popula- tions, even the modest first costs of a new stove are a barrier that can only be overcome with improved access to micro-credit or outright subsidization of the purchase. Information must also be provided about options to encourage consideration on non-traditional designs. For such programs to work well, however, it is necessary to target carefully those who would derive the most benefit from them, as demonstrated by the failure of several programs in the 1970s and early 1980s. Among other reasons, the Chinese National Improved Stove Program, the largest ever undertaken (120 million stoves have been used in rural households) was a success because it concentrated on areas with the greatest shortages of fuelwood (Smith et al., 1993).

There are also numerous opportunities for improvement by reducing distortions in the pricing and allocation of modern energy resources. Taxes on modern fuels are a convenient revenue source, but such taxes also drive many middle-class people into continuing their reliance on wood beyond the point at which they would have normally changed fuels. The tax raises the cap on fuelwood prices, thereby hurting the poor (Box 8.2), while also putting additional pressure on forest areas around cities.

Similarly, policies to limit petroleum imports in many countries imply that people in rural areas may have no chance at gaining access to modern and cleaner fuels for cooking. In an Indian study involving six states, for example, only two of them had significant use of LPG in rural areas. For one of these states—Himachal Pradesh—the policy to target LPG to urban areas had been relaxed to protect the existing remaining forests in the state. Most of the other states had an insignificant percentage of households using LPG for cooking (World Bank, 2002a).

While subsidies can assist the poor, these subsidies also can cause other problems in the energy sector (see Table 8.4). Often, not only the poor but also the

---

Box 8.2 TAXING THE RICH INADVERTENTLY HURTS THE POOR

Haiti is characterized by LPG prices among the highest in the Caribbean, if not the world. This means that fuels like LPG and kerosene are limited to only a small fraction of the population. Massive deforestation over the past 25 years has depleted the country's wood supplies, meaning that the urban poor, most of whom depend on charcoal for cooking, now pay higher prices.

As the graph below illustrates, kerosene and LPG prices have historically been related to that of charcoal. As wood resources have disappeared from rural markets, the price of charcoal for cooking has approached that of alternative commercial fuels. Today there is hardly any price difference, and taxes on kerosene and LPG mean higher prices for charcoal.

Energy Prices in Haiti, 1970–90.
(Current $ per gigajoule adjusted for end-use efficiency).

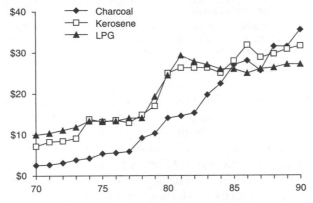

Analysis shows that under normal supply conditions, gas would become the best financial option for the Haitian consumer and the best economic option for the country. Thus, if liquid fuels were taxed lightly instead of heavily, and priced to reflect their economic cost, consumers would also pay less for wood and charcoal, making it easier for the entire country to move toward greater energy efficiency.

Source: World Bank 1991.

---

middle-class and the rich get the subsidy. Thus, in Indonesia, for example, the subsidization of kerosene does help the poor, but it is an unnecessary boon to higher-income consumers and keeps the middle-class from switching to superior fuels such as LPG. Subsidies to household fuels such as kerosene often wind up being diverted to other markets, including transportation. In Pakistan, the government had subsidized kerosene to assist the poor, but much of the kerosene was diverted away from households to the transportation sector. In Ecuador, subsidized kerosene wound up on the black market and was exported to a neighboring country.

Even when subsidies do benefit the poor, they may represent an unsustainable financial burden on the state while creating other burdens. For example, imports

Table 8.4 Impact of energy pricing and supply policies on rural people and urban poor

Supply policy	Energy pricing policy		
	Subsidized prices	Market prices	Fuel taxation
Limited or targeted supply	Subsidy is redirected away from poor to other groups.	Higher-income groups are served first.	Traditional fuel prices are unaffected by those of alternatives.
	Rural and poor people lack access to fuel.	Rural and poor people lack access to fuel.	Rural and poor people lack access to fuel.
Unlimited or untargeted supply	Modern fuel subsidies mean lower prices for traditional fuels.	Traditional fuel prices are capped at price of alternatives.	First costs of service, along with fuel costs, constrain poor from purchasing fuel.
	Rural and poor people can access service, but it is fiscally unsustainable.	Rural and poor people can access service, and it is fiscally sustainable.	Rural and poor people can access service, but it is expensive.
	Poor benefit from lower fuel prices, but other income groups benefit more.	First costs of service constrain poor from purchasing modern fuels.	Traditional fuel prices are often high because of higher-priced alternative fuels.

of petroleum products in limited quantities with subsidies and rationing, as in India, is problematic because the poor have problems obtaining ration cards, and the limited supply means that the fuel has cap effect in capping the price of fuelwood. Market liberalization is usually a far more effective strategy. In Hyderabad, India, for example, only the richest 10 percent of households used LPG in 1980 (World Bank, 1999b). When the Indian government liberalized energy markets and relaxed restrictions on the production and import of LPG, more middle-class households could buy LPG, a more efficient fuel than kerosene. The poor could then afford kerosene. Now more than 60 percent of households use LPG. High taxes on cooking fuels are also usually counterproductive. When LPG and kerosene are heavily taxed, demand for other fuels increases, driving up the prices of all fuels and penalizing the poor. Abandonment of targeted subsidies and loosening of restrictions on imports may be needed to clear the bottlenecks to adoption of transition fuels. Since the fuels are comparatively attractive and efficient, it may be more productive to provide credit to low-income consumers for the purchase of appliances such as stoves.

Improving Access to Electricity for Poor and Rural Populations

In some cases the high initial costs of rural energy services can be addressed by lowering system costs through technology choice and design innovations. Typical power demand in rural areas of developing countries ranges from 0.2 to 0.5kW of power service. Many distribution companies design systems that are capable of delivering between 3 and 7kW hours of service, which means heavier wires, larger transformers, and generally more expensive distribution systems components. The entire system design can be lightened to provide service at less cost.

Technologies involving wind power, solar thermal power (sunlight used to heat air or water), photovoltaic (PV) cells (which produce electricity directly from sunlight), and small-scale hydropower also merit attention in some circumstances. They are in many cases an ideal way to get energy to rural areas and have significant environmental advantages relative to fossil fuels. Costs, once prohibitive, have decreased significantly over the past decade to the point where it is practical to consider these options where grid-based energy options are not an economical option. These technologies may be used at the level of the individual household or in village-scale micro-grid applications. For example, in remote areas that might otherwise be served by using kerosene, LPG, dry-cell and car batteries, and, occasionally, small diesel or gasoline generators, photovoltaic systems have increasingly demonstrated that they can be competitive on cost and service grounds.

Design innovations also are important to the deployment of these small-scale technologies. For example, the standard household photovoltaic system promoted by many development agencies is a 50 watt household system. There is some recent evidence from Kenya (van der Plas and de Graaff, 1988; Nieuwenhout, van de Rijt, Wiggelinkhuizen, 1998) and China (Tuntivate, Barnes, and Bogach, 2000) that people are starting off by purchasing photovoltaic systems of about 12 watts that are more affordable. Just as important, however, is support for development of effective capacities to provide service for decentralized systems (Box 8.3).

Financial innovation also can lower service costs for rural electricity. In particular, costs can be spread over time through enhancing credit availability for both consumers and suppliers of energy services. In particular, credit may be augmented for assisting the poor to pay for the up-front costs that are involved in initiating electricity service. Because the poor gain great benefits from switching from kerosene to electricity for lighting, improved electricity access can yield real improvements in their quality of life, thereby justifying some targeted and judicious subsidization of access. In many developing countries, however, money lenders charge consumer rates of more than 100 percent, which would make purchasing any energy systems unaffordable for rural people. Electricity companies can provide credit for access charges, by spreading payments out over a period of several years and including the charge on regular electricity bills. Some non-governmental organizations are making credit available for the installation of microgrid systems based on renewable energy technologies.

While subsidization of electricity consumption in general is problematic, one subsidy that can be justified in some cases is a lifeline rate for grid electricity (Barnes, Krutilla, and Hyde, 2004). Most poor people use very little electricity (one or two light bulbs and a radio), and their demand for electricity is for basic service only. Thus the establishment of a low price for the lowest electricity

Box 8.3 FINANCING AND SUPPORTING PHOTOVOLTAIC SYSTEMS IN RURAL DOMINICAN REPUBLIC

Since 1984, Enersol Associates Inc., a U.S.-based nongovernmental organization (NGO), has supported the development of indigenous Dominican supply, service, and financing mechanisms and a market-driven demand for household photovoltaic (PV) systems. Enersol's immediate objective is to develop an 'open-ended self-sustainable program for solar-based rural electrification and, eventually, to integrate solar technologies with rural societies in Latin America.' The approach involves using donor grants to train a network of local entrepreneurs to sell and service PV systems; and to develop a community-based solar NGO to manage revolving loan funds that can be used by local people to purchase systems.

Because a standard home PV system costs more than half the average annual per capita income in the Dominican Republic, credit is essential if PV is to penetrate the rural energy market. Accordingly, a key component of the Enersol model is a network of locally managed NGO credit programs to finance systems using revolving loan funds capitalized by external donors. Recipients must repay full capital, installation, and market interest costs with monthly payments over two to five years. The default rate for these credit programs is less than 1 percent, though late payments are not uncommon. Other rural Dominicans have purchased systems with cash or informal three-to six-month loans provided by system suppliers. In addition to building capacity for household systems, Enersol created a program to help communities finance and implement PV water-pumping and community-lighting projects.

Enersol founder Richard Hansen attributes the program's success to several factors: simple, economical, stand-alone systems; emphasis on training and development of local human resources; village-level focus and control; local capital generation to ensure community responsibility and support for the projects; and parallel development of credit programs, service enterprises, and technical and organizational human resources.

Source: K. Kozloff, O. Shobowale, 1994.

consumers (generally poor people) is a direct benefit for poor people. Lifeline rates for blocks of approximately 40 to 50 kWh, or even less for rural areas, will cover basic lighting for the poor, especially for cities in the later stages of the energy transition. It also does not cause a significant financial drain on the distribution company because the revenue lost is very minor when compared to the total revenue from the higher income consumers. The financial losses can even be recovered through slightly higher prices paid by the larger volume, generally higher income customers. However, lifeline rates at the 200 to 300 kWh level should be avoided, since this helps the middle-class and rich more than the poor who use electricity.

Last but certainly not least, effectively and efficiently expanding electricity service to poor and rural populations requires careful attention to institutional and political considerations, including local participation in decisionmaking and attention to incentives for serving higher-cost rural markets in the wake of privatization and restructuring initiatives. Successful experiences in Senegal, Costa Rica and India illustrate the kinds of endeavors that are required (Box 8.4). In Chile, a tax on existing electricity users is placed in a fund for the

---

Box 8.4 RURAL ELECTRIFICATION LESSONS FROM SUCCESSFUL PROGRAMS

Cooperative Rural Electrification in Costa Rica

Rural electrification is one of Costa Rica's success stories. In the 1960s as little as 20 percent of people in rural areas had access to electricity. At that time, despite growing demands from rural areas, rural electrification remained a low priority for the public electricity company. By the early 1970s, with assistance from USAID, four rural electrification cooperatives were set up in Costa Rica. All four of these cooperatives have prospered and now provide electricity supplies to about 20 percent of the country's rural population. In the meantime, most of the remaining rural areas have been provided with electricity by the national utility. By the end of 1995 over 90 percent of the rural population has been connected into the national electricity supply system.

Village Provision of Electricity Near Bangalore, India, South India

The village of Pura supplies household electricity and water through large community biogas digesters. Because grid electricity supply was unreliable, the community decided to establish a system of biogas production for fueling a five-horsepower diesel generator. Electricity from the generator was supplied through a microgrid to households and also powered a deep tubewell pump that supplied water to a local system. Each household participating in the program received a tap with clean water at the front of their house, eliminating long walks to the local tank and significantly improving their health. Each household is charged a fixed rate for the water tap and each electricity connection. Some households now have both a grid and a village connection that some in the village have called 'people's power.'

Public Company Rural Electrification in Thailand

In Thailand the rural electrification was implemented through a public distribution company. In the early 1970s, the task of rural electrification was given to the Provincial Electricity Authority, which was responsible for serving customers in both urban and rural areas outside of Bangkok. The company established an office of rural electrification to carry out the task. The company was required to be financially viable throughout the rural electrification expansion, and this was accomplished by relying on international donors for investment capital, a bulk supply tariff reduction sanctioned by the government of Thailand, and an internal cross-subsidy from urban consumers. Thus, for the most part existing customers with electricity provided much of the financing for new rural consumers.

Source: World Bank, 1996; Foley, 2004; Tuntivate and Barnes, 2004.

---

development of new electricity distribution. Access to the fund has been used mainly to the distribution companies throughout the country, but it is also open for the development of decentralized electricity distribution as well. This fund can only be utilized for extending access to new electricity consumers. The funds are available to communities. But the distribution companies or contractors can assist the communities to apply for the funds. Although the funds are not loans but are straight subsidies, to qualify for the funds both communities and service providers must demonstrate that they are investing much of their own money in the project. Thus, the companies have to match these funds with their own investments based on a set of considerations, including cost of construction and service.

Rural electrification on a large scale, whether through grid extension or through off-grid technologies, generally is not a profitable business based on short-term commercial profit motives or financing arrangements. Historically in almost all parts of the world, private sector businesses have tended not to enter the business of providing electricity service to rural areas. The initial capital costs can be recovered over the long term, but this requires long-term financing or other forms of financial intermediation. On the other hand, the welfare benefits for rural and poor people of having access to electricity are quite high, as already noted. The challenge is to develop privatization frameworks that do not significantly distort efficiency in the energy sector, but does take into consideration societal goals of expanding access to energy services by poor and rural populations.

Improving the Efficiency and Sustainability of the Modern Electricity Sector

As the modern electricity sector grows in importance within a developing country, so does the importance of a variety of policy reforms to promote its efficiency. The converse is also true—reform to promote efficiency and financial sustainability is a necessary condition in many cases for effective expansion of the sector.

Electricity subsidies are a particular problem. In the early 1990s, the average electricity tariff in developing countries was about 4 cents per kWh, while the average cost was about 10 cents per kWh. Such subsidies have left many utilities economically crippled, unable to finance the extension of services to rural areas. Moreover, they distort the market, encouraging consumers to buy grid-supplied electricity and discouraging the development of cheaper ways of generating electricity. Inefficient pricing also distorts plant dispatch and investment decisions by masking the true opportunity cost of different sources of supply (see Wolak, 2003 for illustrations of this).

There is a widespread belief that electricity tariffs need to be extremely low, often well below their true supply costs, if rural electrification is to benefit rural people. The facts do not support this. Rural electrification only makes sense in areas where there is already a demand for electricity-using services such as lighting, television, refrigeration and motive power. In the absence of a grid supply, these services are obtained by spending money on kerosene, LPG, dry-cell batteries, car battery recharging, and small power units, all of which are highly expensive per unit of electricity supplied. Recent surveys in regions without electricity in Uganda and Laos indicate that people spend approx-imately 5 dollars per month on these energy sources. Private suppliers often find a ready market for electricity at more than US 1$ per kwh. It follows that rural electrification tariffs set at realistic levels do not prevent people making significant savings in their energy costs, as well as obtaining a vastly improved service. Charging the right price allows the electricity company to provide an electricity supply in an effective, reliable, and sustainable manner to an increasing number of satisfied consumers.

Improved sector governance more generally is another key step toward improved efficiency of service provision. This contains a number of components. The economic performance of publicly-managed enterprises (generation or transmission and distribution) needs to be improved. Often, however, this is difficult. Privatization can be an alternative, but it will succeed in improving efficiency and acceptability of service only if accompanied by effective regulation and strengthened, independent regulators. This institutional reform also is difficult to achieve. As noted above, moreover, if access to the services by poor households is not improved in the course of privatization, the benefits of such sector reform will materialize mainly to more wealthy households that already have service.

Programs of regulatory reform and promotion of competition are of undoubted importance to the long-term evolution of modern and efficient electricity systems in the developing world. Yet, when these reforms are undertaken they must take account of the particular circumstances of the country or countries undertaking the reform, avoiding a 'one size fits all' approach. This is illustrated by the experience with reform in Central America (Millan and von der Fehr, 2003). Each of these countries has had experience with reform, with varying results. One concern with attempts to institute competitive generation markets, for example, has been the small size of individual country demands relative to minimum efficient plant scale, raising questions of whether enough competitors could effectively enter national markets. Under these conditions, more traditional cost-based plant dispatch may be more efficient. Even more efficient in the longer term may be the promotion of regional market integration, in particular through transmission system upgrading and extension, to enlarge market size and allow for both greater competition and more efficient investment scales. This observation does not obviate the need for attending as well to the need for smaller-scale investment in more isolated markets.

An interesting question in the context of modern electricity sector development is the need for what has been referred to in developed countries as demand-side management. At later stages in the energy transition, people in urban areas increase the number of appliances that they own, and consequently the demand for electricity rises dramatically. This makes the conservation of electricity more salient. While efficient energy pricing and the development of energy service companies are an important part of the development of effective energy conservation, some information and standards programs (such as publishing energy efficiency ratings on appliances) may also be useful in practice.

Concluding Remarks

The energy sector makes an important contribution to both people's quality of life and level of economic well-being for people in developing countries. There is a misconception that the percentage of energy used by households declines with development. However, the reverse is true. The use of modern energy by households increases both absolutely and as a percentage of energy use with development.

As we move beyond the start of the twenty-first century, urban populations will continue to grow at a high rate and rural populations will become more stable. This means that the rural populations by necessity will have to become more productive to meet ever increasing demands for food, fiber and other farm products. They will need energy as an input in this process. Urban populations will switch from the use of traditional fuels to modern fuels as a consequence of changing lifestyles, economic development, and reduced availability of inexpensive biomass around their urban perimeters. However, this transition needs to take place in an environmentally sound and equitable manner. Interfuel substitution, energy conservation, efficient small-scale and large-scale investments in electricity supply, and enlightened policies governing energy pricing and access all will influence how this transition takes place.

References

Bacon, R. W. and J. Besant-Jones (2001), 'Global Electric Power Reform, Privatization, and Liberalization of the Electric Power Industry in Developing Countries,' *Annual Review of Energy and Environment* 26: 311–59.

Barnes, Douglas (1988), *Electric Power for Rural Growth* Boulder: Westview Press.

—— and Willem Floor (1996), 'Rural Energy and Developing Countries: A Challenge for Economic Development,' *Annual Review of Energy and Environment* 21: 497–530.

——, Keith Openshaw, Kirk Smith, Robert van der Plas (1994), *What makes people cook with improved biomass stoves? A comparative International review of stove programs.* Washington, DC: The World Bank.

——, Kery Krutilla, and William Hyde (2005), *The Urban Household Energy Transition: Energy, Poverty, and the Environment in the Developing World*, Washington, DC: Resources for the Future Press.

Brennan, T., K. L. Palmer, R. J. Kopp, A. J., et al. (1996), *A Shock to the System: Restructuring America's Electricity System* Washington, DC: Resources for the Future.

Ezzati, M., H. Saleh, and D. M. Kammen, 2000. The Contributions of Emission and Spatial Microenvironments to Exposure to Indoor Air Pollution from Biomass Combustion in Kenya. *Environmental Health Perspectives* 108: 833–9.

——, and Daniel Kammen (2001), 'Quantifying the effects of exposure to indoor air pollution form biomass combustion on acute respiratory infections in developing countries,' *Environ Health Perspect* 109: 481–9.

——, H. Saleh, and Daniel Kammen (2002), The contributions of emissions and spatial microenvironments to exposure to indoor air pollution from biomass combustion in Kenya. *Environ Health Perspect* 108: 833–9.

Fitzgerald, Kevin, Douglas Barnes, and Gordon McGranahan (1990), *Interfuel Substitution and Changes in the Way Households Use Energy: The Case of Cooking and Lighting Behavior in Urban Java*, Industry and Energy Department Working Paper, Energy Series Paper No. 29, Washington, DC, World Bank.

Foley, Gerald (2004), 'Rural Electrification and the Cooperative Experience in Costa Rica' (forthcoming) in *Meeting the Challenge of Rural Electrification in Developing Nations: The Experience of Successful Programs*. Washington DC, World Bank, ESMAP.

——, Willem Floor, Gerard Madon, et al. (1997), *The Niger Household Energy Project: Promoting Rural Fuelwood Markets and Village Management of Natural Woodlands*. World Bank Technical Paper No. 362, World Bank, Washington, DC.

Hosier, Richard H. (1993), 'Urban Energy Systems in Tanzania: A Tale of three Cities,' *Energy Policy* 21(5): 510–23.

Hughes, Gordon, Kseniya Lvovsky, and Meghan Dunleavy (2001), *Environmental Health in India: Priorities in Andhra Pradesh*. Environment and Social Development Unit, South Asia Region, World Bank, Washington, DC.

Jorgenson, D. W. (1984), 'The Role of Energy in Productivity Growth,' *Energy Journal* 5(3): 11–26.

Joskow, P. L. (1998), 'Electric Sectors in Transition,' *Energy Journal* 19(2): 25–62.

—— (2003), 'Electricity Sector Restructuring and Competition: Lessons Learned,' *Cuadernos de Economía* 40: 548–58.

—— and R. Schmalensee (1983), *Markets for Power: An Analysis of Electric Utility Regulation*, Cambridge, Ma.: MIT Press.

Kozloff, K. and O. Shobowale (1994), *Rethinking Development Assistance for Renewable Electricity*, Washington, DC: World Resources Institute.

Leach, Gerald (1993), 'The Energy Transition,' *Energy Policy* 116–123 (February).

Millán, Jaime and Nils-Henrik M., von der Fehr (eds) (2003), *Keeping the Lights On: Power Sector Reform in Latin America*, Washington, DC: Inter-American Development Bank.

Nakicenovic, N. (1996), 'Freeing Energy from Carbon,' *Daedalus* 125(3): 95–112.

Nieuwenhout, F., P. van der Rijit, and E. Wiggelinkhuizen (1998), *Rural Lighting Services: A Comparison of Lamps for Domestic Lighting in Developing Countries*, Report of the Netherlands Energy Research Foundation, The Netherlands.

Office of Technology Assessment (OTA) (1990), *Physical Vulnerability of Electric System to Natural Disasters and Sabotage*, Report OTA-E-453, June; accessed through http://www.wws.princeton.edu/~ota/.

—— (1991), *Energy in Developing Countries*, Report OTA-E-486, January; accessed through http://www.wws.princeton.edu/~ota/.

—— (1992), *Fueling Development: Energy Technologies for Developing Countries*, Report OTA-E-516 (April); accessed through http://www.wws.princeton.edu/~ota/.

Parikh, Jyoti and Vijay Laxmi (2000) 'Biofuels, Pollution and Health Linkages: A Survey of Rural Tamil Nadu', *Economic and Political Weekly*, vol. 34, pp. 4125–37.

—— and —— (2001), 'Biofuels, Pollution and Health Linkages: A Survey of Rural Tamil Nadu,' *Economic and Political Weekly*, vol. 36.

Ravindranath, N. H. and D. O. Hall (1995), *Biomass, Energy, and Environment*. Oxford: Oxford University Press.

Reddy, A. K. and B. S. Reddy (1983), 'Energy in a Stratified Society: Case Study of Firewood in Bangalore,' *Economic and Political Weekly* 17(1) (October 8).

Reddy B. S. and Amulya Kumar N. Reddy, (1983) 'Energy in a stratified society: A case study of firewood in Bangalore', Economic and Political Weekly, vol. 17, pp. 1757–70.

271

Sathaye, Jayant and Steven Meyers (1985), 'Energy Use in Cities of the Developing Countries,' *Annual Review of Energy* 10: 109–33.

Sathaye, Jayant, and Stephen Tyler (1991), 'Transition in Household Energy Use in Urban China, India, the Philippines, Thailand, and Hong Kong,' *Annual Review of Energy and Environment*, 16: 295–335.

Schurr, S. H. (1982), 'Energy Efficiency and Productive Efficiency: Some Thoughts Based on American Experience,' *Energy Journal* 3(3): 3–14.

Smith, Kirk (1993), 'Fuel Combustion, Air Pollution Exposure, and Health: The Situation in Developing Countries,' *Annual Review of Energy and Environment*, 18: 529–66.

——, S. Gu, K. Huang, and D. Qiu (1993), 'One Hundred Million Improved Cookstoves in China: How Was It Done?' *World Development* 21(6): 941–61.

——, M. G. Apte, M. Yoqing, W. Wongsekiarttirat, and A. Kulkarni (1994), 'Air pollution and the energy ladder in Asian Cities.' *Energy* 19(5): 587–600.

Tuntivate, Voravate, Douglas Barnes, and Susan Bogach (2000), *Assessing Markets for Renewable Energy in Rural Areas of Northwestern China*. World Bank Technical Paper No. 462, Washington, DC, World Bank.

——, ——, and —— (2004), 'Public Distribution and Electricity Problem Solving in Rural Thailand' (forthcoming) in *Meeting the Challenge of Rural Electrification in Developing Nations: The Experience of Successful Programs*, World Bank, ESMAP, Washington DC.

van der Plas, R. and A. de Graaff, Robert (1988), *A Comparison of Lamps for Domestic Lighting in Developing Countries*. Industry and Energy Department Working Paper, Energy Series No. 6, Washington, DC, World Bank.

Wasserman, Gary and Alice Davenport (1983), 'Power to the People: Rural Electrification Sector Summary Report.' AID Program Evaluation Report No. 11, US Agency for International Development, Washington DC.

Wolak, Frank A. (2003), 'Designing Competitive Wholesale Electricity Markets for Latin American Countries'. Working Paper C-104. Washington, DC: Inter-American Development Bank.

World Bank (1991), *Haiti: Household Energy Strategy*, Report No. 143/91, Washington, DC, World Bank.

—— (1994), *Rural Electrification in Asia: A Review of Bank Experience*. Operations Evaluation Study No. 22, Washington, DC: Operation Evaluation Department.

—— (1996), *Rural Energy and Development: Improving Energy Supplies for Two Billion People*, Development in Practice Series. Washington DC: World Bank.

—— (1999a), *Poverty and Social Developments in Peru, 1994–1997*, A World Bank Country Study, Washington, DC, World Bank.

—— (1999b), *India: Household Energy Strategies for Urban India: The Case of Hyderabad*, Joint UNDP/ESMAP Report 214/99, Washington, DC, World Bank.

—— (2002a), 'Energy Strategies for Rural India: Evidence from Six States.' ESMAP Report No. 258/02. Washington, DC, World Bank.

—— (2002b), *Rural Electrification and Development in the Philippines: Measuring the Social and Economic Benefits*, Joint UNDP/ESMAP Report, Washington, DC, World Bank.

—— (2002c), 'India, Household Energy, Indoor Air Pollution and Health.' UNDP/ESMAP Report, Washington, DC, World Bank.

—— (2004), *The Impact of Energy on Women's Lives in Rural India*, Joint UNDP/ESMAP Report, Washington, DC, World Bank.

9

Water Institutional Reforms in Developing Countries: Insights, Evidences, and Case Studies

R. Maria Saleth and Ariel Dinar

Overview

While institutional reforms are critical for developing countries to enhance and sustain the economic and environmental contributions of their water sector, undertaking them is not an easy task in view of binding technical and political economy constraints. Despite these constraints, reforms of varying degrees do occur in the water sector of many developing countries. What is the nature and extent of these reforms? How can we explain the forces that motivate and constrain the reform process? How do countries overcome the reform constraints? What are the policy lessons that these reform experiences offer to other countries at reform threshold? This chapter attempts to address these and related questions by (a) utilizing an institutional transaction cost framework, and (b) relying on stylized facts on water institutional reform observed across countries, empirical evidences on how institutional design and implementation principles are used to circumvent technical and political economy constraints, and case studies on the reform process in country-specific context. Based on the discussion and analysis, the chapter then concludes by identifying key implications for both theory and policy that could contribute to international policy dialogue on the interface between institutional reform and water resources management.

Introduction

Water availability and its quality are emerging as a major development challenge in many countries. Obviously, for countries racing towards their limits

273

to fresh water expansion, such as those in the Middle East, water availability remains a serious development constraint. In other countries with expanding urban settlements, industrial sectors, and intensive agriculture such as those in Asia and Latin America, water quality is emerging as a major health and environmental concern. Because pollution-induced deterioration in water quality reduces the utility of available water resources, water scarcity is also a growing concern even in countries with no apparent limits for fresh water expansion. Even though the nature and severity of water constraint vary considerably across countries, there is one aspect that is common to most countries. That is, water constraint—whether quantitative, qualitative, or both—originates more from inefficient use and poor management than from any physical limit to supply augmentation. This diagnosis certainly raises our hope that water crisis and its economic and environmental consequences can be averted by improving the use and management of the resource. However, the task is not that easy, as the prescription involves wide-ranging changes in water institutions, namely, the water-related legal, policy, and organizational arrangements that together govern the way water resources are developed, allocated, used, and managed. The issues of how to design, initiate, and sustain these changes within the economic, political, and environmental constraints are at the heart of the ongoing water debate both at the national and global levels.

Because water institutions in most countries are dated and deeply rooted, the task of reforming them to the required extent is certainly vast, difficult, and time consuming. Apart from the technical constraints emerging from the stupendous nature of the reform task itself, there are also serious obstacles emerging from the political economy front. Despite the binding nature of these obstacles, water institutional reforms of varying degrees are being observed in countries as diverse as Australia, Brazil, China, India, Morocco, Mexico, South Africa, and Spain. What is the nature and extent of these reforms? How can we explain the forces that motivate and constrain the reform process? How do these countries overcome the technical and political constraints for reforms? What are the policy lessons that the reform experience of these countries offer to other developing countries that are at the threshold of water sector reforms? This chapter attempts to address these and related questions by (a) utilizing a simplified representation of an institutional transaction cost framework as applicable to water sector, and (b) relying on stylized facts summarizing existing knowledge on water sector issues and water institutional reforms, empirical evidences for indicating the way countries exploit institutional features to circumvent reform constraints, and select case studies to derive key insights on the nature of, and motivation behind, the reform process in country-specific as well as cross-country contexts. The chapter concludes with some key messages for research and policy that can contribute to international policy dialogue on the institutional dimensions of managing water resources on an economically, socially, and environmentally sustainable manner.

Institutional Roots of Water Crisis: A Global Perspective

To set the context for our subsequent discussion, let us start first with an institutional diagnosis of water crisis and its economic and environmental consequences. Although water crisis is an immediate outcome of the physical phenomenon of a growing supply-demand imbalance, in a fundamental sense, it is actually an outcome of the pervasive gaps in the economic and institutional dimensions of water resource development, allocation, use, and management. While this fact can be shown in country-specific contexts, the true magnitude and universality of the problem can be understood better from a global perspective.

Water is certainly the most abundant and ubiquitous resource on the planet. However, given its physical properties, atmospheric roles, ecological functions, and spatial distribution as well as our current technical and economic capabilities, annual accessible water can be only about 12,500 billion cubic meters (bcum). This is just 0.04 percent of the global water resources [Food and Agriculture Organization (FAO), 1996: 3]. There are constraints to use even these accessible resources. First, the more ideal sites for the construction of large dams and reservoirs have already been developed. Secondly, the growing demands for fiscal austerity in most countries have resulted in growing concerns with least-cost alternatives for meeting water needs. Thirdly, awareness and concern have increased about the environmental impacts related to the construction of hydraulic infrastructures. And fourthly, increasing competition by various sectors for scarce water resources is the result of growing population and increased economic activity. These changes have caused a fundamental shift in the way that water resources development is considered—a shift from looking to construction as a means for solving water needs to looking to improved management as the means for solving such needs (Cummings, Dinar, and Olson, 1996). Other supply augmentation options such as desalinization and recycling are useful, but cannot add more than a fraction of global water demand (Abdulrazzak, 1995: 230; Gleick, 1998: 30–1).

Water demand, in contrast, is increasing fast due to growing population, swelling food demand, expanding scale of economic activities, and broadening perspective of water in terms of its ecological and cultural roles. The result is an eightfold increase in global fresh water withdrawals, that is to say, from 500 to 4000 bcum/year during 1900–2000 (Gleick, 1998: 6–7). While current withdrawal represents only a third of the accessible water resources, it is expected to reach up to 70 percent by 2025 (e.g. Postel, Daily, and Ehrlich, 1996: Falkenmark, 1999). Since a withdrawal of 30 to 60 percent of the accessible fresh water resources is considered as the practical limit for supply augmentation (Falkenmark and Lindh, 1993), many countries are expected to reach their accessible supply limits within the next 20 years. The tell-tale symptoms of water scarcity are already evident in 80 countries with 40 percent of the global population.[1] Apart from its human and productivity implications, increasing physical water scarcity also leads to serious water conflicts among users, regions, and countries (Beaumont, 1994; Frederiksen, 1998).[2] Water scarcity is also having serious effects on water quality, reducing the utility of available supply and enhancing the severity of environmental and health hazards.

Governments are searching for, and debating on, ways to close the gap between increasing usage of water and its limited availability. Among several policy interventions, one could mention allocation of water use rights (Easter, Dinar, and Rosegrant, 1998), establishment of water user association and management transfer (Johnson, 1997), and applying charges in the form of cost recovery and water prices (Dinar and Saleth, 2005). For example, water pricing is one of the most important policy instruments for integrating supply augmentation with demand management so that an efficient allocation (quantity and quality alike) and use of the already developed resources provide the economic and financial justification for the development of additional supplies from both conventional and unconventional sources.

The improvement of water use efficiency is certainly a promising avenue for supply augmentation via demand management, that too, with an added benefit of minimizing ecological effects such as waterlogging, salinity, and aquifer depletion.[3] Unfortunately, these supply augmentation options are very costly in terms of their investment demand, technological needs, and institutional requirements and hence, they remain infeasible for many countries under current economic and technical conditions.[4]

---

[1] Of these countries, 18 are in the Middle East, which are either nearing or exceeding their renewable water supply limits whereas another 55 countries in Africa and Asia cannot fully meet the basic water needs of their growing population (Falkenmark and Lindh, 1993: 80; Gleick, 1993: 105–6).

[2] Some of these conflicts have the potential to become full-fledged water wars because a large proportion of surface flow in several countries originates outside their borders. In 19 countries, this proportion ranges from 21% (Israel) to about 97% (Turkmenistan and Egypt). As a result, the share of global population that will face the predicament of water conflict in these hotspots is expected to rise from 44 to 75% by 2025 (Postel, 1999: 138–40).

[3] For instance, a 10% improvement in water use efficiency can add 2 million hectare (mha) of additional irrigation in Pakistan (Postel, 1993: 60) and 14 mha of the same in India (Saleth, 1996: 234).

[4] However, desalinization and water recycling are important for countries in the Middle East and North Africa as well as for few coastal regions in other parts of the world. Although the total daily water supply from desalinization exceeds 18 million cubic meters, it is no more than a fraction of total global water demand (Gleick, 1998: 30–1). Similar is also the case with water recycling, though it is growing in countries such as Chile, India, Israel, Mexico, Pakistan, and Tunisia. However, these options are very important for countries such as those in the Arabian Peninsula where desalinization meets 10% of the total water demand and water reuse accounts for 2% of the same (see Abdulrazzak, 1995: 230–2).

The magnitude of the socio-economic consequences of water scarcity can be understood by the central role of water resources in economic growth and development. Water resources support 40 percent of global food production through irrigation and 20 percent of global fish yield through aquaculture (FAO, 1996: 2). Given their role in hydropower generation, water resources also account for 20 percent of global power supply (Gleick, 1998: 70).[5] Water sector has indeed performed well its historical function of supporting a world with an increasing population and an expanding scale of economic activities. But, the positive relationship between water resources and economic development is now becoming increasingly weakened (Orloci, Szesztay, and Varkonyi, 1985). This is because the initially observed linear relationship between water resources and economic development has to now accommodate the circularity of multifarious effects emerging from the society-water-ecosystem interactions (Falkenmark, 1999; Varis, 1999).

The negative consequences such as ecological and social disturbances in project sites, salinity in irrigated regions, aquifer depletion in arid zones, and pollution-induced water quality and health risks in urban areas tend to raise the social costs whereas poor maintenance, inefficient use, and mismanagement reduce the social benefits possible from additional supply.[6] As a result, the net economic and welfare contributions of water tend to decline over time and across countries. Equally serious is the persistence of a negative trend in the financial contributions of water sector in many countries. This negative trend jeopardizes both the quality of existing water infrastructure as well as the potential for future investments in new projects. Given the close linkages among the financial status, physical health, service quality, and economic performance of water sector, the overall process of economic development itself depends critically on water sector performance.

The key issue, therefore, is how to improve the financial and economic sustainability of water sector so as to enhance and sustain its indispensable socio-economic and environmental contributions. The answer lies in the creation of appropriate incentive systems, allocation mechanisms, and management structure, especially with an explicit recognition of the fact that the water sector is no longer isolated but linked closely with the economy, environment, and society. Unfortunately, the water institutions in most countries are unable to promote

[5] The direct economic contributions of water resources can be still higher at the regional level. For instance, irrigation contributes to 70% of food production in China and 50% of the same in India (FAO, 1996: 5). Similarly, in 63 countries, hydropower accounts for more than 50% of total power production and in 23 of them, this proportion is over 90% (Gleick, 1998: 71).

[6] For instance, the area affected by irrigation-induced salinity is estimated to be 20 to 47 mha and the yield loss from these areas is estimated to be about 30% (Postel, 1999: 93; Rosegrant and Ringler, 1999: 11). On the other side, while the total storage capacity of all reservoirs in the world is about 6,000 bcum, the actual storage in these reservoirs is far below this capacity due to siltation, catchment degradation, and irregular flow (FAO, 1996: 8). Such problems are still more serious for countries such as India where a tenth of the created irrigation potential of 90 mha is unutilized and a sixth of the irrigated area is waterlogged/saline (Saleth, 1996: 20).

such arrangements so indispensable for the sustainable management of water resources, as they were developed mostly in an era of water surplus. The predominance of supply-side solutions, engineering approach, bureaucratic allocation, and centralized management are now inconsistent with the requirements of the scarcity era such as demand management, economic approach, user involvement, market-based allocation, and decentralized management. This is why we see only few cases with a comprehensive water sector reform success (Dinar, 2000). Given an increasing inconsistency between existing water institutions and emerging resource realities, the ability of most countries to face their water challenges depends clearly on the extent and speed with which they undertake institutional reforms to create a new governance structure for their water sector.

Observed Reforms across Countries: A Stylized Overview

Countries are increasingly recognizing the importance and urgency of reorienting the institutional foundation of their water sector. Despite the challenges and difficulties, many countries have indeed undertaken significant reforms in an effort to create institutional structures that are more responsive to their current and future economic and environmental requirements. These reform initiatives are visible both at macro level (e.g. declaration of water laws and water policies, preparation of national and regional water plans, and administrative reorganizations) and at sub-sectoral level, for example, irrigation management transfer and urban water sector reforms. Specific reforms observed in many countries include the enactment of water laws, creation of basin-based and user-based organizations, management decentralization to promote stakeholder/user participation, privatization of urban and irrigation water supplies, establishment of water rights system, promotion of inter- and intra-sectoral water markets, reorientation of water prices, and water quality regulations. There is now a rich literature that has reviewed and evaluated these reform initiatives with varying focus and detail, both in country-specific as well as cross-country contexts (e.g. Le Moigne et al., 1992; Brinkerhoff, 1994; Hearne and Easter, 1997; Easter, Dinar, and Rosegrant, 1998; Frederiksen, 1998; Savedoff and Spiller, 1999; Challen, 2000; Shirley, 2002; Dinar, 2000; Saleth and Dinar, 2000 and 2004; Dinar and Saleth, 2005; Bauer, 2004; Gopalakrishnan, Biswas, and Tortajada, 2005). A careful review of this literature allows us to distill a few stylized facts on the overall thrust and common trends of the recently observed water institutional reforms across countries.

Ushering into an Allocation Paradigm

There is a gradual but definite shift from water development or supply-side approaches to water allocation or demand-side solutions. This shift has already occurred in water scarce countries in the Middle East and North Africa as well as in countries such as Australia and regions such as California and Colorado in the U.S. It is also inevitable in countries such as India and Spain that are fast approaching their physical limits for fresh water expansion. Even in countries such as Brazil with no apparent limits for supply expansion, issues related to spatial mismatch between water availability and demand, growing water pollution, and ecological constraints warrant water allocation institutions for an efficient use of both existing and future supplies. While a paradigmatic shift towards water allocation is evident in almost all countries, there are considerable variations across countries as to the extent of creating the necessary institutional arrangements to underpin an allocation-oriented water management system. For instance, countries such as Australia, Chile, and Israel as well as regions such as California and Colorado in the U.S. are already having the institutional capability for an allocation paradigm. While countries such as China, South Africa, Spain, and Mexico can develop their institutional potential faster, others such as India, Brazil, and Egypt have a long way to go to create the necessary institutions for ushering their water sector into the allocation paradigm centered on economic instruments and market mechanisms.

Moving towards Management Decentralization

The dominant trend toward management decentralization is an unmistakable thrust of water sector reforms observed in most countries. The decentralization initiatives include the creation of River Basin Organizations (RBOs), promotion of irrigation management transfer (IMT), and the emergence of utility-type bodies in urban sector. RBOs are being created in most countries with varying levels of effectiveness and success (Barrow, 1998; Bruns and Bandaragoda, 2003).[7] IMT, the program for transferring the managerial, cost recovery, and maintenance responsibilities to legalized water user associations (WUAs), is the main mode of decentralization within irrigation sector. IMT is extensive in Mexico, Turkey, and the Philippines and is picking up in countries like India, Morocco, Indonesia, and Pakistan (Vermillion, 1997). China and Central Asian transition countries such as Uzbekistan have a long-established tradition of involving local communities in lower level irrigation management. Decentralization within urban water sector takes the forms of moving water supply functions to autonomous and financially self-dependent utility-type organizations. Instances of such utility-type organizations can be found in many cities in countries such as Australia, Chile, and Mexico. Although China has no such utilities at present, its 1997 Water Industry Policy mandates the creation of such arrangements.

[7] RBOs are called differently in different countries (e.g. Watershed Committees in Brazil, Water Conservancy Commissions in China, Basin Councils in Mexico, Hydro-geological Federations in Spain, and Catchment Management Agency in South Africa). However, they share a common conceptual basis and functional framework.

Going for Selective Privatization

Another thrust of water sector reforms observed in many countries is an increasing tendency towards water sector privatization.[8] Such a tendency is more visible particularly in urban water sectors as compared to other water sub-sectors. National and international private water companies are now involved in the provision of urban water supply and sanitation activities in countries such as Argentina, Mexico, Morocco, the Philippines, and Thailand. Privatization initiatives can also be seen in the irrigation sector with two notable patterns. In England and Australia, irrigation supply functions were transferred to private irrigation companies. In contrast, in Argentina and New Zealand, the irrigation assets were transferred directly to farmers themselves. Although there is not any actual case of irrigation privatization in countries such as China, India, and Sri Lanka, they are currently pursuing the policy of promoting private sector involvement in irrigation-related water resources development and service provision. Despite the few but striking instances of irrigation privatization, privatization initiatives are confined mainly to the economically attractive and technically viable segments of the water sector such as urban water supply, sanitation, and desalinization.

Espousing an Integrated Approach

Many countries have undertaken significant initiatives to promote integrated water resources management (IWRM). Flow loss from catchment degradations, storage loss from siltation, and productivity loss from salinization are some of the common factors inducing countries to take a holistic approach in the use and management of land, water, and environment resources within an integrated framework. Obviously, the institutional implications of IWRM are vast given the requirements for strengthening the linkages among land, water, agricultural, and environmental institutions and dovetailing various components of ongoing and planned development programs. In this respect, the creation of RBOs by countries augurs well, as it provides an appropriate spatial and organizational context for operationalizing the IWRM approach. Similarly, the fact that many countries have developed their national water plans indicates their informational and technical capabilities for pursuing IWRM. This is true for both countries that are already having their national plans (e.g. Australia, India, Israel, Mexico, and Spain) as well as those (e.g. Brazil, China, Morocco, South Africa, and Sri Lanka) with a mandate to develop such plans under recently enacted or proposed water laws. There are

[8] Although privatization can be linked to decentralization, given the historically established bureaucratic domination of water sector in most developing countries, it is more appropriate to interpret it as an effort towards the debureaucratization of water management. It is also an effort to make the water sector more responsive to market conditions.

also few reform initiatives to firm-up the organizational basis for IWRM. These include the ministerial reorganization to move water from agriculture or power-related ministries to environmental ministries (e.g. Australia, Brazil, Mexico, Spain, and Morocco), organizational streamlining to integrate most water-related functions within one organization (e.g. Brazil and India), and the incorporation of watershed and catchment considerations within basin management plans (e.g. China, South Africa, and Sri Lanka).

Focusing on Financial Viability

There is an international consensus that a phased improvement in cost recovery is the first step toward salvaging the water sector from financial crisis and physical degeneration. Many countries have indeed undertaken concrete steps in terms of water pricing reforms to enhance the financial and allocation role of water rates and pricing methods (see Dinar and Subramanian, 1997). However, these reforms could not always proceed to the needed extent due to political economy constraints and implementation costs (Dinar, 2000). As a result, currently observed pricing reforms across countries evince mixed results. In general terms, cost recovery is relatively better in urban water supply as compared to irrigation and rural water supply. Similarly, cost recovery is better in advanced countries and water scarce regions as compared to developing countries and water surplus regions. While the full recovery of operation and maintenance costs is the stated objective, many developing countries in Africa and Asia are struggling hard to recover even the operational and maintenance costs both in their irrigation and residential water supply projects. This is the case even in countries where water rates were raised substantially. For instance, a few states in India have raised irrigation water rates by 300 to 400 percent, but could not cover yet the full costs, as the raised levels of water rates are still far below the provision costs. In contrast, countries such as Australia and Chile have gone a step ahead of others by going for an annuity-based capital cost recovery in their water projects. Notably, South Africa is planning to recover even the costs involved in activities like water management and water-related research. Despite these forward-looking initiatives, financial subsidies have not been completely eliminated even in countries adopting an economic approach to water pricing such as Australia, Chile, England, Israel, and the US.

Moving from Mere Quantity to Better Quality

Improved financial health can facilitate the physical health of water distribution and drainage infrastructure, but the physical sustainability of the water sector cannot be ensured without controlling the damage that pollution from industrial, agricultural, and urban sources causes to water quality. Added to the effects of pollution are also the water quality impacts of salinization, turbidity, and algae growth. As quality deterioration reduces the utility of available water resources and raises the health and environmental costs, water quality issues are receiving as much, if not more, attention as water quantity in all countries regardless of the stage of water resources development. The common approaches pursued in this respect involve water quality grading, quality standards, and pollution control regulations (Saleth and Dinar, 2000). Although most countries have provisions for a pollution permit system, they are all at different stages of implementation. Australia, Israel, and the U.S. enforce strict quality standards as do all countries in the European Union. The mechanisms for water quality enforcement in countries such as Brazil, China, India, Mexico, and South Africa, though not yet developed fully, are relatively more effective compared to many other countries in Africa, Asia, and Latin America.[9] The undeniable fact, however, is that water pollution and its health and environmental consequences are deeply registered in the reform agenda of all countries.

Outstanding Reform Challenges in Developing Countries

The reform thrusts and trends indicated above are certainly very positive from a long-term historical perspective of water institutional change. However, the reforms undertaken so far are by no means adequate for meeting the institutional requirements for sustainable water resources management, especially in the case of most of the developing countries facing severe water scarcity problems. As we consider the overall nature of the reforms undertaken by these countries, they are mostly at a policy level rather than at the implementation level. For instance, most of the reforms are ceremonial and cosmetic in nature (e.g. declaration of water policies, marginal rise in water rates, establishing inter-sectoral allocation priorities, creation of RBOs, and renaming of organizations) rather than substantive in character (e.g. enactment of water laws, adoption of volumetric allocation, establishment of water rights system, and reorganization of water administration). Some of the significant initiatives (e.g. IMT, water pricing reforms, and water quality regulations) are also undertaken tentatively more as a crisis response than as part of any comprehensive reform package.

As the reform experience of many developing countries shows, the challenge is not so much on enacting allocation-oriented water laws and policies, as on building an allocation-oriented organizational structure out of an outmoded and centralized water administration with insufficient skills and resources.

---

[9] In India, public-interest litigations have played a more effective role in enforcing many of the legal provisions on water pollution as compared to the state organizations mandated with the task of pollution control. The most notable case in this respect is the closure of many polluting industries on the banks of Ganges River, as prompted by a public interest litigation filed by environmental groups in the Supreme Court of India.

While there is a definite commitment to move towards an allocation paradigm, the necessary institutional conditions for operationalizing such a paradigm (e.g. volumetric water allocation, water rights, and water pricing reforms) have not yet been created. The decentralization initiatives have also not achieved their institutional objectives, as they have neither led to decentralized decision structure nor resolved the fundamental centralization–decentralization dilemma.[10] Similarly, with few notable exceptions (e.g. Mexico, Spain, and South Africa), decentralization initiatives have also occurred as isolated exercises without recognizing the necessity of linking them with other complementary institutional arrangements.[11] As a result, the currently observed decentralization initiatives in most countries are inherently unable to accelerate the transition towards the allocation paradigm. While privatization has the healthy effect of infusing economic discipline in water provision and management, it has its own limits, especially in the provision of socially important 'public good' water activities such as flood control and catchment management.[12] What is needed is a governance framework that recognizes the mutually reinforcing complementary roles of the state apparatus, private companies, and user groups and, at the same time, demarcates their respective spheres of influence within water sectors. Certainly, the observed reforms across countries are far from creating such water governance structures.

Considering the water institutional structure and the recent water institutional reforms observed both across developed and developing countries, it is possible to make few generic observations as the ability of these countries in supporting a responsive, allocation-oriented, and forward-looking water institutional arrangement. Obviously, countries differ markedly in terms of the

[10] This actually points to the two caveats for decentralized regional or organizational arrangements such as RBOs. First, regionalization need not automatically ensure decentralized decisions, as some RBOs of the past (e.g. the Tennessee Valley Authority in the U.S. and Damodar Valley Corporation in India) have degenerated into centralized organizations. Secondly, decentralization cannot succeed without a dose of centralization essential for effective coordination (e.g. decentralization initiatives in the Mexican water sector were effective because they were undertaken with the 'big-bang' approach by a higly centralized agency). The challenge lies in carefully crafting the institutional arrangements at different spatial levels so as to achieve both local flexibility and regional coordination in water management.

[11] For instance, when the RBOs, WUAs, and water utilities are viewed from a larger perspective of water sector reforms, they can provide an organizational context for promoting further institutional reforms related to water rights, conflict resolution, accountability, and water pricing. Similarly, their legal and organizational requirements also suggest substantial upstream institutional changes such as water law reforms and the organizational reorientation of national and regional water administration. Unfortunately, the reform programs in most countries have not grasped well the upstream and downstream institutional implications of the decentralization process.

[12] Although privatization and other decentralization initiatives minimize the role of bureaucracy, they cannot eliminate the role of government altogether. Nor is such elimination desirable in view of the need for both the regulatory and the enabling functions that only the state apparatus can perform better in the new context. Nevertheless, since the process of privatization process strengthens the complementarity, and rekindles healthy competition between public and private sectors, it adds a new institutional dimension to water resource management.

historically inherited institutional structure as well as the extent and effectiveness of the recently undertaken institutional reforms within their water sector. From an overall perspective, countries such as Australia and Chile, England, France, Germany, and the US (especially, California, Colorado, and Arizona) are in an advanced, though not yet in an ideal, stage of institutional evolution. Israel, with its technologically advanced and economically sensitive water sector, can be ahead of most countries when its reform proposals take practical shape.

China, Mexico, Spain, and, to a larger extent, South Africa have the organizational potential as well as the water law and water sector reform proposals to strengthen the allocation dimensions of their water institutions. Other countries, such as Morocco, are also favorably placed in terms of national level institutional reforms and its partial success in reforming urban water sector as well as in promoting a basin-based integrated approach in irrigation sector. Although Brazil shows considerable political commitment, followed by concrete actions in the form of water law enactment and administrative reorganization, it is still constrained by the present constitutional division of water sector responsibilities between the federal and state governments. Although India exhibits slow progress in terms of water sector reform at the national level, it does show notable progress, especially in terms of irrigation reforms, at the state and local levels. Other countries such as the Philippines, Turkey, and Sri Lanka have made notable progress in reforming their irrigation sector through IMT, but they are yet to make substantial progress in this sector as well as in other water sub-sectors.

From the perspective of deriving more effective and politically acceptable reform strategies, it is necessary to understand why developing countries are able to undertake certain kinds of institutional reforms but not others that are needed for a durable solution to their water problems. The standard explanation links the reform difficulties with the constraining role of the political economy process and technical factors associated with the nature of institutions themselves (e.g. qualities of stickiness or persistence of institutions, the linked nature of institutions, and the irreversibility of institutional change). The argument is rather simplistic, as many countries have, in fact, advanced their water sector reforms through a clever exploitation of the opportunities and contexts provided by these very factors considered to constrain the reform process. From the recent reform experiences of both developed and developing countries, it is possible to generate a rich set of empirical evidences as well as a few case studies to illustrate how the political factors and institutional features are exploited to initiate and sustain the reforms process. A careful review and understanding of these evidences and cases studies can be valuable, particularly to derive more effective, replicable, and politically viable reform strategies for countries undertaking or contemplating water institutional reforms. To provide a sound and theoretically consistent context for this review, it is best first to understand the relative role that the economic, political, technical, and other factors play during the process of institutional changes within the water sector.

Explaining Institutional Reforms: A Transaction Cost Approach

There are many theories for explaining institutional changes in a general context. They include such well-known theories as evolutionary theory, contractarian theory, public choice theory, institutional transaction cost theory, induced institutional change theory, demand-supply theory, and political economy theories including rent-seeking and bargaining theories. Saleth and Dinar (2004) provide a detailed review of these theories, especially from the perspective of their implications for, and applicability to, water sector reforms. Among these theories, the institutional transaction cost theory has both conceptual advantage in view of its close resemblance with cost–benefit analysis as well as analytical ability to bring together many relevant factors within a common analytical framework. Since it is more inclusive in terms of explanatory factors, it provides a more generic and intuitive approach for understanding and explaining both country-specific and cross-country variations in water institutional changes, as we attempt in this chapter.

Institutional Transaction Cost Framework

The institutional transaction cost theory was originally proposed by Coase (1937) and developed and extended later by Williamson (1975 and 1985). Although the initial version of the theory considered only economic transactions costs, North (1990a and 1990b) has generalized the theory to include also the real and political costs. This generalized theory can be both simplified and specialized to develop a framework for explaining institutional changes within water sector (Saleth and Dinar, 2000 and 2004). In simple terms, this framework identifies first all the major factors affecting water institutions and then traces their effects either on the transaction or opportunity costs of institutional reform. Before seeing what these costs are, it is instructive to consider first the factors having a strong influence on water institutions.

For analytical convenience, the factors influencing water institutions can be grouped into endogenous factors that are internal to both water institutions and water sector and exogenous factors that are outside the strict confines of both water institutions and water sector. The endogenous factors include water scarcity, water conflicts, financial crisis, and infrastructural deterioration, and the internal structure and operational efficiency of water institutions. The exogenous factors, in contrast, represent the general setting within which water sector and water institutions operate. They include aspects such as economic development, demographic growth, technical progress, economic and political reforms, international agreements and pressures, changing social values and ethos, and natural phenomena like floods and droughts.[13] It is the interactive and joint effects of these endogenous and exogenous factors that determine the structure, performance, and change in water sector and its institutional arrangements. Thus, in broader terms, the exogenous factors represent the overall institutional environment facing water institutions whereas the endogenous factors reflect the internal features of water institutions and water sector in a given context and time point.

Although it is difficult to isolate the individual effects of the exogenous and endogenous factors, it is still possible to track them, especially by conceptualizing their effects either in terms of the transaction costs or in terms of the opportunity costs. The transaction costs cover both the real and monetary costs of instituting and changing the legal, policy, and organizational arrangements governing water development, allocation, use, and management.[14] The opportunity costs, on the other hand, cover both the real and economic value of opportunities foregone (i.e. the net social costs of inaction or 'status quo'). In this sense, the opportunity costs are actually the potential benefits of institutional change. That is, when the institutional change cannot be effected, these benefits are reckoned as social costs in terms of the opportunities (or, benefits) sacrificed or foregone to maintain the status quo. These costs are not static but change continuously due to changes in both endogenous and exogenous factors.

A major question is how and by whom the transaction and opportunity costs are reckoned. While these costs can be reckoned *ex-post*, it is of little value for providing predictive inputs into an ongoing and future process of institutional change. What is more relevant is the *ex-ante* evaluation of the transaction and opportunity costs. Such an *ex-ante* evaluation necessarily involves subjective elements including a subjective and adaptive evaluation of even objective factors.[15] As to the issue of by whom these costs are reckoned, these costs are evaluated by various stakeholders such as the state, water bureaucracy, rural and urban communities, water users, non-governmental bodies, and lending agencies and donors.[16] As to the issue of how the decisions on

[13] Notice that it is these exogenous factors that together define the overall institutional environment for the water institutional structure. As such, our analytical framework captures also the transactions costs implications of changing institutional environment as characterized by both economic and non-economic factors.

[14] The real costs also include political risks (Dinar, Balakrishnan, and Wambia, 2004), the net effects of any reallocation of power/opportunities (Bromley, 1989) and the deadweight loss of institutional/bureaucratic redundancy (Dinar and Saleth, 2005).

[15] Subjective and *ex-ante* reckoning of these costs are, in fact, inevitable in view of the dynamic and inter-disciplinary nature of institutional changes, lacking both observed data as well as a unified and trans-disciplinary framework needed to integrate and process diverse information (Saleth and Dinar, 2004).

[16] In trans-boundary resource systems, the stakeholder groups include their counterparts in other riparian countries as well as those representing regional and international arrangements such as river basin commissions and agencies (e.g. those operating in the Mekong and Danube rivers).

reforms and their implementation are taken, the state and hence, the political process, plays an important role. The main factor that prompts such a state role is the convergence in the transaction cost calculus of the majority or the most powerful groups.[17]

Critical Role of Exogenous Factors

Exogenous factors play a major role in changing the transaction cost calculus and political balance toward reforms. For instance, as water scarcity becomes acute due to economic development and population growth, the real and economic costs of inappropriate water institutions tend to rise. Similarly, the economic reforms magnify the fiscal implications whereas natural calamities such as droughts and floods aggravate the political implications of the opportunity costs of institutional reforms. Political reforms involving nationwide institutional changes, on the other hand, reduce the transaction costs of water sector reforms directly because the institutional changes within the water sector form only a small part of the overall reform process. Likewise, technical progress can also reduce the transaction costs of institutional changes. As the exogenous factors tend to magnify the opportunity costs of water crises and reduce the transaction costs of water sector reforms, they often provide a powerful economic urge and political thrust for water institutional changes.

Strategic Role of Institutional Linkages

One crucial endogenous factor pertains to the internal linkages among institutional components. Institutional linkages and their implications are well recognized (e.g. North, 1990a: 83 and 99; North, 1997: 6; Boyer and Hollingsworth, 1997: 445–7; Ostrom, 1999: 38). Besides their effects on transaction costs, institutional linkages also have substantial effects on performance, as they can correct mutual defects among institutional components (North, 1997: 4; Williamson 1994: 18–19). Despite its importance, the effects of institutional linkages are not formally incorporated into the framework of institutional

---

[17] How such convergence occurs and how it leads to institutional change are more fundamental and contentious issues in the literature. In an attempt to explain these issues, Saleth and Dinar (2004) have proposed a subjective and stage-based theory of institutional change. According to this theory, institutional change occurs through four stages: mind change of stakeholders (as induced by subjective and objective evaluation of the existing and future state of affairs); political articulation of such change (due to the role of political entrepreneurs); policy changes and actual implementation (through the process of interest group politics and political bargaining); and performance improvement (as measured against objective criteria and subjective expectation of stakeholders). These stages are not linear but cyclical because when performance improvement is below expectation, the process will again go through the four stages. Depending on country or regional context, the time dimension and quality of the process at each stage can be different.

transaction cost theory. Instances for institutional linkages include the institutional connections among water rights, conflict resolution, accountability, and water markets as well as those among user organizations, cost recovery, volumetric allocation, water rights, and water markets. Still broader linkages also exist both within and across the legal, policy, and organizational components of water institutions as well as between these institutional components and the institutional environment, as represented by the exogenous factors.

From the perspective of water reform strategy, the institutional linkages and their transaction and performance implications are very important, as they form the basis for deriving reform design and implementation principles such as institutional prioritization, sequencing, and packaging as well as reform timing, spacing, speed, and scale. These principles have strategic roles in relaxing the political and technical constraints for reforms. For instance, institutional prioritization and sequencing (e.g. undertaking the reform in politically and technically easier institutional components, sectors, and areas) can bypass the political economy constraints by gradually weakening reform opponents while concurrently strengthening the pro-reform groups. Institutional sequencing (e.g. developing user organizations and volumetric allocation to promote water pricing and water rights systems, and the creation, water rights to promote conflict resolution, accountability, and water markets) can also relax technical constraints by exploiting the path dependency properties of institutions. Similarly, institutional packaging (e.g. combining reform options favoring different groups) can also help in building pro-reform political coalitions (White, 1990). Institutional packaging (e.g. privatization and water pricing or institutional reform and investment programs) can also overcome technical constraints by exploiting the mutual reinforcement and balancing effects of different institutional or reform components. Likewise, changing nature and configuration of exogenous factors (e.g. macro-economic reform, political reconstruction, droughts/floods, or international agreements) can also be used to advance the reform process with an appropriate choice of reform timing, spacing, and scale.

There are also some important features of institutions that can also be strategically exploited to promote institutional reforms. For instance, institutional change, by nature, is not a one-time event but rather a continuum involving gradual changes over time. This means each small and minor change in an institution, though it may look insignificant from a short-run perspective, does matter for the long-term process of institutional change. Likewise, the transaction and opportunity costs vary considerably across individual institutional components (Ostrom, 1990; Saleth and Dinar, 2004). This feature can be exploited to prioritize and target institutional reform and minimize the total transaction costs of reform.[18] There are also considerable synergies and scale

[18] For instance, the transaction costs of changing water policy are far lower and politically less sensitive than those involved in changing water law or reforming water organizations. Likewise, the costs of establishing a water rights system are far higher than the same in undertaking pricing reform or creating a basin organization.

economy effects during the process of institutional change. As the reforms initiated in earlier stages brighten the prospects for downstream reforms, there are intricate and direct linkages between the transaction costs of subsequent reforms and the opportunity costs of earlier reforms.[19] Since each institutional change became the foundation for subsequent and higher level institutional changes, the cost of each subsequent institutional change can decline, suggesting the presence of substantial scale economies in institutional change (North, 1990a: 95).[20] There are also scale economies on the performance side as well. Similarly, since the institutional changes within water sector can also derive considerable synergy from exogenous factors that reflect changes elsewhere in the economy, the transaction costs of water sector reforms can also decline due to scale economies in institutional change.[21] In fact, there are many instances for the fact that the reform programs in many countries have exploited the opportunities and contexts provided by the institutional linkages, exogenous factors, and the synergies and scale economy benefits inherent in the reform process itself. These are addressed in the next section.

How Do Countries Address Reform Constraints?

Let us now provide some empirical evidences to show how countries attempt to overcome their reform constraints by exploiting the design and implementation principles emerging from institutional linkages and political economy contexts. We also provide two case studies—one on India and the other on Mexico—to demonstrate the political economy and transaction cost dimensions of water sector reforms.

Reliance of Reform Design Principles

Based on a carefully conducted study of economic reform processes in several countries, White (1990) has concluded that the way the reform program is structured and packaged has much to contribute to its successful implementation. This result applies to water institutional reform as well. Reform packaging, that

---

[19] For instance, with the establishment of a transferable water rights system, the creation of other institutional aspects such as the conflict resolution mechanisms and water markets becomes easier due to the linkages that the transactions costs of the latter two institutional aspects have with those of the former.

[20] There are also scale economies on the performance side as well. Not only does the performance of lower level rules hinge on the performance of their higher level counterparts but also their synergy and scale economy effects ensure that the aggregate performance implications of a set of hierarchically nested rules are much more than the sum of their individual performance (North, 1990a: 95 and 100).

[21] The scale economies in transaction costs emerge from the fact that the cost of transacting water institutional changes is lower when water sector reform forms part of an overall country-wide economic reform (e.g. China) and political reconstruction (e.g. South Africa) than otherwise (Saleth and Dinar, 2000).

is, the linking of institutional reforms with other economic programs, can also be used to build political coalition (White, 1990) and to minimize, thereby, the political transaction costs. More generally, the issue of packaging involves not only the linking of institutional reform with other incentive programs but also integrating two or more institutional components.[22] In the particular context of water institutional reforms, instances for combining economic incentives within the reform package include the provision of matching grants and a share in the collection of water charges to WUAs during IMT programs.[23] Similarly, an IMT program also involves the component of system improvement and modernization, which, again, has an incentive effect on the transfer process. Both these forms of reform packaging are actually adopted in many countries including India, the Philippines, Turkey, and Mexico.

Instances for the adoption of the principle of institutional sequencing are also a-plenty in recent water reforms observed across countries. An efficiently functioning network of WUAs at various levels is a precondition not just for cost recovery and system maintenance, but equally for the enforcement and monitoring of an effective water right system. Water rights systems can, in turn, contribute to the realization of other institutional aspects such as cost recovery, accountability, conflict resolution, and water markets. The experiences in countries such as Colombia, India, Mexico, Morocco, Turkey, and Uzbekistan demonstrate clearly that WUAs have indeed contributed to cost recovery and improved system management. While WUAs have played a major role in ensuring accountability and resolving conflicts, they have not yet become the organizational foundation for water rights systems and water markets. In order to reach such a high stage of institutional reform, additional conditions such as legalized systems water quotas and volumetric allocation arrangements are essential. While some of the basic conditions for reaching this stage exist in Mexico (e.g. water law and registry of water rights), in the case of other countries listed above, they are still missing.

The experience of Australia shows, on the other hand, that a strong sequential linkage exists among water institutional components such as a rights system, cost recovery, conflict resolution, market-based allocation, and irrigation privatization. The experiences of Australia and California also demonstrate the scope for more advanced forms of institutional sequencing. The existence of

[22] In the latter case, it is useful to combine institutional components with differential levels and gestation periods of impact. While the institutional components with immediate and noticeable performance returns have the tactical role of maintaining the economic and political relevance of the reform process, others are critical to ensure the long-term sustainability of institutional reform through a gradual but concerted effort to strengthen the institutional structure.

[23] The matching grant means that the government will match the amount collected by the WUAs from each of its members (i.e. farmers) for creating an initial fund to support the organization. This grant and the share in the collection of water charges (usually, about 10% of the total proceeds) are used to provide incentives for WUAs, which are in the form of induced collective action initiatives.

a water rights system, and the basin organization such as the Murray–Darling River Commission have enabled the concerned Australian states to formulate and implement what is known as the 'Cap Program' that aims to reduce water diversions to the 1993–4 use level in an effort to reduce soil salinity and water quality in the basins. The same institutional arrangements have also remained a basis for water rights reallocation, irrigation privatization, and facilitating water flow for environmental purposes. In California, the presence of a water rights system and the elaborate organizational framework for water management have facilitated additional institutions such as 'water banks.'

The fact that countries such as Australia, Chile, France, Israel, and United Kingdom, and regions such as California and Colorado, could undertake advanced forms of reforms without too much difficulty, provides a strong evidence for the transaction cost linkages between earlier and subsequent reforms. In these cases, the already prevailing institutional conditions such as water rights, volumetric allocation, economic water rates, and organizational arrangements enable the creation of higher stage institutions such as pricing reforms, water markets, and water banks with less resistance and cost. Similar effects can also be observed, though in a somewhat narrower context, in other countries such as Namibia, Portugal, and Tunisia, where the creations of financially independent corporate entities in urban and agricultural sectors have facilitated downstream reforms such as pricing reforms and organizational changes within water administration. Since these instances show how existing institutions provide scope for undertaking additional reforms or creating new institutions, they indicate how the transaction costs of creating the new institutions are reduced by the presence of appropriate institutions. In this sense, these and similar cases elsewhere illustrate the scope not only for institutional sequencing but also for scale economies in institutional reform. In countries such as Argentina, Chile, and Mexico, water reforms also involved sub-sectoral sequencing in the sense that urban water reforms preceded the irrigation sector reforms. There are also instances of spatial sequencing both in urban and agricultural sectors, as the reforms such as privatization and IMT were focused in some cities and regions. In the case of Mexico, policy and legal reforms have also preceded the organizational reforms.

On the question of scale and dose of institutional reforms, the recent experiences of China, India, Mexico (as well as many other Latin America countries) show that since water reforms form part of the larger program of macroeconomic reform, there were considerable synergy and scale effects powerful enough to neutralize the political economy constraints. The experience of South Africa is similar, as water reform formed part of the political reform. In the case of Namibia, water sector reforms, though limited, have their origin in the country's transition from a colonial system. The irrigation reforms in Mexico as well as in the Indian states of Andhra Pradesh and Madhya Pradesh were based on a 'big bang' rather than a 'gradualistic' approach suggesting both the scale and political economy advantages in undertaking reforms at one go. The scale of reform effort also has a time dimension, as additional reform effort can be undertaken either simultaneously or sequentially with appropriate and strategically spaced time gaps. The issue of when to make the additional reform effort, however, depends not only on the prevailing political climate but also on whether the performance impact associated with the institutional change is immediate or delayed.

The overall institutional environment—as defined by factors such as the cultural traditions, political system, and social arrangement—within which water institutions and water sector interact has a decisive role, not only in determining the nature of reforms, but also the effectiveness of institutions.[24] Performance variations in IMT programs (Johnson, 1997; Vermillion, 1997) and basin level organizations (Kliot, Shmueli, and Shamir, 1997) across countries and regions are notable instances for the powerful role the general environment plays in institutional performance. These instances also show that political and legal commitments to declared policies, though necessary, are not sufficient in the face of administrative inadequacy and other bottlenecks, including the political arrangements (e.g. federal vs. unitary form, presidential vs. parliamentary form, or centralized system vs. multi-party democracy). Based on a review of water institutional changes in 11 countries (Mexico, Chile, Brazil, Spain, Morocco, Israel, South Africa, Sri Lanka, Australia, China, and India), Saleth and Dinar (2000) have established that water institutional reform in these countries is prompted more by factors exogenous to the water sector (e.g. macroeconomic crises, political reform, natural calamities, and technological progress) than due to those endogenous to the sector (e.g. water scarcity, performance deterioration, and financial non-viability). Notably, this observation applies, more or less equally, to both the developed and developing countries.

The water reform initiatives in China and India, as well as in most Latin American countries, can be traced to their macroeconomic reforms of the late 1980s (Savedoff and Spiller, 1999; Saleth and Dinar, 2000). On the other hand, privatization of the water sector in England and New Zealand is linked to their economic liberalization policies. Water institutional changes in Chile and Portugal can also be related to political changes. In contrast, environmental factors including drought, floods, and salinity played a major role in the reform initiatives in cases such as California, China, and Australia. In the case of many European countries, the preservation of water quality and inland water-based ecosystems were the driving forces for institutional reforms in

---

[24] A historical instance can illuminate this point better. That is, the adoption of the U.S. constitution by many Latin American countries and Western property rights laws by many developing countries has not been as successful as expected because 'the enforcement mechanism, the norms of behavior, and the subjective model or models of the actors are not the same' (North, 1990a: 101). Thus, institutional similarity does not necessarily assure performance consistency across contexts.

their water sector. Similarly, international agreements (e.g. the Water Framework Directive of European Union, World Trade Organization, and regional water sharing agreements) also play an equally important role in explaining reform in different countries. The fact is that countries do utilize, though by varying degrees, the political economy contexts provided by the changes in the overall institutional environment of the water sector. Although this happened more by chance than by design, from the perspective of water reform strategy, the experience does point to the advantage of timing reform programs around ongoing and prospective changes in exogenous factors and events.

Water Sector Reform in India: A Transaction Cost Perspective

We have provided some empirical evidences to show how countries use institutional design and implementation principles emerging from institutional linkages, reform processes, and exogenous factors. Let us now turn to case studies of India and Mexico to understand the role that transactions costs and political economy considerations play in explaining the reform process in their respective water sector. The socio-economic consequences of widespread groundwater depletion, ecological costs of large-scale water development projects, storage loss from siltation, and command area loss to water logging and salinity have remained the fundamental factors providing a strong economic motivation for water institutional reforms. Unfortunately, the financial and performance crises of the water sector have failed to gather the political economy thrust needed for prompting concrete actions. From an institutional transaction cost perspective, this means that although the opportunity costs of inaction were high, the perceived political costs of taking actions were still higher to undermine the reform initiatives.

Fortunately, there were a number of developments—mostly exogenous to the water sector—since the mid-1970s that have not only reduced the political costs but also magnified the opportunity costs of water institutional reforms. For instance, the earlier practice of keeping water policy subservient to agricultural policy lost its relevance when India eliminated food imports in 1971 and started building a comfortable buffer stock (often going beyond 20 million tons) in recent years. Although the immediate prompt for the first National Water Policy came from the serious drought of 1987, it is the political and media fallout associated with this natural event that, in fact, galvanized the necessary political will to declare even such a simple and non-binding policy statement. But, the transaction cost calculus changed rather dramatically with the macro economic crisis of the late 1980s and subsequent declaration of the New Economic Policy of 1991 focusing on financial discipline, economic liberalization, and the liquidation of public sector enterprises.

The major impact of the New Economic Policy on the water sector has been a radical decline in its budgetary share. For instance, the share of the irrigation sector alone has declined from 23 percent of the total plan expenditure in the 1950s to 7 percent in recent years. In the wake of such budgetary cuts, water-related departments were forced to take a harder look at the ways of cost saving and internal resource mobilization. At the same time, farm lobbies that were resisting water rate revision have also realized that farm income is increasingly affected by unreliable water supply from poorly maintained irrigation systems. It is these macroeconomic conditions and their microeconomic consequences that have magnified the opportunity costs of reforms from the perspective of both the government and water users. As a result, pressures were building for revising water rates, involving farmers in cost recovery and system maintenance, and contemplating broader water sector reforms. It is in this particular context of economy-wide reforms and sector-specific concerns that the central government constituted the two important committees—one to look into the issues of irrigation pricing and the other to consider private sector participation in the water sector—and few state governments went for options such as the autonomous water corporations and private sector participation.[25]

The revival of interest in many policies that were considered once as anathema or impractical (e.g. irrigation privatization, volumetric water allocation, water rights, and moving water into the concurrent list) indicates the changing balance in water debate. This is certainly a positive development and augurs well for the prospects of more substantive reforms in future. From another perspective, the economic and trade liberalization policies initiated since 1991 have also produced significant scale economies in terms of their synergetic effects on water sector reforms. Since water sector reforms form part of an economy-wide reform, the political economy costs of the former became a small proportion of the latter.[26] Meanwhile, international lending agencies, especially the World Bank and Asian Development Bank, also had considerable influence on the nature and direction of water sector reforms.[27]

The transactions costs and political economy-based explanations apply not only to water institutional changes observed at the macro level but also those occurring at the state and local levels. For instance, groundwater markets and other forms of water-sharing contracts at the local level have emerged because the private costs are lower than their private benefits to individual farmers.

[25] These changes in the case of Andhra Pradesh, Karnataka, and Maharashtra also have an ulterior motive as they use these unconventional means of financing water projects so as to establish their control over water resources in the Krishna basin before the tribunal award comes for renegotiation.

[26] This fact clearly underlines the transaction costs implications and strategic significance of timing and packaging the water sector reform so as to make it coincide with, and form part of, a larger economy-wide reform program.

[27] For instance, most of the organizational reforms, including the promotion of basin-based organizations observed in states such as Andhra Pradesh, Tamil Nadu, Orissa, and Uttar Pradesh were introduced under different World Bank-funded projects.

Although these local arrangements have high social costs such as the implicit/illegal sales of power, violation of proportional sharing principle, and aquifer depletion (Saleth, 1996), they are perceived by the state to be lower than the economic and political costs of creating the institutions necessary for regulating these groundwater markets and water sharing contracts. The irrigation management transfer program implemented both in Andhra Pradesh and Madhya Pradesh also has a perfect explanation within the institutional transactions costs framework. While there are committed change agents on all sides—the state, bureaucracy, donors, research/training organizations, and the users, the actual forces for change, have their origin in the changing political economy realities of these states.

The heavy fiscal burden of irrigation subsidy has convinced the state, the bureaucracy, and the donors of the need for transferring the irrigation system to user groups. The economic threats of an increasing productivity loss from the poorly maintained irrigation system—documented well by research organizations[28] and personally experienced by most farmers—have convinced them of the key role that farmers, as a group, have to play in improving farm productivity and system efficiency. Though it is seldom recognized explicitly, the political groups have also viewed the program as an opportunity to build their grassroots organizations, and local groups found them as an additional avenue for assuming social status and power. Since the program is viewed as a logical part of the process of decentralization centered on the *panchayat* system (particularly in Madhya Pradesh), it is also perceived to have a considerable political mileage for ruling parties, especially during the election years.[29] Thus, from the perspective of all stakeholders, the transaction costs were reckoned to be far lower than the opportunity costs (i.e. the foregone potential benefits) of not implementing this program in the particular institutional environment faced by these states when the program was actually implemented.

While the Indian water sector is gradually emerging from bureaucratic grip and myopic political considerations, it has not yet fully matured enough to be influenced mainly by economic and technical forces. Unfortunately, the divisive role of political factors is likely to increase, especially on the issue of inter-state water sharing, as most rivers in India are shared by two or more

[28] International best practices and research-based knowledge produced by organizations such as the International Water Management Institute (IWMI) have also played a catalytic role in reducing the transaction costs of irrigation management transfer programs, especially in Andhra Pradesh and Madhya Pradesh.

[29] The irrigation management program in Madhya Pradesh was quicker and smoother than in Andhra Pradesh in view of the facilitative role of the decentralization process that was implemented before the transfer program. This is evidence for the advantage of sequencing two different, but operationally related, reform components in terms of the favorable effects of the earlier program on the transaction costs (especially its implementation cost component) of the latter program. But, it is necessary to note that these reform sequencing attempts in both states have happened more by default than by design.

states. As the basin resources are fully appropriated, additional claims will be politically more acrimonious unless institutional arrangements are created to catalyze negotiated settlements and mutual agreements. But, the issue has become complicated by the proposed 'Garland Scheme' for linking most major rivers, especially when the central government lacks the legal powers and political will to implement the Scheme, though it has the technical and finan- cial arrangements to complete most of the feasibility studies for various links (Iyer, 2002).[30] It is in this political vacuum and indecisive environment that the Supreme Court has been invoked to ask the government to report on the feasibility and prospects of this Scheme. This has, in some sense, reduced the political transactions costs for the Scheme, which is one of the long-term but somewhat tricky options for India to address its water shortage problems.

Water Sector Reform in Mexico: A Political Economy Perspective

Recent reforms in Mexican water institutions provide an interesting case for the powerful role of political economy factors (Hearne, 2003). The irrigation and urban water sectors reforms undertaken by Mexico since the late 1980s have two major thrusts: (a) decentralization and user participation, and (b) the adoption of economic instruments for cost recovery and demand manage- ment. As in the case of India, the factors motivating these reforms were external to both water sector and water institutions. For instance, decentralization has a political motivation of accommodating growing regional interests whereas cost recovery was a necessary response to the economic crisis of the late 1980s. Moreover, the factors that influenced the reform process such as urbanization, globalization, political pluralism, changing prices due to North America Free Trade Agreement (NAFTA), changing land use, and fiscal crisis were all external to the water sector (Hearne, 2003). This does not mean that endogenous factors such as declining groundwater table, water shortage, and deteriorating water quality were less significant. What happened, in fact, is that the opportunity costs of these endogenous factors have been magnified by the exogenous factors to give the necessary political economy thrust for reform initiation.

Mexico was able to enhance public expenditures with international borrowing and maintain an overvalued currency with high oil prices during the 1970s. However, this was no longer possible when oil prices fell and the debt crisis emerged during the 1980s. The policies adopted to solve the economic crisis included the signing of NAFTA, enhanced reliance on international trade, and the privatization of certain state enterprises. Since NAFTA has required the

[30] This Scheme aims to link 37 rivers through 3,000 storages and 12,500 kilometers of canals by 2016. This gigantic water grid, probably the largest in the world, will cost $120 billion, but is expected to generate 35 giga watts of hydro-power capacity and 35 mha of additional irrigation.

elimination of subsidies for most agricultural inputs and outputs, and the economic crisis has necessitated a reduction in government spending, the Mexican government was forced to undertake several reforms in the water sector with a larger share of public investment and budgetary subsidies. These reforms include the management transfer of all the irrigation districts and the promotion of private sector and local government in the urban water sector. Water rates both in irrigation and urban sectors were also revised to improve cost recovery.

While the economic crisis of the 1980s has remained a major factor precipitating decentralization within the water sector, the trend towards decentralization started long before, and it has its roots in the changing power balance of various political groups (Rodriguez, 1997). For decades, Mexico had a centralized political system with a dominant presidency coming usually from the Institutional Revolutionary Party (PRI), the single party that dominated Mexican politics from its inception. With a centralized system of political power and fiscal resources, all regional and local governments were dependent entirely on the federal government. Although decentralization was intended essentially to decentralize governmental functions and to distribute jobs and patronage geographically, it was resisted by groups who consider this to reduce their economic and political power. However, with the economic crises of the 1980s and the electoral defeats of the PRI in 1988 and in 2000, other political parties have become powerful enough to claim the presidency and several state governorships. It is the emergence of this political pluralism and the demand for regional autonomy that have deepened the process of political and economic decentralization (Pineda, 2002). The water sector—especially, its water supply and sanitation segments—has, of course, benefited from the synergetic influence of this overall process of decentralization.

Despite the moves to decentralize government functions and decision-making, the Comisión Nacional del Agua (CNA), the apex body that develops and manages water resources in Mexico, has maintained centralized control and federal proprietorship over Mexican water resources. Yet, this centralized arrangement has been conducive to decentralization because the CNA, as mandated by the President, has led the water institutional reform process involving a large scale program of irrigation management transfer and a substantial degree of privatization and localization of urban water services.[31] The water policy reforms that were initiated in the mid-1990s can be traced to the National Water Plans being prepared since 1975 as part of Mexico's periodic National Development Plans (Hearne, 2003). The preparation of these water plans was supported by the United Nations Development Programme and the World Bank.

Water institutional reforms in Mexico are characterized by the establishment of ambitious long-term goals and their gradual and deliberate implementation.

---

[31] This case shows clearly that a dose of centralization is inevitable even in promoting the decentralization program. Otherwise, the decentralization process will not be that fast or effective.

The 1992 National Water Law presented an ambitious reform program that will take decades for its effective implementation. The irrigation management transfer program was initiated with this law and has progressed rapidly and smoothly. Since this program was implemented with a 'big bang' approach, the whole process of transfer was completed within a span of two years. But, a careful look at the way the program was implemented will reveal that there has been a sequencing element, as it was implemented, on a pilot scale, in selected districts and the lessons learned were carried forward when the program was extended to other districts. Meanwhile, the efforts to link the agricultural input-supply, and extension systems with the WUAs provide an instance for institutional packaging during the reform process (Johnson, 1997). Although the irrigation sector reform was guided from above, there has been generally a favorable response from the user groups (Palacios, 2000).

Institutional sequencing has also been followed in other reform spheres. For instance, although the 1992 law authorized the creations of watershed councils and technical groundwater committees, these institutions (57 of them) were created only after the completion of the irrigation management transfer program. This is because the prior existence of WUAs is essential, as some of these councils/committees are to be the members of the WUAs. There is also prioritization and sequencing while creating the watershed councils, as the basins with more severe problems (e.g. Lerma and Rio Bravo) received priority over the remaining basins. The reform in the urban water sector started from Mexico City with a deliberate three-stage implementation of the privatization plan. Since such a cautious and gradualistic approach involved minimal private sector participation with no immediate long-term commitment, it had the advantage of neutralizing political opposition during the initial years of the reform. The same has also been true of the gradual process with which the urban water sector in other parts of Mexico was brought to the management of the regional and local authorities (Hearne, 2003). But, when the reform has reached a mature stage, the changes have already become entrenched, making it very costly to reverse. With these reforms in the irrigation and urban sectors, additional and marginal changes (e.g. water rates revision and cost recovery) also became easier. In this respect, the Mexican reform provides cases for the strategic use of both path dependency features as well as scale economies to counter political economy constraints.

Conclusions and Implications

The quantitative and qualitative manifestations of water crises are a major constraint for economic development and environmental sustainability both at the national and global contexts. Although water crisis is an apparent reflection of a physical gap between water development and utilization, it has its roots in an institutional gap, that is, the gap between the prevailing archaic and outmoded institutional arrangements and those needed for a more efficient and sustainable development, allocation, and utilization of the scarce resource in the future. This institutional gap also characterizes the differences between the two paradigms of water management, that is, the one based on the supply-side approach, physical solution, agency-based bureaucratic allocation, and centralized management and the other rooted in demand-side approach, economic solution, user-based market allocation, and decentralized management. Such an institutional gap is rather serious particularly in the case of many developing countries with a major share of global population and poor people, where the changing resource realities are already creating the economic and political pressure for moving towards an alternative development paradigm for water resources management.

It is true that the extent of institutional reforms undertaken in most of the developing countries is far from adequate to meet the institutional requirements for the alternative paradigm of market and user-based water allocation. However, as we consider the overall nature and thrusts of observed reforms across countries, institutional changes are moving in the right direction as they can foster economic approach, management decentralization, financial self-dependence, and environmental sustainability. There has also been a radical shift in policy dialogue and reform vocabulary in many developing countries. Many ideas that were considered once as anathema or impractical (e.g. paying for water, water privatization, and market allocation) are now considered seriously and also pursued vigorously even in countries such as China, Morocco, and India. These changes certainly augur well for the long-term prospects of reforms. However, current initiatives are still insufficient to take the reform process to advanced stages involving more difficult but critical changes needed for creating the institutional conditions necessary for an allocation-oriented water resources management. The usual reasons advanced for this reform gap are related to the political economy constraints and technical difficulties associated with the institutional reform itself. Yet, the water reform experiences of many countries—both developed and developing—indicate that they are able to circumvent these constraints and could still undertake both peripheral and substantive institutional achieve reforms in their water sector.

The occurrence of reforms in the face of the binding nature of political and technical constraints means that these factors themselves provide valuable contexts and opportunities for reform and many countries are, in fact, exploiting them to advance the reform process either by chance or by design. This is indeed the main policy message of this chapter, which was rationalized both in terms of an analytical framework based on an institutional transaction cost theory as well as in terms of empirical and case-study-based evidences for the way political contexts and institutional features are used by countries to initiate and sustain their reform programs. The analytical framework is very useful for a simple, yet comprehensive understanding of both the favorable political contexts provided by exogenous factors (e.g. macroeconomic reform, political changes, international agreements, and floods and droughts) as well as the strategic roles played by endogenous factors, especially the technical and transaction implications of institutional linkages. These political contexts and strategic factors provide the basis for deriving reform design principles such as institutional prioritization, sequencing, and packaging as well as reform implementation principles such as reform timing, spacing, speed, and scale. The empirical evidences provided in this chapter illustrate how these principles are actually used by various countries in different forms and contexts. Similarly, the two case studies of India and Mexico are provided to explain water institutional reforms from the institutional transaction cost and political economy perspectives.

Let us conclude by identifying some strategies for advancing institutional reforms in the water sector of developing countries. The first strategy obviously involves the promotion and adoption of reform design and implementation principles in a formal and planned manner. As the analytical framework and evidence provided in this chapter have shown, these principles are quite effective to promote institutional reforms through a careful exploitation of the political opportunities provided by exogenous changes and technical possibilities provided by the endogenous institutional features. The second strategy involves the achievement of a critical minimum level of reform from where the transaction cost calculus would stipulate that a reversal direction is costlier than to go ahead on the institutional change continuum. While the reform design principle based on institutional prioritization can help in identifying the key components of such minimum reform program, other design and implementation principles will help in implementing it in a gradual but consistent manner. Although the nature of this minimum reform program can vary across countries and contexts, in general terms, this program should include water law, water rights system, conflict resolution and accountability mechanisms, user-based decentralized arrangement for water allocation and management, value-based water rates, and regulatory arrangements for water quality and environment. Finally, as transaction costs decline and political balance improves along the institutional change continuum, it is necessary to have a logically linked sequential reform strategy, where water sub-sectors, institutional components, and even, regions are prioritized in terms of their performance impact, facilitative roles for downstream reforms, and political acceptability.

References

Abdulrazzak, M. J. (1995), 'Water Supplies Versus Demand in Countries of the Arabian Peninsula,' *Journal of Water Resources Planning and Management*, 121(3): 227–34.
Barrow, C. J. (1998), 'River Basin Development Planning and Management: A Critical Review,' *World Development*, 26(1): 171–86.

Bauer, Carl J. (2004), *Siren Song: Chilean Water Law as a Model for International Reform*. Washington DC: Resources for the Future Press.

Beaumont, Peter (1994), 'The Myth of Water Wars and the Future of Irrigated Agriculture in the Middle East,' *International Journal of Water Resources Development*, 10(1): 9–21.

Boyer, Robert and J. Rogers Hollingsworth (1997), 'From National Embeddedness to Spatial and Institutional Nestedness' in J. Rogers Hollingsworth and Robert Boyer (eds), *Contemporary Capitalism: The Embeddedness of Institutions*. Cambridge: Cambridge University Press.

Brinkerhoff, D. W. (1994), 'Institutional Development in World Bank Projects: Analytical Approaches and Intervention Designs,' *Public Administration and Development*, 14(1): 135–51.

Bromley, D. W. (1989), 'Institutional Change and Economic Efficiency,' *Journal of Economic Issues*, 23(3): 735–59.

Bruns, B. and D. J. Bandaragoda (eds) (2003), *Governance for Integrated Water Resources Management in a River Basin Context*. (Proceedings of an International Seminar, Bangkok, May, 2002), International Water Management Institute, Colombo, Sri Lanka.

Challen, Ray (2000), *Institutions, Transaction Costs, and Environmental Policy: Institutional Reform for Water Resources*, Cheltenham: Edward Elgar.

Coase, Ronald, H. (1937), 'The Nature of the Firm,' *Economica*, 4(2): 1–44.

Cummings Ronald, Ariel Dinar and Douglas Olson (1996) *New Evaluation Procedures for a New Generation of Water-Related Projects*. World Bank Technical Paper 349, World Bank, Washington, DC (December).

Dinar, A. (ed.) (2000), *The Political Economy of Water Pricing Reforms*, New York: Oxford University Press.

—— and A. Subramaniam (1997), *Water Pricing Experiences*, Washington DC, World Bank.

—— Trichur Balakrishnan, and Joseph Wambia (2004), 'Politics of Institutional Reforms in the Water and Drainage Sector of Pakistan,' *Environment and Development Economics*, 9(3) (June).

—— and R. M. Saleth (2005), 'Issues in Water Pricing Reforms: From Getting Correct Prices to Setting Appropriate Institutions' in Tom Tietenberg and Henk Folmer (eds), *International Yearbook of Environmental and Resource Economics*. Cheltenham, Edward Elgar.

Easter, K. William, Ariel Dinar, and Mark Rosegrant (eds), (1998), *Markets for Water: Potential and Performance*. Boston: Kluwer Academic Press.

Falkenmark, Malin (1999), 'Forward to the Future: A Conceptual Framework for Water Dependence,' *Ambio*, 28(4): 356–61.

—— and Gunnar Lindh (1993), 'Water and Economic Development' in Peter H. Gleick (ed.), *Water in Crisis: A Guide to the World's Fresh Water Resources*. New York: Oxford University Press.

Frederiksen, Harald D. (1998), 'International Community Response to Critical World Water Problems: A Perspective for Policy Makers,' *Water Policy*, 1: 139–58.

Food and Agriculture Organization (FAO) (1996), *Food Production: The Critical Role of Water*. Technical Background Document for the World Food Submit: 7, Rome.

Gleick, Peter H. (1998), *The World's Water: The Biennial Report on Fresh Water Resources*. Washington, DC: Island Press.

Gopalakrishnan, Chennat, Asit K. Biswas, and Cecilia Tortajada (eds) (2005), *Water Resources Management: Structure, Evolution, and Performance of Water Institutions*. New York: Springer-Verlag.

Hearne, Robert R. (2003), 'Progress of Institutional Reform in the Water Sector of Mexico,' Paper presented in the *Workshop on Water Reform, Sector Performance, Water Pricing and Water Resource Accounting*, 25th Conference of the International Association of Agricultural Economists, Durban, South Africa (August 16).

—— and K. William Easter (1997), 'The Economic and Financial Gains from Water Markets in Chile,' *Agricultural Economics*, 15: 187–99.

Iyer, Ramaswamy R. (2002), 'Linking of Rivers: Judicial Activism or Error?,' *Economic and Political Weekly*, 37(46): 4595–6.

Johnson, Sam H. (1997), 'Irrigation Management Transfer: Decentralizing Public Irrigation in Mexico,' *Water International*, 22(3): 159–67.

Kliot, Nurit, Deborah Shmueli, and Uri Shamir (1997), *Institutional Frameworks for Management of Transboundary Water Resources*. Water Research Institute, Technion Israel Institute of Technology, Haifa, Israel.

Lazonick, William (1991), *Business Organization and the Myth of the Market Economy*. Cambridge and New York: Cambridge University Press.

Le Moigne, Guy, Shawki Barghouti, Gershon Feder, Lisa Garbus, and Mei Xie (eds) (1992), *Country Experiences with Water Resources Management: Economic, Institutional, Technological, and Environmental Issues*. World Bank Technical Paper No: 175, Washington, DC, World Bank.

North, Douglass C. (1990a), *Institutions, Institutional Change, and Economic Performance*, Cambridge, Ma: Cambridge University Press.

—— (1990b), 'A Transaction Cost Theory of Politics,' *Journal of Theoretical Politics*, 2(4): 355–67.

—— (1997), *The Contribution of the New Institutional Economics to an Understanding of the Transition Problem*, WIDER Annual Lectures 1, World Institute for Development Economics Research, Helsinki, Finland.

Orloci, J., K. Szesztay, and L. Varkonyi (1985), *National Infrastructure in the Field of Water Resources*, UNESCO, Paris.

Ostrom, Elinor (1990), *Governing the Commons: The Evolution of Institutions for Collective Action*, Cambridge: Cambridge University Press.

—— (1999), *Institutional Rational Choice: An Assessment of the Institutional Analysis and Development Framework*. Working Paper, Workshop in Political Theory and Policy Analysis, Indiana University, Bloomington.

Palacios, E. (2000), 'Benefits and Second Generation Problems of Irrigation Management Transfer in Mexico,' in D. Groenfeldt and M. Svendson (eds), *Case Studies in Participatory Irrigation Management*. Washington, DC, World Bank Institute.

Pineda, N. (2002), 'Water Supply Performance, Policy, and Politics on Mexico's Northern Border,' in S. Whiteford and R. Mellville (eds), *Protecting a Sacred Gift: Water and Social Change in Mexico*. Center for U.S.–Mexican Studies, University of California, San Diego.

Postel, S. L. (1993), *The Last Oasis: Facing Water Scarcity*. Worldwatch Institute Environmental Alert Studies, World Watch Institute, New York.

—— (1999), *Pillar of Sand: Can the Irrigation Miracle Last?* New York: W. W. Norton.

——, G. C. Daily, and P. R. Ehrlich (1996), 'Human Appropriation of Renewable Fresh Water,' *Science*, 271: 785–8.

Rodriguez, V. (1997), *Decentralization in Mexico*. Boulder, Co: Westview Press.

Rosegrant, M. W. and C. Ringler (1999), *Impact on Food Security and Rural Development of Reallocating Water from Agriculture*. EPTD Discussion Paper No: 47, International Food Policy Research Institute, Washington, DC.

Saleth, R. M. (1996), *Water Institutions in India: Economics, Law, and Policy*. New Delhi: Commonwealth Publishers.

—— and Ariel Dinar (2000), 'Institutional Changes in Global Water Sector: Trends, Patterns, and Implications,' *Water Policy*, 2(3): 175–99.

—— (2004), *The Institutional Economics of Water: Cross-Country Analysis of Institutions and Performance*. Cheltenham: Edward Elgar Publishing Pvt. Ltd.

Savedoff, William and Pablo Spiller (eds) (1999), *Spilled Water: Institutional Commitment in the Provision of Water Services*. Washington, DC, Inter-American Development Bank.

Shirley, M. (ed.) (2002), *Thirsting for Efficiency: The Economics and Politics of Urban Water System Reform*. Washington, DC, World Bank.

Varis, Olli (1999), 'Water Resources Development: Vicious and Virtuous Circles,' *Ambio*, 28(7): 599–603.

Vermillion, Douglas L. (1997), 'Impact of Irrigation Management Transfer: A Review of Evidence,' IIMI, Colombo.

White, Louise G. (1990), *Implementing Policy Reforms in LDCs: A Strategy for Designing and Effecting Change*. Boulder and London: Lynne Rienner Publishers.

Williamson, John (ed.) (1994), *The Political Economy of Policy Reform*, Institute for International Economics, Washington, DC.

Williamson, Oliver E. (1975), *Markets and Hierarchies, Analysis and Antitrust Implications: A Study in the Economics of Internal Organization*. New York: Free Press.

—— (1985), *The Economic Institutions of Capitalism: Firms, Markets, Relational Contracting*, New York: Free Press.

—— (1999), 'Public and Private Bureaucracies: A Transaction Cost Economics Perspective,' *Journal of Law, Economics, and Organization*, 5: 306–47.

Appendix

Millennium Development Goals and Targets/Indicators

Goal 1: Eradicate extreme poverty and hunger
Target 1: Halve, between 1990 and 2015, the proportion of people whose income is less than one dollar a day
Indicators:
1. Proportion of population below $1 per day (PPP-values)
2. Poverty gap ratio [incidence x depth of poverty]
3. Share of poorest quintile in national consumption

Target 2: Halve, between 1990 and 2015, the proportion of people who suffer from hunger
Indicators:
4. Prevalence of underweight children (under 5 years of age)
5. Proportion of population below minimum level of dietary energy consumption

Goal 2: Achieve universal primary education
Target 3: Ensure that, by 2015, children everywhere, boys and girls alike, will be able to complete a full course of primary schooling

Maria Saleth and Ariel Dinar

Indicators:
  6. Net enrollment ratio in primary education
  7. Proportion of pupils starting grade 1 who reach grade 5
  8. Literacy rate of 15–24 year olds

Goal 3: Promote gender equality and empower women
Target 4: Eliminate gender disparity in primary and secondary education preferably by 2005 and to all levels of education no later than 2015
Indicators:
  9. Ratio of girls to boys in primary, secondary and tertiary education
10. Ratio of literate females to males of 15–24 year olds
11. Share of women in wage employment in the non-agricultural sector
12. Proportion of seats held by women in national parliament

Goal 4: Reduce child mortality
Target 5: Reduce by two-thirds, between 1990 and 2015, the under-5 mortality rate
Indicators:
13. Under-five mortality rate
14. Infant mortality rate
15. Proportion of 1-year-old children immunized against measles

Goal 5: Improve maternal health
Target 6: Reduce by three-quarters, between 1990 and 2015, the maternal mortality ratio
Indicators:
16. Maternal mortality ratio
17. Proportion of births attended by skilled health personnel

Goal 6: Combat HIV/AIDS, malaria and other diseases
Target 7: Have halted by 2015, and begun to reverse, the spread of HIV/AIDS
Indicators:
18. HIV prevalence among 15–24 year-old pregnant women
19. Contraceptive prevalence rate
20. Number of children orphaned by HIV/AIDS

Target 8: Have halted by 2015, and begun to reverse, the incidence of malaria and other major diseases
Indicators:
21. Prevalence and death rates associated with malaria
22. Proportion of population in malaria risk areas using effective malaria prevention and treatment measures
23. Prevalence and death rates associated with tuberculosis
24. Proportion of TB cases detected and cured under DOTS (Directly Observed Treatment Short Course)

Goal 7: Ensure environmental sustainability
Target 9: Integrate the principles of sustainable development into country policies and programs and reverse the loss of environmental resources
Indicators:
25. Proportion of land area covered by forest

26. Land area protected to maintain biological diversity
27. GDP per unit of energy use (as proxy for energy efficiency)
28. Carbon dioxide emissions (per capita) [Plus two figures of global atmospheric pollution: ozone depletion and the accumulation of global warming gases]

Target 10: Halve, by 2015, the proportion of people without sustainable access to safe drinking water
Indicators:
29. Proportion of population with sustainable access to an improved water source

Target 11: By 2020, to have achieved a significant improvement in the lives of at least 100 million slum dwellers
Indicators:
30. Proportion of people with access to improved sanitation
31. Proportion of people with access to secure tenure
    [Urban/rural disaggregation of several of the above indicators may be relevant for monitoring improvement in the lives of slum dwellers]

Goal 8: Develop a Global Partnership for Development
Target 12: Develop further an open, rule-based, predictable, nondiscriminatory trading and financial system. Includes a commitment to good governance, development, and poverty reduction—both nationally and internationally

Target 13: Address the Special Needs of the Least Developed Countries. Includes: tariff and quota free access for LDC exports; enhanced program of debt relief for HIPC and cancellation of official bilateral debt; and more generous ODA for countries committed to poverty reduction

Target 14: Address the Special Needs of landlocked countries and small island developing states (through Barbados Program and 22nd General Assembly provisions)

Target 15: Deal comprehensively with the debt problems of developing countries through national and international measures in order to make debt sustainable in the long term
Indicators:
32. Net ODA as percentage of DAC donors' GNI [targets of 0.7% in total and 0.15% for LDCs]
33. Proportion of ODA to basic social services (basic education, primary health care, nutrition, safe water and sanitation)
34. Proportion of ODA that is untied
35. Proportion of ODA for environment in small island developing states
36. Proportion of ODA for transport sector in land-locked countries
37. Proportion of exports (by value and excluding arms) admitted free of duties and quotas
38. Average tariffs and quotas on agricultural products and textiles and clothing
39. Domestic and export agricultural subsidies in OECD countries
40. Proportion of ODA provided to help build trade capacity
41. Proportion of official bilateral HIPC debt cancelled
42. Debt service as a percentage of exports of goods and services
43. Proportion of ODA provided as debt relief

44. Number of countries reaching HIPC decision and completion points

Target 16: In cooperation with developing countries, develop and implement strategies for decent and productive work for youth
Indicators:
45. Unemployment rate of 15–24 year olds

Target 17: In cooperation with pharmaceutical companies, provide access to affordable, essential drugs in developing countries
Indicators:
46. Proportion of population with access to affordable essential drugs on a sustainable basis

10

Water Quality Issues in Developing Countries[1]

Anil Markandya

Introduction

The Millennium Development Goals

Of all the environmental concerns that developing countries face, the lack of adequate water of good quality is probably the most serious. When the United Nations agreed at the Johannesburg Earth Summit on the set of the 8 Millennium Development Goals (MDGs), Goal 7 was 'to ensure environmental sustainability.' This has three targets and a number of indicators (Table 10.1). It is noteworthy that water is so prominent; it is the only environmental media that has a target of its own as well as being an indicator for the 'improving slum dwellers' target. One can debate whether this priority is justified on social and economic grounds and we intend to do that in this chapter. However, there is no doubting the importance that national governments and international financing agencies place on addressing the water problem.

This chapter looks at the current status of water access for households in developing countries, the consequences of the poor condition of the water they receive and the way they dispose of water effluent. It also looks at other uses of water, which are not picked up in the MDGs, but which may, nevertheless, be important to local communities in developing countries. These include inland rivers and lakes, as well as some coastal zones.

From this brief description, it is clear that the chapter does not cover all water issues. Primary among those not addressed are the questions relating to quantity (e.g. do we have enough water to meet our needs?). Other major

[1] I would like to acknowledge the major contribution of Suzette Pedroso as a research assistant for this paper and helpful inputs from Gayatri Acharya. My thanks also go to Mike Toman and an anonymous referee who made many helpful suggestions.

Table 10.1 The 'Environmental' MDG

Goal 7: Ensure environmental sustainability	
Targets	Indicators
Target 9: Integrate the principles of sustainable development into country policies and programs and reverse the loss of environmental resources	1. Proportion of land area covered by forest 2. Ratio of area protected to maintain biological diversity to surface area 3. Energy use (kg oil equivalent) per $1 GDP (PPP) 4. Carbon dioxide emissions (per capita) and consumption of ozone-depleting CFCs (ODP tons) 5. Proportion of population using solid fuels (WHO)
Target 10: Halve, by 2015, the proportion. of people without sustainable access to safe drinking water	6. Proportion of population with sustainable access to an improved water source, urban and rural
Target 11: By 2020, to have achieved a significant improvement in the lives of at least 100 million slum dwellers	7. Proportion of urban population with access to improved sanitation 8. Proportion of households with access to secure tenure

Source: United Nations (2003).

issues outside the scope of this chapter are the irrigation uses of water and the management of water flows for flood control, and so on. Finally, the chapter does not address issues relating to the management of groundwater. All these important aspects of water use are addressed in other chapters in this volume.

The Use of Water in the Household

Numbers without Safe Water

The reason for the predominance of water among the MDGs is the view that poor quality drinking water and improper disposal of wastewater have serious impacts on human health. Most work on this has been done by the World Health Organization (WHO). It defines 'safe water' and estimates the physical impacts of the lack of such water in terms of premature mortality and diarrhoea. In 2000, the global population without access to safe water was estimated at about 1.2 billion, or 19 percent (World Bank, 2003a). This has come down from about 26 percent in 1990, showing that significant progress has been made in that decade. The majority of those without access are in Asia and Sub-Saharan Africa (Table 10.2). There is, however, some dispute about the accuracy of the estimates. The definition of 'safe water' is oriented towards reasonable access and convenience and not towards quality of supply; although in most cases the two are highly correlated,[2] this is not always the case. In

---

[2] 'Improved' water supply technologies are: household connection, public standpipe, borehole, protected dug well, protected spring, rainwater collection. Also, 'improved water supply' refers to the availability of at least 20 liters per person per day from a source within one

Table 10.2 Population without access to safe water, by region

Regions	Total Population (Mn.)		Population without access (Mn.)	
	1990	2000	1990	2000
EAP	1,597	1,806	460	435
ECA	466	476	n.a.	43
LAC	434	511	77	69
MNA	237	294	n.a.	35
SAS	1,120	1,354	313	211
SSA	509	658	238	275
World	5,251	6,053	1,354	1,165

Note: The regional population does not add up to the world total population because aggregate data include economies for which component population data are not available.
Legends: EAP–Fast Asia and the Pacific; ECA–Europe and Central Asia; LAC–Latin America and the Caribbean; MNA–Middle East and North Africa; SAS–South Asia; SSA–Sub-Saharan Africa.
Source: World Bank (2003a).

Eastern Europe, for example, it is not the case; water is supplied to the house-holds, but the quality is declining and is not picked up in the WHO data (World Bank, 2003b). If the MDG target is met, the proportion falls to around 9.5 percent by 2015. Given the growth in population, that would leave around 675 million people without this essential commodity.

The access to improved water supply and sanitation is also summarized in Figure 10.1, which shows the level of access in each region in 1990 and 2000, along with the trend in *per capita* GDP from 1980 to 2002. The figures show an increase in access going along with an increase in *per capita* GDP in all regions except for Sub-Saharan Africa, where access also improved from 1990 to 2000, but *per capita* income actually declined. It may be useful to empirically examine whether there is a significant correlation between income and progress in access but it is not possible with the current available data.[3]

Environmental Health Risks

In the 2002 World Health Report, seven groups of risk factors to health are identified, one of which is related to the environment. The environmental risk factors are: unsafe water; sanitation and hygiene; urban air pollution; indoor smoke from solid fuels; lead exposure; and climate change. Table 10.3 shows how the environmental risk factors are assessed. Among the environmental risk factors, *unsafe water, sanitation, and hygiene* is the leading cause of mortality

kilometer of the user's dwelling. 'Not improved' are: unprotected well, unprotected spring, vendor-provided water, bottled water (based on concerns about the quantity of supplied water, not concerns over the water quality), tanker truck-provided water (WHO, 2002). Unprotected water sources are vulnerable to elements that may contaminate the water.

[3] Access data are only available for 1990 and 2000. Also, 1990 data may not always be available, especially at the country level.

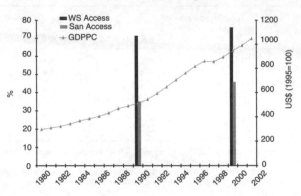

East Asia and Pacific Region

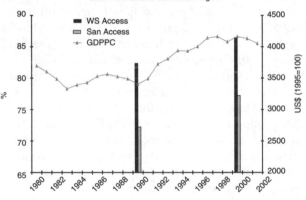

Latin America and Caribbean Region

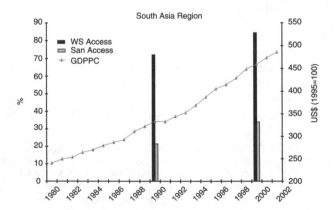

South Asia Region

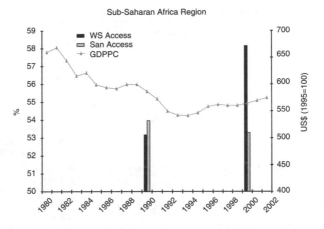

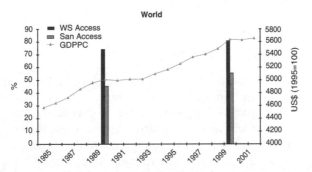

Figure 10.1 Per capita GDP and % population with access to improved water source and sanitation, by region

and morbidity in high-mortality developing countries; and is among the top five of all risk factors (environmental and non-environmental) in the same countries. However, it is second to *indoor air pollution* as an environmental risk factor in the low-mortality developing countries.[4] The measured outcome of the ingestion of unsafe water, lack of sanitation facilities and poor hygiene practices is in terms of diarrhoeal disease and other illnesses related to the risk factor of interest (e.g. schistosomiasis, ascariasis, trachoma, trichuriasis, and hookworm disease).

[4] See Annex I for the list of high and low mortality countries.

Table 10.3 Environmental risk factors to health

Risk factor	Theoretical minimum exposure	Measured adverse outcomes of exposure
Unsafe water, sanitation, and hygiene	Absence of transmission of diarrhoeal disease through water, sanitation, and hygiene practices	Diarrhoea and other illnesses related to the risk factor
Urban air pollution	7.5 μg/m^3 for PM$_{2.5}$	Cardiovascular mortality, respiratory mortality, lung cancer, mortality from acute respiratory infections in children
Indoor smoke from solid fuels	No solid fuel use	Acute respiratory infections in children, chronic obstructive pulmonary disease, lung cancer
Lead exposure	0.016 μg/dl blood lead levels	Cardiovascular disease, mild mental retardation

Source: Adopted from WHO (2002).

The Disability Adjusted Life Year (DALY)

The WHO has estimated the impacts of the lack of access in health conditions by estimating the burden of disease in terms of the number of disability adjusted life years lost (DALYs), attributable to this factor. DALYs combine impacts of mortality and morbidity attributed to a risk factor into a single measure. The DALY has been used as a measure of the burden of disease and it is an indicator of the time lost due to premature mortality and time lived with a disability (mental or physical). It is beyond the scope of this paper to discuss the DALYs in detail but there are various literatures that show different ways of calculating the DALYs (Homedes, 1996; Anand and Johnson, 1995; Pruss-Ustun et al., 2003). Table 10.4 gives the burden of disease attributed to environmental risk factors for the high mortality developing countries in terms of annual DALYs per 1,000 people. These countries account for 29 percent of the world's population but nearly two-thirds of DALYs lost due to unsafe water.

Table 10.4 shows that these high mortality countries face a significant burden from 'unsafe water, hygiene and sanitation'. Overall, it accounts for about half the total environmental health burden, being a slightly smaller share in South East Asia and a higher share in the Eastern Mediterranean and the Americas. Compared to urban air pollution, unsafe water is responsible for thirteen times as many DALYs; and compared to lead exposure, it is responsible for nearly seven times as many. The only environmental risk that comes close is indoor air pollution, which accounts for about 70 percent of the unsafe water burden. Looking at the DALYs across regions, the Eastern Mediterranean

Table 10.4 Attributable DALYs per 1,000 people due to environmental risk factors, high mortality countries, 2000

Countries	Unsafe water, sanitation, and hygiene	Urban air pollution	Indoor smoke from solid fuels	Lead exposure	Total
All Countries	9.0	1.3	6.4	2.1	18.9
High Mortality Countries	18.9	1.4	12.9	2.8	35.9
Of which					
Africa	22.6	1.0	17.6	3.3	44.5
The Americas	11.4	0.8	5.0	4.0	21.2
Eastern Mediterranean	29.7	2.3	12.5	4.0	48.4
Southeast Asia	15.8	1.3	12.2	2.3	31.5

Note: See Annex 1 for the list of high mortality countries.
Source: WHO (2002).

suffers the most, with attributable DALYs of nearly 30 per thousand people due to unsafe water. The region is followed by Africa with about 23 DALYs per thousand people.

These calculations are of course subject to substantial uncertainties and based on many simplifying assumptions. It is not possible to carry out a thorough assessment of the methodology here but it is important to note some of the major problems in making such estimates. One is the state of impact assessment that is undergoing substantial changes in the area of air pollution (see Chapter 6 in this volume). Some of the developments there indicate that the long term impacts of exposure to small particles may be underestimated.

Valuing DALYs

These issues are clearly important and the numbers should be examined more carefully. Nevertheless, even if it is assumed that they are of the right order of magnitude, the WHO study points to unsafe water and sanitation as a major issue to be addressed in terms of development. To put the costs in economic terms, we need to value a DALY in monetary terms. Values for DALYs are hard to come by, but there are two sources from which estimates can be made. One is based on the 'output' approach, which takes the per capita GDP as a lower bound (World Bank, 2003c). This derives its justification from the use of the human capital approach in the valuation of mortality in developing countries (Cropper et al., 1997). Another is to take the recent willingness-to-pay values for a reduction in the risk of death, derived from contingent valuation studies of risks in developed countries (Alberini et al., 2001; Markandya et al., 2003). From these studies, the value of the loss of life expectancy of one year can be obtained and the most recent work indicates that the median value for the European Union is around €50,000, which is about 2.5 times GDP per capita. If we apply a range of values to

Table 10.5 Estimated value of health costs of DALYs attributable to environmental risks

Countries	('000) DALYs attributable to		GDPPC (current US$)	Damage Cost to Health				
				All Environmental Risks			Unsafe water, sanitation, and hygiene	
	Unsafe water, sanitation, and hygiene	All Env. Risk Factors		Low (Bn $)	High (Bn $)	Ave. as % of GDP	Ave. for Unsafe Water (Bn $)	As % of GDP
High Mortality Countries	34,462	65,513	645	42	106	6.3%	39	3.3%
Of which								
Africa	6,916	13,629	490	7	17	7.8%	6	4.0%
The Americas	756	1,403	4,464	6	16	3.7%	5	1.9%
Eastern Mediterranean	8,303	13,557	729	10	25	8.5%	10	4.6%
Southeast Asia	18,487	36,924	449	17	41	5.5%	18	3.4%

Source: WHO (2002) and own calculations.

the countries in question, where *GDP per capita* is the lower bound and *2.5 times GDP per capita* is the upper bound, we obtain the estimates of damages in Table 10.5.[5]

The estimated annual cost of all environmental risks averages $66 billion, with water-related costs being around $34 billion. For the high mortality country group as a whole, the costs are relatively small in percentage terms—around 3.3 percent. One might think that this figure would be greater if we looked at the people most affected, as the loss of DALYs is surely concentrated among them. This does not, however, appear to be the case. WHO estimates indicate that if the risk to individuals with less than $2 a day were to be the same as that for people with more than $2 a day, the 'risk factor' from unsafe water would decline by 51 percent. Given that the population with less than $2 of expenditure per person per day in these high mortality countries is between 15 percent (Algeria) and 83 percent (Madagascar), the costs to them, as a percentage of *their* income ranges from 2.0 to 4.0 percent with the low value of a DALY and 5.0 to 10.0 percent with a high value of the DALY.[6] Although the DALYs are concentrated among the poor, their value per DALY is also lower, with the two

---

[5] There is an underlying assumption that the 'elasticity' of WTP with respect to GDP is one. Krupnick, et al. (1996) have argued for an elasticity of 0.35, based on the work of Carson and Mitchell (1993). Yaping (1999), on the other hand suggests a value of one. Here we take a unit elasticity as providing a lower bound to the costs. Most of the high-mortality countries have a relatively low income, where the gross national income per capita ranges from $140 to $700. Between 1990 and 2002, the average annual GDP growth of this group of countries is about 3.6%.   [6] The calculations are detailed in Annex II to this chapter.

factors pulling in different directions. Even this calculation, however, has an averaging aspect to it and misses the impact on those in the vulnerable groups who actually bear the costs of unsafe water and sanitation, the consequences can be disastrous. Hence, although the share of income represented by these losses is moderate, there is a real distributional and poverty issue to be tackled. Protecting the very vulnerable from unsafe water and sanitation can yield social benefits that are greater than the private benefits estimated above. One way of picking this up would be to use 'equity weights', so a poor person's benefits were given a weight of more than one. This has been used in some analysis by economists, but is criticized on the grounds that there is an element of arbitrariness in selecting the weights. Another way is simply to report the benefits to these groups and leave the judgment as to the value to be attached to them to the decision-maker.

How Much are Safe Water and Sanitation a Priority?

While the discussion so far provides useful information on deciding priorities for action, it does not directly tell us whether it is justified to spend scarce resources on tackling the unsafe water issue. That depends on what options are available to reduce the number who do not have safe water, what these options would achieve in terms of reducing the numbers (the 'avoidable' risk) and what value we attach to that reduction. To see how the benefits and costs stack up, we look at the MDG for water supply and sanitation (Table 10.7). If the water supply target was to be met and the sanitation improvements were to meet a similar target, we can estimate the costs of each target independently, as well as the benefits of both targets. The cost figures are based on an internal World Bank study on the costs of meeting all the MDGs (World Bank, 2003d, e). Table 10.6 and Figure 10.2 summarize the findings. Details of the calculations are given in Annex 3.

The figures indicate that both sanitation and safe water targets of a 50 percent reduction are marginally justifiable. For Africa and South East Asia, the costs are above the upper bound of the benefits of the reduced DALYs. For the Americas, they are below the lower bound thus justifying the targets, and in the Eastern Mediterranean they lie in between. The 'critical' values of DALYs as a percentage of GDP (i.e. the values at which the MDG program just become viable) are: 3.1 times GDP for Africa, 0.4 times GDP for the Americas, 1.2 times GDP for the Eastern Mediterranean and 2.8 times GDP for South East Asia.

The estimates are crude; they underestimate the benefits for two reasons. First, the value of DALYs will increase over the 15-year period due to economic growth and this has not been allowed for (growth rate projections are difficult to make with any accuracy over the period). Nevertheless, with a reasonable

Table 10.6 Estimated benefits and costs of meeting the MDG targets for water and sanitation in high mortality countries ($US Bn)

Region	Cost of Water Supply	Cost of Sanitation	Total Cost	Benefits of reduced DALYS	
				Lower Bound	Upper Bound
Africa	4.1	7.2	11.3	3.6	9.0
The Americas	0.5	0.9	1.1	3.6	9.0
Eastern Med.	2.2	5.8	8.0	6.4	16.1
S.E. Asia	8.1	25.6	33.7	8.8	22.1
Total	**14.9**	**39.4**	**54.3**	**23.7**	**59.2**

Notes:
1. Costs are sum of capital and operating costs.
2. Costs for water and sanitation goals will be mostly for capital costs, which is about 85% of the cost.
3. Capital costs based on a 'levelized' capital cost calculated at a 10 percent discount rate with a 15-year life of the equipment.
4. The annual operating costs are taken as 15 percent of the total investment costs.

Source: Own calculations.

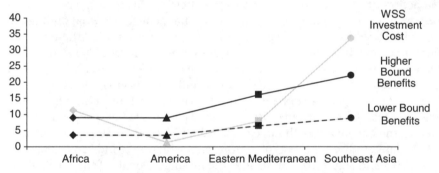

Figure 10.2 Water supply and sanitation (WSS) annual investment cost and benefits by region, US$ Bn

assumption of per capita growth of around 3 percent per annum, the critical value of the DALYs is reduced by a third and all regions' expenditures are justifiable with the upper bound value of the DALYs. The second factor is the non-health benefits of improved water supply and sanitation. Savings in time for collection in the case of the former, and in comfort and ease of use in both cases have not been included. The willingness to pay for these benefits varies widely and depends very much on the nature of the improvement (e.g. public stand posts versus private connection; see Whittington et al, 1990, 2002; Boadu, 1992; McPhail, 1994). It is problematic, however, to add the benefits measured in such studies to the health benefits taken here as the WTP studies also include some element of health benefits.

Separating Improved Water Supply and Sanitation

The assessment provided above is for both water supply and sanitation taken together. The cost justification side of the calculations shows that the sanitation target costs about three times as much as the water supply target. Hence a separate valuation of the two is merited and is provided in Table 10.7. The table shows that while water supply targets are justifiable for all regions (i.e. the costs lie between the lower and upper bounds), the sanitation targets are only justifiable for the Americas. This does not mean, of course, that no programs for improved sanitation are justified in the high mortality countries. Unfortunately we cannot answer the question: if a 50 percent cut is too big, what does pass a cost-benefit test? There are no data on how the marginal costs of the programs change with the target, nor on how the marginal benefits vary. Doubtless, some of the programs will have greater benefits and some will have lower costs. What the analysis does therefore is to draw attention to the need to look more carefully at the individual programs and select those locations and communities where the benefits will be greatest; or scale reductions differently; and/or look at cheaper options. For water supply, on the other hand, a more general commitment to meeting the MDG target is warranted.

Complementary Activities

The prioritizing of water supply and sanitation programs to fund as part of the MDG targets is a reasonable objective. But it is only part of the whole issue of designing such programs and the implementation of complementary activities is critical. In this regard, the role of education for sanitation is paramount. There are several World Bank and other documents that attest to the substantial benefits of careful, well-designed education programs covering basic hygiene practices, such as hand washing. Not only do these activities pay dividends on their own, they also complement the benefits of improvements in sanitation

Table 10.7 Estimated benefits and costs of meeting the MDG targets for water and sanitation individually in high mortality countries ($US Bn)

Region	Cost of Water Supply	Benefits of reduced DALYS		Cost of Sanitation	Benefits of reduced DALYS	
		Lower Bound	Upper Bound		Lower Bound	Upper Bound
Africa	4.1	2.3	5.8	7.2	1.3	3.3
The Americas	0.5	2.3	5.7	0.9	1.3	3.2
Eastern Med.	2.2	4.1	10.3	5.8	2.3	5.8
S.E. Asia	8.1	5.6	14.1	25.6	3.2	8.0
Total	**14.9**	**15.1**	**37.8**	**39.4**	**8.5**	**21.3**

Source: Own calculations.

services. Other areas where the investment and education programs complement each other include: educating people about the use of water filtration and other water quality improvement measures (where necessary), impacts of sanitary landfills on ground water, and so on.

Sustaining Water Supply and Sanitation Services

The comparison of costs and benefits presented above is, of course, only one part of designing and providing systems of water supply and sanitation. Equally important is to ensure that the institutions can provide these services in a sustainable manner. As the 'Camdessus' Report notes, it is critical for the host government to take real political ownership of the targets and to be clear on their strategies and priorities for the water sector. They need to prepare water strategies and action programs for 2015 and to include these in their short- and medium-term development plans (Winpenny, 2003).

The most difficult problem that the program will face is to put in place suitable mechanisms for continued coverage of the costs of provision of improved water supply and sanitation. Typically, water supply and sanitation services in developing countries do not cover the costs—the average level of cost recovery for them is around 25 percent, compared to over 50 percent for power and over 100 percent for telecommunications (Saghir, 2003). This makes private investment in the water sector much less attractive than the other sectors and, furthermore, results in a system that deteriorates over time (capital expenditures are deferred due to lack of funds). That, in turn, makes people less willing to pay for the service and the situation gets progressively worse.

If, therefore, the MDG target of increasing provision of water supply and sanitation is to be met, the issue of cost recovery has to be addressed head on. There are, broadly, only two sources of financing the system: the consumers and the government (local or central). Consumer willingness to pay varies with income (the richer are generally willing to pay more), with quality of service and with their present status as consumers (those already connected to the system may pay less than those who are not). A number of recent studies have shown that the WTP for an improved water supply is considerably higher than current tariffs (Whittington et al., 2002; Brocklehurst, 2003), both for current consumers as well as for those who are not connected. Thus the case for an improved service can be made on grounds of WTP, but exactly what is affordable will depend on the level of income of the population and the distribution of that income. The more costly and sophisticated the system the greater will be the number who cannot afford it. This implies either that they are not connected or that they receive some kind of subsidy. Even with the most basic systems, however, supply will be unaffordable to some households and some form of subsidy will be needed for them. It is key, therefore to carry out careful research on what design is desired by the community and what it will pay for.

What form should the subsidy take? Again recent work at the World Bank has come up with some useful findings. First, 'cross subsidization,' where the 'poor' are subsidized by the 'rich' who pay more than the cost of supply is hard to achieve. The mechanism typically used for this is the increasing block tariff, where the first X cubic meters are charged at a low rate and subsequent amounts charged at increasing rates. Apart from the difficulties in installing meters and monitoring water use, the problem with this method is that consumption is not that strongly related to income. From studies in Bangalore and Kathmandu, it was found that non-poor households consume only about 20 percent more than poor households (Brocklehurst, 2003). Hence a significant part of the benefit of the lower block rate goes to non-poor households and using cross subsidization to cover the full cost becomes virtually impossible. Furthermore a tariff of this kind makes it unattractive for any utility to take on more customers.

The second finding is that a more appropriate form of subsidy may be for connections. Poor households often cannot afford the one-time up-front cost and paying for this can be much better targeted than a consumption subsidy. The data referred to above for Bangalore and Kathmandu were analyzed to show that replacing the consumption subsidy with a subsidy to connections allowed universal coverage to be achieved within a decade.

More generally, subsidizing part of the capital cost and requiring the utility to cover operating and maintenance (O&M) costs, rather than subsidizing the latter is attractive because it provides the utility with an incentive for cost efficiency on the O&M side. On the capital side, a problem that has been encountered, particularly in Eastern Europe, is over estimating the capacity required for an improved system. When tariffs increase as a result of such a change, consumption can fall quite sharply. Utility reform and metering has brought about some astonishing declines in consumption. In Gdansk, Poland, for example, higher tariffs led to a fall in domestic consumption of 33 percent; in Bydgozcz consumption fell from 213 l/c/d to 147 l/c/d (a 30 percent decline). In Rostock, Germany, the French company Lyonnaise des Eaux managed to cut consumption by 67 percent and in the Baltic states higher tariffs led to reductions of around 50 percent (Stottmann, 1999). If such a decline is not planned, the system will be too large and cost recovery will become even more difficult. Indeed it can be shown that if the demand is elastic enough, cost recovery may be impossible, that is, raising the tariff results in even more cuts and even lower revenues (Markandya, 2004a).

The capital financing for water supply and sanitation can come from either the private or public sectors. Given the problems of cost recovery, and the risks associated with obtaining tariff levels that yield a sufficient return on capital, private finance in this sector has been relatively limited. In 2000, for example, just under $60 billion was invested by the public sector in water supply and sanitation and just under $20 billion by the private sector (Saghir, 2003).

Moreover, the usual private sector interest in investing has declined and the supply of 'bankable projects' is declining. This trend will only be reversed through reduced risks in investment in developing countries in general, and through credible legal and regulatory reforms, especially in the regions with the greatest opportunities (e.g. the former Soviet Union, Central Asia and Mekong region and Africa).

To conclude, once investments have been made to provide improved water supply and sanitation services, they have to be sustained. This has not been easy in the past and will continue to be a challenge. It is critical to design systems that meet the affordable needs of the population being served and to design effective systems of subsidy that target those who most need assistance and that ensure adequate funds to the utility, public or private, so it can meet its costs and make a reasonable return on the capital invested.

The Quality of Inland Water

Water Quality and the Environmental Kuznets Curve

Before we look in detail at the issues arising with respect to water quality in rivers and lakes, it is interesting to examine the evidence on the relationship between economic development, as measured by per capita GDP and the quality of water in developing countries (i.e. whether the data support the so-called Kuznets curve). In Figure 10.3, the relationship between real per capita GDP and per capita emissions of BOD is shown for selected 'high mortality' countries from 1980 to 2002, as defined by the World Health Organization (see Annex 1 for a list of these countries). For both series, a five-year moving average has been taken to smooth out year on year cyclical fluctuations. As the graphs show, there is no clear evidence of the Kuznets hypothesis. Some

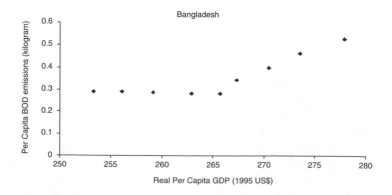

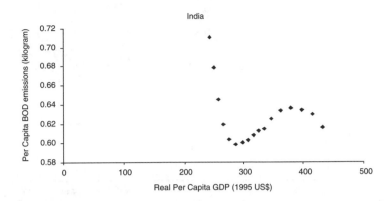

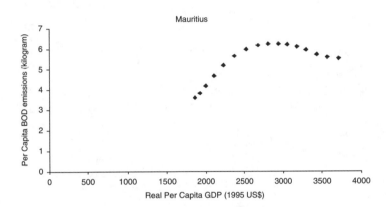

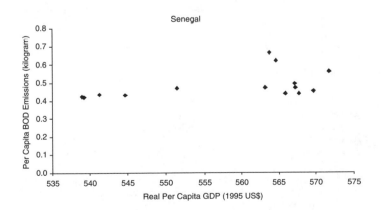

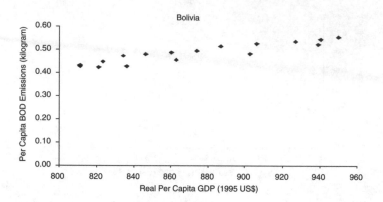

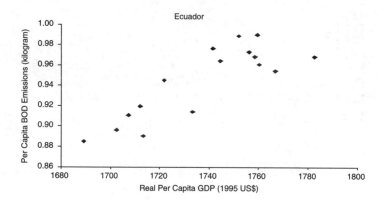

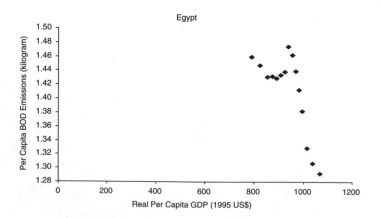

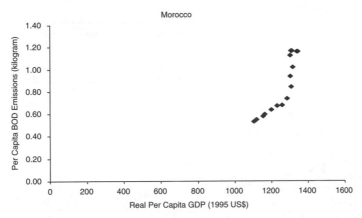

Figure 10.3 Relationship between BOD emissions and GDP, selected high mortality countries (5-year moving average)

countries show the inverted 'U' shape (Mauritius and India, to some extent); some show a 'U' shape, which is the opposite of the Kuznets hypothesis (Bangladesh and Morocco). Others demonstrate no clear pattern.

If, however, the panel data are taken for these countries and some others in the high mortality group,[7] the relationship between water quality and income can be estimated using the simple model of environmental Kuznets curve, as below:

$$BODPC = Intercept + \beta\, GDPPC + \delta GDPPC^2 + error\ term$$

where BODPC is BOD emissions per capita, and GDPPC is real per capita GDP. The following results are obtained (Table 10.8).

Water quality is represented by the variable, *biochemical oxygen demand* or *BOD*, which is the primary indicator of pollution in wastewater. The regression results show that there is a statistically significant relationship between income and an environmental degradation indicator (e.g. BOD emissions), but the relationship does not support the hypothesis of the environmental Kuznets curve. Rather the results suggest that, initially, water quality improves as incomes increase; but when per capita GDP reaches about US$480, the quality of water begins to deteriorate and continues to do so at an increasing rate as incomes increase (Figure 10.4).

---

[7] Fifteen high mortality countries were considered for the estimation because they have relatively more time series data available compared to the others. These countries are: Algeria, Bangladesh, Bolivia, Cameroon, Ecuador, Egypt, India, Mauritius, Morocco, Nepal, Nigeria, Pakistan, Peru, Senegal, and Yemen. The periods covered are from 1980 to 2002, and the data were obtained from the World Bank (2003f). The regression also looked for fixed effects but none were found.

Table 10.8 Regression results using OLS

Variable	Parameter estimate	Standard error	t-Value	Prob
Intercept	0.58745	0.12884	4.56	<.0001
GDPPC	−0.00052	0.00020	−2.53	0.0120
GDPPC^2	5.37245E-7	6.257041E-8	8.59	<.0001

Turning point	0.46 kg (BOD emission), US$ 481.32
R-square	0.6003
Adj R-square	0.5970

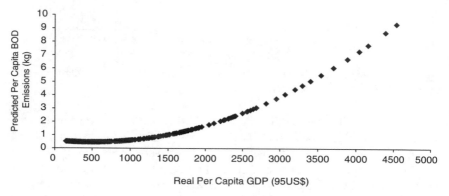

Figure 10.4 Relationship between per capita GDP and predicted per capita BOD emissions

This result, which is contrary to the Kuznets hypothesis, suggests that water quality is a growing problem with development. Of course, the countries looked at are all relatively poor (the highest per capita income here is for Mauritius at $4,500), and there may well be another turning point at much higher per capita incomes (e.g. Egypt). Even assuming this to be the case, however, the evidence does not support a simple Kuznets hypothesis but rather a more complex phenomenon, with multiple turning points, which need further investigation.

Indicators of Water Quality in Developing Countries

In this section, we look at the quality concerns arising with regard to inland water. Frequently, the quality of such water is poor in developing countries. Primarily, as a result of the increased demand on freshwater resources, high environmental costs have been paid. Some rivers no longer reach the sea; 50 percent of the world's wetlands have disappeared in the past century; 20 percent of freshwater fish are endangered or extinct; many of the most important groundwater aquifers are being mined, with water tables already deep and dropping by meters every year, and some are damaged permanently by salinization. Most of the collected wastewater in developing countries is discharged directly to surface waters without treatment. In addressing these problems, however, the focus is on the management of quantity of water, including investment in storage, flood control, and watershed management more generally; and promotion of policies that do not waste scarce water resources. Little reference is to be found in the development literature on improving the quality of freshwater directly. The Water Resources Strategy (World Bank, 2002), for example, discusses various interventions along the lines mentioned above, but has virtually nothing to say about directly improving the quality of the water.

This emphasis on the quantity side may well be justified, given the high costs of ensuring that rivers, lakes and ground water sources are clean. Moreover, the benefits of such investments are probably smaller in developing countries, given that a part of them are derived from recreational uses, for which poorer people are willing to pay less than richer people. Not all benefits, however, are of this kind, and at least some water quality projects include benefits of lower costs of water treatment and use of treated water for irrigation.

There are, broadly, three types of benefits from cleaner water. The first is the *amenity benefit*, which refers to the use of water for recreational purposes and the value attached to it looking and smelling cleaner. The second is the *benefit of lower costs of treatment of the water source* before drinking and the possible benefits to those who use it without treatment. The last are the *benefits attached to cultural and religious values* of some rivers. These may be partly 'use values' but also 'non-use values'; and even for a poor country, these values may be significant enough to warrant investment in clean up. Unfortunately, there is no comprehensive review of projects generating each type of benefit, but there are useful and (probably) representative case studies of each. These are examined below.

Measures to Improve Inland Water Quality

Although the most important contribution to improving water quality is to treat discharges in municipal or industrial effluent treatment plants, there are other measures that can be taken and the combination of measures chosen can make a big difference to the total cost of achieving a given improvement in quality. The general propositions that water quality is a broader management issue than just wastewater treatment, and that quality and quantity are related, are certainly correct and should be borne in mind when designing a control strategy for quality.

Other factors that are relevant include amounts of water abstracted, and discharges from non-point sources, notably agriculture. It is easy to construct examples of situations in which: (a) better management practices or pre-treatment of waste from single industrial or agro-industrial sources would be cheaper than taking the waste to a common treatment plant; (b) policies to reduce agricultural run-off through extension services and/or fiscal incentives such as taxes on pesticides and fertilizers can be a less expensive way of getting a better quality than higher levels of treatment; and (c) prohibiting abstraction in critical low flow periods can make a big difference to water quality during those periods at a relatively low cost.

Notwithstanding these observations, wastewater treatment remains the most important source of achieving improved water quality. Hence the section below looks at the potential benefits of such improvements and compares them to the costs of wastewater treatment. This is not to give such treatment an exclusive role relative to other methods, but to have a benchmark cost with which to compare the benefits.

Arithmetic of the Costs and Benefits of Improvements in Water Quality for Recreation

Before reviewing a number of case studies, it is quite informative to look at the costs and potential benefits of river and lake clean up in simple, 'back of the envelope' terms. The numbers are as follows:

Costs: The capital cost of providing secondary treatment in accordance with the urban wastewater directive of the EU ranges from €89 to €405 per person, depending on the population that is being served. The smaller the population, the higher the unit costs—the lower figure applies to a city of 236,000, while the higher figure applies to a village of 2000. The operational costs have to be added to the capital cost, and the two can be combined by taking the levelized equivalent of the capital cost. In this example we have calculated the levelized capital cost taking a 25-year life for the plant and a 10 percent discount rate. The combined annual costs range from €13.9 to €72.6 per person. Data are taken from the Compliance Cost Study for Bulgaria (World Bank, 2003g).

Benefits: The total benefits will depend on the number of persons who make use of the recreational facilities. In Table 10.9, the total number of such beneficiaries is assumed to range from 10,000 to 150,000 per year. This number may also depend, of course, on the improvements generated in terms of water quality. The costs given in the previous paragraph refer to achieving standards in terms of BOD, COD, suspended solids, phosphorous and nitrogen that would, in most cases, represent a very significant improvement in water quality and allow most recreational uses, including game fishing where this was relevant.

Net Benefits: These will depend on how many urban areas there are that need the treatment facilities. In the calculations in Table 10.9, we allow this figure to range from one town of about 100,000, to ten such towns.

The figures in Table 10.9 give the breakeven benefit values for different combinations of users and polluters whose discharges have to be treated.

As there are very few studies of the benefits of recreational and other use in developing countries, these break-even values have to be interpreted in the light of benefit studies in developed countries plus a few in developing countries. In the U.S., values for improved fishery benefits range between €60

Table 10.9 Break-even values of benefits for improved inland water quality with different combinations of number of users and polluters (€/person)

	No. of Beneficiaries					
	10000	25000	50000	75000	100000	150000
Pop. ('000)						
100	246	98	49	33	25	16
200	492	197	98	66	49	33
300	738	295	148	98	74	49
400	983	393	197	131	98	66
500	1,229	492	246	164	123	82
600	1,475	590	295	197	148	98
700	1,721	688	344	229	172	115
800	1,967	787	393	262	197	131
900	2,213	885	443	295	221	148
1000	2,459	983	492	328	246	164

Note: The population of users is assumed to be located in identical towns of 100,000 each.
Source: Own calculations.

and €380 per household per annum, depending on the exact improvement, the location, and so on (Olsen et al., 1994; Sanders et al., 1991; Hanemann, 1991). In the U.K., Willis and Garrod (1995) estimated the benefits from improved flow rates on a 130 km stretch of river as between €18 and €23 per household per year.[8] In developing and transition countries, the figures are generally somewhat lower. In the Philippines, the benefits of improving river surface water so that it is fit for swimming ranged from €11.1 to €18.9 per user per year (Choe et al., 1996). In Latvia, the benefits from making the Gauja River suitable for swimming and fishing were estimated at €5.7 per person per year (Ready et al., 2002). In Thailand, the benefits of improving water quality so that it moved from 'boatable' to 'fishable' were €28.8 per household per year; and further improvements from 'fishable' to 'swimmable' were €33.2 per household per year (Tapvong et al., 1999). In China, values for water quality for East Lake close to the town of Wuhan were made using CV and travel cost methods (Yaping, 2003). He found that improving quality from 'existing' to 'boatable' gave a *per capita* benefit of €1.2 and €1.8. Going from 'boatable' to 'swimmable' gave a benefit of between €2.2 and €4.7 per person.[9] Finally, we have a study from Hungary where a clean up program was valued in terms of willingness to pay to prevent further deterioration of water quality. The estimate was a WTP of €22.5 per person per year for this benefit[10] (Mourato et al., 1999).

The message from Table 10.9 and these studies is that clean-up projects for rivers and other inland water bodies are unlikely to be justifiable unless the

[8] All benefits figures are in 1999 euros. Original studies have been converted to euros to make them comparable with the cost estimates.
[9] CVM values were the higher of the range of value; travel cost estimates were the lower.
[10] All values have been converted to euros, at the prevailing exchange rates of the year in which the studies were carried out.

number of beneficiaries is large relative to the number of polluters whose waste has to be removed, or unless there are significant non-recreational benefits to improving inland water quality. Just looking at amenity benefits to start with, we can see that, for example, with 150,000 users and only 100,000 polluters, the break-even value is around €16, which might be feasible from some locations in Asia and Eastern Europe. On the other hand, with the number of polluters well in excess of the number of users (which is typically the case), the break-even values are much too high.

Evidence on the Non-amenity Benefits of Cleaner Inland Waters

What evidence do we have on non-amenity benefits of cleaner inland waters? From the ecological perspective, the case has been made for significant impacts of deteriorating water quality on fisheries, health and eco-systems. The valuation of these in economic terms, however, is much more difficult. We consider here the experience of two seas (the Black and Caspian), a river (the Ganges in India) and a lake (Lake Mariut in Egypt).[11]

In the Black and Caspian Seas, for example, fish catches have been declining, and part of the decline is attributable to the impacts of eutrophication, industrial pollution, overfishing and the introduction of exotic species. Quantifying these impacts separately, however, has not been done for the Caspian Sea. One cannot say how much of the loss of the sturgeon is due to the damming of the major rivers flowing into the sea, how much to illegal fishing and how much to the increasing loads of industrial pollution, including the oil spills that occur there regularly (Markandya, 2004b). For the Black Sea, an estimate was made (Knowler et al., 1997) of the increase in profits from fisheries that would arise from investments in eutrophication. The numbers are somewhat speculative, but even if we accept them, they explain between 14 and 21 percent of all identified benefits of the program (Arin, 2001). Of the remaining benefits amenity dominates (60 to 63 percent), followed by health (7 to 14 percent) and agriculture (9 to 12 percent). The resulting calculations marginally 'justify' the World Bank/GEF Strategic Partnership's investment program, although the benefit estimates must be treated with some caution, especially those relating to fisheries and agriculture.[12]

---

[11] Another interesting study on the non-amenity value is that by Emerton et al. (1999) for Nakivubo wetlands in Uganda. It does not value the quality of water in wetlands as such but rather the value of wetlands in purification of sewage loads from Kampala. The savings in sewage treatment account for most of the economic value of the wetlands. As the authors note, however, important non-amenity values, such as non-use values, and the impact of the sewage loads on wetland crops have not been valued and need further research.

[12] The agriculture benefits arise from the improved yields that would result when nutrient applications are reduced as a result of demonstrating to farmers that environmentally friendly practices are actually commercially beneficial as well. Typically, such an assumption turns out to be optimistic about the rate of adoption of the new methods. The other problems with

Another case where non-amenity benefits were examined with some care was the Ganges Clean Up Plan. In this study, it was concluded that (a) fisheries benefits could not be quantified; (b) direct health benefits were small; and, (c) if biodiversity benefits existed, they could not be valued in money terms. More details of this study are given in the next section.

In the case of Lake Mariut, which is immediately south of the coastal city of Alexandria, the authorities decided to divert the city's sewage from the sea to the lake, to reduce pollution on Alexandria's beaches. As a result, the value of its fisheries declined from $8 million in 1950 to 0.5 million in 1985. With the growth in industry, the level of sewage increased to such an extent that the water from the lake, which flows into the sea, is now so polluted that the original objective of the diversion has been lost (World Bank, 2003h).

There are many other studies where non-amenity benefits of better quality water have been cited to a lesser or greater degree but not fully quantified in physical terms and hardly at all in money terms. Examples include the following river, lake and coastal zone projects supported by the GEF:

(a) in Africa: Algeria (El Kala National Park and wetlands), Guinea and Guinea-Bissau (coastal zone management), Kenya (Tana River and Lake Victoria), Malawi (Lake Malawi), Mozambique and Namibia (coastal bio-diversity), Niger (Niger River), Senegal (Senegal River Basin), South Africa (Cape Peninsula), and the Nile River;

(b) in South America: Chile;

(c) in Asia: China (Hai River), Philippines (River Basin Management, Mekong River; and

(d) in Europe: Croatia (Karst ecosystems), Georgia (Kolkheti wetlands), Russia (Lake Baikal), Ukraine (Azov-Black Sea), Lake Orhid, and River Danube.

Non-use Benefits of Cleaner Water

In the case of exceptional water bodies, there could be non-use benefits that justify clean-up. Some of these have been quantified, and a good example is the Ganges study, which is cited below. Other cases where non-use values have been estimated and related to water quality, however, are hard to find. In fact the only studies we could find that came under this category were for the U.S. (see Bergstrom et al., 2001). Hence it is difficult to make a case for clean-up on these grounds[13] in developing countries.

estimating non-amenity benefits arise from predicting the impacts of marginal changes in nutrients when the limited evidence available refers to the impacts of the total loadings that currently exist.

[13] Indirectly, one could argue, however, that support for GEF projects that involve reduced pollution loads in ecologically important water bodies is a reflection of the international non-use WTP. But if the purpose of this kind of assessment is to inform that decision, the argument becomes circular and cannot be used.

Case Studies of Surface Water Quality Improvements

THE CLEAN UP OF THE GANGES IN INDIA

The Ganges is one of the most important river systems in the world, 2,510 kilometers (km) long and with a basin covering 861,404 square km. Currently, half a billion people, almost one-tenth of the world's population, live within the river basin at an average density of over 500 per square km. The local population is projected to increase to over one billion people by the year 2030. There are about 52 cities, 48 towns, and thousands of villages in its basin. Nearly all the sewage from these populations goes directly into the river, totaling over 1.3 billion liters per day, along with a further 260 million liters of industrial waste, run-off from the 6 million tons of fertilizers and 9,000 tons of pesticides used in agriculture within the basin, large quantities of solid waste and, thousands of animal carcasses and several hundred human corpses released into the river every day for spiritual rebirth. The inevitable result of this onslaught onto the river's capacity to receive and assimilate waste has been an erosion of river water quality, to the extent that, by the 1970s, large stretches (over 600 km) of the river were effectively dead from an ecological point of view.

The 'Ganga Action Plan (GAP),' an important environmental project to clean the Ganges, originated from the personal intervention and interest of the late Indira Gandhi. The GAP was launched in February 1985 and was largely completed in 1998. The final cost of the GAP is estimated at Rs11.2 billion ($318 million) in 1995 prices. The operating costs of the program run at around Rs356 million ($10 million).

The GAP has been, perhaps, the largest single attempt to clean up a polluted river anywhere in the world. Although a number of other international scale river basin clean-up programs have been effectively implemented in other countries, none has the full spectrum of geographical, ecological, and socio-cultural complexities that faced the Indian Government during the GAP's implementation. The sums of money referred to above are large by any standards, and were committed with the main objective of raising the river water quality to bathing standard. As a result of GAP, the quality of water in the Ganges has shown varying improvements in absolute terms since 1985. The dissolved oxygen levels have been improving in some areas but in others, particularly the lower stretches, they have continued to decline. Similar improvements in phosphate and nitrate concentrations have been observed since the early 1990s. However, a proper comparison of the water quality 'with' and 'without' the project requires the use of a sophisticated water quality model to account for what quality would have been in later years without the project. The results of such a model in the case of the Ganges show that some improvements in water quality (measured in terms of dissolved oxygen and biochemical oxygen demand (BOD)) were observed everywhere, albeit quite small ones in some places. It is also worth noting that a total stretch of about 437 km still violates the permissible level of 3.0 mg/l of BOD. In terms of dissolved oxygen, the level throughout the river is now more than 5.0 mg/l. Without the GAP, more than 740 km would have violated the BOD limit, with about 1000 km having BOD levels in excess of 10 mg/l. So, in summary, some improvements in water quality have been achieved. The important question is, what are these worth in monetary terms, taking account of the broadest set of values placed on cleaner water?

There are multiple benefits from cleaning the Ganges. There are user benefits accruing to people who stay near the river or visit the river for pilgrimages or tourism. These will be in the form of recreation and health benefits from direct and indirect exposure, and are called user benefits. They will also include benefits to fishermen, farmers and those for whom employment is created as a result of the project. Fishermen get benefits of improved fish production. Farmers get some type of irrigation and fertilizer benefits by using treated water and sludge from the sewage treatment plants of GAP.

The other category of benefits is non-user benefits, accruing to the people who are not staying near the river but gain welfare from knowing that the river is clean. Especially important in this regard is the religious significance of the river to Hindus but also relevant are the biodiversity benefits—the Ganges supports 25,000 or more of species of biodiversity ranging from microorganisms to mammals. There are a number of international species comprising of mammals, reptiles and birds supported by the Ganges ecosystem.

Also, the investment projects for cleaning the Ganges provide employment to unemployed or underemployed unskilled labor in India, and contribute benefits in the form of cost savings to water supply undertakings along the river. Hence, the beneficiaries from cleaning the Ganges can be classified as users, non-users, health beneficiaries, farmers, unskilled labor, and fishermen. Finally, there are the biodiversity benefits not captured in the program.

In a post-project evaluation, an estimation was made of several categories of benefit and these were compared to the costs (for details see Markandya and Murty, 2001) as presented in Table 10.10.

The table shows that overall, the project is viable at a 10 percent discount rate (the official rate used by the Government of India) and yields a rate of return of around 14 percent. It is important to note, however, that the bulk of the benefits come from the non-users (67.2%), principally those who have a religious value for the river, and from the employment creation as a result of the project (18.8%). Without these, the project would never have been viable and indeed the direct benefits are quite small.[14] The study was also instructive in showing that positive net benefits would not guarantee successful implementation of the project. That would require the operational and maintenance costs to be

[14] There is an issue about whether or not the benefits of lower treatment costs should be included in the above. The authors of the study took the view that they should not, because one has already accounted for the improvements in health and other benefits and to include the savings in treatment costs would be double counting.

Table 10.10 Benefits and costs of Ganga Action Plan ($Mn.)

Category	Benefits/Costs		Description
	$Mn.	As %	
Users	0.8	0.3	CV survey of residents within 0.5 km of bank and visitors
Non-users	195.2	67.2	CV survey of literate urban residents in 4 Indian cities
Farmers	16.3	5.6	Estimated benefits of fertilizer value of sludge
Health	23.5	8.1	Epidemiological study of villages near river before and after the program, compared to control group far from the river
Unskilled labor	54.5	18.8	Benefits of job creation reflected in a shadow price of labor of 0.5
Fishermen	N.A	N.A.	It was not possible to estimate these benefits, despite considerable efforts to collect the data.
Biodiversity	N.A.	N.A.	The program did improve natural habitats but a value for these improvements could not be elicited.
Total Benefits	**290.4**	**100.0**	
Industry Costs	42.7	24.8	Industry is required to take an number of measures to treat effluent before release
Public Sector Costs	129.8	72.5	
Total Costs	**172.5**	**100.0**	
Net Benefits	**117.8**		

Note: All costs and benefits are in present value terms, discounted at 10 percent. Note: still marginally have MB>MC even if cut non-use benefit estimate by 50%.
Source: Markandya and Murty (2001).

sustainably financed from one or more sources: the polluters, via a wastewater charge; the beneficiaries, via a charge on non-users and users; or a subsidy from the central government. Unfortunately, this issue has not been resolved and the ongoing operations from the project are in some difficulty as a result.

THE NURA RIVER CLEAN UP

The Nura River in the Republic of Kazakhstan has been the recipient of a significant amount of mercury (about 3,000 tons) from a synthetic rubber factory nearby, which is no longer operating. This has consequences not only for the quality of the water per se, but also on the well-being of the direct water users (World Bank, 2003). Over the operating lifetime of the factory, mercury was discharged from industrial processes and has accumulated at the plant site and in the topsoil of the flood plain, riverbed, and banks. The Nura River project has the following components: (a) clean-up of the Nura River Basin; (b) rehabilitation of the Intumak Dam and Reservoir; (c) capacity building of Basin authorities; and (d) project management and monitoring. The targets of these four components are to reduce the large concentrations of mercury that poses health risks to the local population both through direct exposure and contamination of the Basin's water supply, and to improve flow control within the Basin.[15] These targets translate to security of water supply in terms of it being safe for direct consumption

[15] E.g. for flood management and protection of downstream wetlands.

Table 10.11 Benefits and costs from the Nura River Project

	Cost (US$ Mn.)	Description
Project Cost	54.1	Components: Nura Valley Mercury Clean Up; Intumak reservoir rehabilitation; Nura-Sarysu River Basin Authority Strengthening; Project Management and Monitoring
Beneficiaries	**Benefits (US$)**	
Water suppliers	76.9	Savings in costs of water from a more expensive source
Local water users	2.8	Reduction in health risks from direct consumption of water; Regular source of water
Recreational visitors	1.2	Fishermen, hunters, and tourists, who exploit the recreational services of the Nura River banks and the buffer zone of the Kurgalszhino Wetlands Protected Area, based on interviews of the use of the facilities.
Other community members	0.5	Those who value biodiversity protection by improving the water quality based on a CV study.
Net Benefits	**80.9**	

Notes: All figures are discounted at 12%.
Source: World Bank (2003i). Project Appraisal Document for the Nura River Clean Up Project and background studies.

and accessibility (guaranteed delivery supply at a regular basis). The project is specifically noted in Kazakhstan's Country Assistance Strategy, and meets the Millennium Development Goal on providing access to clean water.

Multiple parties are expected to benefit from the project, such as: the *water suppliers* (in the cities of Astana, Temirtau, and Karaganda), through incurred savings from drawing water from the Nura River instead of the Irtysh-Karaganda Canal, as well as an improvement in the regularity of supply as a result of the project; *local water users*, through reduced health risks and more regular water supply; *recreational visitors* (hunters, fishers, and tourists), through more and cleaner water in the Nura River and Kurgalzhino Wetlands Protected Area; and *other community members*, through improvement in biodiversity levels (i.e. non-use values). Table 10.11 shows the total project costs and the estimated benefits. The positive value of net benefits infers that the project is viable at a 12 percent discount rate. Most importantly, however, the majority of the benefits (95%) are from the savings to water suppliers. Although health issues feature largely in the public discussion about the plant, the direct health benefits of the clean up of the mercury do not appear to be very large. This may partly be the result of problems in identifying the impacts of mercury pollution on the population, and partly the consequence of the fact that people, knowing of the dangers of such pollution, have taken effective avertive action (savings on avertive action are of course a benefit).

THE DAVAO RIVER AND TIMES BEACH IN THE PHILIPPINES

Choe et al. (1996) conducted a study in Davao City, Philippines where they attempted to estimate the economic value that people place to improve the water quality of the rivers and sea near their community. Although the majority of the households have their own water-sealed toilets that drain into large septic tanks, effluent from the tanks reaches the surface waters of the province. The most popular beach in the area is Times Beach, whose quality has deteriorated due to nearby discharge of the Davao River, such as silt, household waste and industrial waste. Due to high levels of pathogens and fecal coliforms found in the water, the city's Health Department issued warnings about the health risks of swimming at the beach. Furthermore, the deterioration of the beach discouraged other recreational activities, such as picnics.

For the study, surveys were conducted through the Contingent Valuation Method (CVM) and the Travel Cost Method (TCM), which intend to capture the respondents' stated preferences and revealed preferences, respectively. The hypothetical scenario is as follows:

There is a city-wide plan to clean up the river and sea (by waste treatment), and make Times Beach safe again for swimming and other recreation activities. The implementation of the Plan would require a monthly fee at a continuing basis to maintain the cleanliness of the surface water body. Assume that other households and industries will do their fair share and other actions would be taken to ensure the accomplishment of the Plan.

The estimated cost of this Clean-Up Plan ranges from $5 to $15 per household per month, but this cost was not revealed to the respondents during the survey.

From CVM, the estimated average willingness-to-pay values of the users of Times Beach for water quality improvement ranges from $1.2 to $2.04 per month. There were also people who were interviewed but were non-users of the beach. The mean WTP of these people for an improvement of the water body's quality ranges from $0.04 to $1.4 per month. These values capture the non-use values for cleaning up the beach, such as significance regarded on enhanced aquatic life and aesthetics. On the other hand, the estimated monthly WTP from TCM ranges from $1.44 to $2.04 per user. Notice that the estimates from both valuation approaches are close to each other. Considering that the average household monthly income is about $204, the WTP estimates are low both in absolute terms and as a percentage of household income. Moreover, since the population of users and non-users is the same as that of the polluters (totaling about 100,000 households), the results do not justify the project at the present time.

Aside from looking at the values people place on improving surface water quality, the study also examined the relationship between income and demand for water quality. Externalities due to lack of wastewater treatment fall largely on the residents of Davao themselves, but their WTP values are low. A closer investigation showed that although people are aware of the poor water quality status, they do not place a high priority on it since there are more urgent environmental issues in the area such as deforestation and, poor collection and disposal of solid waste. The policy message of the study is to wait until incomes and WTP are higher before engaging on large investments (e.g. waste treatment infrastructures).

THE GAUJA RIVER IN LATVIA

Ready et al. (2002) conducted a similar study in Sigulda, Latvia. Latvia attempts to implement Program 800+, which is a package of infrastructure investments in over 800 small- and medium-sized towns. Part of the Program is a project on the modernization of sewerage facilities. The present water and sewerage service charge is $3.6 per month. The annualized cost of the upgrading the sewage treatment plants, under Program 800+, is $1.8 per person per month.

The study employed the CVM approach to elicit the values people place on the improvement of surface water quality. The hypothetical scenario in Sigulda is where the investments on upgrading the sewage facilities would yield an improvement in the water quality of the Gauja River (e.g. reduction in nutrient loads) so that it would be suitable for fishing and swimming, but not for drinking. The payment vehicle used is an increase in the monthly fees for water and sewerage service. Results of the study showed that for an average person, the WTP is about $0.54 per month. However, this is far below the local financing monthly requirement for Program 800+ (i.e. $1.8 per person) and is only 0.7 percent of the average household monthly income.[16]

A similar message was given of delaying the investment which emerges from this study as from the Philippines study. Latvia has to meet the environmental requirements for admission to the EU over a period of time, depending on the particular directives. For the directives related to inland water quality, the time period is 10–15 years after accession—that is, to 2014–19. The authors state that the economic growth of the country will reach its full potential when it integrates with Western Europe. From the study, the calculated income elasticity of demand for water quality was 0.56 for an average person. Further examination of the relationship through econometric analysis showed that the income elasticity will increase as incomes increase, reaching 0.9 at an income level that is twice the current average of $77 per month. Thus, depending on the underlying growth rate in the economy, the programs will be justified at some date in the future. If we take the above elasticities (0.56, rising to 0.9), and assume a 5 percent per capita income growth rate and no changes in populations of users or polluters, the project will only be viable in 2032. With a growth rate of 7 percent, however, it will be viable in 2023 and with a rate of 10 percent it will be viable in 2016.

Conclusions

This chapter has looked at two issues arising from poor water quality: the impact it has on households through their use of such water for drinking and other domestic purposes, and through the facilities they employ for the disposal of

---

[16] As in the Philippines study, the polluters and the users are the same population. Hence a simple comparison of the per household costs and benefits gives the answer to the question of project viability.

household waste; and the consequence of poor water quality in inland rivers and lakes on other water uses (recreation, abstraction for domestic use, etc.).

Regarding the first issue, we have focused on the targets under the Millennium Development Goals, and looked in some detail at developing countries with high mortality rates. According to the WHO, the lack of access to safe water and sanitation is responsible for more than half the DALYs lost due to all environmental factors. The other important one is indoor smoke from solid fuels. Data from 1980 onwards does show access to improved water and sanitation has been increasing worldwide—even in those regions such as Africa, where real per capita income has fallen over this period. There is, thus, not a strong link between increased access and increased living standards over the recent past, although it is undoubtedly true that the countries with higher living standards do have higher levels of access.

In order to see whether the targets under the MDGs are justified in economic terms, it is necessary to compare the costs of meeting those targets with the benefits. For the latter, a value has to be placed on the DALY. We take a range from per capita GDP to 2.5 times per capita GDP, basing this on some of the recent literature that has valued lost life years. On this basis, the costs of achieving the targets by 2015 exceed the benefits for some of the regions (Africa and Asia). For the high mortality countries of America, the costs are less than the lower bound of the benefits; and for similar countries in the Eastern Mediterranean, the costs lie between the lower and the upper bounds.

The above calculations are reported for both the safe water and the sanitation goals. If we separate the costs of each goals and make an estimate of the benefits, we find that the water supply targets are justified for all regions, but the sanitation targets are only unambiguously justified for the Americas. This is the result of two factors: the costs of sanitation connections are about three times those of water supply and the benefits per connection are somewhat lower.

A comparison of costs and benefits is, of course, only one part of designing and providing systems of water supply and sanitation. Equally important is to ensure financial sustainability and here ensuring sustained cost recovery remains one of the most serious problems that need to be addressed. Typical levels of cost recovery are low and utilities find it difficult to operate in an effective manner. A number of recent studies have shown that the WTP for an improved water supply is considerably higher than current tariffs both for current consumers as well as for those who are not connected. Thus the case for an improved service can be made on the grounds of WTP, but care is needed to design the system to recognize the WTP limitations. Furthermore, some subsidy will generally be needed, if the MDG goal is to be met—the poorest parts of the population, who will largely be the focus of the program, often will not be able to afford the services.

Where subsidies have to be provided, recent work has come up with some useful findings. The use of an increasing block tariff is difficult to achieve and not that effective. There are problems in doing the metering and there are not big differences in consumption between the rich and the poor households. It also appears that a connection subsidy is more effective than a consumption subsidy.

Another issue that has to be guarded against is designing systems that are too large. When tariffs increase as a result of such a change, consumption can fall quite sharply and if this not accounted for, the system will be more costly than necessary and have greater difficulty achieving cost recovery.

The overall implications of the analysis therefore are that the water supply targets need careful cost benefit appraisal before they are implemented. In addition, they need a careful analysis of financial sustainability and in this regard affordability is a critical element. The same remarks apply to sanitation programs, but here the cost and benefit comparison is less clearly in favor of the program as a whole. Even if we remain committed to the MDG targets as a whole, the phasing of the investment can still benefit from a careful comparison of costs and benefits. Furthermore complementary activities such as education about hygienic practices have to play an important part.

The second set of concerns relate to the quality of water in rivers, lakes, and other water sources. We looked at an indicator of water quality (BOD), and how it relates to development—à la Kuznets curve. The time series analysis of selected countries for which data are available do not generally support the usual inverted 'U' shape, with quality decreasing in the early stages of development and improving after a certain point. The panel data for 15 high mortality countries in fact come up with a statistically significant 'U'—quality improves up to an income level of $480 and then deteriorate up to an income of $4000 or thereabouts. Beyond that, it may improve again, but this would not represent the usual Kuznets relation.

To ensure that water is clean enough for recreational uses would require significant investments in the treatment of household and industrial effluent and, possibly, some controls on non-point pollution from agriculture. The simple arithmetic of sewage treatment shows that the justification of high level wastewater treatment depends on the: (a) per person WTP for the improvement; (b) number of beneficiaries of the improvement; (c) cost per household of the investment in treatment; and (d) number of households whose waste has to be treated. With plausible values of (b) to (d), we find that the WTP per person has to be quite high compared to the kind of estimates that have been made of this figure in developing countries. Treatment projects are not ruled out in all cases, but their success depends on having a large number of beneficiaries relative to polluters whose waste has to be treated. We also note that most of the data available on benefits of clean water relate to amenity benefits—recreational use and the like. There may also be special cases where non-amenity benefits justify clean-up, but the information on that is very limited—there are hardly any non-use benefit studies and studies of agricultural and fisheries benefits are few and far between.

Hence the viability of cleaning up water bodies in developing countries cannot be analyzed statistically, as the projects are highly individual and depend a lot on local conditions. Instead, we have looked in detail at four case studies from: India, Kazakhstan, Philippines, and Latvia. These studies lead to the following conclusions:

1. In general, water treatment in pursuit of recreational benefits is not justified in developing countries. The benefits rarely exceed the costs and often fall far short of them.
2. An exception is when the water body has special religious or cultural significance, as in the case of the Ganges. Here, an extremely ambitious project was found to be justified largely on the grounds of non-users benefits. Individuals not visiting the river and living quite far away expressed a significant WTP for the clean-up on the grounds that the river held important religious values.
3. Another exception is when the water body is a source of water supply and there are gains to be made from using it as opposed to a more expensive source. This was the case for the Nura River project in Kazakhstan.
4. Finally, clean-up may be justified when biodiversity of international significance is threatened. It is not always possible to value the protection of such natural assets in money terms, but this does not mean that a special case cannot be made for them.

References

Alberini, A., A. Krupnick, M. Cropper, and N. Simon (2001), 'The Willingness To Pay for Mortality Risk Reductions: A Comparison of the United States and Canada', *Fondazione Eni Enrico Mattei*, 92–136.

Anand, S. and K. Johnson (1995), 'Disability Adjusted Life Year: A Critical Review.' Harvard Center or Population and Development Studies Working Paper Series. Harvard, Boston.

Arin, T. (2001), 'Strategic Partnership For Nutrient Reduction in The Danube River Basin and Black Sea: Benefit–Cost Analysis'. *Mimeo*. World Bank, ECSSD.

Bergstrom, J. C., K. J. Boyle, and G. L. Poe (2001), *The Economic Value of Water Quality*. Cheltenham, Edward Elgar.

Boadu, F. (1992), 'Contingent valuation for household water in rural Ghana,' *Journal of Agricultural Economics*, 43: 58–65.

Brocklehurst, C. (2003), 'The Impact of Water Prices on Households and the Importance of Consumer Consultation.' A Presentation to the Conference: The True Cost of Water: Toward Sustainability and Economic Efficiency. World Bank and Agencia Catalana del Agua, Barcelona. On website, http://www.worldbank.org/watsan/Barcelonameeting.htm

Carson, R. T. and R. C. Mitchell (1993), 'The value of clean water—the public's willingness-to-pay for boatable, fishable, and swimmable quality water,' *Water Resources Research*, 29: 2445–54.

Choe, K., D. Whittington, and D. Lauria (1996), 'The Economic Benefits of Surface Water Quality Improvements in Developing Countries: A Case Study of Davao, Philippines,' *Land Economics*, 72(4): 519–37.

Cropper, M., N. Simon, A. Alberini, S. Arora, and P. K. Sharma (1997), 'The Health Benefit of Air Pollution Control in Delhi.' *American Journal of Agricultural Economics*, 79: 1625–9.

Emerton, L., L. Iyango, P. Luwum, and A. Malinga (1999), 'The Present Economic Value of Nakivubo Urban Wetland, Uganda.' IUCN, Geneva.

Hanemann, W. M. (1991), 'Willingness to Pay and Willingness to Accept: How Much Can They Differ?' *American Economic Review*, 81(3): 635–47.

Homedes, N. (1996), 'The Disability-Adjusted Life Year (DALY): Definition, Measurement and Potential Use.' Human Capital Development Working Paper No. 68. World Bank, Washington, DC.

Knowler, D., I. Strand, and E. Barbier (1997), 'An Economic Analysis of Commercial Fisheries and Environmental Management in the Black Sea Region.' Prepared for The Black Sea Environment Programme, Istanbul, Turkey.

Krupnick, A., K. Harrison, E. Nickell, and M. Toman (1996), 'The Value of Health Benefits from Ambient Air Quality Improvements in Central and Eastern Europe: An Exercise in Benefits Transfer,' *Environmental and Resource Economics*, 7: 307–32.

Larsen, B. (2003), 'Hygiene and Health in Developing Countries: Defining Priorities, A Cost–Benefit Assessment.' A Paper presented at the 2nd IFH Conference: Home Hygiene and Prevention of Infectious Disease in Developing Countries—A Responsibility for All, New Delhi, India.

McPhail, A. (1994), 'Why Don't Households Connect to the Piped Water System? Observations from Tunis, Tunisia,' *Land Economics*, 70(2): 189–96.

Markandya, A. (2004a), 'Cost Recovery in Water and Sanitation.' A Presentation to the Lille 4 Conference: Implementation of the Water Framework Directive. Lille, France. http://www.waternunc.com/fr/artoisp8.htm

—— (2004b), 'Gains of Regional Cooperation: Environmental Problems and Solutions,' in R. Auty (ed.), *Energy Resources, Governance and Welfare in the Caspian Sea Basin.* University of Seattle Press, Seattle, Washington.

—— and N. Murty (2001), 'Cost Benefit Analysis of Cleaning Ganges: Some Emerging Environment and Development Issues.' Working Paper Series No. E/218/2001: 1–24, Institute of Economic Growth, India (forthcoming in *Environment and Development*).

——, A. Hunt, A. Alberini, and R. A. Ortiz (2003), 'The Willingness to Pay For Mortality Risk Reductions: A Survey of UK Residents,' in EC NewExt Research Project: WP2, Mortality Risk Valuation, Final Report. European Commission, Brussels.

Mourato, S., M. Csutora, E. Kovacs, S. Kerekes, and Z. Szerenyo (1999), 'Estimating the Value of Water Quality Improvements in Lake Balaton: A Contingent Valuation Study (in Hungarian),' *Gazdaság Vállalkozás Vezetés*, 99(1): 147–71.

Olsen, D. and J. Richards (1994), 'Inter-basin Comparison Study: Columbia River Salmon Production Compared to Other West Coast Production Areas, Phase II Analysis.' A Report to the Army Corps of Engineers, Portland, Oregon.

Prüss-Üstün, A., C. Mathers, C. Corvalán, and A. Woodward (2003), 'Introduction and Methods: Assessing the Environmental Burden of Disease at National and Local Levels,' Environmental Burden of Disease Series No. 1, World Health Organization, Geneva. Also available at http://www.who.int/peh/burden/9241546204/9241546204toc.htm

Ready, R., J. Malzubris, and S. Senkane (2002), 'The Relationship between Environmental Values and Income in a Transition Economy: Surface Water Quality in Latvia,' *Environment and Development Economics*, 7: 147–56.

Saghir, J. (2003), 'The Global Dimensions of the Water Challenge.' A Presentation to a Conference: The True Cost of Water: Toward Sustainability and Economic Efficiency. World Bank and Agencia Catalana del Agua, Barcelona. On website http://www.worldbank.org/watsan/Barcelonameeting.html

Sanders, L., R. Walsh, and J. McKean (1991), 'Comparable Estimates of the Recreational Value of Rivers.' *Water Resources Research*, 27(7): 1387–94.

Shi, A. (2000), 'How Access to Urban Potable Water and Sewerage Connections Affects Child Mortality.' World Bank Policy Research Working Paper No. 2274. World Bank, Washington, DC.

Stottmann, W. (1999), 'The Effects of Metering on Water Consumption and Financial Performance of Water Utilities in the ECA Region.' ECSIN Working Paper No. 7. World Bank, Washington, DC.

Tapvong, C., and J. Kruavan (1999), 'Water Quality Improvements: A Contingent Valuation Study of the Chao Phraya River.' Research Report. Environment and Economy Program for Southeast Asia (EEPSEA), Singapore.

Whittington, D., J. Briscoe, X. Wu, and W. Barron (1990), 'Estimating the Willingness to Pay for Water Services in Developing Countries: A Case Study of the Use of Contingent Valuation Surveys in Southern Haiti,' *Economic Development and Cultural Change*, 38(2): 293–311.

——, S. K. Pattanayak, J. C. Yang, and K. C. Bal Kumar (2002), 'Household demand for improved piped water services: evidence from Kathmandu, Nepal,' *Water Policy*, 4: 531–56.

Willis, K. and G. Garrod (1995), 'The Benefits of Alleviating Low Flows in Rivers,' *Water Resources Development*, 11(3): 243–60.

Winpenny, J. (2003), 'Financing Water for All.' Report of the World Panel on Financing Water Infrastructure. World Water Council.

World Bank (2001), Environmental and Water Resources Management: Strategy Series, No. 2. Environment Department, Washington, DC.

—— (2002), Water Resources Strategy. Washington, DC.

—— (2003a), World Development Indicators. Washington, DC.

—— (2003b), The Environment Millennium Development Goal in the Europe and Central Asia (ECA) Region, Concept Paper. The World Bank, Washington, DC.

—— (2003c), Cost Assessment of Environmental Degradation: Morocco. The World Bank, Washington, DC.

—— (2003d), Progress Report and Critical Next Steps in Scaling Up: Education for All, Health, HIV/AIDS, Water and Sanitation. The World Bank, Washington, DC.

—— (2003e), Water Supply and Sanitation and the Millennium Development Goals (Draft Background Paper). The World Bank, Washington, DC.

—— (2003f), Statistical Information Management Analysis (SIMA) Database. The World Bank, Washington, DC.

—— (2003g), Environmental Sequencing Strategies for EU Accession: Priority Public Investments for Wastewater Treatment and Landfill Site in Bulgaria.

—— (2003h), *Water Resources and Environment: Technical Note G.2: Lake Management*. The World Bank, Washington, DC.

—— (2003i), Project Appraisal Document for the Nura River Cleanup Project. The World Bank, Washington, DC.

—— (2003j), Annual Report. Also available at http://www.worldbank.org/annualreport/2003/challenge.html

World Health Organization (2002). World Health Report. Also available at http://www.who.int/whr/en/

Yaping, D. (1999), 'The use of benefit transfer for the evaluation of water quality improvement: An application in China.' Research Report. Environment and Economy Program for Southeast Asia (EEPSEA), Singapore.

—— (2003), 'The value of improved water quality for recreation in East Lake, Wuhan, China: an application of contingent valuation and travel cost methods.' Research Report. Environment and Economy Program for Southeast Asia (EEPSEA), Singapore.

Annex 1 WHO member states grouped by mortality strata, high mortality, and low mortality (both child and adult), 1999

High Mortality Countries		Low Mortality Countries	
Africa	Eastern Mediterranean	The Americas	South East Asia
Algeria	Afghanistan*	Antigua and Barbuda	Indonesia
Angola	Djibouti	Argentina	Sri Lanka
Benin	Egypt	Bahamas	Thailand
Burkina Faso	Iraq*	Barbados	
Cameroon	Morocco	Belize	Western Pacific
Cape Verde	Pakistan	Brazil	Cambodia
Chad	Somalia*	Chile	China
Comoros	Sudan	Colombia	Cook Islands
Equatorial Guinea	Yemen	Costa Rica	Fiji
Gabon		Dominica	Kiribati
Gambia	South East Asia	Dominican Republic	Lao People's Democratic
Ghana	Bangladesh	El Salvador	Republic
Guinea	Bhutan	Grenada	Malaysia
Guinea-Bissau	India	Guyana	Marshall Islands
Liberia	Korea, Dem. Rep.*	Honduras	Micronesia (Federated States of
Madagascar	Maldives	Jamaica	
Mali	Myanmar*	Mexico	Mongolia
Mauritania	Nepal	Panama	Nauru
Mauritius	Timor-Leste*	Paraguay	Niue
Niger		Saint Kitts and Nevis	Palau
Nigeria		Saint Lucia	Papua New Guinea
Sao Tome and		Saint Vincent and the	Philippines
Principe		Grenadines	Republic of Korea
Senegal		Suriname	Samoa
Seychelles		Trinidad and Tobago	Solomon Islands
Sierra Leone		Uruguay	Tonga
Togo		Venezuela	Tuvalu
The Americas		Eastern Mediterranean	Viet Nam
Bolivia		Bahrain	
Ecuador		Cyprus	

341

Annex 1 (Continued)

High Mortality Countries	Low Mortality Countries
Guatemala	Iran (Islamic
Haiti	Republic of)
Nicaragua	Jordan
Peru	Kuwait
	Lebanon
	Libyan Arab Jamahiriya
	Oman
	Qatar
	Saudi Arabia
	Syrian Arab Republic
	United Arab Emirates

Source: World Health Organization:
http://www3.who.int/whosis/member_states/member_states_stratum.cfm?path=evidence,cea,cea_regions,
member_states_stratum
http://www.who.int/whr/2003/en/member_states_182-184_en.pdf

The 192 Member States of the World Health Organization have been divided into five mortality strata on the basis of their levels of mortality in children under 5 years old (5q0) and in males 15–59 years old (45q15). This classification was carried out using: UN population estimates, and estimates of 5q0 and 45q15 based on WHO analyses of mortality rates for 1999. In this study, High Mortality refers to Stratum E (high adult mortality and high child mortality). Please see the provided Internet links for more details about the WHO's mortality strata.

Annex 2

Estimating the cost of DALYS on the poor

Let
r_p = risks of disease to the poor
r_r = risks of disease to the rich
T = total number of DALYs
T_I = total number of DALYs if risks for rich and poor were equal
P = population that is poor
R = population that is rich
$\alpha = T_I/T$ (the reduction in risk factor if the poor had the same risk as the rich)
V_p = Unit value of DALY to a poor person
VD_p = Total value of DALYs to the poor
Y_p = Average income of the poor
β = share of income of the poor that the DALY loss represents.

The relationship between the risks and the number of DALYs is given by

$$rp + rrR = T$$

Suppose that the poor had the same risk as the rich, then, $rp = rr = \bar{r}$. The number of cases would be αT, where

$$\bar{r}(P + R) = \alpha T$$

or

$$\bar{r} = \alpha T\,(P + R)$$

and

$$r_p P = T - \bar{r}R$$

The left hand side of the last equation is simply the number of DALYs borne by the poor. The value of these DALYs is VD_p where

$$VD_p = r_p P.V_p$$

And the share of their income the loss represents is β

$$\beta = \frac{r_p V_p}{Y_p}$$

For the estimates made in the paper, the following values have been taken

- $T = 34.4$ million

- $P = 15\%$ to 85% of total

- $R = 85\%$ to 15% of total

- Total Population is taken as 1.8 billion

- $\alpha = 0.49$ (WHO estimate)

- $V_p = \$548$ lower bound to $\$1369$ upper bound
  Based on average daily income of $\$1.5$ per day and a value equal to annual income or 2.5 times annual income.

- $Y_p = \$548$
  Based on an average income of $\$1.5$ per day for a group whose income is less that $\$2$ per day.

Annex 3

Estimating the change in DALYs as a result of meeting the MDGs

Since the DALYs in the WHO tables are for both water supply and sanitation, and since the MDG targets involve different additions in the numbers provided with these services, it is necessary to estimate the change in DALYs due to each factor. To do this, the following assumptions have been made:

1. The DALYs lost due to poor water supply are between 1.5 and 3 times those from sanitation. This is based on estimates made by Shi (2000) and Larsen (2003). We take the average of these two, which gives a factor of 2.25.

2. Worldwide, the DALYs lost due to both factors are 0.0542 billion in 2000.

3. The number of people in year 2000 without adequate water supply and sanitation are 1.16 billion and 2.7 billion respectively (World Bank, 2003a).

4. As a result of the MDG target being met, the number of people who will get improved water are 131 percent of the present number without water. Likewise the number of people who will get improved sanitation are 80 percent of the present number without these facilities. Although the target requires a *halving* of the percentage without these services, the greater increases reflect the increase in population between 2000 and 2015.

The calculation is made as follows:

1. Let α be the number of DALYs lost per person per year from a lack of sanitation.

2. Then the total number of DALYs lost are calculated as follows:

$$0.0542 = (2.25). \alpha. (1.16) + \alpha. (2.70) \tag{1}$$
which gives a value of $\alpha = 0.01017$.

From equation (1) it also follows that the share of all DALYs due to lack of improved water supply are about 52 percent of the total, while those due to a lack of sanitation are about 48 percent.

Let

X_1 be the number of DALYs lost due to improved water supply in 2000
X_2 be the number of DALYs lost due to improved sanitation in 2000
X_T be the total number of DALYs lost due to both factors in 2000.
X_S be the total number of DALYs saved due to the MDG program by 2015

Then
$$(1.31) \bullet X_1 + (0.8) \bullet X_2 = X_S$$

Or

$$(1.31) \bullet (0.52)X_T + (0.8) \bullet (0.48) X_T = X_S; \text{ or } (1.06537)X_T = X_S$$

The factor of 1.06637 has been used calculating the total benefits based on the present DALYs. Of this, the share of water supply is 64 percent and that of sanitation is 36 percent.

11

Urban Air Pollution, Health, and Policy Instruments

Alan J. Krupnick

Introduction

Many developing countries have experienced increased urban population and economic growth over the last few decades. This trend brings about increased pressure on public health through air pollution that results from the growth in mobile and stationary sources. At the same time, economic growth may improve the health care system and may result in greater expenditure on cleaner technologies and better pollution abatement equipment, which reduces emissions per unit output. Further, as a country's economy matures, it relies less on manufacturing and more on service sectors, which are less polluting.[1]

The purpose of this chapter is to examine the record of urban population growth, health, and health care spending in developing countries, describe the linkage between urban air pollution and health,[2] and weigh policy responses to reduce stationary and mobile source air pollution, illustrating options through case studies.

---

[1] These factors can be summed up in the environmental Kuznets curve (Andreoni and Levinson, 2001; Millimet, List and Stengos, 2003), which portrays total emissions rising with economic output to a point, where it tops out and then begins to fall as the economy matures further.

[2] The focus on outdoor air pollution should not be interpreted as a judgment that indoor air pollution is less of a problem or a more expensive problem to address. As will be seen in pp. 351 and 352, indoor air pollution is probably a greater problem (and certainly a greater problem for the poor) and there are many low cost ways of reducing it, including through education, increasing ventilation in the home, and stove adaptations.

The Situation in Urban Areas of Developing Countries

Urban Population Growth

Global urban populations have been growing steadily, irrespective of income group, since 1960. The pace has been particularly rapid, however, in the developing countries (low income and lower middle income countries, see Figure 11.1).[3] Underlying this trend are both increases in the general population and increases in the urban share of the national population. The urban population share appears to have leveled out in the high income countries at

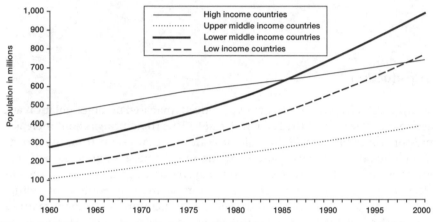

Figure 11.1 Urban population by income 1960–2001

Source: World Bank 2003a.

[3] From World Bank (2003): *Low-income countries*: Afghanistan, Guinea, Nigeria, Angola, Guinea-Bissau, Pakistan, Azerbaijan, Haiti, Papua New Guinea, Bangladesh, India, Rwanda, Benin, Indonesia, Saõ Tomé and Principe, Bhutan, Kenya, Senegal, Burkina Faso, Korea, Dem. Rep., Sierra Leone, Burundi, Kyrgyz Republic, Solomon Islands, Cambodia, Lao PDR, Somalia, Cameroon, Lesotho, Sudan, Central African Republic, Liberia, Tajikistan, Chad, Madagascar, Tanzania, Comoros, Malawi, Timor-Leste, Congo, Dem. Rep, Mali, Togo, Congo, Rep., Mauritania, Uganda, Côte d'Ivoire, Moldova, Uzbekistan, Equatorial Guinea, Mongolia, Vietnam, Eritrea, Mozambique, Yemen, Rep., Ethiopia, Myanmar, Zambia, Gambia, Nepal, Zimbabwe, Georgia, Nicaragua, Ghana, Niger. *Lower-middle income countries*: Albania, Guatemala, Romania, Algeria, Guyana, Russian Federation, Armenia, Honduras, Samoa, Belarus, Iran, Islamic Rep., Serbia and Montenegro, Bolivia, Iraq, South Africa, Bosnia and Herzegovina, Jamaica, Sri Lanka, Brazil, Jordan, St. Vincent and the Grenadines, Bulgaria, Kazakhstan, Suriname, Cape Verde, Kiribati, Swaziland, China, Macedonia, FYR, Syrian Arab Republic, Colombia, Maldives, Thailand, Cuba, Marshall Islands, Tonga, Djibouti, Micronesia, Fed. Sts., Tunisia, Dominican Republic, Morocco, Turkey, Ecuador, Namibia, Turkmenistan, Egypt, Arab Rep., Paraguay, Ukraine, El Salvador, Peru, Vanuatu, Fiji, Philippines, West Bank and Gaza.

about 78 percent. The urban share for the upper middle income group, while starting from a much lower base in 1960, increased at a much faster rate to also reach 78 percent by 2001 (Figure 11.2). Urban shares for developing country groups are much lower than those for higher income countries, and their trends are quite different from each other. Urban population shares increased from 25 percent to 45 percent over 1960–2001 in the lower middle income group but only from 18 percent to 31 percent in the low income group.

Health Care Spending

Data on health care spending for the income groups discussed above are only available from 1990 to 2000 (Figure 11.3). These data give some indication that rising incomes are leading to a rising share of health care expenditures, but the trend is weak. With GDP rising throughout the decade in the low income countries, health care expenditures rose only slightly faster, with the share rising from about 3.5 percent of GDP in 1990 to 4.2 percent in 2000 (a period when expenditures in India were basically flat). In the lower middle income group, however, bolstered by China, expenditure shares rose from 3.5 percent to 5.5 percent. It might be argued that health care expenditures are driven more by increasing population than economic growth in these countries.

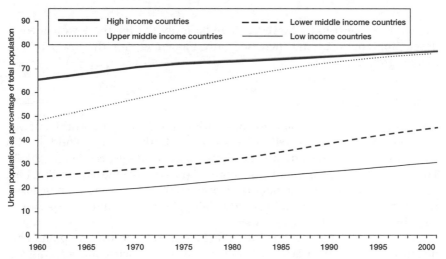

Figure 11.2 Urban population share by income 1960–2001
Source: World Bank 2003.

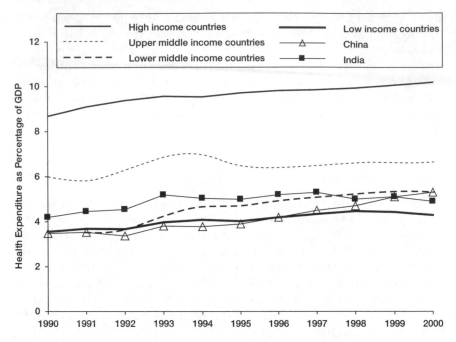

Figure 11.3 Health expenditure as percent of GDP by income 1990–2000
Source: World Bank 2003a.

Expenditures per capita, however, were basically flat for the lowest income developing countries and increased only moderately for the lower middle income group.

Health Indicators

The most comprehensive analysis of health in the developing world, but one unfortunately not restricted to urban areas, is the recent World Health Organization (WHO) study on the Global Burden of Disease (WHO, 2003). This report describes mortality and 'burden' (life-years, adjusted for disability, or DALYs) for regions throughout the world in 2000 and attributes these losses to specific risk factors, including outdoor air pollution and indoor exposure to air pollution from burning solid fuels.

The diseases related to air pollution include chronic obstructive pulmonary disease (COPD), asthma, acute respiratory disease, and ischaemic heart disease, with links to cancer, fetal abnormalities, low birth weight, and other less documented effects. In the high-mortality developing countries, DALYs from

Table 11.1 Top ten leading disease by percentage of regional disease burden

High-mortality developing regions		Lower-mortality developing regions	
HIV/AIDS	9.0%	Unipolar depressive disorders	5.9%
Lower respiratory infections	8.2%	Stroke	4.7%
Diarrhoeal diseases	6.3%	Lower respiratory infections	4.1%
Low birthweight	5.0%	Road traffic accidents	4.1%
Malaria	4.9%	Chronic obstructive pulmonary disease	3.8%
Unipolar depressive disorders	3.1%	Ischaemic heart disease	3.2%
Measles	3.0%	Birth asphyxia and birth trauma	2.6%
Ischaemic heart disease	3.0%	Tuberculosis	2.4%
Tuberculosis	2.9%	Alcohol use disorders	2.3%
Birth asphyxia and birth trauma	2.7%	Hearing loss	2.2%

Source: adapted from Ezzati et al., 2003.

respiratory infections are rated the second highest cause of burden (at 8.2%) behind HIV/AIDS, with ischaemic heart disease ranked 8th (3%) (Table 11.1). The other diseases mentioned above fall far below 1 percent. In the lower-mortality developing countries, respiratory infections slide to third place (4.1%) with COPD (3.8%) and ischaemic heart disease (3.2%) making it into the top ten leading diseases (Ezzati et al., 2003).

The Role of Air Pollution

How does urban air pollution fit into this story? On one hand, the health effects associated with air pollution are arguably the best documented of any environmental problems. For instance, a number of unusually comprehensive and careful epidemiological studies have constructed a link between fine particulate pollution and shortened life expectancy—studies that form the backbone of the U.S. EPA's recently implemented fine particulate matter ambient air quality standard. The concentration-response coefficients from these studies (such as Pope et al., 1995) indicate that mortality rates fall by about 3 percent for every 10 $\mu g/m^3$ annual average reduction of this pollutant. For example, for an urban center with a death rate of 1,200 per hundred thousand people and a population of 10 million, this reasonable reduction could result in the reduction of 3,600 deaths per year. Since these health effects appear to be concentrated in the very young, the old, and the sick, they translate into very high benefits to these groups. Add to these the benefits from reduced hospital and emergency room visits, doctor visits, asthma and other respiratory sickness days, missed work and school, and other effects that must be far more numerous to lead to such a large death rate reduction, and the scope of these health improvements may be significant to the general population.

On the other hand, it would not be surprising to see a relatively small role for air pollution in any story about urban health in low income groups. For one thing, other risk factors, such as HIV/AIDS and smoking, may have a more significant effect. And, in countries with low life expectancy, people may die of other causes before their air pollution exposure catches up to them.

Even here, however, the interaction between various health effects points to a larger role for air pollution. For instance, if one is already sick due to a pollution-induced respiratory disease, the probability of getting sick in other ways may rise. Ozone exposure, for example, has been linked to impaired immune response. Additionally, the relationships can go the other way. If one is already sick from some disease, such as TB, one may be more likely to be affected by air pollution, by, for instance, developing or exacerbating an asthma condition. Further, living in a poor country without good health care means that pre-existing conditions are likely to be more prevalent relative to a developed country.

Based on standard, mostly Western, epidemiological relationships, the WHO data presented in Ezzati et al. (2002) show a very small role for outdoor air pollution in the burden of disease in developing countries. They instead target the role of indoor air pollution from burning solid fuels for cooking and, in some areas, heating. Indoor air pollution is a problem for very poor people in rural areas and possibly a problem for developing countries in cold climates (e.g. China). Then again, outdoor air pollution may be tied more closely to economic growth, concentrated in the cities, and relevant primarily for countries with a high reliance on coal (e.g. China). Specifically, in Africa, deaths from outdoor air pollution are estimated to be only 0.5 percent of total mortality, whereas deaths from indoor smoke make up 4 percent. In the poorest of the poor African countries (with the highest adult death rates), this disparity is even greater. In contrast, in the Western Pacific region which includes China (and has low mortality rates), men are more likely to die from outdoor air pollution than indoor, while women are more likely to die from indoor smoke exposure. In total for that region, deaths from outdoor air comprise 3 percent of total mortality with indoor air at 4.8 percent.

Although urban air pollution plays a relatively small role in affecting health, it is does not follow that countries should not take action to control air pollution. One important criterion for priority setting may be the size of the risk. But another surely is efficiency, that is, the net social benefits from reducing the risks, which depends on marginal costs and marginal benefits from reducing pollution. Air pollution reductions may be far easier and less expensive to achieve than some higher ranking causes of disease burden, such as HIV/AIDS, smoking cessation, and mental illness. More will be said on this topic later in the chapter.

What are the Most Serious Air Pollution Problems?

The contribution of various types of sources to creating emissions, the process transforming those emissions to air pollutants, and the effects of pollutants on health are reasonably well understood in developed countries, but little evidence exists specifically for developing countries.[4] Since the effects of air pollution are probably less potent in developed countries due to better health care, we can assume that the scientific understanding from developed (and some developing) countries holds in general for the rest of the world, but is a conservative estimate for developing countries.[5]

POLLUTANT CATEGORIZATION

The pollutants of potential concern can be classified into conventional pollutants (sulfur dioxide (SO_2), particulates (total–TSP, particulates with a diameter 10 microns or less–PM_{10}, and fine particulates–$PM_{2.5}$), ozone (O_3), nitrogen dioxide (NO_2), and carbon monoxide (CO)), air toxics (including lead, benzene, a number of the diesel particulates), and global pollutants (carbon dioxide, chlorofluorocarbons, and others). Because global pollutants do not harm health directly, they are not addressed in this chapter.

The remaining pollutants mentioned above have all been implicated in health effects of one type or another and to one degree or another. Currently, attention is focused on particulates, particularly $PM_{2.5}$ and several of its constituents, including sulfates (SO_4), nitrates (NO_3) and carbon compounds. Sulfates have been significantly linked to mortality and morbidity risks, as have $PM_{2.5}$, PM_{10} and TSP. Sulfur dioxide has also been linked to health effects, but because the sulfate particles are formed from reactions involving SO_2 gas, it may be impossible to identify separate effects of SO_2 as a gas versus the sulfate particles that result from it. There is very little evidence of links to health effects involving other particulate constituents.

Ozone, which is formed from volatile organic compounds (VOCs) and NO_2 in the presence of sunlight and heat, has been found to affect morbidity endpoints, such as acute respiratory disease symptom days and hospitalizations, but the evidence of a mortality effect is neither strong nor frequent (Figure 11.4). NO_2 is primarily of concern because of its conversion to the particulate NO_3, which counts as a fine particulate and, if one is concerned

---

[4] Eastern European countries have been included in the Air Pollution on Health: A European Approach (APHEA) project and Health Effects Institute's major concentration-response function studies are beginning in Asia (Health Effects Institute, 2003).

[5] This assumption needs one significant qualification. If elderly people are particularly at risk from air pollution and few people live to be elderly in these developing countries, then the public health impact may be relatively low even though the slope of the C-R function may be steeper for developing countries.

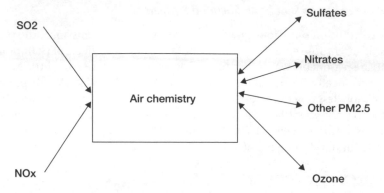

Figure 11.4 Emissions to ambient concentrations

about ozone, through its conversion to ozone. CO is primarily of concern in enclosed spaces, such as parking garages and, of course, indoors. The air toxics are of concern because of their links to cancer, low birth weight and other diseases. With the possible exception of diesel particulate emissions and lead, toxic pollutants are far less ubiquitous and less concentrated in the environment than the conventional pollutants. Lead, even in low doses, has been shown to cause learning disabilities in children and high blood pressure in adults. The U.S. EPA's action level for lead has become increasingly more restrictive as additional epidemiological findings are made.

POLLUTANTS SOURCES OF CONCERN

There are three major categories of sources of air pollution in urban areas: point sources (industrial emissions, power plants), mobile sources (autos, buses, mopeds, motorcycles), and residential and area sources (home heating and cooking, emissions from small businesses, such as dry cleaners and paint finishers).

In developing countries, particularly China and India, coal burning for electricity generation is a major source of particulates and SO_2. Industrial emissions of SO_2 and particulates also come from smelters, coke ovens, and other steel-making operations. Additionally, residential and area sources can, in the aggregate, contribute to a large share of these pollutants.

Mobile sources contribute a growing share of the most troublesome pollutants. Buses and trucks in developing countries have very high per-kilometer emissions of all types of pollutants and, if run on diesel or leaded gasoline, are of particular concern. Low but rapidly growing auto ownership will likely raise VOC and NO_2 emissions from gasoline, raising concerns about ozone and, if the fuel is still leaded, lead.

EVIDENCE ON CONCENTRATIONS

There is surprisingly limited evidence on concentrations of air pollutants in urban areas of developing countries. WHO is the only multi-country source of time-series information, and its data collection efforts are spotty and reporting is late. The current system, Air Management Information System (AMIS; WHO, 2001), replaces the previous system, Global Environment Management System (GEMS; WHO, 1987). Both involve setting up monitors in industrial, commercial and residential areas in each city to measure concentrations of a variety of pollutants. The pollutants measured vary by city, but most measure TSP (and increasingly finer particulates (PM_{10})) and SO_2; some measure NO_2, lead, and ozone. High income countries, as expected, tend to have the most comprehensive reporting of pollutants. There has been some backsliding in terms of the database's coverage. For example, GEMS contained very good data on China in the 1980s, but the AMIS data end for Chinese cities in 1994. In addition, GEMS comprehensively reported the number of days with violations of air quality standards, while AMIS does not.

Thus, to get as complete a picture as possible of the progress (or lack thereof) by urban areas in developing countries in reducing air pollution, we supplemented the AMIS data with country-specific sources where available. Then, we computed annual average values for the periods of 1986–92 and 1993–2000 for each country and took the differences; reporting average differences by pollutant in Table 11.2. For ease of reporting, countries were classified into four categories (according to GDP per capita from the World Bank). Over the two time periods, the poorest countries gained very little ground or got worse. An example is PM_{10}, with annual average PM_{10} concentrations increasing by about 26 $\mu g/m^3$ in the low income countries, while all the other countries gained ground. This situation may not be as dire as it seems. With some economic growth and an increasing population in many of these countries, even holding the line on emissions is an achievement. Interestingly, the largest gains—20 $\mu g/m^3$ reduction in PM_{10}—were experienced by cities in the second poorest group of countries.

What are the Best Solutions?

It is one thing to illuminate the key urban air pollution problems but quite another to identify the best interventions for addressing them—a task beyond this paper. Still, a few comments are appropriate. First, defining what is best is not an easy task, with the efficiency and equity perspectives being the two most easily articulated. However, even if we confine ourselves to an efficiency perspective, what is best can be viewed from a net benefits or a cost-effectiveness perspective. The former involves choosing interventions with the largest net benefits; the latter, choosing an appropriate effectiveness metric and then

Table 11.2 Air pollution change by income

Pollutant by country income category*	Average for 1993–2000	Difference between averages for 1986–92 and 1993–2000**	# cities w/data in both periods
Sulfur Dioxide Annual Mean ($\mu g/m^3$)			
A (low income)	15	3	10
B (lower middle income)	61	16	26
C (upper middle income)	25	13	14
D (high income)	16	13	46
Nitrogen Dioxide Annual Mean ($\mu g/m^3$)			
A (low income)	26	0	10
B (lower middle income)	62	−15	12
C (upper middle income)	42	2	14
D (high income)	42	5	42
PM10 Annual Mean ($\mu g/m^3$)			
A (low income)	127	−26	10
B (lower middle income)	66	20	8
C (upper middle income)	61	4	1
D (high income)	34	13	14
Lead annual Ambient Mean ($\mu g/m^3$)			
A (low income)	0.14	0.05	10
B (lower middle income)	0.37	0.05	8
C (upper middle income)	0.29	0.20	11
D (high income)	0.10	0.13	30
Ozone Annual Mean ($\mu g/m^3$)			
A (low income)	79	–	0
B (lower middle income)	48	−11	3
C (upper middle income)	48	5	3
D (high income)	38	−3	35
SO_2 # days guideline exceeded			
A (low income)	2	1	7
B (lower middle income)	9	2	5
C (upper middle income)	4	16	3
D (high income)	2	7	32
NO_2 # days guideline exceeded			
A (low income)	2	0	8
B (lower middle income)	25	−15	4
C (upper middle income)	11	−17	2
D (high income)	4	3	29
Ozone # days guideline exceeded			
A (low income)	90	–	0
B (lower middle income)	9	−1	2
C (upper middle income)	28	−13	2
D (high income)	18	5	24

* Income categories are based on World Bank World Development Indicators http://www.worldbank.org/data/countryclass/classgroups.htm.

**Negative difference implies that air quality worsened over the time periods compared.

Source: WHO 2001, Air Management Information System.

rank-ordering interventions according to costs per unit of effectiveness. Second, in a limited sense, the choice of policy intervention can be a choice to avoid having to do such rankings. In particular, economic incentive policies can be designed to create incentives for the regulated parties to discover the cheapest ways of reducing emissions (if emissions is the effectiveness measure), or reducing whatever effectiveness measure is operative. For instance, a tradable permit policy with a cap on aggregate emissions will lead to the cheapest interventions per unit of emissions reduced being adopted. This approach is limited, though, because some interventions may need to occur in the public sector or in sectoral areas that do not lend themselves to the application of incentive policies.

For health, a promising effectiveness measure for use in cost-effectiveness analysis is the QALY or DALY, mentioned above. Indeed, the WHO has developed software called WHO-CHOICE, with the purpose of making a wide range of cost-effectiveness calculations and comparisons for each WHO region using the DALY metric (http://www3.who.int/whosis/menu.cfm?path=evidence,cea& language=English). Unfortunately, at the time this paper was written, WHO had not yet developed the tool for air pollution interventions. However, they have developed the tool for childhood illness interventions; among them, case management options for addressing childhood pneumonia, which could be related to air pollution. Table 11.3 provides an example of the model's output for countries in the South East Asia region with high adult and child mortality (Category D). This example shows that extending case management to higher numbers of children has only a modest effect on costs and that the cost-effectiveness is extremely promising. For comparison, Table 11.4 shows some of the interventions to reduce DALYs from poor water quality and highlights how relatively expensive these options are.

The World Bank has also periodically developed cost-effectiveness measures using DALYs. In The World Bank's *Environmental Health Report* (2003b), a variety of interventions to improve health are examined and cost per DALY is estimated. Most of these interventions are low cost, for instance, developing water connections in rural areas at $35 per DALY, instituting malaria controls at between $35 and $75 per DALY, and improving stoves and fuels ranging from

Table 11.3 Region: WHO South East Asia region (SEAR)—high adult and child mortality. *Category:* Childhood pneumonia

| Cluster | Intervention | Average Year Cost (in international [I$]) | | | Effectiveness (DALYs averted: average 1 year) | Average Cost-Effectiveness |
		Programme	Patient	Total		
UFV	Case Management of childhood pneumonia (CM), 50% coverage	38,135,366	176,465,572	214,600,938	2,646,618	81
UFV	CM, 80% coverage	63,218,585	282,387,697	345,606,282	4,234,588	82
UFV	CM, 95% coverage	98,629,429	335,428,693	434,058,123	5,028,574	86

Table 11.4 Region: WHO South East Asia Region (SEAR)–D. *Category*: Unsafe water supply, sanitation and lack of hygiene related risk

Cluster	Intervention	Average Year Cost (in international [I$])			Effectiveness	Cost Effectiveness	
		Programme	Patient	Total	(DALYs averted: average 1 year)	Average	Incremental
WS	Disinfection at point of use with education	523,019,455		523,019,455	3,248,440	161	161.01
WS	Halving the population without improved water supply	585,826,305		585,826,305	951,318	616	Dominated
WS	Halving the population without improved water supply and sanitation	5,907,522,335		5,907,522,335	4,908,162	1,204	Dominated
WS	Improved water supply and sanitation (98%)	11,578,743,777		11,578,743,777	9,627,739	1,203	Dominated
WS	Improved water supply and sanitation with disinfection (98%)	14,184,319,328		14,184,319,328	25,443,560	557	615.51
WS	Piped water supply and sewage with treatment (98%)	39,689,844,066		39,689,844,066	38,442,566	1,032	1962.11

$50 to $200/DALY. But, for reducing urban air pollution, all that is said of the cost-effectiveness of interventions is that they vary from the negative (electronic ignition systems in two-stroke vehicles) to US$70,000 per DALY or more for some pollution control measures.

Policy Response

The purpose of this section is to identify attractive (i.e. efficient and equitable) policies for mitigating the urban air pollution problems caused by point, mobile and residential/commercial sources (not indoor air). This is done by first considering the different types of policies available and then matching the requirements of the various policies to the unique economic, institutional and environmental features of developing countries (what we term 'stylized facts').

Policy Types

In the space of three decades, the popularity of economic incentive approaches to controlling air pollution has gone from virtually nil (i.e. policy dominated by 'command and control' approaches) to the point where, at least in developed countries, tradable permit policies are often the first approach considered by policymakers. In the early 1970s, the only example of economic incentive approaches in the U.S. was the unsuccessful attempt by the Nixon Administration to tax sulfur in fuels. Today, however, there are dozens of examples of serious attempts to implement tradable permit and emissions tax approaches in the U.S. and elsewhere, particularly for taxes in Sweden. While most successful implementations of these approaches have occurred in the developed world, increasingly developing countries are turning to them. In spite of the efficiencies such instruments promise, their successful implementation will be a challenge, due to the complexities of implementation and need for institutional capacity. In addition, these instruments may come with high expectations, being wrongly viewed by politicians as actually lowering pollution, as opposed to reducing the costs of any given pollution reduction.

The available options, as discussed in other chapters, include direct regulation—sometimes termed command and control (CAC), tradable permits, fees or taxes, subsidies and deposit refund systems, voluntary and informational approaches, or the creation of property rights and legal liability. In an air pollution context, command and control policies would include regulations requiring catalytic converters on vehicles and regulations requiring firms to meet certain emissions standards. Note that the latter approach affords more flexibility, giving firms the option of finding the cheapest way to meet the standards, while the former approach is a technology standard.[6] Regulations on vehicle fuel and on fuel economy are other examples of CAC policies associated with air pollution.

Tradable permit (TP) approaches differ from these CAC approaches because they provide more of an economic incentive for firms to find cost-effective methods to reduce pollution. Firms with lower pollution abatement costs find it in their interest to reduce pollution and sell their surplus permits to other firms. Technological change is boosted by TPs because the firm's incentive to innovate extends beyond any given emissions standard, and by reducing emissions firms can actually get paid for their actions by other firms.[7] Probably the

---

[6] Another argument sometimes made for CAC standards approaches is called the Porter Hypothesis, which asserts that a country's tight environmental standards may actually increase competitiveness in the world market. (See Ambec and Barla, 2002b; Smith and Walsh, 2000).

[7] CACs can also boost technology change, however, through their technology-forcing provisions. For instance, by requiring that all cars have catalytic converters, the market and competition to produce such devices cheaply grows.

best-known TP air pollution example in the world, and the first fully specified and well functioning policy, is the U.S. EPA's SO_2 Allowance Trading Program under Title IV of the Clean Air Act.[8]

Fees to raise the price of polluting can be placed on inputs to the polluting process, on outputs produced concurrently with the pollution, or on pollution emissions themselves. By raising the price of polluting (either directly or indirectly), the polluting activity becomes less attractive. Moreover, unlike TPs (if the TPs are distributed for free rather than auctioned), revenues are raised for use elsewhere. This approach can be efficient because firms have the incentive to minimize the cost of reducing their pollution, rather than being subject to arbitrary pollution limitations through standards. Of course, standards and fees can be combined, such as when payments have to be made for any emissions above the standard. The fee in this case functions much like a fine. Examples of fees associated with air pollution are gasoline taxes (a fee on an output with emissions as a joint product), a broader-based fee like an energy tax, fees on fuel sulfur content (as in Sweden), and fees on coal at the mine mouth (a fee on an input).

Subsidies are the opposite of taxes in that polluters are paid not to pollute or are encouraged to produce a less-polluting output by subsidizing the price of that output. Reducing a tax can be thought of as a form of subsidy. Given that there are substitutes for highly polluting activities, one can think of using taxes, subsidies or both to create price gaps between the more and less polluting products. Subsidies to transit (an output-based subsidy) reduce reliance on the more polluting passenger vehicle (per passenger mile). Subsidies to renewable energy discourage producing energy with the more polluting fossil fuels. Taxing unleaded or low sulfur fuel less than leaded or high sulfur fuel encourages purchase of the former. Reducing existing subsidies on highways and on oil production (e.g. the oil depletion allowance in the U.S.) raises the cost of driving

---

[8] Title IV of the (1990) Clean Air Act Amendments initiated an SO_2 emission allowance cap and trade program as a strategy to reduce regional SO_2 emissions from power plants by 50 percent. It is widely believed that Congress would not have imposed the same amount of reductions if not for the prospective cost savings from trading. The program combines an aggregate cap on annual allocation of emission allowances at all large fossil-fired electricity generation facilities with nearly unfettered opportunities to trade or bank allowances. The success of this program stems from the program's simplicity, effective monitoring through continuous emissions monitors, definite penalties and the opportunity for banking.

The cost of the program will be just over $1 billion per year by 2010, but it enabled the industry to fully capitalize on advantageous trends in coal transport and other technology changes, due to the flexibility inherent in allowance trading. Compared to an approach that mandated a specific emission rate at every facility, the allowance trading program is estimated to have reduced program costs by 30–50% (Carlson et al., 2000; Ellerman et al., 2000). However, compared to a prescriptive technology approach, such as a requirement of scrubbers at a certain class of facilities, the savings are perhaps 200% of actual costs.

and producing oil, relative to less polluting (but formerly higher cost) alternatives.[9]

Voluntary and informational approaches are particularly appealing for a developing country because they do not require as sophisticated a monitoring and enforcement infrastructure as other policies. These approaches may rely on public goodwill to push polluters to action. Requiring firms to submit estimates of their emissions for public disclosure can lead to firms abating their pollution to avoid being branded a bad polluter. These programs may be defined in voluntary terms from the beginning. Industry associations may collaborate, with or without government involvement, to change their polluting processes in order to 'spruce up' their image or perhaps to improve the health of their workers. A good example is the attempt by brick kiln manufacturers in Ciudad Juárez, Mexico to change their fuel source from scrap tires to the much cleaner propane (Blackman and Bannister, 1998).

Finally, the creation of legal liability and property rights where none existed can clarify responsibilities and result in pollution reductions.

Point Source Policies

Policies that are appropriate for developed countries may not be appropriate in developing ones. They may require an infrastructure or a legal system that a developing country does not have, or they may emphasize technologies that are too expensive for developing countries. Any discussion of treating developed and developing countries differently, however, runs into a 'political incorrectness' problem for suggesting that developing countries could be satisfied with lower technology and less environmental clean-up because they need to focus more on economic growth. Yet, there is no reason why all types of countries should use a certain set of policies any more than there is a reason to use the same type of policy to address every type of environmental problem. Adaptation and working within the limitations of each country is a must. In this spirit, there are several stylized facts that separate typical developed and developing countries and give rise to a means of notionally ranking some policy types above others.

---

[9] Deposit-refund approaches involve requiring payment up front with the payment refunded once the desired action is taken. This approach is especially applicable to cases where there is a time lag between the purchase of a product and pollution arising from it, such as the purchase of an air conditioner that will eventually leak freon into the atmosphere. Most conventional air pollutants are produced contemporaneously with consumption of the product, so this approach rarely applies.

Stylized Facts

Of the many general differences, six stylized facts are of particular importance to air pollution policy in developing countries (relative to developed countries):

   (i) concerns about minimizing costs overshadow concerns about reducing air pollution to a greater extent;

   (ii) capital is more scarce, relative labor;

   (iii) baseline emissions control is lower;

   (iv) market distortions are more pervasive;

   (v) the infrastructure for implementing an air pollution control system is minimal and transactions with that infrastructure marred by corruption; and

   (vi) revenue needs of governments are more pressing.

What do these differences imply about air pollution policy choice, in theory? Other things equal, the greater ability of incentive approaches to reduce abatement costs argues for their preference over CAC policies. Tietenberg (1985) and many others find such savings in policy simulations and cost–benefit analyses of real programs, with the amount depending on the sophistication of the CAC policy in the comparison. Beyond this distinction, a pricing policy would be favored over a quantity-constrained policy, based on Weitzman (1974), because the former constrains costs while the latter constrains damage.

Having scarce capital and cheap labor in developing countries implies that simple, labor-intensive approaches to reducing air pollution may be more attractive than in developed countries. Additionally, fairly modest incentives (such as a low emissions fee) could bring about emissions reductions at low cost. Other low-cost options could include keeping up with maintenance schedules, purchasing spare parts in advance, and improving worker training. CAC approaches are ill-suited to providing incentives for operations and maintenance improvements because companies have an enormous range of existing conditions and control options. That developing countries have low baseline emissions control reinforces the need for a choice of low-cost approaches; because of rising marginal costs of abatement, the scope for reducing emissions cheaply will be large initially.

Market distortions are more pervasive in developing countries. In particular, energy prices are often kept below market rates.[10] This subsidy exacerbates the lack of internalization of the air pollution externalities and encourages undue reliance on energy-intensive processes. The implication for policy is the need

[10] Generally, damages from pollution are not internalized into the costs of market goods. To internalize the costs from air pollution, a tax or other policy can be used to make these damages part of the input costs.

for the removal of such subsidies, but of course that action is rarely easy from a political standpoint.

The very existence of taxes creates a market distortion (called the dead-weight loss of taxation), which has implications for the use of emissions taxes and marketable permits. Recent research emphasizes that marketable permits should be, at least partly, auctioned off, with the revenues used to offset some of these pre-existing distortionary taxes (Parry 1995 and Parry et al., 1999),[11] and that emissions tax revenues should also be at least partly used in the same way. In practice, however, the ability of governments to initially distribute marketable permits for free is one of the main attractions of this approach. And revenues from environmental taxes are most likely to be used (in developing countries) to support cash-strapped environmental protection agencies rather than to offset distortions.

Weak institutions probably result in the most important differences for policy prescriptions between developed and developing countries. Irrespective of the policy type, strong institutions are needed to carry out basic governmental functions—fighting for scarce resources, writing regulations, establishing an emissions baseline, tracking changes in emissions over time, enforcing the regulations, and monitoring air quality to determine if regulations are effective and at the correct level of stringency. Where strong institutions are lacking, a government can invest resources towards bolstering them before committing to, or implementing, a policy, or can work with the institutional resources available to craft policies that require less-strong institutions. The latter approach could be preferable since establishing strong institutions takes significant time and many environmental problems cannot afford to be ignored in the meantime (Sterner, 2003).

One example of such a policy is voluntary, informational policies, such as PROPER, Indonesia's Public Disclosure Pollution Control Program. Another is setting emissions baselines at default values (say, from U.S. AP-42 documents) to be changed only with a showing by the regulated entity that these defaults are in error. However, this shortcut may blur the distinction between incentive and CAC policies. An alternative option is to focus the policy on the point in the production chain that is overseen by the strongest institutions. In developing countries, the Ministry of the Interior or Commerce is often one of the stronger ministries, with taxing and enforcement powers over the companies it regulates. Thus, using 'blunt instruments,' such as taxes on energy inputs, may be a viable alternative, while sacrificing some efficiency for the gain in enforcement. For instance, a tax on the sulfur content of coal can reduce SO_2 emissions and is easy to document and enforce. Such an approach, however, provides incentive only to

---

[11] A complementary argument is that auctioning emission permits may help correct distortions away from economic efficiency stemming from non-competitive market structure, especially in the electricity sector (Burtraw and Palmer, 2004).

reduce sulfur content, not directly to reduce SO_2 emissions, which might more cheaply be reduced at the point of release.

Weak institutions argue against complex, but conceptually efficient, approaches to reducing air pollution, such as tradable permits. Simpler variants, such as intra-firm bubbles,[12] have some of the advantages of a TP system, although they limit abatement effort allocation changes to within the firm. Simply letting prices rise or adding taxes to highly polluting joint products or inputs seems like the simplest solution if taxing authority and enforcement systems are already in place. Simple, transparent rules may also have the virtue of limiting unpleasant surprises when there is so much uncertainty in how a policy will be implemented and responded to. On the other hand, incentive approaches are favored because weak governments cannot hope to collect and process the information needed to set efficient CAC regulations. Decentralized incentive-based policies that do not require such information have the advantage. In the end, efficiency is but one criterion in deciding the best possible policy for each situation—equity, politics, enforceability, and the need to encourage cooperation and involvement are also important factors (Sterner, 2003).

Recent Examples

TRADABLE PERMITS FOR POINT SOURCE SO_2 EMISSIONS IN TAIYUAN, CHINA

As part of a loan for air quality improvement in Shanxi Province, the Asian Development Bank, in cooperation with the Shanxi Planning Commission, initiated a Technical Assistance (TA) grant in March 2001 to enhance the use of market-based instruments (MBIs) for air quality management in Shanxi.[13] The Provincial capital city of Taiyuan was selected as the site for a demonstration of the use of MBIs for SO_2 control—specifically a cap and trade program involving large stationary point sources.

Taiyuan, with a population of 2.7 million, is located 500 kilometers southwest of Beijing. Topographically, mountains surround Taiyuan on three sides, resulting in a natural smog trap in which air pollutants tend to accumulate. The annual average of daily SO_2 concentrations in Taiyuan was 200 μg/m^3 in 2000, much higher than the People's Republic of China (PRC)'s Class II annual

---

[12] An approach that permits a plant or multi-plant firm to meet its stack-by-stack emissions reduction responsibilities in total rather than at each specific stack.

[13] Resources for the Future led this TA, in cooperation with Resource Consulting Associates, Inc, the Norwegian Institute for Air Research, and the Chinese Research Academy for Environmental Science. Information in this example is based on the project's final report to the Asian Development Bank. In addition, the U.S. Environmental Protection Agency (EPA) provided extensive assistance in the areas of training and capacity building.

362

standard (600 $\mu g/m^3$) and far higher than the U.S. SO_2 standard of 80 $\mu g/m^3$. The Taiyuan city government had proposed more than a 50 percent reduction in SO_2 emissions as part of its five-year environmental plan ending in 2005. MBIs, such as emissions trading, have the potential to facilitate achievement of this very ambitious goal at lower cost than alternative approaches.

Among developing countries, the PRC has been a pioneer in the use of certain economic instruments, most notably the pollution levy system. Although the pollution levy system serves as an integral component of environmental management in the PRC, its principal aim is to fund the regional and local Environmental Protection Bureaus (EPBs) and help finance pollution control measures. In the early 1990s, the PRC began to require emission offsets[14] at selected new facilities. These pilot projects revealed that emission trading was feasible, at least in this primitive form.

The adage that 'Rome wasn't built in a day' aptly describes the challenges involved in introducing a rigorous environmental management system such as emissions trading in Taiyuan. Establishing a program of emissions trading is somewhat like building a complex mosaic: a large number of intricate elements must be fit together. These range from technical components, like air quality monitoring, to policy-relevant and sometimes politically sensitive issues such as developing a viable system design and establishing an appropriate legal framework. The exercise is not merely a matter of mechanically assembling pieces into a working whole. There are a variety of stakeholders and constituents who must understand how such a program might work, who must agree it is in their interests to be part of the effort, and who must be trained to do their share in making it a reality. Thus, an important part of the demonstration in Shanxi Province included capacity building for and with the people, the institutions and the myriad potential participants in the trading program, to develop fluency with, and support for, the principles involved.

In response to the Taiyuan EPB's limited capacity, the TA implemented major improvement to the Taiyuan EPB's emissions monitoring and enforcement system, the heart of any emissions control function. Thus began a multi-year process of establishing facility-specific emission caps for large emission sources for the years 2002–2005, as well as development and demonstration of various computer-based tools designed to facilitate emissions monitoring and verification (the Emissions Tracking System(ETS)).

The ETS collects data on fuel inventories and fuel consumption as a basis for calculating total emissions during the compliance period. In addition to calculating emissions from mass balance formulas, the ETS collects data from the monitoring bureau to facilitate comparison of each enterprise's emission measurements. Data about production levels are also collected to establish

---

[14] This is an approach requiring new polluting sources in a region to obtain emissions reductions from existing sources in the region before they (the new sources) can begin operating.

emission rates (e.g. emissions/unit of output) that the EPB can use to identify possible discrepancies in an enterprise's submission.

A number of additional steps were necessary to move the Taiyuan EPB towards trading:

- education of the government and industry leadership about the benefits of adopting emissions trading in Shanxi province and the city of Taiyuan (including an initial simulation of emissions trading among selected facilities—two large power plants, a small power plant and a heavy machinery manufacturer) as well as on the theory, practice, and management of emissions trading systems;

- promulgation by the city of Taiyuan in October 2002 of a formal regulation on emissions trading and the administrative framework to support the regulation; and

- the building of a computerized Allowance Tracking System (ATS).

The ATS application facilitates allowance accounting, including the creation of allowance accounts, issuance/allocation of allowances to the enterprises, transfer of allowances among enterprise accounts, and allowance deductions to offset emissions during the compliance year. In addition, the data and reports from the ATS can be used to publicize the results of the trading program.

The real challenge is to apply these techniques in a nation where legal and institutional arrangements for environmental management are still in their formative stages. Although the PRC is a rapidly evolving market economy, there is little experience with rigorous environmental monitoring and enforcement or with the trading of intangible commodities like pollution credits. Steady, reliable, fair enforcement and a well-constructed program to detect and act on violations are the basic building blocks of any environmental management system, whether that system uses conventional tools or MBIs. At the same time, analysts from developed countries and western cultures should be alert to the many 'non-policy' avenues (e.g. moral suasion, pressure on Party leaders at the firm, etc.) that a government has to influence firm behavior.

Whether, or when, a TP system 'in the Chinese style' becomes fully operational remains to be seen. Continued support by both domestic and international experts to facilitate the initial operation and help ease the 'growing pains' of the system is recommended, as is a further evaluation of the system when it reaches full-scale operation.

There are many steps still to be taken before Taiyuan has a well-functioning monitoring and enforcement system and before Taiyuan will be able to appropriately use emissions trading. These steps may be divided into technical adjustments, institutional strengthening, and improved coordination and information flow. For illustration, we include three examples of possible steps below.

Increase Compliance Incentives by Lifting the Cap on Total Penalties Article 23 of the *Administrative Regulation on SO₂ Emission Trading in Taiyuan City* sets a yearly cap of 30,000 Yuan on the total penalties that can be assessed against polluters. The obvious difficulty with this provision is that in instances in which the cost of compliance (either installing technology, making process changes or purchasing allowances) is greater than the maximum stipulated by the penalty cap, the incentives for enterprises to come into compliance are dramatically reduced, as the cap limits their overall penalty payments.

Allow Banking of Surplus Permits Without TEPB Approval The emission trading regulation specifies that enterprises must apply to the TEPB for approval before using banked allowances to cover emissions during the compliance period. However, because an enterprise will not know the outcome of its application until after the compliance year is over, there is no opportunity to further reduce emissions or purchase allowances from other enterprises if the request is denied. Therefore, this provision effectively prevents banking of excess allowances. Limiting the use of the banking provision in this manner will raise the costs of meeting the caps without any significant environmental benefits. Concern that the banking provision may allow emissions to increase beyond acceptable levels does not seem warranted.

Establish Realistic but Firm Emissions Reduction Targets for Sources in Taiyuan More than two years of the five-year plan in which SO₂ emissions were to be reduced by more than 50 percent have passed. To date, there has been only limited progress in reducing total emissions. This slow progress should be evaluated and a realistic timetable developed. Without certainty about the outcomes of regulatory, environmental progress will be hampered.

EMISSIONS FEES FOR STATIONARY SOURCE EMISSIONS CONTROL IN METRO MANILA

The Asian Development Bank has supported various initiatives to address the serious air quality problems in Metro Manila, culminating in a multi-component loan and a technical assistance grant (TA) that together make up the Metro Manila Air Quality Improvement Sector Development Program. The Program commenced in 1999 and was originally planned to run for 4 years (1999 to 2002). Previous studies under the TA have recently assessed a broad range of market-based instruments (MBIs) for air pollution control in the Philippines (e.g. Ruzicka et al., 2002). However, it was thought that a research effort was needed to define very specific policies to be applied in Manila. Accordingly, researchers at RFF[15] developed a design methodology for implementing an emissions fee program for stationary sources and a sulfur tax for diesel fuel.

---

[15] This example is based on Fischer et al., 2002.

The intent of the program is to offer efficient financial incentives to reduce particulate emissions and precursors, as well as to raise revenues for important air pollution monitoring and enforcement activities. We recommended beginning immediately with a straightforward fee program, initially targeting the most important emitters, recognizing that the fee level may not reflect full marginal costs. To the extent possible, we felt that distributional concerns should be addressed by means such as standard credits or investment credits, which allow marginal fees to provide stronger incentive effects. These recommendations have not yet been implemented.

Particulate matter (PM) is the main pollution problem in Manila, and monitored readings show some of the highest PM concentrations in the world. Ambient ozone is a lesser problem, with few violations of guidelines/standards. Reducing NO_x and SO_2 emissions is also potentially important since they are precursors to $PM_{2.5}$.

An emissions fee policy is recommended because of its efficiency and its ability to generate revenues to fund pollution control activities. Revenue needs include, but are not limited to, administrative costs of stationary source permitting, monitoring and enforcement. Emission fees are intended to be a major revenue source for the Air Quality Management Fund (AQMF), which has a broad mandate for restoration, research, outreach, and technical assistance, as well as for regulatory activities. Therefore, in designing the fee, we focus first on the direct effects—the marginal incentives and the administrative burdens—and then on the revenue and cost impacts. In principle, efficiency reasons should determine the tax rate, and equity and revenue concerns should determine the exemptions.

We felt that such a proposal was realistic because of Manila's experience with the Laguna Lake Development Authority (LLDA). The LLDA successfully implemented an Environmental User Fee System to reduce the biochemical oxygen demand (BOD) of industrial effluents flowing into Laguna de Bay, the second largest freshwater lake in South East Asia. The total annual fee paid by a facility equals a fixed charge (based on a range of the daily wastewater flow rate) plus, for each pollutant, a variable fee multiplied by the annual load. Emissions are determined using limited sampling and presumptive factors, leaving the firms with the burden of proving actual loads are lower with continuous monitoring.

The program was phased in, initially limited to the top dischargers in the major BOD-contributing industries. It has been credited with helping to reduce the annual BOD inflows to the Lake by almost 75 percent from 1993 to 2000, although the extent to which the reduction can be attributed to the fee has not been formally evaluated.

Legal Basis The Philippines Clean Air Act (CAA) of 1999 (Republic Act No. 8749), explicitly provides for economic incentives as a part of environmental policy.

The Declaration of Principles recognizes that 'polluters must pay,'[16] and the Declaration of Policies encourages the use of market-based instruments.[17] Specifically, an emission fee system is mandated for industrial dischargers as part of the regular permitting system,[18] although the Implementing Rules and Regulations remain broad enough on this point to leave room for interpretation. Fees collected are to be deposited in a special account (the AQMF) established by the National Treasury and administered by the Department of Environment and Natural Resources (DENR). The CAA further identifies the Environmental Management Bureau as the administrator of the AQMF, with funds to be used for environmental restoration and environmental management by DENR, other agencies, and management of local airsheds.

With the legal authority already in place per the CAA, the practical barriers to implementing the emission fee system will be administrative in nature. Capacity must be built so that DENR can perform certain key functions: compiling the specific data needed to calculate the fee; validating the data provided by the firm; billing, collecting, and enforcing penalties for failure to pay the fee; and providing dispute resolution for conflicts emanating from fee computation methods and data inputs. Furthermore, internal accounting procedures will need to be established to earmark revenues for environmental management, program administration, restoration, and rehabilitation.

The other challenges are informational and political. Considerable uncertainty remains over the precise extent and distribution of stationary source and other emissions in Metro Manila. Additionally, although we determined that emissions controls were relatively inexpensive for many of the point sources of particulates and SO_2 in Manila, we could not determine the level of compliance with existing regulations. Perhaps the first challenge to putting the program in place is building support among stakeholders. The fee level, participation rules, and exemptions each have important impacts on the competing interests of government for revenues, of firms for their costs, and of the public interest for the efficiency and efficacy of the program.

Emissions Fee Calculation In the basic design, total emission fees assessed for any plant would equal

$$\text{Total Fee Payment} = \tau_P \text{PM}_{10} + \tau_S \text{SO}_2 + \tau_N \text{NO}_x + X,$$

where the τ's represent the fee rates for each pollutant, and X represents an optional fixed component, which may be positive (a fixed fee, like the current charge for permit processing) or negative (a standard credit or exemption). The fixed component, if needed, represents an adjustment mechanism to achieve the

---

[16] Ch. 1, Art. 1, Sect. 2.   [17] Ch. 1, Art. 1, Sect. 3c.   [18] Ch. 1, Art. 1, Sect. 13.

targeted revenue goals.[19] The fee rates will depend on the relative contribution of the different emissions to PM_{10} concentrations, as well as the corresponding costs in terms of abatement opportunities or health damages.

Both marginal damages and marginal costs seem to lie in the same range of $2,000 or more per ton. Given the uncertainty surrounding these numbers in the Philippines case, we hesitate to recommend a marginal fee that fully reflects these cost estimates. Furthermore, we realize that a fee of this size is not likely to be tenable, given concerns for economic development and the need for stakeholder acceptance of the program. While efficiency should be a goal, it is more important to begin implementing the program. Once started, one will be able to observe how firms actually react to the fee and how the environment is affected by the corresponding changes in emissions. After learning from the responses over time and gathering better monitoring, health, and cost data, the fee can be adjusted in the future to better reflect the policy targets.

Monitoring When properly maintained, continuous emissions monitoring systems (CEMS) are the most accurate means of calculating emissions; however, they are also the most costly. The Clean Air Act requires the installation and operation of CEMS for new and modified sources that have the potential to emit more than 100 tons per year of any pollutant. Currently, only the major power plants (Pabilao, Mauban, and First Gas) are equipped with CEMS. Discussions with the Pollution Control Officer of Pagbilao and Mauban Quezon Power Plants estimates the capital and annual operating costs of CEMS at P2.5 million and P1.0 million, respectively. These CEMS are capable of monitoring SO_x, NO_x, and PM emissions. For medium and small sources, it may not be practical to install CEMS. Thus, most emissions will have to be estimated using emission factor methodology.[20] For those firms not installing CEMS, we recommend that a special emissions tracking system (ETS) be developed and implemented in the Metro Manila airshed, as was done in Taiyuan.

---

[19] The fixed fee can be made to vary according to firm characteristics as well, without compromising the incentive effect of the marginal rate. Differentiation of the fee can make allowances for different abilities to pay of smaller versus larger stationary sources. Another option is to make the fixed fee conditional on certain behavior, e.g. offering rebates for installing pollution control equipment or continuous monitoring systems. This structure would help firms defray fixed capital costs and would be an alternative to funding such projects through the AQMF.

A standard exemption helps mitigate the cost impact while retaining the strong marginal incentive to reduce emissions, particularly if emissions reduced below the exemption are credited. Given the large variation among the sources, we recommend allocating a firm-specific (or possibly industry-specific) exemption based on a share of its historical emissions. If historical emissions data is unavailable, or of poor quality, average industry data may have to be used to calculate the fixed exemption.

[20] The legal basis for the fee assessment is provided in Section 13 of the CAA 'to include, but is not limited to, the volume and toxicity of any emitted pollutant.' There is no prohibition on the use of presumptive emission factors to estimate emissions.

For a credible emissions fee system, the data reporting requirements must be explicit and standardized.[21] Something like an 'emissions tax return' form could be sent out, which would provide the net emissions, fee liability, and the source data used to calculate them. Quarterly self-monitoring reports currently submitted by Pollution Control Officers contain basic information, including data on materials (e.g. fuel) use and production outputs. When coupled with applicable emission factors, these reports could serve as a basis for calculating facility-specific emissions fees.

Selection Criteria for Participants Participation criteria determine which permitted industrial sources are assessed for emissions fees. Different designs for the participation requirement have different revenue implications. For instance, firms below an emissions quantity cut-off could be exempt from full reporting and fee payments, reducing the cost burden, but at the same time creating a financial incentive to stay below the cut-off. Or they could be assessed a reasonable presumptive charge, allowing them to undertake full reporting if they can show their emissions fee payments would be lower.

One could also target sources based on geography. While conditions do seem to vary considerably within the defined Metro Manila airshed, we do not at this point propose differentiating the fee or participation rules within the airshed. The additional administrative complexity is too burdensome. However, geographic variation could be used to prioritize and target enforcement efforts. Furthermore, the fee is not the only emissions policy, and other regulations are available to cope with highly localized hot spots.

Enforcement Previous assessment of the Environmental Management Bureau's (EMB's) enforcement capability (IEMP 1997) revealed that fines by themselves were rarely used to leverage compliance. Further, this assessment revealed that even when assessed, fines were rarely collected. Reasons for low fine collection include: (a) the absence of guidelines on setting fines to account for the seriousness of the violation or the violator's ability to pay, and (b) the lack of institutional incentives for collection since revenues from fines and penalties do not revert back to EMB. However, discussions with two Regional EMB Offices indicated that this trend may be changing, at least for the environmental impact assessment program. The creation of the Environmental Revolving Fund under this program allowed EMB to retain revenues from administrative fines, and assessment and collection of administrative fines and penalties has more than doubled since the Fund's creation.

A review of 33 pollution adjudication cases revealed that it takes EMB an average of 8 months to serve a cease-and-desist order (CDO) from the date of

[21] The U.S. EPA has developed Procedures for Preparing Emission Factor Documents (http://www.epa.gov/ttn/chief/efdocs/procedur.pdf). These procedures may be overly complex for the Philippines case, so opportunities for streamlining EMB guidelines should be assessed, especially for smaller sources.

detection, and 15 months for firms to comply from the date on which compliance activities are initiated. Exceptional cases were documented where it took EMB more than 150 months from the date a violation was detected to serve a CDO. Of the 33 cases reviewed, only seven cases were considered resolved. The types of delays observed in the present system would seriously diminish the effectiveness of the emissions fee system of the type proposed herein.

Timing and Phasing in A phase-in period, where the fee program is announced but collections are not yet begun, can be used to promote understanding among the business community and allow them to take actions that will reduce their emissions and, consequently, their fee payments. For example, in the first year, one could implement the emissions reporting component alone. Firms then learn how to comply with the fee program and observe how it will impact their costs. During this time, they can assess and implement ways to reduce those costs through abatement. The following year, the fee payments would be required.

Over time, as the actual impact on emissions is revealed, the fee can be adjusted to reach ambient concentration targets. Better information about the levels, composition, and consequences of emissions can also lead to adjustments in the fee structure. The standard exemption could also be phased down over time as transitional costs pass and emissions fall. Later, the program could be expanded by reducing the participation threshold or expanding to other airsheds, taking local conditions into account in adapting the program.

Mobile Source Policies

Vehicles in the developing world's megacities, such as Mexico City, Saõ Paulo, Santiago, Bangkok, Bombay, Delhi, Manila, Jakarta and Seoul, have been found to contribute from 40 to 99 percent of some air pollutants (Sterner, 2003). Thus, mobile source control policies must be a part of any urban air pollution strategy.

The data in Table 11.5 illustrate the increasing trend worldwide of vehicle use, as well as the great disparities between income groups. Growth in vehicles has taken off in the middle income developing countries, but is essentially flat in the poorest. Thus, the concern is that unless ownership can be slowed or at least emissions in new vehicles reduced, air pollution is likely to get much worse in these countries. At the same time, ownership in these middle income countries lags far behind that in the high income countries. Another disturbing trend for air pollution is the gradual increase in the share of passenger vehicles in the vehicle fleet (and the corresponding reduction in buses). In China, for example, the percentage of passenger cars in the total vehicle fleet increased from 31 percent in 1990 to 49 percent in 1996, the most recent year that vehicle data are available for China.

Fortunately, the policy menu for reducing mobile source emissions is long and varied. In addition to direct abatement measures, there are transportation

Table 11.5 Vehicles and passenger cars 1990–2000

	Vehicles per 1,000 population		Passenger cars per 1,000 population	
Income category	1990	2000	1990	2000
Low income	9	10*	6	9*
Lower middle income	19	32	11	23
Upper middle income	127	193	114	153
High income	514	586*	396	443*
China	5	8*	1	7
India	4	8*	2	5*

* Data for most recent year available.
Source: World Bank 2003a.

control measures (i.e. measures to reduce vehicle miles traveled and trips) to address congestion externalities (that indirectly reduce emissions) and options to change fuel quality, vehicle design, bus quality, the price of driving, the price of fuel and vehicles, the price of parking, and bus fares, to name just a few.

Most of the stylized facts applying to point sources also apply to mobile sources. Several additional stylized facts that apply to mobile sources include:

(i) leaded fuels and high sulfur diesel fuels are used in higher proportions in developing countries;

(ii) buses are currently a much more important (but declining) part of the urban transportation fleet than they are in developed countries;

(iii) vehicles tend to be older and not as well maintained in developing countries.

We emphasize lead and sulfur in fuels because these pollutants are particularly damaging to human health based on extensive epidemiology research. Since approximately 90 percent of all lead emissions into the atmosphere are due to the use of leaded gasoline, it has become a worldwide public health priority to eliminate lead from gasoline (Lovei, 1997). Developed countries have already phased out lead gasoline, beginning with the U.S., in the late 1970s and early 1980s. Many developing countries, such as Bolivia, Colombia, El Salvador and Guatemala, have done so as well, and many more are in the process. In countries where lead has been phased out, dramatic reductions in both blood lead and atmospheric lead have been observed (Table 11.6). Unleaded gasoline is only available in two of 52 African countries, however, and these countries along with oil-rich areas like the Middle East and Venezuela, have yet to eliminate the use of leaded gasoline (IOMC, 1998).

There are many policy options for phasing out leaded gasoline, and determining which is optimal depends on each country's available technologies, markets, vehicle fleet, and politics. The U.S. phase-out, for example, utilized tradable emission permits whereby refineries that could afford to change their

Table 11.6 Summary of studies on lead in blood, gasoline, and air

Location	Year	Blood lead (μg/dL)	Lead in gas (g/L)	Atmospheric lead (μg/m³)	Population age range tested
Athens, Greece	1982	16.0	0.40	1.76	adults
	1993	5.5	0.14	0.43	
Caracas, Venezuela	1986	17.4	0.62	1.9	15+
	1991	15.6	0.39	1.3	
Mexico City, Mexico	1988	12.2	0.2	NA	0.5–3
	1993	7.0	0.06	NA	
Turin, Italy	1980	21.0	0.6	3	18+
	1993	6.4	0.11	0.53	
United Kingdom	1979	12.9	0.42	NA	Adults &
	1995	3.1	0.055	NA	children
United States	1976	15.9	0.465	0.97	1–74
	1988–1991	2.8	0.00	0.07	

Source: Thomas, et al., 1999; appearing in WRI 2001.

technology did so, and then sold the permits to refineries that could not. Other approaches include direct regulation, eco-labeling, and preferential tax treatment. Many of the eastern European countries, for instance, are using taxes on leaded gasoline to encourage production and use of unleaded gas (Sterner, 2003). Some alternative policies with respect to reducing sulfur in diesel fuel are discussed in the example in this section on Metro Manila.

The current low ratio of autos to total vehicles in lower income countries (Table 11.5) means that there may be opportunities to develop transportation control strategies that might be less accepted once car-commuting habits are formed. The low value of time in developing countries also suggests that the focus should be on transportation controls rather than on new vehicle investment or high cost rail systems. Such controls promise reductions in congestion, an increase in capacity utilization of roads and the vehicle stock, and possibly a reduction in total trips, all of which will reduce pollution. These controls can be CAC, such as banning vehicles from driving on certain days as in Mexico City or placing a quota on new cars as in Singapore; incentives, such as congestion tolls and increased parking fees; or planning, such as designing an efficient mix of public and private transportation routes and urban infrastructure. The city of Curitiba, Brazil, for example, implemented a long-term transportation plan in 1974 that included at its core a privatized express bus service, complemented by designated arteries for traffic into and out of the city. Curitiba now has a high rate of car ownership but no serious congestion, and public transportation carries more than two-thirds of the population each day with an estimated fuel consumption savings of 25 percent (Sterner, 2003).

Stemming the conversion to single occupancy vehicles with rising incomes should be an important part of an emissions reduction strategy. Improving the quality of bus service will be important for this task as incomes rise. While fare increases are always an option, subsidies could also be warranted because of the positive externalities to congestion and pollution that bus use has in comparison with autos—such is the conventional wisdom.

Nevertheless, if buses use diesel fuel and are substituting for gasoline-powered automobiles, the effects on health are unclear. The generally higher sulfur content of diesel fuel as well as the presence of very fine particulates (some of which are carcinogenic) in this fuel, argue for caution in making this particular switch. Conversion of buses from diesel to natural gas, such as the recent program in Delhi (see below), is one method for retaining buses as cheap mass transportation with fewer emissions, although such programs have uncertain effects on costs. On the gasoline side, emissions are mainly VOCs and NO_x, both of which contribute to ozone formation; however, ozone appears from the epidemiological literature to be less damaging to health than the particulates from diesel.

Vehicle maintenance is critical to keeping emissions low, yet bus and vehicle inspection programs are virtually non-existent or largely unenforced in some developing countries. In addition, the average age of the fleet of vehicles in developing countries is 12 to 15 years, compared to 6 to 8 years in OECD countries (US-DOT, 1996). Older vehicles increase emissions by having lower initial design standards, by increasing emissions with age, and by being more likely to be poorly maintained. One of the first steps toward fixing this problem is to remove perverse subsidies, such as tax breaks for older vehicles, and encourage engine replacement, retrofitting of catalytic converters, and 'scrappage' programs to get rid of old cars (Sterner, 2003).

The following are two recent examples of applied mobile source emissions reduction policy.

MOBILE SOURCES EMISSIONS CONTROL IN METRO MANILA

Several recent analyses in Manila (Ruzicka et al., 2002; Larssen et al., 1997 and ENRAP, 1996) develop a menu of economic incentive and command and control approaches that could be applied to mobile sources to begin to lower their emissions. Based on these studies and our own analyses, the RFF team[22] proposed a Mobile Source Control Action Plan involving a pilot diesel retrofit program for utility vehicles (including jeepneys) and a charge on the sulfur content of diesel fuel to encourage meeting the 500 ppm standard and to push refineries harder to reach sulfur content levels compatible with more advanced particulate trap technologies. Here we discuss only the latter recommendation.

---

[22] Fischer, C., A. Krupnick, R. Morgenstern, K. Rolfe, R. Rufo, J. Logarta (2002).

Particulate matter is the main pollution problem in Manila, with ambient ozone being a lesser problem. Thirty-nine thousand tons of PM_{10} are emitted by mobile sources. Forty-nine percent of mobile source PM_{10} comes from diesel utility vehicles, 22 percent from motorcycles and tricycles using gasoline/oil mixtures in 2-stroke engines, and 23 percent from trucks and diesel buses (Fischer et al., 2003). Out of 1.7 million vehicles in Metro Manila, diesel vehicles make up about one-third (543,000), with another third being gasoline autos and the remainder gasoline utility vehicles and gasoline/oil motorcycles. Consequently, a focus on direct diesel emissions (as opposed to gasoline emissions), particularly from non-bus sources, seems necessary and appropriate.

Assigning a low priority to NO_x control in our Plan is a critical element for a diesel emissions control strategy because it permits a way out of the so-called 'diesel dilemma.' Simply stated, the physics of diesel engines creates a trade-off between reducing PM emissions and reducing NO_x emissions. To get both requires very complex and expensive abatement technology, as well as very low sulfur fuel—conditions that are simply not yet practical in the Philippines.

There are several reasons to recommend a sulfur charge aimed at reducing the sulfur content of automotive diesel. Given industry pressure to relax targets for meeting new lower standards, the charge would offer financial, if not mandatory, incentives to meet them. The tax could also encourage overcompliance with the standard, which is desirable because the lower the sulfur content, the more effective the diesel catalyst. Furthermore, to the extent that compliance with the diesel standard is achieved by switching to low-sulfur crude oil imports, the sulfur content of other oil-based fuels (including kerosene and bunker fuel) would be improved as well.

Experience with lead in the Philippines suggests this approach is feasible. The phase-out of lead in gasoline was accomplished quickly with the aid of tax restructuring to offer incentives for consumers to switch fuels. A tax differential equal to the production cost differential of 4.5 cents per gallon was created, with a charge of 2 cents per gallon levied on leaded gas and unleaded gas subsidized by the same amount from an oil price stabilization fund, when prices were still regulated. Upon price deregulation, the excise taxes were restructured to give unleaded gasoline a four-cent per gallon edge at the pump. Started in 1994, the phase-out was complete in 1999. Concurrently, oil prices were deregulated and all prices fell.

The energy department is also concerned about the impacts of new fuel standards and taxes on the viability of the local oil refiners. Figures show that compliance with the current standard of 2000 ppm sulfur (from 5000 ppm prior to January 2001) diesel was achieved mainly through dilution with imported 500 ppm sulfur diesel. If standards can only be met with imported oil, this could drive down local refinery profits.

Some oil companies have officially written the energy department seeking its support for a deferment of the new standard to either 2006 or 2007 (requiring an amendment to the Clean Air Act). If the government is eventually persuaded to defer the new standard on limited protectionist grounds, then imposing a tax differential (between a high-sulfur and low-sulfur grade) would be an attractive option to move policy in the same direction. If transition costs for refineries are a concern, especially for obtaining industry acceptance of the policy, rebates toward installing desulfurization capacity could help defray those costs initially. Alternatively, a type of standard exemption could be included in determining the base for the charge. A fixed exemption would mean that fees would have to be paid on total sulfur exceeding a certain fixed amount. This reduces the total tax liability for the producer while maintaining the marginal incentives (fully so, if the charge is refundable for sulfur levels below the exemption). However, building in such an exemption risks creating a transfer to producers that persists beyond the transition period.

Accordingly, we proposed restructuring the excise tax on diesel fuel into two parts, a base rate and a charge based on the sulfur content. In other words,

Total tax per liter = base excise tax + charge*sulfur rate

Thus, the lower the sulfur content of the fuel, the lower the taxes paid for every liter sold.

In contrast with the recent lead phase-out, consumers will not choose between different grades and prices of diesel at the pump. Rather, producers have the choice of how much sulfur to remove from the diesel fuel that they sell at retail. If a refinery can lower sulfur cheaply, it can do so, and pay less tax; if another finds more desulfurization too expensive, rather than raise its production costs, it can choose to pay more tax.

As with the stationary source fee described in the previous section, the sulfur charge should reflect the costs of sulfur and its removal. A problem common to both designs is a lack of information. One would need to know the marginal reduction costs of all the major participants to determine the tax rate that would achieve the desired reduction (average content = standard). Making the sulfur charge additional to existing excise taxes, instead of lowering the base, would raise additional revenue and raise retail prices. The sulfur charge revenues could be used in many ways, such as to create a fund that can help subsidize purchase of the particle traps for utility vehicles that we advocated in our Plan.

An additional effect of the corresponding price increase would be to reduce some of the differential between gasoline and diesel prices. The relative price change, over time, could induce a switch to gasoline vehicles for new vehicles, or perhaps even engine replacements on old vehicles that, while exacerbating VOC emissions, would result in a large drop in PM emissions. However, if the

375

stock of diesel vehicles improves over time, upgrading to Euro 3 and 4 standards, and sulfur content becomes low enough to make catalysts effective, this switch may not be as desirable given concerns over carbon emissions. Alternatively, one could retain the current excise tax and structure the charge to be paid on sulfur content exceeding some percentage standard (and also credited if below), in effect creating a rate-based exemption. In theory, the price and revenue effects would be the same as in the previous example.[23]

A key question is where the tax should be levied. We recommended that it be levied at the point where the refined products enter the market: sales by refineries and importers of refined products. These actors are limited in number (three refineries, and at least five major importers of automotive fuels). They also have pre-existing regulatory burdens and relationships with enforcement agencies. This 'upstream' point of compliance thus minimizes the administrative and enforcement burden, and has been noted by other researchers such as Harrington and McConnell (2003) as a viable option for some mobile source pollution problems. The price incentives would be similar regardless of the point of compliance. Lower-quality fuels are made more costly, creating pressure to consume and produce higher-quality fuels.

Administratively, the sulfur-content charge should not present much of an increased burden over current practice. Excise taxes are already collected on the volume of diesel sales, and sulfur contents must be certified, so additional reporting requirements are not imposed. It does, however, increase the financial importance of fuel sampling and reporting; thus, verification and monitoring will require greater attention.

Imposing and altering the diesel tax requires legislative approval, so it may be harder to phase it in or adapt it once it is in place. Still, adjustments could be made over time; the reform could perhaps give the Department of Energy (DOE) or another agency with the relevant authority to adjust the sulfur charge on their own. Initially imposed to speed compliance to the 500 ppm standard, the charge will also help provide information regarding the costs and cost-effectiveness of further lowering sulfur in fuels.

By recommending a diesel retrofit program and sulfur charge we are not suggesting that the many other options for reducing mobile source emissions be ignored. With air pollution problems as serious as those faced in Manila, many points of attack are needed. Nevertheless, limited administrative resources demand prioritization, such as putting off consideration of alternative fueled vehicles. Alternative fuel technologies are expensive and not cost-effective, and a policy to promote them will take a long time to pay off. We feel the Philippines should wait for less expensive technologies.

[23] The danger here is that unintended tax credits could be created; in the U.S. lead phase-down policy, which used tradable performance standards (another rate-based scheme), some companies blended otherwise uneconomic fuels (like ethanol) with a little leaded gasoline, just to generate tradable credits.

Similarly, we did not recommend immediately bolstering the gasoline vehicle inspection and maintenance program. Improving enforcement of this program will take a huge administrative commitment and the pollutants emitted may not be contributing very much to Manila's most serious pollution problems. We also recommend putting off consideration of changing vehicle registration fees to make them more environmentally responsive. While responsiveness is a good idea, these fees have just recently been reformed and it may be politically difficult to change them again so soon.

CONVERSION OF BUSES TO CNG IN DELHI, INDIA[24]

Delhi is one of the many mega-cities of the developing world struggling with very high levels of pollution from industrial, residential, and transportation sources. In particular, the latest census shows that the population has grown to 14 million and the number of motorized vehicle registrations grew three times as rapidly as population between 1980 and 2000.

Vehicles were powered largely by highly polluting engines, including buses trailing plumes of black smoke from their diesel engines. In 2002, Delhi's commuters used buses often enough to rank the city in the world's top 20 for use of public transportation. Private vehicles were powered by diesel, gasoline, or two-stroke engines, which use a combination of gasoline and motor oil. The city's huge fleet of 'three wheelers' (small vehicles used as taxis or for light hauling) also used two-stroke engines. Taken together, a 1992 World Bank study estimated Delhi's annual health costs of ambient air pollution to be 10 billion Indian rupees (about US $200 million).

The Delhi government had passed a Clean Air Act in 1981 that authorized a Central Pollution Control Board to 'lay down standards for the quality of air;' 'advise the Central Government on any matter concerning the improvement of the quality of air and the prevention, control, or abatement of air pollution;' and 'perform such other functions as may be prescribed.' Yet, the government was not implementing the Act. Following a 1985 filing by attorney M. C. Mehta, who asked the Court to order the Delhi Administration to enforce its existing laws to reduce air pollution in the city, the Indian Supreme Court began a long process with the government on many pollution fronts, culminating in its now famous July, 1998 Order requiring that public diesel vehicles and three-wheeled vehicles with two-stroke engines be converted to compressed natural gas (CNG). Contrary to popular belief that the Court originated this idea, it had in fact been in discussion from at least as far back as 1988.

In any event, the order began to be implemented in early 2002, with the Supreme Court ordering the immediate installation of 1,500 CNG buses and

---

[24] Information for this example is taken from Bell, Mathur and Narain (2004) and on the web at: http://www.rff.org/rff/News/Features/Clearing-the-Air.cfm.

the replacement of 800 diesel buses per month. It also set up daily fines for buses ignoring the Order and fined the central government 20,000 Rs. (about US$476) for repeatedly delaying the process. By November of 2002, diesel city buses, diesel taxis and two-stroke three-wheelers were completely phased out. Since then, there has been a slight reduction in monitored respirable particulate concentrations in the city. However, a big increase in concentrations the year before makes it risky to attribute such improvements to the policy.

The Court's decision to convert to CNG has been criticized from numerous angles—that it was not cost effective; that the Court did not conduct an adequate inquiry about fuels and ultimately selected the 'wrong' fuel; that rather than set policy, the Court should have set emissions norms and then allowed for multi-fuel and multi-technology options for meeting those norms; and finally that the Court overstepped its bounds by making policy. In addition to fending off fiercely defended positions from powerful interest groups, the Court faced possible policy trade-offs between cost-effectiveness and enforceability: rigid technology standards are likely to be more expensive, but more flexible performance standards could have been more problematic to implement and enforce. The illegal use of kerosene to adulterate the fuel if price instruments were used instead was a major factor in the Court's decision to force the conversion.

Perhaps the most important issue concerning the Delhi program is whether this approach is exportable. Bell et al. (2004) draw out several factors that should be taken into account. First, there must be a 'dependable decision-maker,' a public body, such as the Indian Supreme Court, that is respected by the population, operates independently, and is willing to enforce policy reforms. Second, countries should consider only tools consistent with their institutions and technical capabilities. The Indian Court's decision to order a diesel ban was based on the lack of enforcement institutions to limit fuel adulteration. And third, even with an independent and active judiciary, reforms will not happen unless other institutions support it. In India, a free press and independent NGO community helped keep the spotlight in the conversion issue.

Conclusions

Compared to developed countries, which already have relatively clean water and face arguably less intense trade-offs between economic growth and environmental protection, air pollution may be a lower priority in the developing world. While improving health care systems can result in people living longer and healthier lives, as income grows, energy use grows and along with it, air pollution.

Yet even this attenuated trade-off is not inevitable. The tools and understanding to address air pollution problems in urban areas of developing countries already exist. In developing countries, large stationary sources of air pollutants are easy to identify, document, and target. The stylized facts in developing countries argue for a preference towards applying economic incentive approaches to stationary source problems, but only ones that are sensitive to and accommodate institutional deficiencies in these countries. The growing role of mobile sources is perhaps more troubling, because it brings congestion along with environmental externalities and is more closely tied to income growth. Yet, here, a variety of incentive and CAC policies are available to reduce emissions; those helping to produce cleaner fuels being among the more promising. Further, with the vehicle fleet growing in at least the middle income developing countries, some options exist to embed newer technologies in the fleet at relatively modest cost. In addition, improvements in public transit may slow substitution to private vehicular use.

Lacking, however, is a solid factual basis for defining the type and extent of the air pollution problem—that is, the poor state of air pollution monitoring, and the infrastructure to set air quality goals and implement measures to attain them. The case studies presented here show that NGOs (in this case the Asian Development Bank) have a willingness to bring about such implementation and that analysts can design policies that address to some extent the shortcomings in laws, funding, and experience that afflict developing countries. But, in the end, it is the local and national governments that must be responsible for such goal setting and implementation. The enviable performance of many developing countries in banning lead from gasoline is evidence that progress can be made.

References

Ambec, Stefan and Philippe Barla (2002), 'A Theoretical Foundation of the Porter Hypothesis,' *Economics Letters* 75 (3): 355–60 (May).

Andreoni, James and Arik Levinson (2001), 'The Simple Analytics of the Environmental Kuznets Curve,' *Journal of Public Economics* 80(2): 269–86 (May).

Bell, Ruth, Kuldeep Mathur, and Urvashi Narain (2004), 'Clearing the Air: How Delhi Broke the Logjam on Air Quality Reforms' *Environment* (April).

Blackman, A. and G. Bannister (1998), 'Community Pressure and Clean Technology in the Informal Sector: An Econometric Analysis of the Adoption of Propane by Traditional Mexican Brickmakers,' *Journal of Environmental Economics and Management*, 35(1): 1–21.

Burtraw, Dallas and Karen Palmer (2004), 'Distribution and Efficiency Consequences of Different Approaches to Allocating Tradable Emission Allowances for Sulfur Dioxide, Nitrogen Oxides and Mercury.' Resources for the Future Discussion Paper.

Carlson, Curtis, Dallas Burtraw, Maureen Cropper, and Karen Palmer (2000), 'SO$_2$ Control by Electric Utilities: What Are the Gains from Trade?' *Journal of Political Economy* 108(6): 1292–326.

Ellerman, A. D., Paul L. Joskow, Richard Schmalensee, et al., (2000), *Markets for Clean Air: The U.S. Acid Rain Program*. Cambridge: Cambridge University Press.

ENRAP (1996), 'Philippines Environmental and Natural Resource Accounting Project, Phase III.' Manila, funded by the Asian Development Bank.

Ezzati, M., A. Lopez, A. Rodger, S. Vander Hoorn, C. Murray, and the Comparative Risk Assessment Collaborating Group (2002), 'Selected Major Risk Factors and Global and Regional Burden of Disease,' *The Lancet*, 360: 1347–60.

——, S. Vander Hoorn, A. Rodgers, A. López, et al., and the Comparative Risk Assessment Collaborating Group (2003), 'Estimates of global and regional potential health gains from reducing multiple major risk factors,' *The Lancet* 362: 271–80.

Fischer, C., A. Krupnick, R. Morgenstern, K. Rolfe, et al. (2002), *Air Pollution Control Policy Options for Metro Manila*. Draft report to the Asian Development Bank. Manila, Philippines: Asian Development Bank.

Harrington, W. and V. McConnell (2003), *Motor Vehicles and the Environment*. RFF Report. Washington, DC: Resources for the Future.

Health Effects Institute (2003), 'Update on HEI's Interational Project in Asia— June (2003).' Accessed online at: http://www.healtheffects.org/International/Papa-update2.htm.

Inter-Organization Programme for the Sound Management of Chemicals (IOMC) (1998), *Global Opportunities for Reducing the Use of Leaded Gasoline*. Geneva, Switzerland: United Nations Environment Programme (UNEP Chemicals).

Larssen, S., F. Gram, L. Hagen, H. Jansen, et al. (1997), 'Urban Air Quality Management Strategy in Asia: Metro Manila Report.' Jitendra Shah, Tanvi Nagpal, and Carter J. Brandon (eds). World Bank Technical Paper No. 380. Washington, DC: The World Bank.

Lovei, M. (1997), *Phasing Out Lead From Gasoline: Worldwide Experience and Policy Implications*. World Bank Technical Paper No. 397. Washington, DC: The World Bank.

Millimet, Daniel L., John A. List, and Thanasis Stengos (2003), 'The Environmental Kuznets Curve: Real Progress or Misspecified Models?' *Review of Economics and Statistics* 85(4): 1038–47 (November).

Parry, Ian W. H. (1995), 'Pollution Taxes and Revenue Recycling,' *Journal of Environmental Economics and Management* 29: S64–77.

Parry, Ian W. H., Roberston C. Williams, and Lawrence H. Goulder (1999). 'When Can Carbon Abatement Policies Increase Welfare? The Fundamental Role of Distorted Factor Markets,' *Journal of Environmental Economics and Management* 37(1): 52–84 (January).

Pope, C. A., M. J. Thun, M. M. Namboodiri, D. D. Dockery, and J. S. Evans (1995), 'Particulate air pollution as a predictor of mortality in a prospective study of U.S. adults,' *American Journal of Respiratory Critical Care Medicine*, 151: 669–74.

Ruzicka, I., A. L. Indab, and C. M. Rufo Jr. (2002), 'Coughing up for Clean Air: Incentive-based approaches to controlling air pollution in Metro Manila,' Manila, Philippines: Asian Development Bank.

Smith, V. Kerry and Randy Walsh (2000), 'Do Painless Environmental Policies Exist?' *Journal of Risk and Uncertainty* 21(1): 73–94 (July).

Sterner, T. (2003), *Policy Instruments for Environmental and Natural Resource Management*. Washington, DC: Resources for the Future.

Thomas, V., R. Socolow, J. Fanelli, and T. Spiro (1999), 'Effects of reducing lead in gasoline: An analysis of the international experience,' *Environmental Science and Technology*, 33(22): 3942–3948.

Tietenberg, T. (1985), *Emissions Trading: An Exercise in Reforming Pollution Policy*. Washington, DC: Resources for the Future.

U.S. Department of Transportation (1996), 'Transportation Statistics Annual Report, An International Comparison of Transportation and Air Pollution,' chapter 9. Washington, DC: USDOT Bureau of Transportation Statistics.

Weitzman, M. (1974), 'Prices vs. Quantities,' *Review of Economic Studies*, 41/4.

World Bank (2003a), *World Development Indicators on CD-ROM*. Washington, DC: World Bank.

—— (2003b), *Environmental Health Perspectives*. Washington, DC: World Bank.

World Health Organization (1987), Global Environment Monitoring System, *Global Pollution and Health*. Geneva, Switzerland: World Health Organization.

—— (2001), *Air Quality and Health: Air Management Information System 3.0 CD-ROM*. Geneva: World Health Organization.

—— (2003), *World Health Report*. Geneva: http://www.who.int/whr/(2003)/en/.

World Resources Institute (2001), 'Laden with Lead,' *World Resources (1998)–99*. Originally published (1998), updated October (2001). Accessed online at: http://earth-trends.wri.org/pdf_library/features/ene_fea_lead.pdf.

12

The Economics of Terrestrial Biodiversity Conservation in Developing Nations

Heidi J. Albers and Paul Ferraro

Introduction

Mounting evidence suggests that humans are substantially reducing the diversity of biological resources on the planet (Warrick 1998; Ceballos and Erlich 2002). Some natural scientists predict that a third or more of the species on earth could become extinct in this century. Such losses are encountered in the geological record only as a result of catastrophic events. Moreover, a substantial percentage of global biodiversity can be found in developing nations, including many of the most endangered species. These same nations have limited means for protecting their biodiversity, and myriad other pressing social needs make competing claims on biodiversity. Given that biodiversity loss is fundamentally an economic problem, economic theory and empirical analyses can play an important role in helping to protect biological diversity in developing nations.

Defining, Measuring, and Locating Biodiversity

The term 'biodiversity' is broad but attempts to describe the variety of living things. Biodiversity can refer to variety in genes, species, and ecosystems. For each level, biodiversity can be measured in a range of ways including counting the number of species or determining the 'richness,' the relative abundance, or the degree of similarity among species. Biodiversity also includes several attributes such as compositional, structural, and functional biodiversity (Noss, 1990; Franklin, 1993). Some people view biodiversity as an environmental service although there is growing consensus that biodiversity contributes to the creation of environmental services rather than being a service itself (Millennium Ecosystem Assessment, 2003). Appropriate measures of biodiversity also rely on the spatial and temporal scales for biodiversity. In short, this range of levels, scales, and attributes implies that there is no single number that depicts biodiversity.

It is also not clear how many species or genes exist. Biologists have described approximately 1 million species, of which about 100,000 are well known. Estimates of the total number of species globally range from a few million to tens of millions (May, 2000). Policies cannot, therefore, be based on an actual count of species but are instead based on indicators of biodiversity. These indicators vary with scale but include concepts such as IUCN Red List indicators (lists of vulnerable species), area in protected status, and levels of ecosystem services.

Species, genes, and ecosystems are not evenly distributed across the globe. In fact, approximately half of all terrestrial species are located in 25 areas that cover about 10 percent of land (Myers, 2003; Pimm and Raven, 2000). Approximately 16 of these 25 high-biodiversity areas, and two-thirds of terrestrial species, are located in tropical forests, which fall largely in developing countries, especially in the Amazon, Congo, and South East Asia (Pimm, MEA, 2003). Only 12 percent of the original habitat in these 25 areas remains, which implies significant losses of species already (Myers, 2003). Although the non-linear biological relationship between species and area suggests that more than 12 percent of species remain, the rate of species extinction in recent history appears to be many times—perhaps several thousand times—the natural rate of extinction. Among the most important proximate causes of this biodiversity loss is habitat destruction, although hunting, non-native invasive species and climate change are also important in current and future losses (Vitousek et al., 1997; Pimm and Raven, 2000; Thomas et al., 2004). In our analysis of policy responses to biodiversity loss, we concentrate on habitat destruction, but we will briefly discuss responses to other causes of biodiversity loss as well.

The Value of Biodiversity

The debate over how much and what kinds of biodiversity should be protected is rife with uncertainty. Scientists do not know how much biological diversity exists on the planet, nor exactly how biological diversity supports the ecological services on which humankind depends. Attempts to highlight the importance of biodiversity point to myriad outputs whose production depends on biodiversity: hydrological services, climate regulation, soil management, pollination services, desalinization, biosphere resilience, tourism, pharmaceutical and industrial chemical research, and consumptive outputs like timber, fuelwood, meat, medicines, fruits, nuts, ornamental plants, domestic pets and a variety of other non-timber ecosystem products. Theoretical and empirical work has identified links between changes in biodiversity and the way ecosystems

383

function (Loreau et al., 2002). Economists (Alexander, 2000; Simpson, 2000) and biologists (Wilson, 1984) have also noted that biodiversity can be valued for non-consumptive uses such as spiritual or artistic inspiration. Finally, arguments can be made for protecting biodiversity based solely on our current ignorance: there may be substantial value in retaining the option to discover more about biodiversity's importance and hidden role in our lives before we irreversibly extinguish it.

Given all of these potential values, one might then ask, 'How much is biodiversity worth?' This question is not only controversial (Alcamo et al., 2003: 127–47), but largely unanswered at this point in time. Economists have made modest and incomplete attempts to value ecosystems and related ecosystem services in developing nations (e.g. Pattanayak and Kramer, 2001; Kramer and Mercer, 1997). To our knowledge, no attempt to estimate the value of a specific endangered species has been completed in a developing nation, although a few studies have been completed in the U.S. (see Loomis and White, 1996, Reaves et al., 1999 and references therein). Even if they had been completed, however, the way in which these values should be aggregated and then incorporated into policy decisions is an open question. The exercise of putting a dollar value on a globally-valued ecosystem (e.g. tropical rain forest) or species (e.g. minke whale) puts extreme theoretical and empirical demands on already controversial valuation methods (Carson, 1998).

Given the discussion above about the important benefits of biodiversity protection, one may wonder, 'If biodiversity is so valuable, why do we continue to see declines in biodiversity indicators?' If tourism associated with the visitation of ecosystems and wildlife is so important in many developing nations (Wells, 1997), why doesn't the tourism industry invest in maintaining one of its most important inputs? Why do water users not invest in protecting the biodiversity that contributes to maintaining their water supply? Part of the answer lies in the same attribute of biodiversity that makes it so valuable: it is a global resource from which all humans on the planet derive value.

Biodiversity protection is a classic public good: once it is provided, no one can be excluded from the benefits and one person's enjoyment of these benefits does not reduce the benefits available to other people. However, when people destroy biodiversity through their consumptive use of species and habitat, the benefits from that destruction are then private. Thus people receive tangible private rewards for destroying biodiversity, but people who protect biodiversity have few incentives to offer this protection because they cannot exclude non-payers from benefiting from that protection.

Markets alone will therefore always under-supply biodiversity. Governments and other actors must use programs and policies to provide the socially optimal level of biodiversity. However, the sheer number of individuals and governments who benefit from biodiversity makes coordination difficult and increases the likelihood of free-riding behavior. Moreover, the beneficiaries of biodiversity protection are often diffuse, while the beneficiaries of alternative uses of biodiversity that leads to its disappearance are often concentrated in small groups reaping large private gains from extinguishing biodiversity. The location of substantial amounts of biodiversity in low-income nations with weak institutions, high discount rates, and pressing social and economic needs only serves to exacerbate the loss of biodiversity.

Further complicating matters, many of the benefits associated with biodiversity protection, such as contributions to global ecosystem functions, the potential for pharmaceutical discoveries, and the existence of charismatic species, accrue to people who are far removed from the sources of biodiversity in developing nations. Without institutions that can transfer some of the global value of protecting biodiversity to local and regional decision-makers who bear much of the cost in protecting biodiversity, little progress is likely to be made in stopping the decline in biodiversity in developing nations in the foreseeable future.

Targeting Scarce Conservation Funds

Given the limited funds for biodiversity protection, spending conservation funds in a way that ensures that each dollar goes as far as it can in achieving conservation objectives is essential. To allocate conservation resources efficiently, practitioners and policymakers must necessarily integrate benefit and cost data to make good decisions. This advice holds true whether benefits are measured in dollar values or in physical values (e.g. species or ecosystem attributes). Economic analysis may not be the driving force behind determining the goals of biodiversity conservation investments but cost-effectiveness analysis should inform the decision of where to make those investments (Tacconi and Bennett, 1995).

When prioritizing biodiversity protection investments, however, academics and advocates often focus solely on the benefits that each parcel contributes towards the policy objective, while government agencies often focus solely on acquiring land as cheaply as possible with only a vague notion of the benefits provided by each acquired parcel.[1] In a study of prioritizing investments for

---

[1] Examples of conservation approaches characterized by seeking out the cheapest land can be found in the first nine contract sign-ups of the U.S. Conservation Reserve Program, which attempted to maximize the contracted land area given the available budget, and the establishment of protected areas in Madagascar before 1990, which were overwhelmingly located in steep, marginal lands that were far from infrastructure (Green and Sussman, 1990). Even The Nature Conservancy (TNC), a well-known conservation group, found itself in a situation in which it had been emphasizing maximum land acquisition given its budget. When new TNC president Steve McCormick asked his staff to explain to him how TNC was successful (Knudson, 2001), they responded with the number of acres TNC had protected: 'And I say, "OK, but how does that translate into the preservation of biological diversity? How does it accomplish our mission? And they can't tell me." '

biodiversity conservation in the United States, biologists (Dobson et al., 1997) found that endangered species in the U.S. were concentrated spatially and suggested that conservationists focus their investments on a small number of geographic areas. Economists (Ando et al., 1998) responded by pointing out that variability in economic factors was just as important as ecological variability in efficient species conservation. Ando et al. found that given a target of conserving 453 endangered species, the approach that considers both economic and ecological variability cost less than one-sixth the cost of the approach that only considers ecological variability. A similar debate developed over ecosystem conservation investments at the global scale (Mittermeir et al., 1998; Balmford et al., 2000). Cost-efficient conservation strategies were also examined by Polasky et al., (2001) for the case of species conservation in Oregon. They demonstrated substantial gains could be realized if policymakers considered both costs and benefits simultaneously rather than just costs or benefits alone. Such gains are particularly important when one realizes that economic costs are often positively correlated with political conflict and that reducing political opposition to protecting biodiversity can be just as useful as using monetary budgets efficiently.

Although consideration of costs and benefits simultaneously leads, by definition, to more cost-efficient environmental policy outcomes, data collection and analysis can be expensive. Ferraro (2003) illustrates how the correlation and the relative heterogeneity of costs and benefits across the policy landscape determine the magnitude of the potential gains from integrating cost and benefit data in policy design and analysis. In a specific allocation to biodiversity conservation, he argues that biodiversity conservation efforts would benefit from more investment in research that estimates the costs of biodiversity protection across the globe.

When the trade-offs between different types of environmental services and biodiversity are not expressed in dollar terms, an alternative approach to evaluate biodiversity investments is multicriteria analysis (MCA). MCA enables analysts to find ranges over which the trade-offs between two desired services or biodiversity types are particularly difficult or simple. Any set of parcels that does not fall on the trade-off curves defined in MCA are necessarily inefficient from an economic perspective; the system of protected lands could achieve higher levels of benefits for the costs incurred. In Papua New Guinea, for example, one study compared a plan to achieve a goal of representing 10 percent of all vegetation types to a plan to achieve a biodiversity target using a trade-offs-based approach with a timber volume index and found that a trade-offs-based plan achieved the biodiversity target and cost 7 percent less than the percent-target plan, which achieved only 70 percent of the biodiversity target (Faith et al., 2001).

A final difficulty associated with cost-efficiently targeting scarce conservation funds across the landscape is the dynamic nature of the threats to biodiversity. Conservation funds are raised and disbursed over time. Given the irreversibility associated with ecosystem conversion and species extinction, decision-makers are faced with the question, 'Should current funds be spent on species and ecosystems that are likely to disappear soon or should they be spent on species and ecosystems that are not in danger of disappearing anytime soon?'

At first glance, the choice seems obvious: protect the most endangered. This is in fact the approach of many conservation organizations (e.g. 'hotspot' prioritization by Conservation International; Ecoregion 200 prioritization by World Wildlife Fund). However, the most endangered species and ecosystems are also often the most expensive to save. They are endangered precisely because there is much value derived from extinguishing them. A conservation agent who annually allocates funds to the most urgent cases may find that, at the end of several decades, fewer species and ecosystems were protected in comparison to the approach of a conservation agent who allocated funds to the many more ecosystems and species that are cheaper to protect because they are not yet endangered. Costello and Polasky (2004) present a formal way of thinking about making sequential conservation investments in the face of potential irreversible losses.

Policies to Conserve Biodiversity

Despite the obstacles to raising conservation funds and targeting them efficiently across the global landscape, there has been widespread experimentation with policies to conserve biodiversity in developing nations. We discuss the most popular and promising of these policies below. However, for reasons we discuss at the end of this section, there have been few empirical analyses of these policies. Thus, much of our evaluation of their effectiveness is based on theory, simulations, rough case studies, and anecdotes. Even within developed nations, there is a paucity of empirical work that can guide implementation in developing nations. The evaluation of biodiversity conservation policy there-fore lags substantially behind evaluations of other social policies (e.g. health, crime, labor). Advances in biodiversity policy evaluation represent one of the most critical needs in biodiversity conservation at the beginning of the twenty-first century.

Protected Areas

Defining areas as 'protected' and establishing restrictions on their use is the most common policy to protect biodiversity worldwide. In this classic attempt to provide a public good through government fiat, biodiversity is supplied through 'fences and fines.' In 2003, 10.8 percent of the earth's terrestrial area was designated protected, including 12.6 percent of the land area of developing countries (EarthTrends Data Tables, 2003). Margules and Pressey (2000) state that 'reserves alone are not adequate for nature conservation but they are the cornerstone on which regional strategies are built. Reserves have two main roles. They should sample or represent biodiversity of each region and they should separate this biodiversity from processes that threaten its persistence.' Myers, however, reports that only 37 percent of the earth's 25 biodiversity 'hotspots' (threatened areas with high rates of endemism) are in protected areas (Myers, 2003). Thus, although establishing protected areas is the most common policy to protect biodiversity, much of global biodiversity is outside of protected areas.

As discussed in the previous sections, conservation funds are limited and thus care must be made in allocating them. Which areas to include in a park or reserve system is a complicated choice that should reflect, among other things, the regional distribution of biodiversity, opportunity costs of the land use restrictions, and the impact on rural people. Reserve site selection algorithms exist that determine sets of protected areas that achieve conservation goals under specified constraints (e.g. Rosing et al., 2002). Although these algorithms are rarely implemented in developing country settings, they provide a framework for identifying trade-offs based on the available data and the conservation goals. From the perspective of economics, two factors are critical in determining which areas to include in a protected area system: the goals of the reserve system and the cost effectiveness of plans to attain those goals. In the previous section, we discussed aspects of cost-effective targeting of conservation funds. Thus in this section, we focus on delineating the goals of a protected area system.

Many protected area policies to date are based on conserving fractions of land area rather than conserving levels of biodiversity. The UNEP World Conservation Monitoring Centre (WCMC, 2002) reports, for example, that the IV World Congress of Protected Areas set a target of 10 percent of the earth's land area for conservation. Such area targets say nothing about how much biodiversity is being conserved (Pressey, 1997; Barnard, et al., 1998). In practice, such area targets have often lead to systems of reserves that are made up of lands that are readily available or have low opportunity costs rather than lands that are true priorities for conservation. In some cases, degraded land that provides few biodiversity or environmental service benefits is included in these systems.

Even when protected area establishment is guided by biological criteria, decisions about which land parcels to include and what degree of restriction to place on their use require assessments of trade-offs. The IUCN defines six categories of protected areas, each with a different degree of restrictiveness, beginning with 'strict nature reserves' with no uses other than scientific research permitted (including tourism) followed by 'national parks' which permit recreational activities and ending with areas that are 'managed for sustainable use of natural ecosystems' with various extractive uses permitted (IUCN, 2003). The existence of these categories highlights a fundamental issue with protecting biodiversity in developing countries: people often rely on resources within protected areas and human uses may not be compatible with biodiversity protection. For example, allowing the extraction of fruits might degrade an area somewhat and decrease the amount of genetic diversity, but it may improve local human welfare and help to protect ecosystem diversity. Thus, even with an explicit goal of protecting biodiversity and ecosystem services there are important trade-offs between the types and levels of biodiversity and services that are associated with different patterns of conservation land and with different restrictions on use of that land. Designing effective systems of protected areas also requires recognizing the spatial aspects of the reserve site configuration. The biological conservation literature is strewn with debate concerning whether a reserve system protects more species if the system contains a few large protected areas versus many small areas. The ratio of edge to area is also important for minimizing detrimental disturbances from outside the protected area. Connectivity and interactions across sites are also important, particularly in cases where expanding the size of individual PAs would prove particularly difficult (Beier and Noss, 1998; Sutcliffe and Thomas, 1996; Bennett, 1999). In many cases, spillover benefits from contiguous land parcels and minimum area thresholds add further complications to designing effective reserves.

Economists have rarely weighed in on the debates about the spatial aspects of protected area configuration, preferring to allow biologists to make the decisions. Economists, however, have tools that could contribute to elucidating how reserves should be designed. Albers (1996), for example, created a framework for land conservation decisions in which contiguous blocks of conserved land create a bonus value. Although earlier economic analyses of protected area establishment focused on the simple question of whether to protect an entire area or not (e.g Dixon and Sherman, 1990), more recent work has focused how much of an area to conserve and at what level of use restriction. For example, Albers (2001) takes park-level valuation data for Khao Yai National Park in Thailand, divides the values across park sub-plots based loosely on geographic information, and looks at how management decisions change when the protected area is zoned. Turner et al., (2003) and others have begun to look at how biodiversity and ecosystem services change with different land use restrictions, which provides useful information for determining the trade-offs between conservation goals and land uses.

Economics also has a role to play in helping biologists determine what kind of research would be most useful for making decisions. For example, few biological studies provide information about the changes in probabilities of species survival or other characteristics of biodiversity with marginal changes in the configuration or management of a protected area network, but such information, when incorporated into economic models, could be extremely useful for policymakers and practitioners.

Finally, protected area networks must adapt to changes in economic and biological circumstances over time. Thus site selection should reflect the likelihood of changes within, and between, the sites that may alter those natural processes. Perhaps most pressing in this regard is the impact of climate change on biodiversity. Selecting configurations of reserves that will allow species to move in response to climate change provides one example of how dynamic considerations can be brought into reserve site selection decisions. Conservation biologists have begun to create maps of potential habitats at various points in the future with climate change and some have investigated how biodiversity might be expected to move as climate changes (e.g. Thomas et al., 2004; Peterson, 2002). This kind of ecological information should be brought into site selection decisions to promote long-run biodiversity conservation in the face of change. To date, however, little economic policy analysis, or even feasibility analysis, exists to determine what policies could be implemented to allow for the ecological transitions predicted by natural scientists.

After establishing their protected areas, government landowners must enforce their property rights against those who seek to use the protected biodiversity for alternative uses. As discussed in other chapters in this volume, property rights are often poorly defined and under-enforced in developing countries, and legal systems often fail to adequately support property rights even when they are well defined. For a case study in India, Robinson (1997) demonstrates that imperfect enforcement of a public property right leads, over time, to the complete encroachment of the land. In fact, much of a protected area's budget is often spent on enforcing property rights rather than on other aspects of managing the protected area.

Most protected area managers in developing countries attempt to enforce against land conversion, hunting, and resource extraction within the protected area by patrolling the area and fining (or killing) extractors. Abbott and Mace (1999) collected spatial data on where people extract from forests in Malawi and where the patrols are, and found that fines are so low that they do not deter extraction. In an empirically inspired model, Albers (2003) finds that, for a given budget, larger areas of biodiverse land can be protected if patrols are allocated across space in a manner that reflects the distance costs faced by extractors.

Economic theory on crime (Becker, 1968) offers additional insights into improving the effectiveness of protected area enforcement. Managers can alter the penalty and the probability of detection (in areas in which managers do not have the authority to penalize, they must depend on other agents who can affect the probability of prosecution and conviction if detected). Given the limited budgets of protected area managers, an attractive approach would be one in which patrols were few but the fines of non-compliance were high. Unfortunately, empirical work on tax compliance (e.g. Alm et al., 1995) and fishery law compliance (Furlong, 1991) in developed nations suggest that increasing the probability of detection has a much stronger effect on compliance than does the expected penalty. Beyond these studies, however, relatively little economic modeling or empirical work exists to inform decisions about enforcement of property rights within protected areas to conserve biodiversity. In particular, deadly force is being increasingly applied to wildlife poachers in developing nations (Messer 2000; Mbaria and Redfern 2002), but very little analysis of its effectiveness has been conducted to date.

In many areas of the world, the problem of enforcing property rights stems from the fact that establishing protected areas, like establishing any conservation policy, typically involves curtailing consumptive uses of resources. Given the traditional reliance of local people on natural resources such as fuelwood and wild foods, it is not surprising that some authors have estimated that local people incur substantial losses when protected areas are established (see Ferraro, 2002 and references therein).[2] These losses generate conflict that jeopardizes the achievement of the protected area's objectives and thus protected area managers and other conservation organizations have tried various initiatives to 'bring local people on board.' These initiatives may be implemented within park boundaries or in the neighboring villages and generally involve creating economic incentives to reduce extraction (Wells and Brandon, 1992). We discuss these incentives on pp. 396–9.

We now turn to a more fundamental question: are protected areas effective in achieving conservation goals? Despite how common and long-lived the use of protected areas in biodiversity conservation has been, we have surprisingly little quantitative data on the subject of whether they work or not. In the last two decades, a debate has developed with one group arguing that the 'fences and fines' approach has failed in developing nations (Brechin et al., 2002) and another side arguing that protected areas remain one of the best hopes for protecting biodiversity in developing nations (Oates, 1999; Terborgh, 1999; Brandon, 2002; Bruner et al., 2001). Among the proponents of protected areas, there is a camp of those who believe current parks are 'paper parks' and thus are ineffective without more money (Oates, 1999; Terborgh, 1999; van Schaik et al., 1997) and those who believe that despite funding limitations, existing protected areas have been quite effective in protecting biodiversity (Bruner et al., 2001). There are few empirical studies to inform this debate. Bruner et al., (2001) acquired data obtained from surveys of protected area managers or researchers associated with 93 protected areas around the world. The authors used simple partial correlation coefficients to determine whether protected status affected the level of (self-reported) conservation outcomes within and outside the protected areas, and concluded that clearing, grazing and burning are lower and the abundance of game and commercial tree species are higher within parks

---

[2] The common wisdom that local people incur substantial losses, however, is based on either *ex post* or *ex ante* extrapolations. No one has conducted a 'before-and-after' impact assessment of a protected area's establishment.

than in the adjoining 10-km wide buffer. Cropper et al. (1999) used econometric analysis of a GIS dataset for Thailand and found that land use conversion is lower in nature preserves than in parks, perhaps because of the more restrictive nature and additional enforcement of those restrictions in preserves.

The fundamental problem in evaluating the effectiveness of protected areas is selection bias: there is evidence that many protected areas are located in areas that are not at risk for large-scale ecosystem perturbation (e.g. Green and Sussman, 1990). In other words, protected areas, for political and economic reasons, are often located in areas with few profitable alternative uses of the ecosystem and thus even without protected status, one might not see much degradation in the protected area over time. Furthermore, no one has examined if the establishment of protected areas in developing nations has led to increased pressures on other non-protected ecosystems (some empirical work on this topic has been done in the U.S., e.g. Berck and Bentley, 1997).

Private Provision of Biodiversity

Although establishing protected areas has been a common approach by developing nations to protect their biodiversity, another common approach has been to simply do nothing and depend on the private provision of biodiversity. Although biodiversity protection is a global public good, free riding is not complete because there can be private benefits from actions that, purposely or inadvertently, lead to biodiversity protection. Such actions are common in developed nations. For example, large landowners like Ted Turner own large areas of undisturbed land for their personal use but, in the process of maintaining the land as undisturbed, they provide the public good of biodiversity protection. Non-governmental organizations like The Nature Conservancy (TNC) depend on voluntary contributions from members and other donors to privately provide biodiversity through habitat acquisition. Despite having to contend with poorly defined property rights and enforcement, private landowners and non-profit groups also conserve habitat and species throughout the developing world. Some protect biodiversity for financial gain and others for personal satisfaction, or a mix of both (see, for example, Langholz et al.'s (2000) analysis of motivations of private protected area managers in Costa Rica).

In some regions, private provision of biodiversity protection occurs because firms or landowners are able to capture some of the willingness to pay for the public good by bundling it with private goods (Heal, 2002a). For example in Zimbabwe, ecotourism firms buy land or create incentives for landowners to restore and maintain habitat for the 'charismatic megafauna' (e.g. lions, elephants) that many tourists pay to see on hunting and photographic safaris. By fencing off the property and providing habitat on private land, these individuals and firms provide biodiversity conservation because they capture a significant fraction of the international willingness to pay for that biodiversity. Heal (2002b) notes that southern Africa's property rights system encourages biodiversity conservation because an animal on a plot of land belongs to the landowner. Instead of pitting incentives to protect their crops against regulatory disincentives (such as fines for injuring or killing an animal), this system creates incentives for farmers or grazers to capture the animal (often paying a professional for this service) in order to sell the animal to private game reserves for quite large sums of money. In this way, private game reserves protect biodiversity both within and outside the reserve. Langholz and Lassoie (2001) document a substantial increase in the number of private protected areas worldwide.

Other privately owned land provides biodiversity protection serendipitously because the mode of production is biodiversity-friendly. For example, shade-grown coffee, especially traditional styles of production that maintain nearly closed forest canopies, can provide habitat for a wide range of both flora and fauna. In fact, Mexico's shade coffee plantations provide critical habitat to a large number of migratory birds. Similar systems include other understory crops such as cacao and bananas or planted agroforestry systems of multiple economic species that still provide some habitat. The landowner's incentives to undertake these modes of production may be factors such as the lack of fertilizer and other expensive inputs, the lack of large initial clearing costs, the use of labor-intensive rather than capital-intensive production, credit constraints that prevent the landowners from greatly modifying their land, or simply tradition. In these cases, the farmers do not capture any of the public's willingness to pay for the biodiversity protection they provide on their land (although attempts are being made to capture part of this willingness to pay—see next section).

Other potential sources of private incentives for biodiversity protection include 'bio-prospecting,' the term for the search among diverse natural organisms for commercial products of industrial, agricultural, or pharmaceutical value. A few contracts have been struck between pharmaceutical firms and the government or private agents who control biodiverse ecosystems and at least one paper claims that the value of protecting certain ecosystems for bioprospecting can be quite high (Rausser and Small, 2000). However, other analysts have concluded that the value of biodiversity for bioprospecting is quite small (Simpson et al., 1996) and, most tellingly, the large number of private partnerships originally envisioned by bio-prospecting proponents were never realized.[3]

Although the actions of private agents can contribute to the provision of biodiversity protection, these actions by themselves will not lead to the optimal level of biodiversity protection. When mechanisms for capturing the global willingness to pay for biodiversity are absent or incomplete, outside

---

[3] Costello and Ward (2003) point out that the parameter values chosen in different models of bioprospecting can make huge differences in the estimated profitability of such activities.

incentives for decision-makers who have de facto control over the fate of ecosystems and species will be necessary.

Economic Incentives: Indirect

In our discussion of protected areas and the private provision of biodiversity, we highlighted that conservation practitioners and policymakers have turned to creating economic incentives to reduce resistance to conservation goals among residents around protected areas and to induce potential 'eco-entrepreneurs' to provide more biodiversity than they provide under prevailing private incentives. When done correctly, the incentives align the public's interest in protecting biodiversity with the private interests of those who control the fate of biodiversity. When done poorly, however, such incentives either have no effect on biodiversity protection or, worse, exacerbate the threats to biodiversity (Wells and Brandon, 1992).

Perhaps the most common initiatives aimed at discouraging biodiversity depletion in developing countries are development projects—often called Integrated Conservation and Development Projects (ICDP) or Community-based Natural Resource Management (CNRM) initiatives—located at protected area boundaries or in ecologically sensitive areas. In general, these projects attempt to create a conservation incentive in an indirect way through three mechanisms: (1) by re-directing labor and capital away from activities that degrade ecosystems (e.g. agricultural intensification); (2) by encouraging commercial activities that supply ecosystem services as joint outputs (e.g. ecotourism); or (3) by raising incomes to 'reduce dependence' on resource extraction that degrades the ecosystem (Ferraro, 2001). These mechanisms, however, may not be powerful and may backfire in many settings.

To examine these mechanisms, several studies use household production function models, which were developed to examine decisions of rural households in regions where markets are thin or missing (Singh, Squire, and Strauss, 1986). With re-directing labor or 'conservation by distraction,' an agricultural project, for example, may not reduce the labor allocated to the degrading activity if people can be hired to take advantage of the opportunities the project provides (Muller and Albers, 2004). Agricultural intensification is likely to lead to reduced pressures on ecosystems only in the special case in which residents are subsistence agriculturalists (Angelsen, 1999; even then, one requires the assumption that markets will not develop in the presence of agricultural surpluses).

Encouraging the private provision of biodiversity through support for eco-friendly commercial activities that maintain ecosystem services is another popular form of economic incentive. In these cases, outside aid is often directed towards increasing the eco-output price or facilitating the acquisition of complementary inputs, such as tourism infrastructure, product marketing, and processing facilities. In some cases, the incentive may be successful on a limited basis, but rarely is the demand for eco-outputs, such as for ecotourism or non-timber forest products, large enough to support more than a small fraction of the local population.

Some success has been realized in efforts to market products as 'green' or wildlife-friendly (e.g. shade-grown coffee) and thereby generate a price premium in international markets. If the landowner receives the price premium, it increases his incentives for production through a technology that encourages biodiversity protection. The price premium thus serves as a mechanism with which to capture the broader public's willingness to pay for biodiversity protection and thus encourage its continued protection, but some have criticized the approach for being an inefficient mechanism to transfer funds from beneficiaries to suppliers of biodiversity protection (Ferraro et al., 2003).

The raising of incomes leads to conservation only if the extracted products are 'inferior' goods that are replaced by other, preferable and, by serendipity less degrading, goods as incomes rise. We know of no empirical evidence that suggests that increases in income in developing nations will lead to more biodiversity protection. In fact, the empirical evidence from developing nations suggests otherwise: increased incomes, particularly when investment opportunities are limited to agriculture, leads to increased conversion of habitat and thus biodiversity loss (Foster et al., 2002; Zwane, 2002).

Economic analyses of indirect incentives also reveals other problems with these policies such as implicit assumptions about local people's desire to be nature's stewards, complex issues in implementation, inefficiency and lack of conformity with the temporal and spatial dimensions of biodiversity conservation objectives (Ferraro et al., 1997; Brandon, 1998; Southgate, 1998; Chomitz and Kumari, 1998; Simpson, 1999; Ferraro, 2001; Ferraro and Simpson, 2002; Terborgh and van Schaik, 2002; Muller and Albers, 2004). Despite their widespread use, many assessments of indirect conservation policies demonstrate rather limited success in achieving their conservation and development objectives (Wells and Brandon, 1992; Ferraro et al., 1997; Wells et al., 1999; Oates 1999; Ferraro, 2001; Terborgh et al., 2002). Salafsky et al. (1999) investigated three years of financial data from 37 eco-enterprises subsidized by the USAID-funded Biodiversity Support Program. They found that that the vast majority failed to cover their costs. As with the case of protected areas, however, there has been little formal empirical work in evaluating the effectiveness of indirect incentives on the achievement of biodiversity conservation objectives.

Economic Incentives: Direct

An alternative approach to encouraging the conservation of endangered natural ecosystems is to pay for conservation performance directly. In this approach, domestic and international actors make payments in cash or in kind to individuals or groups conditional on specific ecosystem conservation outcomes (Ferraro, 2001; Ferraro and Kiss, 2002).

In high-income nations, tax incentives, easements, and tradable development permit programs are widespread and useful for inducing private agents to conserve land and biodiversity voluntarily. Despite some issues with the potential for 'conservation overkill,' full-interest acquisitions (or 'fee-simple' acquisitions) are the most institutionally straightforward of all the conservation payment mechanisms and the costs of monitoring and enforcing an agreement are relatively low (Boyd, Caballero, and Simpson, 2000). Conservation easements provide a payment or tax deduction to landowners who extinguish their rights to future land development. Monitored by the conservator, easements involve complex contracting issues but are a legal mechanism with a well-established legal pedigree. Tax credits or other subsidies equal to the difference in value between developed and un-developed uses can also leave land and its biodiversity protected but require monitoring and a well-developed tax administration (Boyd, Caballero, and Simpson, 2000). Tradable development rights (TDRs), which require a restriction on the amount of land that can be developed in a given area, lead to the least-cost development restrictions but are institutionally complex and, as with tax incentives, do not allow for targeting of particularly biodiverse areas. Many low-income countries do not have the legal, property right, and tax institutions to make considerable use of these direct incentives for biodiversity conservation. Still, other methods of direct incentives for conservation, usually in the form of a payment, are underway in several developing countries. Examples include forest protection payments in Costa Rica, conservation leases for wildlife migration corridors in Kenya, conservation concessions on forest tracts in Guyana, performance payments for endangered predators and their prey in Mongolia, and 'contractual national parks' in South Africa and American Samoa (Ferraro and Kiss, 2002).[4]

Proponents of the direct payment approach argue that such an approach is preferable to indirect approaches because it is likely to be more effective, cost-efficient, and equitable, as well as more flexibly targeted across space and time (Simpson and Sedjo, 1996; Ferraro, 2001; Ferraro and Simpson, 2002, 2003; Ferraro and Kiss, 2002). Payments can be made for protecting entire ecosystems or specific species, with diverse institutional arrangements existing among governments, firms, multilateral donors, communities, and individuals.

However, direct payments have also been criticized. They may transfer property right enforcement responsibilities to local participants, which can lead to inter-and intra-community conflict. They, like many indirect interventions, require on-going financial commitments to maintain the link between the

---

[4] For more details and examples, see (Kiss, 2003) and http://epp.gsu.edu/pferraro/special/special.htm.

investment and the conservation objectives.[5] Large sums of financial transfers can exacerbate existing corruption problems and payments to individuals who are threats to biodiversity can lead to a perverse outcome in which individuals attempt to become a threat in order to receive conservation payments. Other authors (e.g. Swart, 2003) worry that by tying conservation outcomes to financial transfers, one loses the moral foundation on which a sustainable conservation ethic can be built. In many settings, a combination of incentives and disincentives, and of indirect and direct mechanisms may prove best (Muller and Albers, 2004). For example, the World Bank's Conservation Trust Fund and Conservation International (CI)'s conservation concession combine direct and indirect approaches.

Although economists have begun to weigh in on the issues surrounding direct payment incentives through theory and simulations, no one has conducted a rigorous and systematic empirical evaluation to assess if an existing direct payment initiative is achieving the conservation and development objectives it purports to achieve. Carefully designed, empirical research on the use of conservation payments to achieve conservation and development goals in low-income nations is a critical next step.

Factors that Affect Incentives

The efficacy of any incentives that are introduced, whether direct or indirect, are strongly affected by the particular market and institutional setting (Muller and Albers, 2004; Robinson et al., 2002). As discussed elsewhere in this volume, markets are notoriously thin or missing in many developing countries. From a theoretical perspective, the impact of improved market access on forest degradation and biodiversity is ambiguous (Omamo, 1998; Key, Sadoulet, and de Janvry, 2000; Robinson et al., 2002). Without access to markets, most resource use will be for home consumption (Sierra, 1999). As market access increases, the impact on the resource base, whether positive or negative, depends on the relative strength of two effects. Some households will increasingly switch from purely subsistence extraction to commercial extraction, whereas other households, especially those with high opportunity costs of labor, may choose to purchase forest resources from the market rather than extract, using their labor for alternative activities (Robinson et al., 2002).

In addition, policies or programs that improve market access to create economic incentives will typically interact with the distribution of labor opportunity

---

[5] We note, however, that social programs in which families are paid for sending their children to school (instead of allowing them to work or skip school) has become a popular and successful program in many Latin American nations (Dugger, 2004). Thus, in a sense, the issue of 'sustainability' is not one of creating self-financing conservation initiatives or waiting until one has a fully financed trust fund capable of making payments well into the future. Instead it is more accurately characterized as an issue of a durable constituency and political will.

costs and so forest managers need to look beyond the pre-policy degree of market interaction to predict a policy's impact on resource extraction patterns (Robinson et al., 2002). The creation or improvement of roads allows a policymaker to reduce market access costs directly (Bluffstone, 1993; Cropper, Griffiths, and Mani 1999; Imbernon, 1999). Resource use incentives change because the roads reduce the cost of accessing and removing resources from threatened ecosystems. Working in the opposite direction, the same roads also reduce the cost of accessing substitutes for forest resources (Robinson et al., 2002). The creation of roads also changes opportunities for labor, which may alter resource management decisions (Muller and Albers, 2004).

One should also recognize that the use of incentives to induce the 'voluntary' provision of biodiversity does not necessarily require, or allow, the abandonment of traditional regulations and enforcement. In fact, most of the incentives discussed in the previous two sections require a strong institutional setting in which rights and responsibilities can be allocated and enforced. Restrictions on resource use may still be required given biological and economic uncertainty, asymmetric information between those who provide and receive the incentives, biological thresholds and non-linear responses to resource use, and the need to induce private agents to innovate in the biodiversity provision 'market.'[6] Bowen-Jones et al. (2002) argue that a combination of controls and incentives will be more cost effective than relying on one or the other, and hence sustainable in the long run.

Economic incentive-based responses alter the relative value of opportunities or constraints and thereby induce change in actions coming from a decision process. How effective a given incentive will be, whether direct or indirect, is determined by the value of the range of possible activities, the market setting, the institutional setting, and other constraints faced by the decisionmaker. In some cases, a response may induce radically different reactions in two settings with dissimilar institutions. The effectiveness of economic incentives for inducing biodiversity conservation is, therefore, strongly dependent on the setting in which the decision is made.

Invasive Species and Biodiversity Protection

Invasive species have been identified as one of the main proximate causes of extinctions (Glowka et al., 1994). Invasive species disrupt important ecological functions and such disruption has substantial implications for economic activities (Heywood, 1995). The growth in the global frequency and abundance of invasive species mirrors the growth in global trade, transport and travel. By the end of the twentieth century, most ecosystems had been affected by invasions

[6] In an empirical analysis of voluntary pollution abatement, Uchida and Ferraro (2003) note that the regulatory pressure in an industry was a strong factor influencing 'voluntary' overcompliance by firms.

(Williamson, 1996; Parker et al., 1999). The economic implications of these ecosystem invasions, however, have yet to be identified (as opposed to the direct costs to agriculture, transportation and recreation; Perrings et al., 2000).

The major approaches to dealing with invasive species and disease are the same within and outside of protected areas: prevent invasion; manual, chemical, and biological agents to eradicate invasive species; and containing the invasive species at some predetermined level. Macro-level initiatives such as trade and transportation regulations have also been applied (Costello and McAusland, 2002). Although there are studies that compare the cost-effectiveness of invasive species policies in high-income nations (e.g. Leung et al., 2002), we know of no such studies for low-income nations.

Among the more important problems for addressing the invasive species problem is that invaders are usually not identified until after they have become well established and thus costly to eradicate or control. Moreover, invasions are associated with a high degree of uncertainty both because they involve novel interactions, and because invasion risks are endogenous. Actual risks depend on how people react to the possibility of invasions (Perrings et al., 2002). Finally, preventing and controlling invasions is problematic because such prevention has the characteristics of a 'weakest-link' public good (Perrings et al., 2002). The provision of such a public good is largely a function of the actions of the least effective provider. Given that developing nations are likely to be the weakest link and they are typically spatially concentrated, solutions to the biological invasion problem in developing nations will be difficult without international institutions that support research and provide incentives for governments and citizens to prevent and control invasive species in developing nations.

Efforts to protect biodiversity from invasive species requires coordination between ecologist and land managers but this type of communication is notoriously lacking even in high income countries (Eiswerth and Johnson, 2002). Most economic policy analysts focus on the dynamic aspects of invasion and policy but the spatial aspects of invasion are increasingly recognized (Leung et al., 2002; Kaiser and Roumasset, 2002). To protect ecosystems from disruptive invasive species, policy must be based on the dynamic and spatial aspects of invasion but such analyses are in the nascent stages. For the protection of biodiversity, appropriate siting and sizing of protected areas paired with restrictions on land use in neighboring areas may eliminate or limit invasion pathways.

Wildlife Damage and Conflict

Human conflict with wildlife is a significant conservation problem around the world (Thirgood and Woodruff, forthcoming). The cost of conserving large and sometimes dangerous animals is often borne disproportionately by rural residents who live closest to wildlife. The risk of wildlife damage to crops, livestock, and human lives provides incentives for rural residents to kill wildlife and to reduce the quantity and quality of habitat on private and communal lands. Conservationists have attempted to reduce these incentives by spreading the economic burden of wildlife damage and moderating the financial risks to people who co-exist with wildlife.

Popular initiatives include compensation to rural residents for the costs of wildlife damage and the introduction of private and public insurance programs. For example, a non-governmental organization in the United States has a program of compensating ranchers for wolf attacks on livestock. According to government agencies who are in charge of wolf recovery efforts, the livestock compensation program has made wolf recovery more tolerable to livestock producers and has made wolf recovery more easily attainable (Nyhus et al., forthcoming).

Few systematic efforts, however, have been made to evaluate the efficacy of these programs or the best way to implement and manage these schemes for endangered species (Sillero-Zubiri and Laurenson, 2007; Nyhus et al., 2003). A recent theoretical and empirical review of these compensation and insurance initiatives (Nyhus et al., forthcoming) points to difficulties in implementing them in any nation, but particularly in developing nations. These difficulties include potential perverse incentives that could lead to greater losses of biodiversity than observed under status quo conditions and obstacles to creating targeted insurance schemes in low-income nations. The authors note that alternative approaches may be more effective in many areas: promoting trophy hunting, building wildlife barriers, providing additional habitat, moving people away from wildlife, or making explicit payment to rural residents that are conditional on wildlife abundance. None of these alternative methods, however, has been empirically evaluated in the field.

Paucity of Empirical Work

A common refrain in the previous sections has been that little is known about the effectiveness of many of the policies we examined. The lack of clear results demonstrating success or failure of a given initiative (e.g. price premiums for eco-friendly products) is not unique to developing nations, but it is particularly glaring in such nations. A recent workshop on International Conservation Finance (UC-San Diego, Dec 2–4) noted that conservation practitioners and donors lag behind their peers in other policy fields (e.g. poverty reduction, job training, criminal rehabilitation, public health) in terms of having well-designed empirical analyses of program effectiveness. The workshop concluded with a consensus agreement among participants that a critical conservation need in developing nations was a substantial increase in well-designed efforts to determine what works and when.

Given that hundreds of millions, if not billions, of dollars have been spent on conservation activities in developing nations over the last two decades and that international research support has been substantial in these efforts, one may wonder how it is that empirical results are lacking. We do not claim to have conducted a formal study on this topic, but our joint experience in the field leads us to several conclusions.

The first and most obvious constraint to well-designed empirical analyses is the lack of conservation researchers who are trained in state-of-the-art empirical program evaluation techniques. Such techniques include randomized field experiments, matching methods and sophisticated econometric analyses. In fact, we know of only one published paper that used such methods to assess a conservation policy in a developing nation. Edmonds (2000) used instrumental variable regressions and propensity score matching methods to assess the effectiveness of devolving control over forest management to local community groups in Nepal. He found that such devolution increased the average availability of fuelwood for local communities.

Moreover, much of conservation investments in developing nations are framed as projects that 'test' an idea in one or several locations. Data collection in these locations is often poor or non-existent and control locations, in which no intervention is attempted, are never formally selected. Without adequate data and controls, one is left with only guesses and vague anecdotes about the effects of the program intervention on the conservation outcome of interest. Donors who fund these projects typically know little about program evaluation methods, and the practitioners who implement the projects typically have few incentives for careful analysis and falsification of hypotheses. Thus there is rarely funding available for more careful policy interventions and analysis.

Furthermore, for empirical analysis to bear fruit, policy interventions cannot be varied in complex ways across space and time. If every village or household is exposed to a different intervention (one gets direct payments, one gets nothing, another gets fish farms, a fourth gets agricultural assistance, etc.) then an analyst is left with few observations for every intervention and thus cannot make any inferences about their effectiveness. We are not proposing that all policy interventions be uniformly applied across space and time, but we are arguing that 'experimental' introductions of policy interventions should be conducted in a way that allows practitioners and decisionmakers to make inferences about their effectiveness.

Conclusion

Scientists report that biodiversity supports critical ecosystem functions and the provision of ecosystem services in a fundamental way. Many governments and policy communities recognize the importance of biodiversity and its value to society. Given that value, the unprecedented loss of biodiversity in this century signals a serious failure of policy to protect biodiversity. This chapter has focused on the use of economic analysis to develop better policy portfolios for biodiversity conservation.[7]

From an economist's perspective, the undersupply of biodiversity conservation globally results from the public good nature of biodiversity and the fact that many of its benefits accrue to communities far from the places in which biodiversity is located. Biodiverse countries rarely capture the full international social value of the biodiversity they contain (see Bulte, Ch. 13 of this volume). In turn, the governments of these countries often fail to create policies that allow the people who bear the costs of biodiversity conservation to capture much of the non-local social value of the local biodiversity. In addition, when the benefits of conservation are not captured as cash, it may be difficult for low-income countries to incur the costs of that conservation. The public good character of biodiversity thus encourages the underprovision of biodiversity conservation at the international, national, and local level.

In addition to this public good problem, several other characteristics of biodiversity complicate the formation of policy. First, the value of biodiversity is largely unknown; most species have not yet been identified or studied, the relationship between biodiversity and ecosystem services is not well understood, and little is known about how biodiversity responds at the margin to various policies. Decisions about conserving biodiversity are made under a high degree of uncertainty. Further complicating policy analysis, losses of biodiversity are likely to be irreversible. Because information about particular species and about biodiversity's role in general is forthcoming, this combination of irreversible decisions under uncertainty calls for performing more biodiversity conservation to prevent irreversible losses (Arrow and Fisher, 1974; Albers, 1996).

Although many millions of dollars are spent by governments and other institutions to protect biodiversity each year, it appears that the current levels of spending fall far short of levels that would provide the socially optimal level of biodiversity conservation from a global perspective. In addition, decisions about what land to target for conservation, and what tools to employ to achieve conservation are rarely made in a cost-effective manner to achieve the most biodiversity conservation per dollar spent. In fact, almost no rigorous social science analysis of biodiversity conservation policy exists to determine which policies are cost-effective in which settings. Protected areas, or a 'fence and fine' approach, are the most common policy to promote biodiversity conservation. The policy issues surrounding protected areas fall into two categories: siting decisions, and management. Historically, protected area siting decisions,

---

[7] Our analysis concentrated on in situ biodiversity protection, but ex situ conservation through gene banks and captive breeding programs also has a role to play in protecting biodiversity. Economics has not yet been brought to bear on contrasting ex situ versus in situ conservation, not has it yet helped to inform ex situ programs in allocating their limited budgets.

have not reflected biodiversity protection itself. In many cases, countries establish targets, such as a percentage of remaining forest land, and set out to meet that target with whatever lands, biodiverse or not, are easily attainable. Protected areas would be a more effective tool in biodiversity conservation if siting decisions better reflected natural science and the goal of maintaining biodiversity rather than the goal of a number of acres of protected land.

In terms of management, protected areas may allow park managers to capture some of the non-local values of biodiversity but that money rarely accrues to the local people who incur the costs of restricted access to natural resources within the protected area. Because local people still have incentives to use, and potentially degrade, the resources within the protected area, protected area management involves patrolling and fining people for illegal extraction. This enforcement of the government property right is quite costly, especially in remote areas of low-income countries where property rights and legal institutions are not always well developed. Many people argue that the amount spent on enforcement is far too low to deter local resource degradation and biodiversity loss, and that these areas are 'paper parks.' Other work suggests that protected areas are successful in conserving biodiversity. The argument rages on because no systematic analysis of the effectiveness of protected area management has ever been conducted despite the widespread use of protected areas worldwide. Properly sited protected areas that receive adequate funding for enforcement and for compensating rural people for the costs they bear are likely to be effective in protecting biodiversity but are rare in practice.

Private provision of biodiversity conservation occurs in many areas but is not a large force in developing countries. Still, many environmental organizations, such as The Nature Conservancy, have begun to buy land in developing countries with the express purpose of protecting biodiversity. Private conservation actions face many of the same issues as government policies but may be better at siting protected areas for biodiversity conservation, have access to more funding, and be removed from political pressures.

Policies that create incentives for biodiversity conservation can be used alone or in combination with protected area policies. Many of the policies employed in developing countries attempt to address poverty or other issues and to use those efforts to create indirect incentives for conservation. Projects that create incentives in an indirect manner, however, are not likely to be as efficient in protecting biodiversity as direct incentive policies. In addition, assessments of many indirect incentive projects reveal widespread failure of these policies. Direct incentive programs are less well-tested in developing countries but provide an under-utilized option for biodiversity conservation. As with protected area enforcement policy, neither direct nor indirect incentives programs have been subjected to analysis to ascertain when and where they are likely to be cost-effective. Some theoretical analysis suggests that the types of local institutions, the opportunities for labor, and the characteristics of the natural environment all contribute to the effectiveness of incentive programs but no empirical analysis exists to characterize settings in which any particular incentive program is likely to cost-effectively conserve biodiversity.

This chapter focuses on biodiversity as a whole rather than on species in particular and emphasizes land management and habitat protection to achieve biodiversity conservation. Two major threats to biodiversity, invasive species and climate change, are not well-addressed by static land use restrictions. Protecting biodiversity from invasive species will require both monitoring and eradication activities in existing reserves. Some aspects of the siting of protected areas and of the management of buffer or transition zones between protected areas and their surroundings can reduce the opportunities for invasive species to take hold. Similarly, the impact of climate change may be mitigated to some degree if the siting of protected areas and the management of nearby land and wildlife corridors allows species to move and adapt gradually to shifts in climate.

The market failure discussed in Erwin Bulte's chapter (Ch. 13 of this volume) identifies some of the reasons why biodiversity is under-supplied by biodiverse countries and calls for increased spending by the international community to protect biodiversity at globally optimal levels. With any level of spending, forming better policy to conserve biodiversity will require using information from natural scientists, to understand the impact of policy choices on natural systems, and from economists, to understand the differences in cost effectiveness of different policy choices. Theoretical analyses and some empirical analyses suggest that current policy is not cost-effective in conserving biodiversity: more biodiversity could be protected for the level of current spending. Only significant efforts to evaluate policies from a natural science and an economic efficiency perspective will insure that monies spent on biodiversity conservation are well spent.

References

Abbot, Joanne I. O. and Ruth Mace (1999), 'Managing Protected Woodlands: Fuelwood Collection and Law Enforcement in Lake Malawi National Park.' *Conservation Biology* v. 13, n. 2: 418–21 (April).

Albers, H. J. (1996), 'Modeling Ecological Constraints on Tropical Forest Management: Spatial Interdependence, Irreversibility and Uncertainty,' *Journal of Environmental Economics and Management*, 30: 73–94.

—— (2001), 'A Spatial-Intertemporal Model for Tropical Forest Management Applied to Khao Yai National Park, Thailand.' RFF Discussion Paper 01–35. 2001.

—— (2003), 'Spatial Enforcement and Extraction in Developing Country Protected Areas,' RFF working paper.

Alcamo, et al. (2003), 'Ecosystems and Human Well-being: A Framework for Assessment. Millennium Ecosystem Assessment.' Island Press, Washington, DC.

Alexander, R. R. (2000), 'Modelling species extinction: the case for non-consumptive values,' *Ecological Economics* 35(2): 259–69.

Alm, J., I. Sanchez., A. de Juan (1995), 'Economic and Noneconomic Factors in Tax Compliance.' *Kyklos* 48(1): 3–18.

Ando, A, J. Camm, S. Polasky, and A. Solow (1998), 'Species distributions, land values, and efficient conservation,' *Science* 279: 2126–8.

Angelsen, A. 1999, 'Agricultural Expansion and Deforestation: modeling the impact of population, market forces and property rights,' *Journal of Development Economics* 58: 185–218.

Arrow, K. and A. C. Fisher (1974), 'Environmental Preservation, Uncertainty, and Irreversibility,' *Quarterly Journal of Economics* 88.

Balmford, A., K. J. Gaston and A. S. L. Rodrigues (2000), 'Integrating Costs of Conservation into International Priority Setting,' *Conservation Biology* 14(3): 597–604.

Barnard, P., C. J. Brown, A. M. Jarvis, A. Robertson, and L. Van Rooyen (1998), 'Extending the Namibian protected area network to safeguard hotspots of endemism and diversity,' *Biodiversity and Conservation* 7: 531–47.

Becker, G. S. (1968), 'Crime and Punishment: An Economic Approach,' *Journal of Political Economy* 76(2): 169–217.

Beier, P. and R. F. Noss (1998), 'Do Habitat Corridors Provide Connectivity?' *Conservation Biology* 12: 1241–52.

Bennett, A. F. (1999), 'Linkages in the Landscape—The Role of Corridors and Connectivity in Wildlife Conservation.' IUCN, Gland and Cambridge.

Berck, P. and W. R. Bentley (1997), 'Hotelling's Theory, Enhancement, and the Taking of the Redwood National Park,' *American Journal of Agricultural Economics* 79(2): 287–98.

Bluffstone, Randall A. (1993), 'Reliance on Forests: Household Labor Supply Decisions, Agricultural Systems and Deforestation in Rural Nepal.' Ph.D. Thesis, Boston University.

Bowen-Jones, E., Brown, D., and Robinson, E. (2002), *Assessment of the Solution-Oriented Research Needed to Promote a More Sustainable Bushmeat Trade in Central and West Africa.* Produced for the British Department for Environment, Food, and Rural Affairs Wildlife and Countryside Directorate.

Boyd, J., K. Caballero, and R. D. Simpson (2000), 'The Law and Economics of Habitat Conservation: Lessons From an Analysis of Easement Acquisitions,' *Stanford Environmental Law Journal*, vol. 19, no. 1: 209–55.

Brandon, K. (1998), 'Perils to Parks: The Social Context of Threats,' in Brandon K., Redford K. H., and Sanderson S. E. (eds), *Parks in Peril: People, Politics, and Protected Areas.* The Nature Conservancy, Washington, DC: 415–39.

—— (2002), 'Putting the Right Parks in the Right Places,' in J. Terborgh, C. van Schaik, L. Davenport, and M. Rao (eds), *Making Parks Work: Strategies for Preserving Tropical Nature*, Island Press, Washington, DC: 443–67.

Brechin, S. R., P. R. Wilshusen, C. L. Fortwangler, and P. C. West (2002), 'Beyond the Square Wheel: Toward a More Comprehensive Understanding of Biodiversity Conservation as Social and Political Process.' *Society and Natural Resources* 15(1): 41–64.

Bruner, A. G., R. E. Gullison, R. E. Rice, and G. A. B. da Fonseca (2001), 'Effectiveness of Parks in Protecting Tropical Biodiversity,' *Science* 291, 5501: 125 (January 3).

405

Carson, R. T. (1998), 'Valuation of Tropical Rainforests: Philosophical and Practical Issues in the Use of Contingent Valuation,' *Ecological Economics* 24(1): 15–29.

Ceballos, G. and P. R. Ehrlich (2002), 'Mammal Population Losses and the Extinction Crisis,' *Science* 29: 904–7 (May 3).

Chomitz, K. and Kumari K. (1998), 'The Domestic Benefits of Tropical Forests: A Critical Review,' *World Bank Research Observer* 13(1): 13–36.

Costello, C. and C. McAusland (2002), 'Avoiding Invasives: trade related policies for controlling unintentional exotic species introductions.' University of California, Santa Barbara Working Paper.

—— and S. Polasky (2004), 'Dynamic reserve site selection.' *Resource and Energy Economics* 26(2):157–74.

—— and M. Ward (2003), 'Search, Bioprospecting and Biodiversity Conservation: A Comment.' University of California, Santa Barbara Working Paper.

Cropper, Maureen, Charles Griffiths, and Muthukumara Mani (1999), 'Roads, Population Pressures, and Deforestation in Thailand, 1976–89,' *Land Economics* 75 (1): 58–73.

Dixon, J. A. and P. B. Sherman (1990), 'Economics of Protected Areas: A New Look at Benefits and Costs.' Island Press, Washington, DC.

Dobson, A. P., J. P. Rodriguez, W. M. Roberts, and D. S. Wilcove (1997), 'Geographic distribution of endangered species in the United States,' *Science* 275: 550–5.

Dugger, C. W. (2004), 'Brazil Pays Parents to Help Poor Be Pupils, Not Wage Earners,' *New York Times* (January 3). Late Edition–Final, s. A, p. 1, col. 1.

Edmonds, E.V. (2000), 'Building Community Institutions to Manage Local Resources: An Empirical Investigation.' Department of Economics Working Paper, Dartmouth College, NH.

Edmonds, E. (2002) Government initiated community resource management and local resource extraction from Nepal's forests. *Journal of Development Economics* 68(2): 89–115.

Eiswerth, M. E. and W. S. Johnson (2002), 'Managing nonindigenous invasive species: insights from dynamic analysis.' *Environmental and Resource Economics* 23: 319–42.

Faith, D. P., H. A. Nix, C. R. Margules, M. F. Hutchinson, et al. (2001), 'The BioRap Biodiversity Assessment and Planning Study for Papua New Guinea,' *Pacific Conservation Biology*, 6, (4) 279–88.

Ferraro, P. J. (2001), 'Global Habitat Protection: Limitations of development interventions and a role for conservation performance payments,' *Conservation Biology* 15(4): 1–12.

—— (2002), 'The Local Costs of Establishing Protected Areas in Low-income Nations: Ranomafana National Park, Madagascar,' *Ecological Economics* 43(2–3): 261–75.

—— (2003), 'Assigning Priority to Environmental Policy Interventions in a Heterogeneous World,' *Journal of Policy Analysis and Management* 22(1): 27–43.

——, R. Tshombe, R. Mwinyihali, and J. A. Hart (1997), 'Projets Intégrés de Conservation et de Développement: un cadre pour promouvoir la conservation et la gestion des ressources naturelles.' Working Paper no. 6. Bronx, NY, Wildlife Conservation Society.

——, and A. Kiss (2002), 'Direct Payments for Biodiversity Conservation,' *Science* 298 (29 November): 1718–19.

—— and R. D. Simpson (2002), 'The Cost-effectiveness of Conservation Performance Payments,' *Land Economics* 78(3): 339–53.

——— and R. D. Simpson (2005), 'Protecting Forests and Biodiversity: are investments in eco-friendly production activities the best way to protect endangered ecosystems and enhance rural livelihoods?' *Forests, Trees and Livelihoods* 15(2): 2–10.

———, T. Uchida, and J. M. Conrad (2005), 'Price Premiums for Eco-friendly Commodities: Are 'green' markets the best way to protect endangered ecosystems?' *Environmental Policy & Experimental Laboratory Working Paper Series #2003–003.* Georgia State University, Atlanta, GA.

Foster, A. D., M. R. Rosenzweig, and J. R. Behrman (2002), 'Population Growth, Income Growth and Deforestation: Management of Village Common Land in India.' Department of Economics Working Paper, Brown University. Providence, RI.

Franklin, J. F. (1993), 'Preserving biodiversity: species, ecosystems, or landscapes?' *Ecological Applications* 3: 202–5.

Furlong, W. J. (1991), 'The Deterrent Effect of Regulatory Enforcement in the Fishery,' *Land Economics* 67(1): 116–29.

Glowka, L., F. Burhenne-Guilmin, H. Synge, J. A. McNeely, and L. Gundling (1994), *A guide to the convention on biological diversity.* International Union for the Conservation of Nature (IUCN), Gland, Switzerland.

Green, G. and R. Sussman (1990), 'Deforestation History of the Eastern Rain Forests of Madagascar from Satellite Images,' *Science* 248: 212–15.

Heal, G. (2002a), 'Bundling Biodiversity.' Columbia University Business School. New York, NY.

——— (2002b), 'Biodiversity and Globalization.' Columbia University Business School. New York, NY.

Heywood, V. H. (ed.) (1995), 'Global Biodiversity Assessment.' United Nations Environment Programme. Cambridge University Press, Cambridge.

Imbernon, Jacques (1999), 'A Comparison of the Driving Forces Behind Deforestation in the Peruvian and the Brazilian Amazon,' *Ambio* 28 (6): 509–13.

IUCN (2003), United Nations List of Protected Areas. IUCN and UNEP-WCMC, Cambridge, UK.

Kaiser, Brooks and James Roumasset (2002), 'Optimal Public Control of Exotic Species: Preventing the Brown Tree Snake from Invading Hawaii.' Draft Paper presented at the WEA Annual Meetings.

Key, Nigel, Elisabeth Sadoulet, and Alain de Janvry (2000), 'Transactions Costs and Agricultural Supply Response,' *American Journal of Agricultural Economics* 82 (2): 245–59.

Kiss, A. (2004) 'Making Biodiversity Conservation a Land Use Priority.' In T. O. McShane and M. P. Wells (eds.) Getting Biodiversity Projects to Work: Towards More Effective Conservation and Development. Columbia University Press, New York.

Knudson, T. (2001), 'Environment, Inc.: Leader steers conservancy in a radical new direction.' Sacramento Bee. (December 29). Available at http://www.sacbee.com/static/archive/news/projects/environment/20011229.html.

Kramer, R. A, and D. E. Mercer (1997), 'Valuing a Global Environmental Good: U.S. Residents' Willingness to Pay to Protect Tropical Rain Forests,' *Land Economics* 73(2): 196–210.

Langholz, J. and J. Lassoie (2001), 'Combining Conservation and Development on Private Lands: Lessons from Costa Rica.' *Environment, Development, and Sustainability* 3: 309–22.

Langholz, J., J. Lassoie, and J. Schelhas. (2000), 'Incentives for Biological Conservation: Costa Rica's Private Wildlife Refuge Program,' *Conservation Biology* 14(6): 1523–739.

Leung, B., D. M. Lodge, D. Finnoff, J. F. Shogren, et al. (2002), 'An ounce of prevention or a pound of cure: bioeconomic risk analysis of invasive species.' Proc. Royal Society of London. FirstCite e-publishing.

Loomis, J. B. (2000), Measuring the Total Economic Value of Restoring Ecosystem Services in an Impaired River Basin: Results from a Contingent Valuation Survey,' *Ecological Economics* 33(1): 103–17.

—— and D. S. White (1996), 'Economic Benefits of Rare and Endangered Species: Summary and Meta-Analysis,' *Ecological Economics*, 18(3): 197–206.

Loreau, M., S. Naeem, and P. Inchausti (eds) (2002), *Biodiversity and Ecosystem Functioning.* Oxford University Press, Oxford.

Margules, C. R. and R. L. Pressey (2000), 'Systematic conservation planning', *Nature* 405: 243–53.

Mbaria, J. and P. Redfern (2002), 'Kenyan in row over Congo elephants,' *Horizon Magazine* (a Thursday pullout in the *Daily Nation* by the Nation Media Group Limited, Kenya) (Thursday, May 30).

Messer, K. (2000), 'The Poacher's Dilemma: the Economics of Poaching and Enforcement.' Endangered Species Update 17(3): 50–72.

Millennium Ecosystem Assessment (2003) http://millenniumecosystemassessment.org.

Mittermeir, R. A., N. Myers, J. B. Thompsen, G. A. B. Fonseca, and S. Olivieri (1998), 'Global biodiversity hotspots and major tropical wilderness areas,' *Conservation Biology* 12: 516–20.

Muller, J. and H. J. Albers (2004), 'Enforcement, Payments, and ICDPs in Protected Areas: What Works Where?' *Resource and Energy Economics.* 26: 185–204, Special Issue on Biodiversity.

Myers, N. (2003), 'Conservation of Biodiversity: How are We Doing?' *The Environmentalist* 23: 9–15.

Noss, R. F. (1990), 'Indicators for monitoring biodiversity: A hierarchical approach,' *Conservation Biology* 4: 355–64.

Nyhus, P. J., S. A. Osofsky, P. J. Ferraro, and H. Fischer (forthcoming). 'Bearing the costs of human-wildlife conflict: The challenges of compensation schemes,' in *People and Wildlife: Conflict or Coexistence?* S. Thirgood and R. Woodroof (eds), Cambridge University Press, Cambridge.

——, H. Fisher, F. Madden, and S. Osofsky, (2003), 'Taking the bite out of wildlife damage: The challenges of wildlife compensation schemes,' *Conservation in Practice*, 4, 37–40.

Oates, J. F. (1999), *Myth and Reality in the Rain Forest: How Conservation Strategies Are Failing in West Africa.* Berkeley, CA, University of California Press.

Omamo, S. Were (1998), 'Transport Costs and Smallholder Cropping Choices: An Application to Siaya District, Kenya,' *American Journal of Agricultural Economics* 80(1): 116–23.

Parker, I. M., D. Simberloff, W. M. Lonsdale, K. Goodell, et al. (1999), 'Impact: toward a framework for understanding the ecological effects of invaders,' *Biological Invasions* 1: 3–19.

Pattanayak, S. K. and R. A. Kramer (2001), 'Worth of Watersheds: A Producer Surplus Approach for valuing Drought Mitigation in Eastern Indonesia,' *Environment and Development Economics* 6(1): 123–46.

Perrings, C., M. Williamson, and S. Dalmazzone (eds) (2000), *The economics of biological invasions*. Edward Elgar Publishing, Cheltenham.

——, E. B. Barbier, D. Delfino, et al. (2002), 'Biological Invasion Risks and the Public Good: an economic perspective,' *Conservation Ecology* 6(1): 1.

Peterson, A. T. et al. (2002), 'Future projections for Mexican fauna under global climate change scenarios,' *Nature*. 416, 626–9.

Pimm, S. L. (2003), 'Contributions to Millennium Ecosystem Assessment'. http://millenniumecosystemassessment.org.

—— and P. Raven (2000), 'Extinction by numbers,' *Nature* 403, 843–5.

Polasky, S., J. D. Camm, and B. Garber-Yonts (2001), 'Selecting Biological Reserves Cost-effectively: an application to terrestrial vertebrate conservation in Oregon,' *Land Economics* 77(1): 68–78.

Pressey, R. L. (1997), 'Priority conservation areas: towards an operational definition for regional assessments,' in J. J. Pigram and R. C. Sundell (eds) 337–57 and 'National Parks and Protected Areas: Selection, Delimitation and Management,' (eds), University of New England, Centre for Water Policy Research, Armidale.

Rausser, G. and A. Small (2000), 'Valuing research leads: bioprospecting and the conservation of genetic resources,' *Journal of Political Economy* 108(1): 173–206.

Reaves, D. W., R. A. Kramer, and T. P. Holmes (1999), 'Does Question Format Matter? Valuing an Endangered Species,' *Environmental and Resource Economics* 14(3): 365–83.

Robinson, E. J. Z. (1997), 'Evolution of property rights with incomplete enforcement.' Ph.D. Dissertation. Food Research Institute. Stanford University, CA.

—— J. C. Williams, and H. J. Albers (2002), 'The Impact of Markets and Policy on Spatial Patterns of Non-Timber Forest Product Extraction,' *Land Economics*. 78: 2: 260–71 (May).

Rosing, K. E., C. S. ReVelle, and J. C. Williams (2002), 'Maximizing species representation under limited resources: A new and efficient heuristic,' *Environmental Modeling and Assessment*. 7, no. 2, 91–8.

Salafsky, N., Cordes B., Parks J., and Hochman C. (1999), *Evaluating Linkages Between Business, the Environment, and Local Communities: Final Analytical Results from the Biodiversity Conservation Network*. Biodiversity Support Program Publication No. 59. Washington, DC.

Sierra, Rodrigo (1999), 'Traditional Resource-Use Systems and Tropical Deforestation in a Multi-Ethnic Region in North-West Ecuador,' *Environmental Conservation* 26 (2): 136–45.

Sillero-Zubiri, C. and Laurenson, M. K. (2001), Interactions between carnivores and local communities: Conflict or co-existence?' in *Carnivore Conservation*, J. Gittleman, S. M. Funk, D. W. MacDonald, and R. K. Wayne (eds): 283–312 Cambridge University Press, Cambridge.

Simpson, R. D. (1999), 'The Price of Biodiversity,' *Issues in Science and Technology* XV(3): 65–70.

—— (2000), 'Economic Perspectives on Preservation of Biodiversity,' in 'Conserving nature's diversity: Insights from biology, ethics and economics,' G. C. van Kooten, E. H. Bulte, and A. R. E. Sinclair (eds): 88–105 Studies in Environmental and Natural Resource Economics. Ashgate, Aldershot, U.K.

—— and Sedjo R. A. (1996), 'Paying for the Conservation of Endangered Ecosystems: a comparison of direct and indirect approaches, '*Environment and Development Economics* 1: 241–57.

Simpson, R. D., R. Sedjo, and J. Reid (1996), 'Valuing biodiversity for use in pharmaceutical research,' *Journal of Political Economy* 104 (1): 163–85.

Singh, I., L. Squire, and J. Strauss (eds) (1986), 'Agricultural Household Models.' A World Bank Publication. Johns Hopkins University Press. Baltimore, MD.

Southgate, D. (1998), *Tropical Forest Conservation: An Economic Assessment of the Alternatives in Latin America*. Oxford University Press, New York.

Sutcliffe, O. L., and C. D. Thomas (1996), 'Open Corridors Appear to Facilitate Dispersal by Ringlet Butterflies (Aphantopus hyperantus) between Woodland Clearings,' *Conservation Biology* 10: 1359–65.

Swart, J. A. A. (2003), 'Will Direct Payments Help Biodiversity?' *Science* 299(28 March): 1981–1982.

Tacconi, L. and Bennett, J. 1995. 'Economic Implications of Intergenerational Equity for Biodiversity Conversation'. *Ecological Economics* 12(3): 209–23.

Terborgh, J. (1999), *Requiem for Nature*. Island Press, Washington, DC.

——and van Schaik C. (2002), 'Why the World Needs Parks,' in *Making Parks Work*, J. Terborgh, van Schaik C. P, Davenport L. and Rao M., (eds). Island Press, Washington DC, pp. 3–14.

——, van Schaik C. P, Davenport L. and Rao M. (eds) (2002), *Making Parks Work*. Island Press, Washington DC.

Thirgood, S. and R. Woodroof (eds). (forthcoming). *People and Wildlife: Conflict or Coexistence?* Cambridge University Press, New York.

Thomas, C. D., A. Cameron, R. E. Green, M. Bakkenes, et al. (2004), 'Extinction risk from climate change,' *Nature* 427: 145–8.

Turner, R. K., J. Paavola, P. Cooper, S. Farber, V. Jessamy, and S. Georgiou, (2003), 'Valuing Nature: Lessons Learned and Future Research Directions', *Ecological Economics*, 46: 493–510.

Uchida, T. and P. J. Ferraro (2003), 'The Adoption of Environmental Management Systems and their Effect on the Environment: Evidence from Japanese manufacturers,' *Environmental Policy & Experimental Laboratory Working Paper Series #2003–004*. Georgia State University, Atlanta, GA.

UNEP WCMC, 2002. UNEP World Conference Monitoring Centre Annual Report 2002. UNEP WCMC, Cambridge, UK.

van Schaik, C. P., Terborgh, J. & Dugelby, B. (1997), 'The silent crisis: the state of rain forest nature preserves,' in *Last stand: protected areas and the defense of tropical biodiversity*, R. Kramer, C. van Schaik, and J. Johnson (eds) Oxford University Press, Oxford pp. 64–89.

Vitousek, P. M., H. A. Mooney, J. Lubchenco, and J. M. Melillo (1997), 'Human domination of earth's ecosystem,' *Science*, 277, 494–9.

Warrick, J. (1998), 'Mass Extinction Underway, Majority of Biologists Say,' *Washington Post* (April 21).

Wells, M. P. (1997), 'Economic Perspectives on Nature Tourism, Conservation and Development'. World Bank Environment Department, Environmental Economic Series No. 55.

Wells, M., S. Guggenheim, A. Khan, W. Wardojo, and P. Jepson (1999), 'Investing in Biodiversity: A Review of Indonesia's Integrated Conservation and Development Projects.' Directions in Development Series. Washington, DC, World Bank (Indonesia and Pacific Islands Country Department).

—— and K. Brandon, with Lee Hannah (1992), *People and Parks: Linking Protected Area Management with Local Communities*. World Bank, Washington, DC, World Wildlife Fund, and U.S. Agency for International Development.

Williamson, M. (1996), *Biological invasions*. Chapman & Hall, London.

Wilson, E. O. (1984), *Biophilia*. Harvard University Press, Cambridge, MA.

Zwane, A. P. (2002), 'Essays in Environment and Development.' Dissertation in partial fufillment of the requirements of Doctor of Philosophy, Faculty of Arts and Sciences, J. F. K. School of Government, Harvard University, Cambridge, MA.

13

Conservation of Tropical Forests: Addressing Market Failure

Erwin Bulte and Stefanie Engel

Background and Motivation

Global forest stocks have fallen only very slightly in recent years. However, behind this reassuring aggregate statistic one can detect conflicting trends in tropical and non-tropical regions, and opposing tendencies in natural forests and plantations. While plantation forests in the developed world are increasing, natural forests in the tropics continue to disappear at a rapid rate. Using the FAO definition of deforestation,[1] the average annual deforestation rate over the period 1990–2000 was 0.2 percent for the world as a whole, but 0.4 percent for South America, 0.8 percent for Africa, 1.2 percent for Indonesia and 1.4 percent for Myanmar (FAO, 2001). Upon converting rates to hectares, annual net tropical deforestation proceeded at an average speed of some 11.8 million hectares for the period 1981 to 1995. Forest loss rates vary greatly across different countries (Matthews et al., 2000), but extensive deforestation has taken place in Asia (e.g. Indonesia, the Philippines, Thailand), Africa (Ivory Coast, Cameroon) and Latin America (Colombia).

Despite these large accumulated losses, considerable areas of tropical forest remain. In 1995, tropical forests were estimated to cover an area of about 1,734 million ha or about 13.4 percent of the globe's land area, excluding Antarctica and Greenland. With sizable tropical forest areas remaining, and with forest stocks expanding in other regions of the world, why should tropical deforestation be considered a problem at all?

---

[1] The FAO defines tropical deforestation as occurring when canopy cover is reduced to 10% or less. Note that not all deforestation is necessarily permanent. For example, when cleared lands are abandoned after a period of cropping, secondary forests may develop (to a greater or lesser extent able to 'substitute' for primary forests).

The gradual disappearance of such forests, whether matched by expansion in plantation areas elsewhere or not, should be alarming to society for at least three reasons. First, tropical forests contain much of the world's biodiversity. Tropical forests, especially wet tropical forests, typically contain far more species than their temperate counterparts, and they are thought to account for perhaps two-thirds of the earth's approximately 14 million species (Hughes et al., 1997). Second, tropical forests represent a considerable store of sequestered carbon which, when released, would contribute to climate change. Third, tropical forests are important for forest dwellers and many rural poor alike, who depend on access to forest services for their survival. In addition to these benefits, tropical forests generate various other tangible and non-tangible outputs, to which we will return in detail later. It is obvious, however, that forest conservation and sustainable natural forest management not only imply benefits—they may also invoke considerable costs. Costs are mainly foregone returns to alternative forms of land use, but may also include nuisance costs of wildlife invading adjacent agricultural fields or negative hydrological impacts by competing for water with other land uses.

A well-known but important observation concerns the spatial and temporal mismatch of costs and benefits. Costs occur often at a local scale and must be borne in the short term. Households, firms, and governments may be confronted with a variety of current costs and restrictions, in some cases impeding the ability to generate income of those who may need extra income most. In contrast, benefits might not materialize until far in the future, and could be shared by many parties, possibly even at a global scale. Globally shared benefits are, for example, the contribution of forests to global climate regulation, or their role in protection of charismatic wildlife. When uncompensated, such benefits might constitute a windfall gain for the rich.

Market imperfections and policy failure frequently prevent an efficient forest management at the national level. Moreover, even if sovereign nations have the institutional capacity in place to allocate their land optimally to various uses, the spatial and temporal mismatch described above implies the following. Unless either a full set of markets exists for all forest ecosystem services or a cooperative outcome can be negotiated, in the long run, sovereign nations will ignore spillover benefits and as a consequence will allocate too much of their land to uses other than forest. While rational from a narrow private or domestic perspective, in light of the inability to capture a reward for spillover or external benefits, this means an efficiency loss from a global perspective. In addition, when the institutional capacity to steer land use is lacking, the mismatch implies that sovereign countries have fewer incentives to establish such an infrastructure. Market failure may therefore result in institutional failure. One possible outcome is that property rights to land and forest resources are *de facto* undefined (or un-enforced), such that individuals will ignore the user cost associated with current extraction or conversion, and refrain from investments in future productivity of the resource. This can result in uncontrolled forest conversion for agricultural uses (as described, for example, by Myers, 1994), but also in large-scale illegal logging for export markets. For example, Mintorahardjo and Setiono (2003) report that in Indonesia, 60 to 80 percent of the timber industry's supplies are obtained illegally.

Recognizing this threat, the international community has developed various instruments to align national and global incentives. Instruments vary from the carrot to the stick, ranging from transfers and debt-for-nature swaps to timber trade restrictions. The international community also does many things that change the incentive structures indirectly by affecting international prices and global investment flows. Ongoing tropical deforestation suggests that these efforts have only been partially successful at best. Upon closer inspection of the available evidence (to which we return later), it is tempting to conclude that 'the North' wishes to free ride on conservation efforts in 'the South,' and fails to develop the appropriate institutions to internalize transboundary and intertemporal external effects associated with current forest conservation. Recent initiatives of direct payments for environmental services appear to be a promising step in the right direction. However, we argue that the implementation of these and other policies needs to take into account the property right regimes in place in the country of concern. Property right regimes have changed considerably over the last decades, with strong trends to devolve rights and responsibilities over local forest resources from the state to communities and private individuals. This has important impacts on the relative importance of different types of market failures and policy effects.

This paper proposes to (1) summarize existing literature on the causes of deforestation and the magnitude of the various forest benefit components (enabling an assessment of the importance of spillover effects in an absolute and relative sense); (2) critically discuss the usefulness of forest valuation exercises for guiding policy choices regarding forest management and conservation; (3) discuss the main market failures underlying deforestation and the policy approaches used to address them; and (4) highlight the relationship between different property right regimes, market failures, and policy effectiveness.

The paper is organized as follows. In section 2 we briefly summarize the existing results on the immediate and underlying causes of deforestation. From our discussion so far, it is clear that deforestation per se is not necessarily inefficient. The socially optimal level of deforestation should equate the social marginal benefits of deforestation to the marginal costs. Therefore, in section 3, we review the various forest functions and services that have been identified in the literature, and critically discuss the potential of forest valuation work as a tool to inform policymakers in the real world. In section 4, we discuss the market failures that are the root cause of many deforestation problems, and various specific policies aimed to address them. As argued above, different property right regimes are affected differently by market imperfections, and thus, effects of policies vary across these regimes. These relationships are discussed in section 5. Finally, section 6 concludes.

Causes of Deforestation

In an extensive review of existing economic models of deforestation, Kaimowitz and Angelsen (1998, ch. 2) distinguish between sources of deforestation (i.e. the agents and actions causing deforestation), the immediate causes of deforestation (i.e. the decision parameters and agent characteristics driving deforestation decisions), and the underlying causes of deforestation (i.e. macro-level variables and policy instruments affecting decision parameters).

Main sources of deforestation include the expansion of cropped area and pasture, logging (particularly in South East Asia) and to a lesser degree fuelwood collection (particularly in Africa). The main agents of deforestation also differ across regions. In somewhat simplifying terms one can say that they are smallholders in Africa, timber companies and plantation agriculture in South East Asia, and cattle ranchers and mechanized farmers in Latin America. Evidence on the effect of agents' time preferences, risk aversion and wealth status on deforestation is generally weak and contradictory (Kaimowitz and Angelsen, 1998, ch. 6).

The parameters driving deforestation decisions include physical characteristics of the forest, agricultural input and output prices, timber prices, wages and off-farm employment, technological change in agriculture, accessibility of the forest, as well as the property regime and strategic behavior. Deforestation tends to be stronger under ecological and economic conditions more suitable to agriculture (e.g. higher fertility, higher agricultural output prices), although changes in relative prices that affect crop composition may have ambiguous effects. The effect of timber prices depends crucially on tenure security. If producers have insecure rights to the forest, higher timber prices are likely to lead to more deforestation because they increase the net benefits from deforestation. With secure tenure, however, higher timber prices may increase the incentive to adopt more efficient harvesting and processing techniques, and to guard against encroachment. Kaimowitz and Angelsen (1998) argue that under most developing country conditions, logging and agriculture have to be seen as complementary rather than competing activities (what they call the 'logging-shifting cultivation tandem') and that higher timber prices will most likely increase deforestation. While these authors conclude that increases in rural wages and off-farm employment opportunities tend to reduce deforestation, the opposite may be the case in situations where labor is abundant relative to land (López,

415

1998) and where communities have to compete with firms for property rights (Engel and López, 2004). Increases in farm implement prices appear to decrease deforestation, but the effect is less clear for fertilizers (Kaimowitz and Angelsen, 1998). Technological change generally has an ambiguous effect on deforestation, with technologies that are particularly suited for land already under cultivation rather than land under forest cover and that are intensive in both labor and capital most favorable to reduce deforestation (Kaimowitz & Angelsen, 1998; López, 1998; Angelsen and Kaimowitz, 2001). Improved access to markets and forests (e.g. through roads) generally increases deforestation. Well-defined and secure property rights reduce deforestation as compared to open access situations. Where farmers obtain property rights by clearing land, improvements in tenure security, however, may increase deforestation (Kaimowitz and Angelsen, 1998).

Potential underlying factors of deforestation include population growth, economic growth, external debt, trade, and structural adjustment, but empirical and theoretical evidence on the direction of the effects is ambiguous and depends on the specific context. Political economy considerations are another type of underlying factor that have received relatively little attention in past research (see also Ch. 4 by Deacon and Mueller in this volume). Often, incentives are distorted in favor of excessive forest exploitation in order to serve vested 'resource mining' interests (Wunder, 2000). The political scientist Ross (2001) has described how, following a boom in timber prices, incumbent politicians may deliberately demolish the institutions that promote sustainable logging. The objective of such politicians is to maximize their own private profits from logging, or the value of bribes associated with allocating timber licenses to favored parties—a process Ross refers to as 'rent seizing.' Again, it is important to note that deforestation per se is not necessarily inefficient. The socially optimal level of deforestation should equate the social marginal benefits of deforestation to the marginal costs. However, evaluating these, especially the benefits from forest services, is not an easy task. We now turn to an assessment of these benefits and the potential for economic valuation to assist policymakers in this regard.

Forest Services and Valuation

It is probably fair to say that without the plethora of services provided by natural ecosystems, mankind would not be able to prosper the way it does. In fact, it is conceivable that it would not survive at all. However, this observation does not imply that every natural ecosystem should be kept intact regardless of the costs. While ecosystem services are presumably infinitely valuable to human society, it may be equally true that conservation of natural ecosystems is a bad investment from society's point of view. This apparent paradox is readily resolved. Generic statements about the value of ecosystems are an assessment of the total value of all ecosystems—how much will mankind lose when all ecosystems are converted or degraded? Of course this is an unlikely scenario in the short run, and one that is therefore essentially irrelevant for policy purposes. Investment opportunities are typically evaluated at the margin—what is the value of one more hectare of boreal or tropical forest, given that there exists a pre-existing stock of ecosystems? If the pre-existing forest stock is large (and the total value of forest services enormous), the value of an additional stretch of forestland may well be negligible. What services do forests provide, at the margin and otherwise?

Ecosystem Services

Many biophysical and biochemical processes take place within natural ecosystems. The outcomes of some of these processes are useful or beneficial for mankind. In what follows, we define such outcomes as *ecosystem services* (ES). There are various ways to cluster or organize the various ES, and any clustering is arbitrary. In this section, we distinguish between production services of tropical forests, regulatory services, and habitat/biodiversity conservation services. Drawing from earlier work by van Kooten et al. (2000) and Nasi et al. (2002), we discuss each of these classes in turn below (see also Pearce and Pearce, 2001 for a more elaborate treatment).

Before starting off, however, a word of caution is in order. It proved impossible to provide sensible monetary estimates for the various ES at the current level of aggregation—the set of tropical forests is simply too diverse. For example, consider the forest service of timber production, one of the key services generating cash income and one for which information is readily available. Rents from harvesting may vary from virtually nothing to some $1,000 per m^3 depending on the location and harvest techniques employed. Similarly, the quantity of timber that can be sustainably extracted from natural forests ranges from some 0.5–2.0 m^3 ha^{-1} (in countries like Costa Rica) to some 20 to 30 times that quantity (in Indonesian dipterocarp forests). Given this broad range of outcomes, presenting monetary estimates for tropical forest management 'in general' serves little purpose. A particular case study, for which a consistent set of data is available, will be provided in section 3.

Production Services of Tropical Forests Tropical rainforests produce tangible products such as timber, fuelwood and non-timber forest products (e.g. rattan, oils, fruits, nuts, ornamental flowers, bush meat), but also less tangible assets such as opportunities for eco-tourism. Timber production is commercially the most significant activity in most forests. There exist huge differences between very selective logging of high value hardwoods, more intensive logging of non-dipterocarp forests, intensive logging of dipterocarp forests, clear felling in natural tropical softwood forests, and clear felling of mixed tropical hard woods for pulp production. The returns per hectare vary accordingly—they not only depend on the type of forest and management regime, but also on discount rates, stumpage prices, management costs, site conditions, distance to markets, infrastructure, and so forth. Vincent (1990) provides estimates of present value ranging from +US$850 down to −$130 ha^{-1}. Selective logging may be a commercially attractive proposition in some areas, but not elsewhere. For example, recent experiences in countries like Bolivia suggest that annual profits from selective logging are smaller than $1 ha^{-1} yr^{-1}; logging firms simply opted to return their concessions when confronted with such taxes (Bojanic and Bulte, 2002).

Fuelwood rarely enters international markets, but is increasingly produced for regional and national markets. It is one of the most important forest inputs in poor households in developing countries. The mid-1970s were marked by a widespread concern that demand for fuelwood and charcoal outpaced supply. This was perceived to result in a 'fuelwood gap' with disastrous consequences for rural poor and forests alike, which triggered interventions aimed at expanding supplies (farm forestry, plantations) and lowering demand (enhance fuel efficiency, etc.). According to the FAO (2001), some 1.6 billion m^3 of fuelwood were extracted in the mid-1990s, a number which is now believed to decline slowly.[2] While an estimated 2.4 billion people continue to utilise wood and other forms of biomass, recent assessments indicate that woodfuels are unlikely to be a major cause of deforestation (Arnold et al., 2003). Urban consumers substitute away from biomass to alternative sources of energy when they can afford it (hence, actual consumption is smaller than predicted), and much of the supply now comes from non-forest areas.[3] While fuelwood collection is expected to remain a major source of income for millions of rural poor households, harvesting will take place in the vicinity of populated areas and its scope for application over extensive areas in natural forests is limited. Wood is a bulky commodity, and the option to gather it profitably is restricted by harvesting and transport costs.

Another potentially important ES concerns the generation of non–timber forest products (NTFP) such as rattan, oils, fruits, nuts and bush meat. Large numbers of forest dwellers depend critically on them for survival, and large numbers of rural and urban poor supplement their income by seasonally moving to the forest to gather commodities like Brazil nuts (Bojanic, 2001). Cavendish (2000) presents evidence for Zimbabwe that suggests some 30–40 percent of household income may derive from NTFPs. NTFP harvesting from unmanaged natural forests has been likened to a 'safety net' to which the poor

[2] Charcoal consumption, on the other hand, is still increasing, and now requires some 270 million m^3 of wood per year.
[3] But deforestation can occur locally in the vicinity of growing urban markets with little purchasing power (typically in Africa).

can turn in times of adversity, but other authors argue that it usually offers little scope for economic development and could perpetuate poverty (Homma, 1994). Regardless, a common finding is that the returns of NTFP gathering on a per hectare basis are very modest (see Pearce and Pearce, 2001). While an early study by Peters et al. (1989) proposed returns that could compete with other commercial uses, many authors have since cautioned against extrapolating 'per-hectare' estimates from sample plots to large stretches of tropical rainforests. Downward sloping demand for NTFP, uncertainty concerning sustainable supply, and increasing costs of production and transportation are all limiting factors. For example, the net annual returns to gathering a major international commodity like Brazil nuts in Bolivia amount to no more than $0.5 per hectare (Bojanic, 2001).

Likewise, eco–tourism is only locally important. Although tropical (moist) forests are generally not very attractive to tourists because of the humid climate and their limited scenic value (compared to, say, East African game parks), recreation and tourism have the potential to generate foreign exchange (for an optimistic case study, refer to Ruitenbeek, 1989). However, the role of eco-tourism in promotion of forest conservation will most likely remain small, and its value will fall on a per hectare basis as more areas are made available for tropical forest re-creation.

Regulatory Services of Tropical Forests Tropical ecosystems provide a wide range of regulatory services. Watershed protection and the provision of hydrological services are clearly important examples in this respect. The surface of denuded forest areas may be compacted by rain—reducing infiltration, increasing run-off and lowering water quality. But exposing areas to the natural elements unprotected is but one possible form of land use after deforestating an area, and possibly not the optimal one. Types of land use other than forests can also provide hydrological services, albeit in varying degrees—compare seasonal cropping where the soil is bare during part of the year versus systems with year-round crop cover offering more protection (extensive livestock ranging systems or fruit tree orchards). Ground cover appears to matter more than canopy from an erosion perspective (Wiersum, 1984; Calder, 1998).

Apart from protection against soil erosion and sedimentation, tropical forests are believed to provide a more balanced supply of water when there are seasonal differences in precipitation because the soil acts as a sponge. However, again, it is important to recognize that tropical forests are not the only ecosystem capable of producing these effects—the nature of the succeeding land use is very important. Equally importantly, as argued by Calder (1998), evapotranspiration rates of forests are high, possibly decreasing water supply from forested areas and lowering water tables. Evapotranspiration rates also have an impact on rainfall patterns, but Calder (1998) argues that it is too simplistic to relate forest conservation to enhanced rainfall. Many other variables will be affected by changes in land use as well, including surface albedo, air circulation, cloudiness and temperature. For this reason, the magnitude and sign of the regulatory effect is unclear a priori, but recent consensus is that this effect is likely to be of minor importance.

Another regulatory service identified in the literature involves <u>pollination</u> services provided by forest pollinators (mainly insects) and pest control by forest 'predators' preying on potential crop pests. Such pollinators and predators depend on forest habitat for their survival, and their disappearance would impact wild ecosystems and agricultural production systems alike. There exist estimates for the value of natural pollination and natural pest control in the U.S. (both run well into the billions of dollars on an annual basis), but there is little information for developing countries (see Reid, 1999). The lack of more information is no surprise, perhaps, as assessing benefits of these services requires insight in potential substitutes for them, which is incomplete at best.[4] Finally, offsetting, and in some regions certainly dominating, the beneficial effects of pollination and pest control are the crop damages caused by forest animals.

A final regulatory service, <u>storage of the greenhouse gas</u> carbon dioxide CO_2, is probably the most important non-market benefit associated with tropical forest conservation. The Intergovernmental Panel on Climate Change (IPCC) provides overviews of estimates of the social costs of CO_2 emissions in different decades (Houghton et al., 1996). It does not endorse any particular range of values for the marginal damages of CO_2 emissions, but cites published estimates of discounted future damage of US$5–$150 per metric ton of carbon emitted, depending on, among other things, the discount rate applied to weight future costs.

Work by Tol (2002a,b) highlights the uncertainty associated with approximating the damages of climate change, and also illustrates the far-reaching distributional effects. Simply put, a $1°$ C increase in global temperature is likely to result in winners (e.g. OECD countries, China) and losers (many developing countries). Depending on how regional impacts are aggregated the net effect of such a temperature increase may be negative, positive or zero. Tol suggests that climate change policy is 'essentially a problem of justice' (Tol, 2002b: 157), and argues that the economics of climate change have hardly progressed enough to be useful for policymakers.

Nevertheless, estimates of the price of carbon are used. Mainstream estimates are typically in the range of US$10–$25 per metric ton of C, and these numbers correspond well with current prices paid on the European carbon trading market (€22 per ton of C in August 2005). Accepting these

---

[4] There is evidence that some substitution possibilities do exist. For example, when a pollinating bee disappeared from a region in China where apples were grown on large-scale apple orchards, farmers switched from natural pollination to hand pollination. Interestingly, they were unwilling to return to natural pollination when that option was offered later.

numbers as the benchmark and assuming a release of some 50–140 metric tons after deforestation, the costs amount to $50 to $3,500 per hectare, or $25–$175 ha^{-1} yr^{-1} (using a 5% discount rate). These estimates may even have to be adjusted upward for some areas that hold larger quantities of carbon (up to 250 tons for closed primary forests), and possibly in light of recent arguments that the shadow price of stored carbon may be as high as $34 per ton (Clarkson, 2000). Assuming that society agrees on a moderately ambitious emissions path, Kopp (2004) argues that the shadow price of C may rise from $20 in 2010 to $50 in 2020.[5]

Habitat, Biodiversity and Non-use Values Tropical forests are home not only to millions of people for whom forests may be an integrated part of economic, social and religious life, but also to millions of animal and plant species, most of which are endemic to the local forest ecosystem. Various species have both use and non-use (preservation) value, and diversity per se may also have a role of play in ecosystem functioning and service provision.

The direct use values of biodiversity have attracted the attention of economists and ecologists alike, not in the least spurred on by the belief that demonstration of high values provides a convincing argument against human intervention in 'vulnerable' ecosystems. Thus Leakey and Lewin (1996), for example, describe how lucrative and important the drugs Vincristine and Vinblastine, alkaloids from the rosy periwinkle from Madagascar, have been in curing acute lymphocytic leukaemia and Hodgkin's disease. The rainforest may be a valuable source of new medicines, and searching for these uses is usually referred to as 'biodiversity prospecting'.

Consider pharmaceutical uses. There are some 250,000 species of higher plants, and approximately 125,000 of these are found in tropical regions. To date about 47 major drugs have come from tropical plants. Simpson et al. (1996) have investigated the (potential) industrial, agricultural and pharmaceutical values of biodiversity hotspots. Even under the most optimistic assumptions, the value of marginal species is small, less than $10,000 at best. As the number of species increases, the value of marginal species falls—from almost $3,000, when there are 250,000 species, to a negligible amount when there are more than one million. If the value of marginal species is small, then, by extension, so is the value of a marginal hectare in biodiversity prospecting.

---

[5] Reiterating our earlier statement: these numbers should be treated with great caution. For example, while the estimates in the text are derived from cost estimates associated with certain pre-determined abatement scenarios (i.e. based on certain assumptions with respect to abatement), there is another approach that advocates a cost–benefit perspective. Nordhaus and Yang (1996) use an integrated assessment model to solve for the 'optimal abatement path' and find that optimal abatement is only slightly more ambitious than 'business as usual.' Shadow prices of carbon along such an optimal path slowly increase from only $4 (in 2010) to $15 (in 2050). However, optimal abatement implies balancing of marginal benefits and costs, and the uncertainty about costs and benefits is daunting (see also Manne and Richels, 2004).

Simpson et al. (1996) have computed maximum willingness to pay for bio-diversity prospecting for a range of 'hotspots' and their upper bound estimates range from $0.2 to no more than $20 (in Ecuador). Barbier and Aylward (1996) also conclude 'the potential economic returns from pharmaceutical prospecting of biodiversity are on their own insufficient justification for the establishment of protected areas in developing countries.'[6]

Obviously, limited direct use value does not imply that the economic value of biodiversity is modest. For example, ecosystem stability and resilience may be positively linked to diversity (Perrings, 1998). However, empirical research on this topic is still in its infancy, with most empirical work focusing on simple ecosystems (e.g. grasslands) under rather controlled conditions.

In addition to direct and indirect use values, 'non-use values' (including cultural values) are also important. Many people derive utility from the knowledge that tropical forests exist and are home to many species with which we share the earth, even though they will never visit these places themselves or intend to 'use' them otherwise. By using stated preference methods such non-use values may be approximated, although this approach continues to be an issue that divides the scientific community. Working with U.S. respondents, Kramer and Mercer (1997) estimated that preservation of global tropical forests had a one-time value of US$1.9–$2.8 × 10^9 ($21–$31 per household), or annual value of only $95–$140 million (using a 5% discount rate). Conservatively multiplying by four to take into account Canada, Australia, New Zealand and Western Europe yields an estimate of annual existence value of $380–$560 million. Assuming constant marginal non-use values and dividing by the total tropical forest area (about 1,750 million ha in 1990), we arrive at an annual per hectare value of approximately $0.2–0.32 per ha. Dividing instead by the total area of tropical rainforest (about 720 million ha), existence value per hectare rises to $0.52–0.78 per year. Since non-use values are likely to decline at the margin as the forest stock increases, the marginal preservation value is even lower than the average preservation value.

Assessment of Outcomes and Methods

How would economists use the information about ES to inform policymakers about land use policies? The standard approach would be to (i) quantify these services and attach a monetary value to them, and (ii) aggregate these values to obtain an estimate of the 'total economic value' of sustainable tropical forest management. Forest valuation, then, enables policymakers at least in theory to make informed trade-offs about the benefits of conservation of forests versus

---

[6] In a more recent paper by Rausser and Small (2000), the implications of the work of Simpson et al. are disputed. By adding efficient search to the theoretical model, Rausser and Small argue that the value of hotspots can be increased enormously. (See Costello, 2003 for a critical assessment of this claim).

those of alternative land use options. We will pursue this approach in Box 13.1, on p. 428–30.

It is noteworthy to point out that while tropical forests provide a wide range of ecosystem services, from the discussion above, the marginal value of forest conservation appears rather modest (something that will be confirmed by the numerical example on p. 429). With the important exception of carbon sequestration, the aggregate per hectare value of production, regulatory and habitat services is small. Hence, tropical forests may have a hard time 'competing for space' even in the absence of market failure.

While forest services are perhaps essential (infinitely valuable perhaps) for mankind, it should be no surprise that a natural upper bound for the value of forest conservation is defined by the budget constraint. But why are estimated values so low? The predominant reason, presumably, is that forest areas are not yet scarce. Rapid deforestation rates notwithstanding, there are still hundreds of millions of hectares of tropical forest. The non-use values generated by these hectares are essentially public goods—hectares of nature serve all. The ecotourism opportunities of distinct forest areas are substitutes in consumption, with different forest areas competing for customers. It is expected that as more of the tropical forest is converted to other land uses, the costs of further conversion (the value of foregone ecosystem and other non-timber amenities) will increase as well. At some point, the marginal costs of additional land conversion will equal or exceed marginal benefits, and no further deforestation of tropical forests should occur.

However, there are several caveats and potential problems associated with the economist's approach and, depending on one's politics, these caveats might well pose insurmountable problems. In this section we will present a brief overview of various relevant issues in an effort to qualify some of the numerical results that follow, and emphasize that current low estimates of the value of forest services should be treated with caution. First, note that distributional concerns have been ignored thus far—one dollar of surplus generated by cattle farming in the hand of a large farmer is considered equally valuable as one dollar of surplus earned with rattan collection in the hands of a forest dweller. This is a straightforward application of the Kaldor–Hicks hypothetical compensation principle—if winners of certain activities (such as deforestation) earn more than enough to potentially offset the losers, then that activity is desirable. Economists then assume that distributional concerns can be tackled later, for example by taxing the farmer and compensating the forest dweller. But if the proper institutions for making actual compensation transfers are not in place in large parts of the world where tropical forests are found, then it is an open question whether distributional issues can really be ignored when we are interested in welfare comparisons. Since hundreds of millions of very poor people rely on access to forest resources for their survival, and alleviation of their poverty is a widely supported objective, this is a particularly pressing concern.

Second, the discussion thus far has severely downplayed the many uncertainties that surround deforestation. Ecological feedback effects can (but need not) have substantial effects at both the local, regional and perhaps global scale. Some ecological systems have threshold effects such that relatively small causes can trigger large consequences. Moreover, such consequences may, to a large extent, be irreversible due to hysteresis effects. It remains to be seen whether such concerns are germane to tropical deforestation, and in the interim it might therefore be advisable to err on the cautious side when converting forests. The precautionary principle certainly suggests this, and conventional economic science has few alternative concepts to guide social decision-making when trying to come to terms with unforeseen outcomes of unknown probabilities. One potentially useful concept in this context may be quasi-option value (e.g. Albers, 1996; Albers et al., 1996).

Third, and related to the issue above, when we account for uncertainty in forest conservation it becomes evident that we are not really interested in how the value of certain forest services may fluctuate over time. Rather, society should care about the overall risk of its total investment portfolio, of which natural forests are only one element. How are fluctuations in the value of forest services correlated to fluctuations in other portfolio components? This issue appears essentially unknown and requires more research.

Fourth, there now exists a large body of experimental literature that suggests that people value gains and losses differently, even though economic theory postulates that gains and losses should be valued identically (apart, possibly, from an income effect). Knetsch (1993) notes that people evaluate gains and losses not strictly in terms of end states, but also in terms of changes from some reference situation—say, the current forest stock. Willingness to pay (WTP) for forest conservation may therefore be quite different from willingness to accept (WTA) compensation for ongoing deforestation. If indifference curves are indeed 'kinked' at the endowment level, as suggested by some of the empirical evidence, then the issue of who owns the forest becomes of paramount importance. Are tropical forests owned by sovereign nations, or are they part of a global heritage for which shared ownership and responsibility applies? WTA for deforestation is unbounded by current income, and could well exceed the gains from further forest conversion.

Fifth, and perhaps most importantly, while the problem of valuing regulatory functions is intrinsically related to the diversity of effects and consequences, and the uncertainties that surround them, a major problem in valuing habitat functions of tropical forests is rooted in ethics. The species-area curve may be used to relate deforestation rates to extinction rates, and it is clear that there exist alternative philosophical stances on trading-off species versus human welfare. Conventional economics need not take pre-eminent status when deciding about nature (Johansson-Stenman, 1998). As argued by Sagoff (1988): 'it is not just a matter of balancing interests with interests, it is a matter of balancing interests with morality, and balancing one morality with another morality.' Common (1995) also notes that economics is particularly important in developing instruments to achieve certain objectives (such that these objectives are reached cost effectively), but not necessarily to determine the objectives themselves.

In addition to these rather generic concerns about valuation of forest services, there are many other practical issues that emerge when balancing the benefits of sustainable forest management against those of other forms of land use—particularly about time trends of key variables. We will consider this in Box 13.1 when we present data for the Atlantic zone of Costa Rica. Regarding this case study it is, however, important to recall that the benefits of carbon sequestration are highly uncertain (the numbers in the case study may be a serious over- or underestimate of reality). With these caveats in mind, it is left up to the reader to decide whether forest valuation represents a useful exercise or not.

Sources of Market Failure and Related Policies

Why do we generally not observe socially optimal levels of forest conservation in reality? Given our knowledge of the direct and underlying causes of deforestation, why do sovereign governments not implement policies and institutional structures to achieve such optimal levels? As we have indicated earlier, excessive deforestation is the consequence of various types of market failures. First, we describe the main types of market failures and potential policy approaches to address them. Given the relative importance of international spillover effects highlighted earlier, our discussion about policies in the next section focuses largely on this particular type of market failure. Some policy issues related to other market failures are also included in the discussion.

Sources of Market Failure

Several sources of market failure in forest management can be distinguished. To begin with, the lack of a complete set of forward markets, in particular, missing markets for forest services accruing beyond the local level may lead to regional and global externalities (i.e. spillover benefits such as carbon sequestration, watershed protection) not being considered in forest management decisions.

Other sources of market failure may induce inefficiencies in forest management even at the local level. A major failure source comes from improperly designed property right regimes and associated problems of tenure insecurity. Ideally, to provide incentives for efficient forest management, property rights should be universal (i.e. clearly defined for all scarce resources), exclusive

---

Box 13.1 UNCOMPENSATED SPILLOVER EFFECTS—AN EXAMPLE FROM COSTA RICA

In this section we will numerically illustrate some of the main issues raised above, and compare the total economic value of forest services to the benefits that can be obtained when converting the land to some other use—agriculture in this case. This obviously requires information on forest values, but also on the benefits of agricultural conversion. We briefly deal with both issues in turn, using data from the Atlantic zone of Costa Rica (a study region of some 320,000 ha, for details and caveats refer to Bulte et al., 2002).

Benefits of Agricultural Expansion

The benefits of agricultural expansion (or the opportunity cost of forest conservation) are approximated by a large LP land management model, discussed at length in Schipper et al. (2000). The model combines detailed agronomic information and economic data (demand for commodities, supply of factors, transport cost, etc.). The total land base L can be allocated to either agricultural land A or remain as forest area F. The focus is on maximizing the present value of net social benefits, or the sum of consumer and producer surplus. We assume a benevolent dictator exists that can freely allocate land to its most productive use—the use that maximizes welfare. It is assumed that those areas most profitable for agriculture are taken in production first. Then, as the agricultural area expands, increasingly less attractive areas are encroached upon. Upon applying a step size of 1,000 ha, the LP model can be used to simulate land use and compute its returns on a per-hectare basis as the agricultural frontier moves out. This simulated output is then used as an input in a regression analysis. We explain the 'shadow price' of land in agriculture P^A as a function of the agricultural land base A. This yields as the preferred specification:

$$\ln(P^A) = 15.8 - 0.89\ln(A), \tag{1}$$

where both coefficients are significant at the 1% level. Plotting equation (1) in a graph illustrates how the value of agricultural land changes as deforestation proceeds.

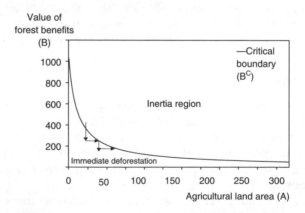

The line in this figure is the estimated shadow price of agricultural land, which is a decreasing function of the land base in production. While the benefits of cropping in prime regions are very high (think of growing bananas or palm heart on preferred soils), it is evident that returns to agricultural expansion drop sharply after the most suitable soils

Box 13.1 (*Continued*)

have been taken in production. The per hectare returns to extensively managed natural pasture systems, the flat end of the shadow price curve, are low.

Benefits of Forest Conservation

We assume the study region in question to be sufficiently small for the marginal value of forest conservation to be constant. We use best available evidence published in the literature. Typically these data are based on average values of the ES discussed above—preferably for the study area but if such information was unavailable we used evidence for Costa Rica or, if that was lacking, for Central America. Bulte et al., equate forest conservation with sustainable forest management (i.e. they allow some timber and NTFP extraction and ecotourism), and as a baseline approximation they assume that the total economic value of forest management amounts to $200 ha^{-1} yr^{-1}. This number can be broken down in its elements as in Table 1. From an economic perspective, the main ES are sustainable timber production and carbon storage.

Table 1 Annual Benefits of Sustainable Forest Management, AZ Costa Rica

Item	$ ha^{-1} year^{-1}
Production Function	**$75**
– Sustainable timber harvests	60
– Sustainable extraction of non-timber forest products	10
– Sustainable ecotourism	5
Regulatory Function	**$105**
– Carbon uptake and storage*	105
Habitat Function	**$20**
– Existence value*	10
– Biological prospecting (incl. Pharmaceutical value)*	10

Source: Bulte et al., (2002). * indicates an international spillover benefit.

The benefits of forest conservation that are external to the domestic country but spillover to other countries are considerable. Costa Rica is able to capture some of the rents associated with bioprospecting (through a deal between INBIO and the pharmaceutical company Merck), but that amounts to only a part of the estimate of the full rent of $10 ha^{-1}. Table 1 suggests that more than 60% of the benefits of forest conservation do not materialize in Costa Rica itself—the country that has to bear the cost of forest conservation in terms of foregone agricultural production.

How much Forest should be Conserved?

Assume that Costa Rica ignores transboundary benefits. Then, the domestic benefits of sustainable forest management are between $75–85 ha^{-1} yr^{-1}, depending on how much of the rents of bioprospecting Costa Rica is able to capture. By balancing the returns to agricultural expansion and forest conservation at the margin, the planner in Costa Rica should *deforest all land* for zero bioprospecting rents, but retain some 120,000 ha of forest for equal sharing with the pharmaceutical company. Two observations stand out. First,

---

Box 13.1 (*Continued*)

while returns to bioprospecting are modest, compared to some of the other items in Table 1, they make a large difference in terms of optimal land allocation. This is due to the fact that the function relating the shadow price of agricultural land to the area under cultivation is non-linear and virtually flat after 100,000 hectares of agricultural land (when additional deforestation is for extensive cattle ranching only). Second, the domestic optimum in the presence of bioprospecting rents is close to the current forest area in the region, which comprises of some 80,000–100,000 ha. In contrast, if Costa Rica is fully compensated for the external benefits of forest conservation, such that these benefits add up to \$200 ha^{-1} yr^{-1}, the economically optimal forest stock is 176,000 ha. From a global perspective, therefore, it is optimal to abandon some of the cattle ranches and let them convert back to forests.

(i.e. all benefits and costs from owning and using the resource should accrue to the owner), transferable from one owner to the other in a voluntary exchange, and enforceable (i.e. secure from involuntary seizure or encroachment by others) (Tietenberg, 1988). As will be discussed in more detail in the following section on p. 436ff, property rights could in principle be allocated to private individuals, local commun- ities and user groups, or the state. In all three cases, however, formal property regimes often degenerate into situations of de facto open access or at least a situ-ation where enforcement is weak. This may be due to policy failure, but it is also a consequence of the fact that forests exhibit inherent characteristics of common-pool resources (e.g. extraction of NTFPs is rival, but exclusion is often difficult and costly), and public goods (e.g. ecological services are often non-rival in consumption and non-excludable). It is well known that open access leads to an over-exploitation of the forest resource as individual users do not take into account the effect of their use on the availability of the resource to other users, resulting in the so-called 'Tragedy of the Commons' described by Hardin (1968).[7] Thus, open access may induce land races as farmers clear forest to prevent others from claiming the land (Angelsen, 1995, 1999) or to benefit from land speculation (Clarke et al., 1993). Tenure insecurity also contributes to favoring short-term benefits over long-run investments. In some cases, property rights are well-defined and enforced, but not transferable, reducing the incentives for forest owners to consider the impacts beyond their own lifespan.

A third source of market failure is market imperfections, including imperfect competition or imperfect capital and land markets. For example, lack of access to credit may prevent local forest users from using efficient technologies (e.g. improved cooking stoves) or sustainable practices (e.g. reforestation, plantations). This is aggravated where tenure insecurity prevents the use of forest land as collateral. As a consequence, local forest dwellers may end up in a vicious

---

[7] The term 'Tragedy of the Commons' is really a misnomer as the situation described by Hardin is one of open access rather than common property.

cycle of poverty and excessive resource extraction to satisfy subsistence needs (the so-called 'fuelwood trap') (Wunder, 2000). Similarly, land market imperfections may prevent farmers from fully internalizing long-run effects of their actions.

A fourth source of market failure related to the above is that private and social discount rates often differ (Tietenberg, 1988). For example, tenure insecurity, poverty, economic and political risks may cause individual farmers or local communities to discount the future more than a social planner. This is not to say that governments will necessarily discount optimally (and it should be mentioned that the 'socially optimal' discount rate is the object of much debate). For example, politicians may take their decisions on the basis of relatively short election cycles. Finally, market failure may also be caused by a lack of information or knowledge about local needs, ecological conditions, and environmentally friendly technologies. Frequently, availability of information is asymmetric, with local people likely to have better information about local conditions, and governments potentially having better access to scientific and technological knowledge (Platteau, 2003).

For some of the above sources of market failures, the definition of appropriate policies is in principle straightforward, but policy failure often prevents their adoption. Rather than correcting market imperfections, government intervention has often aggravated the existing incentives for excessive forest exploitation, for example, through public road-building, settlement schemes, credit and fiscal incentives, and macroeconomic policies (Wunder, 2000).[8]

As stated earlier, probably the most severe source of market failure is the fact that many forest services, particularly the ecological benefits accruing beyond the local level, are not marketed. For example, timber prices in most cases do not reflect the ecological costs of deforestation, leading to excessive logging. Similarly, land use decisions do not consider the ecological impacts of deforestation leading to excessive forest conversion into agriculture or other uses. Resolving this problem is particularly difficult for international spillover effects, as costs and benefits of alternative approaches are distributed very unevenly between individual countries, especially between developed and developing countries. We turn to these issues in the following section.

International Forest Conservation Policies

In the past, policies to address the problem of missing markets for spillover effects have mainly consisted of (i) command-and-control regulations dictating specific land uses, and (ii) remedial measures to reverse or reduce damages (Pagiola and Platais, 2002). Both approaches are problematic. Regulations face

[8] See also ch. 4 by Deacon and Mueller in this volume on the political economy of property rights formation.

severe enforcement problems and impose high costs on poor land users relying on the forest for their livelihood (Pagiola and Platais, 2002; Sawhney and Engel, 2003). Moreover, in the context of international spillovers the scope for the command and control approach is limited in post-colonial times. Remedial measures are often imperfect and far more expensive than preventive measures (Pagiola and Platais, 2002). More recently, three main alternatives have emerged, and together they encompass the entire range from the carrot to the stick.

Turning to the stick first, within the International Tropical Timber Organization (ITTO), consumer and producer countries agreed to ban international trade in unsustainably harvested wood from tropical forests after the year 2000. Many tropical timber countries were opposed to this form of intervention, claiming that trade restrictions are unfair as temperate zone logging faces less stringent restrictions, and because many countries in the temperate zone have already deforested their lands in the past. Moreover, when sustainability requirements are too stringent, it was feared that sustainable forestry becomes less competitive as a land use option, and will be replaced by alternative types of land use (such as plantation agriculture). The claim that trade restrictions are detrimental for development is harder to evaluate. While banning trade might come at a considerable short-term cost for certain underdeveloped regions, it is evident that banning trade might raise welfare in exporting regions when harvesting takes place in a so-called second-best setting (e.g. Brander and Taylor, 1997). In light of abundant evidence of illegal logging (e.g. Kaimowitz, 2003) and legal logging distorted through corruption and rent seeking (Ross, 2001), trade bans on timber from unsustainable practices may be welfare improving for exporting countries—albeit obviously not in the interest of illegal loggers or corrupt politicians.

While some progress has been made to promote sustainable logging, it is clear that most of the forest areas in the world still do not meet the ITTO criteria. Worse yet, even if ITTO meets its stated objectives, it will not stop deforestation. Most tropical deforestation is not caused directly by logging. Logging might badly damage natural forests and compromise their ability to provide some of the functions discussed above, and it might 'open up' closed forests and make them accessible for agriculturalists of various sorts. But Barbier et al., (1990) argue that only a small fraction of the deforested areas, mainly in South East Asia, can be directly linked to the international timber trade. For the political economy behind forest destruction by logging, refer to Ross (2001). Conversion for agriculture (be it by smallholders or cattle ranchers) is typically more important than timber harvesting (e.g. Myers, 1994). To tackle these processes requires implementing policies that go beyond the forestry sector.[9] However, for 'Northern' countries, promoting trade measures that restrict the

[9] Indeed, when sustainable logging policies undermine the profitability of timber harvesting in the South, it could inadvertently promote deforestation by raising the relative profitability of other, more destructive land uses.

flow of 'Southern' timber is relatively inexpensive. Moreover, it is clear that there are parties in 'the North' that actually benefit from such measures.[10]

The second approach to forest conservation consists of indirect interventions.[11] These take the form of either re-directing labor and capital away from destructive activities (e.g. through agricultural intensification or the provision of alternative income sources), or of encouraging commercial activities that supply ecosystem services as joint products (e.g. ecotourism) (Ferraro and Simpson, 2002). At the international level, examples of indirect approaches include forest sector policies, which often occur through financing of projects in the South. During the 1990s, this involved a substantial investment of some U.S.$2 billion. Where did the money go? The forestry assistance portfolio has shifted away from traditional forest sector development, forest plantations and agroforestry towards protected areas and conservation. A large share has been allocated to the protection of specific forests. In general these efforts have met with little success in reversing land use trends.[12] Much of the remaining funds were used to finance pilot projects that provide technical assistance to forest product harvesters and farmers, and localized short-term subsidies for sustainable forest management and sustainable agriculture. Another item that looms large on the budget are activities like preparation of plans and programs, conferences, seminars, public relations activities and information systems. While education and awareness building may be effective in inducing more positive attitudes towards conservation, it is not clear whether these will translate into changes in behaviour in the field (Sawhney and Engel, 2003).[13] Too often these activities are treated as substitutes rather than complements of economic and regulatory mechanisms that may influence actual behavior (Kaimowitz, 2000).

Most of the money has been allocated to either sectoral forestry/conservation approaches, or to rather symbolic activities. This allocation of funds has been largely unsuccessful in containing deforestation rates. Kaimowitz concludes 'it takes a hardy soul or a strong imagination to argue that forestry projects had

[10] Engel (2004) shows that a complete ban on timber from unsustainable logging, given costly monitoring, is optimal for the importing country only under the restrictive conditions of a corner solution. Where these conditions are not satisfied, bans may be motivated by protectionism.

[11] There are various reasons why forest conservation funds have been allocated to a sectoral forest approach, rather than to other uses where they might have been more effective. For example, there are vested sectoral and institutional interests. Technical forestry assistance provides jobs and funds for international experts, and investments in equipment may open up new markets for domestic industries. Political expediency might also have mattered—allocating funds to the forests sends an unambiguous warm-glow signal to the general public.

[12] Efforts to protect specific forests have typically been marginally successful. While there is evidence of somewhat less clearing in protected areas (e.g. Deininger and Minten, 1996), most protected areas also suffer from serious encroachment. Those areas that do not are often just too remote to encroach upon.

[13] In some cases, indiscriminate increases in education and awareness building may even be counterproductive, as they reduce the potential of third-party actors (NGOs, government) to intervene in response to specific local deforestation threats (Engel and López, 2004).

much effect.' This assessment is consistent with evaluations of the international Tropical Forest Action Plan (TFAP, see Winterbottom, 1990) and, more recently, World Bank lending in the 1990s (World Bank, 2000). This begs the question why past efforts have been unsuccessful.

The obvious response is that policies have not been used to directly address the root cause of deforestation: market failure. Very few of the underlying causes of deforestation, summarized in section 2 (see pp. 417–18. (e.g. relative prices, infrastructure investments, credit policies) can effectively be tackled through sectoral forest policies—they require a multi-sector approach rather than a rigid focus on the forest. Moreover, as argued by Ferraro (2001), indirect interventions are often complex to implement and inflexible, and their effects are often hard to predict due to all sorts of context-dependent ambiguities—recall the complex effect of agricultural intensification on forest conversion. Indirect interventions also suffer from a mismatch between policies and temporal and spatial dimensions of ecosystem conservation.

The third policy approach that has been gaining attention recently consists of direct payments for environmental services (PES). This involves monetary transfers for transboundary ecological services. Ferraro and Simpson (2002) demonstrate that PES are likely to be far more cost-effective than indirect approaches. Moreover, given the ambiguous evidence on the effects of agricultural intensification and alternative income provision outlined in section 2 (See pp 417–18, the effectiveness of indirect approaches in combating deforestation remains unclear. In some cases, such approaches may even be counterproductive (López, 1998; Ferraro and Kiss, 2002; Ferraro, 2001; Kiss, 2003). We now review the PES approach in more detail.

Direct Interventions: Payments for Environmental Services

PES are market-based mechanisms for forest conservation. Under this approach, NGOs, governments, or international donor agencies make periodic payments to individuals or groups that supply environmental services (e.g. local communities protecting forests), and these payments are conditional on the services supplied. In this way, externalities are at least partly internalized by local people in their resource management decisions. Moreover, compensating local resource users, which are characterized by a high incidence of poverty and strong dependence on forests for their livelihood, can help alleviate poverty and compensate users for the private benefits foregone from reducing extraction of forest products (Pagiola et al., 2002). PES include, for example, conservation concessions, payments for carbon sequestration under the Clean Development Mechanism, bio-prospecting, land leases and easements, or performance payments and tax relief. Such initiatives have been increasingly implemented in developed countries (e.g. United States, Australia, Germany) and developing countries (e.g. Costa Rica, Mexico, Chile, Guatemala, Madagascar, India). Box 13.2 describes a

---

Box 13.2 PAYING FOR ECOSYSTEM SERVICES; THE COSTA RICA EXPERIENCE

Costa Rica has benefited from its forest resources as a means to attract foreign tourists. Tourism is now the second largest contributor to GDP. Because of this direct and important link between forest resources and income, Costa Rica has a strong incentive to protect its forest base. To this end, the country has introduced a 'market-based' approach, the so-called PSA system, by which thousands of landowners receive direct payments for the ES provided by the forests on their land. PSA is arguably the most elaborate PES system in the developing world, and it took years of policy debate and consensus building to prepare its implementation. Services included in PSA are not only domestic benefits (such as water protection and enhancing scenic beauty of the landscape) but, interestingly, also trans-boundary benefits (carbon sequestration, biodiversity conservation).

The programme aims to reach agreements with private landowners to cover an area of 100,000 hectares. Selected landowners may qualify for three different contracts: forest conservation contracts ($210/ha in 5 years); sustainable forest management contracts ($327/ha in 5 years); and reforestation contracts ($537/ha in 5 years). These numbers are somewhat lower than the estimates of the value of Costa Rican ES as summarized in Table 1, but nevertheless represent a significant first step towards closing the gap between the value of forest services and the income they generate.

The main source of funding for the system is a domestic fuel tax, which raises some $7–9 million annually (Rodriquez Zuniga, 2003). Other important sources of funding for the programme are 'Environmental Service Certificates' (issued for voluntary contributions by the private sector), agreements with hydro-electric companies, and support from the international community. The international community has placed a high degree of confidence in the Costa Rican system and institutional framework. For example, to support the programme and facilitate its implementation, the World Bank has provided a $32 million credit line and the Global Environmental Facility (GEF) has given an $8,3 million grant.

By bundling the various services and base payments on the aggregate value of four key services, the PSA provides 'relatively high payments which are used to promote not only plantation forestry but also regeneration of secondary forests and other degraded landscapes' (Rodriquez Zuniga, 2003). There is evidence that the system is a success as forest cover in Costa Rica is now increasing.

---

leading example of a PES system implemented in a developing country: the case of Costa Rica.

Recent evidence indicates that low-income farmers and communities are more likely to benefit from PES schemes when they have secure tenure rights, and when the schemes support not just pure conservation, but also other environmentally-friendly activities, such as sustainable forestry, agroforestry, or eco-tourism (Rosa et al., 2003). There are, however, important aspects of the implementation of direct conservation payments in developing countries, that still need to be better understood. First, property rights over forests in developing countries are often still weakly defined or poorly enforced. This raises the issue of how PES can assure that the forest will not be degraded by actors other than the contracting party under PES (e.g. industry, other communities). Second, the geographic and infrastructure characteristics of developing countries imply that monitoring of actual environmental services provided is very costly. This implies that there is a potential for moral hazard, which is reinforced by weak property rights and when dealing with groups of individuals such as local communities. Third, rent-seeking is an important problem, both by individuals within the community as well as by local governments. Thus, it is important to consider how an equitable distribution of PES can be assured. Providing environmental services in one area may lead to an increase in environmental degradation in other areas as activities are simply shifted geographically (the so-called 'slippage').[14]

Finally, an important issue concerns whether payments for ecological services should go to governments or NGOs and local communities. The impact of PES on the realization of conservation objectives depends on who controls the management and conversion of forests. When choices of local communities are an important determinant of the fate of forests, then PES must trickle down to the field level to affect behavior and be effective. Under such circumstances, implementing a PES system may align conservation and rural development objectives. In contrast, when national government policies are a key driver of deforestation, it may be more effective and efficient to transfer payments to the central level. This would provide an incentive to consider forests as a legitimate part of the national development portfolio, and gives the government maximum flexibility in choosing how to regulate this asset. Note that such transfers, based on the realized contribution to forest conservation, could result in a conflict between conservation and rural development objectives. This could happen when the government imposes additional restrictions on forest use by rural communities to protect the foreign transfer flow, but fails to plow these transfers back into rural development schemes.

Property Right Regimes and their Relation to Market Imperfections and Policy Impacts

The degree to which market failures occur, and the difficulties associated with implementing different types of policy interventions, depend on the property right regimes in place. Formally, four basic property right regimes can be distinguished: (i) open access, (ii) state property, (iii) common property, and (iv) private property. Mixed forms, such as co-management as a mixture of state and common property also exist.[15] White and Martin (2002) estimate that 71 per cent of

[14] In addition, when demand for ecological services is downward sloping and if certain suppliers of these services have market power, there is an incentive to restrict supplies in order to raise prices or transfers (see Stahler, 1996). PES could, in theory, be bad for conservation if this is the case.

[15] Another mixed form, frequently found in Africa, is 'communal ownership', where primary forests and uncultivated woodlands are owned by the local community and controlled by village authorities, while exclusive use rights over cultivated lands are assigned to individual community members (Otsuka and Place, 2001, ch. 1).

the forests in developing countries are still owned and administered by the government. Fourteen per cent are estimated to be owned by local communities and indigenous groups, and another eight per cent are publicly owned, but reserved for communities and indigenous groups. The remaining 7 per cent of forests are privately held (White and Martin, 2002). In a different study, Scherr et al. (2002) estimate that at least 25 per cent of developing country forests are owned or administered by low-income forest communities.

However, de facto property rights may differ from formal, de jure property right regimes. Particularly, if property right enforcement is insufficient or ineffective, forests under state, common, or private property often degenerate into situations of de facto open access.

The consideration of property rights and their interlinkages with market failures and policy impacts is important because property right regimes have been subject to considerable change over the past decades. While forests have traditionally been considered state property in most countries, the last two decades have shown a strong tendency to either devolve rights and responsibilities over forest management to local communities (resulting in common property or co-management regimes) or private individuals (private property regime).

Property right regimes differ in their ability to reduce transaction costs (such as monitoring, enforcement, and information costs), to internalize externalities, and to deal with market imperfections. They also differ in their susceptibility to policy failure. Moreover, there may be important differences in distributive and social impacts between property right regimes. We now discuss the different regimes and the specific issues they involve.

Open Access

Clearly, open access (i.e. the complete absence of effective property rights) is the most problematic case to be considered. The inherent incentive for exploiting the resource before others do so is unlikely to be altered by any policy intervention aimed at reducing market failure (Otsuka and Place, 2001, ch. 1). Moreover, open access (or generally situations of weak property rights) may induce various types of strategic behavior aggravating deforestation. First, if deforestation by one agent (e.g. the state or the local community) reduces the profitability of forest clearing to the other agent, each agent may aim to 'squeeze the other' by clearing more themselves, leading to higher overall deforestation (Angelsen, 2001). Secondly, if resource users have to invest in costly exclusion of potential encroachers (due to a lack of government enforcement or weak definition of property rights), they may decide to increase the intensity of resource exploitation in order to lower the returns from encroachment (Hotte, 2001, 2002).

In some cases, property rights are made conditional on land clearing, adding a further incentive for excessive deforestation, both by those aiming to claim property rights (e.g. squatters) and those trying to prevent it (e.g. large landowners) (Alston et al., 1999).

Finally, the fact that de facto property rights are endogenous under open access regimes can lead to unexpected policy effects. For example, a rise in off-farm employment opportunities for local community members may increase the community's opportunity costs of fighting off commercial logging companies and thus increase deforestation (Engel and López, 2004). Similarly, a lower discount rate may in some cases increase deforestation by making it more costly for resource users to fight off potential encroachers (Hotte, 2001).[16]

State Property

A large proportion of developing country forests are still under state property. An advantage of the state property regime is that the state is more likely to internalize local and regional externalities as compared to individual households or communities. Governments may also have better access to scientific and technological knowledge. Moreover, policies to internalize international externalities (such as PES) may be easier to handle with the state as a single partner in the transaction, rather than a large number of local communities or farmers. In practice, however, state control has often failed to prevent the degradation of national forests because of the very high transaction costs and information problems associated with the design of effective usage rules, monitoring and enforcement at the local level (Arnold, 1998). Moreover, forest-dependent communities often have customary rights to the forest which cannot be ignored by the state. A lack of formalization of these rights under a state property regime induces a strong degree of tenure insecurity on part of local forest users.

As a consequence of these problems, state-owned forests frequently degenerate into open access resources, particularly in frontier areas that are located far from markets and government administrative centers (Hotte, 2001). There is increasing evidence showing that a large portion of forest conversion and degradation is associated with illegal activities, both by local communities or squatters and by commercial interests. For example, illegal logging was estimated to account for a substantial portion of total log production in many countries, ranging from 90 percent in Cambodia to 34 percent in Ghana (Smith, 2002).[17]

Clarke et al. (1993) shows that governments may optimally tolerate some illegal logging in the face of monitoring and enforcement costs. The failure of governments to enforce property rights is, however, not only due to the costliness

---

[16] A decrease in the discount rate increases the value of a sustainable land use to the first settler as well as the potential contestant. If the latter effect is strong enough, the first settler may decide to mine the resource to avoid a costly conflict with the contestant (Hotte, 2001).

[17] As the author notes these estimates should be taken as 'best guesses' only since derivation and year of estimation vary for the different country sources.

associated with monitoring and enforcement, but also with political economy considerations and policy failure. This is highlighted by recent evidence that illegal activities have not decreased (and may even have increased) in the aftermath of decentralization reforms, although the transfer of forest management responsibilities to local governments should have reduced monitoring and enforcement costs. For example, decentralization in Indonesia has led to an increase in 'illegal logging,' as district governments sanction timber extraction activities that would be considered illegal by the central government in order to generate local government taxes (Casson and Obidzinski, 2002).[18]

In general, reasons for policy failure to enforce property rights include the desire to relieve social pressure through settlement policies,[19] strong lobbying potential of large logging companies, as well as rent-seeking and corruption on part of government officials. Indonesia, again, is a case in point. Illegal logging under President Suharto was associated with several conglomerates and individuals with close connections to central government elite and key military figures (Casson and Obidzinski, 2002). Moreover, the exclusion of local communities from logging benefits during the Suharto era led local people to assist companies in logging outside concession boundaries in return for salary or rents (Casson and Obidzinski, 2004). The general move towards democracy and decentralization following the fall of Suharto has led local governments in the forest-rich provinces to tolerate illegal logging by local communities in times of economic crisis, and the withdrawal of army forces has led to an enforcement vacuum, often resulting in a situation of de facto open access. The informal timber sector, in some cases now legalized, is an important income source of district-level civilian and military bureaucracies (Casson and Obidzinski, 2004).

Clearly, state incentives to monitor and to prevent illegal activities are crucial to the implementation of any policy proposal oriented to internalize international spillovers. As illegal logging is often a symptom of deeper structural problems in the forest sector, potential strategies for combating it include the strengthening of judicial systems and the rule of the law and restructuring forest industries such that processing capacity does not exceed supply (USAID, 2002). Some countries have recently implemented innovative approaches to combat illegal logging. For example, Ecuador has created a Green Surveillance team (*Vigilancia Verde*)—financed with the proceeds from auctioning off seized illegal timber—in which public and private sector institutions cooperate to monitor illegal operations (USAID, 2002). In Cambodia, several international

---

[18] Palmer (2001) estimates that the scale of illegal logging more than doubled during the period of the Asian economic crisis (1996–8).

[19] Settlement schemes and colonization programmes in many countries have played the role of a social 'escape valve' to relieve discontent among the poor and avoid land reform policies in countries with high inequality in land distribution (Dorner and Thiesenhusen, as cited in Wunder, 2000, p. 44).

organizations set up a Forest Crime Monitoring Unit aimed at increasing accountability, transparency, and enforcement through representatives in various government organizations and log tracking. The 1996 policy reforms in Bolivia empower private citizens to inspect forest operations and denounce illegal activities, and reduce rent-seeking opportunities by allocating con cessions through public auctions and reducing forest officials' discretion in setting concession fees (USAID, 2002).

Whether the state will, however, adopt these or other measures to combat illegal logging and land conversion is essentially an issue of governance and corruption (see Ch. 4 by Deacon and Mueller in this volume). The Indonesian case highlights the fact that the local government or agency in charge needs to see a long-run stake in the protection of forests as an asset. The case of decentralized protected area management in Bahia, Brazil, provides a positive example where decentralization and eco-tourism opportunities have led to both environmental and economic benefits from forest conservation (Oliveira, 2002).

Common Property and Co-Management

As a consequence of state failure in sustainable forest management in the past, shrinking national budgets, and a general trend towards decentralization and participatory approaches, many countries have recently started devolving—at least partially—the rights and responsibilities over forest management to local communities or user groups. As Edmonds (2002, p. 1) states: '. . . nearly every country in the world is experimenting with some form of "Community Forestry" '. Devolution may result in a common property regime or some form of co-management. A potential advantage is that the collective management rules, informal courts and sanctions established by user groups can provide a cost-effective alternative to government control (McKean, 1995). Moreover, local communities may have better information about local conditions. Compared to private property, communities may be better able to deal with local externalities, to exploit risk-sharing benefits from exploiting the forest resources jointly, and to provide a more equitable distribution of benefits. Ostrom (1990) describes several empirical cases where communities have successfully managed common-pool resources. Edmonds (2002) provides econometric evidence that devolution of forests to local user groups in Nepal has reduced resource extraction by approximately 14 per cent, while citing evidence that deforestation and forest degradation had accelerated under previous state management.

Conceptual modeling and empirical evidence, however, clearly indicate that community-based forest management is not without problems and risks. First, communities, just as individual households, have no incentive per se to internalize regional or international externalities. Implementing policies to correct this market failure through PES, for example, are however further complicated when dealing with local communities rather than the state or individual farmers, including potential problems of free-riding and moral hazard.[20]

This is related to the second potential problem with community-based management. It is naive to think of local communities as homogenous groups, automatically acting in the interest of the whole. For example, evidence from Indonesia shows that, given rights to negotiate directly with companies over logging agreements, local communities often sell off the forest for short-term financial benefits at high environmental and social costs (Barr et al., 2001; Casson and Obidzinski, 2002; Engel et al., 2003). This is fostered by the fact that devolution is often incomplete in the sense that the state retains some rights over the forest or share of the benefits, leaving communities with reduced or uncertain incentives to consider the long-run effects of their actions. Moreover, achieving even a locally efficient level of resource management requires collective action on part of individual community members, that is, their ability to agree on, and enforce, a cooperative and efficient set of access and use rules (Ostrom, 1990). Otherwise, common property, similar to open access, would result in over-exploitation as each individual does not consider the impact of his action on resource availability to other users. Much literature has focused on the factors favoring the success of common property regimes. Small group size, social and cultural homogeneity, problem severity, high existing social capital, consistent impacts,[21] low discount rates, and low transaction costs are widely seen as conducive for collective action, while the effect of economic heterogeneity (e.g. wealth and asset distribution) remains much debated.[22]

Third, it has been shown that devolution may lead to rent-seeking activities by community elites and prevent the state from exercising an important role in assuring the inclusion of marginalized groups (Abraham and Platteau, 2002; Agrawal and Ostrom, 2002; Platteau and Gaspart, 2003; Platteau, 2003). There is empirical evidence that more powerful actors in the communities manipulate devolution outcomes in their own interest (Shackleton, et al., 2002), at least where the poor are not empowered enough to oppose pressures from the local elite (Platteau, 2003). This is highlighted by empirical evidence from India and Nepal, both countries with major nationwide devolution initiatives. Agarwal (2001) discusses how seemingly participatory institutions often exclude significant sections of the community, such as women. Kumar (2002) shows for the

[20] PES to local communities have been implemented, for example, in Costa Rica, Mexico, Guatemala, and Chile. They are also under development in Indonesia.

[21] 'Consistent impacts' refers to a situation where most individuals will be affected in similar ways by the proposed management changes.

[22] Baland and Platteau (1996) and Agrawal (2001) provide detailed reviews of this literature. Classic references include Runge (1986), Wade (1988), Ostrom (1990), Seabright (1993), Bardhan (1993a/b), Baland and Platteau (1997a/b, 1998). See also Mansuri and Rao (2003) for a detailed review of the evidence on community-based and community-driven development in a wider context.

state of Jharkhand in India that wealthier sections of the communities have benefited from the Joint Forest Management (JFM) program at the expense of the poor. Given a share in total benefits from state timber extraction, community rules now favor long-run timber benefits through forest closure and plantations of high-value species. As a consequence, poor forest-dependent households are marginalized as they suffer from the reduced availability of, and access to, NTFPs (Kumar, 2002). One should be careful, however, to generalize these results as they are likely to depend on initial forest conditions and the type of forest. For Nepal, Karmacharya et al. (2003) found that some communities under community forestry programs have been successful in creating specific pro-poor rules and incentives. By contrast, the parallel program of leasehold forestry which explicitly assigns rights over degraded forest only to groups of poor households has led to serious enforcement problems due to the lack of recognition of these rights by other community members (Karmachraya et al., 2003). The authors thus conclude that the government should share information about existing pro-poor provisions and encourage user groups to adopt similar rules.

The more favorable equity outcomes in the Nepalese case as compared to India, may be due to the fact that timber production for revenue plays less of a role in Nepal. Where community-based forest management involves financial transfers from donor agencies, NGOs, or government, sequential and conditional release of funds may be a useful approach to discipline local leaders (Platteau, 2003). However, for this approach to be effective, funding or implementing agencies need to cooperate to avoid competition among themselves to the benefit of local leaders (Plattean, 2003). Among other things, this would require the systematic reporting of cases of failure, which stands in contrast to current practice by funding agencies (Plattean, 2003).

The case of India also highlights the mixed evidence on the success of community-based forest management. Some studies have shown improvements in outcomes such as increased yields of timber, NTFP, fuelwood, and fodder (Joshi, 1998; Khare et al., 2000; Ballabh et al., 2002). Others indicate a lack of control and management of forests by the communities, despite the fact that communities have de jure rights over the forest. For instance, Jodha's (1986) study of 82 villages in the dry region of the country revealed that not a single village was using control measures such as grazing taxes or penalties for violations of forest use rules. The variety in outcomes of JFM may partly be due to the fact that the degree to which specific rights and benefits were actually devolved from the forest department to local communities differs significantly across states (Damodaran and Engel, 2003). Cynics see JFM as just another way to extend forest department control to new areas, as forest management committees under JFM are mostly still controlled by government staff (Sundar, 2001).

Co-management is often seen as a desirable combination of the advantages of state and common property. The above discussion indicates that the degree to which communities should be given rights and responsibilities over forest management depends on local conditions. Community involvement is crucial where there is a prevalence of indigenous and forest-dependent population, where natural resources are located in remote areas and are locally specific and diverse, and where there is a lack of state funds and monitoring and enforcement capacity. State involvement is crucial where externalities are important, marginalization of groups within communities is an issue, and where resource and user characteristics are such that the expected ability for community collective action is low. To avoid disincentive effects that are common in present systems, co-management would probably work best if the state took on the role of overall planning and assistance, and potentially put some restrictions to community activities, while the communities are allowed to decide freely and obtain full benefits within the areas and limits set by the state (Engel, 2004). At least three necessary conditions for effective co-management emerge from a review of the literature (Ribot, 2002; Larson and Ribot, 2004): (i) secure and well-defined property rights; (ii) transfer of appropriate and sufficient powers to communities, and (iii) downwardly accountable and representative local institutions. Table 13.1 also summarizes important roles stressed in the literature for the state as well as the international community (donor agencies, NGOs, etc.) in a co-management system.

Private Property

Some countries, for example, China and Vietnam, have recently started privatization programs for formerly state-owned forests. Private ownership as an alternative to state or common property regimes has long been promoted by economists who argue that privatization, by assigning all benefits and costs for a particular forest area to one individual, yields the optimal incentives for an efficient resource management.[23] The argument that private property rights satisfying the criteria of universality, exclusivity, and transferability will yield efficient market equilibria, however, relies crucially on four important assumptions: (i) enforcement costs are nil, (ii) property rights are well defined, (iii) markets are perfect, and (iv) markets are competitive (Baland and Platteau, 1996, p. 37). In the context of developing country forests, these conditions are usually not satisfied.

First, the prime criticism of the private property rights school is that it underestimates the transaction costs involved in monitoring and enforcing private property rights (Baland and Platteau, 1996). The very characteristics of common-pool resources that make exclusion of potential users difficult may make it even more difficult to achieve a degree of separation, exclusion, and protection necessary to privatize it (Arnold, 1998). Unsecured de jure rights, which are not enforced or prohibitively costly to enforce, may not improve tenure

---

[23] See, for example, Demsetz (1967), Hardin (1968), Posner (1977), Anderson and Hill (1977).

Table 13.1 Important roles for various actors in common-pool resource management

THE STATE

Setting national environmental priorities and standards (boundaries to community management, zoning)

- Deal with national and regional externalities
- Provide a legal framework which enables communities 'to obtain legally enforceable recognition of their rights and to call upon the state as an enforcer of last resort'
- Legal backing for community-established use and access rules
- Provide conflict resolution mechanisms
- Provide technical assistance, monitoring equipment, scientific information, awareness building
- Provide economic incentives for conservation (e.g. poverty alleviation, payments for environmental services)
- Provide information on best practices, experiences of other communities
- Assure inclusion of marginalized groups, promote pro-poor rules
- Promote grassroots participation and downward accountability (e.g. through popular elections, forums for discussions and negotiations, mandated financial reports, social audits or vigilance committees)

INTERNATIONAL COMMUNITY/DONOR AGENCIES/ NGOS

- Implement mechanisms to translate international externalities into economic incentives for sustainable resource management and conservation in developing countries
- Support state in its functions
- Support horizontal coordination between community organizations (e.g. regional forest user associations) to address broader-scale problems and increase bargaining power vs. the state.
- Support good governance (rule of law, secure land tenure, democratic elections, government accountability)
- Help overcome 'culture of distrust' between communities and the state, build community confidence in its collective action ability, build up or adapt local institutional arrangements for resource management
- Capacity building at local level (financial and administrative management, technical skills, problem-solving)
- Awareness building at local level (providing information on rights, success stories)
- Promote the participation of marginalized groups (e.g. by helping them to raise their voice in defense of their interests and demand transparency and accountability)

Source: Baland and Platteau (1996), Ribot (2002), Larson and Ribot (2004).

security. In developing countries, insecurity, high transaction costs, poor, partial and arbitrary enforcement of rights due to weak judiciary and constitutional laws and lack of infrastructure can thus seriously constrain the efficiency of individual property rights, especially if those rights do not enjoy the support of custom (Feder and Feeny, 1991).

Second, private property rights do not account for externality effects, neither at the global and regional level, nor at the local level (contrary to common property rights which may at least internalize local externalities such as soil erosion). Third, forests often need to be managed in their entirety in order to maintain their ecological functioning. Fourth, common use of a forest can reduce the individual users' risks in areas where the location of the most productive zones can vary from year to year.[24] Finally, privatization usually

---

[24] This is the case, for example, of woodland in arid areas.

implies that some former users are excluded, which may have undesirable equity and poverty implications. Assuming that privatization actually does lead to efficiency gains, Weitzman (1974) shows that if privatization leads to resource ownership by an outsider or if the state sells off competitively the rights to the resource, former resource users (e.g. traditional communities) always lose despite the fact that they may become wage earners and wages increase as a consequence of the efficiency gains. If, on the other hand, former users get their rights recognized and are compensated for losses incurred from privatization, everybody can gain from privatization; but empirically this is often not the case due to political economy considerations and information problems (Baland and Platteau, 1996). Otsuka and Place (2001) present evidence from several African and Asian countries indicating that land distribution under common and communal property regimes tended to be more equitable than in private property regimes.

The optimal property regime may also depend on the type of forest. For example, Otsuka and Place (2001) conclude that common property regimes are effective when NTFPs are the predominant forest products. They argue that management of timber forests (where protection is less costly, but management intensity is high) is more efficient under private land tenure than under common property regimes. However, where protection is costly (e.g. due to a threat from grazing), a combination of private and common property systems may be optimal, where management is carried out individually or by a centralized management committee, and protection is carried out communally (Otsuka and Place, 2001, p. 48).

Conclusion and Discussion

In this chapter we have highlighted the key role of market failure in tropical forest conservation. The mismatch between costs and benefits of forest conservation, both in space and in time, implies that too much forest area will be converted to other uses. Policy failure is a compounding factor, making matters even worse.

We have explored the various policy options that exist for the rest of the world to address market failure. There appears to be a slow trend towards payments for ecological services, a development which we believe is encouraging as it tackles the market failure problem directly, which is likely to be both efficient and cost-effective. North–South transfers also reduce distributional inequality and may help promoting rural development. A recent review found almost 300 examples of marked-based approaches to forest conservation, mainly in Latin America and the Caribbean (Landell-Mills and Porras, 2002). This list is growing, which offers hope that cost-effective and efficient conservation of valuable natural capital may be within reach. This tendency will offer increasing opportunities for the international community to 'put their money where their mouth is,' and reach fair agreements with selected and accountable governments in developing countries. The great challenge for forest conservation in the future may be to move beyond local cases and implement a consistent plan of action that encompasses many countries.

However, while forest conservation expenditures have increased considerably since the 1970s (the total amount involved in the 1990s amounted to some $2 billion—or an average of $200 million per year), it appears as if actual North–South monetary transfers still lag behind the value of the South–North spillover benefit by a few orders of magnitude. It appears that parties in the North simply prefer to free ride on conservation in the South—an attitude that would not only be unfair, but also inefficient and unsustainable in the long run. The suggestion of 'willingness to free ride' is somewhat reinforced when we take the evidence into account that consumers in the North are unwilling to pay a premium for sustainably produced tropical timber, or for biodiversity-friendly shade-grown coffee from forest regions. None of this is surprising given the public good nature of most forest services. Not only may the North free ride on the South, but also each individual country in the North has an incentive to free ride on the others' actions. Given the public good nature, it is unlikely that a true market for international spillover effects will evolve in the absence of international agreements assigning clear property rights and implementing supra-national enforcement mechanisms. The discussion on carbon trade is encouraging in this regard (but difficulties in including all relevant parties to sign the Kyoto Protocol is illustrative). As long as such markets are not in place, however, PES are likely to take the form of bilateral agreements. The theory of public goods clearly predicts that this will lead to an under-provision of forest services. PES are essentially forms of bargaining. The Coase theorem, however, states that such bargaining emerges where property rights are well defined and transaction costs are small. Both conditions are not satisfied in an international context. This may also explain why large PES schemes such as the Costa Rican scheme have emerged from a national rather than international initiative. Again, resolving these issues on an international level will require cooperation and coordination between countries, particularly within the North.

There exists another, more hopeful perspective. The majority of the current efforts to provide direct compensation for forest services deal with local or regional issues—mainly watershed management. While one can be sceptical about the prospects of fully incorporating transboundary services in the future, it could also be argued that the current phase of incomplete compensation for such services is necessary to build the appropriate institutions. Not all countries are like Costa Rica, where payments immediately trickle down to landowners and affect their decision-making. For many countries, this requires considerable challenges in terms of public governance, financial administration and political will.[25] Landell-Mills and Porras (2002) emphasize the importance of secure land tenure, good governance and a strong legal framework to provide an 'enabling environment' in which market-based incentives can prosper.

We have also discussed how market failures and policy impacts depend on the property right regimes in place, an aspect that has been subject to considerable change over the past decades. It appears clear that secure and well-defined property rights are a crucial precondition for any policy to be effective in reducing deforestation. Which property right regimes is appropriate, however, depends on ecological conditions, user characteristics, dominant extractive activities (e.g. timber vs. NTFPs), and political economy considerations. It is now generally agreed that pure state property regimes have performed very poorly in the past, and that it is impossible in a developing country context to simply protect the forest from the local people depending on them for their livelihood. The move towards devolution and the participation of local people in forest management is certainly a move in the right direction. However, common or private property regimes are not without serious problems and risks. If properly designed, co-management regimes could benefit from the comparative advantages of both governments and local communities in managing local forests (Knox and Meinzen-Dick, 2001). However, in reality, it seems that devolution of rights has often not kept pace with devolution of responsibilities, and that government agencies—while increasingly adopting the rhetoric of devolution and participatory approaches—are often reluctant to give up substantial powers, resulting in half-hearted policy change with potentially counter-productive effects.

To improve current systems will also require a better understanding of past experiences. Particularly, the literature on government-initiated community institutions and the outcomes of privatization is limited. As Agrawal (2001) states, we need to go beyond the examination of individual case studies towards more systematic, large-sample studies. Two issues that need particular attention appear to be the importance of fund-transfers for the sustainability of effective community-based forest management institutions and the related incidence of rent-seeking at the national vs. local level (both for local governments and local community elites). Also, current analyses of 'community-driven development', 'community-based management', 'devolution', and 'participation', include many very different types of institutional settings. Therefore, not only do we need a better understanding of determinants of success within a given setting, but furthermore a comparison across projects and countries to improve our understanding of the impact of the overall institutional framework conditions (e.g. the degree to which rights and responsibilities are shared between state and communities under co-management regimes) is required.

---

[25] The Costa Rica example is of course not perfect. Among other things, it has been criticized because of its emphasis on forest conservation (as opposed to providing development opportunities for the rural poor).

References

Abraham, A. and J. P. Platteau (2002), 'Participatory Development in the Presence of Endogenous Community Imperfections,' *Journal of Development Studies* 39(2): 104–36.

Agarwal, B. (2001), 'Participatory Exclusions, Community Forestry, and Gender: An Analysis for South Asia and a Conceptual Framework,' *World Development* 29(10): 1623–48.

—— A. (2001), 'Common property institutions and sustainable governance of resources,' *World Development* 29(10): 1649–72.

—— A. and E. Ostrom (2002), 'Collective Action, Property Rights, and Decentralisation in Resource Use in India and Nepal,' *Politics and Society* 29(4): 485–514.

Albers, H. (1996), 'Modeling Tropical Forest Management: Spatial Interdependence, Irreversibility and Uncertainty,' *Journal of Environmental Economics and Management* 30: 73–94.

——, A. Fisher, and M. Hanemann, (1996), 'Valuation of Tropical Forests: Implications of Uncertainty and Irreversibility,' *Environmental and Resource Economics* 8: 39–61.

Alston, L. J., G. D. Libecap, and B. Mueller (1999), 'A model of rural conflict: Violence and land reform policy in Brazil,' *Environment and Development Economics* 4(2): 135–60.

Anderson, T. L., and P. J. Hill (1977), 'From free grass to fences: Transforming the commons of the American West,' in *Managing the Commons*, G. Hardin and J. Baden (eds). W. H. Freeman, San Francisco.

Angelsen, A. (1995), 'Shifting cultivation and deforestation. A study from Indonesia,' *World Development* 23: 1713–29.

—— (1997), 'State-local community games of forest land appropriation.' Working Paper WP 1997: 7. Chr. Michelsen Institute, Bergen.

—— (1999), 'Agricultural expansion and deforestation: Modeling the impact of population, market forces and property rights,' *Journal of Development Economics* 58: 185–218.

—— (2001), 'Playing games in the forest: State-local conflicts of land appropriation,' *Land Economics* 77(2): 285–99.

—— and D. Kaimowitz (eds) (2001), *Agricultural technologies and tropical deforestation.* CABI Publishing, Oxon, U.K., and New York.

Arnold, J. E. M. (1998), *Managing forests as common property.* Forestry Paper 136. Food and Agriculture Organization of the United Nations (FAO), Rome.

Arnold, M., G. Köhlin, R. Persson, and G. Shepherd (2003), 'Fuelwood revisited: What has happened in the last decade?' CIFOR Occasional Paper 39, Bogor, Indonesia.

Baland , J. M., and J. P. Platteau (1996), *Halting degradation of natural resources: is there a role for rural communities?* Oxford: Clarendon Press.

—— and —— (1997a), 'Wealth inequality and efficiency in the commons Part I: the unregulated case,' *Oxford Economic Papers* 49(3): 451–82.

——, and —— (1997b), 'Coordination problems in local-level resource management,' *Journal of Development Economics* 53: 197–210.

—— and —— (1998), 'Wealth inequality and efficiency in the commons Part II: the regulated case,' *Oxford Economic Papers* 50(1): 1–22.

Ballabh, V., K. Balooni, and S. Dave (2002), 'Why local resource management institutions decline: A comparative analysis of Van (forest) Panchayats and Forest Protection Committees in India,' *World Development* 30(12): 2153–67.

Barbier, E. and B. Aylward (1996), 'Capturing the pharmaceutical value of biodiversity in a developing country,' *Environmental and Resource Ecomomics* 8: 157–81.

——, J. Burgess, J. Bishop, and I. Strand (1990), *The economics of the tropical timber trade*, London: Earthscan.

Bardhan, P. (1993a), 'Analytics of the institutions of informal cooperation in rural development,' *World Development* 21(4): 633–9.

—— (1993b), 'Symposium on management of local commons,' *Journal of Economic Perspectives* 7(4): 87–92.

Barr, C., E. Wollenberg, G. Limberg, N. Anau, et al. (2001), 'The Impacts of Decentralisation on Forests and Forest-Dependent Communities in Malinau District, East Kalimantan.' Decentralisation and Forests in Indonesia Series: Case Study 3. Center for International Forestry Research, Bogor, Indonesia.

Bojanic, A. J. (2001), 'Balance is beautiful: Assessing sustainable development in the rain forests of the Bolivian Amazon,' PROMAB Scientific Series 4, Utrecht: Utrecht University.

—— and E. H. Bulte (2002), 'Financial Viability of Natural Forest Management in Bolivia: Environmental regulation and the Dissipation and Distribution of Profits,' *Forest Policy & Economics* 4: 239–50.

Brander, J. and M. S. Taylor (1997), 'International Trade and Open Access Renewable Resources: The Small Open Economy Case,' *Canadian Journal of Economics* 30: 526–52.

Bulte, E. H., D. P. van Soest, G. C. van Kooten, and R. Schipper (2002), 'Forest Conservation in Costa Rica when Nonuse Benefits are Uncertain but Rising,' *American Journal of Agricultural Economics* 84: 150–60.

Calder, I. (1998), *Water resources and land use issues.* SWIM paper 3, CG System-wide Initiative on Water Management, International Water Management Institute, Colombo, Sri Lanka.

Casson, A. and K. Obidzinski (2002), 'From new order to regional autonomy: Shifting dynamics of 'illegal' logging in Kalimantan, Indonesia,' *World Development* 30(12): 2133–51.

Cavendish, W. (2000), 'Empirical regularities in the poverty-environment relationship of rural households: Evidence from Zimbabwe.' *Mimeo.* London: Labour Party.

Clarke, H. R., Reed, W. J., and R. M. Shrestha (1993), 'Optimal enforcement of property rights on developing country forests subject to illegal logging,' *Resource and Energy Economics* 15: 271–93.

Clarkson, R. (2000), 'Estimating the social cost of carbon emissions.' London: Department of the Environment, Transport and the Regions.

Common, M. (1995), *Sustainability and policy*, Cambridge: Cambridge University Press.

Costello, C. and M. Ward (2003), 'Search, bioprospecting and biodiversity conservation: Comment,' Working Paper, University of California at Santa Barbara, Donald Bren School of Environmental Science and Management.

Damodaran, A. and S. Engel (2003), 'Joint Forest Management in India: Assessment of Performance and Evaluation of Impacts.' ZEF-Discussion Papers on Development Policy No. 77 (October). Center for Development Research (ZEF), Bonn, Germany.

Deininger, K. and B. Minten (1996), 'Determinants of Forest Cover and the Economics of Protection: An Application to Mexico, Poverty, Environment and Growth.' Working Paper, Washington, DC: The World Bank.

Demsetz, H. (1967), 'Toward a theory of property rights,' *American Economic Review* 57(2): 347–59.

Edmonds, E. V. (2002), 'Government initiated community resource management and local resource extraction from Nepal's forests,' *Journal of Development Economics* 68(1): 89–115.

Engel, S. (2004), *Designing institutions for sustainable resource management and environmental protection*. Habilitationsschrift. University of Bonn, Faculty of Agriculture, Germany.

—— (2004), 'Achieving Environmental Goals in a World of Trade and Hidden Action: The Role of Trade Policies and Eco-Labeling.' *Journal of Environmental Economics and Management* 48 (3): 1122–45.

——, R. López, and C. Palmer (2006), 'Community-industry contracting over natural resource use in a context of weak property rights: The case of Indonesia'. *Environmental and Resource Economics* 33(1): 73–98. (Electronically available at http://dx.doi.org/ 10.1007/s10640-005-1706-5).

—— and —— (2004), 'Exploiting Common Resources with Capital-Intensive Technologies: The Role of External Forces.' ZEF Discussion Papers on Development Policy No. 90, Center for Development Research, Bonn, Germany.

FAO (2001), '*State of the world's forests 2000.*' Food and Agricultural Organization of the United Nations: Rome.

Feder, G. and G. Feeny (1991), 'Land tenure and property rights: Theory and implications for development policy,' *The World Bank Economic Review* 5(1): 135–53.

Ferraro, P. J. (2001), 'Global Habitat Protection: Limitations of Development Interventions and a Role for Conservation Performance Payments.' *Conservation Biology* 15(4): 990–1000.

—— and A. Kiss (2002), 'Direct payments to conserve biodiversity,' *Science* 298 (November 29).

—— and R. D. Simpson (2002), 'The Cost-Effectiveness of Conservation Payments,' *Land Economics* 78(3): 339–53 (August).

Hardin, G. (1968), 'The tragedy of the commons,' *Science* 162: 1243–8.

Homma, A., (1994), 'Plant extractavism in the Amazon: Limitations and possibilities. In: Extractavism in the Brazilian Amazon: Perspectives on regional development,' Clusener-Godt, M. and I. Sachs (eds), MAB Digest 18, Paris: UNESCO.

Hotte, L. (2001), 'Conflicts over property rights and natural-resource exploitation at the frontier,' *Journal of Development Economics* 66: 1–21.

—— (2002), 'Natural-resource exploitation with costly enforcement of property rights.' Research series working paper No. 234. University of Namur, Belgium.

Houghton, J., L. Meira Filho, B. Callander, N. Hariis, et al. (eds) (1996), 'Climate change 1995: The science of climate change,' Cambridge: Cambridge University Press.

Hughes, J., G. Daily, and P. Ehrlich (1997), 'Population diversity: Its extent and extinction,' *Science* 278: 689–92.

Jodha, N. S. (1986), 'Common Property Resources and the Rural Poor in Dry Regions of India,' *Economic and Political Weekly*. vol. 21(27), pp. 169–81.

Johansson-Stenman, O. (1998), 'The importance of ethics in environmental economics,' *Environmental and Resource Economics* 11: 429–42.

Joshi, A. (1998), 'Progressive Bureaucracy: an Oxymoron? The Case of Joint Forest Management in India.' Rural Development Forestry Network, Overseas Development Institute, London.

Kaimowitz, D. (2000), *Forestry assistance and tropical deforestation: Why doesn't the public get what it pays for?* CIFOR Working Paper. Center for International Forestry Research (CIFOR), Bogor, Indonesia.

—— (2003), 'Forest Law Enforcement and Rural Livelihoods,' *International Forestry Review* 5: 199–210.

—— and A. Angelsen (1998), *Economic models of deforestation: A review*. Center for International Forestry Research (CIFOR), Bogor, Indonesia.

Karmacharya, M., B. Karna, and E. Ostrom (2003), 'Rules, incentives and enforcement: Livelihood strategies of community forestry and leasehold forestry users in Nepal.' Paper presented at the International Conference on Rural Livelihoods, Forest and Biodiversity. (May 19–23). Bonn, Germany.

Khare, A., M. Sarin, M., Saxena, N. C. Patil, et al. (2000), 'Joint Forest Management: Policy, Practice and Prospects.' IIED, London, and WWF-India, New Delhi.

Kiss, A. (2003), 'Making biodiversity conservation a land use priority,' in *Getting biodiversity projects to work: Towards more effective conservation and development*. T. McShane and M. Wells (eds) Columbia University Press, New York.

Knetsch, J. (1993), 'Resource economics: Persistent conventions and contrary evidence, in: W. Adamowicz, W. Hite, and W. Phillips (eds), *Forestry and the environment: Economic perspectives*, Wallingford UK: CAB International.

Knox, A., and Meinzen-Dick, R. (2001), 'Workshop on Collective Action, Property Rights and Devolution of Natural Resource Management: Exchange of Knowledge and Implication for Policy. A Workshop Summary Paper.' CAPRI Working Paper No. 11. International Food Policy Research Institute (IFPRI), Washington, DC.

Kopp, R. J. (2004), 'Near-term greenhouse gas emissions targets.' Discussion Paper 04-41. Resources for the Future (RFF), Washington, DC.

Kramer, R. and D. Mercer (1997), 'Valuing a global environmental good: US residents' willingness to pay to protect tropical rain forests,' *Land Economics* 73: 196–210.

Kumar, S. (2002), 'Does "participation" in common pool resource management help the poor? A social cost-benefit analysis of Joint Forest Management in Jharkhand, India,' *World Development* 30(5): 763–82.

Landell-Mills, N. and I. Porras (2002), *Silver bullets or fools' gold? A global review of markets for forest environmental services and their impact on the poor*. London: IIED.

Larson, A. M. and J. C. Ribot (2004), 'Democratic decentralization through a natural resource lens: An Introduction,' *The European Journal of Development Research* 16(1): 1–25.

Leakey, R. and R. Lewin (1996), 'The sixth extinction.' London: Weidenfeld &Nicolson.

López, R. (1998), 'Agricultural intensification, common property resources and the farm-household,' *Environmental and Resource Economics* 11(3–4): 443–58.

Manne, A. and R. Richels, (2004), 'MERGE: An integrated assessment model for global climate change,' *Mimeo*. Stanford University, http://www.standford.edu/group/MERGE/GERAD1.pdf

Mansuri, G. and V. Rao. (2003), 'Evaluating community-based and community-driven development: A critical review of the evidence.' Development Research Group, The World Bank, Washington, DC. (September).

Matthews, E., R. Payne, M. Rohweder, and S. Murray (2000), *Pilot analysis of global ecosystems: Forest ecosystems*. World Resources Institute, Washington, DC.

McKean, M. A. (1995), 'Common property: what is it, what is it good for, and what makes it work?' Paper presented at the International Conference on Chinese Rural Collectives and Voluntary Organizations: Between State Organization and Private Interest. (January 9–13). Leiden University, Leiden, The Netherlands.

Mintorahardjo, S. and B. Setiono (2003), 'Banks can stop illegal logging if they want,' *Jakarta Post* (August 15).

Myers, N. (1994), 'Tropical deforestation: Rates and patterns,' in D. Pearce and K. Brown (eds), *The causes of tropical deforestation*. London: UCL Press.

Nasi, R., S. Wunder, and J. Campos (2002), 'Forest ecosystem services: Can they pay their way out of deforestation?' Discussion paper prepared for Global Environmental Facility (GEF).

Nordhaus, W. and Z. Yang (1996), 'A regional dynamic general equilibrium model of alternative climate change strategies,' *American Economic Review* 86: 741–65.

Oliveira, J. A. P. de. (2002), 'Implementing environmental policies in developing countries through decentralization: The case of protected areas in Bahia, Brazil,' *World Development* 30(10): 1713–36.

Ostrom, E. (1990), *Governing the Commons: The Evolution of Institutions for Collective Action*. Cambridge, Cambridge University Press.

Otsuka, K. and F. Place (eds) (2001), *Land tenure and natural resource management. A comparative study of agrarian communities in Asia and Africa*. Johns Hopkins University Press, Baltimore and London.

Pagiola, S., J. Bishop, and N. Landell-Mills (2002), *Selling forest environmental services. Market-based mechanisms for conservation and development*. Earthscan Publications Ltd., London.

Pagiola, S. and G. Platais, (2002), 'Payments for Environmental Services,' *Environment Strategy Notes* 3 (May). World Bank: Washington, DC.

——, Landell-Mills, N., and J. Bishop (2002), 'Market-based mechanisms for forest conservation and development,' in *Selling forest environmental services. Market-based mechanisms for conservation and development*, Pagiola, S., J. Bishop, and N. Landell-Mills (eds) Earthscan Publications, London.

Palmer, C. E. (2001), 'The extent and causes of illegal logging: An analysis of a major cause of tropical deforestation in Indonesia.' CSERGE Working Paper. Centre for Social and Economic Research on the Global Environment, University College London.

Pearce, D. W. and C. G. T. Pearce (2001), 'The value of forest ecosystems. A Report to the Secretariat of the Convention on Biological Diversity,' Montreal: Canada.

Perrings, C. (1998), 'Resilience in the dynamics of economy-environment systems,' *Environmental and Resource Economics* 11: 503–20.

Peters, C., A. Gentry, and R. Mendelsohn (1989), 'Valuation of an Amazonian rainforest,' *Nature* 339: 655–6.

Platteau, J. P. (2003), 'Decentralized development as a strategy to reduce poverty?' Paper prepared for the Agence Française de Développement (AFD). Centre de Recherche en Économie de Développement (CRED), University of Namur, Belgium.

—— and F. Gaspart (2003), 'The risk of resource misappropriation in community-driven development,' *World Development* 31(10): 1687–03.

Posner, R. (1977), *Economic analysis of law*. Boston, Mass.: Little, Brown & Co.

Rausser, G. and A. Small (2000), 'Valuing research leads: Bioprospecting and the conservation of genetic resources,' *Journal of Political Economy* 108: 173–206.

Reid, W. (1999), *Capturing the value of ecosystem services to protect biodiversity*, Washington DC: World Resources Institute.

Ribot, J. (2002), 'Democratic Decentralization of Natural Resources, Institutionalizing Popular Participation.' Washington DC: World Resources Institute.

Rodriguez Zuniga, J. (2003), 'Paying for forest environmental services: The Costa Rican experience,' *Unasylva* 54: 31–3.

Rosa, H., S. Kandel, and L. Dimas (2003), *Compensación por servicios ambientales y comunidades rurales. Lecciones de las Américas y temas críticos para fortalecer estrategias comunitarias* Programa Salvadoreño de Investigación Sobre Desarrollo y Medio Ambiente (PRISMA), San Salvador, El Salvador.

Ross, M. (2001), *Timber Booms and Institutional Breakdown in Southeast Asia*. Cambridge: Cambridge University Press.

Ruitenbeek, H. (1989), 'Social cost-benefit analysis of the Korup project,' Report prepared for the World Fund for Nature and Republic of Cameroon, London: WWF.

Runge, C. F. (1986), 'Common property and collective action in economic development,' *World Development* 14(5): 623–35.

Sagoff, M. (1988), *The economy of the earth*. Cambridge: Cambridge University Press.

Sawhney, P. and S. Engel (2003), 'Forest resource use by people in Protected Areas and its implications for biodiversity conservation: The case of Bandhavgarh National Park in India.' (Forthcoming in G. Gerold, M. Fremerey, and E. Guhardja (eds), *Land use, nature conservation and the stability of rainforest margins in Southeast Asia*). Springer, Berlin.

Scherr, S. J., A. White, and D. Kaimowitz (2002), 'Making markets work for forest communities.' Policy Brief. Forest Trends, Washington, DC, and Center for International Forestry Research (CIFOR), Bogor, Indonesia.

Schipper, R., H. Jansen, B. Bouman, H. Hengsdijk, and A. Nieuwenhuyse (2000), 'Integrated biophysical and socio-economic landuse analysis at the regional level,' in B. Bouman, H. Jansen, H. Hengsdijk, and A. Nieuwenhuyse (eds), *Tools for land use analysis at different scales, with case studies for Costa Rica*. Dordrecht: Kluwer Academic Publishers.

Seabright, P. (1993), 'Managing local commons: Theoretical issues in incentive design,' *Journal of Economic Perspectives* 7(4): 113–34.

Shackleton, S., B. Campbell, E. Wollenberg, and D. Edmunds (2002), 'Devolution and community-based natural resource management: Creating space for local people to participate and benefit?', *Natural Resource Perspectives* 76. Overseas Development Institute, London.

Simpson, D., R. Sedjo, and J. Reid (1996), 'Valuing biodiversity for use in pharmaceutical research, *Journal of Political Economy* 104: 163–85.

Smith, W. (2002), 'The global problem of illegal logging.' ITTO Newsletter 12(1), International Timber Trade Organization (ITTO). http://www.itto.or.jp/newsletter/v12n1/0.html.

Stahler, F. (1996), 'On international compensations for environmental stocks,' *Environmental and Resource Economics* 8: 1–13.

Sundar, N. (2001), 'Is devolution democratization?' *World Development* 29(12): 2007–23.

Tietenberg, T. (1988), 'Environmental and Resource Economics,' ch. 3. Scott, Foresman and Company, Glenview, Illinois.

Tol, R. S. J. (2002a), 'Estimates of the damage costs of climate change, PI: benchmark estimates,' *Environmental and Resource Economics* 21: 47–73.

—— (2002b), 'Estimates of the damage costs of climate change, PII: dynamic estimates,' *Environmental and Resource Economics* 21: 135–60.

U.S. Agency for International Development (USAID) (2002), 'Strategies to combat illegal logging and forest crime.' Forest Trends. Technical forest brief. PN-ACT-288. USAID, Washington, DC. (November) http://www.dec.org/pdf_docs/ PNACT288.pdf

Van Kooten, G., R. Sedjo, and E. Bulte (2000), 'Tropical deforestation: Issues and policies,' in H. Folmer and T. Tietenberg (eds), *The International Yearbook of Environmental and Resource Economics 1999/2000*. Cheltenham: Edward Elgar.

Vincent, J. (1990), 'Rent capture and the feasibility of tropical forest management,' *Land Economics* 66: 212–23.

Wade, R. (1988), 'Village Republics,' *Economic Conditions for Collective Action in South India*. Oakland: ICS Press.

Weitzman, M. (1974), 'Free access versus private ownership as alternative systems for managing common property,' *Journal of Economic Theory* 8: 225–34.

White, A. and A. Martin (2002), 'Who owns the world's forests? Forest tenure and public forests in transition.' Forest Trends and Center for International Environmental Law, Washington, DC.

Wiersum, K. (1984), 'Surface erosion under various tropical agroforestry systems,' in C. O' Loughlin and A. Pearce (eds), Proceeding of Symposium on Effects of Forest Land Use on Erosion and Slope Stability, IUFRO: Vienna.

Winterbottom, R. (1990), *Taking Stock: The Tropical Forest Action Plan After Five Years*. Washington DC: World Resources Institute.

World Bank (2000), *A Review of the World Bank's 1991 Forest Strategy and Its Implementation, Preliminary Report*. Washington DC: The World Bank (January 13).

Wunder, S. (2000), *The economics of deforestation. The example of Ecuador*. London: Macmillan Press Ltd.

THE ROLES OF THE ENVIRONMENT AND NATURAL RESOURCES IN ECONOMIC GROWTH ANALYSIS: AN INTUITIVE INTRODUCTION

*Michael A. Toman**

Introduction

All of the papers in this volume are concerned with linkages between economic development and the conservation and/or use of the environment and natural resources. In this appendix, I first provide a brief historical review of the role of natural resources and the environment in neoclassical economic growth theory. I then develop a simple graphical structure to elucidate the general links between economic growth and 'natural capital' in the neoclassical framework. The material is intended to provide background and grounding for the more rigorous and in-depth treatments in the chapters of the volume. Additional material of the type presented here, including graphical representations of environment-economy linkages at sectoral levels and a simple mathematical representation of the linkages, can be found in Toman (2003).

All of the material covered here is set in the neoclassical framework. A central premise of neoclassical growth economics also underlies the treatment here, namely that *growth is fundamentally a process of investment in various forms by society*, and the rate and quality of growth depend on the size and composition of such investments. The neoclassical approach followed here also builds on a set of familiar assumptions that are often criticized in the ecological economic literature on sustainability (e.g. unlimited albeit imperfect substitution of physical and natural capital, maximization of personal utility of consumption with regard for intergenerational or intragenerational distribution, absence of statistically definable uncertainty or surprises, and so forth). My purpose in this appendix is not to criticize or defend those assumptions. Rather, it is to provide as clear as possible a recounting of what the neoclassical model with natural

* The author greatly appreciates the advice and comments offered by Mike Rock, particularly on research needs, and comments by Russell Misheloff, Kenneth Baum, and David Simpson on earlier drafts. He also is very grateful for excellent research assistance from Barbora Jemelkova. This exposition is drawn from a longer paper (Toman, 2003) written for International Resources Group and Resources for the Future, with funding from the Agency for International Development. The views expressed in the paper are the author's alone.

resources and the environment can incorporate and how the analytical framework developed. Even within this framework there are some interesting gaps between theory and empirical understanding which are touched upon the concluding section of the paper.

The Increasing Role of Environment and Natural Resources in Neoclassical Economic Growth Theory

A complete history of the role of environmental and natural resources in economic growth analysis would go back at least to the nineteenth-century writings of Malthus, Mill, and Jevons. Our less ambitious task here is to provide some brief comments on key developments in the literature over roughly the past 30 years.[1]

When modern theories of economic growth first began to be developed in the 1950s and 1960s, natural resources and the environment were largely absent.[2] Economic output flows and rates of output growth were assumed to depend on the applications of services provided by capital and labor. Capital could be augmented by net investment as a result of domestic savings and external capital flows. There were potential 'limits to growth' identified in growth theory in that as capital per person grew, the rate of growth in output per person declined (because of diminishing returns) until a steady state was achieved. But such limits to growth were not related to natural resources and the environment.

When technology was added to capital and labor as an input to the growth process, technical progress was almost always assumed to be exogenous and not embodied in specific equipment or skills—though more recent developments in growth theory have relaxed this artificial assumption. Output growth with technical progress could be prolonged through (assumed) technical advance. But the role of natural resources and the environment as valuable inputs to the growth process remained outside of growth theory in the earlier stages, including possible constraints from the natural world that could lead to more rapid slowing or even a decline in output per capita over time.

Starting in the late 1960s, awareness of the environment and natural resources as a determining factor affecting growth became more widely appreciated. Much of the attention to the interfaces between the natural and economic worlds initially came from natural resource and environmental economists interested in problems of limits to growth. Growth and development economists also began seriously rethinking simple neoclassical growth models because of the realization that policy recommendations based on these models would be incomplete without reference to natural resource and environmental policy components (see, e.g., Dasgupta and Heal, 1974; Solow, 1974; and Stiglitz, 1974). Over time, theories of economic growth with various kinds of natural resource inputs and environmental implications became more fully developed.

---

[1] In addition to the papers in this volume, surveys by Beltratti (1997) and Smulders (1999), and the papers in Simpson, Toman, and Ayres (2005), provide more complete review of various literatures.

[2] From a historical perspective this absence is somewhat curious, since land had played such a vital role in 19th-century classical theories of economic progress. The industrial revolution and the Walrasian neoclassical economics of the late 19th century both initiated a decline in attention to natural capital that has only recently been partly offset with renewed interest in growth and natural capital.

The analytical paradigm was further altered in the late 1980s to reflect concerns about environmentally sustainable economic growth. Sustainable economic growth policies in this perspective depend on the level, quality, and management of renewable and non-renewable natural resources and on the state of the environment. The state of the environment is dependent, in turn, on the level and growth of pollution, or waste streams, and the natural assimilation of pollution by the environment (as an environmental service) or through clean up expenditures. Pezzey (1989, 1992) presented a simple but well-elaborated 'wiring diagram' and accompanying mathematical analysis showing various linkages between natural resources flows and environmental services on the one hand, and economic activity and natural resource depletion or degradation on the other.

Corresponding to these theoretical developments have been episodic efforts to more carefully explore the empirical linkages. Perhaps the most recognized of these within the mainstream economics literature was Barnett and Morse (1963). They argued, based on careful analysis (using available techniques at the time) of price and cost data, that there was little in the way of economic scarcity being signaled for natural resource commodities. However, Barnett and Morse noted then, and many scholars have subsequently addressed the possibility that scarcity could be much more of a dilemma for non-prived environmental goods. These themes have been revisited in a recent volume by Simpson, Toman, and Ayres (2005).

A Schematic Representation of the Roles of Natural Resources and the Environment in Economic Growth

Our general framework is laid out schematically in a 'wiring diagram' shown in Appendix 1.[3] Since our focus is on investments by society, we emphasize the presence of various forms of capital and possibilities for (net) investment in these forms. We recognize of course that the supply and employment of labor also is a critical part of the economic growth process, but to simplify the diagram, we do not develop this part of the economic system in much detail. Another simplification of the presentation is that we do not distinguish a stock of technological knowledge separately from the basic capital stock. Investments in knowledge embedded in machines or increased human capacities (human capital) certainly are crucial to economic development. In our framework, knowledge is implicitly embedded in capital, and investment in technical progress is reflected as an increase in the flow of productive services generated by physical capital. Both technological knowledge and human capital stocks could be added explicitly to the wiring diagram, at the cost of considerable complication of the picture.

One other simplification to note at the outset is that the framework in Figure Appendix 1 focuses on the links between the natural and economic worlds without attempting to elaborate in detail the allocation of resources within the economic sphere. In particular, we recognize that produced final output in the economy takes many forms—agriculture, manufacturing, household production, and commercial services, for example—and that final output results from the production and application of numerous intermediate

---

[3] This diagram is inspired by Pezzey (1989, 1992) though it differs from Pezzey's set-up in several particulars. As explained further below, to accomplish its purposes, our framework emphasizes some factors at the expense of others; there are many ways to build a wiring diagram and none is perfect.

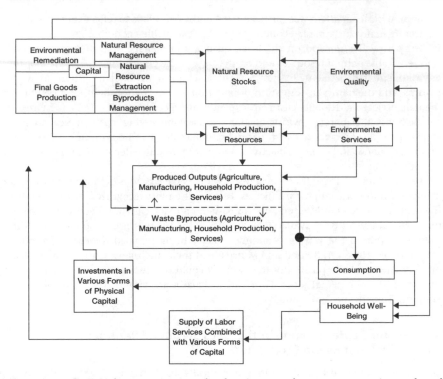

Figure Appendix 1 Links connecting natural and environmental resources, economic growth, and social well-being: the importance of various investments

goods. In practice, growth and development policies must be concerned with these issues of the composition of economic activity—the efficiency of specific sectors, the impacts of trade liberalization, and so forth. Again, the framework can readily be extended to address a richer composition of economic activity, but the substantial complication of the diagram does not add much to the broad understanding of environment-economic linkages at the economy-wide level. Environment-economic linkages for various sectors are elaborated in subsequent parts of the paper.

The large box in the center of Figure Appendix 1 represents the production in the economy of both valued goods and services and the inherent co-production of wastes. In this framework, 'waste' is not a purely physical concept (based for example on materials balance—what goes in must come out). We conceive of waste as flows that reduce environmental quality as broadly defined below.

As shown in Figure Appendix 1, production of goods depends on (a) flows of capital services (and associated labor services), (b) flows of extracted natural materials (biological and geological, renewable and depletable), and (c) environmental services provided by natural systems. The volume of wastes released to the environment depends on the volume of material output and on the flow of services derived from another form of investment by society, investment that is applied to manage the byproducts of production generated within the economic system. We use the shorthand 'byproducts management capital' to summarize these services. Byproducts management refers both to pollution prevention (reduction in unwanted harmful byproducts relative to desired goods), and to end-of-pipe treatment that reduces the damage caused by physical discharges.

At this level of generality, 'environmental services' incorporate a number of productive inputs. Climatic conditions, including temperature and rainfall, are more or less conducive to agricultural and silvicultural production. Water bodies (rivers, lakes, estuaries, wetlands) of certain water quantity, turbidity, flow rate, temperature, and chemical composition provide more or less fruitful habitat for valued aquatic organisms (shrimp, fish, plant life) as well as water resources for human consumption and manufacturing. Biodiversity contributes to ecological stability as well as to tourism, long-term agricultural productivity, and other products such as pharmaceuticals. Air quality and broader climatic conditions affect ambient temperatures, health conditions, and variability of weather in ways that affect the productivity of inputs in various household and manufacturing activities. 'Environmental quality' then can be understood generally as the capacity of the natural system to provide a sustained flow of these various environmental services.

We make the simplifying assumption in this graphical framework that extracted natural resources and the services of capital are the only produced intermediate inputs. Other intermediate inputs, such as environmental quality, are supplied by nature. In practice, of course, the economy has a number of intermediate goods. The flow of extracted natural resources depends on the effective stocks of those resources, as well as on the flow of capital services (and associated labor services) applied to their development and extraction. This is another point of connection between the economic and ecological domains. 'Effective' natural resource stocks also are not a purely physical phenomenon. Society also can invest in what for simplicity we call 'natural resource management capital' to enhance the natural or economic productivity of those resources. Such investments can range from technical progress that enhances the use of lower-grade ores to improved management of biological resources to enhance their regenerative capacity. In Figure Appendix 1, these investments are referred to as 'natural resource management.'

Once final outputs are produced, they are allocated between immediate consumption and various forms of investment. As in standard growth analysis, society can sacrifice some current well-being by reducing immediate consumption to gain greater future well-being through augmentation of capital. Here, however, we recognize multiple forms of investment that are possible, each of which can contribute to future well-being. Investment can increase capacity for final goods production; enhance natural resource extraction; reduce wastes (byproducts management) through pollution prevention and end-of-pipe neutralization; enhance the productivity of natural resource stocks (natural resource management); or remediate environmental harms that do occur, thereby upgrading the part of society's wealth reflected in environmental quality.

Wastes that are produced (taking into account byproducts management activities) flow back into the natural environment and reduce environmental quality.[4] Reduced

---

[4] In this framework we represent wastes as originating only in the production sector. However, in the economy-wide framework of Figure Appendix 1, 'production' can be interpreted to include household production activities—provision of food, shelter, warmth, and so forth—that also include waste byproducts. For simplicity we are not including in Figure Appendix 1 the flow of byproducts

environmental quality negatively affects economic productivity by reducing the flows of various environmental services, as described above, and by reducing the productivity of some natural resources. Reduced environmental quality also has a direct negative effect on household well-being, given a level of material consumption.[5]

The foregoing paragraphs have laid out the various pathways through which natural resources and the environment are related to economic growth and social welfare. Economic output is sustained and enhanced over time through the maintenance and enhancement of various environmental service flows, and through the effective protection and management of natural resource stocks, as well as through the augmentation of natural resource extraction and final production capacity. Stated another way, diminution of the flows of these natural capital services will reduce economic product for a given stock of output producing capital. Such a diminution of production possibilities could only be offset, within certain limits, by increased investment in output producing capital. However, such investments would be subject to diminishing economic returns as well as some inherent natural limits on their efficacy,[6] and in any event they would engender reductions in current consumption that have a social cost. Therefore, investment in the maintenance of natural capital services is one of the important pathways for achieving sustained growth, though the nature of the trade-offs among the various forms of investment in practice is an empirical question.

We can also look at the issue from the perspective of household welfare, the ultimate rationale for sustaining and enhancing growth in any event. We have already noted that household well-being depends on environmental quality as well as material consumption. One way that environmental quality can be enhanced is simply to reduce economic product and the associated environmental degradation from waste flows. Societies can in principle make trade-offs as to how consumption-rich and environment-poor or consumption-poor and environment-rich they wish to be. Fortunately, there are other margins for trade-off through investment as well. By foregoing some consumption in the short term, society can invest in byproducts management and environmental remediation that not only improve the environment but also enhance economic product in the long term. The same logic applies to investments in natural resource management.

Figure Appendix 1 describes pathways and linkages; it does not describe how an actual economic system performs in terms of overall economic efficiency and investment in natural capital in particular. In any economic system, these outcomes depend on what we can call the effective prices faced by agents in the system. These prices depend on the effective

that can originate in natural resource extraction, though it is clear that this is another important source of environmental pressure and the framework can easily be generalized to incorporate this link. The Pezzey diagram represented waste flows as originating exclusively in households as a result of final consumption. Pezzey also divided output into streams of consumption, investments, and environmental clean-up expenditures. In our framework we represent this last claim on output in the accounts as investments in byproducts management and environmental remediation capacity.

[5] The most straightforward way that household well-being is directly affected by environmental quality is health (diversion of productive resources to health remediation being a consequence of the impact). Direct aesthetic impacts also are relevant for household well-being. Other impacts like availability of water or fuel could be seen as part of the production sector broadly defined to include household activities.

[6] To cite the simplest example, the laws of physics do not allow the economic system to run on some negligible amount of energy; at some level energy and capital are complements. Therefore, if depletable energy resources are exhausted and renewable energy resources are not developed, output necessarily suffers.

scarcity of the resources in question, which in turn depends on the state of technology (including human capital as well as technical knowledge); knowledge levels and pre-ferences of the population; the size of the natural resource stock; and the institutions that mediate the allocation and exchange of the resources in question.

Efficiency problems in the allocation of natural capital resources arise because of extern-alities that are familiar to natural resource and environmental economists. If a scarce natural resource is nevertheless freely available for the taking (open access), it will be over-exploited and incentives to invest in better protection and management will be lacking. If social mechanisms for internalizing the costs of environmental degradation are lacking, then waste production will be excessive and investments in waste byproducts management and environmental remediation will be deficient.

Development theory has its own list of growth-retarding market and institutional failures to add to the above list. Prominent examples include excessive investment costs because of capital market failures; under-investment in human capital; inadequate infrastructure provision (by public or private actors); and a variety of product market dis-tortions. There are important potential interactions between the two sets of market and institutional failures. In particular, high costs of other investments, limited employment opportunities, and subsidies to certain output sectors all could accelerate natural capital depletion beyond efficient levels.[7] Both sets of market and institutional failures thus admit the possibility of win-win improvements. Corrections of distortions in the alloca-tion of natural capital can stimulate economic progress and enhance human welfare as well as protecting the environment per se. Correcting other failures can in a number of cases also lower costly pressure on natural capital.[8]

Conclusions and Empirical Challenges

This appendix has attempted to clarify at an intuitive and conceptual level how economic growth and the environment are interconnected. The framework developed here has emphasized that natural resources and environmental quality can and should be thought of as targets for investment by society in promoting an improved quality of life in developing countries, investments that compete against other valued allocations of social savings. Economic growth affects the natural environment, but the natural environment also can affect growth. This implies that concern for the natural environment needs to be a central concern of development policy, though not the only or always the overriding concern. This perspective differs from the notion of a stand-alone environ-mental policy separate from economic development considerations.

By describing investments in natural capital as competing with other uses of savings, we intend to underscore the inherent trade-offs societies face in allocating savings. Investments in natural capital should not automatically be favored over

[7] In other cases, however, high costs of investment could *decelerate* resource depletion by increas-ing the cost of developing extractive capacity. For examples see Farzin (1984) or Rowthorn and Brown (1999).

[8] This connection is not automatically so virtuous. Suppose, for example, that a developing country has been *de facto* subsidizing its manufacturing sector through import protection. In this case trade liberalization could increase demands on natural capital through a shift towards agriculture or natural resource extraction and harvesting. Whether this shift creates inefficient pressure on natural capital depends critically on the nature of the natural resource management and protection institutions in place in the country. (See López, 2000 and Margolis, 2002.)

other uses of resources, as advocated by some activists. Some degradation (depreciation) of natural capital can be appropriate. By the same token, however, we are arguing against the idea that the environment is somehow a luxury good or for some other reason inherently of secondary importance to those interested in economic growth and the well-being of people.

We have noted that natural capital can be inefficiently allocated in practice not just because of market and institutional failures affecting natural resources and the environment, but also because of broader market and institutional failures that simultaneously hamper development and excessively degrade natural capital. In both cases the appropriate policy response must take into account the source and size of the misallocation problem, and the practical constraints of institutional capacity prevailing in the country. Sometimes the best remedy for environmental problems can be found in policies that focus on alleviating institutional barriers to economic growth. But it does not follow automatically that growth policies alone should be pursued to ameliorate environmental problems.

While the conceptual framework we have developed in this paper is grounded in the neoclassical economic theory of growth and the environment, the empirical literature on these interconnections is less well developed. Further investigation through work in the field should put a high priority on reducing these empirical gaps.

A fair amount of empirical work has been done on the collateral effects of development policies on the environment, though this work often has involved case studies of specific policies and countries. For example, non-competitive allocation of forest concessions with low rent capture can encourage concessionaires to economically, as well as ecologically, over-exploit forest stocks. Subsidies for agricultural inputs (water, fertilizer, pesticides) can encourage excessive and inefficient use of these inputs with increases in water pollution and residues on crops. Import substitution policies tend to lead not only to economic inefficiency in manufacturing, but they also can promote excessive development in heavy industries that emit high levels of conventional air and water pollutants; in downstream resource processing that encourages economically excessive exploitation of natural resources; or in agricultural practices that generate excessive land use (soil mining). Policies that foster foreign investment, on the other hand, may sometimes promote some pollution haven effects, but they may also promote cleaner development through access to best technology and corporate practices. While these points have been addressed, there is still plenty of room for more investigation of both the scale of the linkages and the practical options for averting adverse impacts.[9]

Less is known empirically about the effects of environmental quality on economic growth. Some individual studies have described how air and water pollution can reduce agricultural yields and damage materials, as well as forcing industry to invest in costly water clean-up before it uses raw water for industrial purposes. Both water and air pollution seemingly can, through human health effects, reduce labor productivity. Natural resource degradation, of the types mentioned in the previous paragraph, limit long-term productivity in the affected sectors. But the empirical literature at the sectoral level for developing countries remains limited, and the macroeconomic consequences of these impacts in terms of growth are even less well understood.

---

[9] For an older but still useful compendium of analysis related to trade and the environment, see Low (1992); see also Margolis (2002).

One of the least empirically understood connections concerns the effects on growth of investing in natural resource and environmental infrastructure, though infrastructure in general has been an important strand in growth theory recently.[10] A useful broad perspective on the connections between different types of infrastructure and economic progress was provided in the World Bank's 1994 *World Development Report*, which found that whatever the nature of the causality, per capita infrastructure stocks generally correlate highly with per capita GDP levels. However, the reasons for this apparent relationship are not entirely clear, and the specific importance of natural resource and environmental infrastructure is even less well understood.[11, 12] To move ahead in understanding the connections between economic growth and natural capital, deeper probing of both physical and social infrastructure issues ranks as an especially high priority.

References

Barnett, H., and C. Morse (1963), *Scarcity and Growth: The Economics of Natural Resource Availability*. Baltimore: Johns Hopkins University Press for Resources for the Future.

Beltratti, Andrea (1997), 'Growth with Natural and Environmental Resources,' in Carlo Carraro and Diminico Siniscalco (eds), *New Directions in the Economic Theory of the Environment*. Cambridge, Cambridge University Press.

Dasgupta, Partha S. and Geoffrey M. Heal (1974), 'The Optimal Depletion of Exhaustible Resources,' *Review of Economic Studies, Symposium on the Economics of Exhaustible Resources*. Edinburgh, Scotland, Longman Group Ltd.

Farzin, Y. Hossein (1984), 'The Effect of the Discount Rate on Depletion of Exhaustible Resources,' *Journal of Political Economy* 92(5): 841–51.

Ferraro, Paul J. and R. David Simpson (2002), 'The Cost-Effectiveness of Conservation Payments,' *Land Economics* 78(3): 339–53.

[10] Infrastructure is a term lacking precise definition, but for present purposes it can be viewed as embracing two major categories of assets. *Physical* infrastructure comprises such basic capital stocks as electric power, communications, transport, water, and health facilities. In a developing country context, these prerequisites to a viable economy are sometimes labeled 'social overhead capital.' *Institutional* infrastructure comprises a wide range of attributes and conditions that serve as important complements to physical capital in promoting socioeconomic development. Included are financial, legal, and regulatory institutions and policies—e.g. a system of property rights—without which the functioning of a competitive market economy would be severely handicapped. Each category of infrastructure gives rise to, or enables, other sectors to produce a stream of important economic services.

[11] One reason why the relationship can be slippery arises from the difference between indicated *stocks* of infrastructure—paved roads, electric generating capacity, telephone connections, railroad trackage and rolling stock, irrigated land area, access to safe drinking water and sanitation—and the *flow of services* that such facilities provide. The World Bank estimates that across a range of developing countries, 40 percent of installed electric power capacity is in fact unavailable for production (World Bank, 1994, p. 1). The provision of infrastructure services consistent with users' expectations is related to larger institutional failures to which we already have alluded.

[12] One example of the problem relates to the creation of social infrastructure for environmental protection. Developing countries have pursued a variety of policies with very different implications for both environmental impacts and economic costs (Rock, 2002). In Malaysia, the government worked with the private sector to identify low cost, but effective clean-up technologies that enabled oil palm production and exports to grow rapidly while water quality improved. In Singapore, Korea and Taiwan, governments created effective command and control environmental agencies that cracked down on polluters; growth remained high even while ambient environmental quality improved. These examples suggest that the trade-off between growth and environment need not be that severe, even when policies that are less than ideal from a cost-effectiveness perspective are employed.

Hartwick, John M. (1977), 'Intergenerational Equity and the Investing of Rents from Exhaustible Resources,' *American Economic Review* 67(5): 972–4.

López, Ramón (2000), 'Trade Reform and Environmental Externalities in General Equilibrium: Analysis for an Archetype Poor Tropical Country.' *Environment and Development Economics* 5(4): 377–404.

Low, Patrick (ed.) (1992), *International Trade and the Environment*. Washington, DC: World Bank.

Margolis, Michael (2002), 'The Impact of Trade on the Environment.' Resources for the Future Issues Brief 02-28 (August). Accessed at http://www.rff.org/Johannesburg/ Issuebriefs/joburg20.pdf.

Nordhaus, William D. (1993), 'Rolling the "DICE": An Optimal Transition Path for Controlling Greenhouse Gases,' *Resource and Energy Economics* 15(1): 27–50.

Pezzey, John (1989), 'Economic Analysis of Sustainable Growth and Sustainable Development.' Washington DC.: World Bank. Environment Department Working Paper No. 15. Published as *Sustainable Development Concepts: An Economic Analysis*, World Bank Environment Paper No. 2, 1992.

Robinson, Elizabeth J. Z., Jeffrey C. Williams, and Heidi J. Albers (2002), 'The Impact of Markets and Policy on Spatial Patterns of Non-Timber Forest Product Extraction,' *Land Economics* 78(2): 260–71.

Rock, Michael T. (2002), *Pollution Control in East Asia: Lessons from Newly Industrializing Countries*. Washington, DC: Resources for the Future.

Rowthorn, Bob and Gardner Brown (1999), 'When a High Discount Rate Encourages Biodiversity,' *International Economic Review* 40(2): 315–32.

Simpson, David, R. Michael Toman, and Robert Ayres (eds). (2005), *Scarcity and Growth Revisited: Natural Resources and the Environment in the New Millenium*. Washington, DC: Resources for the Future.

Smulders, Sjak. (1999), 'Endogenous Growth Theory and the Environment,' in Jeroen C. J. M. van den Bergh, (ed.), *Handbook of Environmental and Resource Economics*. Elgar Cheltenham, U.K.

Solow, Robert M. (1974), 'Intergenerational Equity and Exhaustible Resources,' *Review of Economic Studies, Symposium on the Economics of Exhaustible Resources*. Edinburgh, Scotland: Longman Group Ltd.

Stiglitz, Joseph E. (1974), 'Growth with Exhaustible Natural Resources: Efficient and Optimal Growth Paths,' *Review of Economic Studies, Symposium on the Economics of Exhaustible Resources*. Edinburgh, Scotland: Longman Group Ltd.

Toman, Michael (2003), The Roles of the Environment and Natural Resources in Economic Growth Analysis. Resources for the Future Discussion Paper 02-71 (May). Accessed at http://www.rff.org/rff/ Documents/RFF-DP-02-71.pdf.

World Bank (1994), *World Development Report 1994: Infrastructure for Development*. New York: Oxford University Press for the World Bank.

INDEX

Items appearing as annexes, appendices, boxes, figures, notes and tables are indexed in bold; e.g. 276n

463